Abridged
ECONOMICS

The Science of Common Sense

Second Edition

ELBERT V. BOWDEN

Professor of Economics
Appalachian State University

H93

Published by
SOUTH-WESTERN PUBLISHING CO.

CINCINNATI   WEST CHICAGO, ILL.   DALLAS   PELHAM MANOR, N.Y.   PALO ALTO, CALIF.

ISBN: 0-538-08930-X

Library of Congress Catalog Card Number: 76-48493

2 3 4 5 6 K 3 2 1 0 9

Printed in the United States of America

Preface

An interesting economics book? With easy conversational style? And with a *solid treatment of theory and issues and applications? Who ever heard of such a thing?*

Yet there were professors at hundreds of colleges who pioneered and used the previous edition of this book. Some of them wrote and told me that their grade distributions suddenly were skewed the other way—that *the majority* of their students were understanding economics in the way that only the few had been understanding before.

So it seems that the previous edition succeeded in doing what it set out to do—that is, to teach the basic concepts and principles of economics to a lot more students. The philosophy and style of this book are still the same as stated in the preface of the previous edition.

The Philosophy of This Book

This book is based on the following propositions:

- that basic economic concepts and principles are for everybody—not just for the scholarly few, but *for everybody who wants to learn them.*
- that the freshman-sophomore economics courses should be among *the most interesting, relevant, rewarding, and popular courses on every campus*—

community colleges, major universities, everywhere;

- that scholarly vocabulary and prose, although delightful to the scholarly elite, is not the language of today's youth—that *economics won't be understood by most students until it is explained in simple everyday language*—that is, in the vernacular of today's young people;

- that *simple explanations do not have to be simple-minded explanations*—that economic principles can be explained with simple words, easy conversational prose and familiar examples, without any sacrifice of depth or rigor or precision;

- that the first objective should be *to get the student turned on to economics* and then *to get the basic concepts and principles thoroughly understood and permanently integrated into each student's way of thinking.*

In short, this book is based on the propositions that *all college students can understand the fundamental concepts and principles of economics* if the explanations are made with familiar language and with examples that each student can see and feel and relate to—and that *the economics textbook writer should try to come as close as possible to achieving a "frictionless communication" of economic ideas.*

If there's any way to make it fun to learn economics, then by all means let's do it!

Changes in This New Abridged Edition

This abridged edition has been designed to provide a balanced coverage of micro and macro theory, problems, and policies for the one-semester or one-quarter course. Many changes (improvements, I hope) have been made in this new edition.

1. Length and Coverage. In this second edition new materials have been added in most chapters.

a. There are *completely new treatments* of kinked oligopoly demand curves, automatic stabilizers, the Lorenz curve, the U.S. banking system, and economics as a science.

b. There's *more than twice as much coverage* on the modern issues and problems of the urban economy and the financial crises of the cities, on poverty and discrimination, and on ecology and environmental externalties.

c. There are *new tabular and algebraic explanations* of the consumption function, the income (investment) multiplier, the deposit multiplier, the acceleration principle, and capitalized value.

2. Reorganization and Repetition. This edition has been reorganized to make it easier to break up the course into convenient exam periods. Also, topics which were somewhat scattered in the previous edition have now been pulled together.

The previous edition contained some unnecessary repetition. I believe all of that now has been eliminated—but without the elimination of the repetition which sometimes is needed for clear and precise understanding.

3. Style and Tone. This edition, just as the previous one, is written in simple conversational style. It's still a very personal book. But I've altered the tone in some places because some students have said that they sometimes felt I was "talking down" to them.

In this edition I've tried to be very careful about using expressions which among friends would be just fine, but which, when coming from a "professor-author" might cause some students to feel "talked down to." I hope that anyone who ever feels "talked down to" by anything in this book will write and let me know, so that I can send a personal letter of apology. I promise I will do that.

4. Masculine Sex Bias. The previous edition used generic masculine words to refer to both males and females. In this edition I think I have succeeeded in eliminating all of that—and without once finding it necessary to resort to such awkward terms as "policepersons" or "fisherpersons"—or anything ridiculous, like "Texas cowpersons."

5. Real-World Orientation. In general, the second edition goes far beyond the previous emphasis on simulated cases and uses a large number of real cases to achieve a much closer identification with the actual functioning of the real world of the 1970s.

Designed for the Student's Success

This edition, like the last one, is designed to help students to succeed. It is not designed for the instructor who wants to "weed out" half of the class. *The purpose of this book is to get students interested and start them off right in economics.*

I've really tried to design this book to *generate a permanent interest in economics and to give an accurate and useful basic knowledge of economics to each student who gives it a reasonable try.* I'm not sure I have succeeded. But I'd rather fail while trying for that than to succeed at something less.

My Sincere Appreciation to All Who Have Helped

Many people helped as I prepared the first edition of this book. Katsuhiro (Ken) Otsuka, outstanding cartoonist, Mrs. Mary Ann Burgess, outstanding secretary, and all of my colleagues and students at SUNY-Fredonia have made lasting contributions.

Now, with this edition, the list grows much longer. To all of the following who have made helpful comments I gladly admit my debt and express my gratitude:

Walter Baumgartner, State University of New York—Oneonta

Clifford Beck, Mount San Jacinto College

Jay Buffenmeyer, Lebanon Valley College

William Cage, Wake Forest University

Brian Carlos, Bristol Community College

Stanley Chipper, Indiana State University

Roger Clites, Glenville State College

Robert Crofts, Salem State College

Miles Eaton, Orange Coast College

Dave Edmonds, University of Southwestern Louisiana

William Flynn, Milwaukee School of Engineering

Paul Forney, Indian Hills Community College

Delmar Frazier, Austin Peay State University

Thomas Holmstrom, Northern Michigan University

Frank Jones, Joseph Lee, and Arlen Skorr, Mankato State College

Richard Ladd, U.S. Coast Guard Academy

R. G. Menefee, Berea College

Ray Roberts, Furman University

Ron Siltzer, Spartanburg Technical College

Herschel Smith, Housatonic Community College

Stella Spiewak, Jefferson Co. Technical Institute

Stanley Steinke, Community College of Philadelphia

G. M. Stone, Jr., University of North Carolina—Charlotte

Jay Stone, Florence-Darlington Technical College

Jack Thornhill, Georgia College

H. H. Ullom and John Dunton, Del Mar College

Peter Watry, Southwestern College

Steve Welch, State University of New York—Fredonia

Earl Williams, Northeastern Oklahoma University

My sincere thanks to all of you. I hope you will be pleased as you see the many ways this edition and the new study guide-workbook have been influenced by your suggestions.

As I prepared this second edition from my temporary United Nations post in the Fiji Islands, I found myself again indebted to Mary Ann Burgess and my other friends at SUNY-Fredonia for supplying me with the many kinds of up-to-date information needed for the revisions.

But my greatest debt of gratitude for this edition goes to Rosemary Jones, my secretary in Fiji, who has typed and retyped everything so many times. Orchids to you, Rosemary, for a job done uncommonly well.

Dispelling the Dismalness

For many years I've been acutely aware that we must do something different for our beginning economics students. We must give them something that's interesting *to them*—something they can really relate to, really understand, really learn from.

I can't be sure this book will be thoroughly successful in doing that. But I am sure that now there's an economics book which really does try.

I hope those of you who agree will join me in trying to dispel some of the inherent (and some of the inherited) dismalness of our "queen of the social sciences"—of our "science of common sense."

Elbert V. Bowden
Appalachian State University
Boone, North Carolina

January, 1978

Contents in Brief

Contents

Prologue: Why Economics?

Why should anybody want to learn economics? Several reasons. There's a lot you just can't understand until you learn some economics. When you get to the end of this book you'll realize just how true that is.

And another thing. Learning economics is a good exercise in mental development. It leads to new ways of thinking about things. You don't understand what that means yet, either. But soon you will.

You Can't Escape from Economics

Economics is everywhere. It's at work all the time, in everything. Once you learn to recognize it you can never escape from it.

When you're doing things or making things, cooking breakfast or washing your car, going places, studying math, playing basketball, using up your time and energy and money and things to do one thing or another—all those things involve economics. If economics is involved in everything, then how can you ever get away from economics? That's the point. You can't. You just can't.

Economics is involved in all the things you've been doing all your life. So how have you been able to get along all these years without knowing any economics? You haven't. The fact is, you know quite a lot of basic economics already. Everybody does.

You already know, right now, 40 or 60 or maybe 70 or 80 percent of the economics you will know when you get to the end of this book. But right now you don't call it "economics." You call it "common sense."

Economics Can Sharpen Your Common Sense

So should you study economics because it can expand and sharpen your common sense? Yes! You're going to be surprised how much it can do that. But it can do much more than that. It can let you see much more deeply into so many things that are going on around you.

This book starts with sharpening your own common sense—talking about how you solve your own personal "economic problem." Then it expands the horizon more and more until the first thing you know you'll be working with and understanding the "economic problem" from the point of view of the society, the nation, the entire world.

You're Always Facing an Economic Problem

I suppose you already know that when you're trying to decide if you'll save your money or spend it, you're facing an "economic problem." Or whether to pay your tuition or go to Ft.

Lauderdale or someplace, that's an "economic problem" too.

But what about deciding whether to study math or play basketball? or cook breakfast or wash the car? an "economic problem" too? Sure. An economic problem is a problem of having to choose—like whether to have your cake or eat it.

When are you facing an economic problem? All the time! Every moment of every day of your life you're having to decide what to do with yourself—with your time and energy and thoughts—and what to do with your possessions—your money and your things.

Right now you're reading this book. But there are a dozen other things you *might have* been doing right now. Right? Sure.

So many, many choices we all have! We're choosing all the time: to do this or that, to make this or that, to use up this or that, to save this or that. There's just no end to it! And now, already, just from reading this first couple of pages you can see your own personal "economic problem." It's your problem of choosing—of deciding what to do with all the different things available to you. That's *your* economic problem.

Does your family have an economic problem? Like who will wash the dishes or the car and who will get to use the car and who will get to spend how much of the money? Sure. What about your church? Your club? Any organization? Do they have an economic problem? Sure.

What about your city? Your local school board? The corner grocery? The burger drive-in? Your college? Do they have an economic problem too? a problem of deciding what to do with what they have? and of who will get to use how much of what? Of course they do.

Every Society Is Always Making Choices

What about the whole society? Does it face a problem of choosing? of deciding who will do what, who will get to have how much of what, which things to use up and which to save and all that? Of course it does!

It's pretty easy for you to see how you decided to spend your time right now, getting started in this book. It isn't so tough seeing how each person decides.

All of us think about the different things we might do and then we try to make the best choices from our own points of view. But what about the society? How does the society decide what to do and what to make? and what to use up and what to save? and who will get to have how much of what?

Seeing how the society solves its economic problem is not obvious. Not unless you understand economics. That's one of the things you'll learn in the chapters coming up.

Society's Problems Are Economic Problems— and More Than That

Every society has always faced problems. As times change the problems change, but some problems always seem to be there. These days people are concerned about the population problem and about environmental destruction.

Are problems of this sort economic problems? Yes. They're economic problems—but not just economic problems. They're economic problems and more than that.

All real-world problems—all the problems that face the human race—are economic problems. Sure. But they're more than that. You'll never find a real-world problem that isn't both an economic problem and more than an economic problem.

Pick any current problem you're concerned about: the crime rate, inadequate housing, drug abuse, unemployment, poverty—all economic problems? Yes. All economic problems and more than that.

What about the problem of international tensions? wars? rising prices? school integration? urban blight? Are these economic problems? Of course. Not *just* economic problems, but economic problems to be sure. *Economic problems and more than that.*

Without "Scientific Economics," Common Sense Can Mislead You

In many chapters throughout this book you'll be reading about real-world problems. When you do, you'll learn to see each of the problems in a new and different light. Each problem will be more clear to you than ever before. That's one of the important reasons why it's a good idea to study economics.

The study of economics is going to let you really understand many things that will concern you all your life—things which your common sense alone couldn't explain. Sometimes your common sense might even mislead you! There are so many things a person really can't understand without some "scientific-knowledge" of economics.

If the study of economics is so important, then it's worth some effort. Right? But what if it would turn out to be fun too? Impossible you say? Not at all. Just you wait and see.

PART 1

BASIC CONCEPTS
AND PRINCIPLES:
AN INTRODUCTION
TO ECONOMICS

YOU CAN'T HAVE YOUR CAKE AND EAT IT, TOO!

1 Economics: the Study of Scarcity and Choice

The problem is: how can I best reach my objectives with no more than I have to work with?

Economics is the study of choosing. Who chooses? Everyone. Each person, each family, each business, each educational or religious or political organization, each society, each nation. Everyone. The successful ones—the ones who really wind up getting as close as they can to their objectives—are the ones who are making the right choices.

Economizing Is Making the Right Choices

Economizing is the science and the art of making the right choices. Which choices are the right ones? Those which best serve the wishes of the chooser. Every person has a "personal set" of desires and objectives. Are your choices helping you as much as possible toward fulfilling your desires and objectives? If so, you are economizing. You are making the best choices for you.

Why choose? We must choose. The things we have to work with are limited. When we use up something in one way, obviously we can't use it some other way. If we're smart or lucky (or maybe both) we will choose the way that does the most to help us to achieve our objectives. That's what most of us are trying to do, anyway.

Most Things Are Scarce

Too bad so many things are scarce. If things weren't scarce it wouldn't be necessary to choose and economize. But people seem to want more than they have of most things. That means most things are "scarce."

In economics, scarce means "the amount available is limited." If cake wasn't scarce then you could have all the cake you wanted, and eat all the cake you wanted, too. We would all be up to our knees in cake! Scarcity is an important concept in economics. Let's talk about it.

SCARCE THINGS ARE WANTED AND LIMITED

To say that something is scarce is not to say that there is a *shortage* of it. Scarcity only means that the available amounts are not completely unlimited. For example, out on the desert, water is very scarce. You wouldn't use up the water in your canteen washing your face and hands before lunch! You *economize*. That is, you make the best choice about how to use your water. You limit its use (conserve it) so it will be used only for the most important purpose—moistening your parched throat.

If your canteen runs dry you will pay all the money you have just for enough water to make it back to civilization. Water is not nearly so scarce in the city as it is out on the desert. But even in the city it's a little bit scarce. People in the city don't economize water the way you would if you were on a desert. But they do pay for water, and they do economize water a little bit. Why? Because water in the city is a little bit scarce.

Economic Value Is the Price You Pay

The more scarce something is the higher will be its economic value (its exchange value, or price) and the more it will be economized. If something is not scarce at all then it will have no "economic value" (no price). It will be free. It will not be economized because there is no need. Enough is available to serve all the possible uses, so there is no need to choose the best use and conserve it for that purpose.

Suppose our desert wanderer stumbles into an oasis and finds a bubbling spring and a big lake. Suddenly water becomes a free good. He will drink it, wash his face and hands, water the donkey, splash around in the lake, then splash some water on the donkey just for fun. Why not? Nobody economizes or conserves or limits the use of free goods!

Marginal Utility Means "Additional Satisfaction"

Suppose, while our happy wanderer is splashing around in the lake, someone comes along and offers to sell him a drink of water. Will he buy? Obviously not. He would not pay a penny for a hundred gallons. Does this mean

that water is of no value to him? Again, obviously not. It only means that *more* water (more than he already has) is of no value to him. Additional water would bring him marginal utility (additional satisfaction) of zero.

Is it true that the best things in life are free? Sometimes maybe so. It all depends on what you like best, and on whether or not the amount of it is *limited*.

We're into an important concept in economics. It's this: the economic value of something to you (that is, the price you would be willing to pay for it) is never determined by the "total usefulness" of it. The value is determined by *how useful it would be for you to have more of it than you already have*.

Free Goods Have Zero Marginal Utility

Suppose you have all of something you could possibly ever use. Would you like to have more? Of course not. Any additional amount would have zero value to you. The more of something you already have, the less important it is to you to get even more of it. What we're talking about is called the principle of diminishing marginal utility.

"Marginal utility" is the "extra satisfaction" you get from having a little more of something. Does marginal utility "diminish" as you get more and more? Sure. As more and more of something is available to you, the additional utility you could get from having even more gets smaller and smaller. If *unlimited* amounts are available, then the marginal utility (the extra utility from having more) drops all the way to zero. You saw what happened to the marginal utility of water when our thirsty wanderer stumbled into the oasis. Right?

If you think about it you'll realize that the price you would be willing to pay for an additional something reflects the importance of that additional something to you. If you think you're going to gain a lot of additional satisfaction (marginal utility) from whatever you're thinking of buying, then you'll be willing to pay a high price. Right? But if you think you'll gain only a little from it, you'll buy it only if the price is low. If you expect the marginal utility to be zero you won't pay anything for it.

What if nothing was scarce? Then everything would be free. There would be enough of everything for all of us to have all we could ever want and some left over. We would have no reason to worry about economics. There would be no need to choose or conserve or economize. But that's just not the way it is. Almost everything is scarce. Scarcity is an inescapable fact of life. So, like it or not, we must choose and conserve and economize.

We are forced to live with economics. We have no choice about that! So we might just as well learn a little something about it—about "the *science* of common sense." That's what you're going to be doing throughout this chapter and throughout this book. First there's a little more about free goods and scarce goods and marginal utility, just to be sure you really understand these basic concepts. Then we'll get into "the economic problem."

Only Scarce Things Have Marginal Utility and Economic Value

Of all the things that people need, air tops the list. Yet, to the individual, air has no economic value. Why not? Because it is not scarce. Would you pay to get any more air than you already have? Of course not. You already have more than you can use! The marginal utility you could get from an additional jugful of air would be zero. Therefore the amount you would be willing to pay is zero.

Why is air not scarce? Because there is so much of it around. Suppose there's only a little bit of something around. Will it be scarce? and valuable? Not necessarily. There probably aren't a dozen No. 2 cans of Mississippi mud in the entire world. The same could be said of cans of mosquito-wings, dried-fleas,

toadstools, apple-cores, broken glass, and rotten peaches. Very, very few. Right? But scarce? No.

Something is scarce only if people want more of it than they can get for free. If people want something enough to pay for it or work for it or trade for it, then it's scarce. To the individual, air is not scarce (and therefore is of no economic value) because no one wants any more of it than is already available. No. 2 cans of Mississippi mud are not scarce (and therefore are of no economic value) because nobody wants any of these things anyhow. Air has no marginal utility and therefore no economic value, for the same general reason that canned mud has no marginal utility or economic value. No one wants any more air and no one wants any more canned mud than is already available. So neither is scarce.

Both of these qualifications must be met if something is going to be called "scarce": (a) people must want it, and (b) the amount of it must be limited. The more it is limited and the more it is wanted, the more scarce it is. As something gets more scarce, it gets more valuable. If only a small amount of something is available and many people want very much to have it, then it is very scarce. Its marginal utility will be high and its price will be high. Its use will be carefully conserved, limited, economized.

Economics Is About Conserving and Producing Scarce Things

Most things are scarce. People are willing to work and pay to get scarce things; people economize the use of scarce things. Also, people work to produce more of the scarce things. Essentially, that's what economics is all about. *Economics is about conserving scarce things, and producing more of the scarce things. It's about choosing—about deciding which scarce things to conserve the most and which to produce the most—which to save, and which to use, and for what.*

THE ECONOMIC PROBLEM: A MATTER OF CHOICE

The economic problem is the problem of economizing—that is, of carefully choosing what to do with our scarce things. The problem faces each individual, each family, each business. It faces each society, each nation. More and more it is coming to face the entire world as a whole.

How are these choices made? How do the individual and the business and the society decide what to do with their scarce things? And what difference does it all make? These are the questions of economics. You'll be finding out the answers all through this book.

The economic problem is simple enough. All we need to do is answer this question: How can we best use what we have to fulfill our desires? To reach our objectives? To achieve our goals? That's what it's all about.

No One Can Escape the Economic Problem

The economic problem—the problem of deciding what to do with the things we have—faces each of us in each of our roles in life: as parent, executive, worker, student, vacationer, spouse, patron of the arts, homeowner, taxpayer, concerned citizen or whatever. All of us must be constantly deciding what to do with what we have—our money, time, mental and physical energies, everything. If we make the best choices we will make the most progress toward our objectives—toward whatever it is that we want most to achieve.

This same economic problem faces every organization—business, religious, social, educational, political, governmental, etc.

It faces every society—totalitarian or democratic, capitalist or socialist, primitive or advanced, civilized or barbaric, Christian or Buddhist, anarchist, communist, utopian, or what have you. The economic problem is truly universal. No person, no organization, no society can escape it. Those who do the best possible job of solving this problem get the most they can of what they want. Those who don't, don't.

What's Your Most Pressing Economic Problem?

For most students the most pressing economic problem is trying to decide how to use their most valuable resources—their time and "mental energy." How about you? Everyone has lots of conflicting objectives. You want to go out and have fun, get plenty of rest, daydream about your new love, and earn enough money to stay in college. Last (hopefully, not least) you would like to get a certain amount of education. Someday you'd like to graduate. Lots of conflicting objectives, right?

You've been struggling with this economic problem all your life. So has every other person, every organization, every society. It's too bad, but you just can't have your cake and eat it too. The resources you use up making, improving, repairing, protecting, enjoying, learning, or doing any *one* thing can't be used for doing, making, improving, learning (etc.) any *other* competing thing. Each time you choose to do one thing or to go one way you give up the chance to do the other thing or go the other way. Frustrating? You bet. But that's economics.

Which Things to Give Up? and Which to Have?

People (and organizations, and societies) want to *do* more and to have more than they can do or have. So what happens? We have to learn to accept the fact that we can't do and have everything we'd like. We learn to forego some of the things we want. But which to forego? And which to have? That's the economic problem. It's the problem of deciding among the alternatives.

The economic problem is inescapable. You can't spend this morning studying for a sociology test and also studying economics. Your father can't be selling insurance policies at the same time he's mowing the lawn. Your parents can't spend all their money on the children's clothes and still have money for school lunches. Your school can't put all its money into the athletic program and still buy library books.

The United States is finding that we can't overcome poverty and pollution and urban slums and crime and all the other major problems of the society and do everything else we might want to do all at the same time. Something must be given up. But what? The space program? Military power? Foreign aid? Low-cost housing? Universal college education? These are really tough questions. Which to give up? and which to have? and how do we decide?

You Choose One Thing and Lose the Other

What about this: Each time you decide to do or have one thing you are denying yourself the opportunity to do or have some other thing. Suppose you decide to go skiing this weekend instead of studying your English. Then suppose your English grade slips down from C to D. You might say that the ski trip "cost you" your C in English. (You lost your C because you went skiing.) But maybe that's not all.

Suppose you had been planning to buy a new speaker for your stereo but you spent the money on the ski trip instead. The ski trip cost you your speaker, too. Right? Maybe the trip also cost you your "true love," who found somebody else to do English (and other things) with. Seems that the "costs" of the ski trip are beginning to get out of hand! Maybe you're about to decide that you made a bad choice.

It isn't always easy to make the best choices. Everyone makes bad choices sometimes. But we all must keep on choosing just the same. If you make a good choice, that means *what you're getting* is worth more to you than *what you're giving up*. It would be just great if all of us could do that all the time!

The Opportunity Cost Is the Opportunity Lost

Suppose a city urgently needs a new firehouse and a new school building. But it has only enough money to build one or the other. If the city builds the firehouse, the "cost" is the opportunity to have the school building; if the city builds the school building, the "cost" is the opportunity to have the firehouse. Can you see why economists call this the opportunity cost concept?

The idea of "opportunity cost" is that in order to have whatever you decide to have you must *give up the opportunity* to have the "something else" you also wanted. If you are craving a chocolate malted and also a maple-walnut sundae, and if you only have enough money for one or the other, what happens? You must choose. If you choose the malted, you give up the opportunity to have the sundae. The "opportunity cost" of the malted is the sundae. If you choose the sundae, the "opportunity cost" of the sundae is the malted.

During World War II the American economy was producing about as much as it could with the labor, materials, machinery, and other things available. More of everything was badly needed. Soldiers were needed. But every time a steelworker became a soldier it "cost" the country one steelworker. Ships were needed. But every time steel was put into making a ship it "cost" the nation the opportunity to make more tanks or guns or aircraft engines.

No Country Can Produce Any More Than It Can Produce

It's obvious that an individual can't be in two different places doing two different things at the same time. The same idea applies to the whole society. The society is limited in how much it can produce. If all the labor is busy and all the factories, mines, railroads, machines, and everything else are operating at "absolute maximum output," then that's all the economy is capable of producing. If that's all it can do, then that's just all it can do!

Suppose a country's economy is clicking along at top speed. Then what happens if the society wants to do more to try to discover a cure for cancer? Or to clean up Lake Erie? Or to send a man to Mars? Or to produce more power mowers and color TV sets? Or to build a new bridge across the Mississippi at Vicksburg? You know the answer. Something else has to go. Whatever goes, that's the *opportunity cost* the society is paying for what it gets.

MANY THINGS IN ECONOMICS CAN BE SHOWN ON GRAPHS

Note: Students who already understand graphs may skip this section and go immediately to Figure 1-1.

There's a very simple graph economists use to illustrate the opportunity cost concept. You know the idea: "the more you get of one thing, the less you can have of some other thing." This relationship—"the more of one, the less of the other"—is easy to picture on a graph.

Graphs really can be a lot of help in economics. Often, two things will be "related to each other." When *one* changes, the *other* also changes in a predictable way. When this

kind of a situation exists, a graph can be used to show the relationship.

One Graph Is Worth a Thousand Words—If You Understand It

It's been said that one picture is worth more than ten thousand words. I'm sure that one good graph in economics is worth at least a thousand words. Maybe more. But a picture is no good unless you take time to understand it. If you aren't in the habit of reading and drawing graphs, now is a good time for you to get started off right.

When you come across a graph for the first time, study it for about five minutes. (Time yourself.) Then close the book and try to draw the graph and explain it to yourself. Keep doing this until you really understand it and can draw and explain it without looking at the book. Pretty soon you'll find that you're completely familiar with graphs.

Now here comes a chance to practice all this good advice. The next page shows a graph illustrating the economic problem—that is, the "opportunity cost" concept. Study the graph, then practice drawing and explaining it to yourself until you have it down pat. You'll be surprised how clearly you can see the concept, once you learn to draw a graph illustrating it.

A Graph Always Shows the Relationship Between Two Things

The "expenditure possibility" graph (Figure 1-1) is only one of the several kinds of graphs economists use. But don't let that worry you. Graphs are all pretty much alike. "When you've seen one, you've seen them all," sort of.

A graph always shows the relationship between two things. One thing is measured along the horizontal line (the "x axis"); the other thing is measured up the vertical line (the "y axis"). Any point in the graph shows a certain amount of "the x thing" and a certain amount of "the y thing."

Fig. 1-1   The Expenditure Possibility Curve

You can't buy any more than you can pay for, so you must choose.

This shows the concept of opportunity cost in spending money. You have five dollars weekly to spend for lunch and you must choose between the "counter-special lunch" and the "giantburger-shake combo."

If you only have $5 to spend for lunches this week, you can only spend $1 per day. This graph shows your choices.

The *expenditure possibility curve* is also called the *consumption possibility curve* and the *budget constraint line*.

Which combination will you choose? You already know the answer to that—the one that best suits your tastes! You'll choose the combination that brings you the most satisfaction from your five dollars.

If you really go for the combos, maybe you will buy *all* combos. But this you know: each day when you order the lunch, it's costing you the combo; each day when you order the combo, it's costing you the lunch—*opportunity cost*, that is.

A "Curve" May Have Positive Slope or Negative Slope

When a line (a curve) is drawn in a graph and labeled, it tells you something. It tells you how much of "the y thing" goes with each amount of "the x thing," or vice versa. A curve in a graph is an "if, then" line. It tells you *"if you have 'this amount' of x, then you have 'this amount' of y."*

Sometimes the curve slopes downward as it moves to the right (as in Figure 1-1). This is called "negative slope." It means that as you get more of x, you have less of y. Or as you get more of y, you have less of x.

Some curves have "positive slope." As you get more x, you get more y. For example, if you make a graph showing "miles traveled" on the x axis and "gasoline used" on the y axis, the curve in the graph will have a positive slope. It will show that if "miles traveled" increases, then "gasoline used" increases also. Can you picture it?

Maybe it would be a good idea for you to draw some graphs showing the relationships between some things you know about. Could you put study-time on one axis and your exam grades on the other? Relate how much you eat to how much you weigh? The number of people you smile at to the number who smile at you? Hours of the week spent on study to hours spent on other things? Time in the sun and amount of suntan? (or maybe sunburn)? Sure. Take a few minutes and draw some graphs. If you learn to draw and read these "pictures" right now, you will gain a valuable tool to work with.

PRODUCTION POSSIBILITY GRAPHS SHOW THE ECONOMIC PROBLEM

In Figure 1-1 you learned about the "expenditure possibility" or "consumption possibility" curve. You had a limited amount of lunch money ($5 a week) and had to choose what to eat for lunch each day. Now you're going to see another graph just like Figure 1-1, only it will show a "production possibility" curve.

A production possibility curve is exactly like an expenditure possibility curve, except that instead of a limited amount of *money to spend to buy something*, now you have a limited amount of *resources to use to produce something*. Now you are going to decide how much of each product to produce. The more you produce of one, the less you can produce of the other.

Opportunity Cost Again?

Production possibility curves illustrate the concept of "you can't have your cake and eat it too," only maybe it would be better to say it this way:

If you use all your flour to make bread, you can't make any cakes. If you use all your flour to make cakes, you can't make any bread. The more bread you make, the less cake you can make.

Obviously? Of course. *Opportunity cost* again? Sure.

Sometimes the Production Possibility Curve Is Curved

Suppose you're running a bakery and you're using all your flour to make bread. Then you decide to produce less bread so you can make some cakes. When you shift from bread to cakes do you get back as much in cake as you give up in bread? Maybe so. But maybe not! Maybe half of your flour and ovens and pans and all are best for making bread and the other half are best for making cakes. Then you have a *curved production possibility curve*.

The graphs on the following pages explain and illustrate different kinds of production possibility curves. Each is explained on the page on which it appears. If you did a good job of learning Figure 1-1 the following graphs will be a breeze. But take your time and learn them well.

Fig. 1-2   The Straight-line Production Possibility Curve

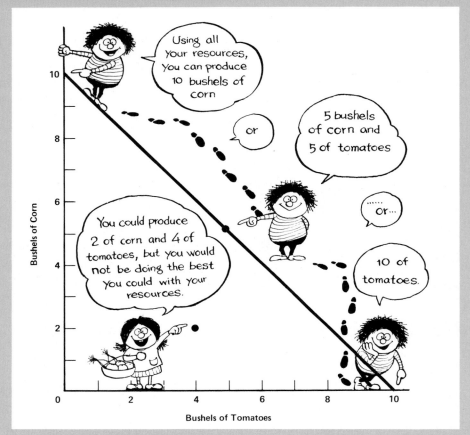

The "transformation ratio" (opportunity cost ratio) between corn and tomatoes is constant.

You have a garden plot, some gardening tools, enough money to buy some seed and fertilizer, and enough free time and energy (labor), to grow a patch of corn and/or tomatoes.

This graph shows your "production possibilities" between corn and tomatoes. It shows that the trade-off ratio (the opportunity cost) is one bushel of corn for one bushel of tomatoes, and that the ratio does not change as you shift output from one to the other. Whenever the "curve" is a straight line, it shows that the ratio does not change. It might be one-for-one, or two-for-one, but whatever it is, if the curve is straight, the ratio will not change as you shift from one product to the other.

The production possibility curve is also called the *"transformation curve"* because it shows how, through shifting your efforts and resources from one to the other, you can (in effect) "transform" corn into tomatoes. In this graph the *transformation ratio* is one for one.

Fig. 1-3 The Convex—In-sagging—Production Possibility Curve

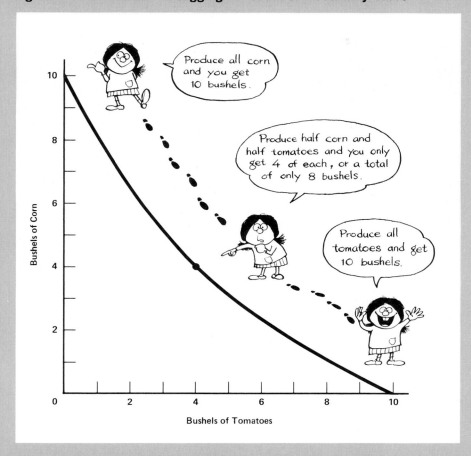

You will get the most product by producing all corn or all tomatoes but not both.

Notice that if you are producing all corn (10 bushels) and decide to produce half corn and half tomatoes, you must give up six bushels of corn (from 10 bushels, down to 4 bushels) in order to get 4 bushels of tomatoes. But then, if you decide to produce all tomatoes, you can get six more bushels just by giving up that last 4 bushels of corn.

This curve shows that you can produce more total product by specializing entirely in one product or the other. There could be several reasons for this.

Perhaps your seed, fertilizer, bug spray, etc. will cost you more if you buy in smaller quantities. Or maybe you need a big patch of one or the other for better pollination. Or maybe you work more efficiently in preparing the land, planting, weeding, and harvesting, if you specialize in one crop or the other. There are many reasons why specialization might increase your productiveness, or "productivity." More on this later.

Fig. 1-4   The Concave—Out-bulging—Production Possibility Curve

You will get the most product by growing corn in the cornfield and tomatoes in the tomato patch.

Sometimes, you can produce most by producing the best combination of products. Here's a case where half of your land and other resources are best for growing corn, and the other half are best for growing tomatoes. You get the most product by producing corn on the best corn land and producing tomatoes on the best tomato land. When your best corn-producing resources are specializing in corn, and your best tomato-producing resources are specializing in tomatoes, your total output is greatest.

Your maximum output combination is 7 bushels of each. Suppose you decide you want 9 bushels of corn. You must give up about three bushels of tomatoes to get the two extra bushels of corn. Then suppose you decide you want *all* corn. To get that 10th bushel of corn, you must give up about four bushels of tomatoes.

The Different Shapes of Production Possibility Curves

Now that you know about the different shapes of production possibility curves, let's talk about them. First, the straight-line curve. The straight-line production possibility (transformation) curve shows that your productive resources and energies are all "equally substitutable" between "product x" and "product y." The "trade-off ratio" between the two is always the same, no matter what comibination of x and y you choose.

On the straight-line curve the ratio might be one x for one y or two x for one y or ten x for one y. But whatever the ratio is, it will always remain the same no matter what combination you choose. Why? The curve is a straight line therefore its slope will be the same at all points along the line—that is at any combination of x and y you choose.

If the production possibility curve is convex—that is, if you are looking at it from the zero point and the curve is sagging down toward you—then it means you have the greatest output if you produce all of x *or* all of y. But if the curve is bulging out (concave when looked at from the zero point) that means you have some resources which are better at producing x and other resources which are better at producing y. If you want to get maximum output you must produce some of x and some of y.

The concave (out-bulging) curve is the one which best describes the production possibility for the society as a whole. Whenever a nation contains a great variety of productive inputs—land and natural resources, factories and machines, skilled and unskilled people, etc.—some of these inputs will be best at producing some things, others will be best at producing others.

The Slope of the Curve Shows the "Transformation Ratio"

Suppose the economy is running along producing at maximum output. It's producing a normal combination of "consumer goods" and "industrial products." Now suppose that for some reason the society decides it wants more output of industrial products. The output of consumer products must be cut back. If the consumer goods output is cut back, inputs will be released. These "released inputs" can be used to produce the extra industrial products the society wants.

How much must the consumer goods output be cut back? Enough to release the needed inputs to produce the extra industrial products. Of course! And how much is that? It all depends on the transformation ratio between consumer goods and industrial products.

Figure 1-5 shows that the more we cut back our consumer goods output (y) and expand our output of industrial products (x), the higher goes the opportunity cost of the extra industrial products. We must forfeit more and more of our consumer goods output flow to get each additional increase in our output flow of industrial products. Now if you'll study Figure 1-5, I believe all this will become very clear.

The Diminishing Marginal Rate of Transformation

Figure 1-5 shows that the nation can produce a lot more total output if it will produce its "usual mixture" of industrial products and consumer goods. As the combination moves away from this "most appropriate output mix," the total amount of output goes down. As we produce less consumer goods we get more industrial output. Sure. But not enough to make up for what we're losing in consumer goods output! Why not?

Why the Marginal Rate of Transformation Diminishes. As we transfer more and more labor, machines, factories, and natural resources out of the production of consumer goods and into the production of industrial products, pretty soon we get to the place where the inputs we are transferring out of consumer goods production are highly specialized. They are especially designed to be

Fig. 1-5   Production Possibility Curve for a Nation

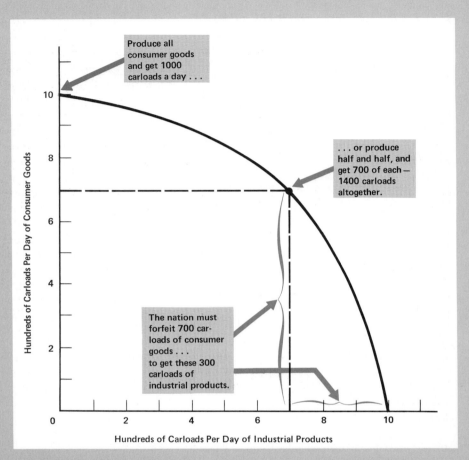

Even the nation can't have its cake and eat it too.

If we want more consumer goods, we must produce fewer industrial products. But if we want to build more factories and machines and college libraries and highways and such things, we must cut back on consumer goods.

If the society uses its best consumer-goods inputs to make consumer goods and its best industrial-goods inputs to make industrial goods, it will get a maximum total output. The further it moves away from this combination of output, the smaller the total output gets. Each move from this maximum output position means society is giving up more of one than it's getting back of the other.

very productive in making consumer goods and they aren't very good at doing anything else. For example, you can stop making canned peas and use the same farms and processing plants and people to make gear grinders. But you will lose a lot more canned peas than you will get back in extra gear grinders!

Economists call this concept the diminishing marginal rate of transformation. As you keep shifting your resources out of the production of canned peas and into the production of gear grinders, you keep getting back less and less extra gear grinders for each truckload of canned peas you give up.

See how the number of extra gear grinders keeps on diminishing? This is the reason why the production-possibility curve for a large nation will always be concave (bulging away from the zero point). The outward bulge shows that the biggest output comes when those workers and machines and resources which are best at producing industrial products are specializing in the production of industrial products. Those which are best at producing consumer goods are specializing in consumer goods.

The total output is greatest when each of society's resources is being used to produce that product which it is *most efficient* at producing—growing corn on the best corn land and tomatoes on the best tomato land; using the dairy farms to produce dairy products; using the canning plants to make canned peas instead of gear grinders.

Sometimes the Marginal Rate of Transformation Increases. Some economic units (individuals, families, businesses, small regions, or even small nations) are not very diversified. For these small units there may not be much variety in the kinds of resources available. Sometimes it might be best for such an economic unit to produce only one product—something it's good at producing—and then trade to get the other things it wants.

By specializing in this way a region or a nation can become more efficient in the production of its specialty. In this situation the production possibility curve would be convex (in-sagging toward the zero). Output would be smaller when a combination of goods is produced. You saw this in Figure 1-3.

The convex (in-sagging) production possibility curve faces most individuals. You can specialize in doing one thing and usually get a higher total output and income than if you try to spend your work time doing a variety of things. There are exceptions, but generally a person who concentrates on one profession or skill is likely to be better at it than someone who is a jack-of-all-trades.

The Transformation Curve Highlights the Economic Problem

The production possibility (transformation) curve is nothing more than an illustration of the economic problem. It highlights the concept of opportunity cost. It shows very clearly that something must be given up in order to get more of something else. The curve can be used to illustrate the basic economic choice for an individual, a business, or a society. It shows how much of one thing we must *not* have, in order that we *can* have the chosen amount of the other. The curve is an illustration of the fact that every choice involves the decision to "not get" or to "not do" or to "not have" something that we might like to get, do, or have.

Perhaps it's a bit sad to realize that all throughout our lives we (as individuals and as a society) are going to have to be constantly deciding to "not get" and "not do" some things, so that we *can* get and do certain other things. But if we always give up the things which are *least* important to us and choose to get (and do, and have) the things which are *most* important to us, then we will have no cause for regrets.

The sadness comes when we fool ourselves into thinking we can have our cake and eat it too—when we move blindly ahead doing and having the things we want without considering the opportunity costs. Then when the opportunity cost comes along and smacks us in the face, we realize we made the wrong choices—we gave up the best opportunities and settled for second best, or third best—or maybe sometimes even worse than that!

Maybe all the kids have expensive new jackets, but there's no money left for school lunches. Suddenly their parents realize that they have not economized. They have made a bad trade-off. They have "traded off" the opportunity for lunches in order to get the most expensive jackets. A little less spent on jackets and a little more spent on lunches would have made everybody happier. (Perhaps their parents need a course in "consumer economics.")

Just as individuals can make bad choices, so can businesses and other organizations. Not everybody understands "the science and the art of economizing"—of using their available resources to maximize their objectives. Not everybody has learned to plan and manage efficiently. Even the society as a whole can (and does) make unwise choices. No society has ever achieved perfection in solving its economic problem. It isn't likely that one ever will.

Some people now are questioning whether or not the United States really should have been putting so much of its resources into urban thruways, instead of building more efficient mass transit systems; some people question the wisdom of using resources in space exploration when the opportunity cost for that is some other kind of progress—maybe cleaning up the environment. Many criticize the use of resources for military purposes, charging that the opportunity cost is the chance to solve some of our pressing domestic problems—maybe the problem of the ghetto areas of big cities. Later in this book you will

get into some of these issues. But for now we must move on to the question of how the "economizing choices" are made: by individuals, by businesses, and by the society. That's what the next two chapters will be talking about. First, though, here's a little more about this new subject you're getting into—about economics.

THE ROLE OF MATH IN ECONOMICS

You probably have heard that math is often used in economics. It is. But in this book, you have nothing to fear from math. The simple graphs you studied and learned a few pages back are as high-powered as any math you will see in this book. You will see some of these graphs again, and you will see a few other mathematical things. But not many. And all will be very simple.

It is essential that you take the time to learn each graph when you come to it. If you have not yet learned the graphs in this chapter, you are now using your time unwisely. Economize your time. Stop reading this and go back and learn the graphs. If you have already learned the graphs and the concepts they illustrate, congratulations! Read on. You are ready to understand what comes next.

The graphs you have seen in this chapter illustrate the basic economic problem—the problem of "you can't have your cake and eat it too." Each of the curves shows the trade-off ratio between one thing and another. By looking at the graph you can see *exactly* how much of one thing you must give up to get an extra unit of the other. Truly, graphs can be very helpful.

Equations Can Deal with Many Variables at Once

Sometimes graphs are just great for illustrating economic concepts. But the usefulness of graphs is limited. Why? Because with graphs, it's difficult to work with more than two things at once—one on the x axis, the other on the y axis. But mathematical equations aren't limited that way. With equations you can deal with many things—with several products and inputs and other things all at the same time.

Suppose we want to deal with many things—not just "consumer goods or industrial goods" but with cars and refrigerators and sofas and raincoats and canned peas and gear grinders and lathes and milling machines and more. If we're growing corn and tomatoes, we might like to see what happens if we simultaneously use less land and more water and less fertilizer and better seed.

Economists like to try to figure out what's going to happen if the local plant shuts down—what will happen to employment, wages, grocery sales, new car sales, apartment vacancies, tax collections, highway traffic, school enrollments, welfare payments, and other things. With equations we can deal with such things. Equations can't give us all the answers. But sometimes they can help.

You Don't Need Math to Learn Economics

Math can be a powerful tool in economics. But what most people need to know about economics can be learned and understood without any more math than the simple graphs you just learned. In this book you will learn the basic concepts and you will get them integrated into your thought processes, not by working with math, but by working with words and examples that you can understand and relate to.

A solid, rigorous treatment of economic concepts does not have to be mathematical. Nor does it have to be dry or heavy or frightening. There's no cause to be apologetic about the non-mathematical approach in learning economics. The "non-math" approach is likely to generate more conceptual depth and a more thorough, more permanent, and more useful knowledge of economics than you

would gain from a more mathematical approach. Why so? One reason is that much "relevant economics" just can't be handled with math. Another reason is that very few people can think and conceptualize as well in mathematical terms as they can with familiar words, and with examples they can see and relate to.

As you are learning the economic concepts, if you have a facility with math you may find yourself translating some of the concepts into mathematical terms in your own mind. If you don't have a facility with math, that's no problem. If you major in economics, eventually you will need to use some math, but most economics majors manage to get by without using much math. What math you will need depends on what specialties in economics you choose and how far you plan to go. Be heartened by the fact that if you major in economics, much of the math you will need will come to you and may make good sense for the very first time in your advanced economics courses. Some students find it exciting to see the ways math can be used to help fathom "the economic problem."

ECONOMICS AND MATERIALISM

Some people criticize economics on the grounds that it is not concerned with human values, but with material things. Yes, economics is concerned mostly with material things—with resources and products and energy and effort and with other valuable and scarce things. But this does not mean that economists are "materialists."

Economics Doesn't Recommend Materialistic Goals

Economics doesn't tell people to go out and be materialistic. Economics only says that if you are using your "scarce things" to best achieve *your* desired objectives, you are making the right choices *for you*. Today, as throughout history, a major objective of most of the people in the world is to have more and better material things—food, clothing, shelter, medicine, transportation, tools, and other things.

It is difficult to pursue any objective, however noble or lofty, without using up some energy and effort and resources—some "material things." In a very poor nation or area (or even family) in which the people have barely enough food and other things to stay alive, *the* major objective will be to get more food and other material goods. Where there's more affluence, more resources will be used for other objectives.

Most of us in the advanced nations have quite a lot of material goods. We can go after whatever objectives we desire. Our affluence lets us do our own thing—go to college, buy luxury things, waste things, goof around any way we please.

Material Things Can Be Used for Noble Objectives

Economics is sometimes defined as "the study of how people earn their daily bread." If the objective is to earn daily bread, then economics is going to be about how people do that. Most of the efforts of most of the world's people are aimed toward satisfying their material wants—that is, toward earning their daily bread!

But what if the objective is to get to the moon or find a cure for cancer or eliminate the slums or get better teachers into the colleges? Then economics will be about how the society uses its scarce resources to try to get to these objectives. Economics has no business telling people what their objectives ought to be. Honest. It doesn't do that.

People do as they do and want what they want for a variety of personal reasons. No one (certainly no economist!) would ever be so foolish as to suggest that all people will find great satisfaction from building up piles of material goods! There are many aspects of human behavior which economics doesn't get into at all. Hopefully, the other social and behavioral sciences are making progress in these other areas.

What the economist says is this: "An individual or family or business or society will most rapidly achieve whatever it seeks to achieve if it will economize—that is, if it will conserve, and direct its scarce resources so as to attain maximum progress toward its objectives." What objectives? You name it: bigger pyramids, more food, successful military conquest, universal college education, faster cars, whatever.

Most "Good Economics" Is "Good Common Sense"

Now that you're coming to the end of your first chapter in economics, how does it strike you? Are you beginning to get the feeling that much of "good basic economics" is really "good common sense"? I hope so. Because it really is.

Economics is concerned with the kinds of choice situations you have been dealing with all your life. Economics will help you to see deeper into the choice situations which people and societies are always struggling with. If you put forth the effort, basic economic concepts and principles will become a permanent part of your way of thinking and will help you to make many of the choices you will have to make throughout your lifetime—for yourself, your family, your society. Economics, learned well, will provide lifetime support for your own good common sense. I'm happy that you decided to learn it. I think you'll be glad you did.

A WORD ABOUT THE END-OF-CHAPTER REVIEW EXERCISES

Each chapter in this book ends with a section of review exercises. Each section of review exercises contains the following:

1. a list of the *major* concepts, principles, and terms explained in the chapter;
2. a list of *other* concepts and terms mentioned in the chapter;
3. a list of all the graphs and curves explained in the chapter (if any); and
4. a few discussion questions
   (a) highlighting some of the most frequently misunderstood concepts and principles, and
   (b) relating some of the concepts and principles to the "real world."

It is likely that the educational value of each chapter (to you) will be very much determined by the amount of effort you put into the review exercises. The chapters are designed for easy reading and understanding. But beware! There's quite a long jump between *reading and understanding* a concept, and *permanently integrating the concept into your way of thinking*.

You won't get much permanent and lasting value out of just reading—not from *this* book or from *any other* book. The review exercises are designed to get you involved—to make this a genuinely educational experience for you. So

what should you do? After reading each chapter, without looking back try to do this:

1. For the major concepts and principles and terms, try to write at least two or three good sentences explaining each.
2. For the other concepts and terms, try to write a brief phrase saying what each one means.
3. For the graphs, try to draw and label each and then write a few sentences explaining what it means and why it's important.
4. For the discussion questions you might try writing out complete answers. But if you don't have time for that, at least jot down the key points which should be included in a good answer.

After you have tested yourself and practiced explaining everything, look back into the chapter to see how well you did. Then study and practice the ones you didn't do too well on. If you'll do all this you'll learn your economics well and it will serve you well. Good luck on the review exercises for Chapter 1!

REVIEW EXERCISES

● **MAJOR CONCEPTS, PRINCIPLES, TERMS** (Explain each carefully.)

economics
economizing
scarcity
the economic problem

opportunity cost
diminishing marginal utility
diminishing marginal rate
   of transformation

● **OTHER CONCEPTS AND TERMS** (Explain each briefly.)

economic value
exchange value
free good
marginal utility
expenditure possibility curve
production possibility curve
transformation curve
budget constraint line

transformation ratio
trade-off ratio
x axis
y axis
negative slope
positive slope
convex curve
concave curve

• CURVES AND GRAPHS (Draw, label, and explain each.)

The Expenditure Possibility Curve
The Straight-Line Production Possibility Curve
The Convex—In-Sagging—Production Possibility Curve
The Concave—Out-Bulging—Production Possibility Curve
Production Possibility Curve for a Nation

• QUESTIONS (Write out answers or jot down key points.)

1. Suppose all the shoe companies made a mistake and produced so many shoes that they had to lower the price to 10¢ a pair to sell them all. Would shoes still be "scarce," according to the "economics" definition of the word "scarce"? Explain.
2. If you inherited ten million dollars, you sure wouldn't have an "economic problem" then. Right? Discuss.
3. What does it mean when we talk about "transforming" consumer goods into industrial goods? That isn't *really* what happens, is it? Explain.
4. When you try to make up an expenditure budget, are you trying to solve your "economic problem"? How about when you work out a time schedule of study hours for each course? How about when the President and Congress try to work out the national budget? Are they working on "the economic problem"? Explain.
5. Can you think of any ways you might shift your own "resource uses" so as to move more rapidly toward *your* objectives? Can you think of any way your *college* might? Your family? Your local city or county government? Your nation? Think about it.

2 How Individuals and Businesses Choose: the Marginal Concept and the Science of Economics

People try to satisfy their wants, businesses try to make enough profits to survive and prosper, and the science of economics can help you to understand all this.

All of us want what we want. We all try to use the things we have—our money, time, and things—to get as much as we can of what we want. People who succeed in doing the very best they can with what they have are optimizing. "Optimizing" is doing the best you can possibly do with the limited things you have to work with. When you are optimizing, you are making as much progress as you can toward your chosen objectives.

EVERYONE WANTS TO OPTIMIZE AND ECONOMIZE

What is "optimizing"? It's using each thing you have in the best possible way—in the way that will help you the most to get to your chosen objectives. Suppose you would rather have your cake than eat it. So you keep it. You go around feeling good all day because you know you have that delicious piece of cake waiting for you. You know you have the *opportunity* to eat it any time you want to.

For you, optimizing means never running out of cake. You never eat the last piece of one

cake until you have another one to take its place. That way you always go around feeling good! See what a personal thing "optimizing" is? Different people optimize in different ways.

Optimizing Is a Very Personal Thing

I'll bet you know people who get greater satisfaction from knowing they *have* something than they could possibly get from using it up. Maybe you are one of those people. Do you always carry a $10 bill tucked away somewhere, just so you will never be broke? Only the most urgent necessity can make you spend that ten! If you are such a person, you always will have "something to fall back on" all your life. Why? Because that is what optimizing means to you. Having the $10 gives you a better feeling than you ever could get from anything you might buy with it.

If you are "optimizing," does that mean you are "economizing"? Yes, that's true. The meaning is the same, but the emphasis is different. Economizing emphasizes the *negative* side of choosing. Optimizing emphasizes the *positive* side.

> *Economizing* says: "No! I will *not* use up my money and time and scarce things for purposes that I don't really care about. I will *conserve*, so I can have things that will mean more to me in the long run."
>
> *Optimizing* says: "Yes! I *will* use each dollar and each hour and each thing I have in such a way that each will carry me as far and as fast as possible toward my objectives."

Every time you use up or spend up something, you do it for some reason. You have some objective and you would like to maximize your progress toward that objective. Economizing and optimizing mean using your scarce money, time and things to try to maximize your progress toward your objectives.

Optimizing the use of your study time means maximizing your progress in learning something. If you are using your money, time, and everything else so as to maximize whatever you want to maximize, then you are economizing and optimizing. For one person, *optimizing* the use of cake (or pancakes) might mean eating a lot. But to another person it might mean *maximizing* the quantity on hand. You'd like whole trunks full of pancakes? Ridiculous.

Each Individual, Business, and Society Tries to Optimize

As each "economic unit" decides what to do with its scarce things, it tries to maximize its progress toward its desired objectives. One person's objectives will be very different from another's. One quits work, buys a used pickup camper and sets out for distant places; another takes an extra job and starts a savings account to be able to send the yet-unborn children to college someday. Both individuals are optimizing. But their objectives differ.

Businesses usually try to make money. Unless they are able to make enough money to cover their costs, they don't survive for very long. When they're deciding which choices to make it's usually the "profit objective" they have in mind.

What about the society as a whole? The society might aim for any number of objectives. One society may produce consumer goods while another may produce more industrial goods for economic growth. A society might work for military supremacy, economic stability, economic equality, maximum individual freedom, flush toilets in every home or whatever else it wants to work for. Ultimately each society will work for the things wanted most by "the people in charge"—that is, by the people who have the power to influence the economic choices.

It's important who gets to influence the economic choices, wouldn't you say? (It sure is!) In some societies, control over the economic resources—that is, the power to decide what to do with what—is diffused among many people. In other societies this control is concentrated in the hands of one, or a few.

Each society has some kind of economic system. It's through the "economic system" that the economic choices are made and carried out. The next chapter talks about economic systems—about the organizations and procedures which different societies use to get their "economic problem" solved—to get their choices made and carried out. The remainder of this chapter explains how the economic choices are made by individuals and families and businesses.

HOW INDIVIDUALS CHOOSE

Everyone has wants and objectives. For one individual or family the wants and objectives may be carefully laid out. Another individual or family may just let things drift along and sort of "happen." How about you? Do you have a list of carefully chosen objectives? And a program for directing all your money, time and things toward your objectives? Probably not.

Still, I'll bet you know of some things you're working for. Right?

Do you mostly go for maximum immediate satisfaction? Or do you sacrifice a lot of present satisfaction and work for long-run objectives? And what are your long-run objectives? These are choices all of us must make for ourselves. That's each individual's economic problem—yours, mine, everybody's.

Individuals and Families Choose Their Own Objectives

Perhaps one family's objective is to have the biggest and nicest house in the city. They all work, deny themselves things, never take vacations. They save their money and eventually they buy the house of their dreams. After that they spend their spare time and money painting, decorating, furnishing, and working on the house. That's their chosen objective.

Another family might have maximum educational progress as their objective. Maybe they spend all their extra time and money on tuition, books, travel, and such things. They read a lot and they only cut the grass and paint the house just often enough to keep the neighbors from complaining.

You probably know people who enjoy acquiring things—automobiles and boats, or paintings and furniture and silverware. You probably also know people who don't care at all about acquiring things. They spend their spare time and money night-clubbing and partying and such. Who's right? And who's wrong? Nobody's right or wrong. These are matters of individual taste, attitude, desire. Chacun a son gout! De gustibus non est disputandum! (Let's all do our own thing!)

Poor People Don't Have Much Choice. For many people there isn't enough income to achieve any very lofty objectives. Some people spend their extra time working on extra jobs trying to make enough to pay the rent and utilities and buy groceries. Sometimes people

seem to just give up on trying to make it. They use each payday as an opportunity to have a little fun at the neighborhood bar, hoping that the finance company won't really repossess the TV set and that the landlord won't really kick them out on the street.

All these individuals and families are *trying* to use their scarce resources to maximize their satisfactions. All of us want to get as much as we can of whatever means the most to us. We all have our own (usually unconscious or partly unconscious) objectives, goals, desires, hungers, wants. All of us (sometimes thoughtfully, sometimes instinctively) use our scarce resources (income, time, tools, all of our things) to try to satisfy our desires. Some people make wise choices and are happy. Some make unwise choices and are miserable.

How Hard Do You Work at Optimizing? We must all decide how much effort we are willing to put into the task of economizing and optimizing (carefully managing) our time and money and things. People who want to get ahead—to have more things and to build some future freedom and security—must manage their resources carefully. But those who don't care so much about the future don't have to go to all that trouble. In a free society each of us gets to decide how hard we want to work and what we want to buy and how much we want to save and all that.

THEORIES OF CONSUMER BEHAVIOR: WELFARE ECONOMICS

Why do individuals make the choices they make? Various theories in economics deal with this question. One theory says that each time a person gets "an additional something," this "additional" or marginal something adds to the person's total "satisfaction," or utility. The theory says that if the marginal utility (extra satisfaction) I can get from spending ten dollars in the local tavern is greater than the "marginal utility" I can get from having the living-room rug cleaned, then I will choose to spend my ten dollars in the local tavern. That seems logical enough. It's obvious that we all would like to get as much "extra satisfaction" as possible for each dollar we spend.

If you get the most you can for each extra dollar you spend, that's the best you can do. RIGHT ?

SUPER MARKET

EXIT

Another theory of consumer behavior approaches the question a little differently. It says that when I decide not to have the rug cleaned so that I can spend my ten dollars in the neighborhood tavern, I am "substituting" (giving up) the opportunity to have the rug cleaned in exchange for the opportunity to spend the evening in the local tavern. The theory says that if I really would rather visit the tavern than have the rug cleaned (and if both cost the same) then I won't have the rug cleaned. I'll spend the evening in the tavern. I'll get the most extra satisfaction that way so that's what I'll do.

You will recognize this concept as another appearance of our old friend, opportunity cost. The opportunity cost of the evening in the tavern is the lost opportunity to get the rug cleaned. The opportunity cost is the opportunity lost. Remember? Since the evening in the tavern was more important to me, I made the right trade-off. I made the right choice for me. (But the other members of my family might disagree violently!)

Both the "marginal utility" and the "marginal rate of substitution" theories of consumer behavior have been developed into detailed complexity by economists. But the logic of the two theories is very similar and very simple.

The Marginal Utility Theory. The *marginal utility theory* says that when you spend a dollar, you'll spend it in the way you think you'll get the greatest additional satisfaction. If product x would add only a small amount of satisfaction and product y (for the same price) would add more, then you'll buy product y.

You will try to spend each dollar (and use each "unit" of your time and things) to add as much as possible to your "satisfaction," or "utility," or "progress toward your objectives." If each dollar you spend carries you as far as it possibly can toward your objectives, then by the time you've spent all your money you've done the best you possibly can! You must be achieving the highest level of satisfaction you can get. That, in a nutshell, is the idea of the "marginal utility theory" of consumer choice.

The Marginal Rate of Substitution Theory. The marginal rate of substitution theory is a way of getting at the trade-offs (opportunity costs) which each of us considers as we are choosing between two things. It says that if you can give up a little of one product and get a little of another product and end up with a higher level of satisfaction than you started with, then you are better off. That was a good move.

This theory says that we always try to cut down spending for those things which mean less to us (bring us less satisfaction, less progress towards our objectives) and increase our spending for those things which mean more to us. The idea is that people are constantly making small marginal adjustments in their spending patterns—spending less for the things that mean less to them and more for the things that mean more to them.

Both the marginal utility and the marginal rate of substitution theories describe an optimal position where the individual cannot make any further changes and come out with more "total satisfaction." When you reach this optimal position it means you have made the best possible choices for yourself. You have achieved the highest level of satisfaction, or "welfare" you can achieve. You are "faring as well" as you can with what you have to work with.

Welfare Economics: How Well the People Fare

Both the "utility" and "substitution" theories can be helpful in understanding consumer behavior. Both are included under that part of economic study usually called welfare economics—the study of what determines how "well" the people "fare." At this point it is only necessary for you to realize that what you would have guessed anyway, is really right. Our choices about how to use money, time and things, are very personal—very individual. We all try to use money, time and things to get what we want the most.

Many people (students, for example) deny themselves things in the present, hoping to build greater future opportunities for more economic choices and a better life. For other people the time horizon is shorter. They want their pleasures in the present so they follow a "live-it-up-now" philosophy. Both are trying to optimize in their own way.

Perhaps both the "miser" and the "squanderer" are making the right choices for themselves. Only they can tell. The one who best succeeds in solving this personal economic problem is the one who, after years have gone by, can honestly say: "If I had it all to do over, I would make the same choices again." But no one ever has the chance to "do it all over." So we all should hope that we luck-out, and make good choices the first time through.

The Income Decision

As we have been talking about consumer behavior we have been going along as though each person's income is fixed. In reality we can all do things to influence the size of our incomes. Each of us has the opportunity to decide how much we are willing to work and sacrifice to get more income. With more income we get the opportunity to make more choices.

More Work Can Bring More Income. Each of us must decide how we want to use our time and energies. How much of our time do we want to spend earning money? How hard are we willing to work? A person can get a quick increase in income by getting a second job "moonlighting" in the evenings or on weekends. A person who is willing to move may be able to go to another part of the country and get a higher paying job.

Another income-increasing opportunity available to the family is for more members of the family to work outside the home. In many families both husband and wife and sometimes older children take part-time or full-time jobs. If employment opportunities are available the family can get an increase in income by increasing the amount of work they do.

Savings and Investment Can Bring More Income.* Most people can increase their incomes by saving money and investing it. The more an individual or family saves and invests, the more future economic choices they will have. The higher the level of economic welfare they will be able to enjoy.

One way of saving and investing is to put money into savings accounts, bonds, mutual funds, stocks, rental housing, a small business, or some other income-producing investment. Another (more frequent) form of saving and investing occurs when people buy furniture, appliances, an automobile, and (most of all) a house. When people buy these things they are, in a sense, "saving and investing." As the years go by they will own more things. They will be able to live better. After their house and all their things are paid off, they will find they have extra income and

---

* The words "saving" and "investing" have a different meaning for the individual than they have for the economist who is analyzing the economic system. You'll find out about this later. For now, just think of "saving and investing" as "not spending up your time and money on 'current consumption' items, but using it instead for some purpose which will bring you more income or more things in the future."

greater freedom to do what they wish with their money.

Education Is One Kind of Saving and Investing. Another important way of saving and investing is by going to college or taking training courses. Investing time and money in getting an education and in developing skills is an important kind of saving and investing. Money and time invested in this way are likely to bring you much larger returns than any other investment you could make.

Further along in this book you will find out that just as the individual can enjoy increased productivity and income from saving and investing, so the nation as a whole can experience *economic growth* (increased capacity to generate output and income) by saving and investing. The "economic growth" of a nation hinges on its willingness to save and invest. But that discussion must wait until later.

In summary, each individual and each family is seeking a unique solution to a unique economic problem. Each must decide how to use up the available time, money, and things.

> How much time and effort to put into earning income? How much in education, training, building job experience? How much in household chores, community improvement, neighborly helpfulness? How much in gossiping and arguing, watching TV, outdoor recreation? Mowing lawns? Sleeping? Other things? How much money to use for food? Clothing? Housing? Education and training? Recreation? Medicine? Religious and charitable contributions? Savings and investments? Other things? Which things to use up? And which to hold on to? Sell the house and move into a mobile home? Share things? Or be stingy with things? Hide the beer when Uncle Bert comes to visit?

All these choices about how to use up the available time and money and things are highly individual decisions. De gustibus non est disputandum. Remember? All individuals and families make their own choices based on their own pattern of wishes, desires, and preferences. If you aren't making the choices which bring you maximum progress toward your objectives, then you can improve your situation by changing the way you use your time and money and things.

Time Is the Coin of Your Life

Are you spending your time and money and things in the best ways for you? Most people seem to be more careful with their money and things than with their time. It's easy to waste a lot of time. That's too bad. The poet Carl Sandburg once referred to time as "the coin of your life." He suggested that you ought to be careful how you spend your time—that if you aren't careful, other people are likely to spend it up for you. That idea is worth thinking about once in awhile. As a student, how you choose to spend your time is likely to be your most important economic problem.

MARGINAL THINKING IS ALWAYS BEST

As you look back over the previous sections of this chapter it may surprise you to find that all the "optimizing decisions"—the choices which bring the most progress toward the chosen objectives—are *marginal* decisions. The same would be true for all economic units—all people, all businesses, all organizations, all societies, all nations.

What's so important about making the right "marginal" choices? Suppose each little choice, each little move, each little bit of something used up, is used so that it does as much good as possible. If each choice leads to the best possible move in the best possible direction, then all these little "best moves" must take us to the best possible place.

If you really optimize each little bit of your time and money and things, then you're doing the best you can possibly do. Wherever you want to get to, you're getting there as fast as you can go. See the importance of making the right "little choices"?

Take Care of Your Little Choices

The wisdom of thinking marginally—of breaking down the big choices into lots of little choices—is not new. Some 200 years ago Benjamin Franklin told us that we should take care of our pennies—that if we did, our dollars would take care of themselves. You can see that the whole idea of "marginal thinking" is just good common sense, anyway. Still, it's a very important concept. Every day small businesses fail and people do foolish things just because they don't know how (or don't bother) to "think marginally."

The Business Manager Must "Think Marginally"

Making "marginal adjustments" is "fine tuning," sort of. The idea is that you start from where you are and then consider making little adjustments to see if you might come out better. Suppose you are running a factory. You ask yourself: "If I expand my output by one unit per day how much will that add to my daily cost? And how much to my daily revenue? If you think the marginal revenue will be greater than the marginal cost, you will expand your output. No matter what your situation was *before*, you are bound to be better off (make more profit) after you expand your output.

Suppose Mr. Bellino, your friendly neighborhood grocer, is thinking about spending $100 a month on advertising. How does he decide? If he thinks he will get enough extra revenue to more than cover the cost (the $100 advertising expense) then he will spend the money. If he doesn't think the advertising will pay off, he won't spend the money.

At any moment, most of a business manager's choices have already been made, at least for the time being. Mr. Bellino has already paid for his store. Most of his equipment is bought and paid for. He hasn't paid his taxes yet, but he's going to. (He doesn't have much choice about that.) What choices can he make on a day-to-day basis? Marginal choices. He makes them every day. Every hour. Every minute, even. These little moment-to-moment choices are the decisions which will determine whether his business will make money or lose money—whether he will prosper, just barely hang on, or go broke.

What are these little choices he makes? He must decide:

> whether to use a little more shelf space for Pepsi and a little less for Coke; whether to run a "special" this week on chicken or on beef; whether to run a little ad or a big one in tomorrow's paper; whether to charge more for cold beer than for warm beer; whether to extend credit to Mrs. Capozza; whether to have part-time help every evening or only on Thursday, Friday, and Saturday; whether to stock the "Bella Maria" brand of bakery products, and if so, what to move out to make room; whether to put a little sign or a big sign in the window announcing the "special" on canned peas; whether to continue to close at 11 p.m., or to stay open until midnight; and dozens of other little decisions.

All of Mr. Bellino's marginal choices are important. Some are critical. His most critical choices are likely to be the same as yours and mine. What choices? The little marginal choices about how to "spend up" each little unit of time.

> Should he spend his next five minutes sweeping the sidewalk? Catching up on his bookkeeping? Being friendly and helpful to the new customer who just came in? Painting a sign to go in the window? Planning next week's promotion? Calling several wholesalers to try to get a better price for

corned beef? Making up "Italian grinders" for the noon rush? Restocking the shelves? Or how?

If Mr. Bellino makes the right choices on most of these little marginal decisions, he is likely to have a successful, profitable business. He will serve his neighborhood well, and for that he will be rewarded with profits. But if he makes too many of the wrong marginal choices, soon his store will be up for sale. Truly, in the success of a business, it's the little things that count.

Good Enough Is Best

It's easy to see how thinking marginally applies to the business manager. It's just about as easy to see how it applies to almost any other "choice situation" you can imagine. Let's take some examples of things you're familiar with.

When you are washing the car, or the dishes, or the kitchen floor, or when you're mowing the lawn, or ironing a shirt or skirt, or studying economics, how much time and effort should you put into each task? That's up to you. But you can be quite sure that you will optimize by thinking marginally. That means *doing a job well enough to meet your own personal objectives.* (And it means *not* doing it any *better* than that.)

Perhaps for your brother an absolutely clean, shining, spotless, dust- and grease-free car, inside and out and under the hood, is just about the most important thing in the world. To him, "good enough" means perfection. Since perfection is impossible, he will never do anything in his whole life except work for and work on his beautiful car. You can't say he's wrong. But you may have a different set of objectives for yourself.

When learning economics, only **very good** *is good enough!*

You may be highly interested in studying economics and making an "A" in the course. You may also be embarrassed about driving a dirty car. So if you have an hour to burn, you will spend fifteen minutes quickly scrubbing down your car. Then you will spend the next forty-five minutes studying economics. Why? Because the "marginal satisfaction" you got from washing the car during the first fifteen minutes was highly important. The "marginal satisfaction" you would have received from spending another forty-five minutes washing the car would be very low—much lower than the marginal satisfaction you can get by spending that time studying econ.

After a person spends a certain amount of time washing the car, the extra progress begins to slow down. The same holds true for almost anything you can think of. You could spend all night studying this one page of this economics book. You could memorize it so you could quote it forward and backward. You could count the words and the letters and the commas and periods, and then diagram each sentence. You could scratch off some of the letters and run a chemical analysis to find out what kind of ink South-Western Publishing Co. uses in its economics books. With your fertile imagination you could think of ways to spend the rest of the semester on this one page! Why don't you? Because your good common sense has already told you that "good enough is best." You're thinking marginally.

How much time should you spend on each page, section, or chapter in a book? Enough to learn each "just well enough." Spend too little time and you don't learn it, so the time is wasted. Spend too much time and you're wasting time.

At first you can get increasing returns as you

study a chapter. When you begin it may not make much sense. Then later you understand it, but you don't really have a solid grasp of it. Finally, you get it all together. You know how to think about and explain and relate to the concepts. That's good enough. Quit. You will get a greater marginal return by spending your next "marginal units of time and energy" on some other subject or some other chapter or some other concept.

How much time and effort should you put into anything you do? As long as "the marginal return" you're getting is worth more to you than "the marginal effort" you're spending, you're doing just fine. As long as the additional "value" or "satisfaction" you're getting from the time and effort you're spending is *greater* than the additional satisfaction you could get from spending that time and effort in any other way, you are optimizing. That's the best you can do. You're making the best marginal choices, for you.

All Intelligent People Think Marginally

Intuitively, all intelligent people think marginally, more or less. It's just good common sense. But once in awhile it's a good idea to stop and remind ourselves that we really *do* have a choice about how to spend each five minutes during each day, how to spend each dollar we have, how to use each thing we have—and that success in college (and in life) depends very much on how wisely we make these little choices.

To "think marginally" means to make each little choice so it will do you the most good. It means each time you spend each extra bit of effort or time or money or anything, make it do the best it can, for you. It means to optimize the use of everything you have to work with. The importance of making each decision "at the margin" and of concentrating on this "marginal trade off" is easy to see, once you start to think about it.

In a business enterprise, "marginal decision-making" is crucial. The successful business manager thinks marginally. You can be certain of that! The next section talks about that—about how businesses make their choice decisions.

HOW BUSINESSES SOLVE THEIR ECONOMIC PROBLEM

Each business is constantly facing choices. The business manager must constantly be trying to use all the buildings, machines, equipment, raw materials, management and workers' skills and everything else in the best possible ways. The *best* ways are the ways that help most to achieve the objectives of the business.

What Are the Objectives of a Business?

A few minutes ago when we were talking about how individuals and families make their choices, we dodged the question of "objectives." Each person's wants and objectives and goals are unique. You chase your rainbow and I'll chase mine. Chacun a son gout, and all that. Remember? So whatever people consider to be most important to them, those are the objectives which will guide their choices.

Suppose we took the same approach in trying to understand how business decisions are made. Would that be bad? You bet it would be bad! A whole major segment of basic economics would collapse! The part of economics we call "the theory of the firm" (the theory that explains "how businesses choose") would collapse. Then our whole "theoretical model" of how an economic system works would go down the drain! Let me explain why.

Businesses are the ones who actually make the decisions about which inputs to use and which products to make. If we can't understand how businesses choose which (and how many) inputs to use, and which (and how many) products to make, then we can't understand what's going on in the economic system! Now take it one more step. If we don't know what the specific objective of each business is going to be, then there's no way we can figure out what that business is going to do—how it will behave in any given set of conditions and circumstances, or how it will respond to changes.

We economists had better be able to fill in the blank in this sentence: "The objective of every business firm is to _____." If we can't, a lot of economists are going to have to "go out of business"! So you may be sure that we *can* fill in the blank. What's the objective of every business? To *maximize profits*. In our "model theory of the business firm" that's what it is, anyway. But is it really?

Do Businesses Really Try to Maximize Profits?

The "profit maximization assumption" is useful. It lets us know exactly what choices a business will make: which (and how many) inputs it will hire and which (and how many) products it will produce.

Business Decisions Reflect Various Objectives. But is maximum profit really the objective of all businesses? Actually, no. Business decisions are based on a variety of different motives. Businesses undertake civic projects, develop playgrounds, install antipollution devices, give guided tours for students, and do other things which add to their costs but which bring them no immediate revenues.

Perhaps we might say that the businesses are trying to maximize their "long-run" profits. Maybe such things as keeping the air and water clean and keeping the employees and their families happy will pay off in the long run. Perhaps so. Still, no matter how we might "nudge it" to try to make it fit our "theory of

the firm," most civic-minded business behavior just can't be explained in terms of the profit maximization assumption.

Large modern corporations are owned by thousands of stockholders. Each corporation is operated by a board of directors and a group of executives who respond (more or less) to the wishes of the major stockholders. Some of the stockholders may want the business to make the highest possible profits, right now. Others may be more interested in long-run stable growth of the firm, of the industry, and of the economy.

Some stockholders and directors and executives and managers may be more interested in seeing a cleaner environment or a general improvement in the employment conditions in the city where the plant or the corporate headquarters is located. Some may even want to maximize the number of Democrats or relatives or blacks or Catholics or pretty girls working in the local office. Some may even want to maximize the number of business trips to Hawaii!

How Badly Are Profits Needed? In the real world the motives which guide business decisions will differ from time to time and from one business to another. A business on the verge of bankruptcy will be much more interested in making immediate profits than will one which is embarrassed by the fact that its profits are already so high that the labor union is demanding a big wage increase.

Some businesses have more leeway than others. But you may be sure that *no business can afford to ignore the question of whether or not it is going to make a profit.* All businesses have costs. The costs are usually almost as high as (and sometimes higher than) the revenues coming in. This means that profit is usually small. Losses are not unusual. Often the owners who have invested in the business do not receive as much return on their money as they would receive in savings accounts or on government bonds. It isn't unusual for business owners, during bad years, to receive no return at all. Also don't forget that thousands of businesses go broke every year.

Business Profits Are Usually Small. Most businesses operate very close to the break-even point. If anything goes wrong, they find themselves fighting for survival. All businesses face this problem. The giant Penn-Central Company went into bankruptcy in 1970. Lockheed Aircraft Corporation was hovering close to bankruptcy during 1971. One of Britain's best known and most highly thought of firms—Rolls-Royce—declared bankruptcy in 1971. How can such things happen? Simply by letting costs get too high or revenues too low.

Making a profit is not the only objective of businesses, true. But the need to make a profit certainly can't be ignored. For the business no other need or objective is as universal, as inescapable, as constantly nagging as the need to make profits and to avoid losses. Why? Because the survival of the business depends on it.

Suppose a business is faced with a choice between using or doing or making or buying or selling one thing ("choice x") or another ("choice y"). If "choice x" looks more profitable than "choice y," which do you think the business will choose? Choice x? Probably. Not always, but usually.

The profit maximization assumption really isn't exactly true in the real world but it's true enough to be very useful. It's closer to the truth than anything else we can think of.

In the *economists'* "model world" each business decision is *always* made on the basis of the expected effect on profits. Suppose a business could expand its output a little and add a little to its profits. Would it do that? Sure! Suppose it could hire another worker and make more profits. Would it? Of course. But what if hiring a worker would *reduce* the profits? Would the business do that? Not a chance! (See how the "profit-maximization

assumption" lets us say *exactly* what the business will do?)

The Idea of "Marginal Profit"

The economist would say it this way: "When faced with a choice, the business will make every move which is expected to bring a marginal profit, and will reject every choice which is expected to bring a marginal loss." *Marginal profits add to total profits* (or subtract from losses). *Marginal losses subtract from total profits* (or add to losses). The more marginal profits the business can get, the larger its total profit will be.

All we have to do is figure out whether a certain move will bring a "marginal profit" or a "marginal loss." Then we can tell right away whether the business will make that move.

The "Choice Decisions" of Businesses. The "choice decisions" of businesses center around such questions as: Which product(s) should we produce? How much of it (of each) should we produce? Which kinds of inputs (labor, resources, machinery, etc.) should we use? How much of each kind? When should we add more inputs? Or cut back some? Should we build a larger factory? Maybe initiate an employee training program?

Most of these choices (and many more) are facing most businesses all the time. How do businesses decide about these things? How do they choose? In our "profit maximizing, model world" they make all of the moves which they think will be *profitable*. They reject all the others.

Each Business Tries to Economize and Optimize

Each business that seeks maximum profit will always try to produce more valuable outputs and use less valuable inputs. Each business tries to achieve a high level of efficiency—that is, to produce as much as possible (the most valuable outputs) while using up as little as possible (the least expensive inputs). This will make the total profit (the value of the outputs minus the cost of the inputs) as high as possible. Obviously.

Each business is constantly trying to optimize the use of its inputs. The most expensive inputs will be used as sparingly as possible. Cheaper, more plentiful inputs will be used whenever possible to replace the more expensive, scarcer inputs. Businesses are always trying to develop better machines and equipment to try to increase their outputs and cut down on their costs.

Marginal "Value Product" and Marginal "Input Cost"

A business is always ready to buy any kind of new machine that will more than "pay its way." The same is true about hiring labor and buying materials or other inputs.

Suppose you're a business manager and you're thinking about taking on an extra input (worker, machine, or whatever). If you expect the extra input to "pay off" (in terms of reduced cost or increased output value, or both) then, sure enough, you will take on the extra input. But suppose you think the input is going to cost you more than it's worth. What then? You won't buy. Common sense again, right?

Suppose you can hire a worker for $20 a day. If the worker will increase the output value by $25 a day, that's a good deal. Will the worker get the job? Sure.

Economists say it this way: If the marginal "value product" you get from hiring another worker ($25) is greater than the marginal "input cost" you pay ($20), then you should hire the extra worker and get the marginal profit ($5). If you do, total profit will be $5 higher (or total losses $5 less) than before.

Why are we talking about "value product"? When a business buys or hires an extra unit of an input, what the extra worker or other input really adds is output—more goods—more

"physical" product, not more "value" product. Right? Of course.

But when you're in business do you care about the number of extra units of the "physical" output? Not really. What you care about is how much value is going to be added. How much will the total revenue go up? That's what you want to know. So that's why we talk about marginal "value product." It's the extra "value product" that pushes up the total revenue and gives you your marginal profit. And that's what the profit-maximizing business cares about.

Suppose the marginal "value product" is less than the marginal "input cost." Suppose the extra worker would only add $15. What then? The extra worker would not be hired because the marginal "value product" ($15) is less than the marginal "input cost" ($20). There would be a marginal loss ($5). Total profit would be $5 smaller (or total losses $5 larger) than before.

When you're running a business you don't mind adding to your costs—not so long as you are adding more to your revenues! You don't mind having your revenues go down, either—not so long as your costs are going down more. It's not how big your total revenue or total cost is that matters. It's the difference between the two—that is, the profit (or loss) that counts.

When is the business maximizing its profits? Think back to the consumer spending decision—about how people keep making little marginal adjustments. As long as there's a chance to make a marginal adjustment and add some satisfaction, you'll keep doing it. And you'll keep moving to higher levels of satisfaction.

When do you get as high as you can? Maximum satisfaction? When you have taken advantage of every opportunity to make a change and add satisfaction. When each dollar is being spent so as to bring you the greatest possible satisfaction, that's the best you can do. What the business does is not so different from that.

The business is maximizing profits only when it has taken advantage of every available opportunity to add marginal profits. Of course! As long as there's a chance to spend $20 and get back $25 (marginal profit $5) the business will do so. The business keeps making marginal adjustments of inputs and outputs as long as the adjustments bring marginal profits. But when there's no more chance to make an adjustment and come out with a marginal profit—that is, when the "marginal profit opportunity" drops to zero—that's when the business is maximizing it's profits.

When a positive "marginal profit opportunity" exists, the business is not maximizing profits. It can get more profits by taking advantage of the marginal profit opportunity. Only when all "marginal profit opportunities" have been taken advantage of—when "marginal profit opportunity" on any move the business might make, would be zero—only then will the business be maximizing its profits. When it gets to that point, that's the best it can do.

Business Managers Need to Understand Economic Concepts

It takes more than an understanding of basic economic concepts to be a successful business manager. On the other hand, no one is likely to be very successful in business without a pretty good understanding of basic economic concepts—either through common sense, or from education, training, or experience. Usually it's good to have some combination of all of these.

Each business will strive for success. The one that produces the right quantities of the right products while keeping costs low enough will succeed. The successful, profitable business will grow, hire more people, build more plant space, buy more machines and add to the growth of the economy. The unprofitable business will fire employees and reduce output. Unless someone finds out what's

wrong and does something about it, the business will go broke.

There are many reasons for success in business, just as there are many reasons for success in life. But in both cases the answer rests to a very large extent on the way the economic problem is solved. Success for each of us (whatever it means to each of us) depends on our making the right choices about what to do with what we have to work with.

The most successful people are the ones who do the best job of economizing and optimizing. They are the ones who make the wisest choices about how to "spend up" their scarce time and money and things. It's true that sometimes people are just plain lucky. But I expect the people who think marginally usually come out ahead of the rest.

The Marginal Approach Doesn't Ensure the Best Choices—But It Can Help

Perhaps Benjamin Franklin wouldn't mind if we borrow his idea and say it this way: "Take care of your little choices, and your big objectives and goals will take care of themselves." That's good economics. But recognize that thinking marginally will not always make things come out the way you expected. The marginal approach is essential in making intelligent choices, but it can't insure you (or a business manager, or your college president, or the President of the United States) against making wrong choices.

Throughout this chapter you've been reading about choosing by people and by businesses. That's important. But the issue of choice-making by the society as a whole is just as important—in some ways maybe even more important. That's what the next chapter is about. But before you go on into that there's something else you are ready for now.

So far in this book you've been getting a very personal view of basic economic concepts and principles. Throughout this book you'll be getting a personal view of economics. I think you'll understand it better that way. But economics can be (sometimes *must be*) approached very impersonally. After all, economics is a social science—and a very highly developed one at that!

Economics has gone farther in developing scientific techniques of analysis than have any of the other social sciences. Since 1969 several distinguished economists have received Nobel prizes for their scientific work in economics. So let's spend a few minutes talking about economics as a science.

A LOOK AT THE SCIENCE OF ECONOMICS

Why must we assume that businesses always try to maximize profits? Because we can't understand the choice decisions of a business unless we know what the *objectives* are. But what about the objectives of individuals?

Economics as a science tries to explain people's economic *behavior*. To do that, we must know (or assume we know) what people's objectives are. So far in this book you've read a lot about consumer behavior—about economizing and optimizing and all that. In fact you have read a lot of economic theory. All this theory is based on certain assumptions.

It's time now to take a look at these assumptions. Then you need to know something about the *techniques* of scientific economic analysis. Also, you need some insight into how the science of economics helps in working out economic policies. And finally you need to be cautioned about some special times when you *really need* the science of economics because otherwise your common sense might (probably would) let you down! You'll be reading about all those things in this section.

Basic Assumptions About How People Behave

Economics begins by assuming that *people want things* and that *the amounts of these things are limited*. That's easy to believe. Secondly, economics goes on to assume that

people try to *maximize utility*—that people *really will try to improve their "satisfaction levels."* That's fairly easy to believe too.

A third assumption is that *people are rational*. For centuries economists have talked about the fictional "economic man." It's the idea of a "perfectly rational person" who always makes all choices so as to maximize utility. Such a totally rational person would always choose the least cost ways of getting or making something and would always spend money in the absolutely most efficient way to maximize utility. Such a person would always budget very carefully—would always optimize and economize all the time.

Our economic theory assumes that *work is unpleasant* and that people will try to avoid it. Also it assumes that our *wants are insatiable*—that we'll always find something to want more of.

In the theoretical world of "total economic rationality" *each person will compete with others* to get ahead. I will offer more to buy something before you get a chance at it; I will undercut you and take your customers. Personal feelings of kindness or thoughtfulness for others never have any influence on a person's behavior in this dog-eat-dog world of "let the devil take the hindmost"!

Pure economic theory of human behavior is based on all these assumptions. Is it all true? No. Not exactly. But is it close enough to the truth to help us to get some understanding of how people behave? Yes. At least we think so. If it isn't, then there goes a big chunk of our scientific economic theory down the drain! You can see how the things you have been reading are based on these assumptions. We think there's enough truth in these "laws of behavior" to help us to understand better why people do some of the things they do.

Natural Constraints

Economics as a science also assumes certain things about nature. Scarcity is the basic assumption. A lot of economic theory is concerned with how people and societies go about overcoming these natural limitations—trying to reduce the constraints of nature.

Back in Chapter 1 you saw production possibility curves. These curves illustrate the economist's conception of natural constraints. If you want to grow more corn you must grow less tomatoes. Remember? If the nation wants more industrial products it must be satisfied with fewer consumer goods. Not only that. The "rate of transformation" of one product for another changes as more of one and less of the other is produced. These ideas are based on the economist's assumptions about these natural constraints—about these natural limitations which *restrict the supply of material things* and keep things scarce.

Are our assumptions about nature accurate enough to provide a base on which to build a science of economics? We think so. Much of what we assume about the nature of things can be proven. But most of what we assume about the behavior of people cannot. Still, it seems that people tend to act the way we assume they act—trying to maximize utility, and all that. Now, what about our techniques of scientific economics?

Techniques of Economic Science: Principles, Theories, Models, Laws

Economic science is concerned with trying to find out what causes what. If you know "what causes what" then you can tell "what will happen if . . . " If you understand the law of gravity (which could also be called the "principle of gravity" or the "theory of gravity" or the "gravity model") then you could figure out that if you drop a cannon ball and a BB shot off the Leaning Tower of Pisa at the same time, unless something happens to interfere, both will hit the ground at the same time.

In economics, if you understand the law of demand (which could also be called the "principle of demand" or the "theory of demand" or the "demand model") you know that if you're selling tomatoes by the roadside and you put up a sign announcing a big price cut, unless something happens to interfere, you will sell more tomatoes than if you hadn't lowered the price.

Economic science tries to find out things like this. It tries to discover systematic patterns of relationships: of what causes what, of what would happen if . . . , of what depends on what. Economists try to find out these cause and effect (or "functional") relationships concerning production, output, prices, buying, selling—about lots of things.

Economic Models

When economic science discovers a relationship between two or more things, then a model (or principle, theory, or law) can be stated. What is an economic model, or theory? It's a simplified picture of reality that tells how some things influence other things. The model leaves out irrelevant variables—that is, it leaves out the "static" of the real world so that we can clearly see what we want to see—so we can see how some things cause other things to happen. All scientists do things like this. For example, the physicists build their law of gravity in a vacuum.

The Ceteris Paribus Assumption. We have our own special "vacuum" in economics. We call it the *ceteris paribus* assumption. Meaning what? Just this: "Everything must freeze!" If everything else remains exactly the same, then we can see how the things we're interested in are influencing each other. Once we understand how one thing (A) influences another (B), then we can predict what will happen to B, if A changes. But that depends on the *ceteris paribus* assumption! Suppose some stronger influences (C, D, and E) all change while A is changing. Then what will happen to B? We don't know.

For example, when you cut the price of your tomatoes we can say "*ceteris paribus*, you'll sell more." Ah, but suppose there's a story on the radio today warning people not to eat local tomatoes because of bugs. So after you cut the price nobody buys any more. People buy less! Does that mean your demand model is wrong? No. It just means "other things weren't frozen." The "other things" had more influence on your customers than the price cut did!

Suppose you dropped a fluffy little feather and a BB shot at the same time out of the little window at the top of the Washington Monument on a windy day. The law of gravity says they'll both hit the ground at the same time. In a vacuum, they would. But will they? Of course not.

Here you can see one of the problems of economic science. The economist may have the best model in the world. But it's always based on assumptions about things staying equal, or about other things changing in a predictable way. But the real world is a very complex place! Things are always changing in unpredictable ways. Some of these changes are bound to cause the results to come out differently than the economist's model would predict.

How Do Economists Build Models? How do economists find out about the cause and effect relationships they need to know to build models about things? We can't easily set up laboratory experiments to find out these things. One technique is to go back and dig up old data about past happenings.

Suppose you want to find out how buyers respond to changes in the price of chicken. You could go back and find a time when the price of chicken dropped from 60¢ to 30¢ a pound, and you could find out how much chicken was being bought before and after the price went down. Then you might build a model saying that when the price of chicken falls from 60¢ to 30¢ a pound, consumers will increase their purchases of chicken by 100 percent.

Of course your model might not work at all next time. Maybe last time the price of beef

was going up. Maybe that was mostly why people bought so much more chicken! But economists, especially with the wonders of modern computers, can take a lot of different things into consideration when they build their models.

I'm happy to report that economists using what we call "econometrics" really are building some good models these days. That's one of the reasons economics is the one social science which has been recognized as a science and why the Nobel Prize has been awarded to distinguished economists! Just in the years since World War II economists really have come quite a long way in learning how to build good economic models.

Exactly What Is an Economic Model? An economic model is the same thing as an economic theory or principle or law, depending on what you want to call it. Economists talk about the "principle of diminishing marginal utility" and the "law of demand" and the "theory of the firm." All of these are models: statements of "what causes what" or "what would happen if . . ." or "functional relationships between dependent and independent variables."

An economic model can be stated in an equation which shows the relationships among the variables. For example, in the case of the effect of a price cut for chicken on the sales of chicken, we might use shorthand symbols and say:

Sales of chicken (Sc)	is =	a function of f	the price of chicken (Pc)

This is a model to predict *sales* of chicken, based on *changes in the price* of chicken.

Suppose you know the price of chicken isn't the only variable you should take into consideration in figuring out chicken sales. Maybe you would also like to include the price of beef (Pb) and the price of fish (Pf) and the rate of employment (E) in your local area. Could the economist build a model which would include all these variables? Sure.

It won't be easy to figure out how much each one of these variables will affect the sales of chicken, of course. So it won't be easy to build an accurate model. Some statistical analysis and some "sophisticated guessing" will be necessary. But it's easy enough to write the model in shorthand symbols:

$$Sc = f(Pc, Pb, Pf, E)$$

This says: sales of chicken (Sc) depends on (f) the price of chicken (Pc), the price of beef (Pb), the price of fish (Pf), and the level of employment (E) in your area.

Economic Models and Economic Policy

In recent years there has been a great increase in the use of economic models, both as a guide to business decisions and as a guide to national economic policy. Businesses use models to try to predict prices and quantities of various inputs and outputs. Surely the models must be useful. Otherwise the economists who build and run them for the businesses wouldn't be so well paid!

In government there are economic model builders just about everywhere you look. They are predicting everything from next year's income tax receipts to the effects of agricultural policies on grain prices. Government economic policies regarding taxing, spending, and the money supply are constantly being guided by economic models. Models help to predict long-range pollution problems, water needs, expenditure requirements for various programs and in fact just about everything you can think of.

Economic models cannot predict with complete accuracy, of course. But usually the predictions are better than we would be likely to get *without* the models. So it seems that "the day of the economist" has arrived! It isn't that

economists and their models are always so accurate—because certainly that isn't true. It's just that what the economists are doing is so much better than nothing!

Now aren't you glad you're in economics? And who knows? Maybe you'll get turned on and become an economist. It seems to me that there are lots of *worse* ways to go through life!

HIDDEN FALLACIES: SOMETIMES COMMON SENSE CAN LET YOU DOWN!

Now we need to talk about one final thing: About hidden fallacies that can slip into economic reasoning and lead people to the wrong conclusions. There are some things in economics that are so tricky that unless you are aware of and very careful of these pitfalls your intelligent common sense is likely to lead you astray. We need to talk about these "tricky pitfalls."

Unconscious Preconceptions

It's almost impossible to begin the study of economics without already having a lot of firm ideas about economic things: maybe about government spending, government debts, business profits, labor unions, taxes, zoning laws, tariffs, immigration policies, minimum wage laws, and lots of other things. Your preconceived ideas will make it difficult for you to understand things in economics which appear to conflict with what you believe. See the problem?

As you study this book, try to understand what's being discussed before you decide to reject it. Ultimately, reject anything you wish. Of course. But please: Try to understand it first. Fair enough? Good. You'll learn a lot more economics that way.

Post Hoc Ergo Propter Hoc

This is a Latin phrase that simply means "it happened *after this* (post hoc) *therefore* (ergo) it happened *because of this* (propter hoc)."

This is bad reasoning anywhere you find it—in economics and everywhere else. But in economics it's especially common—and especially dangerous.

This is the idea of the rooster who wakes up in the morning and crows, and then the sun comes up. He's sure that if he overslept the sun would never rise! Or if a black cat crosses your path and a few minutes later you stumble into a mud puddle, blame it on the cat. Right? No one with a grain of common sense would fall for that brand of logic! But in economics the fallacy isn't always so easy to see.

The problem in economics is that sometimes it's hard to be sure what causes what. Last year the fishing trawlers caught more fish. This year there are fewer fish. Is it because more were caught last year? Without further investigation, no one knows. In 1975 the Federal government gave out some tax rebates. Then the economy improved. Did the tax rebates cause the economy to improve? Without further investigation, no one knows.

It's so easy to say "Look what happened after we did that, last time!" But the trouble is this: *there are so many variables at work all the time.* Unless you know something about the situation other than "one thing followed the other," you really can't conclude anything. So please: Be extremely careful not to fall into the *post hoc ergo propter hoc* trap. And be very careful when someone comes to you with a *post hoc ergo propter hoc* argument about something in economics!

The Fallacy of Composition

In economics there are several things which are true when looked at from the point of view of an individual but which are false when looked at from the point of view of the entire economy, or nation. For example, suppose a farmer clears more land and produces more corn. Does the farmer get more income when the extra corn is sold? Sure. But suppose all the farmers in the country clear more land and produce more corn. What then? The corn price would collapse. All the corn farmers would go broke!

If I can get a lot of money somehow (inherit it or borrow it from a bank or maybe print it up myself in my bedroom) then I can buy more things and live a lot better—bigger house, bigger car, bigger boat, long vacation trips—and I won't have to work anymore. Great! But suppose everybody did this. What would happen then? The economy would collapse. We would all starve to death!

Suppose the government printed up $50,000 in $100 bills and gave it all to you. What a great day for your economic situation that would be! But suppose the government did that for *everybody*. What then? Nobody would be helped. Everybody would be a lot worse off. Probably the monetary system would collapse and the economy would collapse.

This "fallacy of composition" works the other way, too. Free trade can bring great benefits to the people of the society, as you will find out in Chapter 4. But does that mean *everyone* in the economy is going to receive great benefit from free trade? Of course not. It may mean that the people who are working at producing sugar beets or hand tooled leather belts or assembling the movements of watches will lose their jobs. The businesses will go broke!

Here's another kind of example: What about comparing the individual's budget with the federal government's budget? If the government budgeted like an individual, that would be foolish. If an individual budgeted like the federal government, that would be madness! You'll find out all about this later.

Loaded Terms

Another problem is that often the words we use to express things in economics, aren't "pure." Many words have subtle "side effect" meanings. Suppose the government is going to get involved in a new kind of program. The program might be referred to as "government intervention in the free private enterprise system." Or it could be referred to as a "government injection of investment capital for the development of the nation's natural resources." See what a different feeling you get when it's said one way or the other?

Do we "exploit" resources? Or do we "develop them for useful purposes for the society"? Suppose the government levies taxes on high-income people and gives the money to poor people. Is that called "taking money from productive people to support unproductive ones"? Or is it a program of "transfers of money to offset the extremes of income inequality"?

In this book I would like to keep all the words "clean"—no subtle meanings. I don't suppose I'll really succeed in doing it. But I promise to try.

What's True in Prosperity May be False in Depression

Suppose the economy has full employment. It's operating on its production possibility frontier. So if we want more industrial products we must give up some consumer goods.

But suppose the economy is operating below capacity. There's unemployment everywhere. What then? Then it's possible to have more industrial products and more consumer goods too!

What about the people who are printing up money in their bedrooms? If the economy is seriously depressed, maybe their extra spending will be good for the economy! Do you suppose the economy could be stimulated and prosperity regained if everyone would print up a few dollars and go out and spend them? Think about that for awhile!

The "hidden fallacies" in economic reasoning really are good at tripping people up. But after reading about them I'm sure you'll be careful about these tricky pitfalls. When someone comes to you with an important bit of economic truth maybe you'll say: "Okay, so it's true. But: true, assuming what?"

Now you're at the end of Chapter 2. You know quite a lot about what economics is all about. You know quite a lot about the problem of choosing and about how people and businesses choose. You'll find out a great deal more about both these things later in this book. But the next thing you need to know is this: How does the society as a whole get its choices made? That's what you'll find out in the next chapter.

But before you go on, be sure you have a good understanding of the choice decisions of individuals and businesses. And be sure you have a clear picture of the science of economics. Also you might want to spend some time with the Review Exercises. Do, if it helps. Don't if it doesn't. Think marginally.

REVIEW EXERCISES

● MAJOR CONCEPTS, PRINCIPLES, TERMS (Explain each carefully.)

the "marginal utility" theory of consumer behavior
the "marginal rate of substitution" theory of consumer behavior
"thinking marginally"
the profit-maximization assumption
economics as a science
the fictional "economic man"
economic principle, theory, law, model

● **OTHER CONCEPTS AND TERMS (Explain each briefly.)**

optimize	*ceteris paribus*
economize	econometrics
welfare economics	*post hoc ergo propter hoc*
theory of the firm	fallacy of composition
marginal profit	unconscious preconceptions
marginal loss	loaded terms
marginal "value product"	truth in prosperity may be
marginal "input cost"	false in depression

● **QUESTIONS (Write out answers or jot down key points.)**

1. For many people, as the years go by life seems to get a little easier. Do you suppose it might be because they have been "saving and investing"? Explain.

2. Think about "optimizing and economizing" as it applies to your choices
   (a) about using your free time, and
   (b) about using your money.
   Which times do you think you're trying to optimize? Which times do you think you're trying to economize? Discuss.

3. A producer, thinking marginally (as all good producers do), is always thinking about cutting back or speeding up the daily rate of output.
   (a) Suppose the marginal input cost of expanding the present rate of output would be less than the marginal value product. What should the producer do? Why?
   (b) Suppose the marginal input cost would be greater than the marginal value product. What should the producer do? Why?

4. One of the things about a "free society" is that each individual has the right to make the wrong choices. Are you making any of the wrong choices for yourself? Is there any way that you might think marginally and shift some of your own time and energy from one direction to another and come out better? Think about it.

5. Explain what economic models are, how they work, and how economic models can be helpful in developing and revising national economic policies.

3 How Societies Choose: Tradition, Command, the Market Process, and Real-World Economic Systems

The production and distribution choices can be made by social custom, government control, or the market process.

The economic concept "you can't have your cake and eat it too" is as true for the society as a whole as it is for each individual or business. In each society people are busy growing food and making things. These same people at the same time are eating up, using up, and wearing out these things. Which things to grow and make? And then, who gets to have them and use them up? These are the questions every society somehow must answer.

Every Society Must Solve Its Economic Problem

Every society which has ever existed has had to solve its economic problem—has had to face these resource-use questions and come up with some answers. The approach differs from one society to another, and from one time to another. But before we talk about the different ways societies solve their economic problem, let's talk about the three basic questions which every society must answer—the three basic kinds of choices which every society somehow must make. When these three basic questions are answered, then for that society, that gives the answer to their economic problem. It may not be the "best" answer. But it is *that society's* answer.

EACH SOCIETY MUST MAKE THREE BASIC ECONOMIC CHOICES

The economic problem of the society can be broken down into three basic questions. First: the output question—what to produce? Second: the input question—which resources to use? And third: the distribution question—who gets to have what share of the output? Each of these questions needs to be explained. Then we need to talk about ways of getting the answers. That's what this chapter is about.

The Output Question: What Are We Going to Produce?

What are we going to produce? Of all the possible things we might spend our time and resources making, which ones will we choose to make? Will we put more effort into building houses? or into growing food? What kind of food? grain? or beef? Or perhaps we should erect monuments to our ancestors. Or paint beautiful pictures and make beautiful music

What to make? What resources to use? And then who gets to have how much? I dunno....

and write books. Will we produce military tanks? or farm tractors? automobiles? or trucks? if automobiles, big cars? or little cars? school buildings? or hospitals?

The list of possible products could be endless. Yet these choices must be made for each society. The question is: Of all the thousands (or millions) of things we *might* use our scarce resources to produce, which things and how much of each *will* we produce? The quantities of some things—canned mud from Mississippi—will be zero. Other things—perhaps bread—will be assigned higher priority. Sometimes the choices will not be easy. But somehow this question "what to produce?" must be answered.

The Input Question: Which Resources Will We Use?

Which resources will we use in making our chosen products? Almost anything can be produced using different combinations of inputs. Roads could be paved with straw, wood chips, boards, gravel, leather, bricks, concrete, asphalt, steel, copper, gold, economics books, or almost anything you could think of. Ridiculous? Well, for some of the examples, yes. Yet it illustrates the fact that almost everything could be produced in several different ways. Somehow it must be decided which resources will be used to produce which things.

Just as we can use different materials, we can use different sources of power and different production methods. For power we can use electricity, steam, draft animals, internal combustion engines, manpower, the wind, water, or sunshine. If we want to make steam we can use wood, coal, oil, gas, nuclear energy, or buffalo chips. As tools we can use

steam shovels or hand shovels, conveyor belts or wheelbarrows, paint brushes or paint sprayers, farm tractors or hand plows, adding machines or computers. To travel or to move things we can use trucks or boats or railroads or pipelines or airplanes or horses or pogo sticks. Again, the list of possibilities is endless. And again, some of the alternatives are a little bit ridiculous.

No society would have any trouble making the obvious choices. No one is going to pave roads with gold and no one is going to use a steam shovel to plant tulip bulbs. But most choices aren't this easy. Suppose we're trying to decide if we should pave the roads with crushed granite, or natural gravel from the gravel pit, or tailings from the local copper mine—or perhaps some mixture of all three. Now the best choice is not so obvious.

These close choices—where the little marginal "fine-tuning" decisions must be made—are difficult. Should we use a little more land and a little less fertilizer to produce our grain? Should we produce a little more corn and a little less wheat? Should we use migrant labor? or harvesting machines? More account clerks? or a computer?

If the people are going to enjoy the most efficient society—if the uses of all the resources are to be optimized toward the society's objectives—then somehow the society must get the best possible answers to these questions. We must produce just the right amounts (proportions) of just the right *output products*. We must use just the right amounts (proportions) of just the right *inputs* in making each product. You can see that in a modern society these choice questions can get very complex! But before we go into that we need to talk about the third basic choice.

The Distribution Question: How Much Will Each Person Get?

Who's going to get all those products that are being made? How much of the output are *you* going to get? And how much of it will belong to me? Most people are going to want more than they are going to get. But we can't *all* have more. There's just no way!

How will we decide who gets how much? Will the men get the most and the women have to beg the men for a share? Maybe we will share it all equally among everyone who is over 21, and let all the young people beg for their shares. Or why not let a larger share go to everyone who voted for the winner in the last election?

There are lots of ways we could divide up the output. A smaller share for short people and a larger share for tall ones? A larger share for educated people and a smaller share for ignorant ones? A larger share for native-born citizens and a smaller share for immigrants? Larger shares for the diligent ones? the tricky ones? the ones whose mothers or fathers got large shares?

How about larger shares for the ones who produce the most? or for the ones who make the most noise and threats? or for everyone who has a monopoly in something? How are we going to decide?

You can see that the question of "who is going to get how much" can get to be pretty complex! But complex or not, the answers have to be found. Somehow the society must devise some kind of system for getting each person's share figured out.

The Production Questions Involve Opportunity Costs

Now you know the three basic kinds of choices which must be made. Sometimes the first two (the output question and the input question) are lumped together and called the production question. In its broadest meaning, the "production question" is concerned with: (a) choosing the specific products to be produced and deciding how much of each will be produced; (b) choosing the specific resources to be used and deciding how much of each will go into making each product; and then (c) stimulating and directing the people and the other inputs to go to the necessary places and to do the necessary things to carry out the society's production choices.

There are thousands of little "choice decisions" which must be made to answer the society's production question. Which people will build the roads? Will we use rocks and gravel? or oyster shells? Will we haul the rocks and gravel in wagons? or in wheelbarrows? Will the wagons have wooden wheels? or bronze wheels? Who is going to build the wagons? With the lumber we use to build the wagons, we can't also build a house to live in or a boat for catching fish. Opportunity costs are staring us in the face. Which resources will we try to conserve? Which will we use up freely?

The "production question" can get about as complex as the distribution question. But one way or another every society must get the production question answered. There's just no way around it.

There Are Never Enough Resources to Do Everything. There will never be enough resources and products to give all of us enough to fulfill all our wants and objectives and also to permit the society to fulfill all its objectives and goals. Sometimes we like to make-believe about this. We like to think that the reason there are so many factories and power plants polluting the air and the water, and the reason people must work so hard and the reason we use up resources so fast is because "those other people" want too many things.

"Those other people" are too materialistic. They want bigger cars, bigger houses, bigger everything. And electric everything—blenders and can openers and TV's and hair driers and frying pans and air conditioners and you name it. If "those other people" didn't want so much we could all slow down and escape from this rush-rush-rush—produce-produce-produce hangup. Then we would all be better off. But would we?

Most People Disagree with Some of Their Society's Choices. Isn't there *something* each of us wants more of, for ourselves? or for the society? Maybe not an electric can opener or a bigger car—but maybe a new tire and enough gasoline for a trip to the beach? Perhaps more books? Or maybe more books for the college library. Or more college libraries. Or more colleges. Or more libraries. A trip to Singapore? Or France? Maybe better sewage systems in the small towns and villages throughout the nation and the world so we can stop polluting the streams and rivers. Maybe better health and medical care and better food and housing and education and transportation for the urban and rural poor in our country—and in other countries, too. How about a major effort to develop and install antipollution equipment? Or to make automobiles safer? Or to cure muscular dystrophy?

How long is this list? As long as the sheet of paper you have to write it on. Almost everyone sees some desired objectives going unfilled.

Certainly you can disagree with the society's answers to the production question. You can argue that we are producing the wrong things or that we are using up the wrong resources in the process. Probably anyone in any society (anyone who takes time to think about it) will disagree with some of the society's production choices. So long as individuals have different wants, ideas, beliefs, objectives, and different degrees of information and misinformation, how could it be otherwise?

Yes. The production question is difficult. But what about the other basic question—the distribution question. Isn't that difficult, too?

Everyone Seems to Want a Larger Share of the Output

You know that the "distribution question" concerns the decision about who (that is, which individuals) will get what shares (how much) of the things which are being produced.

Now that all these cakes have been baked, who gets to have them? or eat them.

Will everyone share equally? or will the strong get the most? or the wise? or the hungriest? Or will everyone who has royal blood, or is kin to the chief have first claim on the cakes? and on the fish that are caught? the vegetables that are grown? the houses that are built? the horses that are raised? the services of the best physicians?

Most of the people are always going to get a somewhat smaller share of the society's output than they want. Each choice to let one person *have* something is a choice that someone else will *not* have it. These are the very difficult choices posed by the distribution question.*

There is no way of working out each person's distributive share so that all the people will be completely satisfied. Most people are going to want at least a little more than they get. From the time you first argued about the size of your weekly allowance you probably have been trying in one way or another to increase your "distributive share." Throughout your life you probably will go to all kinds of trouble to try to keep your share rising.

Your Money Income Brings You Your "Distributive Share." In all the modern countries of the world, people initially receive their income as *money*. The money a person receives is a claim to a "distributive share" of the output. Your money income lets you "go into the market and claim your share" of the things produced. The bigger your money income, the bigger share of the output you can

---

* The word "distribution" has two different meanings. As used here it is concerned with: "How much of the output each person will receive." A completely different meaning is used in business to refer to the "marketing channel" through which the products are "distributed" to consumers—that is, the movement of products from manufacturer to wholesaler to retailer to final consumer. Be careful not to confuse these two meanings of the word "distribution."

buy. Anything which changes your money income changes your "distributive share."

In every modern economy the distribution question is essentially the question of how much money—how much *income*—each person will get. No matter how the question is answered, you may be absolutely sure that nobody will be completely satisfied with the answer.

There Are Only Three Ways the Society Can Choose

By now you probably are impressed with the fact that society's economic problem is not going to be easy to solve. But somehow it must be solved. There are several ways a society might go about getting the answers to the production and distribution questions. But all the different ways can be grouped into three different categories. There are three different processes the society can use to get the choices worked out: (1) the social process, (2) the political process, and (3) the market process.

All three of these processes are at work in every society. In one society, one process may be dominant. In another society, another may be dominant. But all three processes will be there, influencing the choices (at least to some extent) all the time. Most of the rest of this chapter will be talking about these three processes—social, political, and market—which all societies use for solving the economic problem.

HOW THE SOCIAL PROCESS MAKES THE BASIC ECONOMIC CHOICES

Many of the production and distribution questions in every society are answered by the social process—that is, by the customs and the traditions, the "usual way of doing things" in that society. If you ask why Dad mows the lawn and Mom washes the dishes, the answer

is: "That's the way it is usually done in our society." Why does the husband usually work outside the home to earn income, while the wife usually stays home and uses her "scarce productive energies" (her labor) in domestic duties? It's customary. It's traditional.

Why does the son wash the car and the daughter mop the kitchen floor? Why do the children in the family receive allowances? Why do the children sometimes get more allowances as they get older? Again, because this is the way it is usually done in our society. But wait. Are we talking about the basic production and distribution questions? Of course we are! Mopping floors, washing dishes, mowing lawns and washing cars are all *productive* activities. And children's allowances certainly have an influence on the distribution question!

In our society and throughout most of the world it's the *men* who usually lay bricks, fly planes, collect garbage, fix pipes, fight wars, pass laws, and build highways. Women usually do the typing, vacuum rugs, teach kindergarten, nurse the sick, work as airline stewardesses, cook, clean house, and raise kids. Why? Because it's traditional. Even in the most modern nations people aren't yet free of traditional bonds. Tradition still tries to force people into the customary roles passed down from ancient and medieval times. In the "less modernized" societies the bonds of tradition are much stronger.

The Social Process Is Strongest in Less Developed Countries

Even today, the less developed countries of the world have very strong social pressures which influence the production and distribution choices. In almost all tradition-bound societies there is a hierarchy of royalty or chiefdom, with the highest-ranking chiefs having the largest influence on how the society's resources will be used. The high chiefs receive more of the output than do the others.

In a society which operates mostly on custom and tradition, each individual's life—economic, social, and personal—is largely predetermined by tradition. The people follow the paths of their ancestors. The position and activities of all the people in the society, including the work they will do and the share of the output they will receive, are largely determined by customs and traditions from the past. The same patterns are repeated by each new generation, century after century.

In the Traditional Society, Everyone Shares. In most traditional societies the people share the output on the basis of kinship and bloodlines, but usually there also is some special reward for good work. The one who catches the most and biggest fish usually gets a larger share of the catch than the one who brings in no fish at all. But the one who brings in no fish still gets a share. The situation usually is: "Most of what you produce belongs to the other members of your family, extended family, clan, and society. But something extra of what you produce will go to you as your reward for producing it."

If one person catches a big fish and eats it all, that's the same as stealing from the others. Why? Because according to the rules of that society a share of the fish belongs to everyone! (It's about the same as if you are working on an Aransas Pass shrimp trawler and you steal and sell boxes of the shrimp you catch. They aren't your shrimp!)

The Traditional Society Discourages Saving. The traditional society's way of answering the distribution question keeps everyone fed, but it discourages saving. It's almost impossible for anyone to work hard and build up some savings. Whenever a person saves, the savings "rightfully belong" to everybody—so why save?

In recent years some of the ambitious young people from the traditional societies have moved to other places where they can earn money and keep it for themselves. Those who get away, and save, know that if they go back home, most of their savings will have to be shared with others. Yet, often the feeling of "their just and rightful obligation" is so strong that either they return home or they send most of their money back to be shared. Nobody likes the feeling of stealing from relatives and loved ones. Would you? Of course not.

You can see how a traditional society would discourage savings and investments. There is not much incentive for the individual to try to get ahead. In many traditional societies, "getting ahead" is discouraged. But even if it isn't, anyone who wants to get ahead must pull along the entire family and clan—and maybe the whole society. Not very many people are either able or willing to undertake such a formidable task!

The Traditional Societies Are Eroding (and Exploding!) Away. Much of the political unrest throughout the world today reflects the erosion and breakdown of the traditional societies. Their customs and traditions have maintained social and political stability, solved the economic problem, and held together and maintained these societies over the centuries. But the breakdown is inevitable. The traditional societies are not designed to encourage—or even to permit—the kinds of rapid changes required to bring about the higher productivity and increased standards of living which all people now are demanding.

The day of the traditional society is rapidly passing into history. Sad, perhaps. Anthropologists like to observe them; all of us can learn much from the study of such societies. But not very many of the traditional society's young people (who have glimpsed the "free outside world") seem to want to live in such a society anymore. Most of the people seem to want to have more personal freedom, and more things—better tools, clean water, modern medicine, outboard motors, cars, transistor radios, and Cokes, beer, and cigarettes. But such standards of living for the masses simply are not compatable with the traditional society.

Anthropology and Sociology Explain the Social Process

Economics is not the place to look if you want to understand how the basic economic choices are made through the social process—through custom and tradition. Anyone who is deeply interested in such questions should study anthropology and sociology. It is in understanding the social process—how the society functions—that you will find the key to understanding how the economic choices are made in the traditional society.

Yes, the traditional societies are rapidly eroding away. Still the influence of the social processes on the economic choices will continue to be important in all societies. The diminishing but continuing importance of the family as a "producing, distributing, consuming economic unit" is one good example. The diminishing but continuing economic discrimination against women is another.

HOW THE POLITICAL PROCESS MAKES THE BASIC ECONOMIC CHOICES

Billions of dollars worth of our resources are being used to produce the U.S. interstate highway network. Space exploration, military activities, education programs are all using up billions of dollars worth of resources. How did the society decide that all these resources would be used to produce these things? Governments decided. The federal government, the state governments, and the local governments made the choices.

Governments Make Many of the Economic Choices in Every Country

All countries rely on the political process for many of their economic choices. In the United

States, governmental decisions play a very important role in answering both the production and the distribution questions. You can see the government's influence on the production question everywhere you look— streets and highways, post offices and public buildings, parks and recreation areas, schools and prisons, and B-52's flying overhead.

What about the distribution question? Can you see the government's influence there, too? Sure. The government requires people to forego some of the goods they could buy and to pay taxes with that money instead. When people pay taxes their "distributive shares" of the society's output are reduced. Then when the government gives money to unemployed people, to poor families with dependent children, to disabled veterans, old people, and students, that increases their "distributive shares." That way, people with no income of their own can have a share of the output.

These examples of government influence (and there are many, many more) show that even in a "free economy" such as that of the United States, the political process (government) makes a lot of the production and distribution choices. Yet the United States is one of the countries in which the government has the least influence on the economic choices. Most of the production and distribution choices in the United States are *not* decided through the political process. Political (governmental) control of the economic choices is the exception, not the rule.

In some countries—for example the Soviet Union and Maoist China—political control over the production and distribution choices is the usual thing. In those countries the choices which are *not* made by government are the exceptions. Even in the countries of Western Europe, more of the economic questions are decided by government than in the United States.

Governments Direct the Economy by "Command." Whenever a production or distribution choice is made by governmental decision (through the political processes of the society), this overrules any other choice which might be made—either by tradition, or by "the free individual who wants to do his or her own thing." When the government levies a tax, the people pay. There is no choice. When the State Highway Department says a new highway is going to occupy your front yard, sure enough, that's what happens. (You get paid for the land, of course, but you don't have much choice in the matter.) When the city zones your vacant lot as "open space," not to be used for buildings, then you won't get a building permit, and that's that! (Unless you can get the zoning board to change the decision, or get the city council to change the zoning law.)

When the resource-use choices are made by the political process, this sometimes is called the command method for making the choices. You can understand why. Notice that the word "command" does not have to mean that there is a dictator making the decisions. Your own local city council and county board are making some of these choices every day.

The Command Method May Be Direct or Indirect. Sometimes the command method involves direct allocation: "This piece of land will be used for a naval base; that one for a recreation area. That person will serve in the armed forces." Sometimes the "command" (political process) method uses the *indirect* approach. Resources are induced to move into the uses the government wishes, but not by direct order. The government simply offers attractive prices for those resources which it wishes to control. Thus the people and resources are persuaded (rather than ordered) to do the government's bidding. In the Communist countries, many of the choices are made by direct allocation. But in most modern countries, most of the government-directed economic choices are carried out by the use of wage, price and profit incentives.

If you are thinking about being a school teacher, chances are you are planning to work for some state or local government. School teachers are teaching school because the government pays them enough to induce them (or to let them) keep doing that. If the government stopped paying them, the school teachers would have to quit teaching and find some other kind of work to do.

Contractors build government buildings because they are offered payments to do so. Engineers construct dams, aerospace firms make Apollo moon-landing ships, and police officers try to keep the peace, all because the political process induces them—pays them—to do these things. The political process (the government) makes choices about how it wants some of the resources (human and other) to be used. Then the government carries out the choices by offering income (that is, a distributive share of society's output) to those who will do what it wants done.

Political Science and History Explain the Political Process

To understand how the choices are made by government, you need to understand the political processes of the society. You need to understand how the government functions—how it makes its decisions. Why does the government decide to expand the interstate highway system, to cut back the space program, to raise the tuition at the state university, to put a ceiling on professors' salaries, to build a bridge across Oregon Inlet, or to increase social security payments? Such decisions are all made through the political process. How does it work?

In a country like the United States, each governmental choice usually involves many individual decisions. The decisions are made by elected representatives and by administrative officials and subofficials and assistants and clerks and secretaries and others. No one can ever be quite sure about the reasons why legislators decide and vote as they do. Sometimes the decision may be based on a careful analysis of the issues; sometimes perhaps on personal whim. One legislator may vote "yes" because "the party" is for it; another, in response to pressures from the local voters.

One thing we can be sure of. Any legislator who doesn't respond reasonably well to the wishes of a goodly number of the voters will someday soon cease to be a legislator! In countries with less democratic forms of government, the political process is less responsive to the wishes of the people. But even in the United States where we enjoy some of the world's most democratic governments, the responsiveness of the political process on economic matters is far from perfect.

Economics Explains the Market Process

Just as it is necessary to study anthropology and sociology to understand how the social process makes the economic choices for the society, so is it necessary to study political science, history and the workings of governments to understand how these choices are made through the political process. It is only for the third and final "choice-making process" that you must study economics to understand how it works.

The third choice-making process is called the market process or simply, "the market." The study of "the market process"—what it is and how it works—is a major part of economics. Much of what's in this book—much of what you've already seen and a good bit of what's coming up—is concerned in one way or another with the nature and operation of the market process.

HOW THE MARKET PROCESS MAKES THE BASIC ECONOMIC CHOICES

Suppose the government isn't getting involved in the production and distribution choices. And suppose there are no traditions directing the economic activities and choices in the society. Then neither the political process nor the social process is going to solve the economic problem. But somehow things have to get produced and distributed. Otherwise everyone will starve. So what happens?

Without government or social control over the economic choices, we're all on our own. If you want something you had better make it for yourself. That seems to be the only way. But wait! Perhaps somehow you can *induce someone else to make it for you*. Great idea! But how might you do that? It's easy. Just offer to pay the other person enough. Or offer to trade something the other person wants. Simple? Logical? Natural? Yes. And that, in a nutshell, is how the market process works.

How "The Market" Answers the Production Question

In its barest essentials, this is the way the market process works: Someone is producing the things you want because you are buying those things. You produce something *others* want, because that's the way you get the money to buy what *you* want. The other person wants your money (as income), and the only way to get it is to produce something for you. So, just like that, the society chooses "what to produce." It's automatic! Neither "tradition" nor "command" need to be involved at all. "The market" answers the question "what to produce" automatically.

How "The Market" Answers the Distribution Question

What about the distribution question? How does the market process solve that? That's the other side of the coin. The ones who produce a lot of what I want get a lot of my money. That's their income. With that they can buy their "distributive share" of the society's output.

Where do I get my money? By doing and making things other people are willing to pay for. Of course! The more I produce of the things others want, the more money I get to buy the things I want. That's how I get to claim my "distributive share." See how the distribution question is automatically decided by the market process? Your production—the value of what you produce—determines your income and (therefore) the size of your share of the output. This is called the productivity principle of distribution.

Now you know how "the market" answers two of the basic questions:

(1) What to produce? Produce those things the people want and are willing to pay for. Produce the things the people *demand*.

(2) Who gets to have how much of the product? The ones who produce the most value will get the largest incomes and can buy the largest shares of the output. Those who produce the least will receive the least.

But there's one more question. Which resources will be used for what? The next section tells about that.

How "The Market" Conserves Society's Resources

When I'm making the things other people want, which of society's resources do I use? The cheapest ones I can get to do the job. Of course! I never use moon rocks to pave people's driveways. I help society by conserving its moon rocks. Who tells me to conserve the moon rocks? Or is it just that I am a good guy and am doing my bit for the good of society? Neither. The market induces me (forces me, really) to conserve the moon rocks. Here's how.

Great scarcity puts a high price on moon rocks. The high price convinces me to conserve them—not to use them to pave driveways. Suppose I did buy and use moon rocks to pave driveways. What would happen then? I would be severely punished by the society. I would lose a lot of money on the job, and go

broke. My "distributive share" would drop to zero because I used up more of society's valuable things than I produced for society in return. See what a high price can do? It forces people to conserve the society's most valued things. And, just as with everything else about the market process, it works *automatically*.

The Driving Force Is Self-Interest

What is the driving force of the market process? The desires, hungers, wants of people. All of us are looking out for ourselves. But the only way anyone can get what he or she wants is to produce something the other people want. I make something for you and you reward me with money. Then I can buy what I want from other people. I will reward them with money. And on and on it goes.

All of us are working for everybody else and we get rewarded for how much we do and how efficiently we do it. All three of the "basic economic questions" are being answered all the time, automatically. As each individual, family, and business works to solve its own economic problem, the society's economic problem is automatically solved.

People buy the things they want most. This stimulates other people to go into business and make more of those things. So the output question is answered. The business is interested in making profit, so it uses the inputs which will do the job at least cost. The business, to be successful, must carefully conserve and optimize the use of society's resources. So the input question is answered.

The owners of the most profitable businesses will get the best incomes. Their most productive employees will get the best wages. The people who supply the best resources and equipment and products to the businesses will receive the highest incomes. Everyone who gets a good income will enjoy a good distributive share of society's output. But those who don't produce anything don't get anything. The output goes to the productive ones. In this way the distribution question is answered.

The market process is a very natural sort of thing. We all decide what we want to do (or what we are willing to do) to get enough income to buy the things we want. So what happens? We all wind up doing or making something that someone else wants. How naturally and easily the market process makes the three basic choices! Let's summarize it once more. But first, a word of warning.

In this discussion we aren't talking about "the American economy" or about *any* real-world economy. Far from it! We're talking about the *pure market process*—which does not exist, has never existed, and will never exist in the real world in anything approaching its "pure" form. More on that later. But now, the summary.

Summary Highlights of the Market Process

What to Produce? Produce those things the people are buying. The more being bought, the more will be produced.

Which Resources to Use? Use the cheapest ones to do the job adequately, and optimize the use of each one. The cheap resources are the ones society has a lot of. It's better to use these than to use the more expensive, more scarce, more valuable ones which really ought to be conserved.

Who Gets How Much? The people who produce the most of what other people want the most (and use up the least valuable amounts of society's resources in the process) will get the most income. Your income will reflect the value which society places on what you (either you yourself, or something you own) produce. Your income lets you claim your distributive share of the output.

The market process is really only an extension of the way things work in nature. In nature, each living thing must produce to stay alive. Each animal gets to consume whatever it produces. If it produces much, it lives well. If it produces nothing, it starves. That's the way

it is in nature with all the animals and birds—and even plants!

A tree in the forest solves its economic problem by sending its roots deep and wide to "produce" moisture and minerals and things. However much it produces, that's how much it gets to consume—no more, and no less. If the roots don't go wide and deep enough, the tree doesn't produce and consume enough to stay alive. So it dies. That's the way it is in nature with all living things. The productive ones get to consume and live. The unproductive ones die.

The market process modifies this natural "produce and consume cycle" in only one way: It gives each person the opportunity to produce one thing and then consume a different thing. You produce indirectly for yourself by producing directly for others.

The market process lets you specialize in producing something you're good at, and then trade to get the other things you want. When you get into the next chapter you'll see just how important this is!

The Market Permits Individual Freedom of Choice

The "pure market process" leaves each person free to choose what and how much to produce and what things to buy with the income earned. Each of us is free to influence the size of our income by deciding how productive we want to be. Each of us is free to decide what products we want to buy. As all the individuals make their choices, they automatically determine the choices for the society. The market process just lets nature take its course. Such is the nature of the theoretical "pure market process."

ALL THREE PROCESSES ARE AT WORK IN EVERY SOCIETY

The three processes—social, political, and market—are at work throughout the world today, exerting their influences on the production and distribution choices. All three processes are at work in every society, in every nation. It's interesting the way these intermixed processes are working in the real world economic systems. You'll be reading about that soon.

The Social Process Reflects the Kind of Society. If the economic choices in a society are going to be made by the social process, then it's pretty important what kind of a society (what kind of "social process") exists there. If it is a very rigid society, controlled by taboos and omens and superstitions, economic conditions of most of the people may be less than pleasant. On the other hand, if the society is controlled by love and mutual sharing, the production and distribution choices will look a lot different.

The Political Process Reflects the Kind of Government. What about the political process? Suppose a nation has traditions of high morality and democracy and a high degree of responsiveness of the political process to the wishes of the people. Then the "political process" (command) choices will reflect the wishes of the people. But what if the political process is not responsive to the wishes of the people? Then the economic choices are likely to be very different.

The Market Process Works Independently. With the market process, it doesn't really make too much difference what kind of society or government exists. So long as the market is permitted to make the economic choices, the results come out the same way, regardless of the kind of social or political system. This fact has been a strong argument in favor of the market process as a way of organizing an economic system. As you know, this idea is strong in the "philosophical heritage" of the United States—free enterprise, freedom of the individual, minimum influence by government, and all that.

Do not be worried that you don't yet understand much about the details of how the market process works. It's really all very logical and easy to understand and it will be coming to you little by little, off and on throughout much of this book. For now, all you should really understand is what the market process is, and the bare essentials of how it works.

You should know that the production problem is solved automatically as the businesses produce the things the people are buying; that businesses try to produce these things at the least possible cost and this conserves society's scarce resources; and that each individual's share of the output is determined by the value of what he or she produces. If you really understand this much about the market process, that's enough for now.

THE MARKET PROCESS AND POSITIVE AND NORMATIVE ECONOMICS

Would the pure market process always make "good" choices? Would it always produce the "best" combination of outputs, using the "best" combinations of inputs? Would it always distribute the outputs so that everyone gets the "best," most "rightful" share? No. It really wouldn't always do all these things.

Many times throughout this book you will see examples of the inability of the market process to fulfill the wishes of the society. One of the reasons why no "pure market" economic system exists in the world is because (in its pure form) no society would put up with it! Neither in the "pure model" of the market process, nor in the real world, is the market process (acting alone) capable of making acceptable social choices about everything. About many things, yes. But about some things, no.

In education, antipollution, social security, and in many other areas the market process is "overruled" by the society. The *political process* takes over and tries to do what the society thinks should be done. How do we know what "should" be done? Can economists answer that question?

Positive Economics and Normative Economics

For more than a century economists have been arguing with each other about whether or not economics and economists ought to get involved in questions of "what should be." Should economics try to be a "positive science"? to deal only with scientific laws of cause and effect? with questions of "what is?" and "what would happen if?" and stay away from such questions as "what *should* happen?" and "what *would be best* for the society?"

Or should economics be a "normative" field? Should it deal with some of the "less scientific" (more philosophical) questions of *what should be?* Should economics deal with "value judgments"? and try to figure out how *good* or *bad* one choice or another might be, for the society?

Positive Economics Deals with Economic "Laws"–with How Things "Are." "If you don't pay a person to work for you then that person will not work for you." "If the price of fried chicken doubles and the price of hamburgers goes down, people will buy less fried chicken and more hamburgers." These are statements of positive economics. Positive economics doesn't say it's good or bad—it just tells "what would happen if. . ."

Normative Economics Deals with Questions of How Things "Should Be." Normative economics deals with "value" issues—the issues of good or bad, right or wrong, better or worse—and of how to make better economic choices for the society.

When economists recommend such things as progressive income taxes and social security programs as "just and equitable," then their recommendations are based on normative economics—on an idea, or philosophy of "social justice." But *the economist's knowledge of positive economics makes possible realistic and feasible normative recommendations.* Anyone who really knows the "laws of positive economics" knows the most basic law: you can't have your cake and eat it too. That's a good thing to keep in mind (and so easy to forget!) when we start making "normative" recommendations.

In the past few years, more and more economists have been getting into the normative "value judgment" issues of economics. Normative economics is much less definite, much less "sure and scientific" than positive economics. For example, it's much easier to say what will happen to a family's food budget if the father loses his job (positive economics), than it is to say what the minimum income of a family of four "should be" (normative economics), or to decide who "should be" required to help to support the family when the father loses his job (normative economics). Yet, even in the face of uncertainties, many economists are willing to get involved in the many pressing normative economic issues of our day.

Realistic and effective involvement in the *normative* economic issues requires a basic understanding of the concepts (the "laws") of positive economics. That's why it's good that you are studying economics. When you get to the end of this book you will have a good basic understanding of the concepts (the "laws") of positive economics. So you will be able to think more realistically about the normative issues.

AN INTRODUCTION TO REAL-WORLD ECONOMIC SYSTEMS

Every society has some kind of organization and some procedures for getting the basic production and distribution questions answered. This organized set of procedures is called the economic system. Every economic system is made up of some combination of tradition, command, and the market process.

It's a lot easier to talk about "the three processes" than it is to talk about real-world economic systems! Each process has a precise meaning. But when we get into real-world economic systems nothing is very precise anymore.

Each Economic System Is Unique

Each real-world economic system is unique. All three processes—social, political, and market—are at work all the time. And each economic system is changing all the time, too. But we still keep calling each of these evolving real-world systems by the same names.

We still talk about "American capitalism," for example. How can that be? It's just that the "system names" aren't very precise. So don't get hung up on the names. How we "label" an economic system really doesn't tell you much about it.

Many times you've heard about "capitalism" and "socialism" and "communism." What do these words mean? That's what this section talks about.

The Economic System Called "Capitalism"

What is capitalism? It's an economic system in which the means of production—the factories, tools, equipment, coal mines, oil wells, railroads, etc.—are owned by private individuals, not by the government. Private ownership is the distinguishing characteristic of capitalism.

In a capitalist economic system the owners and workers are free to use their resources, energies, tools, etc. in response to the market process. The workers and owners who respond best—by making the things wanted most—will enjoy the biggest incomes. Of course.

Capitalism has many names. It's called the *free enterprise system* or the *private enterprise system* or the *competitive free enterprise*

system or the *laissez-faire system*. Laissez-faire is a French term meaning that the government lets the people do whatever they want to do.

If we put together all the names describing it, capitalism is a system of "laissez-faire-competitive-free-private enterprise." That's really a pretty good description of what capitalism is. But no "pure system" of capitalism has ever existed in the real world. Some of the effects of such a system would be intolerable!

In "pure capitalism" you're on your own. Entirely. If you break your leg and can't work, unless you've saved enough to get by on, you starve. In "pure capitalism" the government doesn't bail out the ones who can't make it on their own.

With "pure capitalism" we wouldn't have any national, state, or local parks or recreation areas and no public schools or libraries or health and welfare programs. No "public" anything!

Unmodified capitalism would be too harsh to be socially acceptable. Real-world capitalism is always some mixture of capitalism and socialism. Probably a better name for the American economic system would be mixed socio-capitalism. But what does it mean to say it's "mixed with socialism"? What is socialism?

The Economic System Called "Socialism"

The word socialism can mean many things. But it always includes the idea that many economic choices are made and carried out through the political process. If the political process is democratic, then you have "democratic socialism." If the political process is autocratic or dictatorial, then you have "autocratic socialism."

Suppose the people could work out a way of mutually sharing all of the work and all of the output of their economic system. Then they would have an economic system of "utopian socialism" (which is the same thing as "utopian communism"). The words "socialism" and "communism" come from the same idea. Socialism says "society-ism" and communism says "community-ism." But that isn't what these words have come to mean in the world today!

In a real-world system, "socialism" means that the government owns and controls some of the industries and it also provides "welfare programs" for the people. The government may own and operate such industries as electric power, coal, oil and gas, transportation, communications, perhaps steel and chemicals, and perhaps others.

One "socialist" country will have more industries under government ownership than another. Also the welfare programs will be different from one socialist country to another.

Is the U.S. Economy Capitalist? In the United States the federal government dredges rivers, builds dams and bridges, produces and sells electric power and chemicals, manages many kinds of natural resources and operates recreation areas. Since 1971 it even operates a nationwide railroad passenger service (Amtrak). And it regulates and controls transportation, communications, electric power, natural gas and several other industries. Is that socialism?

The state governments in the United States are in the insurance business, the liquor business, and various others; local governments are in transportation, water and sewer service, electric power, and other enterprises. Is that socialism?

In the U.S. economy the influence of government touches everybody. No business can afford to make any important decision without first considering the effect of the decision on the taxes it will have to pay. There are licenses, zoning regulations, building codes, pollution regulations, minimum wage laws, and many other government influences.

"Free enterprise" in the United States is really not so free after all. Yet we still refer to the U.S. economy as a "free enterprise" economy—as an economic system of "capitalism."

Capitalism and Socialism May Be Indistinguishable. If the U.S. economic system (with so much governmental influence and control) can be called capitalism, then what is socialism? The truth is that in most real-world cases it isn't very different from the American economic system of "modified capitalism."

Take the British system for example. A few more of the major industries and resources are owned by the government—coal, transportation, communications, etc. But the British and U.S. economies are really very much alike. Yet we call the U.S. system "capitalism" and the British system "socialism." Why?

Here's one reason: In the United States most people have been taught that socialism is "bad" and capitalism is "good." The Democratic party and the Republican party and the people in general are always doing things to bring about "socialist reforms" in our economic system. But you seldom hear anyone calling the changes "socialist reforms"—not in the United States.

The "Socialist Reforms" of "Mixed Sociocapitalism." We are constantly making socialist reforms: More unemployment and social security benefits, Medicaid and Medicare, public welfare and public assistance, college fellowships with family support, government subsidies for industry, minimum wage laws, Amtrak, TVA, and many other "government interventions" are always chipping away at "raw capitalism."

These changes are really socialist reforms. But "socialism" is a bad word in the United States. So no matter how many "socialist reforms" are undertaken in this country it isn't likely that you'll hear many people calling them that!

If you should happen to make a trip to Western Europe and find the "good old American spirit of capitalism" everywhere you go, don't be too surprised. The difference between the "capitalistic socialism" of the Western European countries and the "socialistic capitalism" of the United States really is not easy to see! The systems are really much more alike than different.

In both places the demand of the people works through the market process to influence most of the production and distribution choices of the society. In both places the political process (government) plays a very important role in making and carrying out the economic choices.

The truth of the matter is this: The U.S. economy and all these other economies are really systems of "mixed socio-capitalism." It would eliminate a lot of confusion if we would all start calling them that!

Economic System?
or Political System?

Be careful. Don't confuse the political (governmental) system with the economic system. The two are always related, of course. But they're essentially different things.

Democracy and dictatorship are forms of government. Capitalism and socialism are forms of economic systems. Either capitalism or socialism could exist in a country with either democracy or dictatorship. Sometimes people tie democracy with "laissez faire-competitive-free private enterprise capitalism," and associate socialism with dictatorship. How absurd!

We call the British system "socialism" and the American system "capitalism." But is the British government any less democratic than the American government? No. In some ways the British government is more directly responsive to the people than is the government of the United States!

And what about the United States? There's much more government control over the economic choices now than there was 100 years ago! But has the government become less democratic? I don't think so. All the evidence points the other way. These days, even people without property, blacks, women, and eighteen-year-olds can vote!

What about Communism? Is that different? Let's talk about that.

The Economic System
Called "Communism"

Communism is a difficult term to understand. It refers to both a political system and an economic system. And there are so many different meanings of "communism"!

Communism (with a capital "C") is the name of a political party. The Communist party is the group that runs things in the communist countries. What's a communist country? One where the Communist party is in control, and running things, of course!

The Communist Philosophy and Predictions. Another meaning of the word "communism" is "the philosophy and predictions of the communist philosophers": Marx, Engels, Lenin, Mao Tse-tung, others.

For some people the philosophy of communism is a sort of religion. There's a strong belief that the communist doctrine is true and that the predictions are really going to happen. So one definition of a "communist" would be "one who believes in communism"—one who believes the doctrine of communism.

The communist philosophy generally holds that the market process really isn't going to work. Pretty soon a few monopolists will gain control and enrich themselves while everyone else suffers.

Then the miserable masses will revolt. They'll kill off all the monopolists and take control. So capitalism will be destroyed. After that the government will be in the hands of the Communist party leaders who will be in control of everything in the nation.

Ultimately there will evolve "an economy of abundance." There will be no economic problem of scarcities of material goods— not for anyone. A beautiful world will evolve in which people will no longer be selfish. The wants of everyone will all be satisfied.

People will continue to produce for society because of their love for society and the government will just "wither away." In such a society of mutual love and trust and respect for each other and where there are no unfulfilled desires, who needs a government? The idea of the coming of the utopian "ideal world community" is where the word "communism" comes from.

The philosophy of communism describes a "heaven-type" situation and offers it here on earth to those who will believe and follow. But you get into "communist heaven" not by being peaceful and loving thy neighbors. How, then? By being destructive. Maybe by killing them!

The most fanatical communists believe that the predictions really are going to come true. They feel duty-bound to help the process along by doing everything they can to weaken capitalism—by causing disruption and revolution in countries where any kind of capitalism exists.

What About Utopian Communism? What about the idea of living in a "communal society" with a group of other people? The clan in some traditional societies and the family in modern societies operates as a sort of economic "commune."

The idea of the commune is that each person works for the group. Each plays his or her role in helping out and they all share things together.

"Utopian communism" (like "utopian socialism") has never existed except on a small scale among groups of a few people. In your studies of "real-world economic systems" you don't need to worry much about utopian communism. It doesn't exist.

The Communist Economic System. The economic system of communism is really an extreme form of socialism. Not just a few major industries but all the factories and farms are government-owned and operated.

The natural forces of the market are not permitted to have much influence on the economic choices. The government owns and directs virtually all of the resources. All the production and distribution decisions are made by the government.

Since the Communist party is in control of the government, the party controls the economic choices. Since the party is controlled by a few people, these few people are really the ones who make the choices for society.

The outputs and inputs of the farms and factories are all determined by the government's economic plan. In the communist system, all of the society's inputs—workers and resources and everything—move according to the government's economic plan.

Industries operate as the government directs. Whether or not the economy will produce more heavy machinery and less consumer goods is not determined by private investors. There aren't any private investors! The government decides.

The number of economic decisions which individuals control is very small. People are free to spend their (small) incomes among the few kinds of consumer goods which the "economic plan" calls for.

In general, people's incomes are determined by the work they do and how productive they are. But it is the important people in the party (in the government) who get the largest shares.

You'll be reading more about the economic systems of capitalism, socialism and communism—about how they work and how they're changing—in the very last chapter of this book. But that's enough about economic systems, for now.

The next chapter talks about that *special advantage* of the market process: It leaves you free to work for yourself so you can get the things you want. But at the same time it lets you *specialize* in producing something you're really good at. That way you can maximize your output and income.

But how can you get all the things you want if you specialize in producing just one thing? You trade to get the other things of course. And that's what the next chapter is all about. I think you'll enjoy it. But before you go on, be sure you're satisfied that you and this chapter have done your bit for each other.

REVIEW EXERCISES

● **MAJOR CONCEPTS, PRINCIPLES, TERMS (Explain each carefully.)**

the three basic questions
the three ways of making the choices
economics of the "tradition-oriented" society
how the political process makes the choices
how "the market" answers the production question
how "the market" answers the distribution question
economic system
capitalism
socialism
communism
mixed socio-capitalism

● **OTHER CONCEPTS AND TERMS (Explain each briefly.)**

the output question
the input question
the distribution question
the production question
distributive share
positive and
    normative economics

the social process
the political process
the market process
command: the direct approach
command: the indirect approach
productivity principle of distribution
laissez-faire
utopian socialism

● **QUESTIONS (Write out answers, or jot down key points.)**

1. What are some of the ways you are dissatisfied with the *production* choices in your society? What about the *distribution* choices? Discuss.
2. You know that there is no country in the world in which *all* of the economic choices are made by either the social process, or the political process, or the market process, but do you think there ever *could be*? Discuss.
3. What are some examples you have run into *today* (since you got out of bed this morning) of economic choice-making by tradition? by command? by the market?

4. Can you think of any choices that are now being made (in your family, at your college, in your society, in your *world*), where you think the "choice-making process" ought to be changed (from tradition, to command, to market, or vice versa)? Think about it.

5. Think about an economic system of "pure capitalism." What are some of the ways in which such a system would be intolerable, from *your* point of view?

6. Suppose you were to rank different real-world economic systems on a scale (from 1 to 10) to indicate how much the "political process" and how much the "market process" was responsible for the choices in that economic system. (Let 1 = pure *political* process, and 10 = pure *market* process.) What number do you think you would assign to the present economic system of the United States? Great Britain? Japan? West Germany? East Germany? the USSR? What number would you assign to the economy of each country, 20 years ago? What do you think the number for each country will be, 20 years from now? Think about it.

4 How the Market Process Fosters Specialization and Trade

With specialization and trade, everyone gets to have more cake and eat more too.

Suppose a society's economic system is operating *entirely* on the "pure market process." (None ever did, but just suppose.) Why do people produce? Because they would get pretty hungry if they didn't. They produce because they want to consume.

Some people may be producing their own food and clothes and shelter and all, but most people will be producing just one thing (or maybe a few things). Why? Because it's more efficient to specialize in producing something you're good at and then trade to get the other things you want. It's "the market" that lets you do that.

All this may seem pretty obvious to you right now. But after you read the next few sections you'll see that there's a lot more to it than you might think. And you'll see how all this "specializing and trading" helps the people to live much better.

HOW THE MARKET PROCESS MIGHT EVOLVE

Let's begin with a "Robinson Crusoe" world. Suppose our "Robinson Crusoe" is living on a big tropical island in the middle of the Pacific Ocean. Obviously he will make all the economic decisions for himself. If he is hungry he will try to "produce" (find, catch, or gather) something to eat. If he wants protection from the sun and rain he will try to "produce" (find or make) something to use for clothing and shelter. Whatever he is successful in producing, that is what he gets to have. If he doesn't produce very much he doesn't get very much.

A "Robinson Crusoe" Makes His Own Choices

Our Robinson Crusoe's production and distribution choices are automatically decided. He solves his production problem by (1) deciding what he wants most, and then (2) producing it in the most efficient way he can. The distribution question is so automatically solved that it's a little ridiculous even to mention it. Obviously he gets a "100 percent share." There's no one else to share with! (I'll bet he wishes there were.)

It's all so simple and easy to see when there's only one person. But when we introduce more people the picture gets more complex. Still it operates essentially in the same way. Let's introduce more people and see what happens.

60

Suppose there are four large families (clans, maybe) living on the island. Each family is located some distance from the others. One family lives on the east side of the island and one on the west side; one on the north side and one on the south side. Each family is entirely self-sufficient. Each produces only for itself—there is no trading between one family and another.

With More People the Choices Are More Complex

Even within each island family the production and distribution choices are somewhat more complex than for one person alone. In one family, father and the boys may be responsible for growing and gathering vegetables and fruits while mother and the girls catch fish from the lagoon. Father may get the biggest and best fish and fruits, mother second best, and the children, whatever is left.

In another family, father and the boys may fish while mother and the girls grow and gather vegetables and fruits, and all share equally at suppertime. The third family may have the women doing all the work and the best of everything going to the father and the oldest son. All these different kinds of arrangements (and many others) have actually existed in various societies at various times and places throughout the world. What we're talking about, of course, is "the production and distribution choices as decided by tradition."

Comparative Advantage Leads To Trade

Now let's suppose that the family living on the east side of the island finds fishing to be very good. But the family on the west side has very poor fishing. Ah, but the westside family has very fertile soil. Coconuts, breadfruit, and other tropical vegetables and fruits are plentiful. You could say that the eastside family has a "comparative advantage" in producing fish and the westside family has a "comparative advantage" in producing vegetables and fruits. And you know what's going to happen. Right?

The westside family will grow things and the eastside family will catch fish and the two families will trade. How do you know? It's just obvious. Nobody is going to keep trying to catch fish where there aren't any fish! No one is going to keep trying to gather breadfruit where it doesn't grow! So the eastside islanders will catch fish and trade for breadfruit; the westside islanders will grow breadfruit and trade for fish. Everyone will benefit. Soon you will see exactly how this "specialization and trade" gets started. But first take a look at the map of our little island. You'll find it on the next page.

Trade Adds to the Complexity

When trade arises, the economy is going to get more complex. Production will become more specialized and much more efficient. The distribution question—the question of which family gets how much fish and how much breadfruit—will get more complex, too. But the most productive families will get most of the output.

Suppose the people living on the south side of the island are not very productive at anything. Either because of poor fishing and growing conditions or their inability or laziness or for some other reason, the southside family doesn't produce very much of anything. Since it doesn't produce much, it doesn't have much to consume. After trade arises it still isn't going to have much to consume unless, with specialization, it can produce a lot more. If it doesn't have much to trade, it won't receive much in return. The "productivity principle of distribution" really works; each family's share of the output depends on how much that family produces. That's the way it is if they don't trade; that's still the way it is if they do.

TUBALAND ISLAND

Northside pass

NORTHSIDE
village

WESTSIDE
village

Westside
pass

CENTER ISLAND TRAIL

EASTSIDE
village

Eastside pass

SOUTHSIDE
village

Southside
pass

The Northside Family Starts Producing Things for Sale

Now let's suppose the people on the north side of the island—an inventive and industrious family—start producing bows and arrows, and "tuba" (a kind of wine made from the sap of the coconut palm). Early one Saturday they begin beating the drums inviting all the other island families to come and try out (and perhaps buy) some of the new products. All the families come. Before noon all the tuba is sold. For the tuba they paid handsomely with tropical vegetables, fruits, and dried fishsticks. But no one bought any bows and arrows.

It doesn't take a genius to figure out what the northside islanders will produce next week. More bows and arrows? Of course not. They are going to make tuba. Why? Because that is what people are buying. The market process is beginning to answer the production question. The northside islanders are seeking profit so they produce tuba. That's what their society wants them to produce. The market tells them so!

Tuba Is a Profitable Drink— to Produce and Sell

The way things are going it seems that the northsiders are going to get very rich. All the island people (the society) place high value on tuba. The northside islanders are the only ones who know how to make tuba. It seems that these inventive and industrious people, by producing and selling tuba, are going to get more fish, vegetables, and fruits than those who catch the fish and grow and gather the vegetables and fruits.

From this simple illustration it's obvious what will happen if the members of the society are free to "let nature take its course." People will make those products which other people want to buy. Through the market process, the individual motive "I will make what I need to satisfy my wants," changes to "I will get more of what I want by making what *you* want, and trading."

The northside islanders are producing tuba and becoming wealthy. The southside islanders aren't producing very much of anything. They are staying poor. With the market working it's almost as though each family is producing directly for itself. But suddenly each family can be much more productive by specializing in whatever it's good at. Still, if a family doesn't produce anything, the market won't help them. Those who produce nothing get nothing.

Now you have seen a simple "market system" arise. But so far, not much trading is going on. The northside islanders are producing and "selling" (trading) tuba. But everything else is going just as before. Wouldn't it be a good idea for the other families to specialize in something and trade? It really would. And that's exactly what's going to happen. Just watch.

THE GAINS FROM TRADE

You know that almost any "economic unit" could produce almost anything if it was willing to work at it hard enough. Any individual, family, business, farm, or nation could use its resources to make a hundred different kinds of things. You could go to Iowa and become a farmer and produce all sorts of things: corn or tomatoes, chickens or eggs, coconuts or bananas or polar bear skins. How would you decide which to produce?

The Producer Specializes in the Most Profitable Product

If the market process is working it's easy. You figure how much it would cost to make each product and how much revenue you would get from it. Then you choose to produce the most profitable product, or the most profitable combination of products. You don't produce bananas (or coconuts or polar bear skins) because the cost would be ten times as high as the value of the product! You might be able to break even on chickens and eggs, or tomatoes. But for *your* farm, *corn* is the thing. You own some of the best corn land in the state. So what will you grow? Polar bears? Ridiculous.

If the market process is working as it's supposed to, if you're a producer you will automatically make the most efficient, most productive (the optimum) use of your (the society's) resources. You will produce the highest-priced outputs (the ones your society values most) and use up the lowest-priced inputs (the ones your society values least). It's a neat system. But from this kind of example you can't see how much good comes from all this. To really see the gains from trade we need to start back at the beginning.

Different "Opportunity Cost Ratios" Generate Trade

Let's go back to our island. Remember that fish are much more plentiful on the east side of the island and breadfruit grows much better on the west side. But both the eastside islanders and the westside islanders like to eat both fish and breadfruit.

Suppose the eastside islanders can work all day and catch five baskets of fish. Or if they wanted breadfruit and worked all day at that, they could gather one basket of breadfruit. So what is the opportunity cost of a basket of breadfruit? Five baskets of fish! So the value of breadfruit is high: one basketful of breadfruit is worth five baskets of fish.

To the Eastside Islanders Breadfruit Is Very Scarce and Valuable. Breadfruit is five times as valuable as fish to the eastside islanders. How do we know? Because the only time they will go after breadfruit (and give up five times as much fish) is when the one basket of breadfruit is at least as valuable to them as the five

baskets of fish they are giving up. Otherwise they would be fishing instead. They will conserve breadfruit and eat mostly fish. At suppertime, an eastside child who reaches for a second slice of breadfruit gets a slap on the hand!

To the Westside Islanders Fish Is Very Scarce and Valuable. Now let's look at the westside islanders where the situation is exactly reversed. In one day's work they can produce five baskets of breadfruit or one basket of fish. When they spend a day fishing, the one basket of fish they catch "costs" them five baskets of breadfruit. Fish are *five times* as valuable to them as breadfruit. They eat mostly breadfruit. Woe be unto the westside child who reaches for another piece of charbroiled fish!

Eastside Fish Will Be Traded for Westside Breadfruit

Let's suppose that both families spend half their productive time catching fish and the other half gathering breadfruit. In their normal twenty-workday month the eastside family will produce 50 baskets of fish (10 days of fishing, five baskets a day = 50) and 10 baskets of breadfruit (10 days gathering breadfruit, 1 basket a day = 10).

Over on the west side the situation is exactly reversed. They wind up with 50 baskets of breadfruit and only 10 baskets of fish. They also get a total of 60 baskets of food per month. Figure 4-1 uses transformation (production possibility) curves to show this situation. You should study Figure 4-1 for a few minutes now.

Trade Permits Specialization and Increased Output for All

There is really a great opportunity for the eastside islanders and the westside islanders to gain from trading fish and breadfruit. If the eastsiders could trade *less than five baskets* of

Fig. 4-1   Production Possibilities for Separate Economic Units

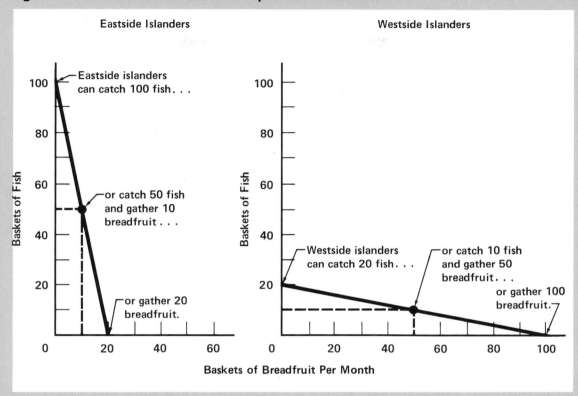

The eastside islanders are great at fishing and the westside islanders are great breadfruit gatherers.

The "opportunity cost ratio" or "transformation ratio" for the eastsiders is 1 basket of breadfruit for 5 baskets of fish, or a 1 to 5 ratio of breadfruit to fish.

The transformation ratio for the westsiders is 5 baskets of breadfruit for one basket of fish, or a 1 to 1/5 ratio of breadfruit to fish.

To the eastside islanders, a basket of breadfruit is very valuable. It is worth 5 baskets of fish; to the westsiders a basket of breadfruit is worth only 1/5 of a basket of fish. To say it the other way, to the eastsiders, fish is not very valuable. It is only worth 1/5 basket of breadfruit. But to the westsiders, fish is very valuable. It is worth 5 baskets of breadfruit. What a great opportunity to gain from trade!

fish and get *one basket* of breadfruit in exchange, they would be better off. Suppose they could trade four baskets of fish for one basket of breadfruit. They would be ahead by one basket of fish. If they could trade *one basket* of fish for *one basket* of breadfruit they would wind up with *five times* as much breadfruit as they are now getting. With a one-to-one trade ratio, breadfruit would become as easy to get and as cheap as fish!

Even if the eastside islanders had to pay four and a half baskets of fish for one basket of breadfruit, they still would be one-half basket of fish better off than if they didn't trade. They could spend a day producing five baskets of fish (instead of producing one basket of breadfruit). Then they could trade four and a half baskets of fish for one basket of breadfruit, and wind up with one basket of breadfruit and one-half basket of fish. That's better than one basket of breadfruit and no fish at all! (which is what they would get if they produced the breadfruit themselves).

The Production Ratio Is Different from the Trade Ratio

For the eastside islanders, the "trade-off ratio" in production (between fish and breadfruit) is 5 for 1. If the trade-off ratio *in trade* is anything *less than* 5 for 1, then they should get their breadfruit by trading—not by producing it. Isn't it obvious? When they *produce* to get a basket of breadfruit the trade-off cost is 5 baskets of fish. If they can *trade* and get a basket of breadfruit for *less than* 5 baskets of fish, then they will come out with more by trading.

Any individual, family, business, or society will get more of what they want if they will follow this general principle: If the opportunity cost is higher *in production* than it is *in trade*, then you should trade to get what you want. You should get what you want at the lowest opportunity cost (the lowest "trade-off" cost) you can arrange. That way you'll get the most

of what you want with what you have to work with.

Now take a look at the westside islanders. They are facing the same kind of situation the eastside islanders are facing except that the "trade-off ratio in production" (the transformation ratio) between the two products is exactly reversed. To the westside islanders the opportunity cost of *one basket* of fish is *five baskets* of breadfruit. If they could trade *less than five baskets* of breadfruit and get back *one basket* of fish, they would be better off. So we have a beautiful setup, just waiting for trade to begin.

The Island Chiefs Discover the Gains from Trade

Suppose that one day the chief of the eastside islanders, King Tuituranga, is walking down Center Island Trail and meets the chief of the westside islanders, Queen Isaleilani. They stop to talk. Soon King Tuituranga begins to brag about the good fishing. Queen Isaleilani responds with stories about the fabulous breadfruit harvest. Each challenges the other: "Prove it!"

Soon they have worked out an agreement to meet regularly, and to trade. They agree that they will trade one for one—one basket of fish for one basket of breadfruit.

Once the bargain is made, the eastside chief hurries home as fast as he can, hardly able to contain his glee. What a great trick he has pulled off! He knows breadfruit is *five times* as valuable as fish. Yet he has arranged for a one-for-one trade! Such a bargain! And at the expense of the westside islanders! He rushes on home to tell his people.

At the same time, guess what the westside chief is doing and thinking? The same things, of course! She knows that fish are *five times* as valuable as breadfruit. But she has talked the eastside chief into trading each basket of fish for only *one* basket of breadfruit! Each chief keeps thinking, "What a steal! What a steal!"

Chapter 4 • How the Market Process Fosters Specialization and Trade   **67**

The Gains from Trade:
More Output for Everybody

The beauty of this situation is that both chiefs are right. It is "a steal." But they're both wrong about where all the extra fish and bread-fruit are coming from. The gains of one obviously aren't coming from the other. Both are gaining equally. Nobody is losing. The "steal" that each chief has made, is coming from the increase in total output!

The "steal" is coming from the gains from trade. A great increase in output of both fish and breadfruit is going to result when each family specializes in the production of the thing they can produce best. "The gains from trade" come from *increased productivity*. The increased productivity comes from specialization. And trade is what makes it possible.

Once the trade arrangement is set up, the eastside islanders produce only fish. They produce a total of 100 baskets of fish per month and trade 50 baskets of fish to the westsiders for 50 baskets of breadfruit. The westsiders produce 100 baskets of breadfruit and trade 50 baskets of breadfruit for 50 baskets of fish. Now both families have much more food than before.

Now all the eastside kids and the westside kids can reach for all the second helpings they want. Even the chickens and pigs are finding that life is easier these days. See the great gains from trade? The entire society benefits. Chickens and pigs too.

BENEFITS OF ECONOMIC
INTEGRATION

Figure 4-2 puts together the production possibility curves of the two families. The "combined" production possibility curve shows the great gains in output which result from the economic integration of the two formerly separate economies. In the production of fish and breadfruit, these two units— the eastside economy and the westside economy—are now integrated into *one* economic unit. The transformation curve in Figure 4-2 shows the production possibilities for this "newly integrated" economic unit. Figure 4-2 builds on Figure 4-1. Perhaps you should review Figure 4-1 first, and then study Figure 4-2 on the next page.

Economic integration permits the free movement of goods and resources (of inputs and outputs) among economic units. The benefits can be really great. In our island example no one is working any harder than before. Yet the total product of the society is almost doubled. Perhaps they will decide to go on a four-day work week, or a six-hour day. Or perhaps they will spend more time building better houses or developing a better water supply. Or maybe they will build a harbor so they can export dried fish and copra (dried coconut meat). Then they will be able to gain even more by trading with other islands and other countries.

The Price System Stimulates Trade

In a society where the market process is functioning, the *price system* automatically gets people to specialize and trade. In our example, if the market process with its automatic price system had been working on the island, the trade would have developed automatically. Here's how it would happen.

To the eastside islanders who catch so much fish, breadfruit is highly valued. It is very scarce, so its *price* (on their side of the island) is very high. But to the westside islanders (the good breadfruit growers) breadfruit is *low-priced*. Fish is the highly valued, very scarce, *high-priced* item. What's going to happen? It's obvious.

One day the eastside islanders will hear about the high westside price of fish. They will start catching more fish and selling them to the westsiders. Big profits! But as fish become more available to the westsiders, what happens? The more available the fish become, the

Fig. 4-2   The Production Possibility Curves Added Together

Much more can be produced when the eastsiders and westsiders specialize and trade.

This concave (out-bulging) production possibility curve puts together the two curves (eastsiders and westsiders) as shown in Figure 4-1. The great outward bulge in the curve shows how much more product it is possible to get by letting each specialize and then trade.

This integrated east-west economic unit can produce 100 baskets of fish *and* 100 baskets of breadfruit per month—a total product of 200 baskets a month. Without trade, each could produce only 50 of their specialty and 10 of the other, for a total of 60 for each family—120 for the two families combined. The specialization and trade doesn't quite double their food output, but it almost does!

less scarce they become. So the less valuable they become. The price goes down.

What about breadfruit? It works the same way. The westside breadfruit growers will hear about the eastside price of breadfruit. They will start producing more baskets of breadfruit and selling them to the eastsiders. As more breadfruit is supplied to the eastsiders some of the scarcity is relieved so the price goes down.

Trade Brings the Prices into Balance

Without trade, eastside fish would stay low-priced and breadfruit would stay high-priced. Westside fish would stay high-priced and breadfruit, low-priced. But the market process will *generate* trade and bring the prices into balance.

If the market process is working, the ultimate result will be the same as what happened when the sly island chiefs outfoxed each other. The *price mechanism* will induce the eastside islanders to specialize in fish and the westsiders to specialize in breadfruit. Then each will sell to the other. See how efficiently the price mechanism can get the right production choices made? Automatically!

COMPARATIVE ADVANTAGE

In our example, both the eastside islanders and the westside islanders have a clear and obvious advantage in something. The eastsiders are definitely more productive in producing fish. The westsiders have an obvious advantage in breadfruit. But suppose one family doesn't have an obvious advantage in *anything*. What then? Can they trade, and gain? To find the answer to that let's go on with our example.

It's the Comparative Advantage
That Counts

Remember the southside islanders? The unproductive ones? Suppose it takes them a *whole week* (5 days) to produce a basket of fish. In one day they can only produce 1/5 of a basket of fish. With breadfruit, things are bad too—but not quite as bad. They can produce three baskets of breadfruit a week (3/5ths of a basket a day).

If the southsiders fish all week they wind up with one basket of fish (1/5th basket a day for 5 days). That's all they get to eat that week. If they spend the week gathering breadfruit they get three basketfuls (3/5ths basket a day for 5 days).

The southside islanders aren't nearly as productive as either the eastsiders or the westsiders. Can they possibly gain anything from entering the on-going trade between east and west? Yes! They certainly can!

Opportunity Cost Ratios Determine Comparative Advantage

The southside islanders' opportunity cost ratio between breadfruit and fish is three for one. Each time the southsiders decide to *not* produce breadfruit for a week so they can produce fish, how much breadfruit do they lose? Three baskets. How much fish do they get? One basket. So whenever they produce their own fish, each *one basket* of fish is costing them three baskets of breadfruit.

Suppose the islanders' "going exchange rate" between fish and breadfruit is still one-for-one. Then if the southsiders produce breadfruit and trade to get fish, how much breadfruit will they have to give up to get a basket of fish? Only one! So can they gain from trading? Of course!

When they *trade* to get a basket of fish, the cost is only *one basket* of breadfruit. But when they *produce* the basket of fish the cost is *three baskets* of breadfruit. When they trade, the cost of fish is only one-third as much as when they produce the fish themselves! By producing breadfruit and trading for fish they can get three times as much fish. Now study Figure 4-3 and you'll see what it looks like on a graph.

Fig. 4-3 Production Possibilities and Trade Possibilities Compared

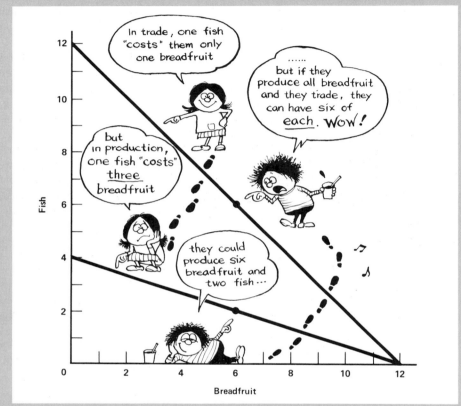

The southside islanders have a disadvantage in everything, but still they have comparative advantage in something.

Their comparative advantage is in the product in which they are "least worse off" relative to their trading partners.

In production, the opportunity cost (transformation) ratio between fish and breadfruit for the southside islanders is 4 to 12 (or 1 to 3). If the southsiders produce their own, the opportunity cost of one basket of fish is three baskets of breadfruit.

Since the "going exchange rate" on the island is one-for-one, the southsiders could trade one basket of breadfruit and get back one basket of fish. So the opportunity cost of one basket of fish *in trade* is only one basket of breadfruit. So by specializing in the production of breadfruit and trading, the southsiders can get three times as much fish as if they had produced their own.

The effect on the southsiders' food supply is the same as if they had discovered some new technique to make them three times as productive in catching fish. All hail the gains from trade!—(even when—or *especially* when— you have a disadvantage in everything).

But maybe it isn't all as bad as it seems. Maybe the southside islanders are a very small family and the eastsiders and westsiders are very big families.

What Is Comparative Advantage?

The southside islanders don't seem to have an advantage in anything. They are very un-productive as compared with the eastside and westside islanders. Still the southside islanders have a comparative advantage in the production of breadfruit. So, what is comparative advantage?

"Comparative advantage" means "the op-portunity cost in production" is less than "the opportunity cost in trade." When you have a comparative advantage in something (like breadfruit) you don't trade to get it. You pro-duce it yourself. Then you trade to get other things (like fish). You trade to get the things in which you have a comparative disadvantage

Comparative disadvantage, quite obviously, means the opposite of comparative advan-tage. It means *"the opportunity cost in trade"* is *less than "the opportunity cost in produc-tion."* You don't produce the things in which you have comparative disadvantage (like southside-island fish). You produce some-thing else (like breadfruit) and then trade.

Let's say it another way. Can you get more of product x by producing product y and then trading to get x? If so, you have a comparative advantage in y. You have a comparative disadvantage in x. You can get more x by pro-ducing y and trading for x than you could get by producing x yourself.

Both Trading Partners Have an Advantage.

Whenever one trading partner (individual, bus-iness, or nation) has a comparative advantage in one thing, the other party automatically has a comparative advantage in the other thing. Anytime it's possible for one "trader" to come out better, that means the other "trader" has the opposite opportunity to come out better also. If the "trade-off ratio" (opportunity cost ratio or transformation ratio) between two products is different for any two economic units—individuals, businesses, or nations—then one of the units will have a comparative advantage in one of the products and the other will have *exactly the same amount* of compara-tive advantage in the other product. Your comparative advantage is my comparative disadvantage; my comparative advantage is your comparative disadvantage. It's the same "comparative situation" looked at from two different points of view.

If the southsiders produce all breadfruit and trade for fish, they can get three times as much fish as they could get by producing fish themselves. You can see that their low total output makes no difference in determining whether or not they can gain from trade. Perhaps the southside islanders will always be poor. But they will be *less poor* if they will specialize and trade.

What About International Trade? Suppose

there are national boundaries separating these island families into different nations. Then all this trade we have been talking about would be international trade. Would that make any difference? No. Not from the point of view of the economics involved.

With international trade, there might be some difficulty working out the exchange be-cause of the different kinds of money used in the different countries. Also, the Westside Fishing Association and the Eastside Bread-fruit Growers Association may scream for pro-tection against "foreign competition."

Or the eastside chief King Tuituranga may not want to become dependent on westside breadfruit because he's planning a war against the westsiders. Or there might be some other complications. But from the point of view of the opportunity for both to benefit, it makes no difference whether the trading partners are in the same city, in different states, or on opposite sides of the world.

The Law of Comparative Advantage

In the real world, every economic unit, every country (no matter how rich or poor) has comparative advantage in some things and comparative disadvantage in others. Each unit will get more output if it concentrates on producing the things in which it has comparative advantage and then trades for the other things it wants. Economists call this the law of comparative advantage.

The "law of comparative advantage" emphasizes the potential benefits of trade. It says that the plumber should work as a plumber, then buy shoes from the shoemaker. The shoemaker should concentrate on making shoes and hire the plumber to do the plumbing. Through this arrangement the society will have more and better shoes and more and better plumbing. Everyone will benefit.

ADVANTAGES OF SPECIALIZATION

People who concentrate on doing the things they can do best usually produce more, receive higher incomes, and enjoy higher standards of living than those who don't have any "specialty." But specialization requires trade. One of the important differences between the poverty-striken economies of the underdeveloped world and the affluent societies of the modern world, is the degree of specialization.

We All Depend on Specialization and Technology

Think about it for a minute. What would you be eating today if all you had to eat was what you produced yourself? What would you be wearing? What kind of house would you be living in? What kind of medical care would you get? What sort of transportation would you use? Things would be sort of primitive, right?

The only way it's possible for people to have more than just the bare necessities of life is through specialization and trade. People concentrate on doing the things they can do best and they become much better at their jobs. But for some people to specialize, other people must want to buy what they're producing. If you're going to specialize in medicine, then you must depend on many people to buy your services. Unless the market demand is great enough to buy up what you are producing, you cannot specialize.

If a 20-acre field is best for producing cotton, its owner will let it "specialize" in cotton. But suppose the market is too small. People don't want to buy all that cotton. Then the field can't specialize in cotton.

Suppose this is a "subsistence type" economy and not much trade is going on in anything. Then the owner of the 20-acre field must use the field to grow some food to eat. See how impossible it is to specialize without markets? without trade?

Business firms are always trying to design better, more specialized machines and tools. The most *efficient machines* are the *highly specialized* ones. Highly specialized machines produce only one thing and they produce it with great efficiency. For example, compare the value of output per hour you could make with a hacksaw to that which you could make running the machine that bores the holes in an engine block—or running the machine that puts the caps on beer bottles. Specialization is really great! But unless there's a big market for engines, and for bottled beer, we can't afford such highly specialized machines.

Specialization and Division of Labor

The word "specialization" is frequently used together with *division of labor*. Both expressions mean essentially the same thing. Both mean that each unit of productive input—each person, each piece of land, each machine—does only a part of the total production job. The total production operation is divided up so that each task can become specialized.

Different people have different skills and abilities. By specializing, most people can become even more productive at their specialities. With division of labor comes the opportunity to use *more advanced technology*— that is, more efficient ways of doing things.

As new technology is discovered, new kinds of machines are built. Workers are trained to use the new machines. Output gets larger. The productive capacity of the economy increases. This is the process of economic growth.

The society gets more output as technology develops. The different parts of the production process become more specialized. It tends to come about all by itself. If you just let people alone in a society where the market process is working, they will figure out ways of specializing and trading to get the things they want.

The effects of specialization and trade are truly remarkable—so remarkable, in fact, that it's almost impossible for us to visualize a world without specialization and trade. It's a basic, essential part of modern society. It influences every moment of the lives of each of us. And the results—in terms of fewer hours, easier work, and more and better things of all kinds—are truly phenomenal. Yet we are so accustomed to it that we just take it for granted.

Specialization is great. Still, there is a cost. What's the cost? Interdependence. Vulnerability. We all become dependent on each other.

With Specialization, Everyone Is Dependent on Everyone Else

A Robinson Crusoe alone on an island does not need to worry about what his neighbor does. But when there are many people all producing and trading with each other, no one stands alone anymore. All of us are dependent on and influenced by what all the other people decide to do. Whatever happens anywhere has an effect everywhere.

The more specialized and interdependent the economy becomes, the more productive it can be. And the more speedily the society can achieve whatever objectives it seeks. But what about the costs of interdependence?

If I produce eggs and you egg-buyers decide you don't like eggs, it hurts me. If I am depending on you to produce the gasoline I use in my car and suddenly you go on strike, it hurts me. If the workers in my steel mill demand a wage increase and I can't raise my price to cover it, it hurts me.

If I do raise my price and then my customers start buying their steel from foreign producers, I go out of business and fire my workers. It hurts me. It hurts my workers. Before it's all over it's going to hurt the grocers and the bakers and the bartenders and a lot of other people in my town.

With specialization and exchange we live much better. We're happy about the easier work and the free time, the warm houses and fast cars, the eyeglasses and dentures and allergy shots. Specialization and division of labor "cost us" our economic independence. But it's quite clear that it's a cost we are willing to pay.

The next chapter will introduce you to the "macro view" of an economic system. There you'll see how the economy is all tied together and you'll see what some of the costs of all this economic interdependence really are. Then in the chapter after that you'll find out about the essential exchange medium without which specialization and trade couldn't develop much. What exchange medium? Money? Of course!

I think you'll enjoy the next two chapters. But before you go on, be sure you have a good understanding of specialization and comparative advantage. And be sure you can explain the gains from trade.

**REVIEW
EXERCISES** ● **MAJOR CONCEPTS, PRINCIPLES, TERMS (Explain each thoroughly.)**

how the "market process" might arise
the gains from trade
the advantages of specialization
trade requires different "trade-off ratios"
how the "price mechanism" generates trade

● **OTHER CONCEPTS AND TERMS (Explain each briefly.)**

economic integration
comparative advantage
comparative disadvantage
the law of comparative advantage
international trade
economic growth
division of labor
specialization and technology
specialization and interdependence

● **CURVES AND GRAPHS (Draw, label, and explain each graph.)**

Production Possibilities for Separate Economic Units
The Production Possibility Curves Added Together
Production Possibilities and Trade Possibilities Compared

● **QUESTIONS (Write out answers, or jot down key points.)**

1. The westside islanders *really* shouldn't be buying their fish from the eastsiders. They should "buy locally" from the Westside Fishing Association. That would be good for the local economy. Support your local businesses! Keep the money at home! Right? Discuss.
2. One impediment to the economic development of the poor nations of the world is that the poor nations can't benefit from the gains from trade. As compared with the advanced nations, a poor, under-developed nation couldn't possibly have a comparative advantage in *anything*. Discuss.
3. Most of the European countries have joined the European Economic Community (the Common Market) to eliminate trade (and other) restrictions on things (and people) moving among the member countries. If it's such a good idea for Europe, why not the whole world? Discuss.
4. Suppose stringent restrictions were imposed on trade between all the states in the United States. What difference do you suppose that would make? Do you think it would have any effect on you *personally*, in your daily life? Think about it.

PART 2

THE MORE WE ALL SPEND
THE MORE WE ALL EARN!

5 Macroeconomics: the Circular Flow of Income and Spending

*The size of the national output
or income depends on how much the
people and businesses are spending.*

What determines whether you will be rich or poor? Is it up to you? Partly, yes. But only partly. In the modern world all our destinies are tied together. Everything you do has an influence on somebody else. And how well-off *you* are depends a lot on what *others* are doing. This is perhaps true in every aspect of life. It is certainly true in economics.

THE ECONOMIC SYSTEM IS ALL TIED TOGETHER

What happens if the economy slows down? Suppose you are working in the stockyards and you are told that because of a declining demand for beef you are no longer needed. Many of your friends receive the same notice. Maybe if the drop in demand for meat products is great enough the stockyards will shut down.

If the stockyards lay you off and shut down, does this mean the economy is slowing down? Maybe yes, maybe no. Maybe people are buying less beef and pork but buying more of other things—maybe poultry. Maybe there is a boom in the egg business and maybe you can get a

job there. You start watching the want ads. But you don't see any jobs available. Suppose one day you are talking to your poultry-farming brother. He's thinking about looking for a job at the stockyards. He tells you that the poultry workers are having tough times. Layoffs. No jobs.

You figure that maybe people are buying less food so they can buy more cars and nicer clothes. So you hitchhike to Detroit to get a job in an automobile factory. Then you find that the automobile workers are being laid off too. So you hitchhike down to Burlington, North Carolina and try to get a job in the textile mills. But there you find the same problem. What's going on?

A New Kind Of Economic Problem: Recession and Depression

What you are seeing now is a new kind of economic problem—the problem of recession or depression—a slowdown of the economic system. The economy never seems to want to run at just the right speed. Why not? And what can be done about it? That's what we're getting into now.

The previous chapters were concerned with the question of choosing *which way* to use our resources. What to produce? Which resources to use? How to share the output? And what to trade for what? Now, suddenly we are looking at a different kind of problem.

Idle factors of production are everywhere. People are trying to sell their labor, but no one wants to buy it. Businesses are trying to sell beef and pork and chickens and eggs but nobody is trying to buy them. The automobile companies would like to produce and sell more cars but there aren't many buyers. The same is true for new clothes and shoes and furniture and airline tickets and almost everything else.

As you hitchhike around the country looking for a job you begin to get hungry. You certainly would like to have a steak! The meatcutters would like to have jobs cutting steaks. The cattle ranchers would like to sell their cattle. The stockyards would like to get back into production again and you sure would like to get your job back. Then you could buy a steak!

All the needed inputs—all the factors of production—are available, itching to go to work. You and many other people are hungering for steak. So why isn't the steak being produced? You don't have any money. So what's wrong? Simply this: The economic system isn't working right. The market process isn't doing what it's supposed to do. The system is suffering from a "partial breakdown."

When One Thing Slows Down, Other Things Slow Down

If people stop buying things, businesses stop producing things. Then factors of production get laid off. So people's incomes get cut off. So they don't buy as much. So businesses produce even less. They fire more workers. The economy goes into recession and then maybe on down into depression.

If people shift their spending from steaks to eggs, there's no problem. The factors of production move from where they are less wanted to where they are more wanted. But if people stop spending for steaks and for eggs and for everything else, then the people who make these things—that means all of us, as workers, business managers, clerks, investors, service and repair people and so on—all of us lose our sources of income. Then we are forced to cut our spending. Can you see how different this new kind of economic problem is from the problem of choosing we were talking about before?

Now we are looking at the economic system as one big unit—as a big production-consumption circle. Let's go back to our island example and see how the production-consumption "circular flow" might develop.

The Circular Flow of Production and Consumption

Robinson Crusoe alone on an island would be producing and consuming at the same time. He climbs a palm tree and gets a coconut, then drinks the juice and eats the coconut meat. He catches a fish and tosses it on the coals. As soon as it is cooked he peels off the charred skin and eats the tender, char-broiled meat inside. By the end of the day he has eaten all the food he has produced.

Robinson Crusoe's "circular flow" of production-consumption is a tight little circle! If he wants more output (food or shelter or fishing spears or whatever) he must speed up his "economic system." He can start working longer and harder and produce more. Then he will get more output so he will have more things to have and to consume—that is, more real income.

In the Robinson Crusoe world it's very easy to see how the production-consumption circle (the output-income circle) works. It isn't quite as obvious, but the same kind of output-income production-consumption circle also exists in a complex modern economic system.

Suppose you could somehow rise up above and look down on a "transparent economic system." Maybe you could go up in a balloon, then lean out and look down. What would you see? People making things and getting money and buying things and spending money. *Things* going from the makers to the buyers. *Dollars* going back and forth and around and around. A person gets some dollars then spends them, then gets them again, then spends them again. It's all sort of like a big circle. For a few minutes let's pretend that the "transparent economic system" you're looking down on, *really is* a big circle.

THE CIRCULAR FLOW OF THE ECONOMY

The total amount of money being spent by everybody—all the people and all the businesses—is the total spending flow. It's flowing for one reason—to buy things. The buyers push the spending into the market.

As the "total spending flow" pours into the markets, the money doesn't just puddle up in the streets! It goes to people. It pours into the hands of the producers and workers and everybody and gets them to keep on producing and working and making the things the spenders are buying.

The people who are working and producing and selling things are the *receivers* of the spending flow. But as they are receiving the money with one hand they are *spending* it with the other. Each person who receives money from the spending flow just turns around and spends it again. This is the way the spending flow keeps on flowing.

Total Amounts Spent Equal Total Amounts Received

How much do all the people and businesses spend in a week? And how much do they receive? Can you see that the two amounts—

the amount spent and the amount received—must be equal?

When a handful of dollars is being spent by somebody, that handful of dollars is also being received by somebody. Obviously! Otherwise the dollars *would* be puddling up in the streets! Every spender must have a receiver. So total amounts spent must equal total amounts received. No doubt about it.

As long as everyone keeps on spending all the money received, the total spending flow will continue flowing at the same speed and the economy will keep running at the same speed. But what if people decide *not* to spend as much as (or to spend more than) they receive? That's when things get interesting (and sometimes, tough)! You'll see more about that later. But now it's time to stop looking at the money flow for awhile and to look instead at the real flows of things. It's time to look at *real* output (goods produced) and *real* income (goods received).

Real Output Equals Real Income

It's obvious that total spending equals total receipts. Each time someone spends a dollar, someone must receive it. The same is true for real output and real income. The total amount of goods made this week must be equal to the total amount of goods received this week.

Why? Because every new thing must have an *owner*!

If nobody makes anything, nobody receives anything. If I produce a thousand dollars worth of corn and tomatoes, the somebody is going to receive a thousand dollars worth of corn and tomatoes. If I sell my output of corn and tomatoes to you then you will receive the thousand dollars worth of corn and tomatoes. If I don't sell my output then I'm the one who receives it as "real income." Maybe I receive it or

Every new thing must be **real income** for somebody!

REAL INCOME

maybe you receive it. But *somebody* must receive it. It doesn't just pile up in the streets!

If we look at it from the point of view of those who produce it, it's real output. If we look at it from the point of view of those who receive it, it's real income. But either way we're looking at the same flow of goods. Real output equals real income? More than that. Real output *is* real income.

Flows of Money Equal Flows of Goods

Now let's tie the *money* flow (total spending equals total receipts) together with the *product* flow (real output equals real income). Your common sense would tell you that the spending flow and the output flow must be closely related. Why do people put money into the *spending* flow? To get some of the things in the *output* flow, of course! Why do people put goods into the *output* flow? To get some of the money in the *spending* flow. Of course!

Do you begin to get the feeling that all these flows must be equal? Everyone is pushing in goods and taking out money and then turning around and pushing the money back in and taking out goods. For every dollar's worth of goods flowing there's a dollar's worth of money flowing. The two amounts must be equal.

Why do people push goods into the flow and take out money and then turn around and put the money back in and take out goods? That seems to be so much wasted energy. But no! They're putting in a lot of one thing—their speciality—and taking out small amounts of many kinds of things—the great variety of things they want.

Specialization and trade is the name of the game. Remember? That's what the "market system" is all about. It stimulates people to produce something they're good at and then lets them exchange what they make for the other things they want. And when we're watching the circular flow of the economic system, that's exactly what we see happening.

People are selling goods and factors of production. In exchange for these goods and factors they are on the "receiving side" of the spending flow. These same people, when they are buying goods and services from others, are on the "spending side" of the spending flow. Here's another way of looking at it.

The Circular Flow Between Households and Businesses

Businesses buy factors of production and use them to produce outputs. The factor owners (households) get paid by the businesses. Then the households use the money to buy the outputs of the businesses. This circle keeps on going and the money keeps on flowing from businesses to households and from households to businesses.

Isn't this a neat way to look at any economy? Really, it's a pretty good picture of what actually is going on all the time: People selling factors to businesses and using the money they earn to buy the outputs of the businesses; businesses paying out money to the factor owners, the factors making things, then the businesses selling the things to the factor owners to get the money back.

In this illustration, don't think of "the business" as being "somebody"—some wealthy person—some "business owner." That isn't the idea. The business is sort of "a place where everybody goes to sell factors and receive incomes." Even the person who owns the business—the buildings and machines and all that—is selling those factors to the business in exchange for an income from the business. The business owner doesn't actually "live in the business." Business owners live in households just like everybody else and sell productive factors—capital and managerial skills—to the business.

Actually, when we say "businesses" what we really mean is "the *buyer's side* of the *input* markets and the *seller's side* of the *output* markets." Businesses buy inputs and sell outputs. So that's a good way to look at it.

When we say "households" what we really mean is "the *sellers' side* of the *input* markets and the *buyer's side* of the *output* markets." Households sell inputs and buy outputs. Of course! All the people who are earning incomes are selling in the input markets. And just about everyone is buying in the output markets. We all have to eat!

Figure 5-1 shows a diagram of this circular flow between households and businesses. If you'll study that diagram now, I think all this will become very clear to you.

The Interdependence of the Circular Flow

The circular flow concept really shows how much we are all dependent on each other. If the flow of money being paid to businesses gets smaller, then the businesses can't pay out as much money to the households. Employment is cut back and output is reduced. As the money flow gets smaller, the real flow gets smaller.

The circle fits together so tightly that if any part of the system speeds up or slows down, all the other parts of the system—both the money flows and the real flows—will be forced to speed up or slow down, too. Once it starts to speed up or slow down, it may go on changing more and more. As you'll see later, that could cause some serious problems.

It's the Total Spending for New Output that Matters

We have been talking about "the spending flow" as though all spending was spent for *new output*, and as though all spending created *new income* for someone. This is not quite true. Here's an example that will explain why not.

If I produce a bushel of corn and sell it to you for $10, then that "sale" is a part of total spending for output. It creates income for me. Then, after you have bought the corn, suppose somebody offers you $11 for it and you sell it to them. The $11 you get does not represent another $11 worth of output, and income. Obviously not. Only one dollar of it would be income for you. That would be your payment for increasing the value of the corn by "buying, keeping, and carrying" the corn to a time and place where it was more valuable—$1 more valuable.

You have increased the value of the output of the economic system by $1, and your income has gone up by $1. But *not* by $11! The value of *your* "output" is the value *you* have added. That's what you get to keep as income. One dollar. Your "value added" is *your* output.

Throughout this book, whenever we're talking about *total spending*, what we'll *really* be talking about is total spending *for new output*. We won't be counting the spending and respending over and over for the same old things. So remember: when I say "total spending," what I really mean is "total spending for new output."

Each "Economic Unit" Influences the Total Economy

Think about the "modern economic system." What a complex piece of machinery it is! Like the inside of a watch. Only instead of dozens of little wheels there are millions of little wheels. Each little wheel is "locked in" and turning with the others. Yet each wheel has its own little engine which it can speed up or slow down if it wants to. But as each tries to speed up or slow down, it influences the speed of all the other little wheels which are "locked in" around it. How fast (or how slowly) the whole machine—the economic system— actually will be going depends on how fast (or how slowly) all the little wheels—the individual economic units—are trying to go.

Fig. 5-1 The Circular Flow Between Households and Businesses

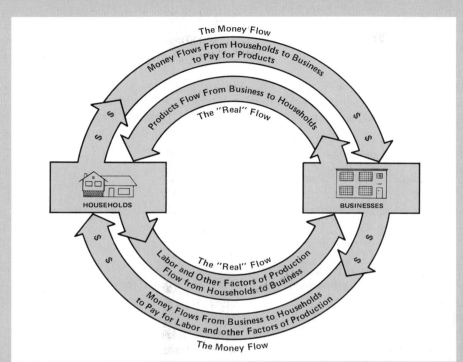

Around and around it goes. Money flowing one way, things flowing the other.

The households own all the factors of production. They sell factors to the businesses. When the businesses pay for the factors, the income goes to the households.

When the households spend the money to buy the products from the businesses, this completes the circle. The households get the goods and the businesses get the money back.

You can see that if anything makes the money flow smaller, the "real flow" will get smaller also. The two flows are completely dependent on each other and are (quite obviously) equal.

The more you work and produce and earn and spend, the more you help to speed up the "total mechanism"—the economic system. If you produce a lot, earn a lot, spend a lot, then you push the system to speed up—and it does! When a business buys more materials, hires more people, and steps up production, that pushes the system to speed up. And it does. But when people or businesses produce less and/or spend less, they slow down the system.

Employment and Unemployment

Sometimes the economic system doesn't *fully employ* all of its "able and willing" factors of production. So sometimes it's possible for us to produce more cake to have or to eat, without giving up anything. No opportunity costs? How could that be possible?

Suppose we are doing nothing with some of our factors of production. Then we start using these surplus factors to bake more cakes. What do we lose? Nothing! We lose only the "nothing" we were producing with these factors before. What a bargain for the society! Why should the society ever let its "able and willing" productive factors go unemployed? go to waste?

If we were all producing just for ourselves like Robinson Crusoe, we could use our productive factors as much as we wanted to. But when we start producing for "the market" this isn't true anymore. Sometimes the market doesn't buy our output. So we stop producing.

Spending Flows Support Employment and Production

How does the market process induce the factors to produce things? By offering them income, of course. Where do people get the money to offer other people incomes? From their own incomes. From selling whatever they have to sell. If anything happens to change one person's spending, that affects everybody else's income and everybody else's spending. A *very interdependent system!*

If anything happens to reduce the total rate of spending, the total output will not be bought, so production will be cut back. We will have unemployed labor, land, capital. People's incomes will fall. People with no income don't spend much. So total spending drops even more.

Are you beginning to get an overview concept of how the total economic system works? Of what keeps it moving? Of what speeds it up and slows it down? If so, you now are ready to understand the meaning of a new term—*macroeconomics*.

AN OVERVIEW OF MACROECONOMICS

Ever since you started reading this chapter you have been aware that we're now in a "different sort of ball game." We haven't been concerned with *which things* to produce.

We have been concerned with such questions as: Will we operate our economic system at full capacity? Will our actual production reach our full potential? That is, will we produce an output which is on the "production possibility curve"? Or will we have unemployed resources and produce less than we are capable of producing? I'm sure you realize that these questions take us into a new area in the study of economics.

You might say that the area of economics we are now talking about is "the economics of full employment and unemployment." Or you could call it "the economics of full production and underproduction." Or you could call it "the economics of over-spending and under-spending." Or you could call it "the economics of inflation and recession." Or you could call it "the study of the overall level of economic activity." Or you could call it "the study of the causes of speedups and slowdowns of the economic system."

You could call it any or all of these things and that would be all right. All these things have essentially the same meanings. But we have a special name for this part of the study of economics. We call it *macroeconomics*.

What Is Macroeconomics?

When we talk about macroeconomics we are thinking about the overall "level" or "rate" of economic activity (employment, production, output, income) and about what might cause it to change. Just like everything else in economics, macroeconomics is concerned with questions about *how* and *why* things happen.

Why is there so much unemployed labor this spring? Why are several of the major business corporations reporting losses instead of profits? Why are department store sales running below the level for this time last year? Why did my boss say unless business picks up within the next two weeks, he will have to let me go? And why did two of my best customers come by yesterday to tell me they can't buy any more corn or tomatoes until they get their jobs back?

These are "unemployment" problems—problems of an economic slowdown—of the underutilization of the society's factors of production. "Macroeconomics" is concerned with the question of what might be causing things like this to happen.

There is another kind of problem in "macroeconomics." Sometimes it goes the other way. Sometimes the problem is one of "over-employment" and "inflation." People try to buy more than the factories and farms can produce.

Suppose demand for eggs is up. The price moves up. Egg producers try to hire more factors of production. They try to get some of the stockyard workers to shift to egg production. But people are also demanding more beef. And pork. The stockyards not only are trying to keep their workers—they are also trying to pull in more workers from the poultry business! The automobile companies are looking for extra workers. So are the textile mills and the airlines and the local taxi companies and everybody else.

The lady next door comes by my roadside stand and finds that I have already sold all my corn and tomatoes. She says she will pay an extra 50¢ if I will be sure to save some for her tomorrow. See what's happening? Shortages are developing throughout the economic system. All the resources are fully employed, yet people are still trying to get more output. But the economic system can't possibly produce any more than it is capable of producing! (That's a safe statement.) So what happens?

People keep trying to buy more. Prices rise. What prices? Prices for all the things the people are trying to get more of—almost everything—all products, all factors of production. What do we call this situation? *Inflation*. Unemployment is one of the problems of macroeconomics. Inflation is the other.

The Key to Macroeconomics Is Total Spending

Macroeconomics is concerned with problems of recession, depression, and inflation. It is concerned with the question of how fast, how fully we operate our economic system. It is not concerned with the question of whether we use our factors to produce eggs or steaks. It is only concerned with the question of whether or not we use our factors to produce *something*. What's the key to keeping production levels high? You already know. Keeping *spending* high. It's the level of total spending that determines whether or not we will keep our factors fully employed, producing things.

If enough people are spending enough money to buy all the things that all of us want to produce, then all of us will produce. If not, then we will not. If enough money is being spent for beef and pork to keep the stockyards and all their employees and cattle cars and everything else operating at full capacity, then the stockyards will operate at full capacity. If people are spending enough to buy my complete output of corn and tomatoes every year, then I will keep on using my factors to produce corn and tomatoes. The same holds true for all producers throughout the economic system.

If anybody ever asks you why so many automobile workers are unemployed, you know how to answer them. They are unemployed because the people are not spending enough money to buy up the "full employment output" of automobiles. If somebody asks you why the stockyard workers are unemployed, you can answer them quick as a wink: because people aren't spending enough money to buy up the "full employment output" of the stockyards.

Then someone asks you a very broad question: "Why are so many people and factories and railroad cars and machine tools and processing plants 'unemployed'?" Your answer: "Because the people and businesses throughout the country are not spending enough to buy up the 'full employment output' of the economic system."

Then your question-asking friend asks you the ultimate question—the really tough one: "Tell me *why* the people aren't spending enough to buy up the 'full employment output' of the economic system. That's *really* what I want to know!" This question stumps you. You admit that you don't know the answer to that one.

Macroeconomics Tries to Explain Why People Don't Buy

You have just discovered another one of those tricky little things that economics has so many of—answers which really aren't answers at all. You've been answering questions by making obvious statements—by stating truisms. When we say that producers don't produce because people don't buy, this doesn't explain very much. But it gives us a start. At least we know the next question to ask: *"Why don't people buy?"* Macroeconomics is concerned with trying to get at

the answer to this question—to *find out* and *explain* why people do, or don't buy.

Any number of things might influence the "level," or "rate" of total spending. One important influence is money. How easy is it to borrow money to build a new factory? To buy a new car? How high will the interest cost be? Another important influence is the general outlook of the people—their expectations. If people think times are getting better, they are likely to spend more freely than if they expect hard times ahead.

If we can understand what determines the level of total spending, we can understand why the level of economic activity is high or low. We can understand *why* we have surpluses and unemployment or shortages and inflation. That is what macroeconomics is all about.

Macroeconomics tries to explain what determines the level of total spending (the *size* of the "total spending flow") in the economic system. Why? Because *in a market-directed economy, total spending is the key to understanding total output and total income.* All of Parts Two, Three, and Four of this book deal with macroeconomics. But now perhaps it's time now to talk about the opposite term: *microeconomics.*

What Is Microeconomics?

"Microeconomics" is what you were reading about until you came to this chapter. Microeconomics is concerned with the question of *how economic choices are made.* Mostly, microeconomics deals with the market process and how it works to make the basic choices for society.

Microeconomics explains how the market process brings improved welfare to the people through specialization, trade, optimizing the use of all of society's factors of production, stimulating the production of the most wanted goods, and all that. Microeconomics is the study of trade-offs, of opportunity costs, of substitution, of transformation, of choosing between this and that. Microeconomics *assumes* that there is full employment. It assumes that the society will be producing someplace *on* its production possibility curve—not *beneath* it.

Microeconomics is concerned with the choice of whether to have your cake or eat it. Whether to have chocolate cake or coconut cake. Whether to bake the cake in an electric oven, in a gas oven, or in a "lovo" (a little pit of hot rocks in the ground). Microeconomics is concerned with choosing which things to do with the scarce resources available to us. Microeconomics is the study of choice.

Microeconomics and Macroeconomics

The terms "microeconomics" and "macroeconomics" are still new. During the past two decades these terms have come into popular use. The terms are very helpful in separating the two basic segments or approaches to the study of economics. But as you might suppose for words which have burst into prominence in an old and established profession, not all economists are in complete agreement as to exactly what the terms mean. You may run across several slightly different meanings for both of these terms. But all the definitions are fairly close to the meanings as explained here.

A Summary Statement about Microeconomics and Macroeconomics

Microeconomics is concerned with choices among alternatives. It concentrates on the economic unit—the individual consumer, the individual producer, the market for an individual product. If we are thinking about the egg market, why consumers demand more eggs, how the price moves in response to that demand, and how resources then shift into the production of eggs—all these issues are a part of microeconomics. If Willie Wonka is deciding how fast to operate his candy factory, how many boxes of each kind to produce per day,

how many workers to employ, whether to pack the boxes of candy in cardboard or wooden cartons for shipment, whether to ship by truck, rail, or airlines—all these are questions of microeconomics.

In the market system, each consumer and each producer makes individual choices. Then it works out so that society's economic choices reflect the choices of the people. How all this happens is the subject of microeconomics.

Macroeconomics, on the other hand, is concerned with the *total level of economic activity—the rate of employment, production, output, income.* You know that all these are tied together, and they all hinge on the rate of total spending. Macroeconomics, then, is the study of what determines the level, or rate of total spending. Anything which influences the overall level of spending (anything which causes people or businesses to spend more, or less) is a part of the study of macroeconomics. If there is not enough spending to keep the economy fully employed, then we will have surpluses and unemployment. But if people are spending to try to buy more than the economy can produce, then we have the opposite macroeconomic problem—the problem of shortages, and inflation.

No society likes either unemployment, or inflation. If the basic causes which influence total spending can be understood, perhaps steps can be taken to stabilize total spending. Perhaps recession and inflation can be overcome; full employment and stable prices can be maintained. As soon as you understand more about the basic principles of total spending, output, income, and employment—that is, about macroeconomics—we will get into these issues of "economic stabilization policy."

But now, here's a different question.

How Fast Do We Want the Economy to Run?

Suppose we are trying to decide how fast we think this "total economic machine" ought to be going. Should it be running at maximum possible speed? At maximum physical capacity? Of course not. People don't like to put in their absolute maximum effort: Sixteen hours a day? Seven days a week? No holidays? No vacations? That's no fun!

It seems that as an economy grows and as output per person increases more and more, there is a tendency for the society to let its "total desired" output fall farther and farther below its "maximum physical potential." People like to take more time off. Young people sometimes don't start doing anything productive until they're in their twenties. Many people retire early.

No economic system has ever succeeded in running at its absolute maximum physical capacity over long periods of time. Very few people would want it to. So except perhaps when there is some sort of national emergency, the question is not whether or not the economic machine is running at maximum possible speed. That isn't the desired objective. We only want to know if it's running "fast enough"—that is, as fast as we want it to run. And this brings us to *the basic questions of macroeconomics*.

THE BASIC QUESTIONS OF MACROECONOMICS

The macroeconomic questions are these: "Is the economic machine running as fast as the people *want* it to run? And no faster? And if so, why? And if not, why not? Does each person who *wants* to work a 40-hour week have a chance to do so? Without being pressured into working weekends too? Do all the factory owners who want to operate their factories on an 8-hour day, 5-day week have a chance to do so? And without being induced to run a night shift?

Is the aggregate demand (total spending) of households great enough to buy all the output the businesses want to produce? And no greater than that? Is the aggregate demand

(total spending) of businesses great enough to buy all the factors of production (labor, land, capital) the households want to sell? And no greater than that? If so, the economy will have full employment and there will be no inflationary "excess demand pressures."

Whenever there are surpluses, this means that some of the outputs and some of the labor and other factors are remaining unbought in the markets. There is unemployment. Whenever this happens the economic system is running too slowly. The unemployed workers and the owners of the other unemployed factors are not very happy about this situation. If you couldn't get a job, how would you feel? You'd say: "Let's do something to speed up the economy so I can get a job!" Right?

Now look at the opposite situation. Suppose the economic system is trying to run too fast. If aggregate demand (total spending) is too great, shortages will appear. Consumers will be trying to buy more goods than are available. Businesses will be trying to get more factors than are available. Prices will rise. As businesses offer more money to get the factors to work harder, faster, longer hours, outputs will increase some. But it's a dangerous situation. The economic system is trying to run too fast.

You can see that "the basic questions of macroeconomics" can be looked at in several different ways. But all the macroeconomic questions are concerned with the same issue—the issue of *how fast the economic system will run.* For a minute, let's take this basic question apart. Let's look at it from two different points of view.

First, we can look at the *normative* question: "How fast *should* the economy run?" Then we can look at the question economists usually talk about—the *positive* question: "What determines how fast the economy actually *will* run?" (If you aren't sure about the meanings of the terms "normative" and "positive," perhaps you should go back to Chapter 3 and review the section headed "Positive Economics and Normative Economics.")

The Normative Macro-Question

The normative macroeconomic question is: "How fast do we *want* the system to run?" "What's the best, the most desirable speed of the economic system, to bring the most good to the society?" "What speed is 'fast enough but not too fast'?"

Each society, somehow, explicitly or implicitly, must answer this question. When the Bible says: "And on the seventh day He rested"—it's talking about the normative macro-question. When the society decides to have an eight-hour workday and a five-day workweek and vacation time each year, it's deciding the normative macro-question. When we decide to (or not to) use schools for productive purposes at night and on weekends, we are making a normative macro-decision.

Custom Influences the Normative Macro-Question. In each society, custom and tradition are very strong in influencing the answer to this normative question of how hard the economy *should* work—how fast it *should* run. You can see that in the *pure market* economy, the socially desirable rate of output would be reflected in the amounts the people were trying to buy, and in the amounts the producers and workers and farmers and everyone were willing to produce and sell.

In the model pure market system, whatever rate of output the society wants, that's the rate of output the society gets. The rate of employment and production automatically reflects the customs, traditions, wishes, and desires of the society. Just automatically!

Even in a completely controlled economy the government planners must build their employment and output goals within the limits of "what the people are likely to be willing to put up with." These limits are mostly determined by the customs and traditions of the society. But even so, if it wants to, an autocratic government can change people's ideas about such things as working on the Sabbath or working long hours or on the night shift.

The Government Can Force More Output. Economic plans, enforced with the power of law, sometimes can result in very large increases in the total rate of employment and output—that is, can push the economy to speed up to a rate much faster than the society "naturally" would seem to want it to go. Very few people seem to want to work a ten-hour day, seven-day week, and forfeit all vacations. But if a government with enough police power decides to enforce this kind of maximum productive effort, it can do so.

The U.S. World War II Experience. During World War II the American economy went on a 24-hour day, seven-day week. Vacations were cancelled. Workers were frozen on their jobs. Many were urged to work a ten-hour day. Every able-bodied person, male or female, was urged to join the labor force and take a job.

During this period, millions of people were moved out of the labor force and into the armed forces. But even so, the value of the total output of the U.S. economy more than doubled between 1940 and 1945: from less than $100 billion in 1940 to more than $200 billion in 1945. Some of this increase resulted from inflation, but very little. Almost all of it came from the maximum effort speed-up of the economic system.

The Soviet Union. In the Soviet Union the planned production goals and constant push for more outputs have speeded things up greatly. Outputs have been expanded and more capital has been produced. This is the way economic growth has been generated in the U.S.S.R. over the past several decades.

The Economic Plan Must Answer the Macro-Question. In a *completely planned economy* (where the political process is in full charge of all the economic choices) *somebody* *must decide on the rate at which the system will run.* In the governmentally planned "sectors" of every economy, these planning decisions must be made.

For example, in the U.S. economy we face the question of whether or not our public schools should go on a 12-month year. We must decide how many class hours and how many students should be assigned to each teacher. These kinds of normative macro-questions must be answered in all of the sectors of the economy which are operated by the political process—like public education, mass transit, libraries, etc.

The Positive Macro-Question in the Planned Economy

From what you've been reading about the *normative* macro-question, a good bit about the *positive* macro-question has already come to light. Suppose we're talking about a completely planned economy. You know that the positive macro-question (what actually influences or determines the speed of the economy) will be answered by government directive. The administrators give the orders and the people respond. Everyone does what he or she is told to do, so the economy runs at the planned speed.

Of course you know it isn't as simple as that. People don't always do exactly as they're told. Administrative controls very often are inefficient. Nevertheless the speed of the planned economy generally is controlled by the economic planners and resource administrators.

A good course in public administration or administrative management, or one on the Soviet economy, will clue you in to how the "planned economy" carries out its micro and macro decisions. It isn't difficult to see how economic controls and government resource management are supposed to work. But what about the market system?

How is the "automatic pure market mechanism" supposed to take care of the positive macro-question? What forces are supposed to determine the overall rate of employment and output and income in the "pure market" system? Then, in the real world where there aren't any *pure* systems (only "mixed economies") how does it work?

HOW THE MARKET PROCESS AUTOMATICALLY ANSWERS THE MACRO-QUESTIONS

In the "model market system" the speed of the economy just takes care of itself. It is automatically determined, just like everything else in the "model market system." The normative question just doesn't arise. In the "pure model," however fast the economy *does* run, that's how fast it *should* run.

If everybody wants to work hard and long, then a lot of output will be produced. A lot of income will be earned by all those industrious people. There will be a lot of spending. If all the manufacturers and farmers and businesses and workers and everyone are really producing as much as they can, pushing hard to make as much income as they can get, then employment and output and income in the society will be high. But if nobody feels stimulated to work very hard or produce very much, the society's output and income will be low. See how the normative and positive macro-questions are automatically answered in the pure market system?

The more people produce the more they sell and the more they earn and the more they buy. If people decide to produce more they get more income and they buy more. No one needs to decide how fast the economy *should* run. No one needs to plan and direct the people to produce at the right speed. It's all determined automatically by the natural market forces— by "the basic laws of positive economics."

Prices Adjust to Prevent Depression

But suppose that for some unexplained reason, suddenly there is too much output for sale in the market. Businesses and farmers are going broke because they can't sell all their products. Many workers lose their jobs. The economy goes into a depression. How does the market process solve this problem of depression?

In the "pure model," it's easy. Prices will adjust themselves until the surpluses are all bought up and until the unemployed workers all have jobs again. Here's how it's supposed to happen.

Product Prices Go Down. The producers who can't sell all their products start offering them for sale at lower and lower prices. As the prices of the surplus products go down, money becomes more valuable. All of us now can buy more products with our dollars. Also, people are more willing to spend, to take advantage of all those good bargains! So as the prices fall more and more, people (and businesses) buy more and more. Soon all the surpluses are cleared out of the market and everything's okay again.

Wages Go Down. At the same time that product prices are falling, wages (labor prices) are also falling. The unemployed workers (the "surplus labor") will be willing to work for lower wages. As wages go down, each dollar will buy more labor than before so the cost of producing products goes down. Therefore profit opportunities get better and better. Businesses hire more labor. Soon the unemployment problem is solved.

Interest Rates Go Down. Also there's another "price" working to help get rid of the surpluses and unemployment: the interest rate. Businesses usually borrow much of the money they need to build their factories and to buy their machines and equipment and raw materials and to stock their shelves with inventories. If business is booming and everybody is trying to expand, then everyone will be trying to borrow money. The "money market" will be very "tight." And the interest rate? High, of course!

But suppose the economy is depressed. Not many businesses are trying to borrow. The money market is very "easy." Interest rates are low. As the economy slows down, interest rates go down. With easy money available, businesses can expand at very low interest cost. This induces them to borrow more and expand. This helps to bring prosperity back again.

It's easy to see how depression is self-correcting, in the "model pure market system." As soon as surpluses and unemployment begin to appear, automatic price adjustments come into play and begin to solve the problem. The price adjustments keep doing their thing until the problem is solved. It's so neat you just wouldn't believe it! So don't believe it. It doesn't work out quite that way in the real world.

Real-World Prices Don't Move Down Easily

In the real world, all these "market tendencies" really do exist. The tendencies really do try to work in the real world, just as the model says. When there are surpluses and widespread unemployment, it is a fact that prices and wages do *try* to go down.

Some prices and wages actually *do* go down, some. But most prices and wages *can't* go down. People won't let them go down. Most often it's the *sellers* (not the buyers) who have the most control over prices. So guess which way the prices of most things are likely to move. Up? Yes. Down? No. All modern nations have such things as minimum wage laws, agricultural price controls, and lots of other "price-fixing" laws. But that isn't the really big problem.

Prices don't fall because sellers don't want them to fall, and most sellers have enough market power to keep them from falling. Both the sellers of products and the sellers of factors of production fight very hard to prevent price reductions for the things they sell. They would rather see less output and more un-employment than lower prices!

Workers don't want lower wages, land owners don't want lower rents, and the owners of capital and businesses don't want lower interest and profits. How bad would the economy have to get before the steelworkers or the autoworkers or the teamsters or the communications workers or the school teachers or anyone else would accept a major wage cut? Pretty bad. Right?

When businesses are faced with declining demands they can cut back output and still survive—sometimes even make profits. But to keep producing and let surpluses pile up to be sold for "whatever the market will bring"—that would be industrial suicide.

In the pure market model, declining demand would have an immediate effect on prices. Prices would fall until the surplus products were bought up and wages would fall until all the workers were hired. (Of course several people might starve while the process was working itself out.) But in the "controlled markets" of the real world, declining demands don't usually push prices down much. In almost all real-world markets, reduced spending results in production cuts and unemployment—not declining prices.

If Prices Won't Move, The Market Model Won't Work

Once prices are frozen, the pure market model is of no help in explaining how to get out of a depression. All it can tell us is this: "With inflexible prices, if everything else stays the same the depression will continue indefinitely." That's no help to the hungry workers, the dispossessed farmers, the bankrupt businesses, or the harassed economist who's trying to advise the governments on what to do!

For the market system to maintain full employment—that is, to prevent depression—wages and prices must be able to move freely up or down to reflect changes in demand or supply. But are all prices flexible? Of course not.

Generally, prices can move upward without much resistance. But downward? No. Not without a long, hard struggle. Many prices would never move down no matter what!

The "Gut Issues" Of Macroeconomics

If we can't depend on *price adjustments* to bring total spending into line with full employment, then *what can* we depend on? What will keep the economy out of bad depressions? or inflations? Now you have your finger on the really tough questions. These are the real "gut issues" of macroeconomics.

In the real world, price adjustments don't work the way they're supposed to, to keep the economy out of depression. So how can we be sure that the economic system will stay out of depression? That's a good question. You don't yet know enough of the macro concepts and principles for me to give you the answer and explain it thoroughly. That will come in Parts Three and Four. But for now let me give you a tentative answer.

We can pretty well depend on a modern economic system like the U.S. economy to stay out of serious and prolonged depression. To the extent that the economy does it by itself, that's fine. But when the economy doesn't do it by itself, the government will enter the picture and do whatever it must to prevent a serious and prolonged depression.

The government has the "tools" it needs to do the job. You may be quite certain that whenever it becomes necessary these tools will be used and that serious depression will be averted. After you have studied Parts Three and Four you will understand how it all works. But first there's a lot you need to know about money. You'll find out some of that in the next chapter, and you'll find out even more in the chapter after that. But before you go on, be sure you understand about macroeconomics and the circular flow of the economy.

REVIEW EXERCISES

• MAJOR CONCEPTS, PRINCIPLES, TERMS (Explain each thoroughly.)

the interdependence of the modern economy
"partial breakdown" of the economic system
total spending equals total receipts
real output equals real income
the basic questions of macroeconomics
the normative macro-questions
the positive macro-questions
how the market process answers the macro-questions
macroeconomics
microeconomics

• OTHER CONCEPTS AND TERMS (Explain each briefly.)

the total spending flow   normative
real output   positive
real income   "value added"

• DIAGRAM (Draw and explain.)

The Circular Flow Between Households and Businesses

• QUESTIONS (Write out answers or jot down key points.)

1. Suppose, next spring, *everyone* decides to really be stingy and save up for a nice long vacation trip, in July. Nobody buys any new cars or appliances or clothes, or goes out to restaurants or shows. Everybody just saves. What do you think will happen? Will all the people succeed in their savings and vacation plans? Discuss.

2. It's interesting to think about how much the normative macro-questions are determined by tradition and custom and habit, even in the highly sophisticated, modern economies of the 1970's. Think about such things as the work-day, the work-week, school vacations—how many of these arrangements have been "passed down" to us by the needs of the agriculturally-based, daylight-restricted societies of the past? Do you think it would be a good idea to make some basic changes in some of these "customary" arrangements? Discuss.

3. Explain how depression is supposed to be automatically prevented, and self-correcting in the "pure market economy." Then explain why it doesn't (can't) work that way in the real world of the 1970s.

6 The Magic of Money: What It Is and What It Does, and the American Banking System

Money is the lifeblood of the market system, and the banking system is the heart.

Money is one of the most important yet most thoroughly misunderstood things in modern society. This chapter tries to give you a real understanding of what money is and how it works. Some of the things you will read on the following pages will be very different from what you have always thought about money. Some of the things may not be easy for you to believe. But it's all true.

Much of what's going on in the modern world is incomprehensible to most people because they don't understand about money. Here's your chance to escape forever from "the ranks of the unaware." Here's your introduction to the magic world of money.

THE MEDIUM OF EXCHANGE AND THE FUNCTIONS OF MONEY

Everyone has heard that money is a medium of exchange. Exactly what does that mean? You know that a newspaper is a medium for spreading the news. We talk about newspapers and radio and TV as being "news media." A truck is a medium for transporting things. We talk about trucks, railroads, airlines, pipelines as "transportation media." You have heard of the spiritualist who acts as a medium for contacting spirits. So what is a "medium"?

A medium is anything which serves as a go-between. It permits or makes it easier for something to happen. A medium lets you accomplish something easier. Money is a "medium of exchange." Money makes it easier to exchange things—to trade things.

Most of the trade in the modern world could not be accomplished without something to serve as the medium of exchange—that is, without something to serve as money. *Whatever serves as the medium of exchange is money.*

Money is not "the medium of exchange" because it is money. It is money because it is serving as "the medium of exchange." No matter what it is, so long as it is serving as the exchange medium, it is money. After I show you some examples you will understand what all this means.

The Need for a Medium of Exchange

I am a fisherman. I just caught a boat load of fish and I want to exchange all these fish for a new suit. Without an "exchange medium" this is very difficult to do. Try to find a suit-seller who wants a boat load of fish! But with an exchange medium it's easy.

What will I accept as a medium to help me exchange my fish for a new suit? I will accept anything for my fish—I don't care what it is—so long as I am sure the suit-seller will accept it in exchange for a suit. If there is any doubt about whether or not the suit-seller will accept it for a suit, then I will not accept it for my fish.

Now let's be more realistic. I really don't want to exchange my boat load of fish just for a suit. I want groceries, electricity and water, housing (rent), and maybe a few glasses of beer and some jukebox music at the local tavern. So whatever I accept in exchange for my fish cannot be something acceptable *only* to the suit-seller. It must be acceptable to all those other people, too. Why might all those other people accept it? Only because they are confident that everyone they do business with will accept it too. See how it all ties together? When everyone is confident that everyone else will accept something as money, then that something becomes *generally acceptable*. Then—and only then—it is money.

Money Is Anything Which Is Generally Acceptable

Now you know what *money* is. Money is anything which is *generally acceptable* in exchange for things. People will accept it for whatever they have to sell—products, natural resources, labor services or whatever. I will accept it for my fish because I am sure other people will accept it for the things I want to buy. It's as simple as that.

In any society or at any given place or time, *anything* which is serving as the exchange medium, is money. It is money because everyone is confident that it is "good money." If people begin to question the acceptability of the money, then they will refuse to accept it. Once this happens it will cease to be money.

If you heard that there was a great flood of near-perfect counterfeit twenty-dollar bills in your neighborhood, you might decide not to accept any twenty-dollar bills. Others also refuse to accept twenty-dollar bills. So twenty-dollar bills cease to be money in your neighborhood. How quickly something can cease to be money when people lose confidence in its general acceptability!

The Functions of Money

As soon as something becomes generally acceptable in exchange for things, it becomes money. Then it begins to perform all the functions of money. There are four functions of money. The first is to serve as medium of exchange, of course. But there are three more functions.

Money serves as the standard for valuing things. People automatically compare the values of things in terms of how much "money" each thing is worth. Is my boat worth more than your car? How can we tell? Just translate both into money. A $3,000 car is worth more than a $1,500 boat. Right? Of course. So money serves as the standard of value, or unit of value for the society.

The "value unit" function and the "medium-of-exchange" function are sometimes called the two *primary functions of money*. The primary functions are the functions which money performs at the present time. You might call them the "current functions" of money—the functions of valuing things and exchanging things *now*.

The two other functions of money serve the purpose of "transferring value" from one time to another. These are called the *secondary functions of money*. You might call them the "future functions" of money.

Money is money because people believe it is money!

WOW! That's crazy!

Whenever a person or a business takes on an obligation and agrees to make some future payment, the obligation (debt) is usually stated in money. The money unit (for example, dollars) is usually the most convenient way to express the amount of the debt. When money is used this way, we say that it is functioning as the standard of deferred payments.

In its other secondary function, money serves as a convenient form in which to hold savings. It is a thing which can be used to "store up value" for the future. When you save money, your money is serving as a store of value. That's the fourth and final function of money.

If you want to save you must have some way to store up the value you are saving. You could buy and hold land or buy and store steel ingots or mahogany lumber or antique furniture or anything else you think will hold its value. Money is a very convenient form of stored up value. If you save money (instead of land or steel or whatever) you can always exchange it for other things in a hurry. You know that you can use the money anytime for whatever you might want to buy. No other kind of asset is as liquid (as easily and rapidly exchangeable into other things) as money.

The four functions which money performs for the society—medium of exchange, unit of value, standard of deferred payments, and store of value—are *vital* in the operation of the market process. Even in tradition or command-oriented societies these functions must be performed. It would be difficult for even a primitive society to operate without something to serve as money. Modern society just couldn't exist without it.

HOW MONEY MIGHT EVOLVE

To illustrate how money might evolve, let's go back to our island economy. Remember when the northside islanders started selling tuba? They were accepting all sorts of things in exchange—dried fishsticks, breadfruit, taro, and anything else the other islanders wanted to trade. But much time has passed since that day. Now the northside islanders no longer accept "any old thing" in exchange for their tuba. Here's what happened.

Fishsticks Become Money

One day the westside islanders took several baskets of breadfruit and taro to the northside islanders to trade for tuba. But it happened that on that day the northside islanders already had all the breadfruit and taro they could use, so they refused to accept the breadfruit and taro in exchange for tuba. They explained that the breadfruit and taro would all be spoiled before they could eat it. Then the northside chief, King Ratukabua, made a suggestion.

"Why don't you trade your breadfruit and taro to someone for dried fishsticks? We will sell you all the tuba you want, for dried fishsticks. Dried fishsticks last forever. If we get too many we can always ship them and sell them in Japan. The Japanese call them "katsuobushi" and value them highly. They pay us with Japanese money (yen) and we can use the yen to buy all sorts of things from Japan."

So the westside islanders go around trying to find somebody who will give them dried fishsticks in exchange for their breadfruit and taro. Sure enough, the eastside islanders are willing to trade fishsticks for the breadfruit and taro. So the westsiders make the trade, then go and exchange the fishsticks for jugs of tuba. In this trade, what function did the fishsticks perform? Medium of exchange? Of course.

Soon the word gets around that the northside islanders will always accept fishsticks in exchange for tuba. Because of this, other people around the island begin to accept fishsticks in exchange for the things they want to sell. Soon everyone realizes that everyone else will accept fishsticks in exchange for things. So no one hesitates to accept fishsticks. Fishsticks have become money? Just automatically? Yes.

Anyone who wants to trade anything can first sell it for fishsticks, then use the fishsticks to buy other things. As long as fishsticks continue to be generally acceptable—that is, as long as everyone is confident that everyone else will accept fishsticks—then fishsticks will continue to be money.

See how easy it is for money to arise? The gains from trade are so great and trade without money is so difficult that some kind of money just naturally evolves. It has actually happened this way in every society—small or large, primitive or advanced. Something always arises to perform the functions of (and therefore to become) money.

Specially Printed Paper Becomes Money

Suppose that over the years the northside islanders become very wealthy from making tuba and selling it for dried fishsticks. They have a great warehouse which they built from hewn mahogany logs, just to hold the fishsticks. One member of the northside family stands guard every night so no one will steal any of their fishstick money. When the warehouse gets too full they export some fishsticks (katsuobushi) to Japan in exchange for better tuba-making equipment and for all kinds of luxury items to enjoy.

These days, when the members of the wealthy northside family travel around the island, they don't carry sacks of fishsticks to use to buy things. If they want to buy something they just give out small pieces of paper saying: "The northside family will pay to the bearer on demand, one fishstick." These "IOU's" of the northside family are beautifully designed in green and gold and carry the signature of the northside chief who had them printed up in Japan.

The "paper money" idea was thought of by the northside chief as a way to make trade more convenient. He thought: "Why should we travel all over the island buying things and paying with fishsticks, when a few days later the people always bring the fishsticks back to us and buy tuba? Why not keep the fishsticks in our warehouse all the time, where they are safe and dry? We can just make payments with slips of paper saying 'the northside islanders owe you one fishstick.' Then when the people come to us to trade the fishsticks for tuba, they can give us back these IOU's." This seemed to be a good idea so they tried it.

At first some of the islanders were wary about accepting pieces of paper in exchange for their fruits and vegetables. But a few tried it and it worked so well that soon everyone wanted to be paid in "paper money." Now, the people have complete faith in the paper money. They are sure that everyone else will accept it and they know it's fully backed by fishsticks—they could always turn it in to the northsiders and get fishsticks.

Now that modern times are here, when the eastside islanders want to buy something from the westsiders they never carry fishsticks with them. They simply use the little pieces of printed paper as money. Printed paper? as money? If we didn't use it ourselves we wouldn't believe it!

Pieces of paper are so much easier to keep, to hide, to use in exchange. How easily and naturally the society has moved from a less efficient kind of money (fishsticks) to a more efficient kind—paper. But even paper is not efficient enough. Watch what happens next.

The Eastside Islanders "Deposit" Their Money

Over the years the eastside family has been very industrious. They have been producing many fishsticks and exchanging them for paper money. Also they have been making other products and selling them for paper money. The savings of the eastside family now amount to many thousands of the fishstick-backed paper bills. The family begins to worry about the possibility of a fire or a robbery.

The northside family has a large stone house with a big fireproof vault in the basement. One day the eastside chief, King Tuituranga, asks the northside chief to please store the paper money in the vault. The northside chief agrees. So the eastside chief delivers the paper money and receives in exchange, a receipt. You might say the eastside islanders have put their money into a "bank account" for safe keeping.

Bank Accounts Become Money

A week or two later the eastside family wants to buy some breadfruit tree logs from the westside family so they can make outrigger canoes. First they go to the northside chief and get (withdraw) some of their paper money from the vault. Then they buy the logs and pay the westsiders. The westsiders don't want to keep all this cash lying around either. So they take it to the northside chief and ask him to keep it in the vault. They "deposit" their money and get a receipt.

A week or two later the eastsiders withdraw more money and buy taro from the westsiders. As soon as the westsiders get the money they take it right back to the northside chief and ask him to put it back in the vault. They "deposit" it again. This sort of thing continues to happen every week or two.

One day the northside chief has an idea. He says to the eastside chief: "Every week or two you come and get some of your money from your vault box and you go and spend it to buy things from the westsiders. Then the westsiders bring the money right back. So I have to open the vault and let them put the money into *their* vault box. That seems to me like a lot

of trouble for nothing. Let me make a suggestion.

When you want to buy something, why don't you just write a note to the westsiders authorizing me to take the money out of your vault box and put it into their vault box? That will save you both a lot of trouble, and I will only have to open the big heavy door to the vault one time for each transaction. Here. Write your authorization on these special pieces of paper I had printed up in Japan. These are called 'checks.' All you do is write who gets the money (whose vault box I should put it in) and how much and then sign your name. I'll take care of transferring the money, and I'll keep a record. I'll send you a statement once a month showing how much you have deposited, how much has been paid out, and how much is left in your vault box. Want to try it?"

The eastside chief thinks this is a little bit unusual, but he decides to give it a try. When he tries to buy something the westsiders are wary about this flimsy way of doing business. But soon they decide to take a chance and accept the eastside chief's "check." Lo and behold, the system works fine! So now whenever the eastsiders want to buy from the westsiders, they write checks. It works so well that soon all the people on the island start keeping their paper money in the northside vault and writing checks when they want to buy things.

An Efficient Money System Has Evolved

Notice how far the island's monetary system has evolved. And how efficient it is! Seldom does anyone exchange checks for paper money. Almost all of the paper money just stays in the vault. The most efficient way of doing business is by writing checks to each other. Paper money is only used for small, day-to-day transactions. No one ever uses the actual fishsticks to make payments. Not anymore. How medieval that would be! The islanders now have a modern monetary system. But it isn't through evolving yet. Just watch.

As the years go by, trade picks up on the island. In a few years it gets so busy that the northside chief, King Ratukabua, has to spend much of his time going into the vault and moving paper money from one owner's box to another. One day he says to himself: "This is ridiculous. All these fishstick bills are exactly the same. Why should I keep moving them from one box to another? Why not count the number of bills in each box and make a record. Then I will know how much belongs to each 'depositor.' After that, I can dump all the bills in the same pile and not worry about which ones belong to which people. Then I won't have to be going into the vault all the time and moving cash from box to box.

"I will keep the account books upstairs in my office. When the westside chief (Queen Isaleilani) comes in with a check from the eastside chief, I will just add the amount to her account and subtract it from the eastsiders' account. How easy that will be! I will also keep some fishstick bills up there in the office safe so that if anyone wants any cash I'll have it right there. I may *never* have to open this big, heavy door to the vault, ever again. (How stupid I was not to have thought of this sooner!)"

Account Figures Begin to Be Used as Money

The northside chief puts his plan into action. It works beautifully. Sometimes someone comes in and wants cash (fishstick bills). But before the wall safe gets empty, someone else comes in and deposits cash and replenishes the supply. Last year just before Christmas, many people came in to get cash because they were making lots of small gift purchases. The wall safe was emptied and the northside chief had to open the vault and bring more cash upstairs. But right after Christmas all the cash came back. The wall safe got overstuffed with cash and the chief had to take some of the currency to the basement and put it back in the vault.

The monetary system is working just great. The dried fishsticks never leave the warehouse. Most of the cash never leaves the vault. People do business mostly by writing checks. Whatever you "spend" is subtracted from your account and added to someone else's account. Whatever checks you receive are added to your account and subtracted from someone else's account.

The account figures are being transferred back and forth. So what's serving as money? Would you believe, the account figures? That's the truth.

How neatly it all works—just like a modern monetary system. And it all came about so naturally! Why? Because the benefits of an efficient monetary system are so great and so obvious, that's why. The islanders couldn't enjoy the full advantages of specialization and trade without an efficient medium of exchange. So one evolved. But look out! A disaster is about to happen.

The "Backing" for the Money Is Destroyed

Let's suppose that one spring the tuna from which the fishsticks are made all migrate away so that no more fishsticks can be produced. Also, that same spring, a midnight fire breaks out in the warehouse. The flames leaping skyward can be seen all over the island. Everyone awakens and hurries anxiously, apprehensively, to see what is burning. When they arrive the entire warehouse is ablaze. They stand dumbfounded, watching the flickering reflection of the flames lighting the circle of sad, tearful faces of their friends from all over the island. The fire is beyond control. Everyone knows that their money—the island's store of treasure—is gone. And they know it can never be replaced.

Almost overcome by grief, the eastside chief speaks: "Woe be unto all of us. Our money is gone. Our savings of paper money now are only paper. Our checking accounts mean nothing. We are all poor again. We must all go back to the hard, primitive life we had to lead before our fishstick money freed us from all that. Truly, this is the saddest day in our lives, and the saddest day in the entire history of this island."

Then the wise old northside chief who earlier had withdrawn from the crowd to think, came forth and began to speak. Everyone's attention was captured by his deep, reassuring voice: "Do not despair, my friends. Truly, nothing is lost. The kindly gods have relieved us of a burden. No longer will we need to waste our energies guarding and repairing the warehouse or producing fishsticks which no one will ever eat.

"You have my word that your paper money and your checking accounts are as good as they ever were. You can't exchange them for fishsticks. But you never wanted to do that anyway. You *can* exchange them for tuba anytime you want to, and you can still spend your fishstick money for anything else you want to buy from us. We will all miss the delicious flavor of dried fishsticks. But except for that, nothing is lost. Your money is still just as good as it was before."

At first the others can't see how "fishstick money" can be any good if there are no fishsticks to back it up. What good is paper money if the *backing* is gone? But then the westside chief announces: "As long as the northside chief will continue to accept this money in exchange for tuba, we will accept it in exchange for breadfruit and taro."

The eastside chief announces: "As long as we are sure we can use this money to buy tuba and breadfruit and taro, we will accept it for smoked lagoon fish, turtle meat, and anything else we have to sell."

The Monetary System Doesn't Need Any "Backing"

The monetary system has been saved by the wisdom and quick, reassuring action of the northside chief. He was wise enough to know that it is not what "backs up" the money that gives it its value—it is what you can *buy* with it.

It is "faith in its general acceptability" which makes money, money. The northside chief knew that if he could assure everyone that the currency and checking accounts were still acceptable then the monetary system would continue to work just as before. But if the people lost confidence in the money, the monetary system would collapse.

It is always true in every society that the monetary system operates on confidence. If the American people, for any reason, lost confidence in the future general acceptability of the U.S. dollar, the U.S. monetary system would collapse. The dollar would cease to be money. Unless something was done quickly to reestablish some kind of money, production would stop. Drastic action would be required to prevent most of the people from starving.

The wise old northside chief saved the monetary system and the island's economy by guaranteeing that the money was still acceptable in exchange—it still had purchasing power. Before he spoke, the monetary system had been destroyed because the people *thought* it had. After he spoke the money was good again. Why? Because everyone was confident that it was.

The only thing the island's fishstick money can now be used for is to buy things. But that is what money is always wanted for anyway! Do people want money so they can turn it in for whatever backs it up? Of course not. They want it so they can buy things.

The value of money is determined, not by the number of fishsticks or grains of gold you could get for it, but by what you can buy with it. This is true in every society. You accept dollars, not because they are backed by gold (which they are not), but because you can use them to buy things. The more you can buy, the more valuable is your dollar.

Most of the Paper Money Is Destroyed

Even though the backing behind the fishstick money is gone, the monetary system functions as well as it did before. Everyone has complete confidence in the money. As time goes on, the northside chief occasionally looks into the big vault and sees the great pile of paper money lying there. One day he picks up one of the aging pieces of paper money and reads what it says: "King Ratukabua will pay to the bearer on demand, one fishstick." Suddenly it hits him.

"These are nothing but my old IOU's! Each one says that I owe the bearer one fishstick. Why should I have to keep and store and guard all these old IOU's? If I could get rid of them we could use the vault space as a wine cellar for aging our tuba. Why shouldn't I just burn up all this old money? If I ever need more of these bills (because people want to carry more cash, like at Christmas time) I can always get a new batch printed up in Japan. So why keep this pile of old paper money?

The chief ponders over this question for quite awhile. But try as he will, he can think of no good reason to keep the paper money. So one day he clears out the vault and burns the money. He is very careful not to be seen. He doesn't think they would understand.

Now the island has no fishsticks backing up the paper money, and almost no paper money backing up the checking accounts. Then one day before long the eastside chief comes and wants to see his money, just to be sure everything is all right. The northside chief opens the account book and shows the eastside chief his balance. But the eastside chief says: "I want to see the *money*, not a *number* in your account book!"

"The number in the account book *is* your money, my friend," says the northside chief. "It's perfectly good money. You can spend it by writing checks. But you can't change it into fishsticks. And you can't change it into paper money either, unless you wait for two weeks while I have the paper money printed up."

The Eastside Chief Demands Cash

The eastside chief is really upset. He has heard of many strange things, but this takes the cake! The idea that the *number* showing his *checking account balance* is his money—the idea that *the number in the account book is the only form in which his money exists*—that is just too much for him to comprehend. He says "I'll be back in two weeks to get my cash and you'd better have it ready for me when I get here. Otherwise, be ready for war!"

The northside chief orders the bills printed. Two weeks later the eastside chief returns, gets his cash, closes out his checking account, and goes home with a big basketful of new paper money. He really doesn't have any more money than he had before. He has just changed the form of his money—from an accounting figure to printed pieces of paper.

As the weeks go by the eastside family finds that using cash is not nearly as convenient as using checks. Also they get worried about theft or fire. One day the eastside chief finally realizes he did the wrong thing. He takes his basketful of cash back to the northside chief, apologizes, reopens his checking account and deposits the cash. Now he has changed the form of his money from paper bills back into an accounting figure.

The paper bills really aren't money any longer. They aren't serving as a medium of exchange anymore. They are old IOU's of the northside chief and as long as they are in his vault they are not serving as money. That night the northside chief discreetly takes the cash out and burns it. The eastside chief has regained his confidence in "checking account" money. Once again everyone is happy and all goes well.

The Island Now Has a Modern Monetary System

Now a modern monetary system has evolved on the island. Most of the money exists only in the account books of the northside chief. The accounts are not fully backed by paper money (currency), and the currency is not backed by anything. People make payments by writing checks. Each check results in a subtraction from one account and an addition to another. That's all. No currency changes hands. Currency representing these accounts doesn't even exist.

What do you think of the island's monetary system? Would you believe that's the way it works in every modern society? This example really does fairly well describe the money system of the United States and of every other modern nation in the world. You will hear more about this later. But first we need to look at the interesting effect which borrowing can have on the money supply.

LENDING MONEY SOMETIMES CREATES MONEY

Suppose the eastsiders want to buy a plot of land from the westsiders but they don't have enough money in their account. The eastside chief goes to see the northside chief who, as you know, is operating as the island's banker. The eastside chief asks if he can borrow 10,000 fishsticks (FS 10,000) to buy some land from the westsiders. The northside chief realizes that the eastside chief doesn't want cash—he only wants the amount added to his checking account so he can write a check to buy the land. Then the westsiders will deposit the check to their account and the "loaned money" (FS 10,000) will be subtracted from the eastsiders' account and added to the westsiders' account.

The northside chief, knowing the eastside chief's credit is good, says "Certainly. We will lend you as much as you would like." The northside chief adds FS 10,000 to the account of the eastside chief, and the eastside chief signs a note promising to repay the money, plus interest.

What has happened to the supply of money on the island? It's FS 10,000 bigger than before! The eastside family now has FS 10,000 which it did not have before. Nobody had it before. It didn't exist! The northside chief,

acting as the banker, simply created that FS 10,000 when he added that amount to the eastsiders' account. Is it *really* money that has been *created*? Yes! It really is.

Look at it this way. Suppose *before* the FS 10,000 loan, you went around the island and found out how much money each person had (in cash and in checking accounts). If you added up all the figures you would come out with the total size of the island's money supply. Then *after* the FS 10,000 loan, suppose you did it again. You would come up with a larger total than before. How much larger? FS 10,000 larger. Where did the extra FS 10,000 come from? It was *created* by the northside chief? That's right.

The eastside family will now buy the land from the westside family and pay them by check. Then the new FS 10,000 will be subtracted from the eastsiders' account and added to the westsiders' account. The new FS 10,000 will become the westsiders' money. Before the eastside chief borrowed it, whose money was it? Nobody's. Where was it? Nowhere. It didn't exist.

All the Money on the Island Is Really "Debt"

All the money on the island consists of debt. It's the debt of the northside chief. The "balance" in each account is the amount the northside chief owes to the owner of the account. And it's those "account balances" which make up most of the island's money supply.

Since the debt of the northside chief serves as money, any increase in that debt is an increase in the money supply. When the eastside chief borrows, he gives the northside chief a promissory note saying, "I owe you FS 10,000." What does the eastside chief get in return? He gets a FS 10,000 addition to his checking account. He gets a "deposit slip" from the northside chief which says (in effect), "I owe *you* FS 10,000."

See what has happened? Each has given the other a debt in exchange for a debt! Each owes the other an additional FS 10,000! But the important thing is that the northside chief's debt is monetized debt—that is, *his debt serves as money*. This transaction creates money because the debt of the northside chief *is* money. When the northside chief is issuing more *debt*, he is issuing more *money*! Get it?

Increasing the Checking Account Balances Creates Money

Whenever the northside chief is lending money to people by adding to their checking accounts, he is adding to the island's total money supply. The people are getting more money to spend. But whenever a person pays back the northside chief by writing a check, that reduces the person's checking account balance and destroys money. It reduces the size of the total money supply of the island.

The total money supply is made up of the checking account balances of the people, plus the paper money they carry around. Anything which increases the size of the checking account balances increases the money supply; anything which reduces the size of the checking account balances reduces the money supply.

If anything happened to cause the northside chief's bank to collapse, all of the checking account balances would be gone so all of the "checking account money" would be gone. That's about the way it is in the real world, too. If the bank where you keep your money suddenly collapsed, your "checking account money" would be gone. But the Federal Deposit Insurance Corporation (FDIC)—the government agency which guarantees the safety of your bank account—probably would reimburse you.

Soon you will see how this simple island example of "creating money by making loans" is more true to life than you might think. Most of the money in the United States and in other

modern nations is actually created by bank loans. It doesn't happen exactly as in the island example, but almost! In the next chapter you will find out exactly how it works. If you understand how it happens on the island you won't have any trouble seeing how it works in the real world.

MONEY IN THE UNITED STATES

To see just how similar the monetary systems of the modern world are to our island example, let's take a quick look at money in the United States. In this country most of the money is made up of checking account balances in the banks. Each depositor has an account balance. Each depositor's account balance is that person's money. Paper money ("currency" or "cash") doesn't exist to back up these checking accounts. If the currency did exist, all the vaults of all the banks in the country would be stuffed full and there still wouldn't be enough space to store all the currency.

People don't like to use paper money except for small transactions. They would rather have most of their money in the form of an account figure at the bank than in the form of paper bills. If there was enough paper money to pay off all the checking accounts in the country, no one would want to hold all that cash.

Nobody wants several thousand dollars in cash lying around the house. The banks certainly don't want several billions in cash lying idle in their vaults! If all this cash existed someone would have to arrange for it to be taken out and burned. That's just what would happen. Just like on the island.

The Federal Reserve Banks Issue Paper Money

In the United States the twelve Federal Reserve Banks are the ones that issue the currency (paper money). As people go to their local banks and cash checks, the banks pay out the cash they have on hand. If they run short they get more paper money from the Federal Reserve Banks which get it from the Bureau of Engraving and Printing of the U.S. Department of the Treasury in Washington, D.C.

The paper money in the United States consists of *Federal Reserve Notes*—simply the IOU's of the Federal Reserve Banks. Just as the northside chief could have a little piece of paper printed up to say: "This piece of paper represents one fishstick," so the Federal Reserve Bank of New York (or St. Louis or Chicago or Minneapolis or Kansas City or Dallas or any other) can have a piece of paper printed up to say: "This is one dollar."

Reach in your wallet and pull out a Federal Reserve Note. The black numbers on the face of the bill and the letter and the printing on the black seal tell you which Federal Reserve Bank issued the note. The number "1" and the letter "A" indicate Boston; 2 and B-New York; 3 and C-Philadelphia; 4 and D-Cleveland; 5 and E-Richmond; 6 and F-Atlanta; and so on to 12 and L for San Francisco.

Currency Is Printed Up As Needed

The number and sizes (denominations) of the notes issued by each Federal Reserve Bank are determined by the currency needs in their district. That depends on the desires of the people and businesses to hold and use "cash money" instead of "checking account money." If people want to hold more cash (perhaps at Christmas time), they cash checks. Then their banks ask for (buy) more currency from the Federal Reserve Banks.

The Federal Reserve Banks get more currency printed up, as needed. If the people decide to change their form of money from "currency" back to "checking account money" they simply deposit the Federal Reserve Notes (currency) in their bank accounts. The banks send the surplus dollar bills back to the Federal Reserve Banks where some (the

newest) are kept for future use and the others are destroyed.

Be careful to say "money" when you mean money, and "currency" when you mean only "the paper kind" of money, and coins. You know that money is anything people will generally accept in exchange for things. And you know that "the paper kind" is only a small percentage of the total. So be careful to say it that way. In the United States and other modern countries, money consists primarily of people's and businesses' checking account balances on the books (or in the computer memories) of banks.

The Present U.S. Money Supply

In the United States in 1976, the total amount of money in existence (the money supply) amounted to something more than $300 billion. More than 75 percent of it consisted of demand deposits—that is, the checking account balances of people and businesses. More than three-fourths of the U.S. money supply is really nothing but little numbers in the account books and computer memories of banks! Total currency (paper money and coins) added up to less than one-fourth of the total money supply. The value of all the paper money amounted to less than $60 billion and the balance (about $7 billion) was in coins. (Many of the coins are not being used as money but are being held by collectors and speculators.) *

---

* Are savings deposits money? Are government bonds money? Strictly speaking, no. But sometimes it is useful to define the money supply to include savings deposits, since it is very easy for a person with a savings deposit to exchange that deposit into "spendable money." The same is true of government bonds held by individuals and businesses.

Economists use three different symbols to refer to their different definitions of the money supply: M_1 means the money supply made up of "immediately spendable money"—demand deposits and currency; M_2 means the supply of spendable money plus savings deposits. Sometimes M_3 is used to

None of the money being used in the United States is backed by gold or silver or anything but the promises (and the assets) of the Fed and the banks. It has been more than forty years since a person could turn in paper money and get gold. It has been several years since a person could turn in paper money and get silver. But no matter. Money is money because people accept it as money—because you can use it to buy things.

THE EVOLUTION OF MONEY IN THE REAL WORLD

Money is so useful and it evolves so naturally that in every society something has evolved into money. Seashells, stones, various kinds of metals, diamonds, cigarettes, fish hooks, grain, bullets—almost every imaginable thing has been money at one place or another at one time or another throughout history.

At First, Money Must Be Full-Bodied

How does something get to become money? Usually it starts out as something useful—some commodity or tool, something used and wanted by most people. At first, people will not be sure whether other people will accept it as money. Still they are willing to accept it because it is "full-bodied." If others will not accept it as money it can always be used for its original purpose anyway.

For many years in the evolution of money, the "money thing" must continue to be full-bodied– that is, it must have as much value as

---

mean spendable money plus savings deposits plus government bonds. And sometimes the Federal Reserve economists even define M_4 and M_5. But you don't need to worry about that.

When you are talking about the size of the money supply, it makes a lot of difference whether you choose M_1 or M_2 or what. There's much more money in savings deposits in the United States than in demand deposits! And individuals and businesses hold more than one hundred billion dollars worth of government securities! But usually when people talk about the "money supply" they mean M_1: demand deposits and currency.

a "thing" as it has as "money." Otherwise people would not trust it and would not accept it.

Over the centuries, precious metals have been valued for their own sake. It was almost inevitable that gold and silver would evolve into money—so convenient, so attractive, so permanent, so easily made into bigger or smaller sizes, and such a little bit can be worth so much! So gold winds up performing the functions of money. People go around with gold dust or nuggets in a little pouch. Before they can trade they must find someone who has a scale to weigh the bits of gold.

Full-Bodied Coins Emerge. One day someone gets the idea that if the little pieces of gold were melted down into carefully measured sizes, with each piece stamped to indicate the weight, trade would be much easier. No longer would everyone need a scale for weighing gold. Gold would become a better medium of exchange—better money. This idea lead to the development of uniform little pieces of metal, each stamped to indicate its weight. But who can you trust to stamp the right weight on the pieces of gold? Not everybody! So before long, coins are being made and certified by the government.

Once the government gets involved, the next step is to reduce the amount of precious metal in each coin. So long as people continue to accept the smaller or less pure coin at face value, the "un-full-bodied" coin (token coin) works just as well as a full-bodied one. Smaller coins are more convenient, anyway. (Did you ever see one of the old full-bodied copper pennies which were once used as part of the U.S. money supply? How would you like to lug around a pocket full of those?)

The next step in the evolution of money comes with the introduction of paper money, backed by (convertible into) the gold or silver coins. Then as time goes on, people stop carrying so many metal coins and begin to use paper money almost entirely.

The Valuable Substance Is Removed from Money. The two final steps in the evolution of a modern monetary system are taken (1) when the precious metals are withdrawn from the monetary system entirely, and (2) when the people begin carrying out most of their exchanges by writing checks. Most of the money supply becomes the checking account balances of the people and businesses. Why? Because the government says so? No. Because this is the form in which the people choose to hold their money. It is the most convenient, most efficient form of money for most transactions.

So now you know the way the monetary systems have evolved in all the nations of the modern world. Interesting, isn't it? Hard to believe? Maybe. But it really did happen that way.

Money Is Essential in Every Society

It would be impossible to overstate the importance of money in the operation of any modern economy. The economy simply could not function without money. The market process just naturally happens. But it couldn't happen without money. Money is the medium which permits the market process to function. Truly, money is the lifeblood of the market process.

Exchange, specialization, division of labor, technological development—these are essential for *any* society which seeks to achieve high standards of living for the people. You know about the gains from specialization and trade. You know that the advantages can't come about without exchange. And you know that the many opportunities for exchange can't be fulfilled without money.

The Banking System Is the Heart of the Money System

Another thing you have learned in this chapter is the critical role of the banking function in an economic system. How important is the banking function? It's this important: *the money function can't be separated from the banking function.*

Think back to the island example. What would life on the island have been like without the northside chief, King Ratukabua, to serve as the island's banker? And suppose he wasn't honest? and prudent? The economic welfare of the people on the island really hangs in the balance! It all depends on a one-man banking system. If you lived on the island, wouldn't that make you nervous?

What if King Ratukabua should die? Then Prince Hafakaloa would take over. And the prince seems to be more interested in playing on the beach with eastside Princess Kasaleilia than in looking after the island's money and banking needs. Don't you think the islanders should do something to ensure the safety of their "money and banking system"? Of course they should. It works that way in the real world, too.

THE AMERICAN BANKING SYSTEM AND THE FEDERAL RESERVE SYSTEM

In every modern society the banking function is recognized as vital in the functioning of the economy. For this reason, every nation takes a lot of interest in what's going on with the banks. Of course!

Banks can create money as you learned a few minutes ago. In the next chapter you're going to find out exactly how that happens. But before we go into that, it would be helpful for you to know something about what the U.S. banking system looks like. And you need to know something about the Federal Reserve System.

Decentralized Banking

There are about 14,000 different banks in the United States. In addition, many banks have branches scattered in various locations.

Most of the banks are small. They are located in cities, towns, little communities, shopping centers, and neighborhoods all over the country. But some are huge, with assets worth billions of dollars.

Traditionally there has been a strong sentiment in the United States in favor of decentralized banking. Most modern nations have only a few banks with many branches scattered throughout the country. But not so in the U.S.A.! The agricultural areas and Western areas have always been a little distrustful of the "Eastern bankers" and have tried to prevent the big city banks from controlling the banks in their areas.

Even the "central bank" of the United States is decentralized! In England they have the Bank of England, in France they have the Banque de France, in Japan the Bank of Japan, in Germany the Deutsche Bundesbank—one central bank in each country. That's how it is everywhere else. But in the United States we have the Federal Reserve System—a decentralized central banking system made up of twelve different banks. How did that happen? Let's take a quick look at the history.

A Brief History

Ever since the beginning, the United States has had recurrent problems with its money and banking system. Most of the time, almost anyone with a few assets (like King Ratukabua) could set up a bank and then do just about anything—hold demand deposits, create money, and all that. There has always been some, but usually not very much government regulation or control.

The states have always been chartering banking corporations. Since the National Banking System was set up during the Civil War, the federal government (the Comptroller of the Currency) has been chartering "national banks." Both the state banking authorities and the Comptroller of the Currency have always examined banks to see if they are being honest with their depositors and prudent in their investment policies—that is, not putting their depositors' money in unproven oil wells or gold mines. Often, the safeguards haven't been good enough. But that hasn't been the big problem.

The big problem has been "financial panics." Every few years there would be a business slowdown or something would happen to shake people's confidence. People would be afraid the banks might fail. So they would hurry to the banks to get their money out. This is called a "run on the banks" or a "panic."

When a panic occurs the banks can't possibly pay off all the depositors, of course. They would have to sell all their investments, and billions of dollars of new currency would have to be printed up first! So the banks are forced to fail. All of the depositors (except the few who got there first) lose their money. When all this money just ceases to exist that's no good for the depositors or for the economy, either!

In 1907 there was a really bad one. Many banks failed and the depositors lost their money. With no money, the people couldn't buy much. The economy went into a depression. A lot of people were fed up with the instability of the American banking system. They demanded that the government do something about it. A commission was set up to study the situation. Ultimately, over the protests of the bankers, legislation was passed (in 1913) establishing the Federal Reserve System.

The Creation of the Federal Reserve System

To satisfy the demands for decentralized banking, Congress divided the country into twelve Federal Reserve districts. A separate Federal Reserve Bank was established in each district. All commercial banks which became members of the Federal Reserve System were required to buy a specified amount of stock in the Federal Reserve Bank in their district. So do these stockholders exercise *policy control* over the Federal Reserve Banks? No. Control rests with the Board of Governors of the Federal Reserve System (usually called the Federal Reserve Board) in Washington.

All national banks (banks chartered by the federal government) were required to join the Federal Reserve System. State-chartered banks could join if they wanted to—that is, they could join if they had enough assets and if they could meet all the other requirements for membership.

What was the Federal Reserve System (usually called the "Fed") set up to do? Several things:
- —to issue currency,
- —to act as banker for the federal government,
- —to hold deposits for the Treasury,
- —to buy and sell government bonds,
- —to aid in the collection of taxes,
- —to act as banker for and to provide banking services to the commercial banks.
- —but most important: the "Fed" was set up *to hold the reserves and regulate the lending activities of the commercial banks.*

Banking Problems of the 1920s and 1930s

You know enough about money and about the role of banks to appreciate the importance of the banking system in the functioning of an economic system. It's just amazing that the United States could wait until 1913 to set up the Federal Reserve System. But as it was originally set up the Fed fell far short of meeting the needs.

One of the things that the new Fed was supposed to accomplish was *safety*. The depositors shouldn't have to worry about the banks collapsing. Another thing was to provide for a *flexible money supply*. The money supply needs to expand when business is expanding to support the prosperity and growth of the economy.

Both of these problems—lack of safety and lack of flexibility—had been serious before 1913. Did the creation of the Fed solve these problems? You know the answer. It certainly did not.

Even during the prosperous years of the 1920s hundreds of banks failed. Millions of dollars worth of depositors' money were lost. And you know what happened in the 1930s.

Between 1930 and 1933 *more than 8,000 banks failed*. Many billions of dollars of "demand deposit money" were destroyed. By 1933 the American economic system hung on the verge of total collapse.

The depression of the 1930s wasn't entirely a "monetary phenomenon." The interrelated causes were very complex and are difficult to sort out. But here's one thing you can be sure of and it's worth remembering: in an economic system, *when money goes, everything goes.*

Banking Changes of the 1930s: Deposit Insurance and Tighter Controls

Since the beginning of the Roosevelt administration in 1933, the role of the government in money and banking in the United States has been quite different from the way it was before. The government now takes the position that it should do whatever necessary to protect bank depositors from the loss of their money. If the bank fails, the government pays back the money to the depositors.

The federal government, through the Federal Deposit Insurance Corporation (FDIC) now insures bank deposits and through the Federal Savings and Loan Insurance Corporation (FSLIC) it insures non-bank savings accounts. So no longer do depositors have to "run on the banks" to look out for their money. They don't have to worry any more.

Control over bank practices has been tightened up. Both the state bank examiners (for state-chartered banks) and the examiners for the Comptroller of the Currency (for national banks) now keep a more careful eye on the banks. In addition there are now two more examining agencies: the FDIC and the Fed. All of these different examining agencies coordinate their activities so that no one bank is hounded to death by examiners. But there's a lot more examining going on now than there was back in the early days of this century. And there's a lot less that banks can get away with.

Present Membership in the Federal Reserve System

Which banks are members of the Fed? All the banks chartered by the federal government (the about 4,000 national banks) are members. That's required by law. How many state banks have joined? More than 1,000. But that still leaves some 9,000 which have not. Most of the non-member state banks are small, but a few are large.

There are now about 5,000 member banks in the Federal Reserve System—much less than half of the banks in the country. But don't forget this: (1) almost all of the big banks are members of the Fed, so more than 75 percent of the bank deposits in the nation are in "Federal Reserve member" banks. And more important: (2) the Fed's policies and actions don't just influence the member banks. The Fed influences the entire money and banking situation in the nation. You'll be finding out a lot more about that later.

Some economists have recommended that all banks be required to join the Fed and meet its standards and requirements. Someday that might happen. It would give the Fed a little more effective control. But whether it ever happens or not, it isn't a critical issue. Banking and money in the American economy already are under the effective control of the Fed.

Structure of the Federal Reserve System

The Federal Reserve System consists of the twelve Federal Reserve Banks, the Board of Governors in Washington, and two committees: the Federal Open Market Committee, and the Federal Advisory Council. The Board of Governors establishes the policies and the policies are carried out by the twelve Federal Reserve Banks.

The Federal Open Market Committee (FOMC) decides when and how much the Fed will buy or sell government securities in the open "bond and money markets" of the country. Later you'll find out all about this. But for now just remember this: The FOMC plays a very important role because its decisions have an important influence on bank lending—and therefore on the money supply of the nation.

The Board of Governors is made up of seven members. Each is appointed to a 14-year term by the President with the advice and consent of the Senate. One member's term expires every two years. The FOMC consists of the seven members of the Board of Governors plus the presidents of five of the Federal Reserve Banks. The Federal Advisory Council consists of twelve prominent commercial bankers, one chosen by the Federal Reserve Bank in each district.

Figure 6-1 shows a map of the Federal Reserve System. Although the System is geographically decentralized, its policies are not. The money and banking policies of the Fed really are *national policies*—not twelve different "regional" policies.

The Functions of the Federal Reserve System

What does the Fed do? It performs the "central banking function" in the United States. You will be hearing a lot more about this in several of the chapters coming up. But for now, here's a quick rundown of the Fed's functions:

1. Serves as a banker for the commercial banks: holds their deposits, and lends money to them.

2. Supplies currency (dollar bills and coins) to the banks, who then supply them to the public.

Fig. 6-1   The Federal Reserve System

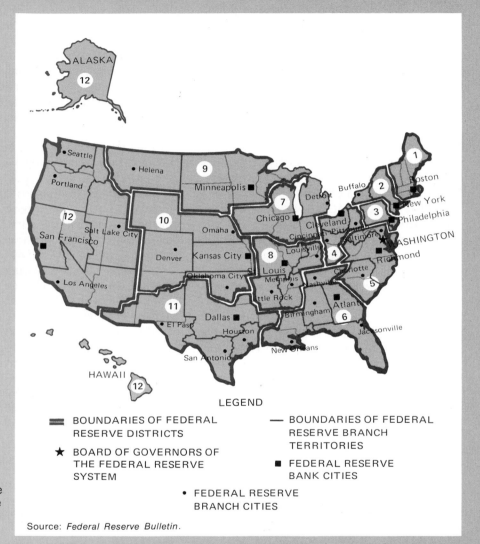

A map of the Federal Reserve districts showing the locations of the 12 Federal Reserve Banks and their 24 branches.

LEGEND

▬ BOUNDARIES OF FEDERAL RESERVE DISTRICTS

★ BOARD OF GOVERNORS OF THE FEDERAL RESERVE SYSTEM

● FEDERAL RESERVE BRANCH CITIES

— BOUNDARIES OF FEDERAL RESERVE BRANCH TERRITORIES

■ FEDERAL RESERVE BANK CITIES

Source: *Federal Reserve Bulletin.*

This map shows the "decentralized" central banking system of the United States. Each Federal Reserve Bank performs banking functions for and holds deposits of the member banks in its district. But policy for the entire system is established by the Federal Reserve Board in Washington, D.C.

The Federal Reserve Banks aren't all equal in size and importance, of course. The biggest and most important one (by far) is the one located in the financial center of the nation, right in the middle of the money market. Which one? The Federal Reserve Bank of New York, in New York City, of course!

3. Helps in the "clearing and collection" of checks—checks deposited in one bank and drawn on another bank.

4. Serves as fiscal agent for the federal government: holds deposits for the U.S. Treasury and aids in the buying and selling of government bonds and other securities, and in the collection of taxes.

5. Supervises, examines, and regulates the activities of the member commercial banks.

6. Sometimes plays an important role in foreign exchange transactions.

7. Finally, and by far most important, the Federal Reserve System exercises control over the money supply of the nation. The policies and actions of the Fed determine whether or not the money supply will be expanding or contracting. The Fed's decisions play a critical role in influencing the levels of employment, the stability of prices and the growth of the economy. To be sure, this final function of the Federal Reserve System places it at the very heart of the American economic system.

Clearly, the Fed is at the center of the financial structure of the nation. But what does the rest of the structure look like? There are the 14,000 commercial banks. Then there are the many thousands of other financial institutions. We need to take a minute and talk about all this.

Commercial Banks and Other Financial Institutions

What is a commercial bank? It's any bank that holds some of the demand deposits (checking accounts) which serve as the nation's money. The commercial banks are by far the most important kind of "financial institution" in the economy. Why? Because they create and destroy money. The nation's money supply depends on what they do!

But the commercial banks aren't the only dealers in the money markets. There are other businesses (financial institutions) which perform important "money market" functions. What's the role of the other financial institutions? Essentially this: to channel money from *savers* to *investors*. A very important function. Think about it.

When you save money and put it in a savings account where it will earn interest, you may think you're "investing." From your point of view, you are. You're making a personal investment. But from the point of view of the economy you aren't investing at all. You're only saving.

Now it's up to the financial intermediary—the savings bank or building and loan or savings and loan association or whoever—to channel your *savings* into *investment*. To become investment (from the point of view of the economy) your savings must be spent to buy capital or to build something or to produce something productive. See the important role of the "financial intermediaries"? A modern economy couldn't function without them.

In addition to the savings institutions there are some other important financial institutions. The "consumer finance" companies gather up savings and use them to make small loans to individuals. Insurance companies gather up money from millions of individuals and businesses and then invest this money in productive ways in the economy. In the big city finance markets there are the so-called "factors" who provide working capital for corporations, and there are "small business investment corporations" (SBICs) which provide capital for (invest in) small businesses. The investment bankers help corporations by selling their stocks and bonds for them. Even companies like American Express and Western Union (and even the Postal Service!) function as financial institutions when they're selling money orders or traveler's checks!

The commercial banks themselves play a very important role as "other financial institutions." Almost all commercial banks have savings accounts. They channel savings into investment. They also sell travelers' checks and money orders and they have "consumer finance" (small loan) departments. Some act as investment bankers too. Some even sell insurance policies!

The point is this: most commercial banks function in both ways: (1) as commercial banks, and (2) as financial intermediaries. But try to keep these two different functions separate in your mind. *It's in their* commercial *banking role that banks create and destroy money.*

That's a very special role. It requires special protection for the depositors, of course. But more than that. It requires special regulations and limitations to make sure that the money supply will adjust in desirable ways—in ways conducive to the economic health of the nation.

Now you know quite a lot about money and banking. Soon you'll be learning even more about it. But I think you've gone far enough for one chapter.

REVIEW EXERCISES

● **MAJOR CONCEPTS, PRINCIPLES, TERMS (Explain each carefully.)**

the meaning and importance of money
how "full bodied" money might evolve
how paper money might evolve
how "checking account" money might evolve
how lending can create money
how repaying loans can destroy money
the functions of the Federal Reserve System
the functions of commercial banks
the functions of financial intermediaries

● **OTHER CONCEPTS AND TERMS (Explain each briefly.)**

medium of exchange	monetized debt
standard (or unit) of value	FDIC, FSLIC
primary functions of money	Federal Reserve System
secondary functions of money	Federal Reserve Bank
standard of deferred payments	Federal Reserve Notes
store of value	demand deposits
liquid	full-bodied money
monetary "backing"	investment bankers
currency	

● **QUESTIONS (Write out answers or jot down key points.)**

1. Do you think *tuba* (instead of fishsticks) might have evolved into money on the island? Explain in detail.
2. During the great U.S. and worldwide depression of the 1930s, not very many people had very much money. A lot of banks had

collapsed—gone bankrupt. Where do you suppose most of the money had gone? Did the rich people have it squirreled away somewhere? Or what? Discuss.

3. If you lend your friend $5 to buy a few glasses of beer, that doesn't create any money. But suppose you were so rich and well known that everybody knew your signature and would accept your IOU. If you write your friend an IOU for $5 and your friend goes and "spends" the IOU at the local bar and the barkeeper uses it to pay the waitress and the waitress uses it to pay the taxi driver and the taxi driver uses it to buy gas. . . Does that mean that your loan has *created money*? Discuss.

4. Describe the American banking system.

7 How the Banking System Creates Money: the Deposit Multiplier

*As banks make loans
the money supply expands
automatically and
people can spend more.*

You already know a lot more about money than most people do. You learned about it back on the island when the fishstick warehouse burned down. And when the northside chief took all the paper money out and burned it. But you need to know more. This chapter takes you step by step, deep into the "magic world of money."

The Money Supply Expands and Contracts Automatically

If the economy is going to speed up very much, the "money supply"—the actual number of "spendable dollars" in existence—must somehow increase to permit the increased spending to occur. So where does the extra money come from? It's newly created. Nobody "creates" it. It just sort of naturally expands itself through the normal workings of the banking system. You saw it happen when the northside chief lent FS 1,000 to the eastside chief. Remember? So you know *what* happens. But *how* does it happen?

First, let me level with you. This is no trick. It isn't some "economics professor doubletalk." It's the honest truth. The amount of money in existence really does expand and contract to meet the "money needs" of businesses and consumers. It really does happen automatically through the normal processes of the banking system.

Most of the money in existence in the United States and in the other modern nations has been created by banks. More is being created every day. Here's a little story that will show you exactly how it happens.

HOW ONE BANK CAN CREATE MONEY

Mr. Zimmer, the local banker, is sitting at his desk one morning musing about the ups and downs in the banking business. "The 'money market' is a strange 'market'," he says to himself. "Six months ago we had more money to lend than we knew what to do with. I was buying government bonds just so we could earn some interest on all the money we had on deposit. But today? It's hard to believe. We're all loaned up and the demand for loans seems to just keep on increasing.

"Interest rates are going up too, but people keep on borrowing. I guess those 'monetary policy' people in Washington are doing something to make money hard to get. Anyway, it's sort of good to be all loaned up. No need to worry about having to keep our money busy by buying government bonds! On the other hand, it's tough to tell old customers, old friends, that you can't lend them any money because you're all loaned up. Ah well, such is life...."

Banks Can't Lend Unless They Have Some Money to Lend

While Mr. Zimmer is thinking all these thoughts, Mr. Baker walks into the bank. He interrupts Mr. Zimmer's thoughts with a shocking request. Mr. Baker had an economics course in college some years ago. He flunked it, but he remembers the part that said the banking system really does create money. So, full of desire to show his sophisticated knowledge about banking (only we insiders know this—wink) he says: "How about creating $4,000 and lending it to me? I'd like to buy a camping trailer that's on sale."

Zimmer calms himself enough so that he says nothing worse than: "Don't be ridiculous! You think I can create money for you, right out of thin air? Preposterous! I can only lend you the money I have available to lend. And I don't have any money available to lend. Money is very tight these days."

Baker is confused. He's *sure* he remembers the part about banks creating money. That's the only question he got right on the final! He's thinking, "No money to lend? Is this guy pulling my leg?"

A New Deposit Creates Excess Reserves. About that time one of Mr. Zimmer's good customers, Mr. Alber, comes striding into the bank, waving a government check, saying: "I

knew the government would finally understand my case and refund all those unjustified taxes I have been paying over the past five years!" The man is carrying a treasury check for $5,000. The check is drawn against the U.S. Treasury's account in the Federal Reserve Bank of New York.

(The Treasury has accounts in the Federal Reserve Banks. Remember? So when the government spends money it can write checks against those accounts. When it collects taxes or sells bonds it can deposit the money in those accounts.)

Mr. Zimmer's bank is not a very big bank. In fact there's only Mr. Zimmer, one teller, and a secretary. Right now the teller is out to lunch so Mr. Zimmer has to interrupt his conversation with Mr. Baker to take Mr. Alber's deposit. Baker doesn't mind the interruption. In fact he isn't too happy about the way things are going so he's getting ready to leave anyway. He heads for the door.

Zimmer calls him back: "Mr. Baker, wait! Now I will be able to lend you the money!"

A Bank Can Lend Its Excess Reserves. Baker looks puzzled. He turns and slowly walks over to the other two men and says, "I'm afraid I don't understand. You just said . . . "

Zimmer interrupts: "I know what I just said. But that was before we received Mr. Alber's $5,000 deposit. Now we have money to lend! Now we have some excess reserves! Let me introduce you to Mr. Alber. Why don't both of you have a seat here at my desk and let me explain to you something about banking procedures." So they do, and he does.

"We keep checking accounts for people. We call them demand deposits because they are payable 'on demand' to anyone the owner tells us to pay them to. Whenever Mr. Alber writes a check to somebody he's just telling us to pay that somebody some of the money out of his (Mr. Alber's) account. Right, Mr. Alber?"

Alber nods.

"Mr. Alber has had demand deposits in this bank for several years. He's one of our best customers. But we have lots of good customers. In fact would you believe that in our little bank we have a total of one million dollars in demand deposits? Don't ask to see the money in our vault. We only keep about $50,000 in the vault. There's no profit made on money in the vault! But on the books we really do have total deposits of $1,000,000. I'll bet that surprises you!"

Baker doesn't look too surprised or too impressed either. In fact's he's a little bit bored listening to Zimmer brag about how "big" his little bank really is. "Okay," he says. "So what's the point?"

"The point I was coming to is this: The only way we can make any money in this business is to lend out the money our customers deposit in their accounts. Mr. Alber just made a deposit. So now we can make you a loan."

"There, he said it again," Baker thinks. "He keeps trying to tell me that banks don't create money when I know they do! And I'm getting kind of tired of all this . . . "

Zimmer continues. "Mr. Alber just deposited $5,000 but we can't lend you all of that. The banking regulations of the Federal Reserve System require that we keep some money 'on reserve.' The more money we have in our demand deposit accounts, the more we must keep 'on reserve.' So how much must we keep?

"Right now the reserve requirement is something less than 20 percent, but let's say it's 20 percent just so that numbers will come out

even. Twenty percent of what? Twenty percent of the total amount of money our customers have in their demand deposits, that's what! So you can see that whenever our customers deposit more money in their demand deposit accounts, we also must keep more in our reserve. Understand?"

Baker nods. "I think I see it, but I'm not sure."

Federal Reserve Banks Hold Reserve Deposits

Baker is beginning to get interested. "You said you're holding a million dollars in demand deposits, and suppose the reserve requirement is 20 percent. That means you must be holding $200,000 on reserve. (20% of $1,000,000 is $200,000.) Right? And you just said you only keep about $50,000 in your vault. Where's the other $150,000? Or are you just pulling my leg?"

"No, no leg-pulling. It's all very true. And you're right. There is another $150,000. It's in our bank account at the Federal Reserve Bank in this district."

"You mean your *bank* has a bank account? Like a demand deposit account? At the Federal Reserve Bank?"

"Right!" says Zimmer.

Banks Pay Each Other Out Of Their Federal Reserve Accounts. Zimmer goes on. "My bank has an account in our Federal Reserve Bank, but we can't write checks to people or businesses on our *Federal Reserve bank account*. The account is only used for making payments to other banks. Whenever another bank has a 'money claim' against this bank— that is, whenever we owe money to another bank—the other bank gets paid out of our account at the Federal Reserve Bank. It's a neat system!"

"But wait!" Baker thinks something's a little bit fishy here. "If you are going to be using that account to pay off other banks, you aren't going to have enough left. You're supposed to keep that $150,000 there on deposit all the time to meet the 'reserve requirement' you told me about. If you pay some of the $150,000 to another bank, you won't have enough left to meet the 20 percent requirement."

Zimmer's eyes sparkle. "Aha! Now you see it! That's why I couldn't lend you the $4,000 you wanted to borrow awhile ago. You would sign a promissory note and I would open a checking account for you. Then what would happen? You would go right over to Mr. Culver, the sporting goods dealer in Tonawanda and spend the money. You would write him a check for $4,000. Then what do you think would happen after that?"

Baker says, "The sporting goods dealer would come right over here and cash the check and get the money out of my account."

No One Ever Cashes a Large Check. "Come now, Mr. Baker," Mr. Zimmer says. "Who would ever cash a $4,000 check? No, Mr. Culver will deposit the check in his own demand deposit account at the bank where he does business in Tonawanda. Then he will have the deposit in his account at the Tonawanda Bank. The bank will have the check. So what do you suppose the Tonawanda bank will do with the check?"

"Come over here and cash it and get their money out of my account?"

"There. You said it again. No. Nobody *ever* cashes a $4,000 check! The Tonawanda bank will send the check (along with a bunch of other checks) for deposit to its account at the Federal Reserve Bank of New York (or Maybe to the Buffalo branch). The Federal Reserve Bank will then deposit your check—that is, add the $4,000—to the account of the Tonawanda bank. But the Federal Reserve Bank is not just going to add $4,000 to the Tonawanda bank's account without getting that money back from somewhere. Where does the $4,000 come from? Can you guess?"

"I'll bet they take that $4,000 out of your $150,000 deposit at the Federal Reserve Bank. Right?"

"Right!"

Insufficient Reserves Must Be Made Up Somehow

Zimmer goes on. "If they take $4,000 out of my reserve account, I'm suddenly in an illegal position. I won't have enough left to meet the 20 percent reserve requirement, to back up my demand deposits. I will have to do something quick to make up the difference. I might *borrow some money from the Federal Reserve Bank* to make up the difference. Or maybe I would *sell some of my government bonds to them, or to somebody. Or when someone comes in to renew a loan I might refuse to renew it. I could make people and businesses pay off their loans right away,* then I could deposit that money in my Federal Reserve account.

"Anyway," Zimmer continued, "I'd rather not have to do any of those things. The Federal Reserve Bank is charging a high discount rate—that is, high interest on the loans it makes to banks—these days. And the bond market is depressed. Bond prices are so low that if I sell my bonds now, I'll have to take a loss. As for refusing to renew loans, I certainly don't want to do that to my good business customers. They would have to sell off their inventories to pay off their loans. They would never do business with me again!"

NEW EXCESS RESERVES PERMIT NEW LOANS

Mr. Zimmer continues. "Now you see why, before Mr. Alber's deposit, I couldn't lend you any money. I had only enough to cover my required reserve. No excess at all. But now, with Mr. Alber's $5,000 deposit I do have some excess reserves. I can lend you any amount you want, up to the amount of my excess reserves. Can you figure out how much excess reserves I have now? Can you tell me how much I can lend you?"

"Let's see. Mr. Alber deposited a government check for $5,000. You're going to send that check to the Federal Reserve Bank and they will deposit it to your account. Right?"

"Right!"

"Then you will have $155,000 in your account. You only need $150,000. So you can lend me $5,000. Right?"

"Almost right, but wrong. You forgot something."

Part of a New Deposit Becomes Required Reserves

"When Mr. Alber deposited his check he added $5,000 to my bank's total demand deposits. So now I must . . . "

Baker interrupts. "Wait! I see it! Now you must have more reserves, because now you have more deposits! You must have enough new reserves to cover Mr. Alber's new deposit. If the required amount is 20 percent (one-fifth) then for $5,000 more of deposits you must have $1,000 more in reserves (20 percent of $5,000 equals $1,000). So you only have $4,000 in 'excess reserves.' You can lend me any amount up to $4,000! Right?"

"Right. Now you understand. So how much do you want to borrow?"

"I'll take the whole thing! That's exactly how much I want to borrow anyway. Let's draw up the loan papers. I have about $6,000 worth of GM and Exxon stocks here to leave with you as collateral. You can open a checking account for me. Then you can just deposit the $4,000 in my new checking account. Okay?"

"Fine. It will only take about ten minutes to get the papers ready for your signature."

While the loan papers are being prepared, Mr. Baker is re-thinking this whole banking process. "They only need a 20 percent reserve to back up their checking accounts. I'm borrowing $4,000 and it's going to be put into my checking account. Well then! All they *really* need to have on reserve to back up my account is 20 percent of $4,000—only $800!"

He thinks about this a few more minutes and then decides to confront Mr. Zimmer with this new bit of logic. "You really only need $800 behind this $4,000 deposit of mine! Why do you insist on having $4,000 in your Federal Reserve account to 'back up' my checking account balance of $4,000? You said you only needed 20 percent. If you're only holding $1,000 behind Mr. Alber's $5,000 deposit, how come you insist on holding $4,000 behind my $4,000 deposit?

"You're holding a 100 percent reserve behind my new checking account, but only 20 percent behind Mr. Alber's. How come? I don't want to borrow but $4,000 anyway. But I sure would like to know what's going on!"

Loaned Money Soon Leaves. Mr. Zimmer seems pleased that Mr. Baker has gotten so interested. "That's an intelligent question! But I'm sure that if you thought about it awhile, you'd figure out the answer. Really, *your* account is very different from Mr. Alber's account. Both accounts look exactly the same on the bank's books, but still they're very different. Mr. Alber's account consists of *deposited* money. Yours consists of *borrowed* money. Let me explain the difference to you.

"You are going to go out and spend that $4,000 right away. When you spend it to buy the camping trailer the check is going to be deposited in the sporting-goods dealer's account in the Tonawanda bank. Then the Tonawanda bank is going to send the check to the Federal Reserve Bank. Remember?

"The Federal Reserve Bank will deposit the check to the Tonawanda bank's account. Then what? The Federal Reserve Bank will take the money away from my account. How much money? $4,000, of course! Then they will send the check back to me and I will take it off your checking account. Then, poof! Your money (account balance) will be gone!

"See what would have happened if I only had $800 in my reserve account to back up your $4,000 demand deposit? When your check clears, I am going to lose $4,000 from my reserve account at the Federal Reserve Bank. So I *must* have a "100 percent reserve," or $4,000 behind your account. Your account was created not by a *deposit* but by a *loan*. That's what makes it different. Do you understand?"

Deposited Money "Never Leaves." Baker is still puzzled. "But then, why do you feel so confident about keeping only $1,000 behind Mr. Alber's $5,000 deposit? Suppose he goes out and writes a check tomorrow for $5,000? When the check clears, aren't you going to be in trouble? What about that?"

"You're right," Zimmer admits. "If that happened tomorrow, and if that's the *only thing* that happened tomorrow, we would be in trouble. But that's not going to happen. Or if it does, it's not going to be the only thing that will happen. I guess you would say that we are 'protected by the law of averages.' Let me explain it this way.

"We have many customers who come in and make deposits every day. These regular customers are also writing checks, spending their deposit balances every day. We know that on the average day in the average month, the number of people coming in and *depositing* money, will be almost exactly equal to the number of people who are going out and writing checks and *spending* their money. So the two balance each other. There's no 'net change' in our Federal Reserve account."

In A Growing Bank, Deposits Keep Expanding. Zimmer continues. "Look at it this way. On November 1 of *last year* we had total demand deposits of about $990,000. On November 1 of *this year* we expect to have total demand deposits of slightly more than $1,000,000. *Next year* on the same day, we expect to have even more demand deposits on our books. Do we need to worry about the fact that any one individual is spending some of his or her demand deposit money, and that some of our reserves are going to other banks?

"So long as the money coming back and being deposited in our Federal Reserve account is more than enough to make up for the money leaving our Federal Reserve account, we have nothing to worry about. As long as we are a growing bank, our deposits will always be more than enough to offset the 'spending withdrawals.' Doesn't that make sense?"

Mr. Baker sort of understands. But he asks, "What about me? Why don't I fall into the same category?

"Because you are borrowing money. Borrowers go out and spend money *immediately*. The amount you borrow will be leaving our reserve account right away. We can be certain of that. There won't be any 'average return flow of deposits' to offset your expenditure. So you don't fit into the normal pattern. Therefore we can't lend you any more money than we actually have free to lend—that is, we can't lend you any more than we have in excess reserves.

"We can only lend you as much as we can afford to lose from our reserve account. Why? Because we know that when we lend it to you, you are going to spend it and we are going to lose it. Right away."

Mr. Baker seems to understand. Anyway, now the secretary has prepared all the loan papers, ready for signatures. Mr. Baker signs the promissory note. Mr. Zimmer signs a receipt for the stock certificates Mr. Baker is leaving as collateral—as security to guarantee that he will repay the loan.

The teller who has returned in the meantime gets Mr. Baker to sign a signature card, then gives Mr. Baker a new checkbook and a deposit receipt for $4,000. Mr. Baker writes down the balance in his checkbook ($4,000), waves goodbye to Mr. Zimmer, and starts walking toward the door. Mr. Alber, who has been quietly listening, walks out at the same time.

Mr. Baker smiles and comments to Mr. Alber that this has been a very educational day. "I always thought banks created money. They taught me that in college. But today I found out how wrong that is. Banks don't create money at all. Banks don't lend money unless they already have that money to lend, dollar for dollar! How about that?"

Lending the Excess Reserves Creates Money

Mr. Alber, who happens to be taking college courses at night working on his MBA, looks back and smiles. "I think you missed something," he says. "Banks really do create money. You just watched this bank create $4,000."

By this time they are in the parking lot. Baker stops for a second before entering his car and says, "No, I think you must have misunderstood."

"No, my friend," says Alber. "It is you who has misunderstood. Open your checkbook and look at your account balance. What do you see there?"

Baker says, "There's no need for me to look. I already know. But let me show you. Here's the balance: $4,000! That's just the amount of money the bank had free to lend. That's not bank-created money. It's real solid money that has existed all the time."

Then Alber says: "Yesterday I had to pay my fall semester tuition and buy books. This morning I was flat broke. My deposit balance was zero. Then I got the tax refund check in the mail. You saw me deposit it. Right?"

Baker nods. He has no idea what Alber is getting at.

Alber continues: "Here. Look in my checkbook and read the balance. See? $5,000. That's my money. Now look in your checkbook there. See? $4,000. That's your money. Between the two of us we have a total of $9,000. Right? Baker nods again.

Alber goes on. "When I walked in the bank I had $5,000. A government check. Now the two of us are leaving the bank and we have a total of $9,000 between us. An extra $4,000 came from someplace. Where do you suppose the

extra money came from? Where could it have come from? Only one place. Our banker friend, Mr. Zimmer, created it."

Baker's jaw drops. He just stands there, looking at the balance in both checkbooks. There's $9,000 all right, and he knows it's true. But he only half believes his eyes. Sort of half-consciously he mutters, "Well, I'll be!"

HOW THE BANKING SYSTEM CREATES MONEY

Yes, the banking system really does create money. Do you see how it happened in the Alber-Baker-Zimmer case? A man brought in some "new money" and deposited it in his checking account. This was a "primary deposit"—a deposit of new money, new reserves flowing into the banking system. The "new money" went into the bank's reserve account.

Only 20 percent of the newly deposited money had to stay in the reserve account to "back up" the new deposit. So 80 percent of the amount deposited is now in "free reserves" or "excess reserves." It can be lent to someone else. It is through this process of *lending the free reserves*, that money is created. Once the process gets started—once the new "primary deposit" enters the banking system—the money expansion can go on and on from bank to bank to bank. The potential expansion of the money supply is limited only by the size of the reserve requirement.

The Lower the Required Reserve, the More the Money Supply Can Expand

Suppose the reserve requirement was 100 percent. Then how much money could be created by Mr. Zimmer's bank? None. All the money deposited would be held in reserves. Suppose the reserve requirement is 50 percent. How much can be re-lent? Half of it.

So the lower the reserve requirement the more the bank can lend. The more money it can create, so the more the money supply can expand. *The whole purpose of having a reserve requirement is to limit the extent to which the money supply can expand.*

We just watched Mr. Alber's $5,000 turn into $9,000. Alber still has $5,000 and Baker has $4,000. The money supply of the nation has been expanded by $4,000. There's no question about that. But all you have seen so far is the first step in the expansion process.

In terms of the nation's money supply, Mr. Alber's $5,000 government check has already grown into $9,000. Before it's all over with, *that check can grow into $25,000!*

How do we know $5,000 can grow into exactly $25,000? Because if the required reserve ratio is 20 percent (that is, 1/5), then $5,000 in new bank reserves can "back up" $25,000 in new demand deposit money. Of course! The supply of money can expand by *five times* the amount of the new $5,000 in reserves.

Suppose the reserve requirement is only 10 percent (that is, 1/10). Then $5,000 in new reserves can "back up" $50,000 in new demand deposit money because $5,000 is 10% of $50,000. The money supply can expand by *ten times* the amount of the new reserves. If the reserve requirement is 25 percent (1/4) the money supply can expand by *four times* the amount of the new deposit.

The Deposit Multiplier

This idea of a new deposit in the banking system permitting a multiple expansion of the money supply is what economists call the deposit multiplier. The idea is that any new reserves introduced into the banking system permits a multiple expansion of demand deposits—and therefore, of the money supply. As you might guess, we have a way of assigning a number to this "deposit multiplier." What determines the size of the number? You already know—the reserve requirement.

If the reserve requirement was 100 percent, the deposit multiplier would be 1. That is, the

new deposit wouldn't multiply at all! In our case, it would mean that Alber's $5,000 deposit would be the only increase in deposits permitted by Alber's new addition of $5,000 of reserves. But suppose there was no reserve requirement. Then the deposit multiplier would be infinite! The money expansion could go on forever.

You know there's going to be a formula to explain this in simple, shorthand form, right? Sure. You could figure it out by yourself. But here it is anyway:

$$\text{Deposit Multiplier} = \frac{1}{\text{Reserve requirement}}$$

This formula simply tells you that the deposit multiplier is the reciprocal of the reserve requirement. In terms most students use: "turn the fraction upside down."

So to find out how much deposits *in total* can be supported by any given addition to reserves' just "turn the reserve requirement fraction upside down" (that gives you the deposit multiplier), then multiply the increase in reserves by the multiplier. If the reserve requirement is 20 percent, change it to a fraction (1/5) and you know the multiplier is 5. You know an increase in new reserves of $1,000 will permit an increase in demand deposits of $5,000. It isn't very complicated, but it's very important in the functioning of the economic system. So it's good that you know about it.

As soon as the initial deposit (Mr. Alber's deposit) brings new reserves into the banking system, the money supply can start to expand. You saw the first part of that expansion, when Mr. Baker borrowed $4,000. From there, the money supply can keep on expanding until all the new reserves are being used to "back up" new demand deposits. If the required ratio of reserves to deposits is 20 percent (*one* to *five*) then every one dollar of new reserves can "back up" five dollars of new demand deposit money. If the required ratio is 10 percent (*one* to *ten*) then every dollar of new reserves can "back up" ten dollars of new demand deposit money. That's all simple enough to see, isn't it? But how does all this expansion come about?

The Money Expansion Process Goes from Bank to Bank

You know all about the first step in the expansion process. Mr. Alber, Mr. Baker and Mr. Zimmer have shown you that. But what happens next? Let's watch.

Mr. Baker drives over to the Tonawanda dealer to buy the camping trailer. He writes a check for $4,000 to the dealer, Mr. Culver. As soon as Baker has hooked up the trailer and pulled it away, Mr. Culver jumps in his car and speeds off to his bank in Tonawanda. He parks in the lot and dashes into the bank waving the $4,000 check in the air saying, "I finally got my money out of that old-model trailer!"

He fills out a deposit slip and walks up to the teller's window to deposit the check. As he is making the deposit he notices a sad-faced young man walking slowly toward the door leading to the parking lot. Then he hears Ms. Yeager, the loan officer, call out:

"Mr. Dover! Come back!" As Mr. Dover comes back and approaches Ms. Yeager's desk, Mr. Culver hears Ms. Yeager say: "Mr. Dover, I think we are going to be able to handle your request for a loan, after all. We have just received a new deposit for $4,000. With a required reserve of 20 percent we only need to keep as reserves, one-fifth of the amount ($800). We will be happy to lend you the other four-fifths. That's $3,200. Isn't that the amount you need to pay the contractor for the new plumbing in your house?"

So Mr. Dover gets his $3,200 loan. That's new money. Mr. Culver still has his $4,000 in his checking account and Mr. Dover has $3,200 in his. And remember, Mr. Alber still has his $5,000 in his checking account. The original $5,000 has now grown to a total of $12,200 ($5,000 + $4,000 + $3,200 = $12,200).

Notice that Mr. Baker doesn't have his money any more. He spent it. The one who borrows it *always* spends it. His money went to Mr. Culver, so Mr. Zimmer's bank's "excess reserves" went to the Tonawanda Bank. That's why that bank can now make the loan to Mr. Dover.

So what's Dover going to do? Spend his borrowed money right away to pay the plumbing contractor, Mr. Elder. And Mr. Elder will go into his bank waving the check in the air, then deposit it in his account. His bank must hold one-fifth of the amount in its reserves ($640) but it can lend the other four-fifths ($2,560) to Ms. Fuller who wants to build an addition and more shelf space so her shoe store can carry more inventory.

Ms. Fuller will write a check to pay Mr. Garner, the carpentry contractor. Mr. Garner will deposit the check in his bank. The bank will keep one-fifth ($512) as reserves and lend the other four-fifths ($2,048). The borrower will spend the money. And on and on it goes. Until when? Until there aren't any excess reserves left to lend!

The money supply can continue to expand until *all* of Mr. Alber's initial $5,000 of new reserves is being used as reserves to "back up" new demand deposits. That is, the expansion can continue until the total of new demand deposits amounts to $25,000. The $25,000 will include Mr. Alber's original demand deposit of $5,000, plus another $20,000 of demand deposit money created through bank lending. Figure 7-1 shows a summary of this money expansion process. It would be a good idea for you to take a few minutes to study that figure, now.

THE RESERVE REQUIREMENT LIMITS THE MONEY EXPANSION

Alber's new deposit sets off a process of lending, spending, and relending which continues from bank to bank. As the excess reserves move from bank to bank they leave a

Fig. 7-1 How Money Expands as Banks Make Loans

A Summary of the Steps in the Depositing-Lending-Spending-Redepositing-Relending-Respending Process

Deposited by		Amount of Deposit		Required Reserve (20%)		Excess Reserve (80%)		Lent to		Paid to
Alber	→	$ 5,000	→	$1,000	→	$4,000	→	Baker	→	Culver
Culver	→	4,000	→	800	→	3,200	→	Dover	→	Elder
Elder	→	3,200	→	640	→	2,560	→	Fuller	→	Garner
Garner	→	2,560	→	512	→	2,048	→	Horner	→	Ilter
Ilter	→	2,048	→	410	→	1,638	→	Joker	→	Keller
Keller	→	1,638	→	328	→	1,310	→	Lester	→	Miller
Miller	→	1,310	→	262	→	1,048	→	Nader	→	Olter
Olter	→	1,048	→	210	→	838	→	Palmer	→	Quaver
Quaver	→	838	→	168	→	670	→	Richter	→	Salter
Salter	→	670	→	etc., etc., etc.						
		_____		_____		_____				
Ultimate Totals (assuming maximum possible expansion)		**$25,000** (total demand deposit money)		**$5,000** (total required reserves)		**-0-** (total excess reserves)		No more loans are possible until new reserves come from somewhere		

This table shows Mr. Alber's original deposit of $5,000 growing into a total of $25,000—that's twenty-five thousand real, spendable dollars of demand deposit money. Mr. Alber has $5,000 of it, Mr. Culver has $4,000 of it, Mr. Elder has $3,200 of it, Mr. Garner has $2,560 of it, and so on.

Only $5,000 existed in the beginning. Where did the extra $20,000 come from? It was created by the banks. The banks created it just by lending their excess reserves.

But don't forget: If times are bad, this expansion in the money supply may not occur. If Mr. Baker and Mr. Dover and Ms. Fuller and those other people ever get pessimistic and decide not to borrow, then the expansion will stop, right there!

You can always figure out what the maximum possible expansion is by using the deposit multiplier. Here, with a reserve requirement of 20% (1/5) the deposit multiplier is 5. So the maximum possible expansion is $5,000 (amount of new reserves entering the banking system) times 5 (the deposit multiplier)—which equals $25,000, of course!

trail of newly created money in their wake. Every bank they pass through has an increase in its demand deposit money.

But in each succeeding bank the addition gets smaller and smaller. Why? Because each bank keeps a part of the "moving excess" as it goes by. Each bank must hold some of the moving excess as new reserves, to back up the new demand deposit—that is, the demand deposit (like Alber's) which brought the excess reserves to the bank in the first place.

If there was *no reserve requirement*, each bank could relend *all* of the excess. The "moving excess" could go on and on from bank to bank, leaving a new $5,000 demand deposit in *each* bank. The money supply could just keep right on expanding. A new $5,000 "primary deposit" could go zooming around, touching banks, creating $5,000 more at each stop. It could create millions and millions!

Unlimited Expansion Would Destroy the Value of Money

Can you see why a reserve requirement is necessary? If we didn't have the reserve requirement the money supply could continue to expand indefinitely! There would be no way to limit the size of the money supply. Each time a bank received a new deposit it could re-lend it all. Each time this happened the money supply would get larger. It would just be a matter of time before the money supply would increase so much that runaway inflation would occur and the monetary unit would be destroyed.

In the "olden days" of gold-backed and silver-backed money, the limited availability of these metals limited the expansion of the money supply. But in modern times, when the account numbers on the books of banks serve as our money, the only effective limit on money expansion is the reserve requirement. The reserve requirement is vital!

For money to have value, its supply must be limited. In the United States and Canada and other modern nations, the supply limitation

rests on the legal reserve requirement. If you want you can go around telling people that *the money supply of the United States is backed by the "legal reserve requirement" of the Federal Reserve System!* That might not be precisely true. But it's a lot more true than telling them it's backed by gold!

In the last chapter you learned that the total money supply in the United States in 1976 was about $300 billion, and that more than three-fourths of it was bank deposit (checking account) money. Where do you suppose all this bank deposit money came from? From bank lending? Most of it, yes. Just like in the illustration you just read about.

New Reserves Come from the Treasury and the Federal Reserve System

Where did all the new reserves come from, to permit the money supply to expand? Most of the new reserves came from the Treasury and the Federal Reserve System. You just saw Alber's $5,000 come from the Treasury and become new reserves, to permit a monetary expansion to begin.

Whenever the government runs a deficit—spends more money than it collects in taxes—it makes up the difference by selling bonds. If people and businesses and insurance companies and other private corporations buy the bonds then no new reserves go into the banking system. But suppose the Federal Reserve Banks buy the bonds. That's different!

What Happens When the Treasury Borrows from the Federal Reserve Banks?

When the Treasury borrows money from an insurance company or a savings and loan association or from individuals and gives them bonds in exchange, that doesn't create any money. All the Treasury is doing is gathering up existing money. When it borrows existing money and spends it there's no expansion in the money supply.

But when the Treasury borrows from the Federal Reserve Banks and gives them government bonds in exchange, that does create new money. In fact it's exactly like what happens when Baker borrows $4,000 from Zimmer. Remember? And it's exactly like what happened when the eastside chief, King Tuituranga borrowed FS1,000 from the northside chief, King Ratukabua. It creates money!

But the money which gets created when Baker borrows from Zimmer is a lot different than the money that gets created when the Treasury borrows from the Federal Reserve Banks. What's the difference? Just this: The money the Federal Reserve Banks create is *high-powered money*. This is money that will become new reserves for the banking system!

What will the Treasury do with its newly created money? Pay it out in government checks to pay the bridge builders and the civil service workers and the welfare recipients and all the others. When all those people receive their checks, what will they do with them? Take them and deposit them in their banks. Of course.

Then what happens? The banks will send the checks to the Federal Reserve Banks. That is, they will deposit the checks in their Federal Reserve accounts. So the Federal Reserve Banks will take the Treasury's newly created "high-powered money" deposits out of the Treasury's account and add them to the member banks' reserve accounts. See what happens? The banking system gets a lot of new excess reserves! So now, new money can be created all over!

Not just Mr. Zimmer's bank. *All* the banks get new excess reserves. So now they can *all start making more loans*. The money supply can begin to expand, and it can keep on until a five-fold expansion has occurred. High-powered money? You bet! A dollar will get you *five*! And is this where most of the U.S. money supply really came from? That's exactly right.

Did you ever wonder where the government would get the extra money if it wanted to run a deficit?—that is, to spend more than it collects in taxes? Now you see how the government can get all the money it wants. It simply creates the money by printing up bonds and "selling" the bonds to the Federal Reserve Banks in exchange for new Treasury deposits! Then it can write checks and spend these new deposits.

The federal government can spend as much as it wants to. It never needs to worry about not being able to get the money! But you can see how such a program pumps new reserves into the banking system and lets the money supply expand. It could create some serious problems. You'll be reading a lot more about this, later.

Excess Reserves Do Not Guarantee an Expansion

Putting new reserves into the banking system is not certain to result in a multiple expansion of the money supply. For example, suppose Mr. Baker is out of a job and has already had to sell his stocks to pay the rent and buy groceries. And suppose no one else comes in to borrow the $4,000 of excess reserves created by Mr. Alber's deposit. What will happen? Nothing. New reserves *permit*, but don't *guarantee* an expansion of the money supply.

The money supply will not expand unless people want to borrow. People will not borrow unless they want to go into debt for the purpose of *spending*. If people don't want to spend these days, no amount of free reserves in the banks' reserve accounts will force an expansion. (Someone once said that trying to force a monetary expansion by pushing excess reserves into the banking system is like trying to push with a string!) Excess reserves *permit* people to borrow. That's all.

When excess reserves are high, banks want to lend. There is no profit in keeping money in excess reserves! If the banks have excess reserves and borrowers aren't borrowing, interest rates will go down. Money will be easy to borrow. This may stimulate borrowing. But it may not. It all depends on how bad things are. How much unemployment? How much overstocked inventories? How many shut-down plants? How gloomy and pessimistic is the outlook? But let's not get ahead of our story. We'll get into all of these issues later.

Loan Repayments
Destroy Money

Now that you know about how the money supply expands through the banking system, it's easy to see how it contracts. When everyone is in debt and business is bad, people try to pay off their loans and get out of debt. Businesses try to sell off their excess inventories and pay off their loans. Each time a loan is repaid, unless someone else borrows an equal amount, the money supply gets smaller. Excess reserves start piling up in the banks' Federal Reserve accounts.

Unless someone wants to borrow, a bank can't lend. Obviously. And who wants to borrow and build inventories during a depression? Nonsense! So what's happening to all the money that used to seem so plentiful back during boom times? It's being destroyed!

The businesses sell hard to get the consumers' dollars. Then they use the dollars to pay off loans. Poof! The dollars are gone! The businesses are gathering back up and destroying the dollars they were creating and paying out, before. The money supply is contracting and total spending is getting smaller. No wonder we're having hard times!

The excess reserves just keep piling up in the banks' Federal Reserve accounts. The banks can always use their excess reserves to buy government bonds from the Fed to earn some interest income. But this doesn't expand the money supply. It doesn't help to generate any business spending or consumer spending. It doesn't help to speed up the economy.

The way money is created and destroyed through the banking system is a fascinating subject. And it's a very real and serious one. The problems of inflation and unemployment which seem to be continuously—sometimes simultaneously—attacking the economies of today's world can't be understood without an understanding of money.

Now you know enough about money to begin to dig in on some of today's real-world macroeconomic problems. But before we get into that, there are some other concepts and principles you need to understand. One thing you need to know about is how to measure the macro-condition of the economy. It's time to introduce that subject, right now.

HOW TO ESTIMATE THE SPEED
OF THE ECONOMY

Suppose the economy is running too fast. Or too slow. How can you tell? What do you look at to find out?

You could go around asking business managers: "How's business?" Or you might go down to the state employment office and see how many people are out of work and looking for jobs. If all the businesses are complaining about slow sales, and if there are long lines of unemployed people at the employment office, then we can say the economy is running too slowly. But suppose the business manager says: "It would take me three years to fill all the orders I have right now!" Suppose the employment office manager says: "Everybody's trying to hire more workers but nobody's looking for a job!" Then you know the economy is trying to run too fast.

There are lots of ways to see if the economy is booming or depressed. If you see lots of trucks on the highway, trains going by, factories running night shifts, crowds of people spending lots of money in the supermarkets and department stores and bars and everywhere, then you know the economy must be booming. If you see a lot of idle factories and glum people pinching pennies and looking for work then you know the economy must be depressed.

But isn't there some more exact way to observe and measure the speed of the economy? Can't we use some *numbers* to show the overall level of economic activity? You bet we can! And we do.

These numbers are very helpful in telling us what's going on in the economy—in telling us that everything is all right, or that it isn't. The numbers can tell us what's wrong and how wrong and where and (to some extent) *why*— and what needs to be done about it. Magic

little numbers! The most basic ones are found in what we call the national income and product accounts. During the depression of the 1930s we didn't have any such numbers to help us to see what was happening and why. But now we do.

By the time you finish the next chapter you will understand all about the magic little numbers—the "national income and product accounts." But before you go on, take your time and be sure you understand how money is created and destroyed through the banking system. It's crucial!

REVIEW EXERCISES

● **MAJOR CONCEPTS, PRINCIPLES, TERMS (Explain each carefully.)**

how banks create money
why borrowed money always leaves
why deposited money "never leaves"
role of the reserve requirement
how the government creates money
how new reserves are generated
how loan repayments destroy money

● **OTHER CONCEPTS AND TERMS (Explain each briefly.)**

the money supply
demand deposits
reserve requirement
deposit multiplier
Federal Reserve account
discount rate
excess reserves
primary deposit
"high-powered" money

● **QUESTIONS (Write out answers, or jot down key points.)**

1. Try to describe in detail the step-by-step process through which money is created by the banking system. Start with a new "primary deposit" coming in from somewhere, and take it from there.
2. Suppose Zimmer's bank finds that its Federal Reserve account is too small to meet its reserve requirement. How might it get more money to deposit in its Federal Reserve account?

3. If the federal government can create all the money it wants just by printing up bonds and selling them to the Federal Reserve Banks, then why don't they do that? Why does the federal government keep making people miserable by collecting taxes all the time? Why don't they just print up the bonds and get the Federal Reserve Banks to create new government deposits as needed? What would happen to the money supply (and to the value of our money and to the economy) if they did that? Discuss.

4. There seems to be a sort of "natural tendency" for the money supply to adjust to the wishes of the consumers and businesses. When buying and spending are picking up, people and businesses are going into debt and the money supply is expanding. When things are slowing down, loans are being repaid and the money supply is contracting. Can you explain just how this all happens? Try.

8 How to Measure National Output and Income: GNP and Price Indexes

The national income and product accounts and price indexes, and the question of economic growth and economic welfare.

What determines how fast the economy will run? That's the most basic question of macroeconomics. The next several chapters will be showing you the answer to this question. But before you get into those chapters you need to know how to look and see how fast the economy *is* running. You need to know how we measure the speed (the "activity level") of the economy. That's what this chapter is all about.

THE NATIONAL INCOME AND PRODUCT ACCOUNTS

There are several things we might look at and measure to find out the level of "total activity" in the economy. We could look at and measure total employment—which could mean "the total use of all the productive factors," or it could mean just "the total employment of labor." Or we could look at any measure "the total amount being produced"—total output. Or we could look at and measure

"the total amount being received as income by the owners of all the factors of production"— total income. Any one of these figures would give us a measure of "total economic activity" and would tell us about the speed at which the economy is running.

Suppose you look at the figures for "total employment" and "total output" and "total income" and see that all three figures are getting larger from month to month. You know that the rate of total economic activity is increasing. Right? But do you really need to look at all three figures? Of course not. All three figures will be moving along together, won't they? Sure. You know that total output is equal to total income. And you could guess that the rate of employment is closely related to the rate of output and income—the more employment the more output and income.

Now you know what to look at. But where do you look? How can a person find out what these "employment" and "output" and "income" figures really are—for the American economy, or for any other economy?

I'm learning some **exact** ways to answer the question: How's business?

NATIONAL PRODUCT FIGURES

127

Most nations of the world actually try to add up their "national output" and "national income" to see how much is being produced in the country. Everyone wants to know "how's business?" You are already familiar with the term gross national product (usually called GNP). Probably you have heard about national income, too. These, together with the "employment" and "unemployment" figures, are the most often used measures of "the overall level of economic activity"—that is, the rate at which the economy is running.

How the Government Gathers the Statistics

How does the government get the "national product" and "national income" numbers? To get the "product" statistics the government statistics gatherers ask each business to fill out forms telling how much they are producing. As Willie Wonka is operating his candy factory, one day he will get a questionnaire asking about the size of his output. They will ask him to send in a report several times a year indicating his "rate of production." They won't ask for his daily or weekly or monthly rate. They want his *annual rate* of output. So instead of telling them he is producing 10 truckloads a week, he tells them he is producing "at the annual rate of 520 truckloads per year" (10 truckloads times 52 weeks = 520 truckloads). But he needs to tell them more than that.

They need the *dollar value* of his "annual rate of output." Why? Because they are going to add up his output of candy together with everyone else's output of everything else. How can they possibly do that? Only by translating each output into its dollar value. Then they add up the dollar values. This gives them one number, a dollar figure, to indicate the "rate of flow of output" for the entire economic system. That dollar figure is called the *gross national product*—GNP.

So Willie Wonka tells them that during the first quarter of this year he was producing at the rate of 10 truckloads of candy a week @ $10,000 worth of candy per truckload for a total of $100,000 worth per week. So he's producing at the rate of $5,200,000 worth of product per year ($100,000 worth per week times 52 weeks = $5,200,000 worth per year).

When they get Willie Wonka's and everyone else's figures for the first quarter, they add them all up. Suppose they come up with a total figure of $2,000,000,000,000 (two trillion dollars). Then the U.S. Department of Commerce publishes a report saying that during the first quarter (January-March) gross national product (GNP) in the United States was being produced *at the annual rate* of two trillion dollars worth of goods and services per year.

The GNP Rate of Flow Changes During the Year

Suppose this rate of output continues for all twelve months of the year. Then the total GNP for the year will amount to two trillion dollars worth of output. But that isn't the way it's really going to happen. The "annual rate of output flow" isn't going to stay the same for all twelve months of the year. During some months people may buy more candy and Willie Wonka may put on an extra shift of workers to produce enough to meet the extra demand. During other months, demand may slack off and he may cut back production.

During July he may shut down the plant for two weeks while everybody goes on vacation. This will cut his July output almost in half. Even if nothing else happens, he won't produce as much candy in the month of February. Why? Because there aren't as many days for him to produce candy or for his customers to buy candy in February!

If this turns out to be a good year for business, then the annual rate of flow of the GNP will probably get larger from month to month.

But if this turns out to be a bad year for business, the flow will get smaller. As the year progresses we can watch these GNP figures and see how fast the economic machine is running and whether or not it is speeding up or slowing down. As the new GNP figures become available they are reported in the *Survey of Current Business* and the *Wall Street Journal* and the *New York Times* and *Business Week* and *Time* and *U.S. News* and in all the news media, including your own home town newspaper. It's easy enough to find the GNP figures!

It's easy to find the product and income figures !

The National Income Figures

So much for the "product" figures. Now how does the government get the "national income" figures? The same way they get the product figures. They ask the businesses how much they are paying out to the owners of the factors of production—for labor, land, and capital.

The government's national income statisticians try to find out the total amount of income being received as wages, rents, interest, and profits. Then they add up all the figures and come up with the "national income." You can see that these figures would not be too difficult to find. All the businesses and several government agencies keep records of all these payments anyway—for income tax purposes and for several other reasons. It's a simple matter for the national income statisticians in the Department of Commerce to get the figures.

Why the GNP and National Income Figures Are Not Equal

Suppose all the figures of "income payments to the factors of production for the first quarter" have been reported. Then all the figures are adjusted to annual rates and added up. And suppose the total comes to $1,700,000,000 (one trillion, 700 billion dollars). The government issues a report saying national income during the first quarter was running at the annual rate of $1,700 billion." But you know that's got to be wrong. A minute ago you found out that the GNP was running at the annual rate of two trillion.

You know that if *output* in the first quarter is being produced at the annual rate of two trillion, then the rate of *income* being received must also be two trillion. Output is *always* equal to income. Right?

Every dollar paid for output must go to somebody as income. There's no other way! Still, the government *does* come out with a two trillion dollar GNP figure, and a figure of only 1700 billion for national income. How can this be? The answer is easy. The GNP figure isn't really the *true value* of the output. The GNP figure is partly fictitious. It includes some make-believe values, and it overstates the "value added" by the output flow. But for the national income figure the government statisticians stick to the true values. So the national income figure is always smaller. Let me use an example to explain.

Suppose you are talking to me about my backyard corn-producing business. I tell you that, using only my own labor, I produced and sold $2,000 worth of corn last year. I produced 200 bushels of corn and sold it all for $10 a bushel and collected $2,000. You congratulate me for making $2,000 of income from my garden. (You know that if I produced and sold $2,000 worth of product I must have received $2,000 of income.) But I say, "No. I really didn't earn two thousand dollars. I only made about $1,700. Let me explain why."

Deduct Depreciation
from GNP to Get NNP

"First of all, I really didn't produce an additional two hundred bushels of corn. I had ten bushels of corn to begin with, which I planted as seed corn. So really, I didn't add two hundred bushels of corn (or $2,000 worth) to the society's output. All I added was 190 bushels, or $1,900 worth. See? My net product was only 190 bushels. That's all the 'value' I really added through my production process."

It's easy to see why the seed corn must be deducted to find the "net product." It's just as easy to see why *all* the capital used up in the productive process must be "replaced in its original condition" before we can start bragging about how much we have produced—about how much product value we have added.

If you wear out a thousand dollars worth of tractor parts producing a thousand dollars worth of corn, or tear up a thousand dollar fish net catching a thousand dollars worth of fish, or wear out a thousand dollars worth of canning machinery producing a thousand dollars worth of canned peas, you haven't added any product value at all! So really, you haven't "produced" *anything*!

So the first reason the GNP figure is inflated is that it's too "gross." (That's why we call it the *gross* national product.) We must take out enough of this "gross product" figure to make up for what we used up, tore up, and wore out in the process of producing the product. We call this deduction the depreciation deduction.

When we subtract the "depreciation deduction" (also called the "capital consumption allowance") from the GNP figure, we get a *net product* figure. We call it net national product (NNP). That's closer to a true measure of the product value added during the year than is the *gross* GNP figure. But even the NNP figure includes some fictitious value. So we're going

to have to subtract something else. Guess what? You'd never guess, so let's go on with the corn example. You'll find out.

Deduct Indirect Business Taxes
from NNP to Get NP = NI

The "seed corn replacement deduction" (depreciation) takes off $100 from the $2,000 I received when I sold my corn. My "net product" is $1,900. But my income from my corn garden was only about $1,700. Remember? So what happened to the other $200? Why did my $1,900 worth of net product only bring me about $1,700 in income? Here's why: The *true* value of the corn I sold really wasn't $10 a bushel. The corn was only worth $9 a bushel. The price was pushed up to $10 a bushel by "embodied taxes" (indirect taxes) of one dollar a bushel. I collected $2,000 from my customers, but the corn I sold them was really only worth $1,800. I only got to keep $1,800, not the whole $2,000. Let me explain.

Last year the local county board levied their "dollar-a-bushel and pass-it-on-to-the-tourist" corn tax. All roadside-stand corn sellers must pay this tax. If it wasn't for the tax, corn would be selling for $9 a bushel. So the corn is really only worth $9 a bushel. The tax pushes the price up to $10 a bushel.

Since I really only added a net product of 190 bushels, the true value of my total output was really only $1,710 (190 bushels @ $9 = $1,710). And that's exactly the amount of income I received from my corn-producing operation! (I had to pay the county $200 for the indirect taxes I collected, of course. And the true value of the seed corn I used up was really only $90: 10 bushels @ $9 = $90.)

I collected $100 in "indirect taxes" for the county by raising the price of my corn from $9 to $10 a bushel. Indirect taxes are meant to be collected that way. Indirect taxes become embodied in the prices of the products people buy. The buyer pays the tax without even knowing it. But because of the tax, the price of the product is higher than the true value of the product. That's the reason why all indirect taxes must be deducted from the prices of things—that is, from the total value (price) of the net national product—in order to get the "true value" of the output of the economy. After we deduct all of the fictitious value added by indirect taxes, then we arrive at the *true value* of the national product—the value of national product which is equal to national income.

Let's summarize for a minute. The gross national product (GNP) is a "partly fictitious" figure. It includes two kinds of "fictional value" which must be taken away before we get down to the true "output value added" of the economy.

First we must deduct an allowance for all the capital being used up in the production process. We call this the *depreciation* deduction. *"Depreciation" simply means "the rate at which we are using up capital in the production process."* It doesn't make much sense to talk about the "additional value of the output we're producing" unless we first replace the things we're using up in the process (like seed corn).

Second, we must get rid of the inflated prices which have resulted from indirect taxes. Indirect taxes get embodied in the prices of things. The prices of almost everything bought—in the United States or Canada or Great Britain or Germany or anywhere else in the world—reflect some embodied indirect taxes. The prices of automobiles, tires, TV sets, furniture and almost everything else are pushed up quite a bit by indirect taxes. For some products—for instance cigarettes and whiskey—the embodied indirect taxes account for more than half of the price! We must get rid of this "embodied tax" if we want to get down to a real, honest value of the product. So that's why indirect taxes must be deducted from the value of net national product (NNP) in order to get to the true value of the national product.

National Income
Equals National Product

After we subtract depreciation and indirect taxes from the GNP figure, what do we have? We have the "real, honest value added by the newly-produced national product." Is this "true value added by the national product" exactly equal to the "national income" received by the owners of the factors of production as wages, rents, interest, and profits? You bet it is!

This national product figure is exactly equal to the national income. The two *must be equal*. Every dollar paid for new output is a dollar received by someone as new income. The income is shared among the owners of the factors—labor, land, and capital—which helped to produce the product. After all the factor owners are paid their shares, any money left over is profit. So all the money received from the sale of the product is distributed: as wages, rents, interest, and profits. All of it goes as income to somebody. The money received for the sale of the national product *is* the national income. Of course!

The national product and income statisticians actually go through this very process we have been talking about. They add up all the payments to the factors of production. They also take the gross national product and subtract depreciation and then subtract indirect business taxes. When they do both of these things—figure "national income" one way, and figure "the real net value of the national product" the other way—do they come up with exactly the same figures for "product" and for "income"? No. Not exactly. But they would if all their figures were precisely accurate.

We know that national product and national income are equal. Any differences in the figures are obviously statistical errors. When the government statisticians do it both ways, the two figures usually come out very close.

Now you know what we look at to see and measure the speed of the economic system.

You know that the government statisticians collect the figures and publish the "national income and product accounts" showing the figures for GNP, NNP, NI and all. This work is done by the Bureau of Economic Analysis in the U.S. Department of Commerce. Their monthly magazine, *Survey of Current Business*, is a good source of information on national income and output. I'm sure you can find it in your library.

The Bureau of Labor Statistics in the U.S. Department of Labor publishes statistics on employment and unemployment. Their *Monthly Labor Review* is an excellent source of labor market information and statistics.

Several other agencies of the federal and state governments and several local governments and regional planning commissions and chambers of commerce and industry groups and labor groups and others are busy gathering statistics to see and measure the speed of economic activity in the various parts of the economy. We don't have time to get into all that. But we do need to go a little further with the "national income and product accounts."

Finding Personal and Disposable Income

The *income and product accounts* do more than show national product and national income. The accounts also show how much of the national income the people actually get to keep, and how much they actually spend for consumer goods.

So I really made $1,710 last year on my corn operation. That was the real value I added to the national product and that was my part of the national income. Did I get to spend it all? Did all of it flow to my "household"? You know it didn't. The government made me pay $340 in income taxes. All I actually got to spend out of my corn crop was $1,370 ($1,710 − $340). That's a lot less than the $2,000 I took in. But I guess it's a lot better than nothing.

You know that all the "national income" doesn't stay in the hands of the people who

earned it—that is, it doesn't all become "disposable personal income." You just saw me pay $340 in taxes. That's one example of why all the national income doesn't become disposable personal income. People must pay taxes.

Anything which prevents you from spending a part of your income *reduces* your disposable personal income. Anything which gives you *more* money to spend, *increases* your disposable personal income. Let's talk about some of these adjustments.

Social Security Taxes. First of all, some of your income never actually gets to you, "in person." Social security taxes for the federal "retirement, survivors and disability insurance, and medicare" programs are taken right out of your paycheck. You never see it. All the social security taxes collected must be deducted from national income before we get to "personal income." But that isn't all.

Corporate Taxes and Retained Earnings. If you own stock in a corporation, the government takes about half of the corporation's income in taxes before you get to see any of it in your dividend checks. It's really your income, but you'll never see it!

Also, most corporations hold about half of their "after tax" income and use the money for growth. We call this "unpaidout" income "corporate retained earnings." Maybe the corporation wants to build a new plant, or install new equipment or something. "High growth" companies sometimes retain *all* their after-tax earnings and use the money for growth. They don't pay out any dividends at all! So the stockholders never get to see the money. Just like the social security taxes, it doesn't get into anybody's "personal income."

So how much of the total national income gets distributed to the people as personal income? Only what's left after the social security taxes and the corporate profits taxes and the "retained earnings" (undistributed profits of corporations) are deducted. All these dollars are pulled out before the people ever get their hands on them. So if you want to find out how much personal income the people in the nation are receiving, just deduct all these things from national income and you will have it.

Transfer Payments to Individuals. But wait! What about the people who are on the receiving end of all those social security taxes? What about the retired people and the dependent children and all the other people who are receiving the government's retirement and welfare and disabled veterans and all the other money-sharing payments? All those people get money from the government as *personal income,* don't they? Sure they do. But that's an easy thing to handle in the national income and product accounts.

After the statisticians finish *subtracting* the social security taxes and the corporate profits taxes and the retained earnings of corporations, then they *add* the amount of money the governments are giving to people. These "government gifts of money" are called "transfer payments." Income is taken from the people who originally earned it and then "transferred" (given free) to other people.

Personal Income. If we take the national income figure, then *subtract* social security taxes and corporate profits taxes and corporate retained earnings, then *add* government transfer payments to individuals—what figure do we wind up with? Personal income, of course! Then what do we do to get to the disposable income figure? Just subtract all the *other taxes* (the direct taxes) the people have to pay out of their incomes. Then you have disposable income. That's what the households *really* get to spend.

Direct Taxes. What taxes are deducted to get to disposable income? All of them. All the taxes you pay directly out of your income. The income taxes are the biggest for most people. But sales taxes and property taxes and all the others take away personal income and leave less disposable income.

You may wonder why the social security taxes are treated differently than the income

taxes. Income taxes are deducted from most people's paychecks. The wage earner never gets to see that money. It doesn't ever become a part of *personal income*. So why the difference? It's just that the national income statisticians decided to do it this way many years ago, back when income taxes weren't being deducted from everybody's paychecks. It isn't precisely logical anymore, but as long as we all understand, it's okay. No harm done.

The Purpose and the Logic of the Income and Product Accounts

Now you understand the U.S. system of national income and product accounting. Other nations have very similar systems. But often other nations call their GNP by a different name: gross domestic product (GDP). But don't let that bother you. It means the same thing.

The important thing is that you understand the purpose and the logic of the national income and product accounting system. The national income and product accounts measure the economic flows—the size of the spending stream—the output and income flows in the economy.

These accounts represent the real-world application of the output and income concepts of macroeconomics. They let us keep an eye on the changing macro-condition of the economy. If something goes wrong they help us to see what the problem is and maybe figure out what to do about it. These accounts can be very helpful. But there's a lot these accounts do not show. You should know something about that, too. That's the subject of the next section.

SOME LIMITATIONS OF THE "GNP APPROACH" TO NATIONAL ACCOUNTING

The national income and product accounts don't do all we might want them to. There are two problems: (1) the accounts really can't accurately measure the value of the nation's output, and (2) the accounts don't reflect the "economic welfare" (conditions of life) of the people. We need to spend a few minutes on each of these problems.

Why The GNP Accounts Aren't an Accurate Measure of Output

It's a pretty tough task to add up the value of everything produced in a complex economy like the United States! Some things are almost impossible to measure.

Homemakers' Services. For example, take the economic value of all the services performed by family members who work in the home—cooking, cleaning, washing, entertaining—and teaching, directing and supervising children. What would be the value of all these productive activities if they had to be bought and paid for in the market? High, of course. But the value of all this production doesn't even show up in the GNP accounts.

Suppose all the homemakers decided to work in each others' houses and pay each other for all that work. Then their services would be sold and paid for and would be included in the GNP figures. So GNP would go up quite a bit! But did national product really go up? Of course not. See the problem?

Government Services. Then there are some kinds of goods to which it's difficult to assign values because they aren't "sold" in the market. Government services are the best example. How do you value the services of schools? police and fire departments? other government services?

Usually the approach is to assume that the output value of the services is equal to whatever the services cost, and just let it go at that. We know this kind of measure isn't accurate. An inefficient and costly school or fire department gets assigned a higher output value than an efficient one! But that's what we do because we don't have a better way to do it.

Year to Year Changes. Other problems arise when we try to compare "the state of the economy" from one year to another. In the real world, things don't always change in an orderly way as the years go by. Prices sometimes do and sometimes do not reflect product changes. And new products are always being introduced. That even further confuses the issue.

One big problem is that prices are always changing (going up). We can use price indexes to eliminate the worst effects of price changes (as you will learn in a few minutes). But these techniques don't give us precisely accurate comparisons from year to year. There are just too many things changing. We can't take all of them into account.

Yes, there are problems with trying to get an accurate measurement of the national product. But that isn't usually the major complaint about the GNP accounts these days. The major complaint is that GNP is not a very good indicator of economic welfare in the nation. If the GNP was increasing would that mean the people were getting better off? that their welfare was improving? Not necessarily.

GNP Doesn't Measure Economic Welfare

There are several reasons why the GNP figures might be going up while economic welfare in the nation was going down. Usually it probably wouldn't work out that way. But sometimes it very well might. The point is this: we just don't know. Why not? Because we don't have any way to measure the level of or changes in economic welfare in the nation! That's exactly the problem.

All Products Count the Same. For one thing, when the GNP figure is being added up there is no distinction between one kind of product and another. The production of cigarettes and fighter planes and porno flicks counts the same as the production of housing and education and hospitals and pollution control.

Surely all these things don't bring "equal national welfare per dollar's worth"! But in the GNP accounts they're all equal.

Negative Utility of Increased Production. Another problem is this: the "negative utility" which is generated as more output is produced is not accounted for. As more products are produced the quality of life can be impaired in several ways. The GNP shows the value of the products but the social costs don't show up.

Air and water pollution, noises, messing up beautiful landscapes, crowding people into towns and cities, destroying the harmony of peaceful neighborhoods and communities, requiring people to commute long distances to work—all these things have very important effects on our quality of life. How many more cigarettes or fighter planes or porno flicks—or for that matter, houses and schools and hospitals and pollution control devices and cars and boats and steaks and stereos and everything else—must we produce to make up for all these social costs?

Over the past 10 or 20 years, GNP has risen quite a lot. But on balance, are we really any better off? Most economists would say: "Yes, on balance we probably are (at least most of us are) better off. But we probably aren't as much better off as the increase in the GNP figure might lead you to believe."

Less Work and More Leisure. On the other side of the picture consider this: the average work week has decreased by almost one half over the last 100 years. Even if people didn't have any more products they would have a lot more free time. And surely that's worth something in human welfare! These days instead of working more than 70 hours a week most people work 40 hours or less. But the GNP figure doesn't in any way reflect this.

Population and Income Distribution. There are a couple of other things you need to think about when you're on the welfare implications of GNP. First, population size must always be considered. If GNP doubles and population doubles, that's no increase in the output available per person! Secondly, income distribution is important. If a large share of the GNP of a nation goes to a few people, then even if *GNP per capita* is high, most of the people still may be living in poverty.

What About an "Economic Welfare" National Accounting Figure?

Most economists agree about the shortcomings of the GNP approach to national accounting. Some economists are now trying to work out a new system—one which can do a better job of measuring economic welfare. Some experimental accounts have been put together which try to take into consideration the factors which the GNP accounts leave out.

NEW and MEW. Economist Paul Samuelson has worked with a new measure he calls "Net Economic Welfare" (NEW). William Nordhaus and James Tobin at Yale University have worked out a system they call MEW—"Measure of Economic Welfare." But so far we still don't have a generally accepted national accounting system that measures economic welfare. Maybe someday we will. But until then, please don't forget: the GNP accounts certainly don't do it.

Here's an interesting question to think about. Could it be that the best things in life really are free? If they are, measuring economic welfare is going to be a tough task! When you stop to think about it, clean air and refreshing surroundings and lots of good weather and sunshine may be more important to our welfare than most of the goods we buy!

What Is GNP Good For? If GNP isn't a measure of welfare, then what is it? What's it good for? Just this: *GNP is a measure of the speed at which the economy is running.* That's all. It isn't a precisely accurate measure but it's pretty good. It's good enough to tell us when the economy is clicking along well and when it's slowing down and by about how much. That isn't everything. But it's a lot. So let's take a few minutes and look at the national income and product accounts of the United States.

National Income and Product in the United States: 1929-1975

Table 8-1 shows the national income and product figures for the United States over the past several decades. Can you see the Great Depression of the 1930s? Sure. And the big boom of World War II? And then the economic expansion of the 1950s and the 1960s? Sure. But one word of warning: much of the increase you see in the table represents rising *prices*—not just rising *outputs*.

So how do we get rid of this "rising prices" illusion? How can we find out how much the output *really* increased over these years? We have to "deflate" the figures to get rid of the effect of rising prices. That's easy enough to do. You'll learn how to do it in the next section. But first, stop awhile and study Table 8-1. Then, on to the next section.

Comparing GNP from Year to Year

Now when a friend asks you "how's business?" you will know how to find the answer. You will be able to say: "During the first quarter of this year, GNP was flowing at an annual rate approaching two trillion dollars. This is an increase of more than ten percent over the rate of flow of GNP during the first quarter of last year. It looks like business this year is doing just fine."

But that isn't quite all. You must also remember to say: "Of course some of this increase in the dollar GNP figure doesn't really represent an increase in real output in the economy. Yes, prices have increased. And yes, we are valuing each unit of output at a higher price. For example, I hear that Willie Wonka's candy output is up from an annual rate of $5,200,000 last year, to $5,720,000 this year.

But guess what? He is still producing at exactly the same rate: 10 truckloads a week. What's the difference? It's just that this year the price is up from $10,000 to $11,000 a truckload. Prices went up and costs went up. If Willie's candy business is any indication, the economy really isn't producing any more this year than last."

So your friend wants to know whether or not Willie Wonka's case is typical. "Has there really been any increase in the rate of output of the economy between the first quarter of last year and the first quarter of this year? How can I find out?" You explain that the way to find out is to "deflate" the GNP figures, using a price index.

Anyone who is going to compare "levels of economic activity" from one year to another needs to know something about price indexes. A price index is one of the world's simplest things. But lots of people don't understand it. In a few minutes, you will.

HOW TO MAKE AND USE A PRICE INDEX

Let's suppose that just for fun you wanted to make your own price index for the cost of mailing first-class letters. Back in 1970 the cost was 6¢. But by 1976 the cost was up to 13¢. Suppose you decided to use 1970 as your base year—that is, your reference point—the year to start from. Then you want to find out what the "first-class postage price index number" was after the cost went up to 13¢. How do you do it? Easy.

Divide the Base-Year Cost into the Present Cost to Get the Index Number

You know how much it cost to mail a letter in 1970 (the base year)—6¢. And you know it costs 13¢ now, (as of 1976). Simply divide the base-year cost (6¢) into the present cost (13¢), and you will have your index number for the current month. (13 divided by the base-year cost of 6, comes out to 2.17 or 217 percent, or an "index number" of 217.) What could be easier than that?

The price index for the base year is always 100. Why? Because you are dividing a number into itself! You must come out with one, or 100 percent, or an "index number" of 100! In our postage case, you would be dividing 6¢ (cost in the base year) into 6¢ (cost in the base year). (6/6 = 1, or 100 percent, or an index number of 100.) In order to show that 1970 is your base year, you might say: "1970 = 100." That simply means that 1970 is the base year.

Table 8-1 National Income and Product Figures for the United States, Selected Years* 1929-1975 (in Billions of Dollars)

	1929	1933	1939	1944	1950	1960	1970	1972	1975
GNP	103	56	90	210	285	504	976	1,152	1,499
−depreciation	8	7	7	11	18	44	84	104	153
NNP	95	49	83	199	267	460	892	1,048	1,346
−indirect taxes (and other minor adjustments)	8	9	10	16	26	45	92	113	136
NI (= NP)	87	40	73	183	241	415	800	935	1,210
−social security taxes	a	a	2	5	7	21	57	74	108
−corporate taxes	1	a	2	13	18	23	37	42	47
−retained earnings	3	−3	1	7	11	13	14	26	22
+payments, transfer (etc.)	4	3	5	7	23	43	109	143	214
PERSONAL INCOME	86	47	73	165	228	401	801	936	1,246
−direct taxes	3	2	3	19	21	51	116	141	169
DISPOSABLE INCOME	83	45	70	146	207	350	685	795	1,077

Source: Economic Report of the President, and Survey of Current Business. (a = less than one billion)

*Some of the figures presented in this table are not precisely accurate because of adjustments made by the author to take care of statistical discrepancies and to make the table internally consistent without introducing confusing and irrelevant detail.

This table shows annual rates of flow of output, income, tax payments, etc. You can see a lot of interesting things by looking at these figures.

You can see that the rate of flow of GNP, NNP, and NI have all increased by about 14 times since 1929. But taxes and government transfer payments have increased much faster. The rate at which direct taxes are flowing to the government has increased by more than 50 times, and transfer payments flowing from the government to the people have increased about 50 times.

Just look how much change there has been since 1960! Almost all the flows just about tripled in only 15 years. Corporate retained earnings is the only big exception.

You might guess that one of the reasons for the big increases in all these numbers is inflation. That's right. You are getting ready, right now, to find out what to do about that.

Divide the Index Number Into Present Cost to Find "Base-Year Cost"

Now that you know how to get an index number, the next question is: "how do you use it?" For one thing, you can use your "first-class postage price index number" to find out how much it *would have cost* to mail your letters, back in the base year. The index number is 217. This tells you that it's now costing you $2.17 to get as much "first-class postal service" as you got for $1.00 in 1970.

Last month suppose you spent $12 for first-class postage. How much would this have cost you in 1970? Just divide $12 by the index number of 217 and you'll see! ($12 divided by an index number of 217 equals $5.53). The value of your "first-class postage dollar" has gone down, all right. In 1970, $5.53 would have bought as much first-class postal service as $12 can buy, now!

Divide the Index Number into a Dollar to Compare "Present Value" of the Dollar

Suppose you say to yourself: "As compared to 1970, what is the present value of my 'first-class postage dollar'?" To find out, just divide the index number into a dollar. You come out with 46¢. ($1.00 divided by an index number of 217 equals 46¢.) So for first-class postage services, the dollar this year is worth only as much as 46¢ was worth in 1970. Sad, isn't it?

Suppose this little exercise intrigues you and you decide to build a first-class postage price index on a 1960 base. In 1960 it only cost 3¢ to mail a first-class letter. So with 1960 as your base year (1960 = 100), what is the first-class postage "price index" for 1976? It is 13¢ divided by 3¢, or 4.33 or an index number of 433.

So to get as much postal service as you are now getting for $12, how much would you have had to pay in 1960? You find this out by dividing your index number into $12. In 1960 it would have cost you only about $2.77 to mail as many letters as you are mailing these days for $12. ($12 divided by an index number of 433 equals about $2.77.)

There's been a big decline in the value of your postage dollar! In order to buy as much postal service in 1976 as you could have bought for $1 in 1960, you must pay $4.33! So what is the value of your first-class postage dollar now, as compared with 1960? It's only worth about 23¢! ($1.00 divided by 433 equals about 23¢). Now that you know what a price index is and how to use it, let's take another look at the problem of trying to compare GNP figures when our "measuring rod" (the value of the dollar) keeps shrinking from year to year.

Divide the Index Number into the GNP Figure to See How Much the Output Really Changed

When the gross national product for the present quarter is added up, it will include a figure for first-class postal services. The figure will be considerably larger now than it was for the same quarter in 1970. Why? A big flurry in first-class correspondence? No. The higher figure comes partly from the higher price charged for postage services, and only partly from the higher volume of mail. How do you get rid of this "fictitious product value" which results from the inflated postage prices? Simply divide the present "value of first-class postal services performed" figure, by the index number (index number 217; 1970 = 100). This will give you a figure which accurately reflects the *real* increase in "the output of first-class mail services" between 1970 and 1976.

You know that postal services make up only a very small part of the GNP. But suppose you could go around and do, for *each* product and service, exactly what you just did for postal services. Then when you got the dollar value of *each* product and service "deflated" you could add up the deflated figures and get a new GNP figure. The new figure would show the present output, not measured by the *inflated* "current" dollar units, but measured by the *same size* "constant" dollar units that were used to measure the gross output back in 1970. The new (deflated) "constant dollar" GNP figure would show how much the output of the economy really has changed since 1970.

Can you see it? If prices go up and output value gets bigger, you don't know if more is *actually* being produced or not. But if prices stay the same and output value still gets bigger, you know for sure that more is being produced. Right? Of course.

So, do the government statisticians make up a price index for postal services and one for tonsillectomies and one for hamburgers and gasoline and tires and heating oil and subway fares and beer and dorm rent and phone calls and textbooks and everything else, and then "deflate" the "present output value" of each, and then add up all the "deflated output values" to get a new (deflated) GNP figure? That's sort of the way they do it.

The Bureau of Economic Analysis of the U.S. Department of Commerce works out the GNP price deflator. This is an index number which reflects the "average change in all output prices." With this index number you can deflate the whole GNP figure in one fell swoop! How? Simply divide the current GNP figure by the index number! That brings the GNP figure down in size so that it's comparable to the base year GNP figure. Isn't that neat?

Remember Table 8-1, where you saw how GNP in the United States has changed so greatly since 1929? How much of the change was caused by increased output? And how much of it was just caused by higher prices? You know how to find out, now. Just go back and revalue the output produced during each year. Only instead of using the "current prices" which existed in each year, use the *same* prices for each year. Use "constant prices"—the prices which existed in the year you choose as your "base year."

How do you do this? How do you convert the "current dollar" GNP figures into "constant

dollar" GNP figures? Simple. Just divide the "current dollar" GNP figure for each year by the "price index" (the "GNP price deflator") for that year. That's all there is to it! Table 8-2 on page 140 shows that when you deflate the GNP figures it can make quite a lot of difference! Take a few minutes now and study Table 8-2. After that we'll get into some other kinds of and uses for price indexes.

The Consumer Price Index (CPI)

There are all kinds of price indexes. One of the most often used is the "consumer price index," also called the "cost of living index." This index is put together by the Bureau of Labor Statistics, U.S. Department of Labor. What they do is make up a list of all the things that the "average consumer" would buy and in what quantities in the average year. This list will include postal services, medical services, tires and gasoline, meat and potatoes, clothing and everything else bought by "the average family."

It isn't always easy to decide exactly how much of which things to put into this list. But the government statisticians make the best estimates they can and go ahead. Once they get the list made up they then assign a "base year" cost figure (say, 1967 = 100) to each item on the list. Then they add up all the costs of all the things. This gives them the "cost of living" of the "average family" in the base year. That's the first step.

The next step is to take the same list of things and assign the *present* cost of each item on the list, then add up the total. This shows the "cost of living" of "average family" at the present time (present month, or week). Then the *base year cost* is divided into the *present cost* to get the consumer price (cost of living) index.

Suppose the list of things would cost $8,000 in 1967, and $9,300 in September of 1971. Then the index number for September, 1971 (on a 1967 base) would be 116. ($9,300 divided by $8,000 equals about 116.) This means that it would have cost the average family $1.16 to buy in September, 1971 what they could have bought for $1.00 in 1967. It means that the "average family's consumer dollar," in September, 1971 was only worth as much as 86 cents would have been worth to the "average family" in 1967. ($1.00 divided by the index number of 116 equals $.86.)

By May of 1974 suppose the cost of the things on the list had gone up to $10,400. Then the consumer price index (CPI) would be 130. ($10,400 divided by $8,000 equals 130.) The May, 1974 dollar would buy only about as much as 77 cents would have bought in 1967. ($1.00 ÷ 130 = about 77¢.)

By September of 1977 suppose the cost of the list of goods and services—that is, of the average consumer's market basket full of things—has gone up to $13,000. What's the price index? On a 1967 base it's 163 ($13,000 ÷ $8,000 = 163.) On the average, the September 1977 dollar would buy only about as much as 66¢ would have bought ten years earlier. ($1.00 ÷ 163 = 66¢.)

Other Price Indexes

Price indexes are interesting, simple, and helpful numbers. The best known and most widely used index is the one you just heard about—the consumer price index. Then there is the wholesale price index which compares prices of things that businesses are buying.

Table 8-2: A Comparison of Current Dollar Values and Constant Dollar Values of U.S. GNP, Selected Years, 1929-1975 (in Billions of Dollars) 1958 = 100

	1929	1933	1939	1944	1950	1958	1960	1970	1972	1975
GNP (current dollars)	103	56	90	210	285	447	504	976	1,152	1,499
GNP (constant dollars 1958 = 100)	204	142	209	361	355	447	488	707	768	785
PRICE INDEX (GNP Deflator)	51	39	43	58	80	100	103	138	150	191

Source: *Economic Report of the President,* and *Survey of Current Business.*

What a difference price changes can make!

The "current dollar" figures show a 14-fold increase in GNP since 1929. The deflated (constant dollar) figures show that the real rate of flow of output has increased by only about four times. That's still a lot of increase, but it's a lot less than 14 times!

The rapid price increases which have occurred since 1960 are easily visible in this table. See how the "current dollar" figure has just about tripled since 1960? But the "constant dollar" figure shows that the rate of flow of real output has increased by only a little more than 60 percent. That's still a lot of increase, but it's a lot less than 300 percent!

There are lots of indexes for individual products, such as the construction cost index, the housing cost index, the medical cost index, the food cost index, the transportation cost index, and so on.

Each of these indexes simply gives a quick and easy way of finding out how much the prices of these things have changed, on the average, since the "base year." You can look at the index and tell immediately how much it would cost you *now* (on the average) to buy what was "a dollar's worth" in the base year. If the index is 130, it now costs you $1.30 to buy what you could have bought for $1.00 in the base year.

If you want to find out how the "real purchasing power" of your present income compares with the real purchasing power of your income in the base year, simply divide your present income by the cost of living index (CPI). Just as the GNP figure can be "deflated" by dividing by an index, so can your own income.

If the price index is 200, it means that your income now must be twice as large as it was in the base year, for you to have as much "real income" now as you had then. Your income must have doubled just to keep you in the same place. Also it means that the pension funds or insurance policies that you contracted for in the base year are now going to bring you only *half* as much real goods and services as you thought you would get when you made the contract. That, of course, is one of the major problems and one of the great social injustices of inflation.

A Dollar's Value Depends on What It Buys

One small word of warning about price indexes. An index number always refers to one thing, or to an "average list" of things. If you are spending your dollars exactly the same way as represented by this "average list" then your dollars will change in value exactly as indicated by the index number. But no one spends

money exactly like the "average list." Let's take a wild example.

Suppose medical services, automobiles, gasoline and related products and meats and bakery products are all items which have increased considerably in price since 1967. But suppose you use very few of these things. You have decided to sell the car and ride a bike. No one in your family has been sick. You and your family are vegetarians and you do all your baking at home. Further, you always go camping on your vacations and you buy winter clothes for the children at the local rummage sales. You make your own wine and your own beer in your basement. So what does the consumer price index have to do with the value of *your* dollar? Not very much!

The value of **your** dollar depends on what **you** buy!

The actual value of each individual's dollar is determined, not by the consumer price index, but by how much that individual gets when spending each dollar. One family may live better on $9,000 a year than another family would on $12,000. Why? Because the people in the first family spend their money carefully and maximize the value of their dollars!

All this does not mean that the cost of living index is not a valuable tool. It really is. But recognize that it doesn't apply in a precise specific way to anyone. You can have considerable control over the value of *your* dollars—if you want to. A good course in consumer economics can help you learn how!

SUMMARY

Now you know how to measure the speed of the economy. You already knew a good bit about basic macroeconomic concepts—about the circular flow and about the equalities between spending and receipts and between output and income. And you knew quite a lot about *money*! From this chapter you now know how the national income statisticians collect, analyze and present these national income and product statistics. And you also know how to make a price index and how to use it to deflate the income and product figures.

Yes, you know a good bit about some of the basic parts of macroeconomics. But there's still quite a bit about macroeconomics coming up. All of the next three chapters are concerned with the basic concepts and principles of macroeconomics—that is, with understanding the size and reasons for changes in the total spending flow of the economy. You'll be reading a lot about the total spending flow: what it's made up of, what influences it, and different ways to visualize and analyze it.

When you finish the next three chapters you'll know quite a lot about macroeconomics. But right now, here are some review exercises for you to practice with.

REVIEW EXERCISES

● **MAJOR CONCEPTS, PRINCIPLES, TERMS (Explain each thoroughly.)**

the purpose of the national product and income accounts
why depreciation is deducted
why a price index is needed
what determines the value of *your* dollar
limitations of the GNP figure

● **OTHER CONCEPTS AND TERMS (Explain each briefly.)**

gross national product	price index
national income	base year
depreciation deduction	GNP price deflator
net national product	consumer price index (CPI)
indirect taxes	cost of living index
personal income	NEW and MEW
transfer payments	

● **QUESTIONS (Write out answers or jot down key points.)**

1. Suppose you produced macrame belts and sold them to people at the concession stand at Seashore State Park last summer, and you took in $1,000. Do you think all of that thousand dollars would be included as a part of the "national income"? Or what deductions do you think would need to be made? Make up a list, and then explain why each deduction would be necessary.

2. I'm sure you don't spend your money exactly like the "average family." Think about the specific things *you* usually buy, and about how their prices have been changing in the past year or two. Do you think you could make up a sort of "roughly estimated" personal price index? and then figure out what has been happening to the value of *your* dollar? (Maybe you've found out how to buy things cheaper—wholesale, maybe—and the value of your dollar is going up!) Want to take a few minutes and try to make up your own personal price index? It might be interesting to see what you come up with!

PART 3

MACRO CONCEPTS AND PRINCIPLES II: ANALYZING NATIONAL INCOME

THE MORE WE EARN, THE MORE WE SPEND—
AND THE MORE WE ALL SAVE, TOO!

9 National Income Analysis I: The Components of the Income-Spending Stream

Consumers, investors, governments, and foreigners all add to the total spending-output-income flow.

Total spending is the key to understanding macroeconomics. You already know that. And you understand about banks creating money. In fact you know a lot about macroeconomics. Let's take a minute and review the total "overview picture."

An Overview of Macroeconomics

It is total spending which supports the total level of employment and production—the total level of economic activity. Total spending pulls forth total output. As spending goes down, total output goes down. As spending increases, output increases—that is, output increases until the economy reaches full capacity. If spending continues to increase after full capacity is reached, there will be shortages and prices will rise. We will have inflation.

The total level of spending must be just right if we are going to have anything approaching "full employment and stable prices." If total spending is too low we will have unemployment and depression. If total spending is too high we will have shortages and inflation. That's it, in a nutshell. But what determines the total level of spending? What makes it just right? Or too low? Or too high? We need to get into that now.

People Spend for Consumer Goods and Businesses Spend for Investment Goods

Who spends? Mostly people and businesses. Why do they spend? To buy things, of course! And why do they want to buy things? People buy things to have, to use, to consume, to enjoy. People buy "consumer goods."

Businesses buy things to use in production, hoping to increase their profits. Businesses usually buy because they think it will be profitable to do so.

So there are two basic motives for spending. One is to consume and gain personal satisfaction. The other is to buy capital and become more productive. People spend for consumption purposes, and businesses spend for investment purposes. And that's all! What other purpose could there be for people and businesses to spend? There isn't any. Now let's look at some of the reasons why consumers spend. Later we will talk about why businesses spend.

WHAT DETERMINES TOTAL CONSUMER SPENDING?

What might make people spend more? Or less? Various things. Anything which gives people more money to spend usually causes them to spend more. No mystery about that! Suppose the economy is depressed and many people are unemployed. Then for some reason business picks up. Unemployed people are hired. The "unemployed" buildings are rented. Idle factories start producing things. So what happens next? You could guess.

The Consumption Function

When the unemployed workers and the factory owners and other people start earning incomes again, what do you suppose will happen to the total level of consumer spending? Do you think people will buy more TV sets? Movie tickets? Frozen lobster tails? All sorts of things? Of course. Consumer spending reflects people's incomes. You know it does.

Economists have a name for this idea—the idea that the more income people are getting the more they will be spending for consumer goods. We call it the consumption function. Why "consumption function"? Because

people's consumption (meaning, in this case: "spending for consumer goods") is a function of (meaning: "depends on" or "is determined by") the size of their incomes. The higher their incomes, the higher will be their spending for consumer goods.

You can see how the idea of the "consumption function" makes sense for each individual. It makes sense for the total economy, too. It can be very helpful in understanding the size of and changes in the total spending flow. As national income gets larger, what happens to consumer spending? It gets larger too. And as consumer spending gets larger, what does that do to national income? Makes it increase even more? Sure?

See how, once total spending begins to increase and incomes begin to rise, consumer spending is induced to increase? And push up total spending even more? Each increase induces a further increase. That's why prosperous times sometimes lead to overspending and inflation! You'll be seeing a lot more about this idea later. But now, here's more about what determines total consumer spending.

Expectations Influence Consumer Spending

Consumer spending also reflects people's expectations. If people are concerned about their economic future they will usually spend less (save more). People will save more if they think they are going to lose their jobs. Or if they think the union is going to call a long strike. Or if they expect that all their teenagers will need some money to help them go to college. Or if they expect they will have to retire early or quit work because of poor health. Or if for *any* reason they expect their incomes to fall or their expenditures to rise. And the opposite is also true.

If people expect to be earning more (or if they expect their spending obligations to go down) they will be willing to spend up their present incomes right away. They may even buy lots of things "on time." Why should they try to save if they think they are going to be earning more and more all the time?

Anything which changes the attitudes or the outlook of people will be likely to have some influence on how much they spend. The level of consumer spending even reflects such things as whether or not it rains on the Fourth of July weekend and whether or not it snows just before Christmas. Consumer spending is influenced by radio, TV, and newspaper announcements of developments at home or elsewhere in the world. Anything which makes people more optimistic or more pessimistic is likely to influence their rate of consumer spending.

Consumers Can Spend Past Income or Future Income

It's important to remember that people don't just spend their current incomes. Most of the big items people buy are not bought with current income. When you buy a new car you are spending either your past income (your savings) or your future income. (You buy on time.) So consumer spending is influenced by how much savings people have and their willingness to spend these savings. Also it is influenced by how much the consumers are already in debt and their willingness to go further into debt.

Consumer spending is influenced by how easy it is to buy things on credit. You probably could go out and buy a $500 TV set today by spending less than $50 (the down payment). Maybe you could buy one with *no* money down. With easy credit you don't have to have very much current income to be able to buy things. But then your future income is already spent before you get it. That will force you to cut down on your future spending.

You can see how consumer spending is influenced by how much savings and how much debt the "average consumer" already has, and

by the availability of easy credit. You can also see why a really big boom in the sales of autos, appliances, and furniture *last* year is likely to be followed by a slump in the sales of these consumer durables *this* year. If everybody bought new things last year, this year they'll all be paying off their debts!

See how the amount of a person's current income doesn't really determine the amount of that person's consumer spending? Sometimes individuals spend more than their incomes. Sometimes they spend less. For this reason it's very easy for shortages to develop (like in consumer durables last year, when everyone was trying to buy new things) or for surpluses to develop (like in consumer durables this year, when everyone is trying to pay off debts).

Taxes Reduce Consumer Spending

When you pay taxes you don't have as much money left to buy things. Income taxes take hundreds (or thousands) of dollars from most people. Social security taxes take some, too. This money is taken right out of your check. You never even get to see it! Then in addition you must pay property taxes and automobile taxes and gasoline taxes and utility taxes and alcohol and tobacco excise taxes and state and local sales taxes and lots of other taxes. Taxes put a real crimp in the amount you have to spend. Taxes reduce your *disposable income.* Remember?

The basic idea behind taxing (by the federal government, at least) is to keep you from spending—that is, to force you to save (not consume) and leave some goods in the market. Then the government can spend money to buy these "leftover" goods and use them to make highways and schools and ICBMs and things. Or it can give money to poor people who can then buy these "leftover" goods for themselves. The whole idea of taxing is to hold down consumer spending—to get all of us not to spend so much, so some things will be left in the market. Then the government can buy what it needs without pushing up total spending and causing inflation.

Summary of the Consumer Spending Decision

In capsule form, we can summarize the highlights of the "consumer spending decision" this way:

The amount the consumers are going to spend will be determined by how much current income they have, as modified by how much taxes they have to pay, how much money they already have saved up, or how far they are in debt, how easy it is to borrow or to buy things on time, and what they expect to happen to their *future* incomes and expenditure needs. Anything which causes any of these factors to change is likely to cause consumer spending to change.

Think about it. Aren't these the things which influence the amount *you* spend for consumer goods?

WHAT DETERMINES BUSINESS INVESTMENT SPENDING?

There are many reasons why businesses spend. But in general, businesses spend whenever they expect the expenditure to be a "good deal." Suppose a business is considering an additional investment of some sort. If the business expects a high enough return (a big enough addition to revenue or a big enough reduction in cost) then it will make the additional investment. If not, then it won't. That's obvious enough, isn't it?

How high does the "expected return" need to be to induce the business to invest in a machine—that is, in a piece of "capital equipment"? High enough to pay off all the expected costs of the machine (including the interest cost) and leave a *reasonable profit* for the business.

Anything which causes the "expected return" to increase (or anything which causes the "expected cost" to decrease) is likely to stimulate businesses to increase their investment spending. Anything which lowers the expected return or raises the cost is likely to slow down investment spending. Of course.

Investment Spending Is Influenced by Expected Returns and Interest Rates

Why would anyone spend money for capital goods? Why would anyone want to buy a tractor to use to produce corn and tomatoes? Why might you buy a machine to expand the output of your macrame belt shop? How do you decide? You consider the "expected returns" you will get from the investment. And you consider the "interest cost" you will have to pay on the borrowed money you will use to buy the machine.

(If you plan to use your own money to buy the machine, the interest cost is still just as real. You must consider the *interest income* you will have to give up—the opportunity cost—when you withdraw your savings or sell your bonds to get the money to buy the machine.)

You already know that capital equipment is *productive*. An extra piece of machinery has a marginal "value product" just as does an extra worker. Whether or not you will buy a piece of capital depends on whether or not you expect the marginal value product of that piece of capital to be greater than the cost of the piece of capital to you. If you think the additional output will be worth more than the cost of the capital, then you will invest in it. But if you don't think the piece of capital will add enough value to your output to justify its cost, then you will not buy it. Nobody pays more for something than it's expected to be worth! Not ever!

John Maynard Keynes and the Marginal Efficiency of Capital

Everyone who is producing something has some "demand for capital." Your demand for capital will be high or low depending on whether or not you think the capital will add a lot or a little to the value of your output (or perhaps subtract a lot or a little from your cost of production). Is your demand for the capital *high*? Then that means you expect a *high return* from the capital. Of course!

This idea of expected return as the thing which determines the demand for capital was developed by John Maynard Keynes (pronounced KAYns) in his famous and somewhat revolutionary economics book, *The General Theory of Employment, Interest, and Money* (1936). Keynes emphasized the importance of expectations as the thing which determines whether or not the business will invest in a piece of capital.

Keynes referred to the additional return the business expects to get from an additional piece of capital as the "marginal efficiency" of the capital. He said that if the capital is expected to be productive enough to more than cover its cost (including the interest cost) then the business will invest in the capital. If it is not, then the investment will not be made.

So really, we're back to the basic principle you've known about ever since Chapter 2. Businesses will spend for (invest in) anything they expect to be profitable. If a new factory or a new gear grinder or a new truck or a new pile of coal is expected to bring a marginal profit— that is, if its marginal "value product" is expected to be greater than its marginal "input cost"—then the business will buy it. If not, then the business won't buy it.*

Keynes developed quite elaborate theories of macroeconomics—theories explaining the different things which influence the total spending flow—things that might cause it to change. As you might guess, he worked out theories explaining both consumer spending

and investment (business) spending. The theory of the consumption function is one of his ideas for explaining consumer spending.

Almost all of the concepts and theories of macroeconomics in this book are based on Keynesian ideas, as those ideas have been refined and modified over the past 40 years. If you can think of something like macroeconomics as having a father, then surely Keynes is the father of modern macroeconomics. The ideas in the next section on the components of the total spending stream are straight from Keynes.

THE COMPONENTS OF THE TOTAL SPENDING STREAM

So far in this chapter you've been reading about the two "basic spending sources" in the economy—consumer spending and investment spending. You now have some understanding of how the level (rate) of each of these is determined. But you haven't yet looked at *all* the components of the spending stream and their relationships to each other. It's time to do that now.

Consumer Spending (C) and Investment Spending (I)

You know that total spending by people for consumer goods (consumption) plus total spending by businesses for capital goods (investment) add up to total spending for the economy's output of consumer and capital goods. The total rate of spending in any day, week, month, or year for these goods must be equal to the total value of the consumer goods and capital goods being bought; and the total amount of money received by the people producing all this output is equal to the total amount being spent by all those buyers.

Expenditures for consumer goods (C) plus expenditures for investment goods (I) equals total spending for consumer goods and capital goods (C + I). It must be so. And it also equals

---

* For those who would like to go deeper into the Keynesian theory of business investment spending, this chapter has an appendix dealing with that subject. You'll find it just after the review exercises.

the total value of the output of these goods and it equals total income received by those who produced these goods. But that doesn't tell the whole story. So let's take another step to complete the picture.

Government Spending (G)

Since all things produced are either produced to be consumed or to be saved and reused later, you could say that all goods produced must be either consumer goods or capital goods. That's all there is! But what about "government goods"?

The governments—*all* levels of government—spend money. They buy goods which would have been consumer goods if individuals had bought them and they buy goods which would have been capital goods if businesses had bought them. But since the government buys them we call them "government goods." So now we add a third "spending source." We simply refer to this as "government spending" (G). The government spends for "government goods." "Government goods" include everything from school buildings and highways and teacher's services to Polaris submarines and the canned peas to be used to feed the crew of the aircraft carrier *Enterprise*.

So now you know that total spending in the economic system (the total spending stream) generates from at least three sources: spending by individuals for consumer goods (C), spending by businesses for investment goods (I), and spending by government for "government goods" (G). We might say that "C + I + G equals total spending, which is equal to the total value of the output, which equals total income in the economy." We could say that. But as you will see in a moment it wouldn't be precisely correct.

Why do we put *government spending* into a separate category? Couldn't we just include government under "investment spending" and only have two categories? Yes, we could do

that. Why don't we? Because it's useful to look at government spending separately. The spending choices (how much to spend, in which ways, at what times) are made *differently* by the government than by businesses or by individuals.

The whole purpose of breaking down total spending is to identify and understand each "spending source." If we can understand why each "spending source" decides how much it will spend, then we will have a much better understanding of how *total spending* is determined. Then we will know much more about macroeconomics. Perhaps sometimes we can even predict what is going to happen. And perhaps then we can establish government policies to bring better macro-conditions in the economy. We hope so. More on this later. But now, *another* (the last) spending source.

Foreign Spending for Our Goods (Ex)

The fourth and final spending source we break out and identify separately is "spending by foreigners for our goods." Just as with the government, this "spending source" could be included in the "C + I" two-way breakdown. But you can see that it might be helpful to separate "spending by foreigners for our goods" into a category all its own. The term usually used to mean "spending by foreigners for our goods" is "exports." We can use "Ex" as the symbol for this.

Suppose Monsieur Champenois in Paris decides he would like to have a case of Del Monte canned peas. He goes to the Bank of France and exchanges some of his deposit account francs in that bank for some deposit account dollars which the Bank of France has on deposit in an American bank. Now he can use those U.S. dollars to buy the Del Monte canned peas. So he does. This adds to total spending in the American economy. And suppose Signor Costanza in Rome decides to buy an Oldsmobile Cutlass. He goes to the Bank of Italy and exchanges some of his lira deposits for some dollar deposits and he sends the American dealer a check to pay for the Cutlass. Suppose Mr. Smythe in London decides to buy an oyster-breading machine from a Baltimore manufacturer. He goes to the Bank of England and trades some pounds for dollars and then sends the manufacturer a check for the machine. Suppose a Japanese business decides to buy a shipload of American chemicals to be used in making plastic toys. The business manager goes to the bank and exchanges yen for dollars and sends a check to pay for the chemicals. (These "foreign exchange" checks may be called "bills" or "drafts" or "orders" or whatever. But they're really checks.)

All purchases by foreigners add spending into the spending flow, stimulate production, add to the value of output, and add to incomes in this country. The effect on spending, output, and incomes is the same as if the canned peas had been bought by someone in Willimantic, Connecticut and the oyster-breading machine by someone in Pascagoula, Mississippi and the chemicals by someone in Rahway, New Jersey and the Cutlass by someone in Snook, Texas! Can you see that from the point of view of the seller of the goods, or of the effect on the total spending stream, it really doesn't make any difference whether the buyer lives in Paris or Poughkeepsie? In Tokyo or Kokomo? Bangkok or Little Rock?

Some of the foreign buyers are buying consumer goods. Others are buying capital goods. But still we lump both together and treat them the same. Why do we do it this way? Only because it's convenient and useful. This gives us our fourth and last spending source: "spending by foreigners for our goods." Exports (Ex).

The Four Spending Sources

Now we have the entire four-way breakdown of the spending stream. Each spending source is identified in the most useful way. Now our "spending flow breakdown" becomes C + I + G + Ex. Now we have the whole thing. Now can

we say that C + I + G + Ex = GNP? Can we say that? Or not? Think about it.

You know that anything which would cause any one of these "spending sources" to get smaller would pull down the size of total spending. That would cause some of the goods being produced not to be bought. This would cut down on the amount businesses would produce. Production would slow down and total output and total income would decline. Reduced spending means reduced output and reduced income. GNP would fall.

You also know that anything which might happen to cause spending by any one of the "spending sources" (C, I, G, or Ex) to increase, would push total spending upward. This would mean that the goods available in the market would be bought up more rapidly. Producers would expand their production and increase their outputs. GNP would rise.

Yes, C, I, G, and Ex are the only sources from which spending can flow into the total spending stream to support total income and total output (GNP). So can we say that C + I + G + Ex must be equal to total spending and total output? to GNP? No. Almost, but not quite. There's another adjustment we have to make, because C + I + G + Ex doesn't *exactly* equal GNP. Why not? Because we must account for the part of the spending flow which is "leaking out" to foreign countries.

THE FOREIGN TRADE BALANCE

Some of C, I, and G is leaking overseas! Some of the spending for consumer goods (C) is *not* for consumer goods *produced in this country,* but for consumer goods produced in foreign countries and imported to this country. Some of the capital goods bought by the investment spending (I) are capital goods *produced in other countries* and imported to this country. Some of the things that the government is spending for (G) are things that are being *produced in other countries.* Do you begin to get the point?

Some of the Spending Flow Is "Leaking to Other Countries" (Im)

You know that this country's GNP (gross *national* product) is pulled forth by the flow of spending in *this* country, spent for *this* country's output. Right? So we must be careful not to include the part of our spending flow which is "leaking overseas"—that is, the part which is going to foreign sellers to pay for foreign-produced goods. Let me say it again, slightly differently.

You know that the "C + I + G flow of spending" is the spending which supports total output and total income. But the part of the "C + I + G flow" which flows to other countries *does not* support output and income in this country. Therefore, that part of the flow which goes to buy foreign-made goods must be subtracted. Then we will know just how much of the total spending stream is being used *to pay for goods produced in this country* (and to pay incomes to the producers and workers and everybody, in this country).

So how do we handle this adjustment? this subtraction for the part of the spending flow which is "leaking overseas"? We could subtract from "C," that part which is being spent for imported goods, then subtract from "I," that part which is being spent for imported goods, then subtract from "G" the part which is being spent for imported goods. That would take care of it. Right?

Yes, it would. But that would be the hard way. It's much easier to add up all the dollars "leaking overseas" (to pay for imports) and then subtract it all at one time. That's just exactly what we do. We call the subtraction item "imports" (Im). What it means is "total spending by buyers in *this* country for goods produced in foreign countries."

You know that the spending flow in this country is always being *increased* by foreign spending for our goods (Ex.) Now you also know that the spending flow in this country is always being *decreased* by the amount that buyers in this country are spending for foreign

goods (Im). So wouldn't it be a simple thing just to subtract the "spending outflow" (Im) from the "spending inflow" (Ex)? Sure. That's exactly what we do. It looks like this:

$$C + I + G + (Ex - Im) = GNP$$

We May Have a Positive or Negative Foreign Trade Balance (F)

You can see that if the *spending outflow* for foreign goods (Im) is *greater* than the *spending inflow* for our goods (Ex), then "Ex − Im" will be a *negative* number. More spending is flowing out than is flowing back in. This holds down the size of output and incomes in this country. In this case we would say that the foreign trade balance (F) is negative.

If the *spending inflow* from foreigners for our goods (Ex) is greater than our *spending outflow* to buy foreign goods (Im) then "Ex − Im" (F) will be a *positive* number. There will be a net addition to the spending flow in this country. The positive "foreign trade balance" (F) will help to support our total employment, output, and income.

If you want to, you can say it this way:

$$C + I + G + (Ex - Im) = GNP$$

or you can say it this way:

$$C + I + G + F = GNP$$

Either way, our equation is now exactly and precisely correct. You know that F can be either plus or minus, depending on whether foreigners are spending more for our goods, or we are spending more for theirs. If imports and exports should happen to be exactly the same, the foreign trade balance (F) will be zero.

OTHER WAYS TO BREAK DOWN THE TOTAL SPENDING STREAM

We can look at the total spending stream any way we want to. We can look at it as one big flow going on all the time. Or we can look at it as thousands of little flows going on all the time. Back in Chapter 5 we looked at the circular flow between households and businesses. There, we were looking at the spending flow as one big flow. When we look at GNP we are looking at it as one big flow. The same is true if we look at "national income." These are ways of looking at the spending flow (and the output flow) as "one big flow."

Then there's the "four-sector" flow you've just been reading about. Each sector is defined by the source of the flow: consumer spending, investment spending, government spending, and the foreign trade balance. That's a useful way to look at the spending flow, too.

Each one of these four sectors could be broken down into much smaller parts. The consumer spending flow (C) might be broken into expenditures for: consumer durable goods (automobiles, appliances, furniture, etc.), nondurables (gasoline, canned peas, paper towels, toothpaste, etc.), and services (auto repair, attorney's fees, doctor bills, airline tickets, motel bills, etc.). The investment spending flow (I) can be broken down into fixed capital (buildings, machines and equipment, etc.), and circulating capital (raw materials, gasoline for the tractor, seed corn, etc.).

Government spending and foreign spending can be broken down in many ways, too. And each of the smaller spending categories can be broken down even more. For example, expenditures for nondurables can be broken down into food and other things. Expenditures for food can be broken down into meats, canned goods, etc., etc.

Why Should We Break Down the Spending Flow?

Why would anyone ever want to break down the total spending flow into all these little component parts? Because we want to try to understand what is going on. Sometimes it's helpful to know *what kinds* of consumer spending are increasing or decreasing, or *what*

kinds of investment spending are increasing or decreasing.

How far do economists go in breaking down the total spending flow? As far as necessary to do what they want to do—to find out what they want to find out. Sometimes the basic "C + I + G + F" breakdown is sufficient. At least that's usually a good way to start. But often it's necessary to go farther. If something is "going wrong" with consumer spending, a more detailed breakdown of the consumer spending flow (C) may help us to see what's going wrong and why.

Sources of "Spending Flow" Statistics

Do government statisticians actually break down the spending flows into these smaller parts? You bet they do! Where do you think you could find the figures? In the *Survey of Current Business* (monthly) from the Bureau of Economic Analysis, U.S. Department of Commerce? Right! Or in the *Economic Report of the President* (annual), or the *Federal Reserve Bulletin* (monthly), or on page two of *Business Week* magazine (weekly), or from time to time in the *Wall Street Journal* (daily), the *New York Times,* or in almost any news magazine or big city newspaper or in any publication or article entitled: "Indicators of Economic Activity." It might be fun for you to look up some of these figures sometime, just to see what's going on in the economy. (Why don't you go to the library and do it right now?)

Another View: The Money Supply and the Velocity of Circulation

All the ways we have been looking at and breaking down the spending stream have been more or less the same. We have been looking at the spending stream as made up of various components, with each component identified by the *source* of the spending: the consumer, the business, the government, or the foreign buyer. But that isn't the only way of looking at the spending flow. There is an entirely different way of looking at it. You can think of the total spending flow as "the quantity of money" (number of dollars) in existence, and the *speed* at which the money (each dollar) is circulating.

For example, suppose the total money supply consisted of $300 billion. If each dollar changed hands (was spent for new output) six times each year, then the total size of the spending flow in the country would be $1.8 trillion a year. ($300 billion in existence, each dollar spent six times a year: $300 billion × 6 equals $1.8 trillion.) The total amount of output bought in the country would amount to $1.8 trillion dollars worth. Total spending for output equals total output. Right?

Can you see that this is another perfectly good way to look at the spending flow? The quantity of money in existence times the velocity at which each dollar is flowing equals total spending. If we wanted to understand what was going on using this approach, we would try to find out (a) what might cause the total money supply to get larger or smaller, and (b) what might cause the velocity, or speed at which each dollar is turning over, to get faster or slower. This "quantity of money" approach to understanding total spending has been used by economists for more than 100 years. You will be reading a lot more about it later.

Other Breakdowns Can Be Useful

There are many other ways the total spending-income flow might be broken down for the purpose of analysis. We might look to see which parts of the country are doing the most of which kinds of spending (geographic breakdown). Or we might look to see how much and which kinds of spending are being done by young people or older people. Or we might find out how much spending is done by cash or on credit.

Several different ways of breaking down the spending stream actually are used. When? Whenever someone thinks such a breakdown will help to find out something, of course! The basic "four-sector" breakdown by spending source (C + I + G +F) and the basic breakdown which focuses on the *quantity* and *velocity* of money, are generally the most useful. Those are the two we will use.

Right now we need to go farther with the four-sector breakdown (C + I + G +F). After that, we'll go deeper into the "monetary" approach and you will learn more about "the quantity of money (M) times the velocity at which it is circulating (V)." But that must wait until another chapter.

INJECTIONS INTO AND WITHDRAWALS FROM THE SPENDING STREAM

People stand on the receiving end of the total spending stream. They get checks in payment for the use of their labor, land, and capital. Each of us receives a little share of this total spending stream as our income. When we receive it, what do we do with it? What are our choices?

Income Must Be Used In One of Four Ways

We have four choices about what to do with our income: spend it for consumer goods (C), save it (S), pay taxes (T), or buy imports (Im). That completes the list. Those are our only choices. Of course we could spend it for capital goods, for business purposes (I). But that's saving—*and then* investing.

The spending-receiving-spending cycle is going on all the time, every moment of every day. The consumers, investors, government and foreign buyers (C + I + G + Ex) are pushing money into the spending stream. The people who are receiving the money are pushing some of it back into the stream to buy consumer goods (C). They are pulling the rest of it out as savings, to pay taxes, and to buy imports (S + T + Im).

Each "Withdrawal" Has an Offsetting "Injection"

Notice that when the income receivers spend their money for domestically produced consumer goods (C), the money goes right back into the income stream. But the parts of their income they use as savings (S), taxes (T), and for imports (Im), do *not* go right back into the stream. So does the stream get smaller? Not necessarily.

You have already noticed that for each kind of withdrawal from the income stream there is a corresponding injection into the stream. Savings are offset by investment (S, I). Taxes are offset by government spending (T, G). Imports are offset by exports (Im, Ex).

Since each withdrawal is offset by a corresponding injection, does it all come out even? Maybe so. The problem is that it doesn't always work out that way. When it doesn't, that can create quite a problem! A problem of people trying to spend too little. Or too much.

If the system is working along smoothly and you look at it at any moment, what you will see is this: consumer spending is flowing at a continuous level, around and around. Taxes (T) are being pulled out of the stream and flowing away to the governments. Savings (S) are being pulled out of the stream and going into idle pools where they may be available for investment. Payments for imports (Im) are being pulled out of the stream and flowing into the bank accounts of foreigners.

At the same moment you will see government spending (G) flowing into the stream to offset the tax withdrawals. You will see business investors pulling money out of the idle pools of savings and from the banks (creating money) and adding spending (I) back into the stream. Foreigners will get some dollars and push them into our spending stream to pay us

for our exports (Ex). All these things are going on simultaneously, every moment, all the time. If you were to look at the overall macroeconomic picture at any moment, that's exactly what you would see.

It's obvious what would happen if the *reinjection* flows (I, G, Ex) should either fall below or rise above the *withdrawal* flows. The size of the spending stream would change—would get smaller or larger wouldn't it? Sure.

The Expenditure and Income Equation

We have an equation which summarizes the spending-income flow. It shows the four ways money can get pushed into the spending stream: people spending for consumer goods (C), businesses spending for investment goods (I), government spending for goods and services (G), and foreigners spending to buy our goods (Ex). And it shows the four ways people can dispose of their incomes: spend for domestic consumer goods (C), save (S), pay taxes (T), or spend to buy foreign goods (Im). *The amounts the spenders are spending* (putting into the income stream) *must be equal to the amounts the receivers are receiving* (taking out of the stream). You recognized this right off as an equality, didn't you? The equation looks like this:

$$C + I + G + Ex = C + S + T + Im$$

Figure 9-1 on the following page explains this equation in detail. You should study Figure 9-1 now.

An Overview of the Injections and Withdrawals

Income (spending) is flowing in a circle all the time. Consumer spending stays in the circle and goes around and around. At each instant, some of the money in the income stream is being pulled out, but simultaneously new spending is being added in. The stream has a stable level only when the amounts being drained off are equal to the amounts being added in. The stream will be the same size if each withdrawal is exactly "neutralized" or offset by a corresponding injection into the stream.

If the amount the investors are adding to the stream is exactly equal to the amount the savers are pulling out, then S = I, and the effect of both is neutralized. But if the investment injection gets *larger* than the savings withdrawal then the stream will get larger. Or if investment spending drops *below* the savings level, savings will be pulling out more than

investment is putting back in. The stream will get smaller. The same thing can be said about G = T, and about Ex = Im.

If the amount people are spending for consumer goods continues constant, and if all savings are offset by investment, all government expenditures are offset by taxes, and all imports are offset by exports, then the spending stream will be stable. The size of the stream cannot change until one or more of these equalities is broken. So long as C = C, S = I, T = G, and Im = Ex, the size of the spending-income stream cannot change. But any time

Fig. 9-1 The Expenditure and Income Equation

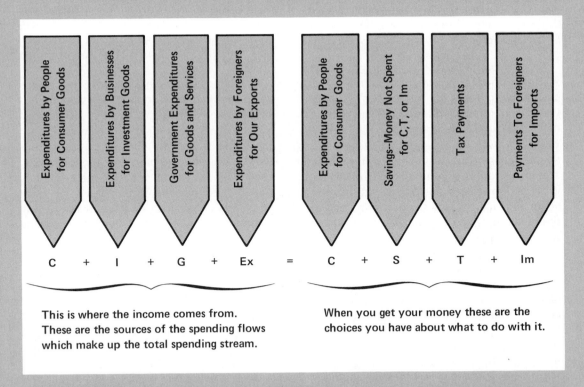

C + I + G + Ex = C + S + T + Im

This is where the income comes from. These are the sources of the spending flows which make up the total spending stream.

When you get your money these are the choices you have about what to do with it.

The expenditure and income equation shows where the income comes from, and then how it is used by those who receive it.

You receive income because consumers, businesses, governments, and foreigners are spending to buy your output. You dispose of your income by spending for consumer goods, or by saving, paying taxes, or buying imports.

these withdrawals and the offsetting reinjections are *not* equal, the size of the spending-income stream *must* change.

Of course, any one of these injections (I, G, or Ex) could offset any one of the withdrawals (S, T, or Im). For example, if investment spending was not great enough to offset savings, the government could spend more. That might offset some of the savings and keep the income and spending flow from going down. The important thing is that S + T + Im (total withdrawals) must be exactly offset by I + G + Ex (total reinjections). Otherwise, the economy will be speeding up or slowing down. No doubt about it. Now, let's look at it another way.

A "Fire Hydrants and Drainpipes" View of the Economy

Try to visualize this total spending stream as a stream of water flowing around in a big circle. There are three big "drainpipes" (savings, taxing, and imports) draining off the water as it flows around. There are three big "fire hydrants" (investment spending, government spending, and exports) gushing water into the stream as it flows around. It's easy to see that if the hydrants keep gushing exactly as much water into the stream as the drainpipes are draining out, then the total size of the stream will stay the same.

The "basic flow" in the stream is consumer spending. That just keeps going around and around. The savings drainpipe drains off some of this basic flow. So do the taxes drainpipe and the import drainpipe. But if the outflow through the savings drainpipe is just offset by the inflow from the investment hydrant, and the taxes drainpipe outflow is just offset by the inflow from the government spending hydrant, and the import drainpipe outflow is just offset by the export hydrant inflow, then the stream will go on flowing around and around. The size, or level of the stream will not change. A lot of water will be gushing in from the hydrants at the top and lot will be gurgling

out through the drains at the bottom. But the size of the stream will stay the same. Can you picture it?

There Are Millions of Little Faucets and Drainpipes

Now that you have the basic picture, let's complicate it a little. You know that in the real world all the savings and taxes and import spending don't really drain off like in one big pipe. All the investment spending and government spending and export payments don't gush in at one place, either. Actually, it's more like millions of little faucets and millions of little drainpipes. Each of us is in charge of regulating the withdrawal flow through our own tiny little "savings drainpipe." Each business is in charge of regulating the reinjection flow through its own little "investment faucet."

With all these people involved in the savings and investment decisions it seems that only a miracle would make the savings withdrawals and the investment injections come out even! The same is true for foreign buyers of our goods and domestic buyers of foreign goods. Each of us decides on our own whether to buy a Saab or a Pinto or a Datsun or a Vega. What we decide determines whether or not we will be draining income out of the U.S. spending stream.

The government's decisions on taxing and spending are not quite as scattered as this. But when you think about all the state and local governments, you'll see that there's a lot of scatter! Governments usually try to adjust the "tax drain" to be about the same size as the "expenditure injection"—but not always. And even when they *try* to "balance the budget," they aren't always successful.

The Federal Government Has a Big Hydrant and a Big Drainpipe

There is only one spending unit which has control of a really big "spending hydrant" and "drainpipe." Which spending unit? The federal government, of course! Even the largest business corporations are not big enough to have a major influence on the total spending flow. But the federal government has control over a big enough injection hydrant (government spending) and a big enough drainpipe (taxes) to have a really big effect on the size of the spending flow if it wants to.

We will talk more about these issues later. For now, just be sure you understand how it all fits together. And remember that all these withdrawals and injections must offset each other to keep the economy in "macro-equilibrium." If the total amounts people are trying to withdraw (drain off) are not exactly equal to the total amounts the people are trying to reinject, then the level of total spending will be changing—will be getting larger or smaller. The economy may be heading for inflation or recession.

Figure 9-2 on page 158 shows a diagram illustrating the injections into and the withdrawals from the total spending stream. It would be a good idea for you to study that diagram now.

SUMMARY

This has been the first of the three chapters on national income analysis. This chapter has had but one purpose: to help you to understand the spending-income stream. If you understand it now, then you've gotten from this chapter what you should have.

The emphasis in this chapter has been on the component parts of the spending-income stream, and on the injections into the withdrawals from the stream. You know about the things that influence consumer and business spending, and you know about the importance of "C" and "I" in the spending-income stream.

Also, you know several ways to picture and explain the spending-income stream. You can use the spending and income equation (Figure 9-1), or the diagram of the spending-income stream (Figure 9-2). Or you can explain the fire hydrants and drainpipes view of it.

One thing you know well, now, is the critical importance of the *equality* between (a) Savings and the other withdrawals, and (b) Investment and the other injections. You know that if the injections aren't large enough to offset the withdrawals, then the spending-income stream will get smaller.

But you don't yet know enough about the things that influence these injections and withdrawals. All of the next chapter is concerned with that. As soon as you're sure you really understand the nature of the spending-income stream and its component parts, go on to Chapter 10 and find out about savings and investment and macroequilibrium. (But first, there's an appendix to this chapter, in case you're interested.)

REVIEW EXERCISES ● **MAJOR CONCEPTS, PRINCIPLES, TERMS (Explain each thoroughly.)**

the expenditure and income equation
what influences consumer spending
what influences investment spending
how investment spending offsets consumer saving
the components of the spending stream
the foreign trade balance
the "quantity and velocity of money" breakdown

Fig. 9-2   A Diagram of the Total Spending-Income Stream, Showing Injections and Withdrawals

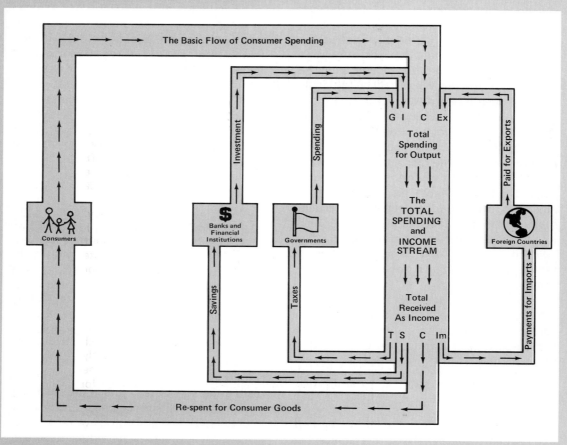

The spending-income diagram is just a picture of
the expenditure and income equation.

The total spending stream is generated by the basic flow of consumer spending, plus spending injections from the investors, the government, and the foreign buyers. All these "spending sectors" are spending to buy outputs of goods and services.

The total spending stream flows as incomes (as wages, rents, interest, and profits) to the owners of the factors (labor, land, and capital) and then is "disposed of" either as consumer spending or for savings, taxes, or imports.

From this diagram you can see what would happen if any of the spending injections got larger or smaller. The spending flow would get larger or smaller. Right? Of course!

● **OTHER CONCEPTS AND TERMS (Explain each briefly.)**

consumer durables
consumer expectations
investor expectations
expected return
John Maynard Keynes (KAYns)
C, I, G, Ex, Im, F
the "four sector" breakdown

● **QUESTIONS (Write out answers, or jot down key points.)**

1. There are several ways in which *optimism* can be very stimulating to the economy. Can you explain several of the ways? Try.
2. What would be likely to happen to investment spending in the economy if the interest rate suddenly went up from 6% to 10%? Can you explain why?
3. If there's too much spending, and lots of inflationary buying in the U.S. economy, then it would be good for the economy if some people would stop buying Vegas and Pintos and Gremlins and Dusters, and start buying Volkswagens and Toyotas and Volvos instead. But if the economy is in a recession, it would help for more people to "buy American." Discuss.

APPENDIX

Business Investment Spending: Expected Returns, Interest Rates, and Capitalized Value

In this chapter you have read a small section about business investment spending. But perhaps that section didn't tell you as much about it as you would like to know. If you want more on that subject, here it is.

Using the Keynesian approach, if we want to understand investment spending in the economy we need to understand expected returns to capital and the interest rate. And we need to know how to use both of these to find out if the business will (or will not) invest. That's what this appendix is about.

What Determines the Expected Return?

What causes a business to think some piece of capital—some machine—will bring a high additional return?—that is, will have a high "marginal efficiency"? Actually, all kinds of things influence business expectations. But there are some fairly straightforward ways of getting at this issue. First, what kinds of "returns" can a capital investment offer? Two kinds. It can add to the output value, or it can reduce the production cost. Often the business expects a new piece of capital equipment to do some of both.

If the local union gets a big wage increase, labor cost goes up. This increases the expected return to capital. The business will be more likely to invest in labor-saving machinery. If the demand and price for the product are expected to go up, this also increases the expected return—the "marginal efficiency of capital." The businesses will be more likely to buy new machines and expand its plant.

Harry Walker owns the local sawmill and joinery shop. Suppose he thinks bad times are coming. He sees the marginal efficiency of capital as being low. His investment spending is likely to be low. Of course!

Some Examples of the Investment Decision

When Mr. Walker sees the expected return of a certain piece of capital as "high," he will have a "high demand" for that piece of capital. But will he buy it? Or not? How does he decide? It depends on the price. Actually, it depends on two prices. It depends on the *cash* price Mr. Walker must pay for the piece of capital. It also depends on the price he must pay for the *money* he will have to sink in the investment. That is, it depends on the *interest rate*. Let's look at some real-world type examples to see how it all works out.

The Seafood Packing House Case. Suppose a small seafood packing house down on the eastern shore of Virginia is considering investing in an oyster-breading machine. This is a "latest technology" piece of equipment. It has a stainless steel breading mixer, then a small conveyor belt to carry the oysters from the mixer through a roller to flatten them and on into the final package for freezing. The minimum wage law has just pushed up the cost of labor and the seafood packing houses have raised their prices for frozen breaded oysters. Several restaurants and hotel chains have complained about the high prices of frozen breaded oysters. Some customers have shifted from Chesapeake Bay oysters to Gulf shrimp and Cape Code flounder fillets. The oyster-dependent economy of the Chesapeake Bay area is hurting.

The oyster-breading machine sells for only $20,000. It is designed for a small operation. Remember your uncle who runs the Seaside Seafood Packing House in Chincoteague, Virginia? He remembers you! And he knows you are taking a course in economics so he writes to you and asks you whether or not he should pay $20,000 for this new stainless steel oyster-breading machine. You are going to have to answer the letter and say something. What are you going to say?

The Iron Ore Pelletizing Case. Before you get too upset about having to make such a tough decision, think of the plight of your roomate's father. He is a high-powered management consultant receiving $500 a day to help a major steel company decide whether or not to install a new iron ore pelletizing plant at Ishpeming, near the Lake Superior shore of the Upper Peninsula of Michigan. The steel company is already operating a pelletizing plant which is less than 10 years old. The present operation crushes the iron ore and tumbles it around and gets the good part—the iron part—to stick together in little pebble-type pellets. Each pellet comes out about 40 percent iron and 60 percent other stuff—"inert ingredients" you might say.

But suppose that a new process has been developed. It would cost $2.8 million to install the new equipment, but it can turn out pellets of 75 percent iron and only 25 percent other stuff. And it operates with only half as much labor. Also, it can handle twice as much iron ore per hour as the present equipment. A shipload of the 75 percent pellets will actually have in it about twice as much usable iron (and only half as much "inert ingredients") as a shipload of the 40 percent pellets. So in addition to all the other benefits, the cost of transportation will be cut almost in half. But remember? The present plant is less than 10 years old!

Should the steel company buy the new equipment and scrap its existing plant which is still working as good as new? Or should they keep using the old plant until it wears out? And then put in the new equipment? Your room-mate's father is going to advise them. Tough task, huh? But these are the kinds of questions on which real world investment spending decisions are based. And you'll see that it's really not so difficult to figure out.

In both the oyster-breading case and the iron ore pelletizing case there is no question that there is a *demand* for the capital. That is to say, there is *some* price at which it would be "good business" to buy the capital. But is the price right? Would it be good business to pay $20,000 for the oyster-breading machine? Or $2.8 million for the new iron ore pelletizing plant?

How Much Will Output Value Increase and Cost Decrease?

How does a business decide whether or not to buy new equipment in cases like these? How complicated is it? Not very. The first step is to estimate each way in which the piece of equipment is expected to reduce the cost. Next, estimate each way it is expected to increase the revenue. Then you put the two together, and you have it. What could be simpler than that?

When you make these estimates you would like to be as precise as you can. But don't try to overdo it. Make-believe accuracy in the face of real-life uncertainty is a luxury which only college professors can afford! (Business managers know better.) Remember that over the life of this piece of equipment, *all* the cost and revenue conditions are going to change in several unforeseeable ways. Some of the changes may be completely unexpected. The situation in three or four years may not even resemble today's situation. So there is no need to really knock yourself out trying to achieve some kind of precise accuracy. That's a waste of energy.

How much cost and effort should Mr. Walker spend in trying to estimate the "expected returns" of a piece of capital? He should follow the marginal principle. Each time he puts any more effort or money into trying to increase the accuracy of his estimates, he should expect the increased accuracy to be worth at least as much as the cost of the extra effort. It would be a waste to try to get more accuracy than that! Good enough is best. Right?

HOW TO FIGURE THE EXPECTED RETURN AND FIND "CAPITALIZED VALUE"

You know that the new oyster-breading machine will bring your uncle some savings in labor costs and perhaps in other input costs—maybe in transportation costs, power costs, or other costs. And you know that the value of the output probably will increase as a result of the new machine. But how much decreased cost and increased revenue will there be? Enough to justify the investment? How can you figure this out?

Just take it step by step. It isn't difficult to work out an "expected return" for the first year. Then you project to the second year,

third year, and so on for the estimated life of the capital. Suppose you figure that during the first year the oyster-breading machine would save about $2,000 in labor costs and other production costs and would probably increase your uncle's output ("value added") by about $1,000 worth. So you estimate that the "expected return" of the machine is about $3,000 in the first year.

Next you might try to guess what is going to happen to wages and to other costs of production and to the prices of breaded oysters in the following years. Then you could make a different calculation for each year, depending on your cost and revenue projections. Or you might take the more practical approach—the easy way—and assume that the return for each year will be approximately the same: $3,000 each year.

Suppose you figure this machine will last about 10 years and its expected return will be about $3,000 each year. Then its total "expected return" over its life will add up to $30,000. Does this mean the machine is worth $30,000 to your uncle? To get at the answer to this question, and to emphasize the importance of the interest rate, let's ask a different question.

The Effect of the Interest Rate

Would you give me $30,000 today if I agreed to give you back $3,000 each year for the next 10 years? You certainly wouldn't! Why not? Because you could put your money in a savings account or in government bonds or in AT&T bonds or in GM stocks or in any kind of investment you could think of and get back *more than* $3,000 each year for the next 10 years! If you could invest your $30,000 at an interest rate of 10 percent, you would get back $3,000 a year *forever!* And always own the $30,000 to boot! See what a bad deal it would be to invest $30,000 when you only expect to receive a return of $3,000 a year for 10 years?

So how much would you advise your uncle to pay for the oyster-breading machine. Certainly not $30,000. But how much? $25,000? $20,000? $15,000? $10,000? How do you figure it out? Let's go on with our example and soon you will see.

Suppose your uncle bought the machine. By the end of the first year it would have brought him an "expected return" of $3,000. Just to make it easy, let's assume that he receives all his "return" on the last day of the year. So looking at it from the point of view of the *first* day of the year, how much is that $3,000 return (to be received on the *last* day of the year) worth? If he had the $3,000 on the *first* day of the year, he could invest it or lend it out, or just put it in a savings account, and by the *last* day of the year he would have the $3,000 *plus* one year's interest. At a 5 percent interest rate, he would have $3,000 plus $150. So: $3,000 to be received a year from now is worth about $150 less to you than the $3,000 would be worth if you had it right now. That is, if the interest rate is 5 percent, "the right to receive $3,000 a year from today" is worth only about $2,850, today ($3,000 minus the $150 you lose by *not* having the money now).

Sometimes people have trouble with this concept because it seems strange at first. But it's really quite simple. For example, suppose your wealthy sister offers you a choice. She will give you $3,000 now, or she will give you $3,000 one year from now. Which would you prefer? You would rather have it now, of course. How strong would be your preference to have the money now? That depends on "the going interest rate" for the kind of investment you are thinking about. If you are thinking about investing the money at an interest rate of 5 percent, then it "costs" you $150 to wait a year. If you are thinking about an 8 percent rate, then it "costs" you $240 to wait a year. (8 percent of $3,000 is $240.)

Future Payments Must Be "Discounted"

Suppose someone comes to you and says: "Here's a piece of paper which says I will pay you $3,000 one year from today. How much will you pay me for this piece of paper (promissory note) right now?" If you're thinking of a 5 percent interest rate you will pay about $2,850. ($3,000 minus $150.) If you are thinking of an 8 percent rate, you will pay about $2,760. ($3,000 minus $240.)

What you are doing is buying a $3,000, one-year promissory note, at a discount. If the interest rate is 5 percent, you will "discount" it about $150; if the interest rate is 8 percent, you will "discount" it about $240. Suppose it is a *two*-year promissory note. At 5 percent per year the discount would be about $150 each year, or about $300, total. The present value would be about $2,700. At 8 percent per year the discount would be about $240 per year, or $480, total. The present value would be about $2,520. (You will notice that these figures are not exactly correct, because of the "compounding effect." But don't worry about that now).

See how the present value of an expected future return goes down more and more as we look farther and farther into the future? Also, notice how much difference it makes whether the interest rate is 5 percent or 8 percent! Maybe you have always thought of the interest rate as something small and insignificant. But as the years go by, the interest rate can become a very big thing. (Find out how much of the average car payment or house payment goes for interest. You may be surprised!)

Discounting the "Expected Return"

Your uncle expects a return of $3,000 at the end of the first year. If the interest rate is 8 percent, the present value of that expected return is only about $2,760. At the end of the second year he expects to receive another $3,000. But the present value of that is only about $2,520. Actually it's a little less than $2,520, because of the "compounding effect"—he's losing the chance to earn interest on the interest!

It's just the opposite of having your money in a savings account. The longer you *have it* in your account, the more you *gain*; the longer you *don't have it* in there, the more you lose. Get the idea? So the *present* value of the $3,000 your uncle is going to receive in the third year, the fourth year, the fifth year and so on, gets smaller and smaller and smaller.

So what do you advise your uncle to do? Should he pay $20,000 and buy the machine? How do you decide? Simply find the discounted value of the "expected return" for each of the years over the expected life of the

		First year	Second year	Third year		nth year
Capitalized value	$(V) =$	$\dfrac{\text{Expected return (X)}}{1 + \text{interest rate (i)}}$	$+ \quad \dfrac{X}{(1 + i)^2}$	$+ \quad \dfrac{X}{(1 + i)^3}$	$+ \cdots +$	$\dfrac{X}{(1 + i)^n}$

machine. Then add them all up. How simple! This little exercise will give you the capitalized value of the machine. It will tell your uncle how much the machine is worth to him, on the basis of your estimates. *The "capitalized value" of any asset is the present value of the asset, as figured on the basis of how much money that asset is expected to bring to its owner over its lifetime.*

Suppose you spent a thousand dollars (or a million dollars for that matter) building a machine, and then found out that it would cost more to run the machine than the output would be worth. What would be the capitalized value of the machine? Zero, of course. The machine might have some scrap value or some "aesthetic value" or something, but capitalized value? No. Anything which won't make you any money doesn't have any capitalized value. The more money it will make for you, the more its capitalized value will be.

You can see that the higher the interest rate happens to be, the greater the discount which must be subtracted from the expected returns. So as *interest rates rise higher and higher, capitalized value gets lower and lower.* At higher interest rates, fewer capital investments appear profitable. High interest rates can have a very discouraging effect on the flow of investment spending. Now you can understand why.

How do you figure out the capitalized value of a machine or of any other asset? First you figure out what you think the expected return is going to be in each year over the expected life of the asset. Then you "discount" the dollar figure for each year. This gives you the present value of each future year's expected income. Then you add up all the *present values* of all the future-year incomes. And what do you have? You have the present capitalized value of the asset. Of course!

Computing the Capitalized Value

By now you could probably figure out what the "capitalized value," or "capitalization" formula looks like. It shows how to discount the expected return for the first year, for the second year, the third year, etc. And once you have done all that you just add up all the figures and you have it!

First, study the formula in the box at the top of this page. Then you'll be able to work through the following examples.

Example (using 8% interest rate)
Present value of $3,000 to be received:

in 1 year: $V = \dfrac{\$3,000}{1 + .08} = \dfrac{\$3,000}{1.08} = \$2,777.78$

in 2 years: $V = \dfrac{\$3,000}{(1.08)^2} = \dfrac{\$3,000}{1.1664} = \$2,572.02$

in 3 years: $V = \dfrac{\$3,000}{(1.08)^3} = \dfrac{\$3,000}{1.2597} = \$2,381.52$

(You can work it out the rest of the way if you want to.)

Sidelight: What about a perpetual income?

Suppose you're thinking about investing in a piece of land which you think will pay you (and your heirs) a rental of "X" dollars a year *forever.* How much would you pay for the land? Here's the formula:

Present Capitalized Value	$V = \dfrac{X \text{ (expected annual return)}}{i \text{ (assumed interest rate)}}$

Examples:
Suppose the annual return is $3,000 and the interest rate is 8%:

$V = \dfrac{\$3,000}{.08} = \$37,500$

Suppose the interest rate is 5%:

$$V = \frac{\$3,000}{.05} = \$60,000$$

Suppose the interest rate is 10%:

$$V = \frac{\$3,000}{.10} = \$30,000$$

(See how much difference it makes which interest rate you choose?)

The easiest way to do the discounting is to look up the figures in a "present value" or "interest and discount" table. (Ask your friendly banker to show you one.) I looked up the present value figures for your uncle's investment problem and found out that at an interest rate of 5%, the present capitalized value of the oyster-breading machine comes out to about $23,000. This assumes, of course, that the machine really will last exactly ten years, and that it really will bring your uncle a return of $3,000 a year. And of course it assumes that the opportunity cost (or the interest cost) of the money he invests in the machine really will be 5 percent. These are big "ifs"!

Should the Business Manager Allow Some "Margin for Error"?

So what do you advise your uncle to do? Should he buy a machine that costs $20,000, when it looks like the machine is going to be worth $23,000 to him? Probably so.

But suppose the interest rate is considered to be 8%. What then? Then the capitalized value of the machine comes out at about $20,000. Should your uncle buy it? Probably not. Not much margin for error! It's chancy at best. Maybe you should just send your uncle all the facts and figures and let him decide. Do you see how uncertain the investment spending decision can be?

Your roomate's father goes through the same process. The only difference is that he deals with bigger figures and he may use a computer to make it easier. Besides, the computer makes everything look so scientific and precise! If he comes up with a "capitalized value" for the iron ore pelletizing machinery *greater* than the $2.8 million it will cost (plus some satisfactory margin for error and risk) then he will advise his client to buy and install the equipment. If not, he won't.

You can see that both of these decisions will be highly sensitive to *changes in expectations* about future returns. Also, the decisions are sensitive to *changes in the rates of interest* in the "money market." So what determines the level of investment spending in the economy? Expected returns and interest rates have a lot to do with it. Higher expected returns are likely to stimulate investment spending; higher interest rates are likely to retard investment spending. Common sense? Sure.

Appendix: New Concepts, Principles, Theories

    capitalized value
    capitalization
    discounted value
    two formulas for finding capitalized value

10 National Income Analysis II: Savings, Investment, and Macroequilibrium

A closer look at the injections into and withdrawals from the spending-income stream.

What determines the macroeconomic level of the economy?—that is, the overall level of economic activity? production? employment? income? It's determined by total spending! Of course.

But what are the conditions of "macro-equilibrium" for an economic system? What determines if the economy (and also total spending, of course) will be just stable? or speeding up? or slowing down? That's what this whole chapter will be talking about.

First I'm going to take you back to the very basics—back to Tubaland Island where you can see the principles working the way the physicists usually like to demonstrate things: in a vacuum. After that I'll "let the air in" and you'll see how it works in the real world.

Meanwhile, back at the island . . .

Things on the island sure are a lot more convenient now that they have a modern money system! No longer is it necessary for everybody to go to the "market spot" on Center Island Trail at 4 o'clock every afternoon to trade things. Now, when people want fish or breadfruit or bananas or tuba or anything else, they just go to the producers and buy it. All of the people can now specialize in exactly what they want to, and then sell their outputs in the market for the going prices. Money is what lets it all work.

But wait! The existence of this efficient medium of exchange (money) can lead to a new kind of problem. Watch what happened.

THE PRODUCTION-CONSUMPTION "CIRCULAR FLOW" CAN BE BROKEN BY SAVING MONEY

Last October when some of the eastside islanders were out fishing they were passing the time talking about Christmas. Soon they were all bragging about the Christmas presents they were going to buy for their friends and loved ones. The more they talked the more they realized that if they really were going to buy all those things they had better start saving some money.

That day, after they sailed their outrigger canoes to shore they sold their fish to the waiting buyers on the beach just as always. But instead of going around the island and spending all their money for breadfruit, bananas, tuba, and other things, they all decided to spend only *half* of their money. They all decided to save the other half—to just deposit it and leave it in their bank accounts.

These good, solid, thoughtful, thrifty eastside islanders are certainly doing a fine thing, saving for Christmas. Right? But that's the start of a chain reaction which is going to develop into a serious problem. Watch.

Savings May Leave Surplus Products in the Market

At sundown that day the westside, northside, and southside islanders couldn't understand why they had so much left over—breadfruit, bananas, coconuts, tuba, everything. Why all the surpluses? You know why. The thrifty eastside islanders didn't spend all their money, so the other producers can't sell all their products. So what's going to happen next?

Maybe the surpluses of breadfruit, bananas, tuba and all will force the prices to go down. At the lower prices, maybe all the surpluses will be bought up and everything will be all right again. Do you think it really will happen that way? Maybe. But probably not.

Over the years the breadfruit gatherers and banana growers and tuba makers have established trade associations and unions. They now insist on "fair and just wages and prices." Each family has made it quite clear that the "going price" is the rock-bottom price they will accept. If the demand for their product happens to drop, they will not permit the price to go down. They will cut back production instead.

You can see that all the sellers on the island have enough "monopoly power" or "market power" to keep their prices from falling. If demand drops they will hold their prices up and just cut back production. They would rather *dump the surpluses in the ocean* than to let their prices go down!

So here we are with the eastside islanders not spending all the money they are getting

from the other islanders. They are saving for Christmas. But as a result of their saving (not respending the money they receive) surpluses develop in the markets for breadfruit, bananas, tuba, and all the other things. Then the westside, northside, and southside islanders cut back their production rather than let the price go down. While all this is going on, what do you think is happening to the demand for fish?

Increased Saving Sets Off a Chain Reaction

Yesterday when the eastsiders decided to save half of the income from their catch, the demand for fish was as great as it always had been. But today, what about it? When the outrigger canoes come sailing in to the beach this afternoon there aren't as many buyers as before. Can you guess why?

Where do the westside, northside, and southside islanders get the money to buy fish? By selling their own products, of course. When they can't sell all their products, they don't get as much money. So they can't buy as much fish.

Today the eastside islanders find that they can't sell all their fish. Several baskets of fish are left over. The eastsiders can't understand what happened. Today the eastsiders face the same problem the others faced yesterday. And today the eastside chief decrees that tomorrow, fewer people will go out fishing. No sense producing more fish than can be sold for the going price!

What's going on, on our happy little island? We have unemployment! The incomes of all the island people are now lower than before. Both their money incomes and their real incomes are lower. What about the eastsiders' Christmas savings plan? That's out the window, too! Their incomes are now so low that *they can't save.*

The economy is depressed. Total economic activity—total production, output, and income in the economy—has declined. The GIP (gross island product) is smaller. The eastside islanders didn't want to cause trouble. They only wanted to save for Christmas. But look at the trouble they caused! Why?

Money Makes It Easy to Defer Spending—to Save

What is "saving"? In *real* terms it means producing something and then not using it up. It means keeping something so you'll have it later when you may need it more. It means to "not-consume" some of the goods you've produced or earned.

In *money* terms "saving" seems to mean about the same thing. It means to "not-spend for consumer goods" some of the income you've earned. So what's the difference? Just this:

> *Real saving* is economizing by "not-using-up" some of the things you've produced—some of the things you own. *Money saving* is "not-spending" some of your income. It's "not buying" things.

Can you see what kinds of problems *money saving* could cause? When you decide to "not-spend," this means you are selling more products and services to others than you are buying back from them. When the eastside islanders started saving ("not-spending") they cut off some of the money which had been going to the other islanders. They stopped giving the others the money needed to buy all the fish!

You know that the economy operates as a big circle. What you have just seen is what happens when somebody doesn't keep the money moving around the circle. Whenever someone receives some of the money from the spending circle and doesn't put it back, soon everyone winds up getting less. Any such withdrawal from the spending circle is felt all the way around the circle.

Back when the eastsiders and westsiders were meeting at 4 o'clock and trading fish for breadfruit, there was no problem. When the fish sellers "sold" (traded) their fish, they automatically "bought" (received in trade) an equal value of breadfruit and took it home with them. There was no way a person could "sell" fish and then "not-buy" an equivalent amount of breadfruit. It always came out even. Obviously!

But once *money* is introduced, this permits a lot of *slack* in the system. When money is used, the people can take their fish to the market, leave their fish, get their money and go home. They don't have to take home the breadfruit! They can leave all the baskets of breadfruit just sitting there in the market! That's the problem.

Money Is a "Claim Check"

Money is really a sort of "claim check," or "credit slip." It's your "right to claim the goods which society owes you." When you place goods in the market or perform services for the market, you get "claim checks." You can use these claim checks to claim whatever other goods or services you want from the market. When you claim the things you want, you pass along your "claim checks" to other people who can then claim the things they want. But when someone gets "claim checks" (money) and doesn't use them, some of the goods in the market will be unclaimed, "surplus" goods.

The owners of the surplus (unsold) goods will not be able to get any "claim checks." So they can't claim the goods they want from other sellers. So the other sellers soon will have surpluses too. The chain reaction just keeps going on and on and the economy slows down more and more. See the problem *money* can cause?

Before money is introduced, the total value of products a person takes into the market must be equal to the total value of products that person takes back out of the market. So long as *things* are being traded for *things*, it must work this way. But with a medium of exchange (money) people can put more products *into the market* than they take back *out of the market*. Some people may decide to hold their "claim checks" so they can claim goods later. That's when the trouble starts.

Say's Law: the Amount Supplied Determines the Amount Demanded

The more a person sells in the market the more that person can buy. When people produce goods and take them to the market, they receive money. With this money they can buy an equal value of goods from the market and take them home.

A Frenchman, Jean Baptiste Say (in the early 1800's), explained this concept, saying that the more a person brings to the market the more that person will take from the market. The more a person supplies, the more that person demands. This principle is sometimes called "Say's Law of Markets," or just "Say's Law."

Say's Law says "supply creates its own demand." If a person supplies more, that person will demand more. Obviously Say's Law is not precisely true. Otherwise there would never be surpluses in the market. The market would always be "cleared"—that is, everything placed in the market always would be bought up and taken away.

If everybody who sells something in the market turns right around and buys something of equal value, the total amount taken to the market will equal the total amount taken home. There will be no surpluses and no shortages. Everything will work out even. But when people take things and leave them in the market and take their money and go home, this breaks the production-consumption circle. Some producers will not be able to sell all their output. This is what you saw happen when the thrifty eastside islanders started saving for Christmas.

The "Secondary Functions of Money" Allow Some Slack

What happened to the economy of our happy island? I suppose you could say that the

island's economy was "wrecked by one of the secondary functions of money." The eastside islanders were using some of their money, *not* as a medium of exchange, but as a *store of value*, instead. That's what created the problem.

It's those *secondary functions*, those "future functions" of money that cause all the trouble. That's what brings the slack in the system and keeps Say's Law from working all the time. The *store of value* function lets people save—to spend *less* than they earn. The *standard of deferred payments* function lets people go into debt—to spend *more* than they earn.

The two "secondary functions" have offsetting effects on the economy, of course. When people spend *less* than they receive, that *slows things down*. When people spend *more* than they receive, that *speeds things up*. If everyone would just use each dollar immediately as a medium of exchange, then Say's Law would always hold true. But people don't. So we have speedups and slowdowns in the economy.

Savings, Economic Growth, and the "Paradox of Thrift"

The island people are facing hard times. Why? Because the eastside islanders wanted to be thrifty and save for Christmas. They were putting more goods into the market than they were taking back out of the market. They were *saving* money. Saving money must be a very bad thing. Look at the trouble it brought to our happy little island!

How can *saving* money be *bad*? Saving is absolutely essential for economic growth. And economic growth provides opportunities for everybody to get more things and not have to work so hard. It sets more people free to go fishing weekends, or to go to college, or to "do their own thing." Economic growth seems to be good. So how can saving be bad?

Just like most of the other answers in economics, the solution to this dilemma is really very simple. Your common sense probably could figure it out for you. But here's the answer: The savings must be *invested* to bring economic growth. If the savings are *invested*, then there's no problem of surpluses or unemployment! But if the savings are not invested—well, you saw what happened.

INVESTMENT IS ESSENTIAL TO TRANSLATE SAVINGS INTO GROWTH

When people save money they leave some of the current output unbought in the market. "Economic growth" occurs when this "left-over output" is then bought up by businesses and used to increase future production. For growth to occur, the surplus which is left because people save must be bought up and used as capital. The unconsumed surplus can't be left lying around in the market! That's what causes depressions!

To have growth, there must be saving. But just saving is not enough. In order to link savings to growth, there must be investment. Savings cannot be translated into growth, without "investment." *People can save as much money as they want to, just as long as investors buy up everything the savers decide to "not-buy."* *

Suppose the economy is clicking along at just the right speed—no unemployment problems and no overspending. As long as investors spend as much money as the savers save, no slowdown will occur. There will be no problem of surpluses or unemployment. And

everything will be fine. The economy can be growing all the time.

Think of "saving" as "leaving some output in the market." "Investing" means "buying up this left over output." If the amount of investing is equal to the amount of saving, then there's no problem. All the markets are "cleared"—no left-over surpluses.

Also, notice this: In order for the investors to be able to buy things, somebody *must* be saving. If there isn't anything left over to be used as capital then the investors won't be able to buy anything!

Let's see what would have happened on our island if investment spending had increased enough to offset the savings of the eastsiders. Suppose, on the day the eastsiders decided to save their money, the son of the northside chief, Prince Hafakaloa, decided he would like to go into the business of producing pearl necklaces. He thinks he could sell a lot of necklaces at Christmas time.

He needs to buy some canoes, underwater goggles, other diving equipment, oyster knives and some other things. But he doesn't have the money to buy all these things. So (just to make it all work out neatly) let's suppose he goes to the eastside islanders to borrow some money. He promises to pay them back (with interest) one week before Christmas. They agree to lend him their savings. They arrange it so that each day they will turn over to him all the money they save that day.

Investment Demand Stimulates Capital Goods Production

When Prince Hafakaloa (our business entrepreneur) takes his borrowed money and goes into the market to buy things, he doesn't buy up the surplus breadfruit and bananas and all. He wants pearl-diving equipment and canoes and such. So he starts spending money for canoes and other capital goods. His spending for capital goods is just great enough to exactly offset the eastsiders' reduced spending for consumer goods. The shift in

---

* Back in Chapter 2 you were reading about "saving and investing" from the point of view of the individual. From one person's point of view, saving money and putting it in a savings account may be thought of as "saving and investing." But from the point of view of the economy: not so! For your deposited savings to become investments in the economy, someone must take those deposited dollars and *spend them for capital goods*. Otherwise your savings withdrawal from the income stream will not be offset by a corresponding *investment injection*. The income-spending stream will get smaller. The economy will slow down and there will be unemployment.

spending convinces some of the people who previously were producing consumer goods—breadfruit, bananas, tuba—to start producing capital goods—canoes, diving masks, oyster knives and other pearl-necklace-making equipment.

See how the factors of production will shift from the production of *consumer goods* to the production of *capital goods*? This is a temporary problem which the "market process" can take care of. There is no problem of unemployment, no drop in outputs or incomes—no hard times at all! Why?

Because the increase in investment spending (for capital goods) is exactly the right size to offset the decrease in consumer spending (for consumer goods). That is, the new rate of investment spending is exactly equal to (and exactly offsets) the new rate of savings. The new injections offset the new withdrawals. See how neatly it works out?

Goods are produced for two reasons: one is to satisfy present consumption; the other is for use in future production. If we are producing goods to be used in future production, those goods will not be bought by consumers. The consumers are saving some income (are "not-spending" for consumer goods) and are leaving some factors of production in the market to be used to produce these "capital goods" for the businesses—for the investors.

If Investment Spending Offsets Savings: No Surpluses, No Shortages *

If the total value of the things people *don't buy* as consumer goods is exactly equal to the total value of things that investors *do buy* as

---

* You will notice throughout this discussion that all of the withdrawals and injections except savings and investment are being ignored. I think you will get a better picture of the critical savings-investment relationship if for the time being we ignore taxes and government spending and imports and exports. Near the end of this chapter all of the withdrawals and injections will be brought back into the picture.

capital goods, then the total size, or "speed" of the circular flow, just stays the same. Total outputs and total incomes do not change. Total economic activity continues at the same level.

But the minute total investment spending for capital goods gets *smaller* than the total amount the people are leaving in the market (saving) then there will be surplus goods in the market. Whenever this happens, output will be cut back. Unemployment will develop. Total economic activity will slow down. Outputs and incomes will decline.

The only way the surplus goods left by the savers can be bought up and cleared out of the market is for someone to get the money the savers took home (or get an equal amount of money from somewhere—like borrowing from banks) and go into the market and buy up those surplus goods. Whenever this happens there isn't a problem. Whenever it doesn't, there is.

As long as the investors are spending as much as the savers are saving, the markets will be cleared and the economy will keep on operating at the same level. No surpluses will pile up in the market because total spending or aggregate demand is great enough to "clear the market." The investors are deciding to spend exactly enough to offset the amount the savers are deciding to "not-spend." All goes well.

Too Much Investment Spending Brings Inflation

Now suppose the investors want to start spending *more* than the savers are saving. What happens? The investors will still be in the market looking for goods after the goods are all gone! What would happen then? Shortages, right?

Maybe producers would try to produce more, to meet the demands of the investors. But suppose we already have a "full employment" economy. The producers are producing all they can produce. Then, no matter how you slice it, that's all they can produce!

Given enough time, producers can build more and better capital. Then they can produce more. But isn't that just what they're trying to do now? They're trying to spend more money to invest in more capital. But the consumers are buying too much! Businesses can't invest any more in growth than the people are saving—that is: "producing but not consuming." So what happens meanwhile? The shortages continue.

The investors who are trying to buy more capital goods than the economy is producing start bidding against each other, trying to get the capital goods they want. They entice some of the factors of production away from making consumer goods and into making capital goods. When that happens *the consumers* start facing shortages.

All the people are employed in good jobs these days, and they want what they want—new cars, new refrigerators, new houses, you name it. And they're spending their money to try to get the things they want. But shortages are everywhere. Prices begin moving up. You know what we call this: Inflation. The investors and the consumers are all bidding against each other, trying to get the available goods and factors of production. Prices go up faster and faster.

Too Little Investment Spending Brings Recession

Now let's take another look at the opposite case. Suppose savings are high. There is a large amount of output that the consumers are not buying. Lots of goods and factors of production are available for the investors. Now, if they want to, the investors can build new factories, buy new machines, order fleets of new trucks—they can get plenty of everything they need. But suppose they decide they don't want to invest very much right now. Then what? I'll bet you know what.

If the businesses don't think this is a very good time to expand, then we have a problem. The amount the consumers are leaving in the market by *saving* (not-spending) is greater than the amount the businesses want to take out of the market by *investing*. So there lie all those goods, waiting unbought in the market. The consumers don't buy them. The investors don't buy them. What happens?

The producers who produced the unbought goods will just hold on to them. Not because they want to, but because they don't have much choice. They are caught with unwanted surpluses. They will cut back production and lay off workers. Some producers will shut down their plants. We will have an economic slowdown. Unemployment. Recession. If it continues and unemployment gets really bad, then we will call it a depression.

With Unsold Surpluses, Does Total Output Still Equal Total Income?

A while ago you saw the eastside islanders catching and selling fish and getting income. The more "dollars worth" of fish they produced, the more "dollars worth" of income they got, of course. The total value of their product was equal to the total income they received when they sold it. Output always equals income. Remember?

Suppose one day the eastside islanders couldn't sell all their fish. Then their *money incomes* would be smaller. They would have to take a *part* of their income in the same way Robinson Crusoe always took all of his income—that is, in goods instead of in money. Their *money income* is equal to the value of the output they produce and *sell*. The rest of their income is made up of *real income*—their unsold fish.

So their total output is still equal to their total income, even though part of their income is money and the other part is fish! It's as though they had invested a part of their money income in fish.

Whatever the value of the unsold fish happens to be, that's the value of that part of the output. So that's the value of that part of their income, and that's how much money they have tied up ("invested") in fish! See how, if the eastsiders can't sell all their fish, they are forced to "invest" in fish? Here's another example of this "forced investment" or "unplanned investment."

Realized Investment Is Always Equal to Savings

When Mr. Hebert the boatbuilder hires labor, buys materials, and builds boats, he is investing in those boats. He hopes to sell them. He doesn't want to keep his money invested in boats. But suppose the boatbuyers decide to save—to "not-buy" the boats? Then Mr. Herbert is forced to take his "income," not in money, but in boats. He is forced to invest in boats.

As the boat-buyers save more, Hebert is forced to invest more in boats. If this sort of thing goes on for very long, what happens? Hebert will stop producing boats. He'll fire his workers, stop buying lumber and screws and paint and things. He'll stop investing in boats and just shut down his boatyard.

If the same thing is happening to lots of other businesses, soon the whole economy will slow down. Outputs and incomes will go down. Unemployment will be everywhere. Soon those boat-buyers who decided to save (to "not-buy" boats) will lose their jobs too. No work. No income. No money to spend. No money to save, either.

Now think about what you just saw happening. Savers saved more and forced investors to invest more. Then pretty soon the investors cut back, invested less, and forced savers to save less. This is a very important principle in macroeconomics. Suggestion: Read this section again and watch how it happens. You'll be

needing a good understanding of this principle, later.

MACROEQUILIBRIUM: A SUMMARY OVERVIEW

The total income is just exactly big enough to buy the total output. So unless all the income is spent for output, some of the output will be left unbought in the market. The producers of the unbought output soon will cut back production. They will fire workers and buy less raw materials. The rate of production will slow down. Incomes will drop. The macro-level of the economy will go down.

If all the *output* is going to be bought, that means all the *income* must be spent to buy it. But we know that some of the people who receive income are *not* going to spend it all for output. Some of the income will be saved. So will we have unemployment? Will a depression come? That depends on whether or not somebody else—the businesses—the investors—will buy up the goods left in the market by the savers.

Investment Spending Must "Clear the Market"

To keep the economy in macroequilibrium, investment spending must be just great enough to "clear the market." The investors must buy up all the goods left by the savers. If the businesses try to buy *more* output than the savers are leaving, then there will be shortages in the market. These shortages will stimulate producers to produce more, up to the point where all of them are producing all they can. Output will expand until the economy reaches full capacity. We could say that the economy will "move up to a higher macroequilibrium."

But suppose the rate of savings is not offset by the rate of investment spending. Some output will be left in the market unbought. The unbought surpluses will result in reduced production and unemployment. The economy will "move down toward a lower macroequilibrium." Perhaps the lower macroequilibrium will be one of widespread unemployment and depression.

You can see that sometimes the issues of macroeconomics could give us some things to worry about. Surpluses, unemployment, and depression; or shortages and inflation—not very pleasant to contemplate! Sometimes these problems can get really serious.

Also consider this: whenever macroeconomic conditions start getting bad, there's a tendency for them to get even worse. Unfortunately, macroequilibrium in the economy is not a stable and dependable condition.

Macroequilibrium Is Unstable— Like a "Perched Boulder"

Macroequilibrium is always sort of shaky. The injections and withdrawals from the spending stream determine the macro-level of the economy. All these injections and withdrawals are sort of unstable.

Macroequilibrium is like a round boulder resting at the very top of a gently sloping mound, or hill. Anything which pushes the boulder off balance is likely to cause it to roll quite a distance before it once again comes to rest—that is, before it finds a new equilibrium. That's the way it is with total spending. So that's the way it is with macroequilibrium.

Do you know what has the most to do with macroequilibrium? It's what you've been reading about so far in this chapter. Macroequilibrium depends mostly on what's going on with *savings* and *investment*. The next section goes deeper into that.

THE QUESTION OF EQUALITY BETWEEN INJECTIONS AND WITHDRAWALS: DOES S = I?

Just about now there's something that may be beginning to bother you a little bit. Something may be beginning to seem illogical about this "spending, receiving, spending" discussion. There's a dilemma here that must be resolved. The next section explains it.

Does "Total Spending" Equal "Total Receipts"? Or Not?

You know that every time a dollar is spent, somebody is receiving it. So total spending must equal total receipts. Right? No doubt about it. If people are receiving dollars, somebody must be spending them. So the amounts being received must be exactly equal to the amounts being spent. That's obvious. But now, the dilemma.

You also know that if all the income received is respent—that is, if *spending* is as great as *receipts* (and no greater)—then the total spending flow will stay the same size—no larger, no smaller. The macroequilibrium of the economy will be maintained.

The only time the macroequilibrium (the rate of spending, employment, output, and income) can possibly change is when the rate of spending changes. And the only way the rate of spending can possibly change is for total injections (I + G + Ex) to be smaller or greater than total withdrawals (S + T + Im).

Do you see what all this means? It means that for us to have an increase in spending (and output and income), total *spending* must be *greater* than total *receipts*! And you know that spending and receipts are (must be!) equal. What a dilemma!

You can easily see that there's something wrong with the logic of this statement:

Since every dollar *spent* must also be *received*, total spending (C + I + G + Ex) must always equal total receipts (which must always equal C + S + T + Im). But whenever the national income flow is *increasing*, spending must be *greater* than receipts (injections greater than withdrawals); whenever the national income flow is decreasing, spending must be *less* than receipts (injections less than withdrawals).

This is a dilemma all right! What's the answer? The key to the dilemma is this: the words "spending" and "receipts" don't always mean the same thing. It's a question of *which* spending equals *which* receipts. Let me explain.

Which "Spending" Equals Which "Receipts"?

As I am standing here receiving income, *somebody* must be spending it. No question about that! People only receive what other people spend. So the amount being spent to generate income must always equal the amount of income being generated. Of course! The amount of income I am receiving is equal to the amount of spending somebody else is doing. But then, as I am receiving the money, am I going to be *spending* the same amount I am *receiving*? Not necessarily! (And that's the point.)

The total income everybody is receiving right now obviously is equal to the total amount being spent (to generate income) right now. But the amount the people are receiving right now as income is not necessarily the amount that they are going to turn right around and spend! We can't say that the total amount of money the people are *receiving today* is necessarily equal to the total amount of money they are going to be *spending tomorrow*! That's the key to the dilemma.

Since the amount being spent today is equal to the amount being received today, savings (and other withdrawals) today must be equal to investment (and other injections) today. Every injector-spender must have a withdrawer-receiver. Of course.

It's obvious that C = C, today. (It's the same thing!) It's obvious, too, that the total of the spending injections (I + G + Ex) must be exactly offset by total withdrawals (S + T + Im). At any moment, spending equals receipts, of course. Therefore, since C = C, total

withdrawals must be equal to total injections. It *must* be so!

How is it ever possible for withdrawals and injections to become unequal? Only when we compare today's injections with tomorrow's withdrawals, or today's withdrawals with tomorrow's injections. That's the way injections and withdrawals can be (and often *are*) unequal. And that's the kind of inequality which explains increases and decreases in the size of the national income-spending stream.

Each Economic Unit Is Locked into the Macro-System

Let's go back to something we were talking about before, back in Chapter 5—the very first chapter that introduced you to macro-economics. Remember how the economic system is a "total mechanism," and that all the "little wheels" are locked in and turning together? Yet each little wheel has its own engine. Each "little wheel," by itself, can try to speed up or slow down. But just the same, all the little wheels are locked in together so they *must* all be turning together! Suppose most of them are *trying* to speed up. What then? The total mechanism will be speeding up. Right? Or if most of them are *trying* to slow down, then the whole mechanism will be slowing down. Do you begin to see what I'm getting at?

Let's forget about the government sector (G and T) and the foreign trade balance (Ex and Im) for a few minutes. Pretend that the only withdrawals are for savings (S) and the only injections are for investments (I). *Whenever investors are "trying to" spend less than the savers are trying to save, the economy will be slowing down. Whenever investors are "trying to" spend more than the savers are trying to save, the economy will be speeding up.* Nevertheless, at any moment the *actual amount* of the investment injection is going to turn out to be exactly the same size as the *actual amount* of the savings withdrawal.

This will be true whether the investors and the savers like it or not!

Increased Investment Can Force an Increase in Savings

If the investors are trying to invest *more* than the savers are trying to save, the increased investment buying will *force* people to cut back on their consumer buying—that is, to save more. At any moment, suppose the investors are buying more of the output. How is that possible unless the consumers are buying *less* of the output? And to say that people are *buying less consumer goods* is just another way of saying that people are *saving more*.

As it actually turns out, S = I. But look. *Because* the investors are *trying* to spend more for investment than the savers want to save, there are shortages. Producers expand output. The total spending flow begins to increase. There is more employment, more output, more income.

As long as the investors are trying to spend more than the savers want to save (want to "leave in the market for the investors") there will be some "forced saving." The people can't spend as much for consumer goods as they want to, so they are *forced* to save. Shortages exist, and output, employment, and incomes expand. The pace of the economy quickens.

What If "Planned I" Exceeds "Planned S" at Full Capacity?

As long as the economy has "excess capacity" (unemployed workers and machines and things) output can continue to expand. But when all the people and factories and machines are busy producing all they can, then if the *desired rate* of spending by the investors ("planned I") continues to be greater than the desired rate of saving by the consumers ("planned S")—that is, if the investors are still trying to buy more than the savers want to leave in the markets for them to buy—

then the shortages can't be overcome. Output cannot be increased because the economy is already producing all it can produce. So what happens?

The consumer-goods buyers really want what they want. They offer to pay more for consumer goods. They try to "bid things back" from the investor-buyers. But the investor-buyers want what they want, too. They offer to pay more for the investment goods they want, to "bid things back" from the consumer-buyers. If there aren't enough goods for everybody, then somebody is going to come up short. The ones who will pay the most will get the goods. What's happening? Inflation, of course.

Why are we having all these shortages? and inflation? Because the economy is producing as much as it can and still "planned I" is greater than "planned S." The investors are trying to buy more goods than the savers want to leave in the markets. The investors are trying to buy more of the output than the consumers want to release. Total "spending pressure" is too great. Prices go up.

Increased Savings Can Force an Increase in Investment

Now you know what happens when "planned I" is greater than "planned S." You already knew about what happens when "planned S" is greater than "planned I." You saw it happen back on Tubaland Island when the eastsiders tried to save (planned S) for Christmas.

And you saw it when Mr. Herbert found himself with an unplanned investment in boats, and then shut down his boatyard. But here's a review of the principle, and then some real-world examples.

Suppose the consumers start leaving more things in the market than the investors want to buy. This means that some of the businesses can't sell all the output they have produced. So what happens to the unsold output? The businesses are forced to keep it. That's called "forced investment." "Unplanned investment."

An Example of Unplanned Investment

Suppose Chrysler Corporation discovers one day that its cars are piling up in the dealers' lots. The dealers are saying: "Don't send any more cars! We have already invested to the limit in our new car inventory! People just aren't spending enough for cars these days."

It seems that people are *saving* too much. So Chrysler Corporation finds itself with a lot of cars it can't sell. It has unwillingly *invested* a lot more than it had planned to in its "stock of new car inventories."

See how, if the consumers decide to save more—that is, to leave more in the markets than businesses want to buy up—that *forces* businesses to increase their investments? Sure. And you know exactly what is going to happen next. The economy is going to slow down.

Chrysler Corporation isn't going to keep on producing more cars and pushing them into its new-car inventory. Of course not! It has invested more in its new-car inventory than it had planned to already. So what does Chrysler Corporation do? It cuts back production. It puts some of its plants on a four-day work week. It may even close down some of its plants altogether.

See what's happening? Output and employment and incomes are getting smaller. Total spending is going down. Why? Because people are trying to save more than the businesses want to invest; "planned S" is greater than "planned I."

All this time, while Chrysler Corporation is having its problems, what's going on at GM? and Ford? and American Motors? The same thing: unplanned investment in new car inventories. What's happening at RCA and Magnavox and GE and Westinghouse and Whirlpool and Maytag? The same thing. Unplanned investments in inventories of new

TV's and refrigerators and stoves and washing machines and things. Why? Because consumers are saving too much for the level of planned investment; "planned S" is greater than "planned I."

It's obvious what's going to happen. All these producers are going to cut back production. The economy (total spending and production and output and employment and income) will slow down. When? Immediately!

The Economy Begins to Adjust Immediately

As soon as the unplanned investments (in new product inventories) begin, the producers begin cutting back. When consumers save more (spend less) it doesn't take long for the companies to see that their sales are slipping!

The moment the consumers begin to save more, that's the moment the unplanned inventory investments begin. It doesn't take long after that for the companies to start cutting back their production. The economy slows down.

The response is just as fast when the opposite occurs—when the investors are trying to spend more than the savers want to save—when "planned I" is greater than "planned S." As soon as shortages begin to show up in the markets (that is, as soon as the businesses see their new-product inventories being completely sold out) they quickly order more. The producers begin to produce more. The economy can start speeding up very quickly whenever "planned I" is greater than "planned S"; it can start slowing down very quickly whenever "planned S" is greater than "planned I."

Planned Savings and Planned Investment: an Overview

At any moment, the amount the savers are *trying* to (want to) pull out of the spending stream may be *greater* or *less* than the amount the investors are trying to (want to) pour back in. So "planned S" may be *greater* or *less* than "planned I."

If "planned S" (withdrawal) is greater than "planned I" (injections), surplus products will be left in the market. Businesses will cut back. Total spending will get smaller. The economy will slow down. But if "planned I" (injections) is greater than "planned S" (withdrawals), total spending will get larger. There will be shortages of things. The economy will speed up. If the economy is already working at "full capacity," there will be inflation.

Does "S" always equal "I"? Sure. It always comes out that way. But if by "S" you mean "the amount people are *trying* to (want to) save" and if by "I" you mean "the amount businesses are *trying* to (want to) invest," then S doesn't equal I unless the economy is in macroequilibrium.

Whenever "planned I" is *greater* than "planned S," the spending flow will be increasing and the economy will be speeding up. Whenever "planned I" is *less* than "planned S," the spending flow will be decreasing and the economy will be slowing down. If anybody ever asks you if savings are equal to investment, tell them: "Yes. Or maybe no. It all depends on what you mean by 'savings,' and 'investment'."

Planned Withdrawals and Planned Injections: an Overview

Now, just to be sure it's all tied together, let's bring all three kinds of "withdrawals" and "injections" back into the picture. You can be sure that at any moment the total flow of injections (I + G + Ex) into the income stream is exactly equal to the total flow of withdrawals (S + T + Im) out of the income stream. You can be *perfectly sure* of that. If it wasn't true, it

Well, does S=1? or not?

If you don't know for sure, better read this whole section *again*. Right now!

would mean that someone was spending money and no one was receiving it—or that someone was receiving money and no one was spending it. And that, obviously, is too ridiculous to contemplate!

However, as people, businesses, governments, and foreigners are *receiving* their money, they are *planning* the amounts they are going to save and to spend, and the ways they are going to spend it. In this *planning process* there's no assurance at all that the planned injections (I + G + Ex) will be equal to the planned withdrawals (S + T + Im).

If the planned injections are greater than the planned withdrawals, the size of the total spending flow will be increasing. The economy will be speeding up. But if the planned injections are less than the planned withdrawals, the size of the total spending flow will be decreasing. The economy will be slowing down.

Macroequilibrium Depends on What the Spenders Are Trying to Do

Just think of all those little wheels, all locked in and turning like the wheels inside a watch. They're all moving along together. For one to speed up, all must speed up. There's no doubt about that. But if several of them are trying to go a little faster (*planned* injections greater than *planned* withdrawals), the whole mechanism will speed up. If several of them are trying to slow down (*planned* injections less than *planned* withdrawals), the whole mechanism will slow down.

Macroequilibrium works like that. It depends on what the various economic units—consumers and investors and the government and the foreigners—are *trying* (planning) to do. If they are trying to withdraw more than they are trying to put back into the spending

Macro-equilibrium is a sort of chancy thing!

stream, then the economy is going to slow down. But if they are trying to inject more, then the economy is going to speed up. Get it?

It is the *equality* or *inequality* between what the "injectors" (I, G, and Ex) and the "withdrawers" (S, T, and Im) are *trying* to do, that determines whether the economy will be speeding up or slowing down. *Macroequilibrium requires that the injection plans are exactly large enough to offset the withdrawal plans.*

Really, that's all there is to it. Now, how would you like to see it on a graph?

THE KEYNESIAN NATIONAL SPENDING AND INCOME GRAPH

As you might have guessed, economists have a graph to show the relationship between spending and income. We call this a "Keynesian" graph after John Maynard Keynes.

The Keynesian national spending and income graph shows total spending on the vertical axis (the y axis) and total income on the horizontal axis (the x axis). Think about that: spending on one axis; income on the other. What kind of a curve will that make on the graph? As spending goes up, what happens to income? As income goes up, what happens to spending? Both go up together? Sure! When one increases, the other increases, and *by exactly the same amount*. Of course!

The curve is going to be *positive* (sloping upward) and linear (a straight line). And more than that. If the vertical (y) axis and the horizontal (x) axis are marked off on the same scale, the straight line will be rising at a 45-degree angle, exactly. You can see why, can't you? (When you increase by one unit on the

spending (y) axis you must increase one unit on the income (x) axis.)

There are two of these graphs shown on the next two pages. You should study and practice drawing them now. Then, when we start to really use them in the next chapter, you will be ready. Now look at Figure 10-1 and you will see that it looks exactly the way you expected it to.

The Keynesian national spending and income graph doesn't tell you very much yet. It isn't supposed to. But you will soon see that it's a very useful tool for analyzing the total spending flow.

Now, spend a while studying the graphs on the next two pages. Then, come back and read the summary to this chapter.

SUMMARY

Now that you have completed another chapter on macroeconomics, you should begin to feel comfortable with the idea of "spending flows and income flows." Much of what you have been reading about in this chapter is just good common sense.

Now that you think about it, isn't it sort of obvious that as people are out spending money, they are adding to total spending? and to the incomes of other people? Sure. And if all of us suddenly decide to take our paychecks and go home and hide them in the bureau drawer, pretty soon the economy is going to be very depressed. Right? We all might wind up losing our jobs!

The equalities between spending and receipts and between injections and withdrawals are all very logical. They really do work that way, too. I hope you have a "comfortable feel" about all these *spending flow* concepts and principles now. That's important, because unless you do the next chapter may be confusing. If you know this chapter and the last one well, the next one will be a real breeze! See you there.

**Fig. 10-1   The Keynesian National Spending and Income Graph:
the Total Spent for Output Always Equals
the Total Received as Income**

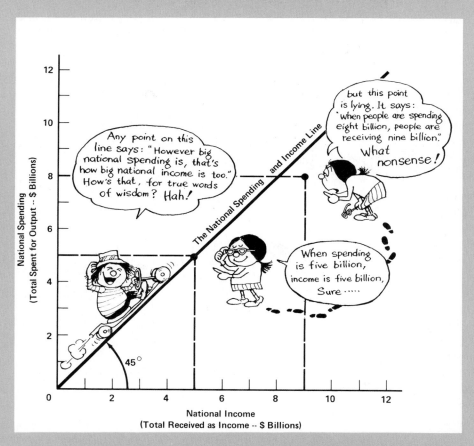

This is just another way to show that spending equals income.

This graph is a simple illustration of something you already know so well—that the total amount being spent for output is always exactly equal to the total amount being received as income. Of course! It's the same flow.

This is such a simple graph and it illustrates such simple and obvious things that you may wonder why I would ask you to learn it. The reason soon will become obvious. Before long we are going to start breaking down the total spending flow into its component parts (C, I, G, and F). Then you will see just how helpful this graph can be.

Fig. 10-2 The Keynesian National Spending and Income Graph: a View of the Equalities

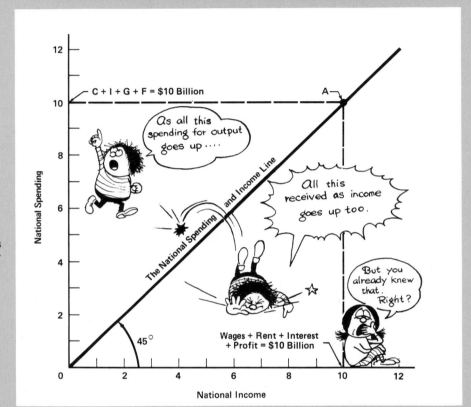

This graph ignores the adjustments for depreciation and indirect taxes.

At "Point A," national spending (C + I + G + F) is $10 billion, and national income is $10 billion. That's all you can read from this graph.

If all spenders (C, I, G, and F) are *trying* to spend more than $10 billion, then spending and income will be moving up along the line. If all the spenders are *trying* to withdraw more (spend less), then spending and income will be moving down along the line. But there's no way you can look at this graph and tell which is happening.

Soon we will draw in more curves. Then you *can* answer these questions. But no matter what lines we draw in, you may be sure that national spending and national income will always be shown by a point somewhere along the "national spending and income" line. Obviously!

**REVIEW
EXERCISES**

● **MAJOR CONCEPTS, PRINCIPLES, TERMS (Explain each carefully.)**

the concept of macroequilibrium
how investment spending offsets saving
how increased investment can force increased saving
how increased saving can force increased investment

● **OTHER CONCEPTS AND TERMS (Explain each briefly.)**

John Maynard Keynes
full capacity
planned investment
planned savings
planned injections
planned withdrawals
unplanned investment

unplanned saving
Keynesian
Say's Law
paradox of thrift
money as a claim check

● **CURVES AND GRAPHS (Draw, label, and explain each.)**

The Keynesian National Spending and Income Graph

● **QUESTIONS (Write out answers, or jot down key points.)**

1. What does it mean to say that macroequilibrium is sort of unstable, like a "perched boulder"?
2. If people could really understand and predict the *planned injections into* and the *planned withdrawals from* the spending-income stream, then they would be able to tell with certainty whether the economy was going to speed up or slow down. Explain.
3. Total spending must equal total receipts because every dollar spent must have a receiver. But total receipts are not necessarily equal to total spending. The only time national spending and income can change is when the two are *not* equal. Can you explain this apparently illogical statement?
4. Suppose "consumer spending" at your macrame belt concession stand at Seashore State Park dropped off, and you got caught with a lot of money tied up in belt-making materials and in finished belts you couldn't sell. Is that "unplanned investment"? Do you think you would slow down your future investment spending? maybe all the way to zero? If this sort of thing was happening all over the economy, what do you suppose the result would be? Explain.

11 National Income Analysis III: Keynesian and Monetary Theories

How to use Keynesian and monetary techniques to analyze the spending and income flows.

You already know what this chapter is going to be about. You're going to learn how to use the "Keynesian national spending and income graph" to find the macroequilibrium of the economy. I told you in the last chapter that we would do that in this chapter.

There's another thing this chapter is going to do, too. Remember about the other important way of looking at the total spending flow? about "the size of the money supply" and "the velocity at which the dollars are being spent"? In this chapter you will learn more about that, too.

First we will analyze the spending flow in a new way, using the Keynesian national spending and income graph. This approach will emphasize the four "spending sectors": C + I + G + F.

In macro-economics, how you **see** it depends a lot on how you choose to **look at** it!

Next, we will look at the spending and income flow the other way: as the quantity of money (M) times the velocity at which each dollar is being spent (V). Now, the Keynesian analysis.

KEYNESIAN NATIONAL INCOME ANALYSIS

What determines the total size of the national income? Total spending, of course! What determines total spending? Lots of things. Consumers spend for one set of reasons, investors for another, and governments for another.

If we could just know for sure why the spenders in each sector behave as they do, we could understand the whole thing. But we don't. Too bad. Still, we do know quite a lot about it. Let's start with the *basic flow* in the spending stream, and build up from there. What's the basic flow? You already know. It's "spending for consumer goods" (C).

The Propensity to Consume

What determines the rate of total consumer spending (C) in the nation? It's influenced by several things. One of the things is the level of national income.

You know that if people are receiving high incomes they are likely to be spending more for consumer goods—more than if their incomes were low. That's just common sense. But also there are statistics to prove it. As people's incomes get larger they really do spend more for consumer goods. As their incomes get smaller they really do spend less for consumer goods. Usually people with more income buy more things. I'm sure that doesn't surprise anybody.

We know something else about how consumer spending relates to income, too. We know that as a person's income gets higher, that person is likely to save a larger share—a larger percentage of it. People with very low incomes usually don't save anything. They spend all the money they earn and maybe even go into debt to pay their bills.

How about you? If you are like most college students you're spending more than you're receiving in income. How is that possible? Well, maybe you worked awhile and saved some money and now you are living off your savings. Or maybe your parents are helping you out. Or maybe you borrowed money so you can make it while you're going to college. But one way or another, almost all college students are consuming more than they are receiving as income.

If the income of the whole nation was very low, most people probably would be trying to spend more for consumer goods than they were receiving as income. That makes sense, doesn't it? Then if the national income moved higher and higher, most people would spend more and more for consumer goods. Right? Of course!

Suppose your income (disposable personal income) was only $5 a week. Would you spend it all for consumer goods? and save nothing? I'll bet so. I'll bet you'd be trying to borrow, too, so you could spend more. Most people would.

People With High Incomes Usually Save More

Suppose your income was $1,000 a week. (That might be a little difficult for you to imagine, but try to imagine it anyway, just for a minute.) What would you be doing with all that money? Most people could live pretty high on $1,000 a week! Most people would save some of it. But pretend that somehow you managed to spend your whole income ($1,000 a week) for consumption. No savings.

Then suppose your income suddenly *doubled*, to $2,000 a week. What then? Would you double your rate of consumer spending? Would you spend the whole $2,000 for consumer goods and services? I doubt it. But suppose you did. Then suppose your income doubled again. Do you suppose your spending for consumer goods would double *again*? And suppose it happened again? and again? How far can this thing go?

Do you get the point? The idea is that the higher a person's income is, the more likely it is that he or she will save some. That isn't too hard to believe, is it? As a rule, a person with a large income will save a larger proportion (percentage) than will a person with a low income.

What happens when you get an *increase* in income? What proportion (fraction) of the increase will you spend to buy consumer goods? Suppose you're almost starving. You may spend it all! Suppose you're very wealthy. You may save it all.

The Propensity to Consume Is an "If . . . Then" Concept

What we are talking about is something economists call the propensity to consume. "Propensity to consume" is a sort of "what would you do if . . . " kind of thing. It talks about: "If your income was such and such, what fraction of it would you be spending for consumer goods?"

Keynes suggested that if the national income was low, then the "propensity to consume" (the proportion or fraction of it that people would spend for consumer goods) would be high. If the national income was high, then the propensity to consume (the fraction of it that people would spend for consumer goods) would not be so high. See how "the propensity to consume" is a kind of "if . . . then" concept? It doesn't tell us what fraction of the national income *is* being spent for consumer goods. It tells us what fraction *would be* spent for consumer goods at all the *various levels* of national income that *might* (sometime) exist.

For each level of national income you might choose, there would be an average propensity to consume—that is, some fraction (percentage) of the total income would be spent for consumer goods. For example, if national income was $10 billion and total consumer spending was $8 billion, that would mean that out of every ten dollars being received as income, eight dollars were being respent for consumer goods. Then the average propensity to consume (APC) would be 8/10ths (or 4/5ths). The average propensity to save (APS) would be 2/10ths (or 1/5th). Out of every five dollars of income being received, one dollar would be saved—that is, not spent for consumer goods.

Let's take another example. If the national income was $8 billion and consumer spending was $7 billion, then the APC would be 7/8ths. The average propensity to save would be 1/8th. Get it?

The APC Determines the Size of "the Basic Spending Flow"

What does all this have to do with total spending and total output and macro-equilibrium and all that? Quite a lot! Just

think. Consumer spending is the basic flow in the income stream. The average propensity to consume (APC) tells us, for any level of national income, just how big that *basic flow* would be!

Let's take an example. Suppose, at a national income (NI) of $10 billion, consumer spending would be $8 billion (APC would be 8/10ths). Then the only way the NI could *ever* get up to $10 billion would be for $2 billion of spending to come from someplace to *add* to the "basic consumer spending flow" of $8 billion. See how important the APC is?

Suppose I told you that if NI was $5 billion, then APC would be 5/5ths, or "100 percent." That means that if NI was $5 billion, consumer spending would be $5 billion. Consumer spending would support the entire national output and national income, right by itself!

With APC of 100%, the average propensity to save (APS) would be zero. There would be no "savings withdrawals." So if the APC is 100 percent when the national income is $5 billion, then NI can *never* drop below $5 billion! How about that? (That is, it can't unless taxes or a negative foreign trade balance are draining off some of the basic consumer spending flow. But we don't have to get into that. So let's don't.)

See the importance of the average propensity to consume? It has a lot to do with setting the macro-equilibrium level of spending for the economy. At any level of national income the APC tells how much of the income received will be *automatically* returned to the total spending flow (as consumer spending). So it tells you (implicitly) how much "spending injection" (investment) would be required to bring national spending (and income) up to any level *above* the size of the basic consumer spending flow!

These relationships can be shown very clearly on the Keynesian national spending and income graph—the one you learned in the last chapter. We'll get into that in just a minute. But first we need to talk briefly about one other concept: the marginal propensity to consume.

The Marginal Propensity to Consume

Suppose national income went up just a little. Do you suppose the basic flow of spending for consumer goods would go up too? Of course.

The "marginal propensity to consume" (MPC) is concerned with the question of how much consumer spending (C) would go up if national income (NI) went up. *The MPC tells you what fraction of an increase in income, would be respent for consumer goods.*

Suppose NI increases by $4 billion and C increases by $3 billion. Then MPC would be 3/4ths. So you know implicitly that the marginal propensity to save (MPS) would be 1/4th. Right? If 3/4ths of the increase is respent for consumer goods then the other 1/4th *must* be saved.

Now, to get some practice with this new idea, look at the marginal propensity to consume (MPC) from the point of view of an individual. You. Suppose you were receiving an income of $1,000 a week. Not bad!

And suppose your average propensity to consume (APC) was 8/10ths. That means you would be spending $800 out of your $1,000 income for consumer goods, and saving $200. Then suppose your income increases by $100, to $1,100 a week. How much of the *extra* $100 will you spend for consumer goods? Maybe none of it. Maybe $800 a week is all you want to spend for consumer goods. See how MPC is likely to be low if your income is high?

But let's guess that you would spend an extra $50 a week for consumer goods. That means you're spending half of the extra $100 and saving the other half. So your marginal propensity to consume (MPC) is 1/2 and your marginal propensity to save (MPS) is 1/2.

The MPC Causes a Spending Increase to Multiply

What does your MPC mean from the point of view of the total spending-income stream?

Quite a lot! If your marginal propensity to consume is high, then when you receive an increase in income you will respend a lot of the increase to buy consumer goods. That way you will pour most of your new income right back into the basic spending-income flow.

If your MPC is high it means that when you receive an increase in income, you "pass it along." The basic spending-income flow expands. If everyone has a high MPC, any increase in income will have a high "multiplying effect." So the initial increase will just keep on pushing up total spending more and more.

Suppose that when you receive an increase in income, you decide to save most of it. That means your marginal propensity to consume is low. You won't pass along much of it. You don't put much of it back into the basic spending flow. Instead, you withhold it as savings. Can you see the difference it could make if everyone had a high MPC? or a low MPC?

A person with a low income is likely to have a high MPC. At high levels of income, marginal propensity to consume (MPC) is likely to be low. *The higher your income the higher your marginal propensity to save (MPS) is likely to be.*

So far we have covered a lot of ground in this chapter. Maybe we should stop right now and see what all this looks like on the Keynesian national spending and income graph. There are four of these graphs coming up, all four showing the same picture in slightly different ways. The graphs show exactly the same things we've been talking about.

You probably could understand all of this from only one graph. But I think it's better to show it in small, comfortable steps. So what's coming up now is really only one graph, looked at four times in slightly different ways. Take your time and study each one and learn it well.

Fig. 11-1   The Consumption Function: How Large We Expect the Basic Flow of Consumer Spending to Be at Different (Assumed) Levels of National Income

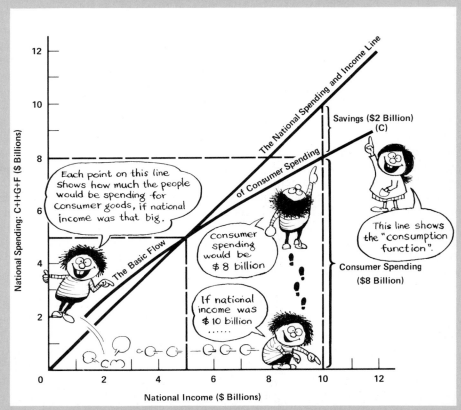

The "consumption function" line shows what fraction of the income will be spent for consumer goods.

The basic flow of consumer spending would be larger at the higher levels of national income. But also, notice how much more the people would *save* if the national income was high!

The higher the national income, the smaller the proportion (fraction) that would be spent for consumer goods. At very low levels of national income the people would be trying to spend more than they were receiving. At high levels of national income the people would spend less than they were receiving. They would save some.

Just look how high the savings withdrawal would be if the national income was $12 billion!

Fig. 11-2   The Consumption Function: The Average Propensity to Consume (APC) Would Be Smaller at Higher Levels of National Income

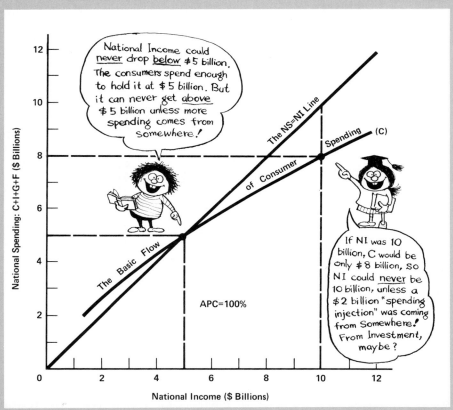

The higher the national income, the smaller the fraction spent on consumer goods.

You can see that as long as the "consumption function" line stays where it is, the only way national income can ever get above $5 billion is for some *other* source of spending to be added to the income stream.

If the consumers are spending only $5 billion and if they are the only ones spending, then total spending will be $5 billion. And that's all. So national income will be $5 billion. And that's all!

Fig. 11-3 The Consumption Function and the Savings Function: Two Different Ways of Looking at the Same Thing

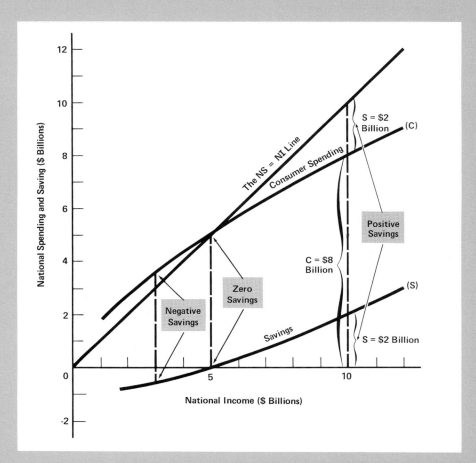

As income gets higher, the "savings gap" gets larger.

The relationship between the "savings function" (S) and the "consumption function" (C) is obvious. The two together must always add up to "100 percent" of national income. For example, if C = 80% (8/10ths), then S = 20% (2/10ths). If C = 100% (10/10ths), then S = 0.

What about "negative savings"? If S = − 10% (people are borrowing, and spending more than they are earning) then C must equal 110% of national income—which means: "Total *consumer* spending is 10% bigger than total spending"—which you know has got to be nonsense!

Some people can spend more than their total incomes, but *all* people can't. If they tried, NI would be forced up by the amount of the increased spending. Of course!

Fig. 11-4   The Marginal Propensity to Consume and the Average Propensity to Consume

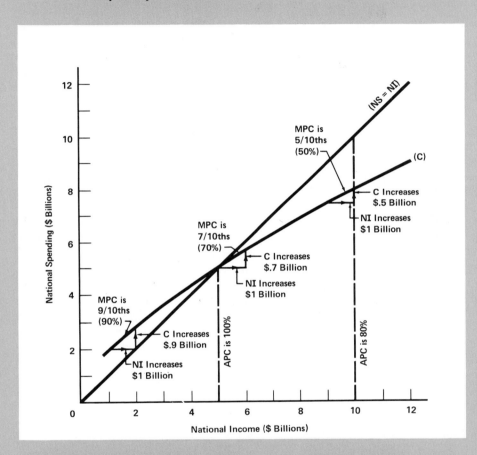

A prosperous nation requires a lot of investment spending.

For any level of national income, the *marginal* propensity to consume is not as high as the *average* propensity to consume. So no matter what the existing consumption rate (APC) might be, an *increase* in NI is going to bring a lower consumption rate (a higher savings rate) than before.

Therefore: the higher the national income, the higher the *savings* rate; and therefore, the higher will be the *investment* rate required to sustain the high level of national income.

So therefore: a very prosperous nation must depend on investment spending (reinjections to offset the savings withdrawals) to sustain its prosperity. How about that!

The graphs you've just been studying are all hypothetical, of course. They show the macro-economic picture of a small hypothetical country—one with a national income of only around $10 billion. But these graphs could be drawn (not precisely, but with some degree of accuracy) for a nation like the United States.

You can look at "national income and product" figures for several years and you can get some idea of what the consumption function and the savings function have looked like in the past. But the real purpose of these graphs is not to plot curves and show an accurate dependable macroeconomic picture of the economy. Things change too fast for that anyway.

The purpose of the graphs is to illustrate some principles which *are* dependable: as incomes increase, consumer spending increases, but savings increase faster, and it requires higher rates of investment to support higher levels of national spending.

The graphs also show that an increase in investment spending has a "multiplying effect," or "multiplier effect" on national income. You probably didn't see the multiplier effect as you were studying the previous graphs. So let me first give you a numerical example of how it works; then I'll show it to you on a graph. In the numerical example I'll use exactly the same figures as shown on the four graphs you just studied. It might be helpful for you to keep looking back at the graphs as you read along.

The "Full Employment" Level of National Income

Suppose this little make-believe nation we're talking about needs to have a national income of $10 billion. Let's say that a $10 billion NI would bring full employment, an acceptable rate of economic growth and no problems of shortages or inflation. But if NI was $10 billion, the average propensity to consume (APC) would be only 8/10ths ($8 billion). Remember?

If NI was $10 billion, the people who received the $10 billion would only be spending $8 billion of it for consumer goods. If the consumers are the only ones doing any spending, the national income can't be $10 billion. That's obvious. Unless $2 billion of spending is coming from somewhere else—from investment spending or government spending or from a positive foreign trade balance—NI can *never* get up to $10 billion.

Now, for the next step, there are two questions which need to be answered:

Question one: In this little make-believe nation if the only people doing any spending were the consumers then the national income would be just $5 billion. Right?

If NI was $5 billion, APC would be 100% ($5 billion). All the national income received would be poured back into the basic spending flow. National spending and national income would be in equilibrium at $5 billion. That would continue to be the macroequilibrium level of NI until some new spending injections were introduced from somewhere—or until something happened to cause the consumption function (the APC) to change. Nothing to worry about yet. So, on to the next question.

Question two: Suppose our little nation was dragging along with a national income of only $5 billion, and then the businesses decided to start spending at the rate of $2 billion a year. That would push national spending and national income up to $7 billion. Right? No. Wrong. It would push national spending and income up to *more than* $7 billion because of the multiplier effect. Let me explain.

Investment of $2 Billion Increases NI by $5 Billion: the Multiplier Effect

Remember how much investment spending it would take to reach the desired level of NI ($10 billion)? Look at Figure 11-3. Only $2 billion, right? But $5 billion (the NI with zero investment injection) plus $2 billion (the investment injection) only adds up to a total spending flow of $7 billion. Where does the other $3 billion of spending come from?

[$5 billion (C) + $2 billion (I) + $3 billion (?)
= $10 billion (NI)]

I think you know the answer already. The extra $3 billion comes from *more consumer spending*. It comes from the *marginal propensity to consume* (MPC). Remember? There is one level of NI (and only one level) at which consumers would spend exactly $5 billion. What level of NI? NI = $5 billion. Look at the graphs again and you'll see.

At any level of NI *higher* than $5 billion, consumer spending will be *higher* than $5 billion. As incomes rise, people spend more for consumer goods. Of course! So it's nonsense to talk of NI = $7 billion and consumer spending of only $5 billion. That just couldn't be.

If the NI was $7 billion, the people would *not* be spending *all* of their incomes on consumer goods (as they would be if the NI was $5 billion). But they certainly would be spending more than $5 billion! Let's say they would be spending $6.5 billion and saving $.5 billion. (That's what it looks like on the graphs.) So can we say that the new level of national spending and income will be:

[$6.5 billion (C) + $2 billion (I) = $8.5 billion
(NI)]?

No, we can't say that, either. Why not? Because if NI was up to $8.5 billion, spending for consumer goods would be up to *more* than $6.5 billion. See how NI and C seem to be working back and forth on each other, pushing each other up higher and higher? If NI was $8.5 billion, C would be up to about $7.4 billion. The graphs show that. So can we say that the new equilibrium level of national spending and income will be:

[$7.4 billion (C) + $2 billion (I) = $9.4 billion
(NI)]?

By now you already know the answer. No, we can't say this either. It just can't be true! If NI was $9.4 billion then C would not be $7.4 billion any more. Therefore $9.4 billion can't be the new level of national spending and national income!

When the rate of investment spending is $2 billion a year, what will be—what *must* be—the macroequilibrium level of national spending and national income? It *must* be that level which will induce the people to want to *save* $2 billion.

With *investment spending* of $2 billion, the national income automatically will move up to the level where the *savings withdrawals* become $2 billion. The national income must expand to that rate of flow at which the savings withdrawals are equal to the investment injections. Remember? Of course! So here it is:

[$8 billion (C) + $2 billion (I) = $10 billion (NI)]

How do we know that this is the equilibrium level? Because we know (that is, we assumed in the beginning) that APC would be 8/10ths ($8 billion) when NI was $10 billion.

(*Note:* We "assumed" (decided to use) these round numbers so that it would all come out nice and even. Whenever you're using numbers to illustrate things, on graphs or anywhere, be careful to "assume" some round numbers that are easy to work with. It's so much easier that way. But more important, it lets you concentrate on the important things—on the *principles and concepts*, instead of the numbers.)

The Macroequilibrium Level of National Income

It's all as simple as 1, 2, 3.

1. If we know what the average propensity to consume would be at each "might exist" level of national income, and
2. if we know how much "injection spending" (investment) there is going to be, then

3. we can see right off what the macro-equilibrium level of national income must be—where withdrawals (savings) are equal to injections (investments).

Isn't that neat? You can see it on the Keynesian national spending and income graph, too.

In the Keynesian graphs you have already studied (Figures 11-1, 2, 3, and 4) the only equilibrium level of national spending and income you can see is NI = $5 billion. If consumer spending is the *only* kind of spending in this nation, then $5 billion is just where NI is going to be. That's where it *must* be! If the consumers are the only ones spending and if $5 billion is all they're spending, then $5 billion is all there is.

We know that the consumers really aren't the only ones spending. So we know that the macroequilibrium for our little nation will come out at a higher national income than just $5 billion. But how much more? That depends on the size of the *injections*. Let's introduce some investment spending and see what happens to national income.

First there's a table and then two graphs all showing exactly the same picture you've been reading about. When you finish studying Figures 11-5, 11-6, and 11-7, I think you will really understand about the multiplier effect—that is, about the income (or investment) multiplier. Now would be a good time for you to study those three Figures 11-5, 6, and 7.

We've been going along talking about investment injections as though the investors were the only ones who ever inject anything into the income stream. But you know that's not true. So what about the other kinds of injections? How would they influence the macroequilibrium? And how would it look on the graph? Just exactly like the investment injection looks, in Figures 11-6 and 11-7. Exactly. Government spending (G), or a positive foreign trade balance (F) would shift the curve upward, just as the "investment injection" did. Then NI would expand to a new level of macroequilibrium.

What about withdrawals? The savings withdrawal is already shown in the graph. But how would taxes or a negative foreign trade balance influence the picture? Just as you would guess. These withdrawals would pull down the basic consumer spending flow. The "consumption function" curve would shift downward. The withdrawals would cause the macroequilibrium level of NI to be smaller.

Fig. 11-5   The Income Multiplier (or Investment Multiplier)

The NI will keep increasing until S = I (planned S = planned I, that is!)

If NI level is		Then basic consumer spending will be		If investors inject		Then NI will be
$5	→	$5	→	0	→	$5
5	→	5	→	$2	→	7
7	→	6.5	→	2	→	8.5
8.5	→	7.4	→	2	→	9.4
9.4	→	7.7	→	2	→	9.7
9.7	→	7.9	→	2	→	9.9
9.9	→	7.95	→	2	→	9.95
9.95	→	etc., etc., etc. . . .				

until the new level of macroequilibrium is reached, where:

$10	→	$8	→	$2	→	$10

Once we assume a "consumption function," then the size of the basic consumer spending flow is determined by the size of the national income. An investment injection into the income stream increases NI, so it causes C to increase. But the increased C pushes NI up even more.

As C increases, NI increases. And each NI increase causes a further increase in C. For how long? Until a new macroequilibrium is reached. Until NI increases to where the consumers are withdrawing as much in savings as the investors are injecting as investment spending.

**Fig. 11-6   The Effect of an Injection of Investment Spending
(the Multiplier Effect)**

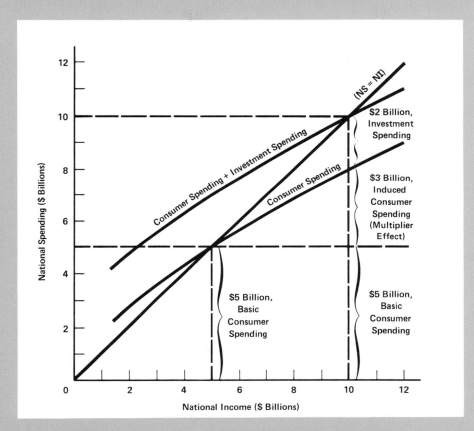

Investment spending has a "multiplier effect" on national income.

Investment spending of $2 billion brings an increase in national spending and income of $5 billion. Why? Because of the income multiplier!

National spending and income are increased by 2½ times the amount of the investment spending. How? By causing (inducing) consumer spending to increase by $3 billion.

This multiple effect of an increase in investment spending (caused by the induced consumer spending) is called "the multiplier." In this case the multiplier is 2.5. [$2 billion (I), times 2.5 (the multiplier) equals $5 billion. This $5 billion is the *total* increase in spending, resulting from the initial increase of only $2 billion. The initial increase, times the multiplier, always gives the total increase in spending and income.]

Can you see that the size of the multiplier depends on the size of the marginal propensity to consume (MPC)? The MPC is "the responding effect" of an increase in income. The more respent, the steeper would be the "consumption function" line in the graph, and the higher would be the multiplier.

**Fig. 11-7   More Investment Spending Induces More Savings;
Macroequilibrium Is Where S = I**

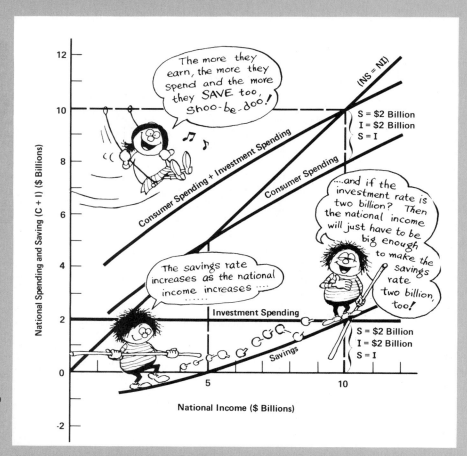

More investment
spending causes
national income to
increase, which
causes savings to
increase.

National income must continue to increase until the size of the flow of the savings withdrawals is great enough to equal and offset the size of the flow of the investment injections.

When investment spending is zero then the savings rate also must be zero. That means APC must be 100%. All income received is spent for consumer goods. The economy is in macroequilibrium at a very low level of employment, output, and income (NI = $5 billion).

With the injection of $2 billion of investment spending, NI must rise—not just by $2 billion, but by enough to induce the income receivers to withdraw from the consumer spending flow (that is, to save) $2 billion, to offset the investment injection. National income must rise to that level at which the income receivers will be saving $2 billion—that is, to where NI = $10 billion.

What about the "consumption function" curve itself? Is that a stable, dependable thing that just stays where it is until some injections or withdrawals push it up, or pull it down? Not really. But it doesn't usually jump around too much.

During times of high expectations and optimism we would expect the consumption function curve to shift upward. There would be more consumer spending at any level of NI you might choose. But during gloomy times, or when everyone is deep in debt and trying to get things paid off, we would expect the average propensity to consume (APC) to get smaller. The curve would shift downward.

The Keynesian Graph Provides a Useful Approach

It would be good, just for practice, if you would stop for a few minutes now and draw a few of the Keynesian graphs and move the consumption function curve around. If you do, you will notice that anytime you move it there will be a multiplier effect. (The "induced respending effect" will see to that!)

By now you're getting a real feel for this Keynesian national spending and income graph, right? See what a helpful framework it gives for illustrating and analyzing the effects of all these different kinds of withdrawals and injections? As soon as you're sure you have it down pat, move on into the next section and learn about the quantity and velocity of money—but first, be sure!

A MONETARY APPROACH TO MACROECONOMICS

All this time we have been looking at total spending as the sum of its parts. We have defined four basic parts, or sectors, or spending sources: consumers (C), businesses (I), government (G), and foreigners (F). Now we are going to do something entirely different. We are going to look at total spending as "a big mass of dollars flowing around and around."

The Spending Flow Is a Mass of Moving Dollars

Total spending can be looked at as "the total amount of money in existence in the nation" and "the speed at which it is flowing." You can see that if the total money supply is a billion dollars and if each dollar is spent to buy some output once each month, then the total size of the spending flow will be one billion dollars each month. Right? Or $12 billion a year. Nothing very mysterious about that.

Economists use the symbol "M" to mean "the supply of money in existence" (the money stock), and the symbol "V" to mean "the velocity of circulation of money" (the number of times each dollar is being spent). It is obvious that the quantity of money in existence (M) times the velocity at which "the average dollar" is being spent (V) equals total spending. So we can say that M times V (or just "MV") equals total spending.

If each dollar is turning over one time each year, then total spending during the year is equal to the size of the money supply. The velocity of circulation is one. If each dollar is spent three times during the year, then the velocity is three and the total spending flow is three times as large as the total money supply. Simple. Right?

Remember that in this discussion we are not going to count all "spending velocity." We are only going to count the velocity of spending for *new* output—that is, only the "output velocity" or "income velocity" will be counted. We will ignore spending and respending for the same *old* goods. Economists frequently use the "MV" approach and consider *all* transactions in figuring "velocity of circulation." But for our purposes it's best to count only the "output and income" velocity because we're looking at national output and income.

Why should anyone ever look at the total spending flow as a big mass of dollars flowing around? What is the purpose of this MV way of looking at the spending-income stream? It's just that when we look at it this way we can see things that otherwise we couldn't see. The "MV" breakdown lets us concentrate on the *size* of the money supply (the money stock) to see how the *quantity of money* (and changes in the quantity of money) might influence (and be influenced by) the rate of spending in the economy.

What Determines the Spending Velocity of Money?

What determines V? What influences the number of times each dollar will be spent during a week, month, or year? Several things. Some of the things are built into the system. If people get paid once a week, then each dollar will turn over faster than if people get paid once a month. If everyone in the economy was on a weekly pay period, the money stock would support a higher rate of total spending than if everyone was on a monthly pay period. Each dollar would be changing hands more often, "doing more work"—buying more things.

If your uncle earns $100 a week but only gets paid every four weeks, then it takes four-hundred dollars of "money stock" to pay him for his four weeks of work. But if he earns the same wage and is paid at the end of *each* week, then only $100 of money stock is needed to pay him. When he gets paid $100 at the end of the first week, he spends it. Then he could get paid the same $100 at the end of the second week, then spend it, then get it back again, spend it again, and so on.

Of course he wouldn't get back the *same* dollars, week after week. But I think you get the idea. It's simply that the more frequently people get paid, the more work each dollar will do. If people get their money once a week, they usually spend it by the end of the week. If they get it once a month they usually spend it by the end of the month. On a monthly payments system, some of the dollars may sit idle all month long—until the last day of the month.

If the economy was on a *daily* payments system, each person could get paid and then spend all of that money every day. Then the velocity of circulation would be really high! A small money supply could support a great amount of spending.

Velocity Is Fairly Stable

At any moment the velocity of circulation is fairly stable, not likely to change very much. It is sort of like the consumption function we were talking about a while ago. It has a tendency to stay where it is, but many things can cause it to change—to move up or down, in response to people's moods or expectations. Still, it isn't unrealistic to think of V (the rate at which dollars are changing hands) as being fairly constant and stable.

The Money Stock Is Closely Related to Total Spending

If we can think of the velocity of money (V) as being fairly stable, then we can say that the size of the money stock is very important when we are trying to understand the size of the total spending flow. If V stays the same, then if the money stock is increasing, total spending also must be increasing; if the size of the money supply is decreasing, total spending must be decreasing. This really is what happens!

Since the velocity of circulation of money is fairly stable, it's obvious that *an increase in the size of the total spending-income flow requires an increase in the size of the money supply!* Also, *if spending and income are slowing down, the money supply must be contracting.* That's just what happens. How? Automatically. Through the banking system. Remember?

In order for the economy to speed up, bank loans (and therefore, the money supply) must expand. But as the economy slows down, bank loans are repaid and the money supply contracts. See how important the money supply can be? And see how it can be useful to look at the total spending flow as "a mass of moving money"?

Since the spending velocity stays fairly constant, if the money supply also stays fairly constant then the total spending flow will stay fairly constant. But if "M" increases, spending increases; if M decreases, spending decreases. So, if we want to, we can say that *all* increases or decreases in spending can be "explained" by increases or decreases in the money supply!

As "M" Increases, Total Spending Increases and Vice Versa

We can say that *no matter what the consumers and investors and the government spenders and the foreign buyers are doing, as long as "M" is gradually increasing, total spending and output and income will be gradually increasing and everything will be just fine!* So why don't we just forget about C + I + G + F and just concentrate our attention on the money supply? Wouldn't that be easier and neater? Sure. But it may not be wise. Perhaps we should talk a little bit about the question of "cause and effect."

The whole purpose of our macroeconomic analysis—taking the spending flow apart—is to try to find out what *causes* changes in the size of the spending-income flow. So we know that the size of the money supply and the size of the spending flow move very closely together. That's important. But here's the real question: Is it changes in the size of the money stock (M) which *cause* the spending flow to expand or contract?

Do you see the problem? Spending doesn't increase unless "M" increases. But M doesn't increase unless spending increases! What causes what? Do you suppose that each could have some causal influence on the other? Sure. That's why it's a good idea not to ignore either "MV," or "C + I + G + F" as ways of looking at the total spending-income flow.

Economists Disagree About the Causal Role of M

Many economists these days disagree about the best way to look at and analyze the macroeconomic forces at work in the economy. The "monetarist school of thought," which includes Professors Milton Friedman, Paul McCracken (former chairman of the Council of Economic Advisers under President Nixon) and others (the "Chicago school of thought") emphasizes the necessity of keeping our eye and our finger on the size (and changes in size) of the money supply. The monetarists emphasize the importance of the "money stock" as the key to understanding economic conditions and prices in the economy. *"Keep your eye on the money supply!"*

On the other side of this argument stand the followers of Keynesian economics (the "new economics"). These economists focus their attention directly on the spending sources which contribute to the total spending flow. This group includes Professors Paul Samuelson (Nobel prize winner in economics in 1970), Walter Heller (Chairman of the Council of Economic Advisers under President Johnson), and many others. They believe that the supply of money is primarily a responsive (dependent) rather than a causal (independent) force. They believe that in order to understand and/or influence macroeconomic conditions it is necessary to focus on the "Keynesian components" of the total income-spending flow: C + I + G + F.

Who is right? The monetarists? The Keynesians? Until a few years ago the Keynesian approach was clearly dominant in macroeconomics. But the monetarist philosophy has gained headway in recent years. The monetarist

philosophy had a dominant influence on economic policy during the Nixon administration—especially during the first two years (1969 and 1970).

Perhaps we are about to see the development of a "new" new economics, integrating the best from both the Keynesian and monetarist schools. Or maybe something else, better than either or both, is just over the horizon. Who knows? (Maybe YOU would like to become an economist and help us to get this thing figured out. If so: Welcome! But you needn't decide yet. You'll be getting a lot more involved in these issues in the next few chapters.)

Another Way to Look at "Output": Price Times Quantity

Now you know two ways to look at the total spending flow: by "spending sector" (C + I + G + F) and by "money supply times velocity of spending" (MV). So now it's time to look at *output* a new way. How? This way: as "the number of units produced" times "the average price per unit."

Let's take an example. Suppose we are producing a thousand units of output per day. Suppose the average price (per unit) is one dollar. Then the total value of the output flow will be one thousand dollars per day. Right? Then suppose the total output flow increases to *two* thousand units and the average price is still one dollar. Then the total value of the output flow will be two thousand dollars per day. Obviously.

Let's say it this way: total output value is equal to the total quantity (number of units) produced (Q) times the average price per unit (P). You can see that "Q" times "P" is really "the value of the national product." It's gross national product (GNP) stated in a slightly different way. Now that we have the output flow defined in this way (Q times P) we can put together what economists call the "equation of exchange."

The Equation of Exchange

The equation of exchange is another way of showing that the total spending flow is equal to the total output flow. We say it this way:

$$MV = PQ$$

This only tells us that the total spending flow (looked at as the total money supply times the average velocity at which each dollar is being spent for output) is equal to the total value of the output (looked at as the total quantity of units produced times the average price per unit). The statement is obviously true. Isn't this an interesting way to look at the total spending-output flow of the economy? Interesting, yes. And different. But what can we do with it? Just watch.

The velocity of circulation (V) is fairly constant and stable. Remember? But what about the quantity of output (Q)? Sometimes that can decrease and increase quite a lot when the economy is speeding up or slowing down. But as a rule the economy may be expected to run along on a fairly stable course most of the time. If so the quantity of output (Q) is not likely to change greatly in any short period of time. Now do you see where this leaves us?

If V is fairly constant and Q is fairly constant, this gives us a direct tie between M (the money supply) and P (the average level of prices). It tells us that if the money stock (M) does not increase, then "prices in general" absolutely cannot rise. Inflation is impossible! Now do you understand the monetarists' position on fighting inflation? "Don't let M increase any more than Q increases; then there can be no inflation!"

The following chapters will go further into these interesting issues of how to fight inflation and unemployment. But for now, let's stop and be sure all this is tied up right.

THE COMPONENTS OF THE SPENDING FLOW ARE ALL LOCKED TOGETHER

You can think of the spending flow as made up of the four spending components (C + I + G + F), or you can think of it as a total quantity of money circulating at a certain rate (MV). Either way you look at it you are looking at the same thing. If any one of the "spending components" slows down (unless something else speeds up) spending and income will get smaller. If this is happening it means that either M or V (or both) are getting smaller. These things must move together because they are exactly the same thing—just looked at in different ways.

You can look at the output flow as the quantity of units of output (Q) times the average price per unit (P). Or you can look at it as "GNP." GNP, really, is figured up by adding the outputs of things times the price of each. Remember? So in both cases you are looking at the same thing: output times prices. The two *must* be equal. Obviously.

If anything happens to cause the total spending flow to increase, then the value of what the spending flow is buying (the output flow) must also increase. There can be no other way. Either the size of the output must increase, or prices must rise. But one or the other (or some combination of both) must increase. See how all this is "locked-in" together? Everything moves together. So it's impossible simply to look at what is happening and *decide what is causing it* to happen. Let's take an example.

What's Causing What?

Perhaps I look and see an increase in investment spending. The investors borrow money from the bank (which expands the money supply) and spend the money to buy more goods. But if the economy is already fully employed, output cannot increase. So prices are forced up. What I see is: "increased investment spending bringing inflation."

Someone else looks at the same situation and says: "the expansion in the money supply resulted in inflation." Was it the increase in investment spending? Or was it the increase in the money supply which brought the inflation? The answer is obvious. It was both! The increased investment spending could not have occurred without the increase in the money supply; the increase in the money supply could not have occurred without the increased borrowing and spending by the investors!

If it happens that next spring consumers start going into debt and are spending more for appliances and automobiles and things, the money supply will increase. The economy will boom and prices may rise. What's responsible? The increase in the money supply? Or the "upward shift in the consumption function"? See the problem? It's difficult to separate inseparable things!

Changes Are Likely to Be Cumulative

Another problem is that these macroeconomic variables are so closely interrelated that any change is likely to set off a chain reaction. If total spending begins to increase for any reason, this may bring a wave of increased spending. If consumers spend more, businesses may think this is a good time to make profits. So they spend more. So incomes rise and consumers spend even more. The money supply expands. Employment and output increase. Probably prices rise, too.

It works the other way too. If businesses start cutting back spending and paying off loans, the money supply gets smaller. Workers receive less income. Some lose their jobs. Consumer spending drops. So businesses cut back even more. The money supply shrinks farther. More jobs are lost. Things get worse and worse.

See how macroequilibrium is sort of like a "perched boulder"? You'll find out even more about that in the chapters coming up in Part Four. But we have been covering a lot of solid ground. Maybe it's time to stop now and give you a chance to catch your breath. Maybe you'd better not go into Part Four until after you spend some time thinking about the concepts and principles explained in Part Three.

This Part (Three) has spelled out the basic macroeconomic concepts and principles— money, spending, macroequilibrium and all that. You know quite a lot now about national income analysis. Part Four will show you the kinds of bad times (depression and inflation) which sometimes develop, and then explain what can be done to try to overcome these macroeconomic problems. Review first. Then, on to Part Four.

REVIEW EXERCISES

● **MAJOR CONCEPTS, PRINCIPLES, TERMS (Explain each carefully.)**

the propensity to consume
the multiplier effect
why money times velocity (MV) equals total spending
why output times prices (PQ) equals GNP
why MV = PQ
the problem of "what causes what"

● **OTHER CONCEPTS AND TERMS (Explain each briefly.)**

average propensity to consume (APC)
average propensity to save (APS)
marginal propensity to consume (MPC)
consumption function
full employment
the money supply (M)
the velocity of money (V)
"income (or output) velocity"

Milton Friedman
Paul McCracken
the "Monetarists"
the "Chicago school
  of thought"
the Keynesians
Paul Samuelson
Walter Heller
the "new economics"

● **CURVES AND GRAPHS (Draw, label, and explain each.)**

The Consumption Function
The Consumption Function and the Savings Function
The Effect of an Injection of Investment Spending
Macroequilibrium, Where S = I

● **QUESTIONS (Write out answers, or jot down key points.)**

1. Can you think of anything that might cause *your* "consumption function" to shift up or down (either temporarily or permanently)—that is, things that might cause you to spend more or less for consumer

goods, even though your income didn't change? Can you think of things that might cause the consumption function to increase or decrease for the entire nation? Explain.

2. What do you think of the "relative usefulness" of the Keynesian and monetary approaches to understanding macroeconomics? For which purposes would you prefer to use the Keynesian approach? the monetary approach? Discuss.

3. Using the "MV = PQ" approach (and thinking back to things you learned in the previous chapters) it becomes pretty obvious why it's necessary to prevent unlimited expansion of the money supply, and why the government must be very careful about how much it finances its spending programs by creating new money (high-powered money) by selling bonds to the Federal Reserve banks. Right? Explain.

PART 4

MACRO PRINCIPLES, PROBLEMS, AND POLICIES: INFLATION, UNEMPLOYMENT, AND ECONOMIC STABILIZATION

IT'S FEAST OR FAMINE, DROUGHT OR FLOOD; WHENEVER IT RAINS, IT POURS!

12 Business Cycles: the Income Multiplier and the Acceleration Principle

The process of economic fluctuations: why the economy speeds up too much and slows down too much.

By now you know a lot of the most basic theory of macroeconomics. In this chapter you're going to see some of these things working in "real-world type" examples. By the time you finish this chapter, you'll have a lot better feel for some of these things.

The Process of Macroeconomic Change

What makes the economy speed up and slow down? What's the *process* of economic expansion and contraction? What is it that makes total spending increase so much sometimes? And decrease so much at some other times?

You already understand how an increase or decrease in spending by anybody has a tendency to result in further increases or decreases by others. You saw that in the Keynesian national spending and income graph. Also, remember when the eastside fishermen reduced their spending to save for Christmas? Soon everybody was forced to spend less. Yes, all

When business is good, it's **very very** good and when it's bad -- yeuck! How come?

these things really do move together. Here's a "real-world type" example.

A Spending Increase Must Come from Somewhere

Suppose there are lots of students in your area who would like to have part-time jobs. They all want some income. Now suppose a national toy manufacturer hears about the great supply of low cost part-time labor available in your area. A "plant location team" visits your area, and decides not to build an automated plant, but to design a toy factory requiring a lot of cheap unskilled labor, and build it in your area. So they build the plant halfway between the college and the shopping center.

Soon they start running ads in the college paper saying that students who want to work can come in and put in a few hours any day they want to. All you have to do when you work there is sit on a swivel-stool between two moving "assembly line" belts. You pick up the pieces you need to assemble a toy from the moving belt in front of you. You put the pieces together, then put the finished toy on the belt behind you. It's really simple to do. Not much variety and challenge, but it's a job and it pays money. To those who need money, that's important!

Many students go down and work in the plant between classes and in the afternoons. Would you say that this new plant is resulting in increased economic activity in your area? Is total output increasing? Is total income increasing? The answer, quite obviously, is "yes." An increase in spending by the toy business brings an increase in total spending in your area.

It results in an increase in output, and an increase in income. That's very easy to see. But this is just the beginning. Now the spending increase is going to *multiply*.

THE INCOME MULTIPLIER IS THE "RESPENDING" EFFECT

Everyone seems to be glad about the new toy factory in the area—except perhaps the few who used to like to go and sit and study under the trees in the field where the toy factory now is. Now the trees are gone, but such is sometimes the cost of economic growth. Many students have more income than before. They are happy.

What happens now? Is that the end of it? Or is this new toy plant going to have additional effects on the local economy? Are all of the students going to keep all that extra money they're making? Save it? Put it into savings accounts or stocks and bonds or real estate or some such? I doubt it. They will probably spend it at the snack bar, at the student union, at the college bookstore (ugh!), and at the shopping center and downtown. Right?

Employed People Spend More

You students are spending more for consumer goods these days. Why? Because the toy business decided to spend more in your area, that's why. See how an increase in spending is cumulative? The initial spending increase by the toy manufacturer seems to multiply throughout the community.

First the toy company's rate of spending in the area increases. The company pays wages to the student-workers. Then the student-workers' rate of spending in the area increases as they spend more each week at the shopping center and downtown. The rate of total spending is multiplying, all right! That's why economists call this "the income multiplier," or just "the multiplier." In the last chapter you saw how this looks on the Keynesian spending and income graph. Now you're seeing what it looks like in the real world.

New Spending Starts the Ball Rolling

Now let's back off and really look at the big picture. Let's suppose that the toy manufacturers are hiring because they expect a big boom this year. They think the bicycle boom is going to continue to expand. And they think all kinds of toys for "children-children" and for "adult-children" are going to be in strong demand this Christmas. So all around the country new toy factories are springing up.

In many places the manufacturers follow the same pattern started in your town. Instead of automated plants, they design their plants to use lots of low cost, part-time labor. So we see all these new toy factories and all these students working there, producing things, making income. We know the additional income they receive will let them spend more for consumer goods. Some of them will save some of the money they earn. But it's a pretty good bet that most of them will spend most of it.

You can see what's happening. The boom in your hometown is being repeated in lots of places. All these new jobs and new wages are not just in your town. They're everywhere!

The Extent of the Responding Effect

Wonder how much the rate of consumer spending throughout the country will increase as a result of the increased spending by all these toy companies? We really don't know. But we know what it depends on. It depends on how much each of you spends out of your new income. That's the marginal propensity to consume (MPC). Remember?

If all of you increase your weekly consumer spending by as much as your weekly income goes up, that means your MPC is 100 percent. When you spend all of your new income you turn it into new income for other people. Then if all those other people spend all of it, they turn it into just that much more new income for still more people. Then if those people spend it all and the next people spend it all and if this continues over and over, the consumer spending stream will just keep getting bigger and bigger! The rate of spending will keep going up and up.

The "investment hydrants" are pouring in more money but the "savings drainpipes" don't open up to drain any of it off. So what happens? The income flow keeps getting bigger and bigger!

Income Expands Until New Withdrawals Offset the New Injections

Could the MPC be 100 percent? Under some circumstances, for some people, sure. But for the total economy, with incomes increasing rapidly? No. As the national income increases, people will start to save some. The more the income increases the more the people will save. So how far will the national income increase? Just to the level where the amount the people want to withdraw (to save) is equal to the amount the businesses want to inject (to invest).

Now let's talk about the opposite example. Suppose all the students who received new income from the toy factory were so proud to get the money that they dashed down to the bank, cashed their paychecks (traded them for paper currency) then went home and hid the currency in the closet.

What's the multiplier now? It's one. Why? Because the new spending created new income only *one time*—just for the student workers. Then the money *immediately* leaked out of the spending stream and turned into savings. The "savings drainpipes" were immediately opened wide enough to offset the effect of the new injections from the "investment hydrants."

From these two extreme examples you can see what determines the size of the multiplier. If people save all the extra money they receive, the multiplier will be one. It doesn't multiply at all! If people spend all the extra money and everybody who receives it after that also spends it all, the multiplier will be infinite. The spending stream will keep getting bigger and bigger and bigger. But in the real world neither of these two extremes is likely to happen. The real situation, as you probably already have guessed, is going to fall somewhere between these two extremes.

At Higher Incomes People Save More

With the increased spending by the toy companies the income stream will get larger and larger. But as incomes get larger, people will save more. Eventually the "savings withdrawal rate" will increase enough to exactly equal (and exactly offset) the new "spending injection rate." You saw this in the Keynesian national spending and income graph in the last chapter. Remember how fast savings increased as national income increased?

Usually a person who receives an extra $10 a day as income doesn't run right out and spend it all! Most people would spend part and save part.

Most people in the "new-income-receiving line" will withdraw a little of the increase (open up their "savings drain valves" a little) before "passing it along." As each person does this the "moving excess of the $10" gets smaller and smaller until finally there is nothing left to pass on—nothing left to multiply. That means the "savings withdrawal rate" has increased by $10. The total income-spending stream will expand no farther. Macroequilibrium has been reached.

Suppose you're receiving the extra $10 a day and you decide to hide $2 (one fifth) of it each day in your closet. Then you spend $8 more each day for gas and picnic supplies and things. Suppose that when the gas people and picnic supply people and others all start getting this extra $8 a day in income, they also decide to save one-fifth and spend the rest.

Each time the multiplier effect (of the $10 a day increase) pushes someone's income up, it pushes up their savings. Eventually, savings withdrawals are increased enough to exactly offset the initial $10 a day increase—the new income you received from the toy company. Then the income stream is again stable, but at a higher level. Ten dollars a day higher? No. More like $50 a day higher! Why so high? Because of the income multiplier. Of course.

You already know that economists have figured out a way to assign a number to the multiplier. We call the number "the multiplier." What it tells you is how many times total income will increase as a result of the initial increase in spending injections.

If everybody saves all of every increase in income, the multiplier will be one. The increased spending increases the income only one time. Then it's all saved. But suppose everybody saved half of the daily increase and spent the other half. Then the multiplier would be two. But suppose the marginal propensity to save (MPS) is very low—say one-tenth. Then the marginal propensity to consume is very

high—9/10ths. And the multiplier? It's 10! The higher the marginal propensity to consume (MPC) the higher the multiplier. Obviously. It's the "consumer respending effect" (that is, the MPC) which is the multiplier!*

Another Table Showing the Multiplier

In the last chapter you saw a table showing how the multiplier works itself out in relation to the Keynesian national spending and income graph. Now, how about a table showing the spending injections and the savings withdrawals? And illustrating the effect of a high (or low) marginal propensity to consume?

That's exactly what Figure 12-1 shows. If you will take a few minutes now and work your way through that table I think you will be able to see these concepts very clearly. It would be a good idea for you to do that right now.

A Summary Overview of the Multiplier

The concept of the multiplier simply says that when businesses (or governments or foreigners—or consumers, for that matter) increase their spending, this immediately increases people's incomes by the amount of the increase in spending. But ultimately, incomes will be increased by *more* than the amount of the initial increase in spending.

The multiplier concept is simply a way of looking at the "respending effect." If the people respend almost all of the increases in

---

* If you would like to know the formula for the income multiplier, it's: "the reciprocal of the marginal propensity to save:"

$$\left(\frac{1}{\text{marginal propensity to save}} \right),$$

or $\left(\dfrac{1}{1 - \text{marginal propensity to consume}} \right).$

The MPC plus the MPS equals one, of course. So 1 − MPC = MPS! (Think about how similar this is to the formula you learned for the deposit multiplier back in Chapter 7.)

Fig. 12-1 How the Multiplier Effect Pushes Up National Income

Examples of how a higher level of daily spending injections have a multiple effect in pushing the economy up to a higher macroequilibrium.

Example 1. Assume that spending injections by businesses increase by $100 per day and that the MPC is 100%. MPS is zero. The multiplier is infinite! Watch:

Day	Total induced daily increase in consumer spending	Daily addition of new spending injections	Total increase in the daily income-spending stream	Spending increase over the previous day	Additional savings induced by today's income increase	Total induced daily increase in savings (withdrawn from income stream)	Additional consumer spending induced by today's increase	Total induced daily increase in consumer spending (carried forward and added to next day's income flow)
(1)	(2)	(3)	(4)	(5)	(6)	(7)	(8)	(9)
Day 0	0	+ 0	= 0	→ 0	→ 0	→ 0	→ 0	→ 0
Day 1	0	+100	=100	→100	→ 0	→ 0	→100	→100
Day 2	100	+100	=200	→100	→ 0	→ 0	→100	→200
Day 3	200	+100	=300	→100	→ 0	→ 0	→100	→300
Day 4	300	+100	=400	→100	→ 0	→ 0	→100	→400
Day 5	400	+100	=500	→100	→ 0	→ 0	→100	→500
Day 6	500	+100	=600	→100	→ 0	→ 0	→etc.	→etc.
		(spending would increase by $100 per day forever!)						
Day n	∞			∞				∞

This example illustrates that when no savings are withdrawn to offset the new larger size of the daily flow of injections, the income-spending flow keeps getting larger and larger, day after day. So the multiplier is infinite!

Example 2. The opposite case. Spending injections increase by $100 per day and the MPC is zero. MPS is 100%. The multiplier is one.

(1)	(2)	(3)	(4)	(5)	(6)	(7)	(8)	(9)
Day 0	0	+ 0	= 0	→ 0	→ 0	→ 0	→ 0	→ 0
Day 1	0	+100	=100	→100	→100	→100	→ 0	→ 0
Day 2	0	+100	=100	→ 0	→ 0	→100	→ 0	→ 0
Day 3	0	+100	=100	→ 0	→ 0	→100	→ 0	→ 0
Day n	0	+100	=100	→ 0	→ 0	→100	→ 0	→ 0

In this case, the savings withdrawals are increased by exactly the amount of the increase in the spending injections. The total income-spending flow increases by the amount of the increase in the size of the spending injections. And that's all. The economy is immediately at a new macroequilibrium, $100 higher than before. The investment injection is $100 higher and the savings withdrawal is $100 higher. The multiplier is one—meaning the $100 increase in spending really doesn't multiply at all.

Example 3. Halfway between case. Spending injections increase by $100 per day and MPC is ½. MPS is also ½. The multiplier is 2.

(1)	(2)	(3)	(4)	(5)	(6)	(7)	(8)	(9)
Day 0	0	+ 0	= 0	→ 0	→ 0	→ 0	→ 0	→ 0
Day 1	0	+100	=100	→100	→50	→50	→50	→50
Day 2	50	+100	=150	→50	→25	→75	→25	→75
Day 3	75	+100	=175	→25	→12.50	→87.50	→12.50	→87.50
Day 4	87.50	+100	=187.50	→12.50	→ 6.25	→93.75	→ 6.25	→93.75
Day 5	93.75	+100	=193.75	→ 6.25	→ 3.12	→96.88	→ 3.12	→96.88
Day 6	96.88	+100	=196.88	→ 3.12	→ 1.56	→98.44	→ 1.56	→98.44
Day 7	98.44	+100	=198.44	→ 1.56	→ etc.	→ etc.	→ etc.	→ ètc.
Day n	100	+100	=200	→ 0	→ 0	→100	→ 0	→100

When MPC is ½, that means one half of every increase in spending will be respent again as a part of the basic consumer spending flow. The other half will be withdrawn from the spending stream as savings.

How much must the income stream increase to induce savings withdrawals to increase enough to equal the new spending injections? It must increase by *twice* the amount of the new spending injection.

Savings go up by half the amount of the injection. So income must go up by *twice* the amount of the new injection to get the savers to pull out an amount equal to the injection. The new injection was $100 a day and the savers pulled out $50 a day of it. But the income-spending stream had to increase by $200 a day to get the savers to increase their withdrawals by $100 a day. That's where Planned S = Planned I, and that's the new level of macroequilibrium!

Example 4. A more likely real-world case. Spending injections increase by $100 per day and MPC is 4/5ths. MPS is 1/5th. The multiplier is 5, so total daily spending will increase by $500. But it takes a few days to work itself out. Watch:

(1)	(2)	(3)	(4)	(5)	(6)	(7)	(8)	(9)
Day 0	0	+ 0	= 0	→ 0	→ 0	→ 0	→ 0	→ 0
Day 1	0	+100	=100	→100	→20	→20	→80	→ 80
Day 2	80	+100	=180	→ 80	→16	→36	→64	→144
Day 3	144	+100	=244	→ 64	→12.80	→48.80	→51.20	→195.20
Day 4	195.20	+100	=295.20	→ 51.20	→10.24	→59.04	→40.96	→236.16
Day 5	236.16	+100	=336.16	→ 40.96	→ 8.19	→67.23	→32.77	→268.93
Day 6	268.93	+100	=368.94	→ 32.77	→ 6.55	→73.80	→26.21	→295.14
Day 7	295.14	+100	=395.14	→ 26.21	→ 5.24	→79.03	→20.97	→316.11
Day 8	316.11	+100	=416.11	→ 20.97	→ 4.19	→83.22	→16.77	→332.88
Day 9	332.88	+100	=432.88	→ 16.77	→ 3.35	→86.57	→13.42	→346.30
Day 10	346.30	+100	=446.30	→ 13.42	→ 2.68	→89.25	→10.74	→357.04
Day 11	357.04	+100	=457.04	→ 10.74	→ 2.15	→91.40	→ 8.59	→365.63
Day 12	365.63	+100	=465.63	→ 8.59	→ 1.72	→ etc.	→ etc.	→ etc.
Day n	400	+100	=500	→ 0	→ 0	→100	→ 0	→400

Notice how the new induced consumer spending gets smaller each consecutive day, and national income increases by a smaller amount each consecutive day. The additional savings withdrawal gets smaller each day too. But the *total daily savings withdrawal* keeps creeping up toward $100. When it gets there, that's the new macroequilibrium, where Planned S = Planned I. That's as far as the expansion will go.

their incomes, then "the multiplier" will be high because the marginal propensity to consume is high. (The marginal propensity to save is low.) But if people don't spend much of the increase—that is, if they save most of it—the multiplier will be low.

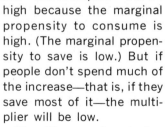

The "income-increasing effect" of an initial increase in spending will continue for how long? Until the daily rate of savings withdrawals increases enough to offset the higher daily rate of spending injections. Once the "savings withdrawal rate" increases enough to exactly offset the new "spending injection rate" the spending flow will be stable again—at a higher level than before.

Let's look at the big picture again, going back to the beginning. Suppose the economy is moving along with a lot of unemployed student labor—people who really would like part-time jobs. The economy is in "macro-equilibrium"—that is, it isn't expanding or contracting. But we have productive capacity that is not being used. So what happens?

The toy manufacturers invest in capital and hire the unemployed students. This increases total output and total income. But that's not the end of it. As the students' incomes increase from working in the toy factories their rates of spending also increase. They add more dollars to the spending stream.

The toy factories keep on paying the higher incomes. The students keep on buying more things. Those who sell things to the students keep on receiving more income and spending more themselves. The income stream is increased by (a) the amount of the initial spending injection plus (b) the amount of the new "multiplier-induced" spending.

The multiplier carries total income to a higher level, where it stabilizes. The new sta-

ble level must be the level at which the new (induced) rate of planned withdrawals (savings) is equal to the new rate of planned injections (investments).

Now you really understand the multiplier. That's good, because this is one of the things which really does work in the real world. It isn't always as neat and predictable as I have described it, but it really does work. The multiplier can be very powerful. But the multiplier is only half of the "induced spending" picture. Here's the other half. We call it "the acceleration principle."

THE ACCELERATION PRINCIPLE IS THE "INDUCED INVESTMENT" EFFECT

One afternoon you go by the new toy shop and work a few hours to earn some income. Then you go on down to the shopping center to spend your earnings. You go into the shoe store to buy a new pair of sandals. All the clerks are busy so the store manager, Mr. McCoy, waits on you. He seems to be in a very good mood. He tells you that his business is better this month than ever before. Can you guess why? You know very well why. It's the multiplier effect of the new income generated by the toy factory!

The "Multiplier" Can Set Off the "Accelerator"

Students now have more money to spend, so they're spending more for shoes. That shouldn't be a surprise. You're spending money at the shoe store today. That's what the multiplier says you will be doing. When you spend your money for sandals that's going to increase the incomes of a lot of people, each a little bit. Mr. McCoy will get to keep some of it for his own income, but not much of it.

Some of the increased spending goes to the shoe store employees. Some goes to the wholesaler who supplies the shoes. The wholesaler gets to keep a little of it, and some goes to the wholesaler's employees. Then some goes to the shoe manufacturer. The manufacturer keeps a little bit of the income and some goes to the workers. Then some goes to the leather company. The leather company gets to keep a little bit and some goes to the workers. Some goes to the bank as interest on loans. The banks keep a little and pay the employees a little. Some goes to the electric company, and to their suppliers and employees, and on and on it goes.

Ultimately, all of the increased spending for output must go as new income to somebody. Each person who receives some of it, respends some. All this new income is being generated by the multiplier. *The multiplier is the respending effect*, don't forget. But something else is getting ready to happen. The multiplier is going to set off the acceleration principle. Watch.

As Sales Increase, Inventories Increase More

While you are in the shoe store trying on sandals you hear a lot of hammering going on in the back. You ask Mr. McCoy what's going on. He says he is expanding his shelf space. He is going to expand his inventory of shoes, especially sandals. He explains that when sales are faster, he likes to have a larger inventory. That way he can be sure he won't run out of particular styles or sizes just when sales are going best.

"Each time you run out of someone's style, or size, you lose a customer," he says. "In the past, we have been selling at the rate of about $1,000 worth of shoes per week and we have been keeping about a $10,000 inventory of shoes on hand. But now our sales are up to almost $2,000 per week, and we think we should keep a much larger inventory, maybe even as much as $20,000 worth." That seems reasonable to you. You commend Mr. McCoy for his quick response to the increased demand for shoes. Then you pay for your sandals and go on your way.

As you are leaving you happen to think about the shoe *manufacturers*. How happy they

must be to get Mr. McCoy's order! He has been ordering about $1,000 worth of shoes a week through the wholesalers, from the factory. Now, suddenly Mr. McCoy is going to place an order for $12,000 worth of shoes all at one time! What an order! He needs $2,000 worth to cover his (larger) weekly sales volume, and he needs another $10,000 worth to build up his inventory.

You say to yourself, "Just think. His sales of shoes increased from $1,000 to $2,000 a week. That's an increase of 100 percent. But his order for more shoes from the manufacturer is going to *more* than double, or triple, or quadruple, or even quintuple. His order is going to increase by *1200 percent*! He is going to order *12 times as many shoes* as he did before. Wow! I'll bet the economists have some word—some strange sounding term—to describe a situation like this!"

And so we have. What you have just seen happening is what we call the acceleration principle. If you think about it for a minute you can guess exactly what's going to happen next. Shortages? Right!

A Tidal Wave of Derived Demand

Throughout the economy, students are working at toy factories earning extra money. Then they are going to the shoe stores and buying twice as many shoes as before. So shoe stores all over the country are sending in big orders to the shoe manufacturers—orders suddenly *12 times as great* as their previous orders. Now I ask you, how in the world are those shoe companies going to fill all those orders? They aren't. They just can't! There's just *no way* they can produce all those shoes. So what do they do? They hire all the extra workers they can find. They start working three shifts a day. They try to lease more buildings and buy new shoe-making machines.

The shoe machinery people are next to get hit by this tidal wave of derived demand. When a Wilmington manufacturer calls in a rush order for more machines, the shoe machinery people respond by saying: "You have been ordering only two machines a year from us, just to replace your old machines as they wear out. Now, suddenly you want to buy twenty new machines so you can set up a new factory. And you want immediate delivery? Would you believe that every shoe manufacturer in the country has called us and tried to buy 20 new machines? There's just *no way* we can produce all those machines.

"We will go on overtime, hire all the extra labor we can get, and expand our plant as quickly as we can. We will do everything we can to produce the machines as fast as we can. But we should warn you that we can't ship you more than one new machine every three months until we get tooled up to expand our output. That may take more than a year. Please understand that *we can't get the machines we need* to expand our plant, either!"

See how the "acceleration principle" blows up an increase in consumer demand, all out of proportion? Of course this example is a little bit exaggerated—I hope you will forgive me for that. Used with discretion, exaggeration sometimes can serve a useful purpose as "the microscope of the social scientist." (But *always* with discretion!)

Shortages Appear in Almost All Industries

Now look back to the day you bought your sandals. Suppose you had gone into the local appliance store or hardware store or sporting goods store or music store or automotive accessories store or almost anywhere else. You would have seen the same thing going on. Fast sales. Expanding orders for inventories. Then, shortages. It's happening everywhere!

Here's the pattern: Consumer demand increases some. Why? Usually because of the multiplier. Increased consumer demand is what triggers the acceleration principle. Retailers will increase their orders *much more*

than consumer demand increases. Then wholesalers and manufacturers "accelerate" the demand even more. *Total demand* goes right out of sight!

If only shoes were involved, resources could be shifted out of other things and into shoe production. But when *everything* is in short supply there's nowhere to get the needed resources. There's just no way all this inventory buildup can happen in a week or a month or even in a year! So there will be tight markets, waiting lists, and people offering extra money to get on the top of the lists. And inflationary pressures? You bet.

What started all this? The increased spending by the toy companies, that set off the multiplier. Remember? Then the increased consumer spending (multiplier effect) set off the accelerator. Consumer demand has gone up. *Derived demand* has gone out of sight! But that's not all. There's more.

THE ACCELERATOR, THE MULTIPLIER, AND THE BUSINESS CYCLE

What kind of "spending" do we call it when the shoe store spends for inventory? "Investment spending," of course! People buy shoes as *consumer goods*, but retail shoe stores buy shoes as *investment goods*, for investment purposes. So when the shoe store increases its spending for shoes, this is an increase in investment spending. Also when the shoe manufacturing company leases and renovates the building next door and buys new machines, what kind of "spending" is all this? "Investment spending," of course!

Remember what happens to incomes and to consumer spending when investment spending increases? If the initial increase in spending by the toy companies caused all this havoc, what do you suppose will happen when all these retailers and wholesalers and manufacturers and everybody else start increasing their spending by leaps and bounds? Talk about an uptight economy!

What's going to happen? How long can these high demand, shortage, inflationary conditions last? You could guess. *Until total production has caught up with and satisfied the pent-up demand* for factories and machines and inventories. But this could take quite a long time.

Each increase in consumer demand works up through the retailer and wholesaler and manufacturer and further accelerates the demand for inventories and factories and machines.

At the same time, each increase in investment spending for inventories and factories and machines works down through the multiplier to further increase consumer demand. Things are really tight. They're going to stay tight for a long time.

When Shortages End the Boom Ends

The boom doesn't keep on going this way forever. One day Mr. McCoy heaves a big sigh of relief and says: "Finally I have my inventory built up to the right size. I have been trying to do that for almost two years. Finally, I've made it. My sales of shoes are now up to $5,000 per week and my inventory is up to $35,000 worth of shoes. All my shelves are full. My sales seem to be stable at $5,000 and I think I will just let my inventory stabilize at the $35,000 level."

Mr. McCoy notifies the wholesaler and the manufacturer that in the future he will be satisfied with $5,000 worth of shoes per week. No longer will he write nasty letters saying that he must have another $15,000 worth. So the pressure is off, at least from Mr. McCoy's store.

What's the situation throughout the rest of the economy? The same. The level of sales is much higher than before and inventories are much larger than before. Everywhere you look, outputs and incomes are much higher than before. Spending is high. People are buying shoes and everything else like crazy. Prices of everything are higher, too.

But one thing is different now. There is no longer a need for the shoe store to build its inventory. So it cuts back its demand for shoes. What's going to happen when every shoe store and clothing store and appliance store and music store and furniture store and paint store and all the others stop building inventory? The manufacturers are going to be in for a real jolt!

Manufacturers Are the First to Feel the Slump

It took the manufacturers a long time to build up enough productive capacity to meet the "accelerated" demand. But now things are different. The wholesalers and retailers don't want to buy but a trickle anymore! The shoe manufacturers start closing down some of their plants. Other manufacturers do too. Soon it happens to several manufacturing firms. See what kind of a problem is sneaking up on us?

What do the manufacturing workers do when they get laid off? They buy less shoes and things. Is this the multiplier going the other way? It sure is. The manufacturers are reducing their spending for labor and other inputs. Down go incomes. So down goes consumer demand. How about the acceleration principle? Does it work in reverse, too? I'm afraid so. It looks like the boom is all over. The economy is on the brink of a recession.

Here's how it happens. First a few manufacturing workers are laid off. They reduce their spending for consumer goods. With less sales, retailers don't need as much inventory. So they stop ordering from the manufacturers for awhile. They just sell out of inventory. When this happens the manufacturers' sales drop to *zero*!

What do the manufacturers do? They close down their plants and lay off their workers for a few weeks. The laid-off workers don't have any income, so they don't spend much. That means retail sales drop even more. So the retailers decide to reduce inventories even more. No sense in carrying the expense of high inventories if it isn't necessary! More manufacturers have to close down.

How far does total spending (aggregate demand) go down? Is this a really bad recession? a depression? Who knows? We could exaggerate it enough to show a time when *all* retailers would be trying to sell out of inventory and *nobody* would be ordering anything from the manufacturers. Then nobody would be making any money working in the factories, so nobody would be buying very much from the retail stores.

If nobody is buying much of anything, how long is it going to take the retailers and wholesalers and manufacturers and everybody to get rid of all their overstocked inventories? A very long time. Such a depression would last a very long time. This is the kind of situation that existed in the United States in the 1930s. The inventory problem wasn't the only thing that caused the Great Depression of the 1930s to be so bad and to last so long. But it was one of the important things. I'm sure you can understand that now.

Economic Instability: the "Business Cycle"

It's easy to see how the multiplier and the accelerator reinforce each other. Any increase in spending by businesses (or by anybody) triggers the multiplier. Consumer spending increases. The increase in consumer spending triggers the accelerator and pushes investment spending up. The two work together, first to speed things up too much, then to pull the rug out from under us.

The boom keeps going until the plant and inventory expansions have been completed. Then everything turns around. The investment spending cutback brings consumer spending cutbacks which bring more investment spending cutbacks—down, down, down we go.

This "boom and bust" we are talking about is sometimes called the business cycle. The multiplier and accelerator reinforce each other and create a natural tendency for the economy to overexpand and then overcontract—to go from boom to recession. Sometimes this tendency is referred to as "the problem of the instability of capitalism." It really can be a problem.

This business cycle of "boom and bust" really isn't desirable from anybody's point of view. The times of declining demand, recession, unemployment and low incomes are usually thought of as the worst times. But the times of shortages and upward pressures on prices really aren't satisfactory either. I don't need to tell you that depressions and inflations are undesirable. Everybody knows that. But maybe it won't hurt, just for a few minutes, to talk about some of the undesirable effects of depression and inflation.

THE GREAT SOCIAL COST OF DEPRESSION AND INFLATION

Think for a minute. What's the purpose of "the economy"? What is the "economic system" supposed to do, anyway? Why should all these people be working and burning up energy and using up resources and making things and all that? The purpose is to feed and clothe us and to try to improve our lives—to let us live better. Right? We produce for the good of ourselves. We do and make what "we the members of the society" think will benefit us—will bring us better lives, or a better world. Anyway, that's what we're *trying* to do, I suppose.

The Tragedy of Unemployment and Depression

When we say "there is widespread unemployment," exactly what does that mean? It means that there are people who want to be productive, to produce something of value for the society. But because of some hang-up, some snag, some flaw in the way the economic system is working, these people don't have the opportunity to produce things for the society. When there's a lot of unemployment, there's a lot of waste. Labor is being wasted. And not just labor. Factories are sitting idle, getting rusty. Trucks, railroad cars, machines, all sitting around, doing nothing. Becoming obsolete. While there's so much that needs to be done!

When unemployment exists it means that the economic system somehow is failing in its job. The things society could be doing for its own benefit are going undone, while the society's productive resources are wasting away. Really tragic.

If we decided to produce less—maybe to conserve natural resources or to go on a 32-hour work week or to slow down the economy for some other reason, that's okay. But that's different! When we are talking about unemployment and depression we are talking about people *wanting* to be productive and society *wanting* and *needing* the output, but nothing happens. The pieces just aren't fitting together.

People are walking the streets looking for jobs, suffering the shame of having to admit failure. People having to accept handouts, losing their self respect. Sometimes just giving up. Sometimes turning against the society which has done this to them.

How would you measure the "social cost" of depression? We can't, really. But everyone knows that the cost is great. Not just *economic* costs, but *many kinds* of social cost. The breakdown in family harmony. The rise in the crime rate. Delinquent taxes. State and local governments facing fiscal crises. The quality of education, health, hospital, social welfare, other services, going down. The list goes on and on. The social costs of widespread unemployment are appalling. Intolerable.

Persistent Depression Is No Longer Tolerable

You can understand why people refuse to put up with depression. If any modern nation began to experience serious depression, the government would be forced to do something about it. If it was necessary to change the economic system to solve the problem, then you may be sure that the economic system would be changed. An economic system which would permit persistent depression and widespread unemployment is no longer acceptable in today's world.

The American economic system has been greatly changed during the past four decades. Much of the change has resulted from the people's feelings of economic insecurity. People really fear the threat of unemployment. They demand that the economic system be set up to do something positive to prevent it whenever necessary.

The following chapters explain what the government can do. But first, what about inflation? What's so bad about inflation?

Inflation Tears the Society Apart

What's inflation? Prices are going up. That's all. Is that so bad? Yes. It's very bad. Much worse than you think. It hurts the society. It brings really serious injustices to people. It actually *robs* people of the economic assets the society owes them. It forces people who, by all rights, deserve a comfortable retirement, to live their retirement years in poverty. But that isn't all. Not by a long shot.

Inflation really does tear the society apart. It forces every one of us to fight to see that the value of *our incomes* and the value of *our assets* keep going up at least as fast as prices are going up.

Inflation forces workers to fight for "exorbitant" wage increases. It forces businesses to announce "exorbitant" price increases. It forces the state and local governments to pass "exorbitant" tax increases, while costs of government services surge forward even faster. "Austerity budgets" are forced on the public schools, colleges, health and welfare services, highway departments. College students are forced to pay higher tuition and fees. People feel more and more cheated, and get more and more angry.

What does inflation do? You can see how it tears the society apart! Everyone must fight as hard as possible just to stay in the same place—to keep from being left behind. Inflation breeds unreasonableness, dissension, mistrust, unhappiness, and even hate among otherwise reasonable people.

If inflation continues, people lose interest in saving money. Nobody wants to hold money. Spend it! Hurry, before prices go up any more! Buy a new car. Buy land. Or stocks. Anything. But don't hold on to any money.

Once the people get afraid to hold money, they spend fast. Then prices really skyrocket! The next step is the complete collapse of the markets of the economy. People just *refuse* to accept money. Suddenly, there is no medium of exchange. The markets collapse. When the markets collapse, production stops. The economy collapses. Depression!

Gouge Thy Neighbor

Inflation instills in all the people—children and adults, workers, investors, business managers, police officers, teachers, college professors, everyone—the philosophy: "Gouge thy neighbor because thy neighbor is certainly out to gouge thee!" We are all forced to get involved in bargaining and pushing and trying to get our own incomes up enough so that (if we are lucky) we at least stay in the same place.

We might all be surprised if we knew just how many of today's economic and social problems are born of the distortions and injustices of inflation. Inflation distorts the economic relationships among all the people of the society. Businesses which sell in markets where they can raise their prices can come out all right. Workers who work where they can keep their wages rising fast can make out all right too. But many people have incomes which are not easy to adjust upward. They are seriously hurt. Usually the burden falls most heavily on the ones who are least able to carry it.

It isn't "just a few people" who are hurt by inflation. Most of the "ordinary people"—those of us who make up most of the society—are depending on some savings, some insurance policies, perhaps some government bonds, and a retirement program of some kind to bring us the things we need in our later years. For many years, most people produce and contribute more to the society than they consume. They save. The extra value they produce for the society (but don't consume) is supposed to flow back to them (as goods and services) so they can help their children through college, and so that in later years they can live decently. But what happens?

Inflation robs them of what the society owes them. If the inflation rate is high, the people simply aren't going to be getting the things they've saved up for. The things that rightfully belong to them will be going to the businesses and workers and governments and all the others who have the opportunity and the power to "increase their take" enough to come out on top. Everyone else gets left behind.

Do you begin to understand what inflation does to a society? If so, then you can understand why it is essential that inflation be held in check. If it isn't, soon it begins to run away. The further it goes, the more the people push to get their prices and wages up. So the worse it gets. Ultimately it can destroy the economy, the government, the entire society.

The problem of inflation is very real. It is much more serious than most people realize—potentially as dangerous as depression.

Neither inflation nor depression can be ignored. But what can be done?

The Necessity of Economic Stabilization

In the following chapters we will be talking about "monetary and fiscal policy"— techniques used by the government to stabilize the economy. While we're talking about what these policies are and how they work, try not to lose sight of the *vital purpose* of economic stabilization. Modern society somehow must prevent the intolerable social costs of both depression and inflation.

Now, before we go on into the issues of preventing and overcoming depression and inflation, there's one more thing we need to talk about. We need to ask this question: When the multiplier and the accelerator get going and everything is speeding up, where does all the *money* come from to finance such a boom?

THE MONEY SUPPLY MUST EXPAND TO FINANCE A BOOM

What role does money play in this whole "boom and bust" cycle of economic instability? The money supply must expand, or else the boom couldn't occur! Remember the toy manufacturers? Where do you suppose they got the money to pay the students for all that part-time work? Where do you suppose Mr. McCoy got the money to build up the value of his shoe inventory from $10,000 to $35,000? What about the money to lease and renovate buildings and to buy all those shoe machines and to pay for all the labor and other things? The multiplier couldn't get going very well without some new (bank-created) money to finance all those payments. Right?

Now think of the consumer goods boom. Where do you suppose all those people got the money to buy all those TV sets and new automobiles and furniture and all those things? All this buying, building, and stocking up of things just couldn't be going on unless a lot

more money was coming from somewhere. Where did it come from? It was being created through the banking system.

Could the money have come from savings that consumers are making out of their current incomes? Obviously not. The consumers are spending up their incomes and going into debt! Maybe the consumers are spending up the money they have been saving for a rainy day? Not a chance. Who is paying cash? Nobody. Well, almost nobody. Everyone's buying on time. How about the money the businesses have saved up? Or the money they're taking in from current business profits? No chance. The businesses are all going into debt, too. And selling things on credit. So *where could* the money be coming from? It's newly created. Of course.

The money to finance the boom is newly created, just for the purpose of financing the boom. It's created by the banking system, to meet the loan demands of businesses and consumers. You learned exactly how it happens back in Chapter 7, from Mr. Alber and Mr. Baker and Mr. Zimmer. Remember?

But what about the new excess reserves needed to let the money supply expand? Where did they come from? Do you suppose the government or the Federal Reserve System permitted bank reserves to expand? Of course. What if they hadn't? Suppose they didn't want this boom to go so far, so fast. Could they have held down the money expansion and slowed down the boom and relieved some of the shortages? You bet they could! And they would, too.

The "monetary control tools" can be used to work against both inflation and depression. In the next chapter you will find out what these tools are, and how they work. The next chapter is all about "monetary policy." As soon as you're sure you understand all about the multiplier and the acceleration principle and the other concepts in this chapter, you'll be ready to go on into "monetary policy."

REVIEW EXERCISES

• MAJOR CONCEPTS, PRINCIPLES, TERMS (Explain each carefully.)

the multiplier
the acceleration principle
the business cycle
the tragedy of depression
the injustice of inflation
a boom requires a monetary expansion

• OTHER CONCEPTS AND TERMS (Explain each briefly.)

macroeconomic change
inflation
depression
derived demand
the "consumer respending effect"
the "induced investment effect"
economic stabilization

• QUESTIONS (Write out answers, or jot down key points.)

1. Can you explain the relationship between the marginal propensity to save and the multiplier? Try.
2. Why is it that when the *shortages* end, the boom ends? Explain.
3. The multiplier and the accelerator always tend to work together and to reinforce each other, yet each one is a *distinctly different thing* than the other. Can you explain the distinct difference between the two principles?
4. When prices continue to rise year after year (as they have been in recent years in the United States and in the other countries of the world) the continuing inflation affects the lives of everyone in the society. What are some of the ways inflation has touched *you personally*? Explain.
5. If the business cycle really does try to work the way it's explained in this chapter, and if recurrent depression and inflation really are as bad as this chapter says, then it's pretty obvious that we can't let the economy just go its own way, and "let nature take its course." It's pretty obvious that the government must play an active macroeconomic role—that it must carry out some policies of "economic stabilization." The next two chapters will be talking about that. But already, right now, you should be able to think of some of the things the government might do. Can you?

13 Monetary Policy, the Bond Market, and the Stabilizing Role of the Fed

How policies of easy money or tight money can be used to try to stabilize the economy.

How would you like to be President of the United States? Maybe just for awhile? I wouldn't either. But would you be willing to make believe? Do you have enough imagination to think of yourself as the President?

This chapter is concerned with "economic stabilization." We'll be talking about the government's efforts to influence total spending, income, output, and employment in the economy. If you could visualize yourself as the President—as "the one who's really in the hot seat," you really might be able to get into it. You might get a feel for the techniques and tools, and for the difficulties and frustrations involved in economic stabilization. So will you try? Then okay, Mr. or Ms. President let's have a go at it!

As President, You Want a Healthy Economy

Now that you're the President you realize what a tough job it is trying to run the government. But you've become sort of attached to the White House and you really would like to be elected to another four-year term. You know that if everyone is happy about everything that's going on in the nation, you probably will be voted in again next November. But if the people are unhappy they will blame you and out you will go! So is there any problem? Yes. The economy is sort of depressed.

The average unemployment level throughout the country is about 7 percent. That means that 7 out of every 100 people in the labor force are out of work and looking for jobs. In some sections of the country the unemployment percentage is more than 10 percent. For some segments of the labor force—young, unskilled, minorities—the percentage is over 20 percent in some areas. You know that these people aren't going to be very happy with your administration. Neither are their families or their friends or the grocers who sell them groceries or any of the others who are hurt by all this unemployment. Unless something can be done to improve conditions in the economy before election time, you may find yourself out of a job!

How Do You Get People to Spend More?

Mr. or Ms. President, do you remember from the Econ 201 course you took in college many years ago, that total spending supports total employment, total output, total income, and all that? Sure. So you know that if you could get the people to go out and buy more refrigerators and vacuum cleaners and automobiles and clothes and shoes and household furnishings and fishing rods and things, everything would soon be all right.

Or maybe you could get some of the businesses to build new plants and order new equipment or start building up inventories. All the new investment spending would solve the problem. But how do you get the people and businesses to start spending more? There are several things you might try. Perhaps monetary policy would help.

WHAT IS MONETARY POLICY?

The first thing you think about is: "Maybe we could stimulate the economy by using monetary policy." You think: "If we had 'easy money' (all the banks with lots of excess reserves, and low interest rates for borrowers, and low down payments and easy credit terms for autos and appliances and all) then maybe people and businesses would borrow and spend. Then the economy would speed up. Unemployed people would be able to get jobs and the spending-output-income flow would be all right again." (And if all that happens, you will be reelected in November!)

You call together your top economic advisers: Chairman of the Council of Economic Advisers, Chairman of the Board of Governors of the Federal Reserve System, the Secretary of the Treasury, and the Director of the Office of Management and Budget. You ask them,

"What can we do with monetary policy to stimulate the economy, *quickly?*"

Depressed Conditions Call for Easy Money

Everyone agrees that there is only one thing you can do with monetary policy to stimulate the economy: make it easier and cheaper for people to borrow money and to buy things on credit. That is, see to it that the banks have plenty of excess reserves and that the interest rates are kept down low.

Your advisers agree that there will be some danger of inflation if you follow this policy. But they also agree that a policy of "easy money" at this time would probably stimulate both business spending and consumer spending. Then this initial spending increase would increase employment, output, and incomes, and perhaps would set the economy on the path to prosperity.

That sounds good to you, Mr. or Ms. President, so you urge your four top economic advisers to do whatever they can to bring about "easy money." You try to impress on them the need for haste. The political future of a great national leader is at stake!

When the meeting breaks up, your four economic advisers go their separate ways. The Chairman of the Council of Economic Advisers goes back to his office in the building next door to the White House and starts preparing some reports which he thinks will make banker's more willing to lend. But he recognizes that there really isn't very much he can do to help. There isn't very much the Director of the Office of Management and Budget can do either. He can say the right things and hope to help to get the people in the right mood. But he really doesn't have any "monetary policy tools" to work with.

With "easy money" people will spend **more**.

Maybe!

The Secretary of the Treasury has some direct dealings in the money market. The Treasury "markets" the government debt, so it is constantly dealing in the "money market." But it is the Chairman of the Board of Governors of the Federal Reserve System who really is in the driver's seat when it comes to monetary policy. First, let's talk a little bit about what the Treasury does, then we will be ready to really dig in on the Federal Reserve and its role in "monetary policy."

The Treasury Deals in the Bond and Money Markets

The Treasury is dealing in the bond and money markets every day. It must do this to "manage the government debt." In 1976 the U.S. government debt was about $600 billion and was increasing by $20 or $30 billion or more each year. If you want an up-to-date figure of the size of the debt you might check the *Economic Report of the President* or the *Federal Reserve Bulletin* or maybe the *Statistical Abstract of the United States*. You'll find them all in your library.

The government debt is made up of government securities: bonds (long-term) and Treasury "notes" and "bills" (short-term). The people, banks, insurance companies, business corporations, local governments, Federal Reserve Banks, and others hold these government securities. The securities are sold by the Treasury in the "open market"—that is, to anyone who wants to buy them.

Where does the Treasury get the billions of dollars to pay off the securities (bonds, notes, and bills) as they come due? By selling more securities, of course. Where does it sell these new bonds, notes, and all? In the bond and money markets, of course. Where else? And where are these bond and money markets? Scattered around the country in cities and towns, wherever there are banks and securities brokers. Securities brokerage companies and banks deal in government securities. The "money market headquarters" (if there is such a thing) is in New York City.

So what can the U.S. Treasury do to bring easy money? It might try to pay off more of its bonds. It could create some new money by selling bonds to the Federal Reserve Banks, and then use this newly created money to pay off bonds held by individuals and businesses. That would increase the money supply.

For example, suppose Mr. Alber cashes a bond. He receives a government check and goes into his bank, waving it in the air shouting: "Look! A new primary deposit! Some new excess reserves for the banking system! High-powered, five-fold, multiple expansion money! Happy days are here again!" Well, maybe he doesn't do all this. But you get the point.

What else can the Treasury do to bring easy money? It might start issuing bonds that pay lower interest rates. This might help to push down interest rates in the bond and money markets of the country. The Treasury could sell these bonds to the Federal Reserve Banks and create more money. But wait.

See how the Treasury must keep leaning on the Federal Reserve if it wants to do anything to bring easier money? Suppose the Fed doesn't want to buy all these new securities? What could the Treasury do then? Not much, I'm afraid. So you see, it's really the Fed which holds the key to monetary policy in the United States. So before we go on, here's a little review of what you learned about the Fed back in Chapter 6, and then more.

THE FED HAS MUCH INDEPENDENCE

The Federal Reserve System is the "central banking system" of the United States. It is controlled by a seven-member Board of Governors appointed by the President of the United States. The major function of this board is to decide on and carry out monetary policy for the nation. Although regulating the money supply is a governmental function, the

Federal Reserve System isn't a part of either one of the "three branches of government." The system was set up as "an independent watchdog agency" to keep an eye on the nation's money. The Board does not "report" to anyone—it isn't under anyone's direction and control. If it wants to, it can be as free and independent as the Supreme Court! (Well, almost.)

Maybe the Federal Reserve won't go along with the Treasury. It doesn't have to buy all those bonds if it doesn't want to. Maybe the Federal Reserve Board won't even go along with your policy, Mr. or Ms. President! They may decide that the advantages of easy money look too small and that the dangers of inflation look too great. If that's what they decide, then unless you can persuade them or pressure them into changing their minds, there isn't much you can do to bring easy money. Oh, the frustration of it all!

Maybe you can persuade Congress to pass a law to change the Federal Reserve System and give you more control. Some people have suggested that. Others strongly disagree. But no matter. It would take forever to get such controversial legislation through Congress, anyway. If it ever did pass, by then it would be too late to do *your* program any good.

So, Mr. or Ms. President, the success of your proposed "easy money" policy—and of your economic recovery plan, and perhaps of your bid for reelection—seems to hinge on the decision of the Federal Reserve Board. If you want things to go your way, now would be a very good time for some of your very best aides to start to do some gentle but persuasive arm-twisting!

The Fed Usually Goes Along With the President

As it turns out, Mr. or Ms. President, you didn't have to be concerned about the Fed's decision after all. Following your meeting, the Chairman of the Board of Governors called a meeting with the other six members of the Board. After some arguments they agreed to go along with your suggested "easy money" policy. They decided that they will take the necessary action to make money readily available to borrowers, and at low interest rates.

Can the Fed really do it? Can they bring easy money if they want to? Yes, they really can. And luckily, you know enough about money to be able to understand the entire process with no trouble at all.

How do they do it? They have several techniques—several "tools of monetary policy"—which they can use to make money easy (or tight). Most of the rest of this chapter will be talking about what those tools are and how (and how well) they work.

HOW "CHANGING THE DISCOUNT RATE" AFFECTS THE MONEY SUPPLY

Perhaps the first thing the Fed would do is to announce that they are going to lower the discount rate. What does that mean? Think back. Remember when Baker was first trying to talk Zimmer into lending him $4,000? Zimmer's bank didn't have any excess reserves. One way to get excess reserves is to borrow the extra money from the Federal Reserve Bank. The "discount rate" is the "interest rate" the Federal Reserve Bank would charge Zimmer's bank for "borrowed reserves." That's all.

Lowering the Discount Rate Brings Easier Money

You can see how a lower "discount rate" could make it easier and cheaper for people and businesses to borrow money. This "easy money" can stimulate more spending, output, and employment.

Flashback, Mr. or Ms. President, to when you were a college student. Suppose you had an uncle down in Chincoteague, Virginia, who was thinking about buying an oyster-breading machine. He has been to see his banker three different times to talk about borrowing the money. But he doesn't think the investment would be feasible unless he can borrow the money at 7 percent or less.

His banker keeps telling him that the lowest available rate for this kind of a loan is 8 percent. So your uncle has not borrowed the money and he hasn't bought the machine. Many people agree with your uncle on this. Nobody is buying oyster-breading machines. The breading machine plant in Baltimore closed down last month.

If Banks Can Borrow at Lower Rates, They Can Lend at Lower Rates

When the Fed decides to lower the discount rate, the picture changes. Suppose the discount rate was 5 3/4 percent and the Fed lowers it to 4 percent. Now your uncle's bank calls and offers your uncle a 7 percent loan. Your uncle borrows the money and orders the machine. Other seafood packing houses do the same. Soon the Baltimore plant may be working three shifts and there may be waiting lists and delayed deliveries. When the economy turns around, sometimes it turns around very fast!

Look at what's going on in upper Michigan and Wisconsin and Minnesota. Several iron and steel companies have borrowed money and are building new pelletizing plants. The lower discount rate has eased money all right! Many businesses are taking advantage of the lower rate of interest. They're buying and building the capital they have been thinking about for the past several months, or maybe years. They were poised and ready to go! The multiplier effect of the new investment spending is beginning to set off a consumer spending boom. Soon we may be worrying about the opposite problem. Shortages! Inflation!

It's easy to see how lowering the discount rate makes money easier to borrow and lowers interest rates. The lower rate at the Fed's "discount window" pushes down the interest

rates in every nook and cranny of the economic system. Even the corporations which are borrowing money by selling their own bonds don't have to pay such high interest to get people to buy their bonds. This makes expansion cheaper, so they may sell more bonds and expand more. When the Treasury issues new securities and sells them to get money to pay off maturing securities, the interest rate on the new issues will be lower. The lower rates will be reflected throughout the entire money market.

When the Fed offers to make loans to banks at a lower discount rate, this amounts to an increase in the supply of money available for loans. Money becomes easier to borrow, and at lower cost. In the case described here, this "monetary policy tool" (adjusting the discount rate) has been very effective. There doesn't seem to be any need to use any other "monetary policy tools." But it doesn't usually work out quite this way. Let's look at an opposite example.

When Times Are Really Bad, No One Will Borrow

Suppose your uncle just closed down his seafood packing house last week. Sales had been on a downtrend for more than a year. Labor costs, packaging costs, transportation costs, electric power costs, repair costs, taxes, and all other costs had been rising constantly. And the federal, state and local health and sanitation regulations and antipollution regulations and working hours regulations and minimum wage laws and bookkeeping requirements and all the other regulations and restrictions were getting more costly and time consuming and annoying all the time.

In the letter you got your uncle said " . . . and I dumped every penny of my savings into trying to keep the thing going. It will be *one cold day in July* before I ever put another penny into that money-leeching white elephant! I swear to that!" Things are bad in Chincoteague. And all over.

Your roommate just got a letter from home. His father was consulting for a steel company about investing in a new iron ore pelletizing plant in Ishpeming, Michigan. Well, that company is now in receivership (bankruptcy). All the steel companies are facing serious financial problems—sort of like your uncle, only on a much larger scale. The same is true for the railroads and the automobile producers and for textiles and petrochemicals and building supplies and food processing and wholesale and retail trade and automotive services and everything else. Talk about depression! This really is a bad one.

How much will it help to lower the discount rate when things are this bad and everyone is really pessimistic about the future? How low must the interest rate go before your uncle will borrow and buy the oyster-breading machine? Or before the (bankrupt) steel company will borrow and build the new pelletizing plant? Or before all the other businesses will start buying new equipment and expanding?

What banker would be so stupid as to lend money to all these "broke and going broker" businesses anyway? Mr. Zimmer, the banker, figures that anybody who tries to borrow and expand under such frightening circumstances has got to be some kind of a nut! Certainly such a person would not be a good credit risk.

Under such miserable circumstances, Mr. or Ms. President, the "easy money" tool of lowering the discount rate is not going to work. Better urge the Fed to bring on another tool.

HOW "OPEN MARKET OPERATIONS" AFFECT THE MONEY SUPPLY

A second and even more important technique the Federal Reserve uses to bring "easy money" is called "open market operations in government securities," or just "open market operations." This is a neat and simple little trick for pushing more money into (or

pulling money out of) the economy, and into (or out of) the reserve accounts of the banks.

You can see that if this tool lets the Fed put money into or take money out of a bank's reserve account (whether the bank likes it or not!) then it's a very powerful tool of monetary policy. Right? Yes. And that's what it does. So it is. It's *the most useful tool* the Fed has for controlling the money supply.

You'll see exactly how it works in just a minute. But first, here are a few things just to be sure you're familiar with "bonds" and "the bond market."

What Are Bonds? And What's the Bond Market?

A bond is a piece of paper which brings interest income to its owner. There are many billions (really trillions) of dollars worth of these pieces of paper in existence in this country. They are owned by individuals and banks and insurance companies and savings and loan companies and businesses and just about everybody. The Fed holds a lot of them.

Where did all these bonds come from? Mostly from governments (federal, state, and local) and businesses (mostly large corporations). There are a lot more corporation bonds than government bonds, but government bonds are the ones the Fed uses in its "open market operations." But don't forget this: whatever the Fed does with government bonds will influence what's going on with all the other bonds.

How does it work? The governments and the businesses have bonds printed up, then they sell them. That's how governments and businesses borrow money. Each bond has printed on it a face value (usually $1,000), an interest rate, and a maturity date. Each bond is a "promise to pay" two things to the owner of the bond: (1) interest each year, and (2) the face value at the maturity date.

Why do people and banks and insurance companies and all buy bonds? Because bonds pay income to their owners, of course. How much income? That depends on the interest rate printed on the bond! The higher the rate, the more it pays. The more it pays the more it's worth to its owner. Obviously? Sure.

What's going to happen someday when all these billions and trillions of dollars worth of bonds reach maturity and have to be paid off? All these people and banks and insurance companies will get all that money back? And the governments and the businesses will all go broke trying to pay off their debts? No. That isn't the way it works at all.

Billions of dollars worth of bonds are maturing and have to be paid off every week! Ah, but guess what? Billions of dollars worth of new bonds are being printed up and sold every week, too. So it all works out about even.

New Bonds? Or Old Bonds? When people buy bonds do they have to hold them to maturity to get their money back? No. And when they buy bonds, do they have to buy new bonds just being issued? No.

When people or banks or businesses buy bonds they usually aren't buying newly issued bonds and they usually aren't thinking of holding the bonds to maturity. They usually buy old bonds "in the bond market." They just call a stocks-and-bonds broker and place a "buy" order. Where do the bonds come from? From the previous owners who decided to sell—who called in "sell" order to their brokers!

It works just like buying and selling stocks. You can buy as many as you want of any kind you want any day you wish—just so long as you're willing (and able) to pay the price. And you can sell your bonds any time you please if you're willing to accept the existing price in the bond market. That's the way old bonds are being bought and sold all the time.

Banks, businesses, and individuals buy and sell millions of dollars worth of bonds every day. Some buy, and plan to hold them for a while. Others (speculators) buy because they think the prices of the bonds they're buying will go up. If so, they can sell and make a profit.

From the point of view of the buyer in the bond market, a bond is an investment like any other investment. You might consider putting your money into rental housing or building lots or a small business or bonds or stocks or antique furniture or whatever. How do you decide? You choose the one you think will bring you the most suitable combination of risk and income—and profit when you decide to sell it.

If people don't think much of bond investments these days, then a lot of them will be selling bonds. Prices in the bond markets will go down. Or maybe just now people would like to shift more of their investments into bonds. Demand for bonds will go up. Bond prices will rise.

See how the bond markets work? Just like other markets. And now that this little "familiarization tour" is complete you are ready to understand the Fed's "open market operations."

What Is Meant by "Open Market Operations"?

"Open market operations" means planned, purposeful, manipulation of the bond and money markets, by the Fed, through the buying and selling of government securities. That is, the Fed changes the supply of or the demand for (and therefore, the prices of) government securities. Then the effect spreads all throughout the money market and makes money easy or tight, and interest rates high or low. It's really neat how it works.

You already know that the Federal Reserve Banks hold billions of dollars worth of government bonds. The Federal Reserve Banks can make interest rates move up or down and can make money "easier" or "tighter" just by buying or selling these bonds "in the open market."

The bonds are bought and sold through "normal investment channels" including banks and stock and bond brokers. If the Federal Reserve is selling government securities (bonds), then anybody who wants to can buy them. If it's buying, it buys from anyone who wants to sell. That's why it's called "open market operations." The Fed is buying or selling bonds in the "open market"—in the regular, normal bond and money markets of the economy. But how does all this make money easy or tight? and interest rates low or high? Watch.

The Fed Buys Bonds, Pushes Bond Prices Up, and Increases the Money Supply

Back at the White House, you, Mr. or Ms. President, are very concerned about the sad shape of the economy. You want to follow a monetary policy of "easy money." You think that with low interest rates and easy credit, more people will borrow and spend. That will stimulate the economy and touch off a rapid recovery. So what should the Fed do with its open market operations at a time like this? Buy bonds! What good will that do? Let's take an example.

Remember Mr. Alber? The businessman who's going to night school working for his MBA degree? Well, he owns five $1,000 marketable government bonds. Each bond pays 6 percent interest on its face value. That is, each is a 6 percent, $1,000 bond, so it pays its owner $60 a year in income. (6% of $1,000 equals $60.) Mr. Alber thinks these bonds are a pretty good investment. That's why he bought them in the first place. But now the Fed is buying bonds in the open market. Will Mr. Alber sell his bonds? That depends on how much the Fed is offering to pay, of course!

Suppose the Fed offers to pay $1,200 for each of Mr. Alber's 6 percent, $1,000 bonds? Do you think he will sell? Perhaps. Let's suppose he does. So Mr. Alber turns his five bonds over to his banker or a local "stocks and bonds" broker. Then the banker or broker sends the bonds to the Federal Reserve Bank and the Federal Reserve Bank sends Mr. Alber a check for $6,000 (for 5 bonds @ $1,200 each). (The broker gets to keep a little bit of the money as a commission, but we won't worry about that.)

The Fed's Payments for Bonds Become New Money and New Bank Reserves

What does Mr. Alber do with the $6,000 check he just received? What *can* a person do with a $6,000 check? Deposit it in his bank account, of course. When Mr. Alber does that, what does the banker, Mr. Zimmer, do with the $6,000 check? What *can* a banker do with a $6,000 check drawn on the Federal Reserve Bank? He sends it to the Federal Reserve Bank for deposit to his reserve account, of course.

See what has happened? Just automatically the amount of money in that bank has gone up by $6,000 (Mr. Alber's account, which he can now spend). The money supply is now $6,000 bigger than before! But that's not all. The bank now finds itself suddenly having about $4,800 in excess reserves in its account at the Fed!

Now Mr. Zimmer has to worry about what to do with all that excess money—how to use it to bring in some income. He would like to lend it to someone. You can see why. See how the Fed's "open market operations" are bringing easy money?

Mr. Zimmer is going to try to expand his loans so he can start earning interest on the $4,800 he has in excess reserves. He hopes Mr. Baker will come in and borrow the $4,800. Then Mr. Baker will go out and spend it and the increased spending will help to stimulate the economy. Then Mr. Culver, who receives the $4,800 check from Baker, will deposit it in his bank. Then Culver's bank will have excess reserves. You know how this process can continue until the money supply expands to five times the amount of Mr. Alber's $6,000 deposit.

Yes, the money supply can expand by as much as $30,000, or maybe more, depending on the exact size of the reserve requirement. But will it? Maybe not. If conditions in the economy are really bad maybe nobody will want to borrow and spend.

It's easy to see how the Fed, by buying bonds, places new money in the hands of the people who are selling the bonds. Also it's easy to see that this new money is "high-powered money." It flows directly into the reserve accounts of the banks. It permits a multiple expansion of the money supply to begin.

If the Fed is buying bonds it is pushing new excess reserves into the accounts of banks all over the country. Does this bring easy money? You bet it does! But wait. You don't know the whole story yet.

To see the full effect of open market operations on the bond and money markets (or interest rates and bond prices and easy credit and all that), you first must know about the interesting relationship between *interest rates* (in the money markets of the economy) and *bond prices* (in the bond markets of the economy). (Both "markets" are the same market, of course!)

BOND PRICES AND INTEREST RATES

Open market operations provide a very neat way to adjust the availability of credit and to push interest rates up or down. A banker with excess reserves would be likely to offer loans at lower interest rates. Excess reserves push interest rates down. But there is another, more direct way that buying bonds in the open market pushes interest rates down.

To understand this, you only need to understand this fact: When the market price you have to pay for a bond increases, the "interest yield" you will get if you invest your money in that bond decreases. Therefore, as the open market prices of bonds go up, the interest yields earned by the buyers of those bonds go down. A bond pays interest (say 6%) on its face value (say $1,000). If you pay $1,200 for

the bond, *you still only get $60 a year*! That's only 5% on your $1,200 investment. This idea is really simple, but sometimes it seems confusing. Let's go through it step by step.

Market Prices of All Kinds of Bonds Rise and Fall

First of all, we aren't talking about the "savings bonds" (E and H bonds) that most individuals are familiar with. The E bonds and H bonds are special, *non-marketable* bonds. They don't fit into this discussion.

When the Fed is trying to ease money it buys "marketable" government bonds and pushes up the prices of these bonds. This entices people, banks, insurance companies and others to sell their bonds. As it pushes up the open market prices of government bonds, the prices of *all* bonds react the same way.

All the money and bond markets are very closely tied together. When the prices of government bonds are being forced up, this pushes up the prices of AT&T bonds, U.S. Steel bonds, General Motors bonds, Amoco bonds, Tenneco bonds and all other marketable bonds in the country. As the bond prices in the market go up, what happens to the actual interest you receive on your money when you buy one of the higher priced bonds? It goes down.

Bonds Paying the Highest Interest Sell for the Highest Prices

The face value of a bond may not be very close to its market price. For example, a 20-year, $1,000, 3% bond would not bring as much in the open market as a 20-year, $1,000, 9% bond. That's obvious, isn't it? When the 3 percent bond was issued, interest rates were low. But as interest rates (interest rates on new bonds) got higher and higher, the market value of the 3 percent bond got lower and lower.

That's the way it always is. *If interest rates are rising, bond prices are falling.* Or we can say it the other way and it's just as true: *if bond prices are rising, interest rates are falling.*

Suppose we are talking about a $1,000 bond which pays 6% per year. The owner of that bond will receive $60 a year. Now suppose you paid $1,200 when you bought the bond. How much income would it pay you per year? Only $60, of course. That's what the bond says. It says it will pay 6 percent on $1,000 to its owner. Even if you paid $1,200 when you bought the bond, you still aren't going to receive but $60 annual return on your $1,200 investment. That happens to be a return of only 5 percent. (5% of $1,200 is $60.) The bond is still paying 6 percent on its face value ($1,000). But *you* paid $1,200 so you're only getting a 5 percent return on your investment.

Why would anyone ever pay $1,200 for a $1,000 bond? Because they think it's the best investment for them available in the bond market, that's why! Suppose the new bonds being issued these days carry an interest rate of only 4 percent. Would you be willing to pay $1,200 for a long-term $1,000 bond that pays 6 percent? I would!

Very-Long-Term Bond Prices Reflect Only the Interest Return

Just to make the point, let's suppose we are talking about 500-year bonds. The only reason a person would want a 500-year bond is for the interest return, right? So suppose you are considering buying some 500-year, $1,000 bonds. You can get 3 percent ones for $500 each or 6 percent ones for $1,000 each or 9 percent ones for $1,500 each. They're *all* $1,000 bonds, but they are selling at such different prices! Which ones would you buy? It really wouldn't make any difference, would it?

You are going to earn 6 percent on your money, no matter which bonds you buy. Guess what the going rate of interest is on new bonds being issued these days? It's 6 percent, of course! The 3 percent bonds were issued sometime back when money market interest rates were low. So what happened to the value of the 3 percent bonds when the money market interest rate went up from 3 percent to 6 percent? The bond values dropped from $1,000 to about $500.

The 9 percent bonds were issued sometime back when money market interest rates were high. So what happened when the money market rate went down from 9 to 6 percent? The bond values went up from $1,000 to $1,500. If you hold marketable bonds while the money market rates of interest are *rising*, chances are that the open market value of your bonds will be *falling*. But if money market rates of interest are *falling*, the market value of your bonds will be *rising*.*

Now you can see that whenever the open market values of existing bonds are being forced up, interest rates are automatically being forced down. Whenever interest rates are moving down, open market values of existing bonds are moving up.

When interest rates are *falling*, people want to buy the high-interest, *old* bonds and they will pay a *premium price* to get them. When interest rates are *rising*, people want the high-interest *new* bonds. Anyone who wants to sell low-interest, *old* bonds must sell them at a lower price, below "par." Otherwise no one would buy them. Would you? Of course not.

---

* In real world markets at any moment this relationship may not be *precisely* true. Why? Because not only *current* conditions but also *expected future* conditions affect open market bond values and interest rates. But don't worry about this—not unless you're planning to speculate in the bond markets—in which case, please get some professional advice!

People Hold Bonds to Get the Interest Income

This is an essential concept and so often misunderstood. Let me say it just one more time, one more way. People buy bonds because they get income from owning bonds. How much you will pay for a bond depends on how much income you will get from owning that bond.

How much income do you insist on getting when you invest your money in bonds? The *going rate*, of course! Suppose the "going rate of interest" is getting lower. If you want to buy one of the old, high-interest bonds, you expect to pay more for it. If the *new, low-interest bonds* are selling at *face value*, then the *old, high-interest bonds* will be selling at a *premium*. Why? Because they pay more interest.

Suppose the "going rate of interest" is getting higher. If I want to sell you one of my old, low-interest bonds, you expect me to offer it to you at less than face value. Right? Otherwise, would you buy it? Of course not. You would buy one of the new, high-interest bonds instead. As market rates of interest change, market values of existing bonds also change—but always in the opposite direction. It must be true, and now you understand why.

Open Market Operations Directly Influence Bond Prices and Interest Rates

From all this discussion of the relationship between bond values and interest rates, you can see what happens when the Fed goes into the market and pushes up the value of government securities—like when it paid $1,200 each for Mr. Alber's $1,000 bonds. Mr. Alber's bonds have a face value of $1,000 each, and they are 6% bonds, so each bond pays its owner $60 a year. Those bonds will *always* pay $60 a year to their owner.

Now suppose Mr. Turner pays $1,200 for one of Mr. Alber's $1,000 bonds. Mr. Turner still only gets $60 a year. So how much interest is he making on his $1,200 investment? Only 5 percent! So when the Fed goes into the open market and pushes the price of $1,000, 6% bonds up to $1,200, it automatically pushes "the effective rate of interest on government bonds" down to 5 percent. But that isn't all. When the effective rate of interest on government bonds is pushed down, the rate of interest on everything else goes down. All interest rates move together (more or less).

Now you can see that as the Fed forces up bond values, interest rates throughout the economy automatically are forced down. At the same time, high-powered money is being pushed into the reserves of the banks. You, Mr. or Ms. President, are hoping that the lower interest rates and the greater availability of loanable funds in the banks will induce more businesses and consumers to borrow and spend. This could set off the multiplier and the accelerator. Then soon the economy would be booming again.

Will the open market operation of "buying securities" really work? Nobody knows for sure. If conditions are really bad, then no. It won't work. It might help a little but it will not be likely to bring a quick recovery. But if conditions aren't really *too* bad the open market operations may work very well. It's never possible to be sure just how much effect a given amount of open market operations will have.

One of the best things about the open market operations approach to monetary control is that the policy can be adjusted gently and quickly as circumstances change. The Fed has an "open market committee" which meets frequently to consider what the Fed's open market policy should be. This flexibility adds to the effectiveness of this

The Fed buys bonds, pushes up bond prices, and pushes down interest rates. Easy money!

most important monetary control tool— open market operations.

OTHER MONETARY POLICY ACTIONS

Now you understand the two most frequently used tools of monetary policy— "discount rate changes" and "open market operations in government securities." A third "tool" consists of changing the reserve requirement itself.

Suppose the amount required in reserves to back up the banks' demand deposits is 20 percent. Remember Mr. Zimmer and his bank? He had $1,000,000 in checking accounts and $200,000 in reserves. If the reserve requirement was 20 percent then Zimmer's bank had just enough reserves to be "legal." What would happen if the reserve requirement was changed?

Changing the Reserve Requirement

Suppose the Fed wants to ease money, so it decides to lower the reserve requirement to 19 percent. Suddenly Mr. Zimmer's bank has $10,000 in excess reserves. So do other banks all over the country. Every one dollar of these excess reserves can support an expansion of about five dollars in the nation's money supply.

Billions of dollars of lending power have been created at one fell swoop! Talk about a meat cleaver effect! Reserve requirements can't be changed or adjusted as easily and sensitively as the other monetary policy "tools." For this reason, this "tool of monetary policy" is used only infrequently and with caution.

For Tight Money, Use the Same Tools the Other Way

We have been talking about using monetary policy to bring "easy money" to overcome unemployment, recession and depression. Now

let's look at the opposite kind of problem. What kind of monetary policy should we use to slow down a runaway boom? Suppose the people and businesses are trying to buy more than the economy can produce. Shortages and waiting lists are everywhere. Inflationary pressures are serious. Prices threaten to break loose and skyrocket.

What would be the proper monetary policy to slow down total spending? That's easy to figure out. Tight money! Make money difficult to borrow, and push interest rates up. How? Raise the discount rate. Sell bonds in the open market. We might even consider raising the reserve requirement. That would be a shock!

Raising the discount rate will discourage banks from lending and it will cause them to charge higher interest rates on their loans. Selling bonds will push down open market bond prices. That will push up interest rates. You know exactly how that works now. Right? Furthermore, the checks people write to the Fed to buy the bonds will be taken right out of the banks' reserve accounts at the Fed! This will pull down bank reserves. Banks will have to restrict their lending.

When people and businesses pay off their loans the banks will have to deposit this money (the repayment money) in their reserve accounts at the Fed. They can't use the money to make more loans. So the money supply will get smaller. People will have less money to spend and it will be more difficult to borrow or to buy things on time. Will total spending slow down? You bet it will!

Open Market Operations Can Force Down Lending and Spending

Let's look at the process of tightening money using open market operations. Suppose our friend Mr. Alber has some excess cash in his bank account. He has been thinking about buying some government securities but he just hasn't gotten around to it yet. Today he hears that $1,000, 6-percent government bonds are available for a price of

$800 each. This seems like a good deal so he decides to buy some.

He buys five of the bonds—total par value of $5,000—for $4,000. He writes a $4,000 check. The check goes from the bond broker to the Federal Reserve Bank. There, $4,000 is deducted from the reserve account of Mr. Zimmer's bank. Then the check is sent to Mr. Zimmer's bank where $4,000 is deducted from Mr. Alber's account. The bank has lost $4,000 in deposits and also $4,000 in reserves. Is it in an illegal position? Yes!

That is, unless it had some excess reserves. The bank needs less reserves because it has less deposits. But *how much* less reserves does it need? Only $800 less. But it has $4,000 less!

The bank must get another $3,200 from somewhere to make up the "illegal deficit" in its Federal Reserve account. Where can it get the money? It could borrow the money from the Fed. But remember? As a part of its tight money policy the Fed has just raised the discount rate. So borrowing from the Fed is expensive!

Zimmer's bank might sell some of their securities to get more money to deposit in their reserve account. But that's expensive, too. Bond prices are depressed now. Remember? What the bank is more likely to do is to reduce its lending. As old loans are repaid the bank just won't relend the money. They'll put the money in their reserve account instead. That will get their reserve account built up again. Meanwhile they will temporarily borrow from the Fed to avoid being in an illegal reserve position.

As the bank cuts back on new loans and refuses to renew old loans, businesses will not be able to expand so much. Some may have to sell inventories, reduce their expansion plans and pull in money to pay off their loans.

The higher interest rates will reduce the demand for machines and equipment and materials, and for inventories. At the higher interest rates it becomes more expensive to carry inventories and it's more costly to buy

new machinery and equipment and things. Another thing. The capitalized value of everything goes down. You learned about high interest pushing down capitalized value from your uncle in Chincoteague. Remember? It sounds like this tight money policy is going to succeed. Will it? Maybe. That's what we'll be talking about next.

HOW EFFECTIVE IS MONETARY POLICY?

Considering all the approaches, all the tools, how effective can monetary policy be? The Fed has several decades of experience. How well have they done? Sometimes, apparently all right. Sometimes not so well. We can't really be sure. Everything the Fed has done with monetary policy has been criticized by someone or other.

The Fed has been accused of moving too slowly and doing too little. It has been accused of doing too much, of doing the wrong things, and of doing things at the wrong times. Even looking back with all the wisdom of hindsight it's hard to be sure which times the Fed did the right things, and which times it didn't. It's difficult to be sure just how effective the tools of monetary policy have been.

Our Picture of the Economy Is Always Late

One of the frustrations in trying to use monetary policy (or any kind of stabilization policy, for that matter) is that we really don't know what's going on in the economy at any moment. We can't see what's going on today. We only see what was going on some weeks ago. Trying to prescribe stabilization policies in the real world is sort of like a doctor trying to prescribe treatment for a patient who hasn't been examined for several weeks.

Try to picture this situation: You don't feel very well so you go to "a council of doctors" for tests in mid-June. Then you wait. In late July the doctors figure out what was wrong with you back in June. But the opinion is not unanimous. Several eminent doctors disagree with the diagnosis. But anyway, medicine is ordered. By the time the medicine starts you may be well again. Or you may be dead! But once the medicine starts coming, you must take it.

It may be several months before anyone can tell for sure if you're getting better or worse. Can you see why monetary policy—and all economic stabilization policy—is sort of chancy? Only when conditions in the economy *really get serious* do the economists begin (more or less) to agree on what needs to be done and how.

People Will Spend the Easy Money Only If They're Ready

In general, we can say this: If businesses and consumers are about ready and have been waiting for some little additional nudge to shake them loose, then "easy money" is likely to have a quick effect. But if businesses are very pessimistic about the future and if the people are out of jobs and deep in debt, then no amount of "easy money" is likely to induce very much increase in spending. No business is going to buy a new machine unless the owner expects to be able to sell the output! I'll bet that even if someone offered to lend your uncle the money *interest free*, he still wouldn't buy that oyster breader!

If things are really bad, consumers won't start borrowing and buying things. Who would lend money to an unemployed person who's already facing overdue debts, anyway? See how difficult it is to try to figure out what monetary policy to recommend—or which tool(s) to use? And just think how unresponsive the economy might be when things get really bad!

What about the opposite kind of macroeconomic problem—the problem of overexpansion and inflation? How effective can monetary policy be in tightened down on an "overheated economy"? We know for sure that if money gets tight enough, people and businesses will spend less. Very tight money can definitely slow down spending in the economy. There is absolutely no question about that. But what we don't know is *when* to tighten and *how much*. And still more serious, we don't know whether the induced *slowdown in spending* will have most of its effect in *reducing inflation* or in *reducing production and employment*.

Tight Money Could Result in "Overkill" and Recession

How much "tight money" do we need to "just do the job and no more"? A little bit of "overkill" when we are trying to curb the boom could result in a serious downturn in the economy. Then the multiplier and accelerator, working downward, could bring widespread unemployment and depression. We just don't know how sensitive the economy will be, when we start to tighten money.

If a slight increase in the discount rate happens to shatter business optimism, the economy could move into an immediate recession. On the other hand, the business community may completely ignore a small change in the discount rate. If the business community overreacts it may be impossible for the monetary policy to be changed back in time to avoid a recession. With your knowledge of the accelerator and the multiplier, you know how hard it is to stop a cumulative expansion or contraction once it gets going!

Economic stabilization is always sort of chancy. But the modern world economies require that the government be concerned with this issue. It can't be ignored. Sometimes problems arise which *require* action. At those times you may be sure that some action will be taken. If things don't soon improve, more (and maybe different) actions will be taken. I think you can be sure of that.

The tools of monetary policy are being used all the time. That's right. Every day, even! You will be hearing about and feeling the effects of these things all your life. When you buy a house or a car or borrow money or use your "revolving credit account" or put your money in a savings account you will be feeling the effects of monetary policy.

Monetary policy is very important in every modern economy. But it isn't the only approach to economic stabilization. Fiscal policy is another approach. You'll learn about that in the next chapter. But first Mr. or Ms. President, if I may venture a suggestion: Before you go on, maybe you should find a quiet spot out by the White House rose garden and spend some time reviewing and thinking about monetary policy.

REVIEW EXERCISES

● **MAJOR CONCEPTS, PRINCIPLES, TERMS (Explain each thoroughly.)**

> monetary policy
> changing the discount rate
> open market operations
> bond prices and interest rates
> how open market operations affect bank reserves
> how open market operations affect interest rates

● **OTHER CONCEPTS AND TERMS (Explain each briefly.)**

> easy money
> tight money
> government securities
> the "money market"

> the bond market
> "old bonds"
> the discount rate
> the "overkill" problem

● **QUESTIONS (Write out answers, or jot down key points.)**

1. For many years there has been a continuing controversy among some economists over the question of the "independence" of the Fed. Some say independence of the Fed is essential to insulate the nation's monetary policies from the whims of politicians. Others say the president is supposed to be responsible for the health of the economy, but because the Fed is independent he is denied control over the monetary policy tools he needs to do the job. What position do you take on this issue, Mr. or Ms. President? Why?

2. Under what kinds of economic conditions in the nation would you expect monetary policy to be most effective? or ineffective? Explain.

3. Can you explain how open market operations work, *both* (1) through the direct effect on the money supply and bank reserves *and* (2) through the direct effect on bond values and interest rates? It's important that you be able to do that.

4. After all is said and done, how effective do you think monetary policy really is in stabilizing the economy? Do you think it's more effective in overcoming depression? or inflation? Explain.

14 Fiscal Policy, the Automatic Stabilizers, and the National Debt

Changes in government spending or taxes can be used to speed up or slow down the economy.

How do you like pretending you are the President of the United States? A little credibility gap? Well, I guess so. But now that you are experienced at it, please stick with it a little longer. Okay?

Let's go back to where we were at the beginning of the last chapter. The economy is depressed. You, Mr. or Ms. President, are looking at the high unemployment figures and thinking, "Something must be done quickly!" You think: "The depressed economic conditions somehow must be overcome. We must get the recovery going and get those unemployed people back to work soon. At least before election day!"

If Easy Money Doesn't Work, What Then?

You have already discussed this matter at length with the Chairman of the Council of Economic Advisers, the Secretary of the Treasury, the Director of the Office of Management and Budget, the Chairman of the Federal Reserve Board and with some bankers and business people and economics professors. You are quite sure that the Fed is going to do something to bring "easy money" to the economy. But you aren't quite satisfied with that. You are still worried.

Remember at your last meeting with your advisers, you said: "Monetary policy may be just fine. But I don't trust it. All we are doing is pushing money into the banks and into the hands of the people and making it easy for businesses and consumers to borrow and buy things. *Suppose nobody wants to borrow and buy?* Suppose all anybody wants to do is put the money into a savings account and just let it sit there? Then what good will all this monetary policy do? No good! So that's why I'm worried."

USING FISCAL POLICY TO INDUCE PROSPERITY

All the economists agree that monetary policy is a sort of indirect approach to the problem. It depends on what the people do. Are they going to borrow, and spend? Mr. Alber's new bank deposit certainly isn't going to increase the money supply any further unless Mr. Baker or somebody comes in and borrows the new excess reserves. If everyone is as pessimistic as your uncle in Chincoteague, there isn't going to be much borrowing and spending, easy money or not!

Fiscal Policy Can Be More Direct Than Monetary Policy

You are impatient, Mr. or Ms. President. You say, "Isn't there some way we can take *more direct* action to solve this problem? Can't we just take the bull by the horns and do something that doesn't depend on what a lot of consumers and businesses decide to do?" Yes, there is something. Your economic advisers agree that you could *increase government spending*. That would be *sure* to put more spending into the total spending flow of the economy.

How obvious! Instead of trying to do something to induce the consumers and businesses (C + I) to increase their spending, why not just come in and increase government spending (G) directly? Once you think of it, how obvious it is! The surest way to increase total spending is to increase it yourself! So you decide to do that. You decide to go to Congress and persuade them to pass some new spending bills—some new "appropriations legislation."

Increase Government Spending or Cut Taxes

You might try to persuade Congress to appropriate enough money so the government could *hire all the unemployed people*. That certainly would be the most direct way to solve the unemployment problem! Or you might get the Congress to appropriate money to build new school buildings and post offices and highways and recreation areas and military bases. That would create more jobs, more incomes, more spending. Maybe the multiplier and the accelerator would catch on and take it from there. Do you try it? Maybe not.

Maybe you decide that this is not a good time to try to get Congress to increase government spending. Maybe you decide to try to get them to cut taxes instead. If the government takes less taxes out of my paycheck, I get to keep more money and very likely I will spend more. If enough people spend enough more,

that will solve the problem. Or maybe the government will cut taxes on business profits. Then businesses will be likely to spend more for investment and hire more people and produce more. That might do the trick.

So which will you do, Mr. or Ms. President? Why not try some of both? Increase spending some and cut taxes some. Use both "tools" of compensatory fiscal policy. When you adjust taxes or spending to "compensate" for too little (or too much) spending by consumers and businesses this is called "compensatory fiscal policy." Suppose you decide to try it. First you plan to cut personal income taxes and leave more money in everybody's paycheck. This should push total consumer spending up and help to get things going again. So you get some of your friends in Congress and some lawyers to start drafting a tax-cut bill.

The Program Must Meet Political Realities

While the tax-cut bill is being prepared, you begin working with a group of Congressional leaders drafting a program of expenditures for federal public works projects—new highways and streets, water and sewer systems, public buildings, things like that. Each senator wants several projects "for the old home state." All the members of Congress want one or more projects in their home districts. All the "party faithful" governors and mayors throughout the country expect to be rewarded for their party loyalties.

This could get out of hand! They can't all have everything they want. Too much government spending would create much more factor demand than there are factors available. *Surplus* would suddenly become *shortage*. Total spending or "aggregate demand" would be too great for the productive capacity of the economy. Prices would break loose and go up. You don't want that to happen. You want to do enough, but *not too much!*

Finally, after many precious weeks have been lost in haggling, your legislative program for compensatory fiscal policy" is ready to be offered to Congress. You go to Congress and give an impressive speech in support of the tax cut and the "public works" spending program. You urge Congress to take speedy action on these high priority measures. But then what?

The weeks drag by and nothing much seems to happen. Several leaders of Congress express concern about your program. "Spend more, and tax less? Blatant fiscal irresponsibility!" Some of your own party, but mostly the opposition, keep making noises about the "government deficit" which your proposed program is going to bring about.

Other members of Congress (and their economic advisers) say the program is one of overkill. They say: "The economy is about ready to start booming anyway. This big push by government will bring shortages and inflation for sure!"

Still others say the opposite: "We are really on the verge of a serious depression. Inventories are high and general confidence is low. Just look at the recent stock market slide, for example! The President's proposed program is too little and too late. It's only a drop in the bucket. Let's build a public works program big enough to do the job!"

How Much Fiscal Action Is Needed?

Who is right? Is your program the right size? With the right emphasis? Or not? What about your economic advisers and the economist-statisticians (econometricians) with their highly refined computerized models of the economic system. Can't they tell you the answer? No. Unfortunately they can't. They can make very scientific-looking guesses, but there's no way they can tell what the people and businesses are going to do, once your program gets started. They can *estimate*, but they can't tell for sure.

Suppose inventories are down to low levels and businesses are looking for some little excuse to begin restocking their shelves. Suppose consumers only need some little indication that things are going to get better. They are just waiting for some excuse to run out and start buying new vacuum cleaners and refrigerators and stoves and furniture and TV sets and automobiles and flared hip-hugger jeans and all. The multiplier and the accelerator are lying just under the surface, poised for action. In these conditions not much government spending or government hiring or tax cutting will be needed to speed up the economy. But under different circumstances, things could be quite different.

The More the Economy Is Overstocked, the Slower the Recovery

Suppose most businesses—manufacturers, wholesalers, retailers—are overstocked with (and are deeply in debt for) excess inventories. And suppose most consumers have just recently been on a buying binge. Every family has a new car, new refrigerator, new furniture, new everything and is up to their ears in debt. Now how much must the government cut taxes and increase spending to get the economy to speed up? Quite a lot!

When taxes are cut and government spending increased, people and businesses will just take the extra money and pay off their debts. Nobody will start buying new cars or TV sets or things. Businesses won't hire anybody. The toy factory is so overstocked with toys that it would be able to meet the Christmas boom without hiring anybody to make another toy!

The economy is overchoked with inventory, with excess manufacturing capacity, and with debt. The multiplier and accelerator are buried deep under all this mass of inventory and excess plant capacity and debt. Until some of the inventories and debts are cleared away the "multiple expansion process" will work only very sluggishly, if at all. That's what happens in a big-big boom. We build big inventories and big debts. Now you can see why a very big boom is likely to lead to a very bad depression.

Is there any way that you, Mr. or Ms. President, can find out whether or not the economy is about ready to surge forward? Or if it is buried in excess inventories and debt? Luckily, there is. During the past few decades great progress has been made in keeping tabs on what's going on in the economy.

Reports from the Departments of Commerce, Labor, Agriculture and others, from the Fed, and from many other sources tell how much the consumers are in debt, how old the average automobile is, how much inventory is being carried in each industry, what the businesses and consumers are buying these days, and all sorts of things. These statistics help a lot. But they can't tell you everything.

Reactions of Consumers and Businesses Are Hard to Predict

The statistics can't tell for sure how businesses and consumers will react to changing circumstances. It's much easier to tell how old a person's car is than to tell whether or not that person will buy another car this year if taxes are cut by 8 percent. It's much easier to tell the level of debt in an industry than to tell how much sales must increase to set off an inventory expansion.

Individuals make their economic choices on the basis of their outlook—their expectations. They seem to all move at the same time. Now you know how a cowboy feels when he's trying to figure out how much noise it will take to move the cattle without stampeding the herd! It's the same kind of question. Sometimes the cattle are spooky and poised for a quick move. How much noise? Just a little! At other times the cattle are feeling overfed and lazy. It takes quite a lot to make them move.

We take all kinds of surveys and opinion polls to find out what people and businesses *think* they are going to do. This information helps. But sometimes people don't really know what they're going to do until the time comes. People and businesses have a tendency to do whatever the people and businesses just down the street are doing. This makes "economic forecasting" very hazardous.

So what now, Mr. or Ms. President? Want to change your mind and withdraw from the race? You really don't know how much or what kinds of "fiscal policy" action to take. Cut taxes? How much? Increase spending? Spend for what? How much? You can see the problem. You face the real possibility of "ineffectiveness" or of "overkill." The very best program you and your advisers could design might hit far from the mark. But no matter. The program you design isn't going to get through Congress anyway.

Congress Doesn't Always Cooperate

Tax cuts and spending projects are of *great* interest to Congress. So no matter what you do, Congress is going to have the last word on this taxing-spending program. Some members of Congress will be fighting for what they see as "the good of the nation." Others will be fighting for reelection or to pay back a political favor or for some other reason. Some of them may even be fighting for your job! But all of them will be fighting.

Which taxes will be cut? and by how much? and what projects will be undertaken? and where? and when?—all of these matters will ultimately be decided by Congress. Not by you. Political considerations are likely to outweigh the economic considerations in *every one* of these taxing and spending decisions. Even though you and your advisers had known with absolute certainty what *should* be done, it is almost an absolute certainty that your "perfect program" couldn't have gotten through Congress anyway!

You, Mr. or Ms. President, are facing a tough problem. I suppose the best thing you can do is, first: be sure you have good economic advisers. Then work with them to design a program which you think will be effective and which you think Congress will pass. Then cross your fingers and go ahead. If you do everything carefully (and if you're lucky) maybe you will get to have a second term in the White House after all.

What we are talking about is "compensatory fiscal policy," or just fiscal policy. It's a powerful tool if you get it to work right. You can adjust taxes and spending to overcome depression. You can also use fiscal policy to hold down a boom and fight inflation.

USING FISCAL POLICY TO CURB INFLATION

Suppose almost everyone is trying to buy a new TV set and a new car and a new washing machine and new furniture and new hip-hugger jeans and other things. And suppose every manufacturer of automobiles and home appliances and furniture is trying to double plant capacity and every wholesaler and retailer is trying to expand inventory. Can all these demands be met? Obviously not. There's just no way!

Everybody is working overtime, making lots of money and trying to buy things. But everywhere you look there are shortages, waiting lists, people standing in line—delayed deliveries for everything. Some people have the attitude: "I want what I want and I want it now!" People are bidding against each other,

trying to get the available things. Prices are being forced up.

Automobile dealers are making big profits. Many dealers start paying extra to try to get more cars than their normal allotments. The same thing is going on in the TV markets, in furniture, appliances, and in everything else. The manufacturers are twisting every arm they can twist, paying extra to try to get more machinery, more steel, more delivery trucks, more coal, more labor, more everything.

The Threat of Inflation

Do you see the picture? It's a booming economy, all right. The acceleration principle is working full force. An economy booming at this pace is headed almost certainly for two disastrous results. The first is rapid price inflation which will eat up a lot of the purchasing power which is now making Mr. and Ms. Average Consumer feel so wealthy. They're going to find out that they won't really be able to buy the cars and the appliances and all the other things that they thought they were going to buy with all of their money. They're going to pay higher prices than they thought and run out of money sooner (and/or be in debt deeper) than they expected.

What's the situation with the business firms? All businesses are trying to expand as fast as they can. They're ordering more inventories, machines, factories, everything. The railroads have ordered thousands of new railroad cars but deliveries are very slow. The steel companies have ordered several new iron ore pelletizing plants to be installed in upper Michigan, Wisconsin and Minnesota. But the installations are being delayed by shortages of labor and materials. The seafood producers and packers—shrimp on the Gulf, oysters in the Chesapeake Bay area, flounder fillets and lobsters in New England—all have ordered the most modern labor-saving machinery and equipment. But deliveries are very slow.

These are "good times" from the point of view of employment. Everybody who wants a job gets a job. Income is good. Producers are begging workers to work overtime. That's great. But shortages are everywhere. Prices and wages are under serious pressure to break loose and start leap-frogging each other until they go out of sight over the horizon!

The Threat of Overbuilding then Collapse

In addition to the inflation threat, another disaster is threatening. Everybody is ordering things, stocking up. Businesses are buying machines and equipment and inventories and going into debt. Consumers are stocking up on cars and refrigerators and other consumer durables and going into debt. Manufacturers are expanding their plants and installing new machines and going into debt. This rate of expansion can't possibly be sustained for very long.

If this big boom continues, soon there will come a day (in the next year or two) when everybody will have everything they want and be head over heels in debt. Consumers will have new cars, furniture, appliances, well-stocked freezers and be head over heels in debt. Businesses will have all the inventory they could possibly want and be head over heels in debt. Manufacturers will have all the plant capacity they could possibly want, and be deep in debt. Then what will happen? Recession? Of course.

Eventually the inventory buildup will cease. "Normal" levels of demand will return. The factories which have been producing to meet the boom-time demand for the build-up will no longer be able to stay busy. They will cut back production. Overtime work will cease. Some unemployment will develop. You know what happens next.

The unemployed people stop buying as much. So retail stores stop ordering as much.

Soon the wholesalers and retailers stop ordering altogether and just sell out of their overstocked inventories. Spending slows down even more. Unemployment spreads. Businesses and consumers stop spending and start trying to pay off their debts. Here comes our depression again! Scary, isn't it?

See why we want to hold down total spending in this supercharged economy? We want to keep from getting hit by the one-two punch of runaway inflation followed by economic collapse and depression. How do we cool down this excessive boom before it's too late? You already know about the monetary policy tools of raising the discount rate and selling bonds in the open market to pull money out of the economy. But what about the *fiscal policy* tools?

Cut Government Spending or Raise Taxes to Hold Down the Boom

One way to curb the boom with fiscal policy is to increase taxes on businesses and consumers. This will force them to cut back their spending. The other way is to cut back on government spending. Delay all new government projects and slow down or stop ongoing projects. This reduces the demand for labor and the other factors of production. Reduced government spending will release factors of production so they can shift to (and relieve shortages in) the "private sector" of the economy.

Would this "counter-inflationary fiscal policy" (increasing taxes and cutting back government spending) really work? Yes, it really would. Except that you will have all the problems you had before. Here are some questions to be considered:

How much to raise taxes? Which taxes? How much to cut back spending? Which projects to stop? Slow down? Delay? Which government employees to lay off? Which private business contracts to cancel? How do I get the answers? And then: how do I get the Congress to go along?

Cutting Spending and Raising Taxes May Mean Political Suicide

Suppose you could get the "exactly right" answers to all these questions (which you can't). Would you then prepare a message and go to Congress urging the tax increases and the spending cuts? Do you want to go down in history (or into the next election) known as the tax-raising, project-cancelling boom-killer? Suppose you're willing to take that chance. How many members of Congress do you think will go along with you?

Later, when you're out stumping the country campaigning for the next election, you will explain to the people why it was necessary to raise taxes and cut back their favorite projects.

- You will explain that the tax increase didn't take nearly as much of their purchasing power away as the *inflation* would have taken, so they're really better off paying more taxes!
- You will explain that the reason you canceled all their government projects—the new hospital and the pollution-free sewer system and the manpower training program and the promised bridge across the river—is that "they, the people" were spending so much for new cars and appliances and things that there weren't enough factors of production left over to keep the government projects going.
- You will tell them all about opportunity costs—that "You can't have your cake and eat it too. The economy can't produce any more than it can produce."

You will teach them all sorts of good lessons in sound economics. Guess what they'll tell you! (I'm sure you can guess.) Even if they

know you're telling the truth, this isn't the kind of truth people like to hear.

They might ask why you didn't cancel the foreign aid programs instead of the domestic programs, and why you didn't cancel any of the programs in *your own* home state. Can you begin to see the difficulty of raising taxes and cutting government spending to fight inflation? It can be made to work, yes. But it isn't easy.

Even if you didn't have to worry about the political repercussions and even if you could get Congress to go along with your program, counter-inflationary fiscal policy is tricky business. How much should you increase taxes or reduce spending? That's hard to say. You always face the problem of choosing the right "dose"—between ineffectiveness and overkill.

THE AUTOMATIC STABILIZERS

By now you know for sure that fiscal policy is not an easy, quick way to stabilize the economy. But wait. Here's some good news for a change. To some extent, compensatory fiscal policy works automatically!

Some Government Spending and Taxes Adjust Automatically

So the economy is speeding up too much and you, Mr. or Ms. President, are worried about an over-boom, shortages, inflation— and then recession. Maybe depression. You would like to increase taxes and cut back government spending. Why? To slow down the rapid increase in the spending stream!

But you're nervous about calling for higher taxes and spending cuts. And you don't think Congress would go along with that idea anyway. But take heart! *Taxes are going to go up automatically! Some spending programs are going to be cut back automatically, too!*

The Progressive Federal Income Tax. The federal income tax is "progressive." That is, the tax rate gets higher as your income gets higher. So as the economy booms and people get more income they automatically pay higher tax rates. As the income stream gets larger and larger the government keeps pulling more and more money out of it. Just automatically! Here's an example.

Suppose Mr. Snyder is a construction worker, but construction has been slow. He only managed to earn $6,500 last year. Considering that he has a wife and three children, he had to pay only about $200 in federal income taxes. That's only about 3% of his income.

This year things are much better. Mr. Snyder's income is up to $13,000. That's twice as much income. And his federal income taxes? Up to $1,400. That's seven times as much! This year his taxes are up to about 11% of his income. But that's not all. For every additional dollar he earns (over $13,000) he's going to have to pay 22% of it in taxes!

Suppose the economy really goes into a boom next year and Mr. Snyder gets higher wages and works a lot of overtime. His income doubles again—up to $26,000. He will have to pay about $5,000 (about 3½ times as much as this year) in federal income taxes. Now his tax rate is up to almost 20% of his income. For each additional dollar he earns now (over $26,000) he's going to have to pay 32% in federal income taxes.

See how the federal government automatically pulls a lot more money out of the spending-income stream when the economy starts to boom? It works the other way too, of course. When the construction boom slows down and Mr. Snyder's income goes down, his "effective federal income tax rate" will automatically go down, too. If his income ever drops down to $5,000, his "effective tax rate" will drop to zero!

Is this "automatic tax adjustment" big enough to really have any effect on the economy? It sure is! It results in billions of dollars of extra tax withdrawals when the economy is expanding. Sometimes the effect is so strong that it prevents the economy from expanding as much as it should. When this happens it's called fiscal drag. Sometimes a tax cut may be needed to cut down the "fiscal drag" and let the economy continue to expand toward full employment!

Spending for Unemployment Compensation and Welfare. It's obvious that payments for unemployment compensation and for welfare programs will work against the business cycle. When times are bad more people draw unemployment compensation and more people go on the public welfare rolls. When business picks up, most of these people become self-supporting again.

Is this "unemployment and welfare" expenditure adjustment great enough to do any good? Yes, it sure is. When the economy slows down, billions of dollars of new government spending flow to individuals and families who need it and who will spend it right away. Their marginal propensity to consume (MPC) is likely to be high so the impact of this spending on the economy is likely to be high. The "induced consumer spending" (and therefore the income multiplier) is likely to be high.

Over the years, as the welfare and unemployment programs have been increased, the "automatic stabilizing effect" of government spending has increased also. Probably these "automatic stabilizing" expenditure programs will be increased even more in the future.

Later in this book you'll be reading about ideas for a "negative income tax"—that is, automatic payments to people whenever their incomes fall below some minimum size. If the negative income tax is ever established in this country—and someday it probably will be—

that will provide an even further increase in the automatic stabilizing effect of government spending.

People's Spending Doesn't Adjust Quickly to Their Earnings

You've spent a lot of time in this book learning about the consumption function. You know that people's spending for consumer goods is determined by the size of their incomes. Right? Well, the purpose of this little section is to tell you "It ain't necessarily so." Not exactly, anyway. Not for any short period of time.

It usually takes people a while to adjust to a new "income situation"—especially if the new income is a *lower* income. People who are hit by hard times usually try to hang on to their old standard of living as long as they can, hoping things will soon get better. For a while they can spend their savings or sell some things or go into debt to keep up their old standard.

If hard times continue long enough, sooner or later they must learn to get by on less expensive housing, food, clothing, transportation, recreation, medical and dental care, etc. But the important thing is this: during times when people's incomes are falling, consumer spending tends to stay high—at least for a while. This "consumer spending buoyancy" helps to support the economy, to use up excess inventories, and to get the economy on the upswing again. If the recession is short, people may get their jobs back soon enough so that their consumer spending doesn't have to be cut back at all!

What about an over-boom? You know how savings increase as incomes increase. Suppose people's incomes are going up fast. Some people will spend it as fast as they get it. Sure. But many people won't.

Many people will let some savings pile up before they move into a better place, buy another car, start wearing more expensive clothes and eating steak and lobster twice a day. See how these savings withdrawals could hold down the boom? They really do, too. It's hard to say just how much this "consumer spending stability" helps. But it's for sure it helps a lot.

Many Corporations Follow "Stabilized Dividend" Policies

There's another automatic stabilizing influence that needs to be mentioned: corporate dividend payments to stockholders. In the mid-1970's corporations are paying out between $30 and $40 billion a year in dividends. That isn't a "massive amount" when compared with a national income of well over a trillion dollars! But it's at least big enough so that its "marginal stabilizing effect" can be important. How does it work? Like this.

Suppose there's a big boom and big profits. Do corporations pay out more in dividends? Usually, yes. A little more. But not *much* more. They just hold most of the extra profits as "undistributed profits," to reinvest.

Suppose the economy slows down and the corporations don't make much profits. Maybe many of them have losses. Do they pay out less in dividends? Usually, yes. A little less, but not much less. Usually they pay out some of the "undistributed profits" from previous years.

What's the effect of all this? It pulls some "consumer spending money" out of the spending stream during boom times and pushes some extra "consumer-spending money" into the stream when things are slack. The net effect is to help to stabilize the economy.

How Effective Are the Automatic Stabilizers?

The "automatic fiscal policy stabilizers" (automatic spending and taxing adjustments) can help a lot. When aided by the stabilizing effects of consumer spending stability and corporate dividend policies, they can go a long way toward bringing economic stability.

The economy has been more stable since World War II. Has it been because of the automatic stabilizers? No one can say for sure. But there's no question that they deserve some of the credit.

But this we do know for sure: the automatic stabilizers are not enough. Sometimes discretionary stabilization policy—like monetary policy and compensatory fiscal policy—is going to be required. That is, when things get bad enough, Mr. or Ms. President, you have to make up your mind that it's time to do something and you have to decide what to do and then you have to do it. That's "discretionary stabilization policy." So now that you know something about the automatic stabilizers, let's go back and talk about the effectiveness of "discretionary fiscal policy."

HOW EFFECTIVE IS "DISCRETIONARY COMPENSATORY FISCAL POLICY"?

So what can we say about "discretionary compensatory fiscal policy?" Is it effective? Maybe. Sometimes. If we are willing to take enough fiscal policy action during depression—cutting taxes, increasing expenditures, hiring people on government payrolls, buying up surplus outputs and so on—we can definitely overcome the depression. If the government adds enough spending to bring the economy up to full employment, then we will have full employment. Obviously!

We can also be sure that if we are willing to take enough fiscal policy action during times of shortages and inflationary pressures, we can cut back the inflationary pressure. But in both these cases we run the risk of "overkill." Each time we move to overcome depressed conditions we run the risk of driving the economy into inflation. Each time we move to hold down inflationary spending we run the risk of generating unemployment and recession. How stabilization works out *depends so much on expectations.*

Fiscal policy is not a "fine-tuning knob" for economic stabilization. We can't hope to use it to maintain "just the right level" of spending, employment, output, and income. When we try to solve our macroeconomic problems with fiscal policy, we go after them not with a surgeon's scalpel but with a meat cleaver. Any time "meat cleaver action" is justified, fiscal policy will work. It may work too much or it may work too little, but it will work.

Whenever serious depression threatens, you may be sure that Congress will take some fiscal policy action. And you may be sure that *it will work.* For this reason you may be sure there will never be another disastrous depression in the American economy. The government will not let it happen.

We might overdo it and run into inflation. But no doubt we will take that chance. We might have to establish wage and price controls—maybe government rationing, even. But it seems clear that the people would prefer widespread economic controls to widespread unemployment. The point is this: there are, today, *known alternatives* to serious depression. It seems to be a safe bet that fiscal policy will be used to whatever extent necessary to prevent serious and prolonged depression.

Yes, the government will use fiscal policy sometimes—and it will work. Not perfectly, but well enough. If it doesn't work well enough at first, then more and different things will be done *until it does work* at least "well enough."

The government will unbalance the budget and run deficits and add to the debt as much as necessary to get things going again. But what will all these deficits and debts do to the economy? Let's talk about that.

FISCAL POLICY, THE UNBALANCED BUDGET, AND THE NATIONAL DEBT

Maybe you haven't thought about it yet, but "discretionary compensatory fiscal policy" really is a policy of *unbalancing the federal* budget on purpose! The idea is that if total spending is too small, let's increase government spending (that will *directly* increase the size of the spending flow in the economy) and let's reduce taxes (that will *indirectly* increase the size of the spending flow in the economy). But increasing spending while cutting taxes obviously means "unbalancing the budget." It means "deficit financing." It means "increasing the national debt." What about that? Isn't that bad?

A Budget Deficit
Increases the Debt

When the budget is unbalanced and all of the tax revenues coming in don't provide enough money to support the government's spending, how does the government make up the difference? It sells bonds, of course. If it sells the bonds to individuals and businesses and banks and insurance companies and all, this pulls money out of the economic system. Then when the government spends the money it puts the money back into the economic system. When the government does this the federal debt gets larger. The government owes the debt to the people who are holding the bonds.

Suppose the government did not sell the bonds to individuals and businesses and banks and insurance companies and all, but sold them to the Federal Reserve Banks instead. What difference would that make? Quite a lot! A "Federal Reserve financed government deficit" would be much more stimulating to the economy. Why? Because then the government would be *creating new money* and putting it into the economy. New *high-powered* money!

When the Fed buys new treasury bonds, the Fed simply creates the money. It creates a new demand deposit (treasury deposit) for the government (just like Zimmer's bank created a new demand deposit for Baker). With the new deposit the Treasury can write checks to hire

people or can buy up surplus things or can start new programs or whatever.

Borrowing from the Fed
Creates High-Powered Money

When the Treasury borrows from the Fed, it works like this: the Federal Reserve Banks receive newly printed government bonds (just as Zimmer's bank received Baker's newly written promissory note). Then the Federal Reserve Banks add the amount to the Treasury's deposit. It's as simple as that! The Treasury now has more money—a bigger deposit balance—in the Federal Reserve Banks. The national debt is bigger, and the Treasury has that much more money to spend. See how easy it is for the government to get all the money it wants?

Soon the Treasury will start spending the new money. Checks will be paid to people and businesses throughout the country. What do you suppose all those people and businesses are going to do with their government checks? Deposit them, of course! Then when each check clears, see what happens? The new money is pulled out of the Treasury's deposit at the Fed and goes into each bank's reserve account at the Fed. The new money soon becomes *new reserves for banks* all over the country!

See how a government deficit, financed by borrowing from the Federal Reserve, creates new money? The new money is paid to people and businesses by government checks. Then the checks are deposited in the banks and the money becomes new reserves for the banking system. Then a multiple expansion of the money supply can result.

When the government uses deficit financing and "covers the deficit" by selling bonds to the Fed, that can have a very stimulating effect on the economy. The increase in government spending pays money to people and businesses. That's the initial increase in the total spending flow. Then if the people have an MPC greater than zero (that is, if they respend *any* of their new income) there will be a multiplier effect. Spending will increase even more.

This kind of fiscal policy has a strong "easy money" monetary policy locked into it—but only when the government sells the bonds to the Federal Reserve Banks. When the government sells the bonds to individuals and businesses and banks and insurance companies, that just gathers up existing money—money they wanted to invest in government bonds. Then when the government spends the money, that just pushes the money back into the economy again. No money is created. See how much difference it makes whether or not the deficit is financed by the Fed buying the bonds?

Is the Government Debt Good? Or Bad?

From what you know about the government debt, what do you think of it? Do you think it would be good if we could just "wish it away"? Would we be better off? To get at this question, first let's think about debt, in general. Surely I'd like to "wish away" the mortgage on my house! If you owe anybody money I'll bet you'd like to "wish away" that debt too!

But suppose somebody owes you money. Do you want that debt "wished away"? Do you have a savings account? Or a checking account? Then the bank or savings and loan *owes you* your money. Right? How would you like it if their debt to you was suddenly "wished away"? Not so good, huh? If the mortgage debt on my house was "wished away" then your savings account in the savings and loan that lent me the money would have to be "wished away" too. So when we look at it from both sides, maybe debt is not such a bad thing.

Is the debt on my house a good thing? I must think so or else I wouldn't have agreed to create it. I would not have borrowed. The savings and loan company must think it's a good thing too, or else they wouldn't have agreed to create it. They wouldn't have lent me the money. The people who sold the house to me thought the debt was a good thing, because it enabled me to buy the house. I wouldn't have been able to buy the house unless I could borrow the money and create the debt. That's for sure! So, all things considered, I guess the mortgage debt on my house must be a good thing.

All of Our Money Is Debt*

What do we use as money in this country? Debt? That's exactly right. Nothing but debt. *Absolutely* nothing but debt! The money supply is made up of demand deposits and currency. The demand deposits are the debts of the banks. If you have a checking account in a bank, that bank *owes you* your money. It's their debt to you.

What about the currency in your pocket? Currency is issued by the Federal Reserve Banks. Each one-dollar bill or ten-dollar bill or fifty dollar bill is a debt (a "liability") of one of the twelve Federal Reserve Banks.

What do the banks use to "back up" their demand deposit money? You remember: their Federal Reserve accounts. More debt? Sure. Where did all those Federal Reserve deposits come from, anyway? Where did we get all that "high-powered money" to back up all these billions of dollars of demand deposit money? Can you guess? From the federal debt, maybe? Of course.

The government printed up bonds and "sold" them to the Federal Reserve Banks. That gave the Treasury new deposits, which they spent. The money went to businesses and people and then was deposited in the banks. Next the new money became new reserve deposits at the Federal Reserve Banks. That's exactly what happened.

---

* Economists sometimes define money as different from other kinds of debt—but no need to get into that issue here.

The Government Debt Supports Money Supply Expansions

The growth of the money supply in the United States (and all in other modern countries) has come about through the creation of new government debt. The government debt becomes "monetized." It becomes money! The newly created money moves into the banking system and creates new reserves. Then the new reserves support the multiple expansion of the money supply.

So is government debt good? Or bad? Would you like to "wish away" that part of the government debt which is supporting our money supply? You wouldn't want that any more than I would.

Furthermore, as the economy grows, national income and national product grow. More people and more businesses are doing and making and buying and selling more things. So do we need a larger money supply? Of course. How do we get it? From the expansion of loan-created demand deposit money? Sure. And where do the new reserves come from to permit all these new demand deposits? The new reserves are created by the expansion of "monetized government debt."

So some of the government debt helps to support (and through the Fed's open market operations, helps to regulate) the money supply. That's okay. But what about the part of the federal debt which wasn't sold to the Fed? What about the "non-monetized" part of the debt—that is, the bonds and notes which were sold to the people and banks and insurance companies and all? What effect does that have? Would it be good if all this part of the debt suddenly could be "wished away"?

Non-Monetized Government Debt Serves a Purpose, Too

One thing is sure. The two government bonds I own are not going to be "wished away"! (Not if I can help it.) And my bank holds millions of dollars worth of government bonds. If that part of the debt is "wished away" my bank is going to go broke and all my money (deposits) will be wiped out. I'm not in favor of that! The insurance company that I am depending on to help me in my retirement years or to pay my survivors if something happens to me—that company holds millions of dollars worth of government securities, too. If that part of the debt is "wished away" the company is going to go broke and my retirement years will be lean and hungry!

I suppose the government could collect more money in taxes and then use the money to pay off (buy back) all those privately-held bonds. But that would take a lot of taxes. A lot of money would have to be pulled out of the spending-income stream. I don't think we want to do that. You can guess what the economic (and political!) consequences of that would be!

The people and companies holding the bonds don't want to get rid of the bonds. They own government securities because they've decided that's the best thing for them to do with their money. That's the best kind of "asset" for them to invest in. If they wanted to they could get cash for their bonds any day. Since they don't, it's pretty obvious that they don't want to.

So what do you think about the government debt? Is it good? Or bad? By now I think you can see that it is more good than bad. It's certainly a lot better to have it than it would be to get rid of it!

As time goes on the federal debt is going to get bigger. I think you can be sure of that. But there's no reason to get excited about that. When people get excited about the size of the government debt it's usually because they don't understand it.

Federal Debt, GNP, and Private Debt: A Comparison

If the size of the federal debt is alarming to you, perhaps it will be comforting for you to look at these comparisons:

1. At the end of World War II (1945) the federal debt was about the same size as the gross national product. It totaled about $200 billion. At that time, total private debt in this country was about $150 billion.
2. By 1960, the federal debt had increased by 25 percent (to about $250 billion). The gross national product had increased by 150 percent (to $500 billion), and total private debt had almost quadrupled (to almost $600 billion).

See what's happening? The federal government debt is getting larger, but not nearly as fast as either GNP or total private debt.

3. From 1960 to the early 1970s, the federal debt increased by more than 60 percent (to more than $400 billion), gross national product increased by more than 100 percent (to more than $1,100 billion), and private debt *almost tripled* again (to about $1,500 billion).
4. By the mid-1970's the federal debt was approaching $600 billion, GNP had passed $1,500 billion and private debt had long since passed $2,000 billion.

Just look at the growth in that private debt! Should we be worried about that? My home mortgage is a part of that. Should we be worried about that part? Suppose the total size of the private debt started coming down? Would that be good? What would that mean?

It would mean that people were paying off their home mortgages and that fewer people were buying houses. Or it would mean that businesses were paying off their loans and were not re-borrowing to expand and produce more. It would mean that the economy was slowing down. Unemployment would be high. Hard times would be here.

Private debt and government debt are very different in many ways. But both are functioning parts of our economic and monetary systems. It just doesn't make sense to look at the size of either and be alarmed.

The "Burdens" of Debt

Aren't there any burdens of debt? Of course there are. Debt sometimes can be very oppressive to people. When people try to consume at a higher rate than they are producing, they go deeper and deeper into debt. If they keep it up, someday their past will catch up with them. They may have a miserable time trying to pay off all those debts! But government debt and the great mass of private debt in this country and in all the other modern countries aren't that kind of thing at all. Debt is an essential part of the market system. It is a part of the exchange mechanism. As the economic system grows, debts will grow.

If anyone ever asks if debt is bad, ask them these questions: Is money bad? Are government bonds bad? Are savings accounts bad? Are mortgages bad? Debt isn't bad. Back in the early chapters of this book you saw how efficiently debt can provide for the monetary needs of the society. You saw the wise old northside chief create all that money. Those checking accounts. Those "bank debts." Remember?

To be sure, debt can create problems. The "borrowing privilege" can be (sometimes is) abused. This is as true for the federal government as it is for an individual. But consequences of "debt abuse" by the federal government are different—are in fact *completely unrelated*—to the consequences of debt abuse by an individual or a family or a business. That's one reason why there's always so much misunderstanding about the federal debt.

The Consequences of "Debt Abuse" by the Federal Government

There are several kinds of problems associated with the federal debt. But the greatest danger results from the *opportunity to be irresponsible*—to go to extremes. A rapid increase in the debt can generate too rapid an increase in the money supply. This can generate inflation and do serious harm to the economy.

Some members of Congress may try to use government debt to "make political hay." Congress can run a large deficit, create money, and undertake many projects to "woo votes" from the people back home. When a member of Congress comes up for reelection (every two years) if he or she can show the people back home lots of government projects and increased jobs and incomes—with no increase in taxes—you can guess who is likely to get the votes! See how great the temptation might be?

It isn't the *existing size* of the federal debt that creates the problem. It's the rapid expansion in the money supply and in total spending which can result from the *rapid expansion* in the size of the debt. Of course, if the economy is depressed, the increase in total spending will help the economy to get going again. And that brings us back to the idea of unbalancing the federal budget *on purpose*, to overcome depression or inflation.

More Spending May Bring More Jobs, and More Tax Revenues

"Deficit financing" (spending more than is collected in taxes) can support public works projects and reemploy people. This can increase incomes and spending. If it does, it will generate more tax revenues for the government. If the "deficit financing fiscal policy" is completely successful, the economy will regain its prosperity. People will have good incomes and will pay a lot more taxes. All those extra tax revenues may bring the government budget back into balance—or even generate a surplus!

When people pay taxes, the money goes into the Treasury accounts at the Federal Reserve Banks. If the government runs a surplus, the extra money can be used to "buy back" the bonds from the Fed. So the new money, initially created by the deficit, can be pulled back

out of the economy as tax revenues, and destroyed. Isn't that neat? Here's how it might happen:

The deficit spending brings an economic expansion. People get jobs and earn more incomes so they pay more taxes. All this extra tax money creates a government budget surplus. The government then can use this surplus money to pay off some of the money-creating (Fed-held) debt. So the money which was created in the first place is gathered up out of the economy (by taxes) and then destroyed. (It doesn't usually happen this way. But sometimes it does.)

THE "CHEER UP" APPROACH TO OVERCOMING DEPRESSION

You know about the importance of expectations in influencing the economy. Expectations influence the amount businesses will spend for factories, equipment, inventories, everything. Expectations play a big role in influencing consumer spending for new cars, TV sets and other consumer durables.

If everyone expects high employment and good times, the spending rate is likely to be high. But people who expect unemployment (and surpluses and special sales and price-cuts) tomorrow, will not go out and spend today. They will wait until the surpluses and price cutting begin. They may also be waiting to see if they still have jobs!

Optimistic Expectations Bring Good Times

See how important expectations are? If everyone thinks there is going to be high employment and a great demand for things and rising prices, then that is exactly what will happen. Everyone goes out and buys before the shortages occur and before the prices rise. So what happens? All this spending *creates* the shortages and rising prices the people are *expecting!* Maybe if they hadn't expected it, it wouldn't have happened.

Here's a specific example: In February, 1976, the Chinese lunar Year of the Dragon began. Well-informed Chinese know that the dragon will bring financial success and prosperity. The prophets prophesied profits. So what happened? As the Year of the Dragon began, Asian investors began buying heavily. Stock prices soared in Hong Kong, Singapore, Taipei and Manila!

We can say it this way: If people expect rising prices and shortages and high levels of employment, that is exactly what they will get. But if people expect unemployment, surpluses, and widespread price cutting, then everyone waits. Because of the waiting and the drop in spending, the people get exactly what they expected! Many lose their jobs. The economy goes into recession. It's sort of a "self-fulfilling prophecy." Whatever the people *expect* to happen, that's what *will* happen.

If you're still playing the role of President and trying to overcome a depression, maybe this discussion of the importance of "expectations" will give you some ideas. Perhaps if some very important person (maybe the President of the United States) makes optimistic announcements, maybe the people will start spending more.

Maybe you should arrange for some prime time and go on radio and TV and try to convince all the people that a big boom is about to begin. Tell them there will be shortages, lots of jobs, and overtime for everybody. Tell them if they want to buy anything they should go out and do it *tomorrow*. Tell them about the Year of the Dragon! Maybe everyone will believe you and go out and borrow and spend. If they do, sure enough, it will turn out that you were right. But if they *don't* believe you it will turn out that you were wrong.

Hoover, Roosevelt, and Nixon Used "Cheer Up" Speeches

Back in the very early part of the depression of the 1930s President Herbert Hoover announced to the nation: "Prosperity is just around the corner." If all the people had really believed him he would have been right. But they didn't, so he wasn't. Then, in 1933, President Franklin D. Roosevelt in his "fireside chat" radio broadcasts told the people: "All we have to fear is fear itself." That was about right. But we had plenty of fear to fear. Until we got rid of some of the fear we weren't going to have much prosperity.

Then in the 1969-70 recession and stock-market crash President Richard Nixon repeatedly assured the people that economic expansion was almost ready to begin and that stocks were excellent buys at such low prices. But the people and businesses didn't believe him, so unemployment continued high, the stock market was in no hurry to regain its huge losses, and the vexing problem of inflation continued unabated.

All these presidents tried to "psych" the people into spending more. Why shouldn't you? Really, the most powerful force for economic downturn and depression or for economic upturn and prosperity is the psychology of the people. If the people are convinced that the economy really is getting ready to go soft, then it will. If they are convinced that it is getting ready to improve, then it will.

The People Need Confidence in the Government's Policies

Suppose the people are really confident that the government has the necessary tools and can guarantee prosperity. Suppose everyone is sure the government knows how to take care of any serious economic problem. Then this confidence is likely to make it unnecessary for the government to use the tools.

If you, Mr. or Ms. President, have been able to inspire confidence in all the people to such an extent that they are *sure* that you can and will handle any serious economic problem which may arise, then the people will not be spooky or gun-shy. They will all just keep going along, doing things in the normal way. No big "rush for the hills" for security and no big "dash for the valley" to make a killing.

If people expect stability and long-term growth in the economy, then they will act as though stability and long-term growth are going to occur. As long as they *act* that way, stability and long-term growth are *exactly what will occur*.

If the people are confident that the government can prevent or quickly overcome depression or inflation, then *the confidence of the people* will take care of the situation. But if there's serious doubt in the minds of the people, the stabilizing tools are not going to work very well. It's almost like this: If the people believe you can handle the situation, then you can, quite easily. If they think you can't then you can't, no matter how hard you try!

We can't use fiscal and monetary policy to smooth out all the little ups and downs in the total spending stream. Anyone who thinks we can "fine tune" the economy on a perfectly stable course—either with fiscal or monetary policy or with any other approach—simply doesn't understand.

When you get into the next chapter you'll see more about how difficult this stabilization problem can be. There you'll get into some of the current problems of inflation and unemployment. And you'll find out about the question of wage and price controls. As soon as you've had a chance to review this chapter—see you there!

REVIEW EXERCISES

● **MAJOR CONCEPTS, PRINCIPLES, TERMS (Explain each carefully.)**

fiscal policy
how expenditure adjustments work
how tax adjustments work
the automatic stabilizers
the "burden" of the federal debt
the "cheer up" approach

● **OTHER CONCEPTS AND TERMS (Explain each briefly.)**

the "excess inventories" problem
the "excess debt" problem
the "excess manufacturing capacity" problem
public works programs
government deficit financing

fiscal drag
progressive tax
unbalancing the budget
monetized debt
self-fulfilling prophesy

● **QUESTIONS (Write the answers, or jot down key points.)**

1. Suppose you were a member of Congress and the President was trying to get you to vote to cut off the money for a planned (and badly needed) interstate highway in your home district. Also, the President wants you to vote to increase taxes. (You're up for reelection, of course.) Do you think you will vote for the President's program? In

view of such problems, do you think it's politically feasible to use fiscal policy to fight an "over-boom" or inflation? Discuss.

2. The government can get all the money it wants just by printing up bonds and "selling them" to the Federal Reserve Banks, but this is a dangerous procedure because a multiple expansion of the money supply is likely to result. Explain what this means and how it happens.

3. Write an essay on "the government debt"—what's good about it and what ought to be done about it, if anything.

4. What do you suppose President Franklin D. Roosevelt meant (in 1933) when he told the people "The only thing we have to fear is fear itself"? Was it true? Do you think the same thing could be said of *all* periods of economic recession and depression? Or are there some *basic economic causes* to blame (totally, or partially) for recession and depression? Discuss.

5. After all is said and done, how effective do you think fiscal policy really is in stabilizing the economy? Do you think it's more effective in overcoming depression? or inflation? Explain.

15 Unemployment with Inflation: the Stabilization Dilemma and Wage-Price Controls

How do we keep the economy running fast enough without letting wages and prices run away together?

Suppose someone asked: "What do you think will be the world's most serious issues, the most pressing problems of modern society during the next five or ten years?" What would you say? To be sure you would mention several things you keep hearing about these days— things you will be reading about later in this book: the environmental crisis, the population crush, the problems of the cities, and what to do about poverty, etc. Of course. But isn't there something, else?

THERE'S NO ESCAPE FROM THE MACROECONOMIC DILEMMA

Do you think the basic *macroeconomic* issues—the problems of inflation and unemployment—are important enough to be included in the list of *major problems*? You bet they are! The basic macroeconomic problem—the dilemma of stabilization—is always with us. It's never completely solved.

Since you're going to be living with it all your life, you might as well understand it. That's what this chapter is all about.

You already know a lot about this stabilization issue. You've just been reading about inflation and unemployment and about how monetary and fiscal policy are used to try to keep things running right. And you've found out that things don't always work out as we might wish.

You've heard a lot of news about unemployment and inflation, too. You always will. Why? Because it's a continuing, unsolved dilemma. It's always there. It plagues every modern, market-directed economy. If it's under control it isn't so bad. It's tolerable. But out of control? Disaster!

Nobody knows what the answers are. In the "pure market model," sure. There, the answers are easy. But answers that will take care of the economic stabilization problem in the unpredictable real world? No. We don't have those answers yet. That's why we're going to have to put up with some unemployment and with some inflation. Too bad. But that's just the way it is.

What's So Bad About Unemployment? or Inflation?

You've already read about the great social cost of unemployment and inflation. Remember? Unemployment wastes resources —valuable human resources and other resources too. It frustrates and degrades people. It leads to poverty, lack of self-respect, family breakdown, crime, social and political stress.

If unemployment gets bad enough it spells collapse for the economic system. Sooner or later the hungry people will likely revolt. That's what has happened in several places in the world just during this century. It almost happened (to some extent it did happen) in the United States during the 1930s. Read Steinbeck's *Grapes of Wrath* if you want to get a feel for what it was like.

What about inflation? It robs most people of the things they have worked for, saved for, planned for. Then it gives those things to other people (or sometimes to the government). It forces everyone to get the "gimmies." Anyone who can't do something to keep up gets robbed the most.

Inflation doesn't let people be "reasonable, good neighbors" about things. It breeds clash between unions and management, between businesses and their customers, between government officials and their constituents. It forces teachers and police officers to unionize and go on strike. It destroys the careful plans and programs of the school boards. It creates financial crisis in all the programs of the state and local governments. It turns

college administration into a financial nightmare. It makes people buy more foreign-produced goods because they're cheaper than the high-priced domestic goods. It creates problems and generates stresses and disharmony in every nook and cranny of the society.

If inflation is moderate—say, if prices rise only two or three percent or maybe even four or five percent per year—we can work out ways to live with it. But if it runs away, inflation destroys the "general acceptability" of money. What happens then? Without money, trade stops. Production stops. Employment stops. Income stops. Complete collapse of the economic system? Right! That's what happened in Germany in the 1922-23 inflation. Here's an example of what it was like.

An Example of Runaway Inflation

Suppose you go camping up in the mountains for a few weeks. Then when you get back to your car and back on the highway heading home, you stop at a drive-in for a double-decker burger and a chocolate shake. The counter girl says: "That'll be fifty dollars."

"FIFTY DOLLARS! Don't be ridiculous!" You leave the bag on the counter and go stomping out to your car, get in, slam the door and drive away. Soon you stop at a gas station and say: "Fill'er up."

"You got the cash? We don't take checks from out-of-staters and we don't take credit cards anymore. We have to have cash so we can spend the money *today*. Prices are going up too fast to wait until tomorrow."

You are confused. "Sure, I have the cash. It won't be all that much anyway. I only need about ten gallons."

"Let's see. Ten gallons, at twenty dollars a gallon, that'll be two hun-

Nobody knows for sure **what** to do about unemployment and inflation!

dred dollars. You got two hundred dollars on you?"

This nonsense is really beginning to get to you! "What do you mean, twenty dollars a gallon? What is going on around here?"

Prices Go Up Several Times a Day

Then he explains it to you, step by step—about how prices have broken loose. How every hour the oil company calls in a new price list. Prices are getting higher and higher, faster and faster.

While he's talking the phone rings. He answers it, then comes back shouting, "Ten gallons will cost $220 now. The price just went up again!"

You don't have $220. You ask him how much he'll give you for your spare tire. He offers you a thousand dollars. You think, "It's good that this inflation works both ways." So you sell the tire and get your tank filled.

Then you think: "By tomorrow, gas is going to cost a lot more. I'd better buy some gas cans and spend up the rest of my money right now. That way I'll be sure to have enough gas to make it home." So that's what you do. It was a wise thing to do, too. Why? Here's why.

This time next week gas is going to cost $140 a gallon! And next month it will cost $2,400 a gallon. A couple of months later it will cost *seven million dollars* a gallon. A few weeks after that it will go to a hundred million dollars a gallon, then to a billion, then to a hundred billion, then to a trillion—but long before then the economy will be in a state of total disruption—total collapse.

The German Inflation of 1922-23

The kind of runaway inflation you've been reading about is an example of exactly what happened in Germany in 1922-23. In the fall of 1923 a new administration took over in Germany. They called in all of the old, inflated

marks and issued a new kind of marks in exchange. Would you like to try to guess what the exchange rate was? Would you believe *a trillion to one?* That's right.

Suppose you had lived in Germany then and had a million dollars worth of marks in your savings account before the inflation. What would all that money be worth in the fall of 1923? Think of it this way: Suppose there were ten thousand people and each one of them was a millionaire—each one had a million dollars worth of marks before the inflation. Then in the fall of 1923 if *all ten thousand* of those millionaires turned in their money on the same day, what would they get back? At the exchange rate of a trillion to one? They would get back *one penny's worth of marks* to split between them. Each million dollars, reduced to one ten-thousandth of a cent!

Suppose something like that happened in the United States today. If you had enough money to buy the whole GNP of the United States before the inflation, then you'd have just about enough to buy a double decker burger and a chocolate shake afterwards. Such is the nature of runaway inflation. Is it any wonder it disrupts the market process and brings the total collapse of the economic system?

The Problem: Moderate but Chronic Inflation and Unemployment

It doesn't seem likely that either runaway inflation or serious, prolonged depression will occur in the United States or in any of the other advanced economies. Not that it's impossible. It's just that I think we will do enough of the right things to prevent any such catastrophe.

No, what we have to worry about is not total collapse of the economic system. It's the continuing, eroding effect of moderate but chronic inflation and moderate but chronic unemployment, both going along together.

THERE'S NO "FULL EMPLOYMENT AND STABLE PRICES" RATE OF SPENDING

What supports (holds up, or pushes up) total employment and output and income in the economy? Total spending? Of course. And what supports (holds up, or pushes up) prices in the economy? Total spending? Of course. Aha! See the problem? That which pushes up employment also pushes up prices. There you have it. That's the reason for this basic dilemma of economic stabilization.

In the pure market model there would be no "stabilization dilemma." A level of spending just great enough to bring full employment would not bring inflation. A level of spending just low enough to prevent inflation would not bring unemployment. In the pure market model there's a level of spending which will bring "full employment with stable prices"— no unemployment, no inflation. But in the real world I'm sad to say, it never works out quite that way.

The Inflation-Unemployment Overlap: the Basic Dilemma

In the real world there is a wide "overlapping area," where "inflationary-level spending" and "full employment-level spending" overlap. What I mean to say is this: Suppose total spending expands enough to eliminate unemployment. Then that rate of spending is already too high for stable prices. As total spending speeds up, inflation gets going before full employment is reached. See the problem? It works the other way too.

As total spending slows down, unemployment starts increasing even before all the inflationary pressures are cooled down. So if we're using monetary or fiscal policy (or both) to slow down total spending to cure inflation, long before we ever get the inflation problem under control we're likely to have more unemployment than we can tolerate!

And what's so difficult about it is this: Whatever you do with monetary or fiscal policy to try to make one better (say, reduce unemployment) is likely to make the other worse (increase inflation). That's the basic macroeconomic problem—that's *the basic dilemma of economic stabilization*.

Here's another way to say it. A level of spending *too low* to support full employment is still *high enough* to support inflation. What we wind up with is a level of spending that gives us some of both evils—unemployment and inflation both at the same time! So what can we do with monetary and fiscal policies? Try to speed up spending to reduce unemployment? We get more inflation. Try to slow down spending to reduce inflation? We get more unemployment. Oh, miserable dilemma!

There's no easy answer. But there's one thing that's fairly obvious. Just this: When this "unemployment-inflation" dilemma exists, *we're going to have to use something in addition to monetary and fiscal policy* if we're going to get it straightened out. That's for sure. But before we get into that, here are some graphs that will help you to see the problem more clearly.

It's too bad that in the real world there is no "full employment and stable prices" rate of total spending. But that's the way it is. We are constantly between these two "evils."

There are two figures coming up that will show you two very different situations. The first (pure model) figure shows a level of spending which brings "full employment and stable prices." The second (real world) figure shows some unemployment and some inflation *at any level of spending* you can choose.

Why doesn't the real world look like the model? Essentially, for this reason: There are things *other than total spending* which are always pushing upward on unemployment, and on prices. More on that in a minute. First, here are the graphs.

Fig. 15-1 Total Spending, Employment, and Prices: the "Model" Case

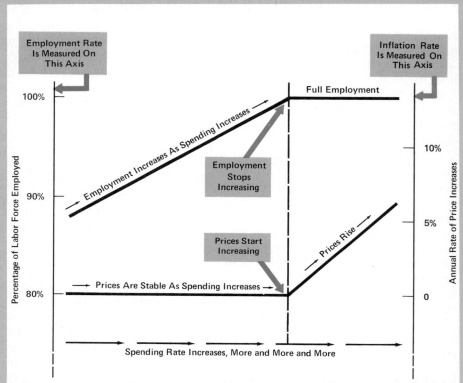

In the "model pure market system" there is no "inflation-unemployment overlap."

In the "model pure market system," as spending keeps increasing, employment and output will keep increasing but prices will remain stable until full employment is reached. Prices will start to go up, bringing inflation, only if total spending keeps increasing after full employment has been reached.

If the real world worked like the model, stabilization still wouldn't be all that easy. Finding out exactly what the right level of spending would be and then getting total spending to stabilize at that exact level wouldn't be quite as easy as falling off a log! On the other hand it would be comforting to know that a "full employment and stable prices" rate of spending really did exist, somewhere.

In the real world, no such rate of spending exists. The next graph shows you how it looks in the real world.

Fig. 15-2   Total Spending, Employment, and Prices: the "Real World" Case

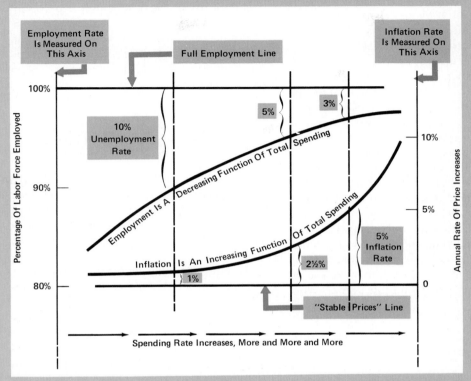

In the real world, inflation speeds up before unemployment gets slowed down.

In the real world there is no level of total spending which will bring full employment and stable prices. If the spending rate is already high, a further increase in spending will add only a little to employment, but a lot to inflation!

In the real world, as spending increases, employment increases, but the employment increase gets smaller and smaller as spending gets higher and higher. You could say: "Employment is a decreasing function of total spending."

What about the inflation rate? As spending increases, prices rise faster and faster. You could say: "The inflation rate is an increasing function of total spending."

If you wanted to sound more like an economist, you could talk about the "increasing marginal rate of inflation" and the "decreasing marginal rate of employment." Say it any way you want to, just remember that as spending increases more and more, each extra increase in spending is likely to add less and less extra employment and more and more inflation.

Everyone Is in the "Upward Price-Inching" Game

In the real world, almost all sellers can do things to push up the prices of what they sell. This is true of consumer goods sellers and it's true of the sellers of the factors of production—labor, land, capital. Each seller wants to be sure not to get left behind in the game of "upward price-inching." All of us are "price-inchers"! We give all sorts of reasons for pushing our prices up—some of our "reasons" are excuses, and some are valid.

Labor cites the increased cost of living and increasing output per worker and other things. Businesses cite increased costs of labor, materials, transportation, utilities, interest and other inputs. Both labor and businesses have the power to push up their prices—so that's just what they do. How much would total spending have to be cut back to make everybody stop this price-inching game? Who knows?

Low-Wage Workers Are Pushing for Higher Wages

These days, everyone is pushing for more money. Low-paid workers are getting unionized and pushing for higher wages. Civil service workers, teachers, those in the fire and police departments, sanitation workers, other government employees have been paid low wages for a long time. But now people are becoming less willing to accept the idea that the person who performs one job—say in manufacturing or construction—should receive a lot more income than the person who performs some other job—say teachers or postal workers. The lower income people are getting organized and are pushing hard for higher wages. Can you see how wages might be going up even in the face of declining total spending? Sure. There's great pressure for wage and price increases and great resistance to wage and price decreases.

What about the unemployment problem? It's easy to see how prices might keep on inching up by themselves. But surely people don't want to "inch themselves out of their jobs"! So if there's unemployment, when spending increases why don't employment and production and output increase until full employment is reached? That's easy to figure out too, if you think about it.

Some Unemployed Workers Aren't Suited for the Available Jobs

Just as the "inflationary bias" in the real world can be explained in terms of one thing: "upward price-inching"—also the "unemployment bias" in the real world can be explained in terms of one thing: *all labor is not alike.*

As total spending increases, more people get jobs. True. But the ones most suited to work in the expanding industries are hired first. As spending increases more, only as prices go higher will people be hired at jobs they aren't well suited for. Total spending would have to go very high for all the unemployed teachers to be hired as bricklayers! or bricklayers as teachers!

Another real-world consideration is that some businesses are always cutting back while others are always expanding. Some people are always changing jobs for one reason or another. While they're between jobs they're unemployed. But this kind of temporary unemployment is not a real problem. It's only when the "between jobs" period stretches on and on—that's when some action needs to be taken to get things going again—and hopefully, without throwing gasoline on the fires of inflation.

You already know from Figure 15-2 what it looks like when spending is increased to overcome unemployment. If total spending is already high, an increase in spending is likely to bring a little more employment and a lot more inflation. Remember? It's a trade-off. You give up some price stability to get some added employment. Do you think this "trade-off ratio" could be shown on a graph? Sure. All trade-off ratios can be shown on graphs. The curve we use to show the "inflation-unemployment trade-off" is called the "Phillips Curve."

The Phillips Curve Shows the Inflation-Unemployment Trade-Off

The Phillips Curve is named for the British economist, A. W. Phillips, who developed the "curve" in the latter 1950s. What Professor Phillips did was to look back over the years and see, for different times, what the rate of inflation had been and what the rate of unemployment had been. He found out that when unemployment was high, the inflation rate was low, and when unemployment was low the inflation rate was higher. You can understand that and you can understand why.

More spending brings more employment, sure. But it also brings a better chance for workers and businesses to raise their wages and prices. So that's what they do, and the rate of inflation picks up. When total spending slows down that brings more unemployment. But when things are slow, there are fewer opportunities for workers and businesses to raise their wages and prices. So when unemployment gets higher, inflation slows down.

The Phillips Curve illustrates this idea: *We can have a smaller unemployment rate, only if we are willing to accept a larger inflation rate.* It's a "trade-off" situation, where we would like to have *minimum amounts* of both—minimum unemployment and minimum inflation. But to get less of one, we know we must put up with more of the other.

Is this the "real-world dilemma of economic stabilization"? You bet. It's one of the really tough economic problems of our time. We keep trying to learn to live with it and to devise

better ways of solving it or coping with it. But so far it's still a dilemma. A very serious one.

A Production Possibility Curve for Unwanted Products?

Now that you understand what the Phillips Curve illustrates, what do you suppose it will look like? Negative slope? Of course. As you give up some of one thing (inflation) you get back more of the other (unemployment). This curve is going to look like a "production possibility" or "opportunity cost" curve. Right? Sure. But in a way, it's very different from the production possibility curve.

The production possibility curve shows you *how much you can get of the good things you want,* and how much of one you must give up to get more of the other. You would be happy if the production possibility curve would shift upward and outward. You could then have more of either product or a larger combination of both.

What about the Phillips Curve? It shows you *how much we must take of the bad things we don't want*—unemployment and inflation. Would we be happy if the Phillips Curve shifted upward and outward? Certainly not! More unemployment, or more inflation, or a larger combination of both? Not if we can help it!

We would like for the Phillips Curve to shift downward and inward. In fact we would be most happy if it would shift all the way down to zero and disappear! Then we could have full employment and stable prices and the whole dilemma would be solved. *We all wish that would happen.* Of course.

Figure 15-3 shows the Phillips Curve. It's just another way of looking at the same picture you saw in the employment-inflation graph a few pages back. In fact this Phillips Curve was derived from the two curves in Figure 15-2. Compare the two figures and you will see that both graphs are telling the same story. Also, take time to study Figures 15-3 and 15-4.

Fig. 15-3 The Unemployment-Inflation Trade-Off: The Phillips Curve

It's a dilemma all right. You can't have your cake and eat it too. But it's bad when you can't have either!

The Phillips Curve says that when the inflation rate is low the unemployment rate is high; when the unemployment rate is low, the inflation rate is high. If we use monetary or fiscal policy to get less of one, we get more of the other.

The Phillips Curve you see here was derived from the "employment function" and "inflation function" curves shown in Figure 15-2. Nobody knows just exactly where this Phillips Curve will be for any economic system at any particular time. All sorts of things might cause it to shift.

The Phillips Curve illustrates the fact that something *other than* total spending must be influencing (holding up or pushing up) wages and prices. Whenever these "other than" influences get stronger, the curve shifts upward and outward; whenever they get weaker the curve shifts downward and inward.

Whenever the "other than" influences are changing, it may be more helpful to try to understand why the curve shifts than to try to understand why it is shaped as it is. The next graph shows you a real-world example of "the shifting Phillips Curve."

Fig. 15-4 Sometimes the Phillips Curve Shifts Outward

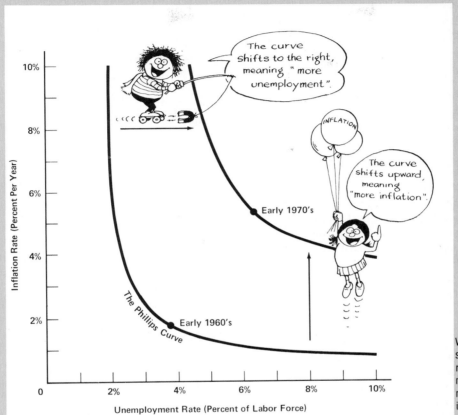

When the curve shifts up and to the right it signals more unemployment and more inflation too.

In the early 1960s the unemployment rate in the United States was less than 4 percent and the inflation rate was less than 2 percent. Then in the early 1970s the unemployment rate was about 6 percent and the inflation rate was more than 5 percent. A big shift in the Phillips Curve, upward and outward!

In the inflation-recession of 1974 the unemployment rate went up to more than 7 percent and the inflation rate went up to more than 12 percent! Picture what that would look like on this graph!

If the Phillips Curve is going to be shifting around all over, what good is it? Just this: It illustrates a concept—the concept of the basic dilemma of economic stabilization—of the unemployment-inflation trade-off. We really don't know where the curve is going to be or exactly how it will be shaped. Still, it's a useful way to illustrate an important concept.

THE PHILLIPS CURVE AND THE U.S. STABILIZATION DILEMMA

The Phillips Curve *illustrates a concept.* It can't *predict* what unemployment rates will go with what inflation rates. But it does suggest that sometimes, if the curve is high up and far out (as in the early 1970s), some approach *other than* monetary and fiscal policy to influence total spending must be used.

When both the unemployment rate and the inflation rate are high, cutting back on total spending to curb inflation may bring a disastrous depression. But increasing total spending to overcome the unemployment may bring a disastrous inflation!

When the Phillips Curve gets itself shifted way up and way out, that's when the stabilization dilemma is really serious. That's when the economic theorist's indirect tools of economic adjustment and stabilization get pushed aside by the policymakers. That's when the last resort approach of "good old American pragmatism" takes over and aims *directly* at the visible conditions—the unemployment and the inflation—and goes to work on them. Direct controls are established to try to stop increases in wages and prices. Direct action is taken to create new jobs for the unemployed. Is that what happened in the early 1970s? Yes.

The Wage-Price Freeze of August, 1971

In August of 1971, after more than two years of trying to stop inflation by using "tight money" policy and after repeatedly vowing that he would never impose direct controls on wages and prices, President Nixon imposed direct controls on wages and prices. Why? Because after waiting so long for the "indirect medicine" of tight money to show that it was working, he reluctantly concluded that he had no choice but to impose direct controls. When the domestic economic problems were compounded by the international financial crisis of the U.S. dollar (which you'll be reading about in Part Nine) he really didn't have *any* choice. He had to do something.

But why? What had happened to bring such a high rate of unemployment and a high rate of inflation? What had made the Phillips Curve shift up and out so far? And how is it possible to get it shifted back down? Or, to say it differently, how can we solve this inflation-unemployment dilemma?

What Causes the Phillips Curve to Shift?

Anything that would get people to stop playing the "upward-price-inching" game would shift the curve down. If everybody would stop trying to play "wage-price leapfrog," always jumping to try to stay ahead of everybody else, that would really help a lot. Then we might be able to have a high level of total spending with a low level of unemployment and a low level of inflation at the same time. It could do a lot of good if we could just get people to quit pushing all the time for higher wages and prices.

It could do a lot of good if we could make it easier for people to be employed, too. That would shift the Phillips Curve to the left and give us less unemployment—and with no more inflation. Anything that could be done to help the unemployed people become more productive or more mobile or more aware of available jobs or more responsive to the changing demands for labor in the economy—anything like that would help. Even lowering the wage rate for inexperienced, untrained, unskilled workers would help. Anything which would reduce the "natural resistance" to full employment, would reduce unemployment without pushing up prices—that is, would shift the Phillips Curve to the left.

It isn't difficult to figure out that manpower training and job placement programs are needed to reduce the resistance to full employment and to shift the Phillips Curve to the left. But what about the inflation problem? How do we get the people and businesses to stop playing the "wage-price leapfrogging game"? How do we get rid of these "built in" inflationary pressures which push the Phillips Curve up? Can anything be done about that?

You know that if it were not for the economic power held by all the big businesses and small businesses and labor unions and the government and just about everybody, then wages and prices would respond a lot more to the "natural forces" of supply and demand. But nearly everybody has some power to push up the prices of what they sell. So what are we going to do about it? Eliminate big businesses? and labor unions? and everyone else who has any power to influence wages or prices? I don't think so.

President Nixon Outlawed the Wage-Price Leapfrogging Game

What can we do? I guess we can do exactly what President Nixon did. We can outlaw the wage-price leapfrogging game! We can establish controls to limit the "wage-price increasing powers" of businesses and unions and other organizations. If wage and price controls can succeed in holding down wages and prices, that means the Phillips Curve shifts down close to the "zero inflation" line. Inflation is controlled without forcing unemployment to increase.

Now you have an overview of the problem. The Phillips Curve shifts *upward*, showing more inflation, whenever everyone gets in the upward price-inching game—when wages and prices start leapfrogging each other. The curve shifts *outward* (to the right on the graph) whenever people aren't prepared for the kinds of jobs available—when a lot of young, untrained people are entering the labor force, and especially if there's a high minimum wage for new workers.

What made the curve for the U.S. economy shift so far upward and outward in the early to mid-1970s? Why didn't the serious problems of unemployment and inflation begin to show up back in the 1950s and early 1960s? Why did the crisis wait so long to happen? To understand the answer to this question, you'll need to know a little bit about what was going on in the U.S. economy in the 1960s.

Some Causes of the Recent Inflationary Push

Why did the Phillips Curve for the U.S. economy shift upward in the late 1960s and early 1970s, bringing more inflation? Several reasons. During the mid and latter 1960s, government spending increased rapidly. Tax increases were delayed and more and more money was created through the banking system. Total spending in the economy kept increasing. The economy was running along just about as "fully employed" as it could get. So what happened as spending kept increasing? Inflationary pressures began pushing prices up. Of course.

Was this a shift in the Phillips curve? No. Not at all. It was just a move along the curve—a move which brought a little more employment and a lot more inflation. Once the inflation was triggered off, it began to get worse and worse. Each time wages in one industry would move up, the workers in other industries would push for higher wages, each trying to outdo the others. Each time one business would raise prices, others would do the same. As wages increased, prices increased; as prices increased, wages increased. Everybody kept on fighting to stay ahead, while blaming everybody else for causing inflation.

In some industries, demand and productivity were increasing, so prices and wages increased. But then everybody (whether they happened to be in high productivity, high-demand industries or not) started pushing to get just as much increase as the other guy. When the auto workers get a wage increase, the school teachers want one, too—and increased productivity be damned! The auto worker's wage can go up, yet the cost of each car may stay the same. How? Because of increased productivity per worker.

But if wages for school teachers go up, unless each teacher teaches more students the cost of education per student goes up. That's inflation. And that's what was happening throughout the economy. Once inflation gets going, everybody gets on the band wagon. The high-demand, high-productivity industries may be the pace-setters. But soon, throughout the economy wages and prices start leapfrogging each other across the landscape until both go out of sight over the horizon!

See what's been happening? Increased spending sets off the inflation. Total demand is too great for the total supply, so shortages develop and prices start going up. Then soon everybody starts trying to get ahead of everybody else. The inflation speeds up more and more. Inflation begets inflation. Once it gets going it tries to run away.

Kinds of Inflation:
Demand-Pull, Cost-Push, Structural

Once inflation gets going, there are three kinds of inflation that all start working together, reinforcing each other. Demand-pull inflation results from too much total spending. Cost-push inflation occurs when businesses raise their prices because their *costs* are going up—usually because the wage rate goes up. Structural inflation can occur when the "structure" (the industrial make-up) of the economy is changing (as it always is, of course).

"Structural inflation" can result from shifts in the buying patterns of the consumers. As demand increases in one segment of the economy (say, the automobile tire industry) this pushes up prices and wages in that industry. But in the industries where demand is declining (say, the wagon wheel industry), wages and prices don't go down to offset the increases in the expanding industry. Of course not! What really happens is that the people in the declining industry fight to get their wages and prices to go up, too! Cost-push inflation, triggered by a structural shift in the economy? Sure.

President Nixon and the Monetarists

When President Nixon took office in January, 1969, he brought in a new group of

economic advisers—economists with a different idea about what ought to be done and how. Several were "monetarists," members of "the Chicago school" of economic theory, anti-Keynesians, allies of Milton Friedman. They believed in carefully limiting the size of the money supply. But except for that, they were for *a hands-off policy toward the economy on issues of both micro- and macroeconomics.* "Let the money supply increase a little each year, and leave everything else alone. Never fear. If you'll do that, the natural economic forces will make everything work out all right."

President Nixon's economic advisers, alarmed by the rapid rate of increase in the money supply and the high rate of inflation, called for tight money. "Stop the money supply from expanding. That will hold down total spending. Soon prices will stop rising." The Fed tightened money so tight that interest rates went up higher than they had been in the United States for more than 100 years! The stock market went into its worse crash since the depression days of the 1930s. For more and more businesses, demand fell off. Profits turned to losses. Bankruptcies increased. The economy went into recession. The unemployment rate increased from less than four to more than six percent of the labor force. And what about prices?

Prices and wages just kept right on going up. Month after month the President and his advisers continued to assure the nation that the "Nixon game plan" was working and that the anti-inflationary tight money policy was just about to take hold. How long did this go on? Until August 15, 1971. For two and one-half years! It continued until the eve of the dramatic Sunday night television address in which President Nixon announced a complete reversal of his previous economic policies, and ordered a freeze on all wages and prices.

What had happened? What had gone wrong? The tight money policy had succeeded in holding down total spending, sure. But instead of the inflation rate slowing down, employment slowed down. Prices just kept right on going up. Why? Once the wage-price leapfrogging game started going it wasn't easy to stop. Or you could say it another way: the Phillips Curve shifted.

The Phillips Curve Shifts

What made the Phillips Curve shift? Once the inflation got moving, more and more people were left farther and farther behind. So they tried harder and harder to catch up. Each time one more group would get its wages or prices jumped out ahead, that would leave that many more that much farther behind and that much more determined to forge ahead. And as all this "cost push" inflationary pressure built stronger and stronger, the Phillips Curve was moving higher and higher, showing more and more inflation for any level of unemployment you might choose.

Cost-push inflation and structural inflation don't have much respect for tight money—or for increased unemployment either, for that matter. And inflation begets inflation, remember? The longer the inflation continued, the harder it was to stop.

What could be done? Just what was done. The leapfroggers could be frozen in their tracks for awhile (for 90 days) during which time someone could try to figure out who was behind and who was ahead when the freeze came. Then after the 90 days were over, in "Phase Two," some adjustments could be made to let the hindmost move up with the rest of the pack. Then after that no more leapfrogging. No more giant steps. Only little baby steps. (And don't forget to say "May I?" to the wage-price control board!)

What happens next? What's the long range outlook? Nobody knows for sure. Of course not. But here's a guess. Most of the time, we won't have to say "May I?" but there probably will be some guidelines, some "rules of proper wage-price conduct" or some such. The government controllers won't be out on center stage, but they'll be watching from the wings.

If the leapfrogging game looks like it's about to get started again, I don't think it will take very long, next time, before the wing-watchers will pounce. It's so much easier to stop it when it's just getting started than after it gets going good.

Tight Money: Necessary, But Not Always Sufficient

Tight money really can't always do the job of preventing inflation—not in the real world. That doesn't mean we can ignore the need to limit the size of the money supply. Of course not! Remember what happened in Germany in 1923? What could wage-price controls have done then? Nothing! Government incomes policies or wage-price guidelines designed to hold down the wage-price leapfrogging game couldn't possibly work if the money supply was permitted to expand unchecked.

If total spending is permitted to expand more and more, the pressure for "demand-pull" inflation gets greater and greater. The longer the "price control lid" is held on, the harder it is to keep the prices from breaking loose. People start to offer more money "under the table" for the things they want. When this "black marketing" gets widespread it becomes impossible to stop. It becomes the name of the game. Everybody does it. All the goods disappear from the controlled markets. The natural market forces take over. When this happens, the sooner the government recognizes it and abolishes the price controls, the better it will be.

No, controls can't replace the need for responsible monetary and fiscal policies. On the other hand, neither can responsible monetary and fiscal policies replace the firm hand of government controls in dealing with the wage-price leapfrogging game. The classic argument against wage-price controls has been this: "If we want to keep the pot from boiling over we must turn down the fire under the pot (tighten money), instead of trying to clamp the lid on (control prices)!" That's a good analogy. It makes very good sense, whenever we're dealing with demand-pull inflation. But when we're dealing with the upward price-inching, leapfrogging game, the analogy doesn't fit very well.

Perhaps it would make more sense to think about a pot of live fiddler crabs, each one trying to crawl over the backs of all the others and get out of the pot. It might help to put the pot in the refrigerator to cool them down. But to be sure it would be more *effective* to clamp the lid on! Whenever many big businesses and labor unions and professional associations and other organizations have enough economic power to set their own wages and prices—and I'm sure you know that many do—then tight money, acting alone, is an insufficient tool for inflation control. Some way to "clamp the lid on" is also going to be needed from time to time. When those times come, the sooner the incomes policies are instituted and enforced, the better it will be for everyone.

It seems to be a safe bet that we will be living under some sort of actual or potential wage-price restraints most of the time, from now on. Suppose it turns out that way. Is that good or bad? And good or bad *compared to what*?

DIRECT CONTROLS ON WAGES AND PRICES

It's good to hold down inflation. So unless there is something bad about direct controls on wages and prices, why not have direct controls all the time? You already know the answer. There's something bad about wage-price controls. Wage-price controls block the operation of the market economy!

Controls Prevent the Market Process from Working

Suppose the government would set up rigid incomes policies—saying that each business should get a certain amount of profit and no more. Each worker should get a certain wage and no more. Every product price should be

no higher than it was last June. What would happen?

If everything in the economy is in a sort of "general equilibrium" when the controls are established, then the "set" prices and wages and profits will all be in line at that moment. There won't be any immediate problem. But the longer the controls stay on, the more things are likely to get out of line. Demands change. Production costs change. Technology changes. As these changes occur, prices will need to adjust to the new conditions. If the adjustment can't be made then shortages will begin to show up in some markets and surpluses will pile up in others. The longer the prices stay frozen, the worse the distortions will get. Shortages of some products will get worse and worse while surpluses of other products will get bigger and bigger.

Unrealistic Prices Generate Black Markets

Suppose prices were frozen when there was an oversupply and very low price of corn. So the corn price is fixed at 10¢ a dozen. Everybody quits producing corn. Soon the shortage of corn is very great. But some people like corn very much—enough to be willing to pay $2.50 a dozen! Suppose I'm growing some corn for myself in my backyard plot and someone sees it growing there, ready to harvest. One night I hear a knock on the door and a voice says "If I leave a $5 bill under the doormat will you look the other way while I steal two dozen ears of corn?" What temptation! I just might look the other way.

As times goes on, the word gets around that you can "steal" corn from my field without anybody catching you if you will leave $5 under the doormat for every two dozen ears you "steal." Soon I'm making lots of money and people who really like corn are getting some. But what about the price controls? They aren't working anymore. Not for corn, anyway. And not for lots of other things, too.

When the "black markets" (free markets) begin to develop, they catch on like wildfire. If the controlled prices are very far out of line with the "real-world supply and demand conditions," then black markets are almost certain to arise. So if controlled prices are going to work for very long, there must be some kind of system for staying in touch with supply and demand and cost conditions in all the markets for all the products in the economy. The controlled prices will have to be adjusted to reflect the changing market conditions. But isn't that hard to do? Yes. It sure is.

Political Influence May Distort the System

There's another problem, too. All sellers want their prices to go up a little bit. All workers want their wages to go up a little bit. Every business wants its profit to go up a little bit. Everybody is putting pressures on their members of Congress, Senators, and local political party representatives, and writing letters to the President, doing everything possible to try to get some "special consideration." Everybody can think of some very special reason for a favorable price adjustment. How does a system which responds to political pressures withstand this sort of thing? It doesn't, of course. As time goes by, *politics* is likely to decide more price adjustments than *economics*!

Wage and price controls are a bad thing—a real no-no for the "free enterprise system." They're hard to design, hard to administer, hard to police. So what are we going to do when the wage-price leapfrogging game begins? We'll use wage and price controls. We have no choice.

During 1969 and the early 1970's we suffered through a very unhappy experience. Tight money was used to try to control the inflation, but serious unemployment developed and inflation just roared on. After that unhappy experience, it is likely that from now on the American economy will always live in the shadow of some kind of incomes policies—some kind of limits or controls (actual or potential) over wages and prices.

Most "Free Market" Systems Use Some Direct Controls

Before the latter 1960s and early 1970s, had inflation ever been a serious problem before in the United States? And what about in other countries? You know the answer. In every healthy, prosperous, growing economy, inflation is *always* a threat. Over the past few decades, most of the time the United States has experienced less inflation than most other countries. But I'm sure you know that in the U.S. economy, prices for most things have been going up all along—sometimes faster, sometimes slower, but they are always trending upward.

Over the past three decades, in most countries most of the time there has been some attempt to use *direct restraints* to hold down wages and prices. Practical, real-world politicians have known for a long time that the unlimited creation of money will force up prices, and that the powerful thrust of a massive surge in total spending can't be held in check by wage-price controls. But they also have known that inflation cannot satisfactorily be held in check simply by tightening money to hold down total spending. There are just too many "fiddler crab" prices crawling over each other trying to get out of the pot!

Of course if money can be made tight enough, total spending can be cut back so much that the economy can be forced into a depression. That would cool down the autonomous enthusiasm of the fiddler-crab prices, all right! But is that really an acceptable solution? Of course not.

When Has the U.S. Used Direct Controls?

In the United States, as you know, a system of "total wage-price controls" was established in August, 1971. That was the first time that had happened since the early 1950s during the Korean War. It had happened during World War II also, and during other wars, of course. But what about the period from the mid 50s to August of 1971? Were wages and prices completely free to seek their own levels? Sometimes, yes. Sometimes, no.

In the early 1960s, President Kennedy set up wage-price guideposts spelling out the "appropriate conditions" for wages or prices to be increased, and by how much. The guideposts were not "legal requirements." They were only "urged upon" the industries and the labor organizations. But both President Kennedy and President Johnson used the power of the presidency to "twist some arms," to convince some businesses and labor leaders to go along with the guideposts. This "arm-twisting"—this unofficial but sometimes quite powerful technique for holding down wage-price increases—is known as *jawboning.*

The "jawboning" policies of the Kennedy-Johnson era were continued until the beginning of the Nixon administration in 1969. Then, responding to the urging of his monetary theorist-advisers, President Nixon instituted a "tight money" policy and openly denounced all other approaches to the inflation-control problem. Repeatedly he announced that he would never use the power of his high office to try to impose "wage-price guideposts" on American businesses and labor.

So what happened in 1969? Interest rates rose rapidly and the economy headed into a recession. But the rate of inflation didn't slow down. Instead, it speeded up. The upward price-inching, wage-price leapfrogging game was taking over? Of course. The "fiddler-crab prices" were crawling out of the pot!

The President was cooling down the pot, all right! The economy was slowing down. Unemployment was increasing. But the fiddler-crab prices kept right on crawling out. For

how long? Until the President decided to ignore his monetary theorist-advisers and put the lid on. That's what he did on August 15, 1971.

What do wage-price controls, or wage-price guidelines, or "incomes policies" accomplish? They don't accomplish anything unless they work. But if they're flexible and sensitive, and supported by appropriate monetary and fiscal policies, they can be made to work. If they work, they shift the Phillips Curve downward. They can give us a reduced inflation rate (a rate we can live with) corresponding to an unemployment rate we can live with. That's a goal worth seeking.

THE PROBLEM OF UNRESPONSIVE UNEMPLOYMENT

We've been talking a lot about the problem of inflation—about how, once it gets started, it's hard to stop. It tries to run away. With everybody pushing for higher wages and prices and with structural changes always going on in the economy and all, it's easy to see why an inflation rate of zero would be pretty difficult to maintain. That's why the Phillips Curve never gets down to the horizontal axis—down to where the inflation rate would be zero. But what about unemployment? Why doesn't unemployment ever go all the way to zero? Why doesn't the curve go all the way over to touch the vertical axis?

There Are Always Some People Changing Jobs

Just as some kinds of *inflation* don't respond very well to *reductions* in total spending, some kinds of *unemployment* don't respond very well to *increases* in total spending. One kind of unemployment which total spending could never bring down to zero is *frictional unemployment*. People who are changing jobs for one reason or another don't "flow smoothly and instantaneously" from the old jobs to the new ones. Sometimes the person may be unemployed only a day or two. Other times he or she may be unemployed for a week or two or maybe longer.

Sometimes the "frictional unemployment" results from structural changes in the economy. Remember about structural inflation? What about *structural unemployment*? What do the old line, highly skilled wagon-wheel workers do when the demand shifts to automobile tires? They get unemployed. If total spending in the economy picks up, will they get new jobs? Most of the younger ones will. Some of the older ones may. Others, no. Their "day in the sun" has passed. That's the way it is with structural unemployment.

There's another kind of unemployment you hear a lot about these days: technological unemployment. That's what happens when people are replaced by machines—"automated out of a job," so to speak. That's what's happening to the migrant farm workers. Everywhere you go you see more "mechanical pickers" instead of "hand pickers" harvesting crops. In every modern economy, jobs are constantly being eliminated by improved technology. As wages get higher, more capital is introduced. "Technological displacement" speeds up.

The more the economy is dynamic, growing, introducing new technology, the more serious structural and technological unemployment will be. What can be done about it? Manpower training and development programs? Job training subsidies? Helping people to find new jobs? Yes. All these and some other things too. But one thing's sure. An increase in total spending can't solve the problem by itself.

New People Are Always Entering the Labor Force

Another kind of unemployment which can't be eliminated is the unemployment of the young and inexperienced people who are constantly joining the labor force. In the early 1970s when the average unemployment rate for the nation was a little less than 6 percent, the unemployment rate for teenagers was more than 16 percent. In several places in the country it was much higher than that. But the unemployment rate for married men was only about 3 percent.

If all the members of the labor force were identical, how simple it would be to solve the unemployment problem. Just get total spending to increase, that's all! Soon everyone would have a job. But the labor force is very diverse—young and old, male and female, skilled and unskilled, black and white, educated and uneducated, brilliant and stupid, industrious and lazy, and on and on and on. So it's obvious that just increasing total spending would create a lot of inflation before it would ever bring unemployment down near zero!

Unresponsive Unemployment Keeps the Phillips Curve Out

What happens to the Phillips Curve as more young, unskilled people join the labor force and as more people get trapped by structural and technological and other "unresponsive" kinds of unemployment? The curve shifts to the right. After the shift, the curve shows that at any "inflation rate" you choose, the "unemployment rate" is larger than before.

IS DIRECT ACTION NEEDED TO HOLD THE PHILLIPS CURVE DOWN?

What does the Phillips Curve say? It tells us that even if total spending keeps increasing, unemployment persists; even if total spending is held down, inflation persists. The Phillips Curve is a graphic picture of the unemployment-inflation dilemma.

Anything that is going to succeed in solving the inflation-unemployment dilemma is going to have to succeed in shifting the Phillips Curve downward and to the left. In the real world, that means taking *direct action* to prevent some kinds of wage and price increases—increases which are not very responsive to adjustments in total spending. And it means taking *direct action* to overcome some kinds of unemployment—kinds which are not responsive to increases in total spending. That's a big order. It won't be easy to do.

Direct programs to overcome unemployment are widely accepted these days. Manpower development and placement programs have been expanded rapidly in recent years, and with a good bit of success. But direct controls to limit big increases in wages and prices? Is that a widely accepted idea these days? Certainly not!

People Disagree About the Need for Direct Controls

To bring the long arm of government bureaucracy into the very heart of the "free market place" by setting up wage-price guidelines? or incomes policies? or some such? to expose the price mechanism to the continuous threat of all sorts of political manipulations and shenanigans? and to do this on a *permanent* basis? Who wants that? Nobody. Of course not. That is, nobody wants it if there's some realistic and feasible alternative.

Several outstanding economists disagree about the need for continuing wage-price guidelines or controls. But of this much we can be sure: The problems of unemployment and inflation are going to have to be approached in the real world. If it turns out that some system of continuing controls is essential, we will have to accept that fact. Then we will have to turn to the task of devising a system that will work.

A WORD OF FAREWELL TO MACROECONOMICS

Now that you're at the end of the last chapter in Part Four, how do you feel about macroeconomics? Do you understand what keeps the economy running? Sure. Total spending. And what makes the economy speed up and slow down? Anything that influences total spending. Of course.

If you've been carefully working your way through all these macroeconomic chapters I think you really understand it now. That's good. Macroeconomic issues are going to be staring you in the face, off and on, all your life. It's good to be able to understand what's going on.

We're leaving the subject of macroeconomics now. We're moving on into a new part of the book—into microeconomics again. Remember about the natural forces of "the market"? About how these forces automatically get the people and resources to go to the right places and do the right things for the good of society? Sure. It's time to get back into that now. So as soon as you're sure you and this chapter and this Part have really done your bit for each other, on to Part Five and to new and interesting things about the subject of MICROECONOMICS!

REVIEW EXERCISES   • **MAJOR CONCEPTS, PRINCIPLES, TERMS (Explain each carefully.)**

the basic macroeconomic dilemma
runaway inflation
the inflation-unemployment overlap
the inflation-unemployment trade-off
the Phillips Curve

● **OTHER CONCEPTS AND TERMS (Explain each briefly.)**

demand-pull inflation

cost-push inflation

structural inflation

the monetarists

the "Chicago School"

Milton Friedman

incomes policies

wage-price guideposts

jawboning

frictional unemployment

structural unemployment

technological unemployment

● **CURVES AND GRAPHS (Draw, label, and explain each.)**

Total Spending, Employment, and Prices: The "Model" Case

Total Spending, Employment, and Prices: The "Real World" Case

The Unemployment-Inflation Trade-Off: The Phillips Curve

When the Phillips Curve Shifts Outward, That's Bad

● **QUESTIONS (Write out answers or jot down key points.)**

1. Can you think of any specific examples (examples you are personally familiar with) of wage and/or price increases which are *not* likely to be stopped by a slowdown in spending? Discuss.
2. Can you think of any specific examples of unemployment which aren't likely to be overcome, even if total spending increases? Discuss.
3. Explain how the Phillips Curve is similar to, and how it is different from, a production possibility curve.
4. Mention and explain as many things as you can think of that would be likely to make the Phillips Curve shift up or down, or to the right or left.
5. What is the basic position of Milton Friedman and the monetarists regarding stabilization policy?
6. There are many reasons why wage-price controls are undesirable in general, and why it's very hard to make them work. But under the right circumstances they *can* be made to work. Try to explain all this, in as much detail as you can.

PART **5**

MICRO CONCEPTS
AND PRINCIPLES:
DEMAND, SUPPLY,
PRICES, AND INCOME
DISTRIBUTION
IN THE MODEL
MARKET SYSTEM

THE PRICE MECHANISM CAN TAKE CARE OF
EVERYTHING, JUST LIKE MAGIC!

16 Essential Micro Concepts: the Market, Private Property, Inequality, the Factors of Production

The market process could not work without free markets, private property, inequality, and responsive labor, land, and capital.

Welcome back to microeconomics—back to the study of scarcity and choosing—back to the study of how the market process automatically "senses" and then carries out the choices of the society. That's what all of Part Five will be about.

First there are some basic concepts you need to understand: Markets. Private property. Inequality. Factors of production. That's what this chapter is about. First "the market."

"THE MARKET" IS A CONCEPT

What is the market? a place? a thing? Neither, really. It's a concept. If you are growing tomatoes in your backyard "for sale," you are producing "for the market." You might sell some to your neighbor and some in your little stand by the roadside and some to the manager of the local supermarket. But in either case, you are producing "for the market." Your efforts are being directed by the market. If people stop buying tomatoes you will stop producing them.

If you mow lawns to earn money, you are producing a service "for the market." If your father is a steelworker or a bricklayer or a truck driver or a dentist or a grocer he is "producing" goods or services "for the market." Probably he is selling his labor services in the "labor market." When you spend your income you are buying things from "the market." You may spend money in several stores, supermarkets, gas stations, and restaurants. Still you are buying from "the market." When the local grocer hires you to drive the delivery truck he is buying your labor in the labor market.

The Market to You Is All Your Buyers and Your Sellers

To say that you are selling "in the market" simply means that whoever is able and willing to pay the price can buy what you are selling. If you are "buying in the market" you are buying the things you want from whatever seller has them available. If you are a seller of tomatoes or of lawn mowing services or of your skills at running a bulldozer, you see the market as *all those buyers who might want to buy what you have to sell.* If you are a buyer of anything—a business buying a bulldozer operator's services or a shopper buying tomatoes—you see the market as *all those sellers who might offer to sell what you want to buy.*

The market may seem to be a fuzzy sort of thing. But for each person (or business) who is making and selling something, it's very real. If the market doesn't want what the seller has to offer, the seller gets the message, pronto!

If nobody will buy your tomatoes it won't take you long to get the message! The market is telling you something. It's telling you that you are using your energies and other resources to do something "the market" doesn't want you to do with those resources.

If the market system is working, then if you want an income you must do something that the market wants you to do. The market is difficult to visualize, "in general." But whenever it needs to send you a message, you may be sure that sooner or later you will get that message. The sooner you do, the better for you!

The "Market Structure": How Many Buyers and Sellers?

Even though "the market" doesn't usually exist in any one place, it is still useful to think of it as being "structured," or "built up" of *buyers* on one side and *sellers* on the other. When economists talk about the market structure they're talking about the *number* and the *relative sizes of the buyers and sellers* in that market.

Are there many buyers? many sellers? or only a few? Are some buyers and sellers big and powerful while others are small and insignificant? Or are the buyers and sellers all small? And is it easy for new buyers and sellers to come into this market and start buying and selling? or not? These are the questions you would ask if you wanted to find out about the "market structure."

Market Structure, and Monopoly and Competition. Sometimes there may be only one seller and many buyers (for example, the local electric company selling electricity). Or there may be only one buyer and many sellers (the local electric company buying the services of—that is, hiring—electrical workers).

You can see that the kind of competition existing in any market will depend a lot on the kind of "market structure." When there's only one seller there isn't going to be much competition on the seller's side of that market! A market which has only one buyer certainly won't have much competition on the buyer's side, either!

If there is only one seller we call that kind of market structure monopoly. If there are only a few buyers or sellers, each will have a considerable amount of market power (which means the same thing as monopoly power). If there are many small buyers and sellers, no one will have any "market power" or "monopoly power." With many small buyers or sellers, each will simply respond to market conditions. No buyer or seller will be big enough to have any noticeable influence on market prices, or on the quantities of things being produced and exchanged.

Is "the market" the idea of people buying and selling the things they want to buy and sell?

Pure Competition: a Very Special Market Structure. Now and then throughout this book you have seen (and many more times you will see) references to the "model pure market system." One essential condition of this "model system" is that each market throughout the system must have a market structure of pure competition.

"Pure competition" is a market made up of so many buyers and so many sellers that no one buyer or seller can have any noticeable influence on the market—either on the amounts being supplied or being demanded, or on the price. Each buyer and each seller is so small in the total picture that no one (acting alone) can create any noticeable surplus or shortage either by supplying or by demanding more, or less. No one buyer or seller can push the price up or down. Why? Because there are so many other buyers and sellers.

Or ....
is "the market"
the idea of people
producing and
selling things
so they can get
more money and
have more
things?

With pure competition no one can do anything but just accept the existing market conditions. You buy what you want to buy or sell what you want to sell at the going price, then go home. That is all you can do in a market of pure competition!

In a market of pure competition you can freely enter the market as either a buyer or a seller anytime you wish. You can buy or sell as much of the product as you want anytime you want to. But you must accept the "going market price." There's no way you can change it.

The concept of pure competition is very important in understanding how the market process works. You will be hearing about it and seeing examples of it several times in the following chapters. But for now it's enough that you just remember what it is.*

Later, when we get into the issues of competition and monopoly you will find out a lot

more about pure competition and about other kinds of market structure. But for now just be sure you have a clear understanding of what these terms mean and why they are important. Then, here's another important concept: private property.

PRIVATE PROPERTY

The market process couldn't work unless people had the right to keep the things they earned. That right is called the private property right. The "private property right" is a "social institution." It exists to some extent in every society. But it does not exist to an absolute or complete extent in any society.

The concept of private property—the idea that people have a governmentally protected right to own things—is very basic. There are several different ways you can look at and think about this social institution called "private property."

What Is Private Property? The concept of private property is simply the idea that you, as a private individual, have the right to own and to do whatever you please with anything which is "yours"—your house, your land, your car, your guitar, your money, your anything. Your right to have and to use "your things" is supported by law. Anyone who interferes with another person's property rights is breaking the law.

In order for "private property rights" to exist in the society, there must be some strong, stable, dependable force in the society—either government, or tradition, taboos, or something—to protect the "property rights" of each individual. Otherwise the things owned by some people would be taken over by other greedy, more powerful ones.

Your Wealth Is Your Private Property. If you were to add up the value of everything you own (that is, all your private property), you would

---

* The term "perfect competition" is sometimes used instead of pure competition. Sometimes "perfect competition" is used to mean exactly the same thing as pure competition. Other times perfect competition refers to a theoretical market model where the numbers of buyers and sellers is infinite and where other "perfect model conditions" exist. If you run across the term "perfect competition," usually you can tell which meaning applies.

arrive at a figure showing the total value of your wealth. As you make more income, you add to this "wealth." As you use up your income, or wear out your car or your shoes or whatever, you subtract from this wealth. Your "wealth," at any moment is the total value of your private property at that moment. Your *private property rights* are the rights you have to keep the things you own and to use them any way you wish.

The Market Process Requires Private Property

The market process could not work without private property. Why do most people work for income or make things for themselves or plant trees in their backyards or undertake any other kind of productive effort? Usually because these efforts add to the total value of their private property—their money, and things—their wealth. Unless the northside chief is going to be able to keep the money he earns or live in the house he builds or eat the fish he catches or drink the tuba he makes or keep the money he gets when he sells his tuba—then he probably would rather not work to produce these things.

People work and produce things so they can have more private property. When you have property you can enjoy having it. Or you can enjoy using it up. People work so they can get more cake to have, or to eat.

The government decides how "complete" your property rights will be. Then it guarantees and protects your property rights. Stealing is punished in every society!

Anything which interferes very much with a person's private property rights is likely also to interfere with the person's incentive to work. When government collects taxes from people, this reduces the "private property" (income) the people get from working. This may reduce their incentive to work. It is sometimes argued that if income taxes in the United States (and in other nations) are increased much more,

the high taxes may reduce the people's work-incentives so much that the functioning of the economy will be impaired.

Property Can Bring Perpetual Income to Its Owner

A person with some wealth can invest the wealth and receive income. With investments you can get a *continuing, perpetual income* that you don't have to keep working for! If you keep your money invested in bonds or in a savings account *you can keep getting income from it forever!*

Or . . . . is "the market" the idea of people trading things they have to get things they would rather have?

If you invest in a house to live in or a car to drive, you are still making an "investment" from which you will receive a continuing "income" for several years—not more "money income," but your "real income" will go up because you own the house or the car.

Once you own your house or your car "free and clear," you get the real income of using it without having to make any payments to anyone. You no longer have to pay out your "money income" as rent, or mortgage payments, or car payments. You can use your "money income" to buy more of some other kinds of "real income"—more steaks or lawn furniture or a new stereo system or a trip to Daytona or Lahaina or Acapulco.

Or . . . . is "the market" all those things, and more? *Of course it is.*

Yes, your income *really is* higher when you own useful, productive property. This is true if you get money from someone else for the use of your property; it is also true if you use your property yourself.

The Right to Receive Income without Working for It. The basic "private property right" can be thought of in many ways. One interesting and useful way is to think of it as "the right to receive real income (today) without having to work for it (today)."

Most people save up for vacations. Some people save up all of their working lives so they can enjoy a high level of "real income" after they retire. What they are doing is storing up some "private property" (money or bonds or real estate or whatever) so that later they can enjoy some real income *without having to work for it.*

The More You Own, the Less Work You Must Do. Any person who gets wealthy enough—that is, who gets enough private property—will never have to work again. Some people are born wealthy. They could go through life living on the income from their property if they wanted to. Some do. But most of them wind up working *harder* because of all their important economic choices—all the important decisions which most wealthy people must make. They must decide:

> Which businesses to expand? to contract? Which manager to promote? to fire? Which investment to shift? Which worthy cause to support? Which political candidate to endorse? and hundreds of other choices.

Want to be a millionaire? No. But want to have enough property to be able to take a good long vacation and travel next summer? Or to have an extra bedroom or an extra bath? an extra car? a boat? Yes! Most people have a strong incentive to acquire just a little more private property—*just a little more* "real income"—than they already have. Don't you? *This is the driving force that makes the market process work.*

Some Private Property Exists in All Economic Systems

The desire to get and have a few more things is so strong an incentive for most people that even in the governmentally controlled societies of Communist China and the Soviet Union, individuals are permitted to own some personal, private property. They usually receive income and products as rewards for their productive efforts.

Throughout history, every successful economic system, every successful society has had some arrangement for giving people "as their own private property" at least some share of the value of the output they produce. If the "pure market system" was working, the person who produced something would get to keep it all. But no society has ever worked quite that way.

The "productivity principle of distribution"—the idea that how much each person receives depends on how much that person produces—is a vital part of the market process. And it depends on the existence of "private property." If you are going to receive a share according to the value of what you produce, then whatever you receive as your share must become your "private property"—to keep and to use as you wish.

Private Property Rights Are Always Limited

If you think about it for a minute it becomes obvious that no society could give individuals "complete, absolute, unlimited private property rights." For example, suppose Mr. Pascal who runs the local junkyard has a pile of old rubber tires in the corner of his lot. He needs the space for junk cars so he decides to dispose of the pile of tires. That is his "private property right." The cheapest way to get rid of the tires is to burn them. So that's what he does.

The stinking smoke from the burning tires blows in the windows of the school down the road. All the children turn green. Before the day is over, many scientifically prepared, well-balanced lunches get flushed. By seven p.m. that day we find that the County Board is meeting in special session. (The daughter of the Board Chairman was one of the victims.) By 7:15 p.m. a new law has been passed removing the "property right" of a person to dispose of rubber tires in this county by burning. A property right has been removed "by due process of law."

Maybe Mr. Pascal should not have had the "right" to burn the tires in the first place. Maybe everyone should have had the governmentally protected "public property right" to breathe clean air all along. Certainly as more people get crowded closer together it becomes more necessary to limit the freedoms of individuals to do whatever they please with their property.

Property Can Be Taken by "Due Process."

The U.S. Constitution says that your property rights cannot be taken away except by due process of law. But what this also means is that your property rights *can* be taken away— so long as it is done by due process of law!

When the State Highway Department decides that a new highway is going to go across the corner of your front lawn, the fact that the land is your private property does not stop the highway. The land is taken by "due process" and "just compensation" is paid to you for your loss. Each time the government collects taxes from you, this takes some of your private property. When a wealthy person dies, the government takes a sizable share of that person's property.

Many limits on private property are imposed by the government to protect the community. People cannot own certain firearms without governmental consent. No unauthorized person is supposed to own or to transport certain drugs. No one can build anything on his or her property unless the structure is in keeping with the local zoning laws. We are all told what we must and must not do with our automobiles. And on and on the list could go.

Private Property Rights Are Becoming More Limited.

Already we live within a complex network of restrictions on our private property rights. In the coming years, with larger population, new technology, increasing demands for goods, crowding of more people into the cities, more pressures on the environment and all the other complex conditions which are advancing toward us over the horizon, you may be sure that more restrictions and limitations on our private property rights are on the way. It seems inevitable.

How far can the local, state and national governments go in limiting private property rights without upsetting the functioning of the market process? No one knows for sure. The important idea is the obvious one: if the market process is going to work, the people must be permitted to have, to keep, and to use at least *some* of what they produce. But *just how much?* No one knows.

The market process operates on *rewards*. And with rewards we get inequality. That's what the next section talks about.

THE ESSENTIAL ROLE OF INEQUALITY

Did you ever stop to think about how "reward-oriented" we all are? Why does a person struggle out of bed in the morning and hurry to get to work on time? What gets the taxi driver to keep fighting the rush-hour traffic? What gets farmers up at dawn to plow, sow, harvest? What gets people to save and invest? Why are people willing to work overtime? nights? weekends? Why would a family pull up stakes and move to some distant city where better jobs are available? You know the answer. The promise of rewards. The promise of higher incomes—a larger share of the output—more and better things. Of course.

We Are All "Reward-Oriented." Even our approach to education is highly "reward-oriented." We professors offer (and most students seem to want) academic rewards, almost on a day-to-day basis. Schools give rewards in the form of grades, quality points, course credits, semester hours, Dean's list, scholarships, degrees, cum laude, and other such "contrived" rewards. Most of us admit that emphasis on these rewards often diverts attention away from the real purposes of being in college. Yet most people seem to insist on them.

Some people suggest that working for money, trying to get ahead, to pay off the mortgage, to gain some financial security—that these objectives divert attention from the real purposes of life. Perhaps so. Nonetheless, this is the way most people are. This is the way the world is organized.

Is Reward-Orientation a Natural Thing? Perhaps all this emphasis on "seeking rewards" appeals to the basic nature, the survival instinct, of all living things. It isn't just true of people. All animals and all plants are seeking, reaching for rewards. The most successful ones get the biggest rewards. The least successful ones may get no rewards at all. The result? Inequality.

Inequality is essential in any system which offers incentives, or rewards. The "market system" in its pure form operates entirely on the basis of incentives. Rewards. Inequality is essential to the functioning of the system.

A Reward-System Requires Inequality

If you are going to be rewarded for performing some task, that means that you must *not*

receive the reward unless you perform the task. Obviously. If you are going to get the reward anyway (task or not) then it isn't a reward anymore!

There aren't very many ways to get the people of the world to do the work that is necessary to keep society fed, clothed, housed, doctored, transported, taught, protected, entertained, etc. One way to get people to work is to reward them. Another way is to order them to do it and punish them if they don't. If rewards are used, inequality results—some people get more than others. But if rewards aren't used, any other system results in a loss of individual freedom of choice. So which system are we going to use? That's the kind of tough dilemma every society must face.

Either we put up with the inequality and use rewards as incentives, or we use something like the military draft to force people to do what the ones in charge tell us to do. Under the draft laws, all "able-bodied men" are equal. If the system is working as it should, there's absolutely no inequality—except as to sex and age and abilities. But notice also that no one is free. Even the "direct command" economic systems are likely to exhibit a high degree of inequality. Unproductive people don't get very much income in those systems, either. And the ones in charge somehow seem to wind up with quite a lot.

Inequality Exists in All Economic Systems. The market process absolutely requires that economic inequality be permitted to exist. Neither the political process nor the social process *absolutely requires* economic inequality in order to get the economic problem taken care of. But in every past or present real-world economic system, a high degree of economic inequality has always existed.

The "market system" is sometimes criticized because inequality is an essential part of the system. Certainly great inequality is not the most desirable human condition. No one likes to think of wealthy people feeding milk to their cats while on the other side of town children are suffering of malnutrition because they don't have enough milk. But in every economic system throughout history we can find examples of waste by the wealthy, while the poor suffer.

Dramatic Examples Don't Help Much. Probably such dramatic contrasts will always be discoverable in every society. But dramatic examples of economic injustice serve very little purpose—except to fuel the emotional fires which demogogues try to build to hypnotize otherwise intelligent people. The real issues hinge on the actual extent of deprivation of the poor, and waste by the rich—and on finding *practical* solutions to the problem—solutions which will do more good than harm.

In recent years all market-directed systems have been undergoing changes to reduce inequality. The political process has been making more and more of the distribution choices. The governments collect taxes and then give money to the unemployed, sick, aged, dependent children and others who cannot support themselves. Such income redistribution programs are now working in all modern societies, both in the market-oriented countries and in the Communist countries too.

How Much Income Redistribution Is Possible?

In every market-oriented economy, the governments take property "by due process of law" (taxes) from the people who have earned it as income (as rewards for their production) and then "redistribute" this property (as money, goods, services) to other people—people who did not earn it. At what point does this "redistribution" process destroy people's incentives to work?

At what point do the productive people say "Why work more (or risk more) when I will get to keep so little of the extra income I earn?" At what point do the unproductive ones say "Why try to get a job? I am already receiving about as much as I would get if I went to work."

No one knows the answers to these questions. No one knows how much the existing redistribution programs are interfering with incentives. If people think marginally (and of course people do think marginally—marginal thinking is just common sense!) any redistribution of income will have *some* effect on *some* people's behavior.

Suppose your older brother is faced with a decision and he's "right on the fence." He just can't make up his mind about whether or not to work overtime, or maybe to move somewhere else to get a higher-paying (more productive) job, or maybe to take a training course to improve his income. Is the income tax likely to influence his decision? Of course. If he's going to get to keep all the extra money he makes, he is more likely to do the extra work. If the government is going to take away about half of his extra income in taxes, your brother may decide to forget the whole thing!

Some people are always on the "threshold of reaction" (right on the fence), so surely our present-day income redistribution programs must be having some effect on some people's choices—to work or not to work, to invest or not to invest, and all that. But how much effect? On how many? We just don't know.

The Great Dilemma of the Market System—Inequality

If the market process is going to work, incentives are essential. Rewards must be used. So inequality can never be eliminated. To eliminate inequality would require that rewards be eliminated. And to do that would be to "kill the goose that lays the golden egg."

It is the *incentive of reward* which works in the market process to make the total output high enough so that there is enough for some people to waste things. It is the *incentive of reward* which generates enough total output so that some of it can be redistributed from the original producer-earners to the unproductive ones. As society evolves, maybe rewards will become much less important, much less necessary as a technique for motivating people. But that hasn't happened yet.

Waste by some while others go hungry? That isn't good. So we have a dilemma. Right? Yes. There's a flaw in the system. But as yet, no method anyone has ever devised for getting the world's work done, for stimulating people to produce the needed output—has come out any better. Actually, most of the tried alternatives seem to have turned out worse.

All this doesn't mean that we should stop seeking better answers to the distribution question. But it does suggest that maybe we shouldn't completely destroy the "incentive and reward" approach until after we have figured out something else that might work. That's the tough part. It's a lot easier to protest or support things than it is to understand them! But you've already found that out. Right?

Market Incentives Really Do Work

Incentives, rewards, and the resulting inequality are essential in the operation of the market process. These are the conditions which stimulate and capture and harness and channel the energies of the society and aim them toward the desired objectives. The incentive of reward stimulates and directs the economy and keeps it going and growing.

Would you be just as interested in a college degree if you knew it would have no effect on your lifetime income? Some people would. But many wouldn't. The market process stimulates and directs most of us. As we try to get ahead, automatically we are working for the entire society. The next section goes further into that.

THE INCOME-SEEKING FACTORS OF PRODUCTION

Whenever something is going to be made, some "inputs" are going to be needed. Obviously. To really see how the market process operates, you need to know more about "inputs"—that is, more about the factors of production.

There are hundreds—even thousands of different kinds of factors of production—everything from the electricity that runs the machines to the paper that packages the products. I'm sure you could list a dozen different kinds of inputs without even thinking about it. But with all these different kinds of inputs, these factors of production buzzing around, how do we ever make sense out of what's going on? Easy. We combine and simplify.

When we economists talk about the "factors of production" we have something very specific and precise in mind. You will need to grasp these special meanings so that what comes later will make sense to you. So let's talk about the "factors of production": labor, land, and capital.

Labor, and Wages

People are not factors of production. They are people. But the effort or manpower they exert to make something, is labor. "Labor" is a factor of production. Perhaps your father sells his labor to a business in exchange for income. Or perhaps he uses his labor himself to grow corn and tomatoes in his backyard field. In a market-directed economy he is free to sell or to use his labor any way he chooses. He owns his labor. He can sell it to the highest bidder, use it himself, or just rest—not use his labor to produce anything at all. Labor, then, is one of the factors of production. Some of the factor "labor" is required as an input for almost any kind of production you can think of.

Wages are the payments people receive when they sell their labor. The wage rate is "the *price* of a unit of labor." As you know, there are many different kinds of labor. Some kinds sell for low prices, others sell for high prices. Doctors and lawyers sell highly skilled labor and receive high "wages." The efforts of unskilled mill workers and migrant farm workers are not valued nearly so highly. Their labor sells for a much lower price (wage rate). But both are selling labor—their own time, energies, and efforts—in the "labor markets."

Land, and Rents

A second factor of production is land. But, like labor, "land" isn't exactly what you would think it is. Actually it's what you would think it is plus a lot more. In order to simplify things and limit the number of different "factors of production," economists usually consider "land" to include all the natural resources—all the "free gifts of nature." When we say "land," then, we include the minerals in the land, the trees in the natural forests, the natural lakes and streams, and even the fish swimming in these lakes and streams, the deer in the forest, and the wild buffalo roaming on the plains. (I don't know why it is that the only thing buffalo ever seem to do is "roam." I suppose it's because "roam" rhymes with "home." But roaming or not, wild buffalo are "land.")

Why do economists include the roaming buffalo and all the other "free gifts of nature" in our definition of "land"? Only because it's useful to do it that way. More on that, later.

Most of the land in the world is scarce. It has economic value and is owned by somebody—individuals, businesses, other organizations, or governments. Just as people can sell their time and efforts (labor) for a price (wage), so also can the use of land be sold for a price.

The price paid for the use of land (that is, the income received by the owner of the land) is called rent. If you own a very productive oil well or gold mine or half an acre just off Times Square, the "rent" you receive will put you on easy street. But if you own a barren plot in some secluded spot, better not quit your job and plan to live it up on your "rent" income!

Capital, and Interest

The third and final factor of production is capital. Like land and labor, the chances are this term doesn't mean exactly what you thought it did. Capital is the only one of the three factors left. So this term must include all the inputs *except* labor and land. And so it does!

If "land" includes all the natural resources (the "free gifts of nature") and "labor" includes all human effort, then what's capital?

"Capital" must include all the inputs *except* "human effort" (labor) and "natural things" (land). What's left? All the "things" other than the "natural things." The man-made things!

All the "man-made inputs" are called "capital." There are thousands of different kinds of "produced" things which are used as inputs—ranging from factories and machines and trucks to electricity and note pads and paper clips. All these different things are lumped together and called "capital."

Produced Things to be Used in Further Production. We define "capital" as *produced things which are going to be used as inputs for further production.* Capital is anything which has been produced and which is not available for the immediate satisfaction of someone's desires. A machine, a building, a shovel is capital. Even a can of peas on the grocer's shelf is "capital" to the grocer. But to the person who buys it to eat, the can of peas is a "consumer good."

Someone must *invest* to make capital. If you invest your income or your efforts in building capital, you can receive more *future* income because your capital is productive. Capital helps you to produce more things. If you start using more efficient machines and tools you will produce more product. Then when you sell this marginal product you will get more revenue. See? Your capital has a marginal "value product," just as your labor does!

When you receive income from the capital you have invested in, this income is called *interest*. The "interest" is the money you receive because your capital is productive, just as your wage or your rent is the money that you receive because your labor or your land is productive.

Two Meanings of the Term "Capital." The economist's use of the term "capital" will be a bit strange to you at first. *When a business manager uses the word "capital," he or she usually means the "money" needed to operate the business*—to buy the machines and raw materials and other things. But when we economists say "capital," we don't mean the money. We mean the factory, machines, equipment, materials, and other things the business will buy with the money. To avoid confusion, economists frequently say "capital goods," or "capital equipment" to make it obvious that they are not talking about the money. It isn't really the money that's productive, and that produces the interest income. It's the machines and equipment and things—the *real* inputs—the capital.

Some capital is essential for almost any kind of production. Even if you are going into the business of selling hot dogs on the beach, you need some capital. You need a little hot dog stand, a grill, a box of rolls, an oven to heat the rolls, a package of wieners, some mustard and relish and a few other things. All these things are your capital.

If you are going to grow corn or tomatoes you need a shovel or a hoe or a plow or a garden tractor or a sharp stick or some kind of tool (capital), and some seeds (capital), fertilizer (capital), some bug spray (capital), and a basket (capital) to use in gathering your harvest. It

wouldn't hurt if you had a couple of hard-working people to help you (labor) and a naturally fertile garden plot (land). But some capital is essential.

Capital Good? Or Consumer Good? Various kinds of capital are being produced all the time. All the things that are being produced, if they are going to be used as inputs for further production, are capital. All the things being produced are being produced for one of two reasons: either to be consumed (used to satisfy people's wants) or to be used to help to produce something else (used as capital).

"Consumption" is the ultimate objective of all production. "Final goods" are the things that come out at the *very end* of the "production pipeline." Final goods are used by "final consumers" for the ultimate purpose— to provide "satisfaction" or "pleasure" or "utility"—whatever that means to each consumer.

Everything that is being produced is aimed either directly or indirectly toward the ultimate objective of "final consumption." If a good is aimed *directly* toward final consumption, it's a consumer good. If it's aimed *indirectly* toward final consumption (if it's going to be used to produce something else) then it's a capital good. All along the "production chain" (like from iron ore to an automobile) everything being produced is capital *except* for the good bought by the final consumer (the automobile).

Whether something is a capital good or a consumer good often depends on how it will be used. A small private twin-jet aircraft used by a millionaire movie star to go zooming around the country visiting friends, is a consumer good. An identical aircraft used by a business manager to more efficiently serve distant customers is a capital good.

The tank of oil a person is going to use to heat the house this winter is a consumer good; the tank of oil the power company is going to use to fire its boilers is a capital good. If your "aggie agent" (your county agricultural agent) convinces you to feed your chocolate cake to your cow so she will give chocolate milk, then your chocolate cake becomes capital!

A Fourth Factor of Production? And What About Profits?

Now you know about the three factors of production—labor, land, and capital. And you know about the three kinds of income (distributive shares) the owners of these factors can earn—wages, rent, and interest. You also know that we have defined each factor in such a way that everything is covered.

All human effort is "labor." All *things* used in production are either man-made, or they aren't man-made. If they *are* man-made they're capital. If they aren't man-made, they're land. So everything is covered.

A fourth factor of production? How could that be? Maybe there can't. But then again, maybe there can. Why? Because something seems to be missing. People earn wages, rent, and interest by selling the services of their labor, land, and capital. Fine. But what about *profits*! What factor of production gets the profits?

Suppose your neighbor, Mr. Hawkins, is a very successful (and lucky) businessman. In a good year he may earn a very high profit. What is he getting paid for? Not for the use of his land or his capital. If it was for that, we economists would say: "What he's earning is really rent and interest and he only *thinks* it's profit." It's not for the use of his labor either. If it was we would say: "He's really only earning wages and he thinks it's profit." No, it's something else.

Over the years, economists have had trouble trying to decide what profit really is. Or to say it differently, we've had trouble deciding the *most useful way* to conceptualize profit. What is the true nature and role of profit? How does it operate? What does it do in the "model pure market system"? And what does it do in real-world economic systems?

The market system couldn't work without profit. (If this isn't obvious to you now, you'll see why later.) But is profit a payment to some factor of production? If so, what factor? And if not, why is profit so necessary to the functioning of the system? What is it a payment for? You can see the confusion that arises when we let profit just "hang loose" without any factor of production to attach itself to.

The Entrepreneur, and Profits. Economists, neat- and orderly-minded as we are, don't like for things to be "hanging loose." So we invented a factor of production to go with profit. What factor? The entrepreneur—the farsighted resource-manager who brings together the other three factors, gets them organized, and directs them into socially desired production.

The entrepreneur is the one who decides what to produce and how much, which inputs to use, and all that. In our example, your neighbor Mr. Hawkins is the entrepreneur. He is the one who hires and pays the owners of the labor, land, and capital. He hopes that when he sells the product he will get all his money back, *plus* some profit. If he produces the right amounts of the right things and does it efficiently, he will make a profit. If he doesn't, he won't. So *we can think of profit as being the payment which goes to the fourth factor of production: the entrepreneur.*

Risk and Uncertainty and Profits. Another way is to explain profit as the "incentive payment" which is necessary to induce people (factor-owners) to take risks. Uncertainty is everywhere. Unless a lot of people were somehow induced to take some chances the market system couldn't work.

Without the profit incentive, who would quit a steady job at a steady salary and start an auto-repair shop? Who would invest their savings in a McDonald's drive-in? or in an organic food store? or in a reverb amp for Friday night gigs? Who would spend money drilling for oil? Who would go hungry and work in a basement trying to invent a better antipollution device? or TV tube? or vaulting pole? or pool cue? Probably nobody.

Profit can be looked at as the reward you get for taking a chance for society, and winning. If you hire some factors of production and make something the people want, and if you do it efficiently, you will be rewarded. Your profit is your reward. But if you guess wrong you get no reward. You lose. Your loss is your "punishment" for using society's resources in ways the society didn't want its resources to be used.

Either way you look at it you can see how important profit (and loss) is. It is essential to the functioning of the market process. It can be regulated and taxed and manipulated without destroying the system—but only within limits. Just as private property, wages, rent, and interest are essential, so too profit is essential for the market process to work. In some ways profit might be considered the most essential of all.

You Can Define as Many Factors as You Wish. Sometimes it may be helpful (and neat and orderly) to think of four factors: labor, land, capital, and the entrepreneur; and four sources of income: wages, rent, interest, and profit. There are times when it is helpful to break down the factors even further. The labor factor can become several different factors: unskilled, semi-skilled, skilled, service, clerical, professional, young, old, male, female, and so on. And capital and land can each be broken into many separate factors.

How many factors are there? As many as you want to define. Use the most useful breakdown—the one that will help you most to observe what you want to observe. For a basic understanding of the market process you can think of either three factors (with profit going to any factor-owner who takes a risk), or four factors (with the risk-taker, resource manager thought of as a separate, profit-seeking factor). You can see the market process working just fine, either way.

The Factors of Production Respond to "The Market"

The factors of production—labor, land, and capital—are the "essential ingredients" in the production process. These factors provide the productive base of every society. These input factors are what the society tries to optimize. The production question for the society is really the question of choosing the way each of these factors will be used.

Which land, which labor, and which capital will we use in which ways? to produce which things? Will we use our factors to produce more consumer goods? Or more capital goods? Whichever ones we produce, will we use a lot of labor and a little capital and land? or much land and capital and only a little labor? Which input combinations? How do we decide? When all these questions are answered, the production question for the society is answered.

Owners Move Their Factors to the High-Paying Jobs. If the market process is in charge, the answers to all these questions will emerge automatically. The owners of the factors of production will be free to use their factors in any way they wish, so they will move their factors into the uses which offer the highest incomes! Of course.

Each kind of labor tends to flow towards its highest-priced (most valued) use. The same is true for land and capital. As the factor-owners try to increase their incomes they automatically move their factors into the uses society values most.

If the specialized labor needed to do some important task is very scarce, that means the society has a great need for more of that kind of labor. The price (wage) offered for it will be very high. The high wage will induce some people in other occupations to study or retrain so they can get one of these specialized, high-paying jobs. As more people respond to the high wage, the great scarcity will be relieved. The wage will move down. See how the market automatically moves the factors of production to where the society most wants them to be?

The Very Efficient "Factor Market." What a neat system it is! Each factor is moved (by its owner) into that activity which society most wants it to perform. This happens automatically. Why? Because the owner of each factor is trying to get more income. The highly efficient "factor market" accomplishes these three objectives:

1. it moves the factors of production from one activity into another;
2. it stimulates the development of new labor skills and new kinds of capital in the areas and activities on which society's demands are greatest; and
3. it discourages people from using their labor, land, or capital in the kinds of work society *doesn't* want done.

The Market System Is Really Efficient!

The great efficiency of the market system in directing the factors of production results from the fact that everything happens so automatically. No one needs to run a survey to find out what things need to be done, and where. No one needs to be assigned the job of going around contacting the individual workers, or the owners of land or capital, trying to induce or force them to move their factors of production from one job or one place to another. The market process handles it all automatically.

This process automatically solves the distribution problem, too! Remember? Each person's "income share"—wages, rent, interest, or profit—depends on how well that person responds to the society's wishes—that is, on how successful that person is in using his or her factors to do what the society most wants those factors to do. A factor of production— labor, land, capital—will only bring income to its owner if it is used to produce something people want to buy. Why did the northside family shift their efforts (labor) and natural resources (land) and tools (capital) out of the production of bows and arrows and into the production of tuba? Because people were buying tuba! Nobody was buying bows and arrows. That's how demand works through the market process. That's how demand induces the input factors to produce the things the society wants most—and not produce the things society doesn't want. But how does it all get worked out? Exactly how do the factor owners know where to go and what to do with their factors? They respond to *prices*, of course! And how do the prices get worked out?

Prices respond to demand. When the demand for something increases, its price goes up. You've known about this ever since Chapter 3. But there's a lot more about it that you don't know yet. The next chapter is all about demand and supply and prices. When you finish that chapter you'll know a lot more about how it all fits together.

But before you go on, take time to review. There's a lot in this chapter: about the market, market structure, private property, inequality, the factors of production. You'll need to know these concepts well as you go on into the next chapter and learn about the theory of "demand, supply, and price."

REVIEW
EXERCISES ● MAJOR CONCEPTS, PRINCIPLES, TERMS (Explain each carefully.)

the market
market structure and competition
the role of "private property"
the factors of production
the role of profits

demand directs the factors
the role of competition
the role of inequality
the "inequality dilemma" of the market system

● OTHER CONCEPTS AND TERMS (Explain each briefly.)

market structure	labor
monopoly	wage
market power	land
monopoly power	rent
pure competition	capital
the concept of private property	interest
private property rights	profit
wealth	capital good
real income	consumer good
money income	the entrepreneur
income redistribution	

● QUESTIONS (Write out answers or jot down key points.)

1. Suppose there's only one dealer in your city who can repair your small foreign car. What kind of a market structure would you say that is? Suppose you don't like that dealer's repair work or prices. What can you do? Discuss.

2. What are some of the ways in which the rights of private property have become more restricted over the past several decades? (If you can't think of anything, ask your parents, or grandparents. They'll tell you!) What additional restrictions do you expect will be imposed over the next decade or two? Discuss.

3. Some colleges now let students take some courses on a "pass-fail" basis.
   (a) Do you think the "pass-fail option" is a move toward greater "equality," and less emphasis on the "reward approach" as a method of getting students to learn?
   (b) Do you think you would be learning more economics, or less, if you were taking this course "pass-fail"? How about if there were no grade and no credit and no college degree? Nothing to stimulate you but your own "yearning for learning." What about that?
   (c) How far do you think colleges can go in eliminating their artificial "incentive reward" systems? And give "equal rewards" (or no rewards) to everybody?
   (d) How far do you think a modern economic system can go toward eliminating pay incentives, and giving equal incomes to everybody? Nobody knows, really, but what do you think?

4. What's so *efficient* about letting the market process direct the factors of production?

5. The *production question* for every society is really a question of what to do with the available inputs—with the available factors of production. Explain how the *market process* gets the question answered and gets the society's wishes carried out.

17 Demand, Supply, and Price: How the Pure Market System Works

The theory of how consumer demand activates the price mechanism and directs the economic choices in the "Model Pure Market System."

You already know a lot about the market process. You know that as all the individuals and businesses are making their choices, the production and distribution choices for the society are being made. It all happens automatically. How? By demand and supply and prices working together.

The study of the market process is essentially the study of supply and demand. Demand reflects people's choices; supply reflects scarcity. Demand works through the market process to pull forth the output (the supply). The people who produce (who supply) the demanded output, get rewarded with income. See how the "supply and demand" idea sort of ties it all together?

Economists have a great body of economic theory dealing with supply and demand. And curves? Yes. But only two basic curves: the demand curve and the supply curve. These two curves are sort of fun to play with. And they sure can help to see how the market process works! So after waiting so long and getting so ready, here it is at last: supply and demand! First, demand.

THE CONCEPT OF DEMAND

Each of us buys something because we want to. We would rather have the "something" than to have the money it costs. To say it another way: We would rather have that "something" than to continue to have the opportunity to spend the money for some *other* "something." The more we *want* something the more we are likely to *pay* to get it. The more we would pay for it, the higher is our *demand* for it.

If you are ready to give up a lot of money for something, then your demand for it is high. If you aren't ready to give up anything (any money) for something, then you have no demand for it. You may have some *desire* for it. But if you aren't ready to pay a price to get it you do not *demand* it.

If you want something but still wouldn't pay to get it, there must be some reason.

The key to microeconomics is SUPPLY and DEMAND... Don't forget okay?

289

Perhaps you want to keep your money for some other purpose. Or maybe you just don't have any money! Either way it makes no difference in the operation of the market process.

Unless you are *ready, willing and able to pay a price* for something you do not demand it no matter how much you may *want* it. Desire? Yes. Demand? No. You aren't going to influence any of society's choices through "the market process" just by wanting something. Unless you are able and willing to spend some money to buy something, your *wants* won't have any effect.

Demand Is "the Propensity to Buy"

Demand, as we economists use the term, is another one of our "if . . . then" concepts (like the consumption function you were working with a few chapters ago). The consumption function doesn't tell how big the basic flow of consumer spending *is*. It only tells "how big it would be if. . . ." For example, we might say: "If national income (NI) happened to be $5 billion, then consumer spending (C) would be $5 billion; if NI was $10 billion, then C would be $8 billion." This is the same way we use the term "demand."

The "demand" for something doesn't mean "how much of it people are buying." It only means "how much of it people *would be buying if* . . . " If what? If the price happened to be $5 or $10 or $30 or maybe 50 cents. So "demand" in economics, doesn't mean what it normally means to most people. In economics it really means "propensity to buy." It means "how much I would buy, if. . . ." Let's make a comparison.

The "consumption function" relates "propensity to buy" (for consumer goods in general) to the different possible sizes of the national income. Remember? The "demand function" relates "propensity to buy" (for some specific good) to the different possible *prices* which might be charged for that good.

If you have a "demand" for something (a "propensity to buy"), whether or not you *actually will buy* depends on how high the price is. You may be willing to pay to get something, but you may *not* be willing to pay a price which you think is too high. If you have been buying something regularly (say, a dozen eggs a week) and then the price goes up, that changes the picture.

If the price goes up you must give up more money to buy your usual weekly dozen eggs. Maybe you decide you would rather buy something else instead. Perhaps breakfast cereal looks like a better deal than eggs, now. And here's something else. Your "consumption possibility" gets smaller if you keep on buying the high-priced eggs.

At Higher Prices, Your "Consumption Possibility" Is Smaller. When you spend your money for the high-priced eggs, you don't get as much for your money as you did before. Each dollar you spend for eggs buys less than it bought before. Suppose the high price turns you off so you just quit buying eggs altogether. Suppose you decide to buy only things which haven't gone up in price. Then your money buys just as much as before! Your consumption possibility is just as large as it was before. (The value of *your* dollar depends on what *you* buy with it. Remember?)

There are always some people who are undecided about which product to buy. They are "right at the margin." If the price of one thing goes up even a little bit, they will stop buying that thing and start buying some other thing instead.

Demand Is a Functional Relationship. You could say that demand is the "functional relationship" between the various prices which might exist and the various quantities people would buy. The quantity people would actually buy is "a function of price." That is, the quantity bought depends on how high (or low) the price happens to be.

Once you *demand* something, whether or not you will actually go out and try to buy it (and how much per week you will try to buy) depends on the price. I wonder how many eggs you would buy if the price went up to $10 a dozen! (You would still have a demand for eggs—a "propensity to buy"—but would you *actually* buy any? I doubt it.)

The "Substitution Effect" of a Price Change

When the price of something goes up, people buy less of it. There are two reasons why people buy less. The first reason is that they decide to stop buying the high-priced good and to spend their money for other things instead—that is, they *shift* their spending to other goods. Maybe they buy breakfast cereal instead of eggs. They *substitute* cereal for eggs. Whenever the price of something rises, the people who are right at the margin—sort of undecided—will stop buying the higher-priced good and substitute something else. Economists call this the substitution effect of the higher price.

The "substitution effect" of a price change also works when the price goes down. If eggs get cheaper, people will buy fewer breakfast steaks and corn flakes and pancakes and start buying more eggs. They "substitute" the (cheaper) eggs for the pancakes and things.

The "Income Effect" of a Price Change

The second reason people buy less of something when it gets more expensive, is this: When goods are higher priced your "money income" can't buy as much "real income" as it could before. Suppose you are buying eggs and the price of eggs goes up. If you keep on buying eggs, the higher price actually reduces your "total purchasing power." Your real income (the things you get to have and enjoy each week) gets smaller. Here's an example.

If you have only two dollars to spend for breakfast foods this month and all you really like in the morning is scrambled eggs, then if the price of eggs goes up from 50¢ to $2 a dozen, you are in trouble. Before the price increase, your $2 bought four dozen eggs. Now it will only buy one dozen eggs.

Your purchasing power for eggs has dropped from four dozen to one dozen. You might still want four dozen and you might be willing to buy them even at a price of $2. But you just don't have the money. So when the price goes up from 50¢ to $2, the quantity you buy drops from four dozen to one dozen—not because you "substitute" other goods for eggs, but because your purchasing power has been reduced by the price increase. Your "real income" has been reduced.

Whenever the price of something goes up, the people who keep buying the good at the higher price actually experience a reduction in "real income." This causes them (really, *forces* them) to buy less. Economists call this the income effect of the price increase. The "income effect" also works when the price goes down. People who are careful to buy the goods they want only when the goods are on sale can enjoy more "real income." (Of course this doesn't mean that you can save money by buying lots of things you don't *usually* buy, just because the things happen to be on sale!)

To summarize: There are two reasons why people will buy more of something as its price goes down (and less of it as its price goes up): (1) the *substitution effect,* and (2) the *income effect.* Think about it. Don't both of these "effects" influence your buying choices? (They do mine.)

Consumer Demand Depends on Wants, and Income

If you have a demand for something, that means two requirements are being met: (1) you want it, and (2) you are willing and able to spend some money to get it. If these two conditions are met, you have a "demand." You have a "propensity to buy." Then, the higher the price, the *less* of it you will *actually buy;* the lower the price, the *more* of it you will *actually buy.* This little capsule statement explains about all there is to the basic concept of "consumer demand."

The Law of Demand

Economists make up "demand curves" to show the relationship between the various prices that might exist and the quantities people would be trying to buy at each of those various prices. Think about it. Will the demand curve show larger quantities bought at high prices? Or larger quantities bought at low prices? See? You already understand the demand curve. And you already know the *law of demand*.

The law of demand says that people would buy more of something at a lower price than they would at a higher price.

You know this is true, because of the substitution and income effects. You know it is true from your own personal experience, too. Right? The demand curve (Figure 17-1) illustrates the law of demand. Take time now to study it for a few minutes.

HOW THE PRICE MECHANISM WORKS: THE FUNCTIONS OF PRICE

The demand curve shows how the buyer responds to price changes. But don't be misled. It isn't the market which directs and controls the economic choices of the people. It's the other way around. The people, as consumers, direct and control the society's choices through the market. But the market does let the consumer know how scarce each thing is, so that the consumer will know which of society's goods need to be most carefully conserved and economized.

Prices Conserve Scarce Things: the Rationing Function

If the price of something goes higher, people don't buy as much of it. The substitution effect and the income effect see to that! We can say, then, that one thing which the *price* of something does is to convince the people (the consumer-buyers) to conserve, to limit the use of scarce things. We call this role—the role which price plays to discourage the use of scarce things—the rationing function of price.

The more scarce something is, the higher its price will be. The higher the price of something, the more it will be conserved and economized. That's what is meant by "the rationing function of price."

The demand curve is a *graphic picture of the rationing function of price*. Look at the demand curve for eggs (Figure 17-1). It shows that at a price of $2 a dozen, only a few eggs would be bought—less than one carload per week. Only those people who really like eggs (or people with lots of money to spend) will continue to eat two eggs for breakfast every morning when the price is $2 a dozen! See how much more carefully eggs will be conserved at $2 a dozen than at 50¢ a dozen?

If the price of eggs would suddenly go up to $2, this would tell us that eggs must have suddenly become very scarce for some reason. People who are really crazy about eggs will probably go around scowling and muttering all the time about the high price of eggs. But they really should be very thankful that the price went up to $2. At a price of $2, every Tom, Dick and Harry will not be eating up all the very scarce eggs!

A price of $2 a dozen saves the eggs for the true egg-lovers. If for some reason the price of eggs had not been allowed to go up—if some "consumer protection committee" had convinced the legislature to pass a law holding the price of eggs down to 50¢—the eggs soon would all be used up and *nobody* would get any more eggs for awhile. You can see how the high

Fig. 17-1   The Demand Curve Illustrates the Propensity to Buy

The lower the price of eggs, the more people will try to buy

Think of this as the weekly demand for eggs in your local metropolitan area.

The demand curve illustrates the "law of demand." It shows that at lower prices people would buy more. For example, if the price moves down from $1.00 to 75 cents per dozen, the quantity people will buy increases from 6 carloads to 10 carloads per week. This shows that the quantity people buy is very responsive (stretches a lot) when the price goes down.

The economist would say that the demand for eggs in this example is *relatively elastic*, or *price elastic*. Elasticity means *sensitivity*, or *responsiveness* to price changes. When the price changes, if the quantity bought does not respond very much we say the demand is *relatively inelastic*, or *price inelastic*. The responsiveness is low.

The concept of elasticity of demand is very helpful in understanding how the market process works. It means "responsiveness of buyers to price changes."

price performs a use-limiting, "rationing" function. As the price moves up, it notifies the people who don't really care very much about eggs that they should stop buying eggs and leave the eggs in the market for those who really go for eggs!

Free goods have no prices. They are used freely. No one tries to conserve or economize or limit or ration the use of free goods. But once a good is scarce it needs to have a price. Then the use of the good will be automatically rationed. If a price had been charged for killing the buffalo on the plains we would have saved many roaming buffalo herds!

The "rationing function of price" limits the use of scarce things. Only those people who want something badly enough to pay the price will get any. Things will be used *only* for those purposes which someone considers *important enough* to be worth the price. Are you beginning to be impressed by this thing we call "price"? Be impressed. It's truly the key to understanding the market process.

Prices Direct Resources and Induce Output: the Production-Motivating Function

While the high price is conserving the use of eggs it is also doing something else. The high price is *pulling in factors of production*—more labor, land, and capital into the production of eggs. At a price of $2 a dozen, big profits can be made in the egg business. Of course! So anyone who can get some laying hens and start producing eggs can make a bundle!

It's easy to see why high prices motivate production. What we are talking about is called the production-motivating function of price. And we're running into the other half of our discussion of "supply and demand." We're getting into the concept of *supply*.

THE CONCEPT OF SUPPLY

If, in the precise world of economics, demand means "propensity to buy," what do you

suppose supply means? Maybe "propensity to sell"? Exactly!

We have been talking about people buying things—you buying bananas and people buying eggs and all that. Goods are flowing out of the market to the buyers. But where are the goods flowing into the market from? From the sellers, of course.

Supply Is "the Propensity to Sell"

Is "supply" the amount flowing across the market from the sellers to the buyers? Is that it? Nope. The supply is an "if . . . then" concept just like demand. The supply tells how much the sellers would be trying to sell if the price was $1, or $5, or $10, or $30, or whatever. It is *"the propensity to sell."*

Supply Is a Functional Relationship. The word "supply," like the word "demand," has a very precise meaning in economics. You could say that supply is the *"functional relationship"* between the various *prices* which might exist and the various quantities the producers would be trying to sell. Once the "supply" (the "propensity to sell") exists, then the *actual quantity* each producer will offer for sale will depend on the *price*. At higher prices, producers will offer more for sale; at lower prices they will offer less.

Now we're about ready to look at the supply curve. Do you know what it's going to look like? Of course. Positive slope. At higher prices greater quantities would be offered for sale. Does the supply curve illustrate the "production-motivating function of price"? Sure! Look at Figure 17-2 and that's exactly what you'll see.

What Price Is the "Right" Price?

If the price of something goes down, people will try to buy more. The "law of demand" tells us that. Remember? But what about the sellers? They don't want to sell as much if the price is low. Only at higher prices would the

Fig. 17-2   The Supply Curve Illustrates the Propensity to Sell

The higher the price, the more eggs people will try to sell

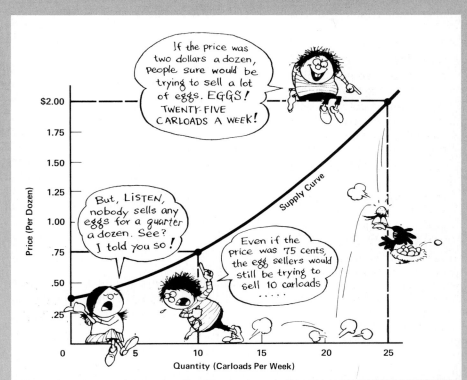

Weekly supply of eggs in your local metropolitan area.

The supply curve shows that at lower prices, smaller quantities of eggs will be offered for sale. How much the quantity offered for sale expands as the price rises (or how much it declines when the price falls) depends upon the elasticity of supply.

This supply curve only makes sense in the "short run." It could not apply to the industry in the long run because in the long run more producers can enter the industry. Or some of the present producers could leave. If more farmers entered the egg-producing business, or if some left, the curve would shift. More on this later.

As output expands, cost goes up. As price goes higher and higher, businesses will produce more and more. The higher price covers the higher cost and makes the higher output profitable. More on this later, too.

sellers like to sell more. But at higher prices the buyers won't buy as much.

So how does it all work out? There must be some "just right price"—a price just high enough and just low enough so that the buyers want to buy just exactly as much as the sellers want to sell. Is there such a price? Yes. We call this "just-right price" the equilibrium market price

Think of supply as "a potential daily flow of the product into the market." Think of demand as "a potential daily flow of the product out of the market." Producers are producing so much per day in response to the price. Buyers are buying so much per day in response to the price. The goods are flowing across the market from the sellers to the buyers. If the price is just right, the flow being pushed into the market by the sellers will be just equal to the flow being pulled out of the market by the buyers.

Now that you know what the supply of eggs looks like, you know that it doesn't make any difference how many eggs people *would be* trying to buy at a price of 25¢ a dozen. Such a low price has got to be a make-believe price anyway. The demand curve in Figure 17-1 shows us that the buyers would like to buy 25 carloads a day at 25¢ a dozen. But that could never happen. Look at Figure 17-2 now and you will see that at such a low price (25¢ a dozen) the suppliers are not willing to sell *any* eggs. None at all!

At a price of 25¢ a dozen, the egg producers would put the eggs in cold storage and wait for better times. If better times didn't come, a lot of egg-laying chickens would soon become stewing chickens and a lot of poultry farms would soon become potato farms or hunting preserves or something else. That's the way it's supposed to happen when the society isn't willing to pay the cost of keeping the factors of production working in the egg industry. So eventually the egg industry will disappear.

What about a price of $2 a dozen? The demand curve shows us that people would buy less than one carload a week. But the supply curve tells us that at a price of $2, the egg suppliers would ship in 25 carloads a week. Soon we would all be hip-deep in eggs! So $2 can't be the right price, either.

The demand curve from Figure 17-1 and the supply curve from Figure 17-2 are shown together in Figure 17-3. This "supply and demand graph" shows that there is a price (but only *one* price) where the weekly flow of eggs being pushed into the market by the sellers is exactly equal to the weekly flow of eggs being pulled out of the market by the buyers. At what price are the supply flow and the demand flow equal? At the "equilibrium market price" of 75¢ a dozen.

Figure 17-3 shows that the equilibrium market price *must be* 75¢ a dozen. At any other price there's either too much *supplied* (a surplus) or too much *demanded* (a shortage). You should spend a few minutes studying the "supply and demand" graph now.

The Equilibrium Market Price

Only one price can exist for long in our hypothetical egg market—or in any market. It is the *equilibrium market price*. It is the price where the quantity supplied equals the quantity demanded. The quantity flowing into the market from the sellers is equal to the quantity being pulled out of the market by the buyers. Each seller is selling all he or she wants to sell at that price; each buyer is buying all he or she wants to buy at that price.

No one is *completely happy* with the equilibrium price. The buyers would rather get eggs cheaper. The sellers would rather get higher prices. But at this "equilibrium market price" the flow of eggs across the market is just the right size. There is no shortage and no surplus.

As long as the supply and the demand remain the same, the "equilibrium market

Fig. 17-3 The Supply and Demand for Eggs

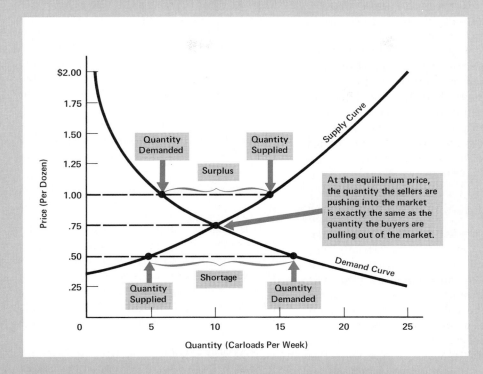

It is obvious from the graph that only the price of 75¢ a dozen can be the real price. Any lower price would leave demanders trying to buy more eggs than would be available for sale. Any higher price would have suppliers shipping in more eggs than people would buy.

If the price was too low (say 50¢ a dozen) buyers would be trying to get more eggs than the suppliers would offer. There would be a *shortage*. Some of the buyers would not be able to get any eggs from anywhere! Soon these unhappy buyers trying to get some of the very scarce eggs would start offering more for eggs. They would push the price up.

If the price was too high (say $1 a dozen) sellers would be offering more eggs than people would buy. There would be a *surplus*. Some of the sellers would not be able to sell their eggs. These sellers trying to get rid of their overly-plentiful eggs would start offering them at lower prices. This would push the price down.

Everyone who wants to sell at the equilibrium price can find a buyer. Everyone who wants to buy at that price can find a seller. That's what is meant by "equilibrium market price."

price" (75¢ a dozen) and the "equilibrium quantity flow" (10 carloads a week) will continue indefinitely. But something will always happen to change either the demand or the supply or both. Soon we will talk about the kinds of things which might happen to change the picture. Then you will see how the market system responds to changing conditions. You will see how the market process works—how price and quantity move toward a new equilibrium, and how each new equilibrium brings with it a new set of "production and distribution choices" for the society.

The General Equilibrium Situation

Suppose the market process is working perfectly. Society is making all its choices through the *price mechanism*. All the prices of everything are "in equilibrium." Just the right amounts of all goods are flowing across all the markets from the sellers to the buyers. There are no surpluses of anything and no shortages of anything. Can you picture that, in a sort of "model situation"?

In the "general equilibrium" situation, all the people are carefully conserving the most scarce, most expensive, highest-priced things because of "the rationing function of price." Producers are working hard to produce more of the most scarce, most wanted, highest-priced things because of the "production motivating function of price." All of us are free to do our own thing, and we get rewarded (receive income) according to how highly the market values what we "sell." Our "reward" depends on the price we get for the product we make or for the services of our labor, our land, or our capital.

This view of the market system "in general equilibrium" shows the neat "model system" with all the choices being made automatically. But suppose something happens to disturb the equilibrium. What happens then? Suppose the people decide they want a larger "output flow" of something. Maybe they want more eggs each week. What happens?

HOW DEMAND DIRECTS THE ECONOMY

Suppose the egg market is in equilibrium as shown in Figure 17-3. The price is 75¢ a dozen and 10 carloads a week are flowing across the market from the sellers to the buyers. Then suppose a respected scientist makes a startling announcement: "Eggs, if eaten regularly, will maintain your youthful appearance and your vim and vigor and will add ten years to your life!"

Increasing Wants Increase the Demand and Upset the Equilibrium

This idea of "eggs for perpetual youth" causes many people to want to eat more eggs. The "propensity to buy" increases. People who always hated eggs suddenly become egg-eaters. With all these people trying to buy more eggs, the weekly supply of 10 carloads gets sold out in a hurry. A shortage of eggs develops.

Everybody's trying to buy eggs but there are no eggs to be found. The disappointed buyers go around offering to pay extra to get some eggs. This pushes up the price. As the price goes up the rationing function of price will squeeze some of the buyers out of the market. The production motivating function of price will pull more eggs into the market. As the price goes up these two "functions of price" work together to force the quantity supplied and the quantity demanded into a new state of equilibrium.

How high will the price go? It will continue to go up until the market moves into a new equilibrium. This situation is shown in the supply and demand graph in Figure 17-4. Take a few minutes and study that graph now.

Increased Demand Pushes the Price Up. The graph shows that the price must go up to $1 a dozen. At that price, a lot of buyers are squeezed out of the market by the rationing function, a lot more eggs are pulled into the

Fig. 17-4 Increased Propensity to Buy: the Demand Curve Shifts

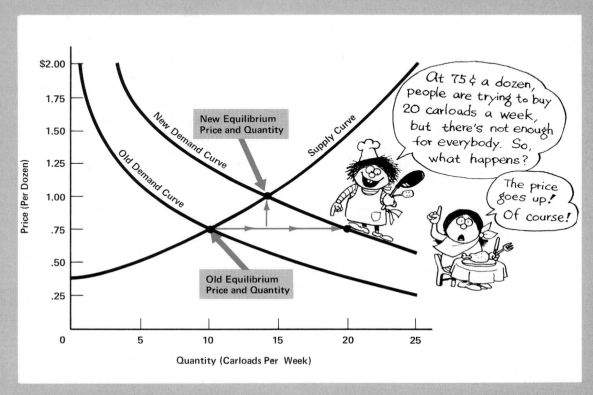

When demand increases it creates a shortage, forces the price up, and the high price pulls in more eggs.

When people think eggs will bring "perpetual youth," the demand for eggs increases. At any price you choose, the quantity people would buy is greater. The demand curve shifts to the right to show that a larger quantity would be bought at each price. The "propensity to buy" has increased!

Seventy-five cents can no longer be the equilibrium price. At that price people now want to buy 20 carloads a week but the sellers only ship in 10 carloads. A serious shortage! The buyers, trying to get eggs, push up the price.

The new "equilibrium market price" is $1 a dozen. This higher price (a) squeezes some of the buyers out of the market (the quantity demanded goes back down from 20 to 14 carloads) and (b) pulls forth more output from the sellers (the quantity supplied increases from 10 to 14 carloads).

market by the production-motivating function, and a new market equilibrium is reached. Fourteen carloads of eggs will be sold by the sellers and bought by the buyers each week. But this new equilibrium price of $1 a dozen can't last for long. Can you guess why? Competition, of course!

Remember I said that everything was in stable equilibrium back when the price of eggs was 75¢ a dozen. So a price of 75¢ must be high enough to convince the egg producers to keep on producing eggs. This means that a price of 75¢ was high enough to cover the production costs and pay enough profits to the producers to keep them satisfied to stay in the egg business. If that's so, then think what a good deal $1 a dozen must be! Big profits in the egg business? Right!

A High Price Brings Big Profits. Suppose you are producing frying chickens. You're doing okay, just making "normal profits." Then one day you see your egg-producing neighbor drive by in his new Cadillac. He's on his way to the airport to fly to the Virgin Islands for a three-day holiday. You suddenly realize that you should be producing eggs instead of fryers! So what do you do? As soon as you can you'll shift into the egg business where the big money is. Your neighbor doesn't mind. He knows that one more little egg producer won't hurt the egg market at all.

Big Profits Attract More Producers. What's going to happen? You have already guessed it. You aren't the only farmer who likes to make big profits. It isn't long before everyone who can shift into the egg business starts to do just that. Everyone wants to get some of the big profits from those dollar a dozen eggs!

This is competition in action. Soon, turkey producers, cotton farmers, beef ranchers, vegetable growers and others start producing eggs. Every day more people become egg producers. Each time a new producer enters the egg industry and starts shipping eggs to the market, the total quantity of eggs going into the market increases a little more. Can you see what's going to happen?

More Producers Bring More Supply. It isn't long before the quantity offered for sale at a price of $1 a dozen increases from 14 carloads to 15 carloads a week. But at $1 a dozen, buyers will only buy 14 carloads. The demand curve in Figure 17-4 already told us that. At a price of $1 a dozen, with 15 carloads a week coming into the market we have a surplus of one carload of eggs a week.

Some of the egg sellers can't sell all their eggs. So what do they do? They start cutting prices to get people to buy up all the eggs. See it? The "production motivating function of price" is still working! The high price is causing the egg industry to expand. Each time a new producer enters the industry, the supply increases. In terms of the supply and demand graph, the *supply curve* is now shifting to the right—a delayed response to the *initial* shift to the right, of the *demand curve*!

More Supply Pushes the Price Back Down. How long will new producers keep on entering the egg business? That's easy. As long as it is more profitable for them to produce eggs than it would for them to produce turkeys or broilers or beef or whatever else they might produce *instead* of eggs. This means that the egg industry will continue to expand and the supply of eggs will continue to increase (the curve will keep shifting to the right on the graph) until the price of eggs is pushed *back down* to "*normal*."

The Normal Price Brings Normal Profits. You remember that in the beginning the normal price for eggs was 75¢ a dozen. The "normal price" is the price that brings the producers normal profits—that is, enough profits to keep them from leaving the industry, but not enough to entice other firms to stop producing other things and shift into this industry.

At the "normal price" with "normal profits" being made, an industry will be stable. At prices and profits higher than "normal" the industry will be expanding. At prices and profits lower than "normal" the industry will be contracting. Businesses are always moving into or out of one industry or another, trying to make more profits, or to eliminate their losses.*

As the egg industry expands, this may cause egg production costs to go up. If so the new "normal price" will be higher than before (maybe up to 80¢) because of the higher costs. But let's just suppose that the "normal price" stays at 75¢. How long will the egg industry continue to expand? Until the price is pushed all the way back to 75¢ a dozen. Obviously? Sure.

The New "Long-Run Equilibrium"

There's a graph coming up that shows the new "normal" or "long-run" equilibrium situation in the egg market in your metropolitan area. The price is back down to 75¢ a dozen. But now, instead of the original quantity of ten carloads, there are *twenty carloads* a week flowing across the market from the sellers to the buyers. Where did all those extra eggs come from? and why? It all happened through the automatic adjustments of the market process. The price mechanism took care of it for us.

---

* Sometimes economists explain that it might be better not to think of "normal profit" as being "profit" at all. Since the "normal profit" is necessary to keep the firms from leaving the industry, "normal profit" is really a part of the cost of production—a "necessary cost" required to keep the product flowing to the market. It's only when the profit gets higher than "normal" that profit becomes a "surplus" and serves the purpose of attracting new firms into the industry. What's the point? Just this: Be sure to recognize the distinct difference between "normal profit" and "excess" or "surplus" profit. Really, they're different kinds of things and they perform different functions in the operation of the market process.

First, people heard that eggs bring perpetual youth. So right away they started trying to buy more. The demand increased. So there was a temporary shortage of eggs. The disappointed egg-seeking buyers went around offering more for eggs and pushed the price up.

The higher price (a) conserved the use of the very scarce eggs, (b) induced the present egg producers to increase their outputs as much as possible (to go out and stroke the hens to get them to lay more eggs), and (c) made the egg business very profitable and attracted many new producers into the business.

As each new producer came in and added more output to the market, the supply increased a little. A little surplus developed. The egg-sellers had to cut prices a little to get rid of all their eggs. But more and more producers kept on going into the egg business and pushing the price down. For how long? Until the price finally got back down to "normal" (back down to 75¢ a dozen).

Once the price gets back to normal that's as far as it goes. Until there is some new change in demand or supply, 75¢ a dozen will continue to be the price and 20 carloads a week will continue to be the quantity exchanged in the egg market in your city.

See how the people through their demands make the choices about which things will be produced? and how much? An increase in demand pushes up the price. The higher price discourages consumption and brings forth more output in the short run. Then in the long run, after there has been enough time for the industry to expand, more output comes forth and the price goes back down to its "normal" level. Then people are no longer severely discouraged from eating eggs. Everyone who is willing and able to pay the "normal price" (covering the cost of production plus a normal profit) can buy all the eggs desired.

Now you know how the market process directs more of the society's scarce resources into egg production. You know how the market automatically carries out the decisions of the people. That's the way it works in the "pure model" of the market system.

Figure 17-5 shows each step in the process: (1) the increased demand, (2) the higher price, (3) the increased supply, and (4) the new long-run equilibrium price and quantity. Be sure to spend enough time with Figure 17-5 to learn each of the steps. This graph is very important. It shows the "market process" and the "price mechanism" in action. It shows, in a "model system," how the market process directs society's productive resources into the desired uses. You should spend a few minutes studying Figure 17-5 now.

The Essential Role of Pure Competition

Think back over the egg example you've just been reading about. Everything worked out just right—very neatly in fact. Why? Because all of the necessary "assumed conditions" existed. The most necessary assumed condition is that pure competition exists.*

What's so important about pure competition? Consider this. After the demand for eggs increased, who put the price up from 75 cents to $1 a dozen? Nobody. The "natural market forces" just took care of it. New buyers entered the market. That's what made the shortages develop. And that's what made the price go up.

Then following the price increase, who decided that a lot of the society's resources

---

* There are several other assumed conditions too. But I won't bother you with those until after you understand more about how the "model system" works. When you get into the following chapters of this book you'll see a lot more about the underlying assumptions of the model system. And you'll find out a lot about how well (or how poorly) these assumptions are likely to hold true in the real world. For now, just concentrate on learning how the model system works. But be forewarned: It doesn't work out quite that way in the real world. (But you probably already knew that.)

should be shifted into egg production? Nobody. The natural market forces took care of it. Farmers saw the opportunity for high profits in the egg business so they started producing eggs. They entered the egg market as sellers. That's what made the surpluses develop. And that's what pushed the price back down.

You can see the essential role of pure competition in all of this. Without large numbers of small buyers and small sellers, and without free and easy entry into the market by anyone who wants to buy or sell, it just wouldn't work. What if there were only one or a few egg sellers? or buyers? or what if there were restrictions on who could produce and sell eggs? or who could buy and eat eggs? The system wouldn't work—at least not the way it did in our example.

How would it work out if the market structure of the egg market was something other than pure competition? Later in this book you'll get into that question. For now just remember this: (1) it would depend a lot on *what kind of market structure did exist*—and (2) it would be likely to work out quite differently than in the "model egg market example" you just read about.

CONSUMER SOVEREIGNTY AND THE INVISIBLE HAND

In the "pure model market system" who holds the choice-making power? The consumers of course. The consumers are *sovereign*. Consumers have the final control in deciding what will be done with society's scarce resources. Their decisions about how to spend their money ultimately determine all the economic choices for the society—all the production choices and all the distribution choices. Consumers have the "ultimate control." That's what "consumer sovereignty" means.

Anyone who has money and spends it, will influence "what is produced." Anyone who

Fig. 17-5 In the Long Run, the Supply Increases

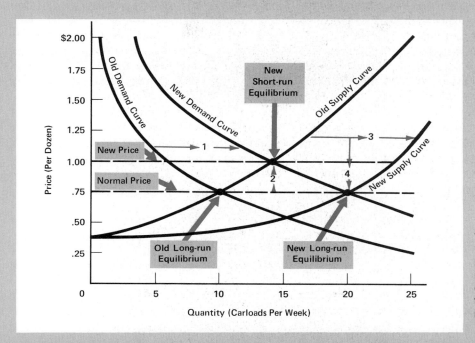

The high price pulls more producers into the industry—a delayed response to the demand increase.

(1) The demand increases. At a price of 75¢ a dozen the quantity the buyers want to buy increases from 10 to 20 carloads a week. This creates a shortage.

(2) The buyers, bidding against each other for the limited eggs, push the price up to $1. At the higher price the new quantity demanded moves back from 20 to 14 carloads per week, and the quantity supplied increases from 10 to 14 carloads. At the price of $1 we have a new short-run equilibrium.

At the price of $1, big profits are made in the egg business. New producers come in and start producing and selling eggs. Each time one more producer adds output to the market this increases the total market supply a little bit. As the supply increases bit-by-bit, the price inches downward.

(3) The supply continues to increase and the price drops until the "normal price" is reached. Then (4) the industry is again in stable long-run equilibrium. The price is again 75¢, but the quantity crossing the market has increased to 20 carloads per week.

produces (or who owns productive factors which produce) will receive money to spend and can influence "what is produced." Of course we never have all the necessary conditions for a "model market system" to work exactly right. But if we did, then consumers really would be "sovereign." They would have complete control over the economic choices of the society.

You may have heard about Adam Smith. Back in 1776 he wrote an economics book called *The Wealth of Nations*. Adam Smith was the first to give a good explanation of how the market process could work automatically to serve the needs of the society. One of his most famous statements was that if you leave people alone to follow their own personal interests, each will be guided "as though by an invisible hand" to do the best things for the society.

The idea of "the invisible hand" is the idea of the market process at work. It's the idea that society's economic choices will be made automatically, in response to the wishes of the people. The "sovereign consumers," through the market process, will cause the labor, land, and capital to do the things society wants done—as though all were guided by "an invisible hand."

Consumer Spending Really Does Influence the Economic Choices

In the real world, no economy could work just like the model of "consumer sovereignty and the invisible hand." Still, in the economic systems of most countries, the consumer's choice (about what to buy) really does exert a major influence. The consumer really does have an important say in deciding what will be produced, which resources will be used for which purposes and how much each person will get. "Consumer sovereignty" in the real world is far from pure. On the other hand, it is far from dead.

The more a nation allows for and protects open and free competitive markets and private property rights, the more "sovereign" the consumer will be—the more "ultimate power" the consumer will exercise over the society's economic choices. I'm sure you realize that the "ultimate power of the consumer's choice" is much greater in the economy of a country like the United States or Canada or West Germany or Great Britain or Japan than it is in the Soviet Union or Mainland China. But even in the communist countries consumers' choices cannot be ignored completely.

SUMMARY OF DEMAND, SUPPLY, AND PRICE

This chapter has carried you a long way forward in your understanding of the precise way in which the "pure market process" works. You know how a change in demand can move the price around. And you know how the price *rations* (conserves the use of) existing goods and *motivates production* of more goods. The higher goes the demand, the higher goes the price and the more the good is rationed and the more its production is motivated.

You know, also, that a high price (higher than "normal") will cause an industry to expand. Producers enter the industry seeking some of the big profits. As the industry expands, more supply is pushed into the market. Soon the greater supply begins to create some surpluses.

Some of the sellers can't sell all their goods so they start cutting prices. More sellers keep entering the industry, expanding the output and cutting prices until the price is pushed all the way back down to "normal." It's really neat!

Of course, it doesn't work out exactly this way in the real world. You'll be seeing this later. But first, before you go on, be sure you've really learned about how supply and demand work, and about the functions of price. Be sure you can draw and explain the curves. Then you'll be ready to go on into the next chapter and find out about how prices are determined in the input factor markets. By supply and demand? You bet! See you there!

REVIEW EXERCISES

● **MAJOR CONCEPTS, PRINCIPLES, TERMS (Explain each carefully.)**

demand
the two effects of a price change
the two functions of price
supply
demand, supply, and price
the essential role of pure competition

● **OTHER CONCEPTS AND TERMS (Explain each briefly.)**

consumption possibility
substitution effect
income effect
law of demand
elasticity of demand
rationing function of price
production-motivation function
  of price

equilibrium market price
change in demand
change in supply
normal price
normal profits
price mechanism
consumer sovereignty
the "invisible hand"

● **CURVES AND GRAPHS (Draw, label, and explain each.)**

The Demand Curve Illustrates the Propensity to Buy
The Supply Curve Illustrates the Propensity to Sell
The Supply and Demand for Eggs
Increased Propensity to Buy: the Demand Curve Shifts
In the Long Run, the Supply Increases

● **QUESTIONS (Write the answers, or jot down key points.)**

1. Explain how supply, demand, and price work together in the "model pure market system." Use supply and demand curves to show how *first price* and then *supply* respond to changes in consumer demand.
2. When you're trying to explain how supply and demand work, it's not easy to always keep it straight whether you're talking about
   a. a change in the *demand*—that is, a change in your overall propensity to buy (a shift of the demand curve) or

  b. a change in the *quantity bought,* which results from a change in
     the price (that is, a movement up or down along the demand
     curve, to a higher or lower price and a smaller or greater quantity
     bought).

  Can you see what would happen to your explanation of how the
  market mechanism works if you let these two things get mixed up?
  Think about it and try to explain.

3. The only price that really could exist in a free market would be the
   equilibrium market price. In the supply and demand graph, all prices
   above or below the equilibrium price and all quantities greater or less
   than the equilibrium quantity are really irrelevant. There's only one
   price (the equilibrium price) and one quantity (the equilibrium quantity) which would exist in that market at any moment. Can you explain
   why this is true? What forces guarantee that it must be true?

4. Students sometimes get mixed up between
   a. the two effects of a price change, and
   b. the two functions of price.

   Can you clearly explain the difference between the two? Try.

18 Income Distribution: How Prices Are Determined in the Input Factor Markets

The price you get for the factors you sell determines your income and your share of the output.

What determines your income? In the model market system it depends entirely on what productive inputs you have to sell and how much they sell for. If you own a lot of high-priced inputs you'll get a big income. If you don't you won't. It doesn't work exactly that way in the real world. But it's pretty close.

Income Distribution: Factor Ownership And Factor Pricing

In the pure market system, your share of the output would be determined entirely by the value of what you sell "in the factor markets"—that is, by what you sell to the businesses that buy in the factor markets. Your share is determined by *how much you sell* and *the price you get* when you sell it. So the question of income distribution in the pure market system is one of "factor ownership" and "factor pricing."

In micro-theory we don't deal much with the question of factor ownership. We can sort of take it as "given." We can assume that everyone owns some labor to sell and that the hard-working and thrifty people (and maybe some lucky ones) will own some land and capital, too.

So now with the "factor ownership" question assumed away, the question of income distribution becomes entirely a question of what determines the *prices* of labor, land, and capital in the factor markets. We'll be talking about that throughout most of this chapter. Mostly we'll be concerned with "what might cause" the price of an input to be high or low, or to go up or down.

The firm's **cost** is the factor owner's income!

Suppose you can find out *why* the labor of a cherry picker is priced lower than the labor of a bulldozer operator and why the labor of a school teacher is priced lower than the labor of a bricklayer or an accountant or a pediatrician. Then you will know why cherry pickers and school teachers don't get as large an income and as large a share of the society's output as do bulldozer operators and bricklayers and accountants and pediatricians.

SUPPLY AND DEMAND
DETERMINE FACTOR PRICES

What determines the price of what you have to sell in the factor markets? Assuming we're still living in the pure model world, it's supply and demand, of course.

If you want to understand the pricing of productive factors (or the pricing of anything else) you need to understand what determines the supply and what determines the demand. In fact, just about all you need to do to understand the question of income distribution in the pure market system is to understand factor demand and factor supply.

Factor Demand Depends on Marginal "Value Product"

Who demands input factors? Businesses, of course. And what determines the demand for (the propensity to buy) a productive factor? The value of what it produces, of course! It depends on the *value* the factor *adds* to the output.

If the marginal "value product" of the factor is high, the demand for it will be high. The price paid for the factor will be high. Whoever owns it and sells it will get a high income and will be able to claim a large share of the society's output.

Marginal Value Product Is MPP Times Price. If a factor of production has a high marginal "value product" exactly what does that mean? It could mean that the factor is responsible for producing a small amount of additional product (MPP) but each unit of the MPP sells for a very high price. Or it could mean that the factor is responsible for producing a large MPP. Or it could mean that the factor produces a large MPP and the MPP sells for a high price, too! Then the marginal "value product" (MVP) really would be high!

What's the point? Just this: the marginal "value product" (MVP) of (and therefore the

demand for) a factor of production depends on (1) the amount of physical product the factor produces, and (2) the price per unit the business gets when it sells the MPP.

For a business producing and selling in a market of pure competition, we can say it this way: the marginal value product (MVP) is equal to the marginal physical product (MPP) times the price (P). Or, if you like to say it the short way: MVP = MPP × P.

So you can see that anything which would cause the MPP of a factor to increase would also cause that factor's MVP to increase. Also, anything which would cause the *price of the product* to increase would cause the factor's MVP to increase.

How much you are worth to a business depends not only on how much you produce, but also on how much what you produce sells for!

Factor Prices Have Special Names: Wages, Rent, Interest

As you know, the price of each factor of production has a special name. But it's only a price just the same. If labor is being sold we call the price "the wage rate." For land we call it "rent." For capital it's "the interest rate." The fourth distributive share—the one the business gets to keep after everyone else has been paid their wages, rent, and interest—is called "profit."

Profit is the only one of the "distributive shares" which is not really a "price." Profit is what's left over after the prices of all the "hired factors" have been paid. Profit is determined by (1) the value of the output, as compared with (2) the cost of the inputs (wages, rent, interest).

The size of the wages, rent, interest, and profits will determine which people will get large incomes and which ones will get small incomes—which ones will be rich and which ones will be poor.

Most people work for wages. If the average wages received by the people in a country are low, then most of the people in that country will be poor. If the average wages received by the people are high, most of the people will enjoy a high standard of living. But what might cause the average wage rates in a country to be high? Or low? *That* is the question.

An Overview of Factor Pricing

You already have a general understanding of what would make the wage rate high, or low. If there's a high demand and a low supply of labor then the wage rate will be high. Of course.

Factor Demand. A high demand for labor would keep the price (wage rate) high. Or you could say it another way. You could say that if the *productivity* (marginal value product) of labor is high the wage rate will be high. Both these statements are true.

Either high demand or high productivity will support a high wage rate. So right away you know there must be a close relationship between high *demand* for labor and high *marginal productivity* of labor. Of course! Labor is demanded only because it is productive! The more productive it is the greater the demand for it. Obviously!

The prices of the other factors (land and capital) are determined in the same way as the price of labor. High demand (high productivity) will bring high prices (high rent or interest). The owner-sellers of the highest priced factors (labor, land, and capital) will receive the biggest incomes and will be able to claim the biggest shares of the economy's output.

Surely there's nothing surprising to you about this little overview of factor pricing. Chances are you already knew this much about how the market process distributes the income. But that's just the surface. What influences marginal productivity and demand for factors? And what determines factor supply? Those are the questions we need to get into now.

Why does a business firm demand (want to hire) any productive factor? Because it's productive, that's why! The more productive it is, the more business will demand it. All we need to do to understand the *demand* for *any* productive factor—labor, land, or capital—is to understand what determines its *productivity*. That's easy enough to see. We will get into that in just a minute. But first, what about supply?

Factor Supply. Factor *demand* is determined the same way for all the factors. But not so for factor *supply*. The supply of each factor is unique. Think about it. Do you think the labor supply is determined by the same things that would determine the supply of land? or capital? Of course not.

The same concept of demand applies to all the factors. We'll deal with that first. For the time being we'll just assume that supply is fixed—that is, unresponsive to price. Then later we'll look at each factor individually to find out about the unique determinants of the *supply* of each. But now let's dig in on factor demand.

WHAT DETERMINES FACTOR DEMAND?

Understanding factor demand is an essential step in understanding income distribution in the market system. But again, a word of warning: *No society distributes income entirely according to the "pure market forces."* Still, it can be very helpful to understand how pure market forces work in the model. Later on we'll get into the question of how all this gets modified in the real world.

Factor Demand Reflects Marginal Productivity (MVP)

Suppose you are running a factory producing hip-hugger jeans. How many workers will you hire?—that is, how many "units of labor per day" will you buy?

If you think an additional unit of labor will bring you more "value product" than it costs (if it adds more to your revenue than it adds to your cost) you will buy it. So your "propensity to buy" a unit of labor is determined by your estimate of its marginal "value product." You first learned about this in Chapter 2. Here's an example.

Hiring Marginal Workers: an Example. Suppose the kind of labor you use in your plant cost $20 a day. You are currently employing 25 people (using 25 "units of labor" per day). Should you increase your daily rate of labor input by one unit? Should you hire 26 people a day? That depends on how much more revenue you expect to get. Right?

Suppose with one more worker (without increasing any of your other costs) you could produce enough more to increase your total revenue by $25 a day. Would you hire one more person? At a wage rate of $20 a day? Sure you would!

Marginal Value Product and Marginal Input Cost. When you increase your labor input and that adds more to your revenue than it adds to your costs, that increases your profit. That's good business.

You will continue to hire more labor and expand your output as long as the marginal value product (MVP) is greater than the wage rate— that is, as long as the marginal "value product" is greater than the marginal "input cost" (MIC). But as you hire more labor, the MVP of labor goes down. When the two become equal (when MVP = MIC) that's the "rate of production" where your profit is at a maximum. You won't hire any more.

Suppose you have adjusted your output to the most profitable daily rate. That means you are using the most profitable amounts of labor and other inputs. If, for each factor of production, the marginal "input cost" is equal to the marginal "value product" then you are operating at your maximum profit position.

A Higher Output Price Increases MVP. Now suppose the market price of hip-hugger jeans goes up, say from $100 a carton to $150 a carton. What happens to the productivity of the labor you're hiring? and to the productivity of your land? and capital? It goes up!

When the price goes up for the product, suddenly the output of each factor becomes more valuable. Suddenly your demand for input factors goes up! See how an increase in the demand (and price) for your output can bring an increase in your demand for inputs?

Your demand for labor or for any other input factor depends on (1) the amount of physical product added by the marginal factor and (2) the amount of *money* the extra physical product adds to your revenue. Remember? So when the output price goes up, that increases each factor's MVP. So it increases your demand for all of the input factors.

Factor Demand Is Always Derived Demand

You demand labor and other inputs for your jeans factory because somewhere, consumers are demanding hip-hugger jeans. If consumers were not demanding hip-hugger jeans, you certainly wouldn't be demanding labor (or denim or machines or electricity or anything else) to make hip-hugger jeans. Obviously not. You remember this from previous chapters. But a brief review won't hurt.

There are only two reasons for demanding something: (1) for *consumption* (to bring "final satisfaction"), or (2) for *production* (to be used to produce something else that is wanted). The *production demand* (demand for input factors) always reflects the fact that somewhere there is a consumption demand. If there was no consumption demand for a product then there would be no *production demand* for factors to be used to make it.

When we talk about the *productivity* (marginal "value product") of an input factor we are talking about *the value a unit of that factor* adds to the output. *All that value derives from the demand for the final product.* If there's no final product demand, there's no derived demand. Nobody will hire a worker to produce something that no one will buy! That's just common sense.

Marginal Productivity Reflects the Law of Diminishing Returns

What determines how much more output you will get if you hire one more unit of labor? The most important thing is this: "How much *other factors* is the new worker going to have to work with?" If the worker is going to have lots of efficient machinery and plenty of materials to work with, then that worker will add a lot of extra product.

But suppose all the machines and everything else are already being overused. All there is for the new worker to do is to go around and clean up and straighten up a bit. Then the extra worker isn't going to add much product.

We're talking about what economists call the law of variable proportions—the law of diminishing returns. The law of diminishing returns says that if a factory or a farm (or any kind of productive activity) expands its output more and more without adding any more land or buildings, sooner or later some overcrowding and inefficiencies will occur. The variable inputs won't have enough fixed inputs to work with. Costs will go up.

You can increase your output some by adding more "variable inputs" (say labor) even though the amounts of some other inputs are fixed (say the size of your jeans factory). But there's a limit to how far you can go. Sooner or later the extra output you get when you hire each successive "unit of the variable input"— labor, materials, etc.—will get smaller and smaller. The returns (extra product) received from the extra variable input, will diminish.

You can see why the law of diminishing returns is also called the law of variable proportions. It is talking about varying the proportions of the inputs. The reason the returns

(extra outputs) diminish is because there is too much of the variable input (labor and materials and all) in proportion to the amount of the fixed input (the factory and machines). Each worker has too little of the fixed input (machines) to work with. So the extra output you get when you hire an extra worker isn't very big.

A Flowerpot Wheat Farm?

The law of diminishing returns is obviously true. If it was not it would be possible for you to grow enough food for the world in your backyard garden (or in a flowerpot!) just by adding enough labor, seed, and fertilizer. Being ridiculous, let's suppose one worker is growing wheat in a flowerpot and another worker decides to come along and help. How much added output do you suppose will result from the added efforts of the second worker? Zero? I guess so.

The economist would say: "The marginal 'physical product' of the second worker is zero. Therefore the marginal 'value product' must also be zero." Say it any way you wish. But the fact is, the second worker doesn't add any output at all.

Why is the marginal product (the additional product obtained from the efforts of the second worker) zero? Because of laziness? Incompetence? No. It's because of the law of diminishing returns. It's because not enough of the needed fixed inputs are available to work with. That's what makes it impossible for the second worker to produce anything.

What About Adding More Fixed Inputs?

Suppose the second worker could manage to find another flowerpot someplace. Then the second worker could produce just as much as the first! How so? What about the law of diminishing returns? The law of diminishing returns wouldn't be working anymore. Why not? Because nothing is fixed anymore. All of the input factors have become variable!

A silly example, sure. But it illustrates something. It tells us that the more and better land, machines, and other things a worker has to work with, the more productive that worker can be.

Suppose you are already running your hip-hugger jeans plant at its maximum efficiency and then you decide to hire more workers and produce more. The law of diminishing returns tells you that the more extra workers you hire the less extra output per worker you're going to get—and therefore the more each extra unit of output is going to cost you.

If you expand your output of hip-hugger jeans beyond the maximum efficiency rate (say, 10 cartons a day) the marginal physical product (MPP) of the added variable factors will go down. Why?

The MPP diminishes because you are trying to produce faster than your plant is designed to produce. The extra workers don't have enough fixed inputs to work with. So they aren't very productive. You probably wouldn't hire extra workers and push your output beyond 10 units anyway. But then again, you might.

Would You Add Factors When MPP Is Low? What might cause you to hire additional workers even when you know they aren't going to add very much output?—that is, even when you know they won't add very much marginal physical product? Either one (or both) of two things: (1) a very high price (per unit) for the output (MPP), or (2) a very low price (per unit) for the input (labor). We could say it this way:

(1) The demand for your product in the market might go up and push the price up so high that the little bit of extra product added by an extra worker would bring in enough extra revenue to more than cover the extra cost of hiring the worker; or

(2) The price of labor might go down so low that even though the additional worker doesn't add much output, the output

value is still great enough to more than cover the very low wage cost.

How Many "Variable Factor Units" to Employ? As the product price goes higher or as the price of the variable factor goes lower, you will employ more of the factor. How much more? Enough to push down the marginal productivity (MVP) of the factor to where it is no longer profitable to hire any more—that is, to where the cost to hire an extra unit of the factor (MIC) ia as great as the extra output is worth to you (MVP). Once you get to this input (and output) rate (where MIC = MVP) you don't hire any more.

The law of demand applies in the factor markets just as it applies in the consumer goods markets. The lower the price of the factor the more the businesses will buy. Why does the law of demand hold true in the factor markets? Partly because of the *law of diminishing returns*. As more variable factors are hired, marginal value product goes down. So the price of the factor must go down to get more to be hired!

How Fast Does Marginal Productivity (MVP) Diminish?

Suppose the price of your hip-hugger jeans goes up a lot. You will hire more "units of the variable factor." How many more units of the variable factor will you hire before the new (higher price) MVP is brought down equal to the cost of a unit of the variable factor (MIC)? *It depends on how fast the returns diminish as you expand your output.*

Can you see that the elasticity of the demand for "units of the variable factor" depends a lot on the law of diminishing returns? As new units of the variable factor are hired, if the returns (that is, the MPP) go down quickly, then not very many more units of the factor will be hired. But if the MPP diminishes only slowly, then quite a lot more of the factor will be hired.

If the productivity of the variable factor diminishes rapidly as more units are added, then the demand for the variable factor will be very inelastic. That means, if the price of the factor goes down, not much more of the variable factor will be hired.

But suppose you add units of the variable factor and each unit you add brings almost as much MPP as the previous unit. Then suppose the price of the variable factor goes down. Will you hire a little more? or a lot more? A lot more, of course. So the demand will be very elastic.

In a few minutes you'll be reading more about the elasticity of the demand for *specific* variable input factors. Here we are talking about "the demand for variable inputs in general."

The Effect of the Elasticity of Final Product Demand.

You know that the faster its MPP diminishes the less elastic the demand for a variable input will be. But what about the elasticity of the demand for the final product?

Suppose the product demand is *highly elastic*. If the price of the final product drops a little, people are induced to buy a lot more so a lot more inputs will be demanded.

It works this way. When input prices go down, cost of production goes down, so producers find it profitable to produce more. So the supply increases. The increased supply pushes the selling price down and (if the product demand is highly elastic) a lot more output will be bought. So a lot more output will be produced and a lot more inputs will be hired.

See how the lower input cost causes a lot more output to be bought? And that causes a lot more inputs to be bought? Sure. That's how the highly elastic *product demand* causes *input demand* to be highly elastic too.

Factor Demand is More Elastic In the Long Run.

Firms will respond to factor prices *much more* in the *long run* than in the short run. Suppose the wage rate goes up. You may cut back a little and release two or three workers. But in the short run you can't cut back very much. It would be better to shut down instead. Either way, if the wage rate goes up very much you're going to lose money. What are you going to do about it?

All you can do in the short run is try to minimize your losses. But as soon as you can you'll either get out of this business or else install labor-saving machinery and fire a lot of workers. See how the demand for labor is more elastic in the long run? The quantity bought will respond a lot more to the price increase if you'll just wait until the industry can adjust!

Factor Prices Can Influence Economic Growth.

In all modern nations of the world, wages have been rising for many decades. As the wage rates have gone up, businesses have brought in more capital. With more capital to work with, labor has become more productive. The higher productivity has justified even higher wages.

Each *higher wage rate* has made it profitable to bring in *more labor-saving capital*; each increase in the "capital-to-labor ratio" has made *labor more productive* and has supported *even higher wage rates*. This is an important part of the "economic growth" process which has brought such big increases in the standards of living for most of us in the advanced economies. See how important the *long-run elasticity* of factor demand can be?

The Factor Demand Curve

Would it be possible to draw a curve to show the demand for a productive factor? No question about it. We could call it a "diminishing returns curve" or a "marginal value product curve," or a "factor demand curve." Either way, it's the same curve. After you finish studying Figure 18-1 you will understand it better. Right now would be a good time for you to do that.

Fig. 18-1   Demand for a Factor of Production: the Marginal Value Product

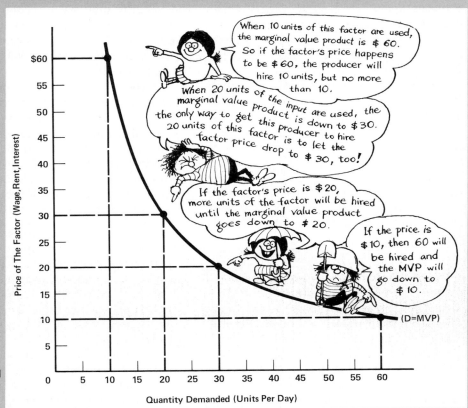

The law of demand works in the factor markets too!

If the price of the factor goes down, the business will use more. So, as the law of diminishing returns tell us, the MPP will go down. So therefore the marginal value product will go down too. *How much more* of the variable factor the business will use depends on *how fast* the marginal value product goes down. And that's what the curve shows you.

If the price is high you will add only a few units of the factor so the marginal value product of the factor will be high (high enough to be worth the high price). As the price goes lower you will add more units of the factor. Its marginal value product will diminish. The lower the price of the factor the more you will use and the lower its marginal value product will be.

This curve will shift only if there is a change in "the marginal value product situation" for this factor. The curve will increase (shift to the right) if (1) the selling price of the product goes up, or if (2) more of the *other* factors become available for this one to work with, thus increasing the marginal physical product of this factor.

How Elastic is the Demand for a Productive Factor?

What determines the elasticity of a firm's demand for a variable factor?

It depends a lot on how easy (or how difficult) it is to substitute one factor for another. Elasticity of demand always depends a lot on the availability of acceptable substitutes. How critical are the ratios (proportions) among the input factors?

Is there much variability in the "input factor mix"? or not? Is each factor an absolutely essential ingredient? Maybe like flour when you're baking a cake? Or is there more variability? like whether to use butter or margarine? or whether to beat the cake by hand or use a Mixmaster? or to use more or less eggs? or if it's a fruit cake, more candied cherries and less raisins?

You can see that in some kinds of production and for some inputs there is a lot of variability. For others there is less. But there is almost always some (and usually quite a lot) of variability (substitutability) in the "input mix."

How "Fixed" or How "Variable" Are the Input Factor Proportions?

Suppose that in order to produce anything at all, each worker's position in the plant *must* be filled. Then the factor proportions of labor and capital are absolutely fixed. The plant's short-run demand for workers will be absolutely inelastic, right up to the "shut-down factor price" (where the factor price gets so high it would be cheaper for the firm to shut down than to operate).

On the other hand, suppose we're talking about a trucking company that can lease more trucks and hire more drivers at a moment's notice. There really isn't much "fixed factor" in this case, so the returns don't diminish much. The trucking company can hire a lot more "variable inputs" with very little "diminishing" of the marginal value product, so the firm's demand for the variable inputs (trucks and drivers) probably would be elastic.

The short-run demand for labor and other variable factors would likely be inelastic for most manufacturing plants. Whenever the marginal cost of expanding the output rises rapidly, that means the marginal value product diminishes rapidly. The demand will be highly inelastic.

Most plants are designed to use a certain amount of labor and other variable inputs. If the price of any one of these inputs goes up or down the quantity can be adjusted some— maybe some of one variable input can be substituted for some of another—but it isn't likely that the "input mix" will be changed very much in the short run. But what about in the long run? That's a different matter!

Long-Run Factor Demand Is Much More Elastic: Substitution Is Much Easier.

In the long run new plants will be built. The new plants will fully reflect the relative prices of all the inputs.

When a business is designing a new plant it insists on using minimum quantities of the highest-priced factors and substituting more of the lower-priced factors. This is where the demand for each factor becomes really elastic. So this is where the rationing function of price really works to conserve the scarcest, most valuable of society's inputs.

As time goes on the higher-priced factors will be conserved more and more. They will be carefully economized—used only for their most highly productive uses, and with lots of other input factors to work with. So what happens? They become even more productive! So the demand for them increases (shifts to the right) even more and their price goes up even more. And the process continues. This is the process of economic growth you were reading about a few minutes ago.

The scarcest, most productive, highest priced factors tend to become even more "relatively scarce," more productive, and higher priced as time passes. This is what has happened (and is happening) to labor in all of the advanced countries in the world.

Employment Effects of Factor Demand Elasticity. Suppose, for example, the demand for labor is highly elastic throughout the economy—especially at low wage rates. What does that mean? It means that businesses have a choice. They can hire low-priced labor or they can use labor-saving machinery and equipment instead. A small increase in the price of labor would cause many businesses to hire less labor and use more capital instead.

In this situation, what do you suppose would happen if the government passed a minimum wage law, pushing up the minimum price for low-priced labor? Do you suppose there would be a lot of unemployment among young inexperienced people? and among high-school dropouts and high school graduates and college students looking for summer jobs? You bet there would.

This is the argument that McDonald's hamburger chain has been using to try to get an exemption from minimum wage laws. The management of McDonalds has been saying that if they must pay the minimum wage, then they must use less labor and more automatic equipment, instead. They argue that the minimum wage is going to force them to stop hiring the many young people who come to them looking for jobs.

Can you see that the whole idea of minimum wages doesn't make sense if the demand for labor at low wage rates, is highly elastic?—that is, if capital is going to be used instead of labor, once the wage rates are pushed up? Yes, elasticity of demand can be very important in the labor market. It should be carefully considered when public policies on wages are being discussed.

Let's look at it a different way. Suppose there's a lot of unemployed labor throughout the economy. If the short-run demand for labor is highly elastic, then a small drop in the wage rate will induce businesses to hire a lot more people. So if wages go down a little, unemployment can be eliminated. But what about the opposite case? If the short-run demand for labor is highly inelastic, then what happens when the wage rate goes down? Businesses don't hire very much more labor. The wage rate must go down quite a lot to induce the businesses to hire all of the unemployed labor.

Yes, the elasticity of the demand for productive factors (that is, the responsiveness of businesses to factor price changes) is very important—not only in the model, but in the real world, too.

The more elastic the demand for the factors of production, the more businesses will adjust to changing factor prices. Elasticity means responsiveness to price. If the businesses are highly responsive to changes in factor prices then the price mechanism is working just great. But if they aren't very responsive to factor price changes, then the market process (the price mechanism) isn't working as responsively.

Suppose nobody responded at all to price changes. Elasticity would be zero. Nothing would shift around in response to price. What about the market process then? It wouldn't work. As you already know, elasticity is essential if the market process is going to work.

SCARCITY AND HIGH PRICES MAKE A FACTOR MORE PRODUCTIVE

The greater the marginal value product of a factor, the greater will be the demand for it. Of course. But did you know that *the high marginal value product of a factor may simply be a reflection of the high price of the factor?*

The rationing function of price will cause a high priced factor to be carefully economized—to be used very sparingly. If a factor is used very sparingly its marginal value product will be high! So a factor's price can be the cause of (not just the *result* of) its high marginal value product. Causality goes both ways!

The Scarcest Factor Has the Highest Marginal Productivity

The productivity of an additional unit of any factor of production depends on the availability of "other factors." If a lot of capital and land are available then an added unit of labor will be highly productive. If a lot of labor and land are available then an added unit of capital will be highly productive. As the quantity of any one factor is increased, it becomes increasingly important to get more of the other factors to work with it.

Suppose a farmer is running a big farm and has lots of land and labor but only one tractor. That farmer will be much more interested in getting another tractor (more capital) than in getting more land or more labor. Why? Because an additional tractor would be much more highly productive—would add much more value to the output than would more land, or labor. Why? Because the tractor is the ralatively scarce factor, that's why!

Which factor are you willing to pay the most to get more of? The relatively scarce one, of course. Your demand for the relatively scarce factor is higher because of its higher productivity. An extra unit of the relatively scarce factor would add more to your "value product." That's why you will pay more to hire it. And that's why its owner will receive a high income.

These concepts apply just as much to *specific* factors as they do to "labor, land, and capital *in general.*" If the *kind* of capital or land you own is relatively scarce or if the kind of labor you have for sale is relatively scarce, then the marginal value product of your kind of capital or land or labor will be high. So the demand for your inputs will be high and your income will be high. You will get a large share of society's output.

An Example Of "the Relatively Scarce Factor"

Suppose you live in the "Grape-belt" area of Chautauqua County in western New York State and you're the only person in the county who has a grape-picking machine. When harvest time comes you will have plenty of opportunity to keep your machine running day and night! Your relatively scarce piece of capital will have high productivity. It will be in very high demand. You will be able to make a lot of money with it. One more grape-picking machine would have a high marginal value product in Chautauqua County! Chances are somebody else (maybe everybody else?) will buy one soon. Maybe *very soon.*

Now, suppose every grape farm in Chautauqua County finally has its own grape-picking machine. But suppose you are the only person in the county who knows how to repair one. You may be sure that the marginal productivity of your labor services will be very high! Your efforts will be in great demand. You will make a lot of money.

The marginal value product of an additional grape-picker mechanic in your county would be very high. Chances are that pretty soon someone else will learn to fix those monsters. Or else some skilled mechanic will move in from Canandaigua or Bass Island, or maybe even from St. Joseph or Roseburg or Fresno or Yakima! Why? You know why. Because the "production motivation function" of the high price for this specialized kind of labor will pull this new mechanic to Chautauqua County. That's why!

What about the marginal productivity of grape-picking machines in Chautauqua County now that everybody has one? It's much lower. Still, if the cost of buying and owning capital is low enough (as compared with the high price of labor), more machines will be bought. The reason all the farmers in the United States and Canada and in the other advanced nations are using so many of these mechanical harvesters—grape-pickers and corn-pickers and tomato-pickers and bean-pickers and cotton-pickers and pickle-pepper-pickers—is because of the relative scarcity (and the high price) of labor. Each time farm workers get higher wages, more "mechanical pickers" take over.

The high-priced factor is conserved. It's used very sparingly. An extra unit would have high marginal productivity (like skilled grape-picker mechanics in Chautauqua County). The low priced factor is used more freely and abundantly. It is used so freely and abundantly that the marginal productivity of another unit of it would be low (like grape-picking machines in Chautauqua County).

High Prices Make Factors More Productive

Remember what happened to eggs when the price went up to $2 a dozen? Only the true egg-lovers (or the filthy rich) kept on buying eggs. To them, eggs are really valuable. How valuable? Worth $2 a dozen of course! When eggs are *priced* at $2 a dozen then you can be sure that eggs are *worth* $2 a dozen to all the people who are still buying them. That's obvious isn't it? The same principle holds true for the business which is buying labor, land, and capital.

In the real world is it true that you always get what you pay for?" In one sense, not necessarily. But in another sense, yes. Some people spend their money more carefully than others and they get more "value received." I'm sure you know that. But you also know that whenever you buy something you *think* what you're getting is going to be worth as much to you as you pay for it! Otherwise you wouldn't buy it. Obviously! Nobody would pay more for something than they think it will be worth to them!

The "rationing function of price" will restrict the purchase of everything (every re-source, every good, every input) so that *nothing will be bought for any purpose (consumption or production) unless the buyer thinks the use is going to be worth at least as much as the cost.*

In the factor markets it says this: No business will pay a dollar for a unit of input unless the unit of input is expected to add at least a dollar's worth to the output. If a factor is selling for $10 then you can be quite certain that the marginal value product of the factor is at least $10. If not, the factor wouldn't be hired. The $50 factor has a marginal value product of at least $50. It will be used sparingly enough to *ensure* that its marginal productivity is at least $50.

High-priced factors will be used very sparingly. They will be used only in highly productive uses, and they will be used together with an abundance of other factors. *So a high price for a factor will guarantee high productivity for that factor.* It is true in the model market system and it is true in the real world. (Exception: Short-sighted administrators sometimes forget this principle and let a $20,000 a year professor or executive do the work that a secretary or student assistant could do.)

In a nation or any area where wage rates are high, labor will be conserved. Lots of labor-saving machinery will be used. The productivity of labor will be high. If the wage was high and the productivity of labor was not high enough to cover it the labor would not be hired. If it was hired the businesses would go broke.

Factor Prices Influence Production Techniques

The organization and techniques of production in a society always reflect the *relative scarcities* and the *relative prices* of the productive factors. In the United States and other advanced nations we use steam shovels and conveyor belts. In countries where labor is very cheap, they use hand shovels and wheelbarrows.

If lumber is plentiful and low-priced while steel and other building materials are very scarce and high-priced, the society will cut down the forests and build things out of wood. But if lumber is very scarce and high-priced and other building materials are plentiful and low-priced, lumber will be used sparingly and other building materials will be used instead.

You can think of all kinds of ways that production would be organized differently if we had different prices on our labor, natural resources, and capital. If you look at a highly developed country and compare it with a less developed country, you will see immediately many differences in the way production is organized. In each case the production organization reflects the relative scarcities, the relative prices, and therefore, the *relative productivities* of the factors of production in the economy.

The LDCs Use More Labor; Labor Productivity Is Low

If you look at the way production is organized in the less developed countries (LDCs) it's easy to see the difference. It's evident in agriculture, mining, manufacturing, transportation, and even in the way the households operate. The most striking difference is the abundant use of labor and the limited use of capital in the LDCs.

If we did things in the advanced nations the way things are done in the LDCs, that would be highly inefficient—very wasteful of our scarce and valuable labor. But if the LDCs organized their productive activities the way we do, that would be highly inefficient for them—very wasteful of their scarce and valuable *capital*. We're doing it the right way for us; they're doing it the right way for them.

Different "factor scarcities" have a big influence on labor productivity (that is, on output per person) and on how much income most of the people get. Where labor is in great supply (relative to the other input factors) wages are low and "the people in general" don't get very much product. When there isn't much product per person it isn't possible for each person to *have* much product. Obviously! There's just no way!

Why is labor productivity so low in the LDCs? Because labor isn't combined with much highly productive capital and resources. Since labor is so plentiful it isn't carefully conserved. Its marginal value product is low and the incomes (and output shares) of the workers are low.

(Note: *Highly skilled* labor—maybe tractor mechanics or grape-picker mechanics—may be more scarce and more productive and higher-priced in the LDCs than in the more advanced nations. The LDCs need to develop capital, sure. But they also need to develop the *kinds* of labor needed to operate and maintain the complex, highly efficient machines and equipment.)

Demand for One Factor Reflects the Supply of Other Factors

By now you are already aware, at least implicitly, of the importance of *factor supply*. All along we have been talking about factor demand. But *supply* seems to keep creeping into the discussion.

The demand for an input is determined by its marginal productivity. But its marginal productivity is determined by how much of it is being used already (relative to the *other* factors it's working with). How much of it is being used already is determined by whether or not, over past years, it has been a relatively "high-priced" or "low-priced" factor. And its past price reflects *relative scarcity*—that is, its past *supply*. See how the supply and the demand are interrelated? all tied together?

It is the productivity which determines the demand and puts the price on the factor, yes. But what is the most important thing that determines the productivity (and the demand) for a factor? The relative scarcity! If one factor is *relatively plentiful,* then it will be used in abundance. Its productivity will be pushed down *low.* Its price will be low. But if a factor is *relatively scarce* it will be used sparingly and its productivity and price will be *high.*

Suppose the price of a factor is high. If the supply of the factor is free to expand, then as time passes the supply will increase and the price will fall. The marginal productivity of this factor will get lower and lower. That's what has happened in the case of capital in the United States and in the other highly developed nations. Capital has become more plentiful, so labor and natural resources have become more scarce. Labor and resources are now higher priced (and are economized more) than in the past.

You can see that it could be difficult to separate completely the supply from the demand for productive factors. But it is useful (for some purposes, essential) to make the distinction. As we get into this next section, you will understand why.

THE SUPPLY OF INPUT FACTORS: LABOR, LAND, CAPITAL

How much of each factor (labor, land, capital) will be available and offered for sale in each market, at each price (wage, rent, interest)? That's the "factor supply" question. The answer is different for one factor or another and it depends on several things. Partly it depends on how we choose to look at the question.

Factor Supply to the Individual Business. Suppose a small business wanted more labor or land or capital. If it offered to pay more, could it get more? Sure. So the supply of any factor to any individual business is likely to be highly elastic. The quantity offered for sale to an individual business (or to any one *industry* for that matter) probably will be quite responsive to a change in the price.

If a firm or an industry is expanding, it must be pulling in more input factors from somewhere. Factors shift from one industry to another. When higher prices are offered in the egg industry, more inputs are supplied.

But we can't understand the income distribution question for the society as a whole by looking at the individual firm, or industry. For example, if we want to find out what market forces are setting "wages in general," we can't figure it out by looking at the egg industry. To get at the issue of "factor price determination" for the economy as a whole, we must look at the nation's *total supply* and *total demand* for each factor.

A minute ago we were talking about what influences the "total productivity" and "total demand" for a factor. You saw why the "total productivity and demand" for labor in the LDCs is so low. Remember? So now let's talk about what determines the *total supply.* When we finish that, you will be able to begin to see how the income distribution question for the society is worked out.

Factor Supply for the Entire Nation. For the nation as a whole the supply of each input factor is *highly inelastic.* At higher prices how much more *total* labor or *total* natural resources or *total* capital would become available? Not very much. The total supply isn't very responsive to price. In a short period of time the total supply may not be responsive to price at all!

The Supply of Labor

The nation's total labor supply might respond a little bit to increases or decreases in the wage rate, but we aren't sure about that. Higher wages may induce more married women to join the labor force. On the other hand, higher wages might induce more women to quit their jobs and live on their husbands' incomes. Higher wages may convince more students to quit college and take jobs; but higher wages may make it possible for students to make it through college by working only part time, or on their parents' high income. Low wages might even force students to quit college and take full-time jobs. (The "production motivating function of price" may work in reverse!)

In High Wage Countries, People Work Less. It's hard to say anything definite about how "the total quantity of labor offered for sale" responds to *price*. As the wage rate gets higher some people will offer more of their labor for sale. But others will offer less.

In the low-wage countries, people work longer and harder than in the high-wage countries. In the United States where wages generally are higher than in any other country in the world, a large number of adults are not even in the labor force (wives, students, retirees, etc). Those who are in the labor force work fewer "hours per year" than in low-wage countries. So we can't say that our high wages are inducing people to offer more labor for sale. It seems to be working the other way!

A Backward-Bending Supply Curve for Labor? We really don't know very much about how the "quantity of labor supplied in the nation" would change if all wage rates went up or down. Some studies suggest that if wages start out very low and then increase a little bit, more labor will be offered. But then if the wage continues to increase, after awhile people start dropping out of the labor force, or demanding a shorter workday or workweek and more time off. This leads to the idea of the "backward-bending supply curve for labor."

Figure 18-2 shows a "backward-bending supply curve." It shows how the wage rate in this "hypothetical nation" would be determined. But don't put too much stock in this backward-bending supply curve. The truth is

that we really don't know much about the relationship between "the wage rate in general" and "the quantity of labor that would be supplied." So, remembering this word of warning, it's time now for you to study the graph.

The Supply of Land and Natural Resources

It's easy to see that the nation's supply of labor is not to be very responsive to wage rate changes. It's more or less fixed by the size, age, skills, habits, economic conditions (etc.) of the population. What about the nation's supply of land and natural resources? That's even more fixed and unresponsive than labor. The production motivating function of price will not have much influence on the *total quantity offered*— either of labor, or of land and natural resources. On labor or land for a *specific purpose?* Yes. But on the *total quantity offered?* No.

What about the nation's supply of capital? Does that respond to price? Capital is made up of *produced* goods. So surely it would seem that a higher price for "capital in general" would soon bring forth more capital. Right? Well, don't be so sure. Better think about that one for a minute, too.

The Supply of Capital

How does a nation increase its supply of capital? By saving (not consuming) and investing (building capital). Capital formation requires less consumption. What would make people consume less? and businesses invest more? That's the key to capital formation.

If capital is bringing a high return to its owners, that means the interest rate is high. Will that induce more people to "not consume"? To save? Maybe so. Then again, maybe not. A high return to capital, just like a high wage rate, might work either way. Some people might save more (to build more capital to get

Fig. 18-2 The Supply and Demand for Labor: Does the Supply Bend Backward?

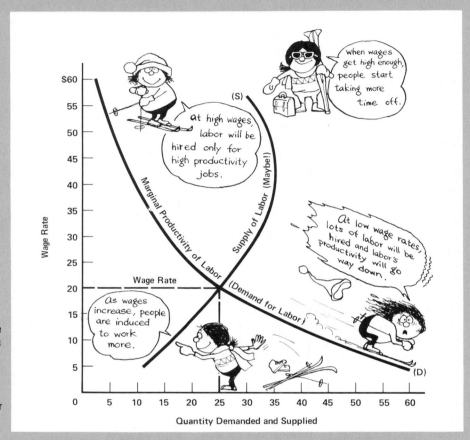

After the wage rate gets just so high, a higher wage rate may cause a decrease in the amount of labor people will offer for sale!

If "the wage in general" goes up for "labor in general" this may get more people to take jobs and workers may be willing to work overtime and to forego vacations. But if the general wage rate in the nation keeps on going up, after awhile some people may start cutting down on their work time so they can take time to enjoy all those things they can buy with their high wages.

the high return); others might save less (the capital they already have now brings them enough income, so they're all set).

For capital in any particular industry, or for any one *kind* of capital—grape-pickers or IBM computers or shoe machines or gear grinders—the supply will be very responsive to demand changes (to the production motivating function of price). But for the nation's *total supply* of capital, it isn't at all certain that the price (interest rate) is all that important. Why do people save more (or less) this year, than last? Many reasons. Some of the other reasons may be much more important than the "price" they get paid for saving—that is, the interest rate.

How to Handle the Problem of Factor Supply

Here we are, faced with a dilemma. If we're going to understand the market forces which influence income distribution then we must understand factor pricing. We must understand factor demand and factor supply for each factor. But we don't know much about factor supply. About all we really know is that for the economy as a whole, factor supply is not very responsive to price changes.

Neither the supply of labor nor land nor capital responds much to factor price changes. But wait! Take heart! Maybe that's all we need to know! Maybe there's no dilemma after all. Let's see.

Suppose we assume that the elasticity of the nation's supply of each of the "factors in general" is *zero*. That would mean "zero responsiveness of the total quantity to a price change." *Absolutely inelastic supply*. The quantity available would be the same whether the price was high or low.

We know this assumption isn't exactly true. Still, it isn't so far from the truth, either. If it will help us to understand factor pricing— that is, income distribution in the market system—then it's a good assumption. And

it does, so it is. Just watch how neatly all the pieces now fall together.

If the supply of each input factor is absolutely fixed, then what will determine the price of each of the factors? *Demand,* or course! You know that the demand for each factor is determined by its productivity. But (as you so well know) *the productivity of each factor is determined by the availability of other factors*.

The productivity of *labor* is determined by the amounts and kinds of land and capital available. The productivity of *land* is determined by the amounts and kinds of labor and capital available. And the productivity of *capital* is determined by the amounts and kinds of labor and land available. See where all this is leading us? It's taking us directly to the answer to the distribution question!

If one factor is relatively scarce, that means that the other factors are relatively plentiful. The productivity of the relatively scarce factor (and the demand for it) will be high. And the price? High, of course! The strong demand and the limited supply will keep the price high. Whoever owns and "sells" some of this relatively scarce factor will receive a large income and will get to have a large share of the output of the society.

Demand and Supply Curves for Factors of Production

Now look at Figure 18-3. It shows the factor demand and the "absolutely inelastic" supply. This graph could apply to any one of the factors. But it makes a lot of difference which one has the largest and which one has the smallest amount of fixed supply!

From studying Figure 18-3 you can see why many people in the less developed countries are so interested in building capital and developing their natural resources. If the people of those countries (or of any country) are going to receive high wages, then there must be an abundance of good land (resources) and/or capital for the people to work with.

Fig. 18-3   The Supply and Demand for a Factor of Production

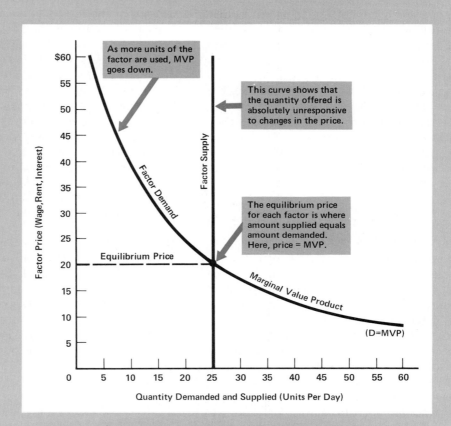

The total supply of a factor of production usually isn't very responsive to price. That is, it's highly inelastic.

The factor supply wouldn't really be a straight vertical line. But this is a useful approximation, at least for prices not too far from "the equilibrium price." (At very low prices the factor owners might not offer any of their factor for sale!)

Any increase in the amounts of other factors available would cause this factor's demand curve (MVP) to shift to the right. The price of the factor would increase.

Anything that would cause the supply of this factor to increase (shift to the right) would lower the price of this factor and would automatically increase the productivity of (and demand for) the other factors.

Anything which would cause the supply of this factor to decrease (shift to the left) would raise the price of this factor and would decrease the productivity of the other factors. For the economy as a whole, *the productivity of each factor depends on the supply of the other two factors.*

Economic development, which the less developed countries are relentlessly striving for, is the process of building capital and developing and making use of the nation's resources. With more capital and resources to work with, labor will be more productive. Output per person will be higher. The people will be able to have more things.

THE MARKET MODEL AND THE REAL WORLD

Figure 18-3 can help you to understand why the general level of wages, rent, or interest in one economy or another, would be high or low. But you know that this doesn't answer all of the "real world" questions. Not by a long shot. It just gives us a place to start.

There Are Many Kinds of Labor, Land, and Capital

Each particular kind of labor, land, or capital has its own relative scarcity, its own marginal value product, and its own "supply and demand situation." One kind of labor or land or capital may be highly productive while another may be of no value at all in the production process. While the total supply of labor or land or capital may not respond at all to a change in demand and price, *each kind* of labor, land, or capital may be quite responsive to price changes. If the price of one kind of labor is unusually high (like grape-picker mechanics) this will "motivate the production" of more of this kind of labor. But in the meanwhile, the owner of the high-priced kind of labor will enjoy an especially high income.

In this "constant shifting about" within the various factor categories the production motivating function of price really does its work. It entices the factors to do the kinds of things most valued by the society. It stimulates the development of new and better labor skills and new and better capital. It even stimulates the discovery of more of the most productive kinds of natural resources. The person who is most successful in developing the kind of labor which is highly valued in the market (or the person who gains ownership of the kinds of land or capital which are highly valued) will receive a high income—that is, a high distributive share of the society's output.

The Normative Question of Income Distribution

In this chapter, most of the time we have been talking about income distribution in the pure market system. The theory of the model system really does relate to what goes on in the real world. But it doesn't answer all the questions. It doesn't get into the issues of extreme affluence or poverty. It doesn't talk at all about how the society's income and output *should* be distributed.

Most people in every society seem to agree that the distribution of income in their society is something less than perfect. How bad is it? What should be done about it? Why isn't a better distribution arrangement being worked out?

Most societies are working on this problem constantly. Each price change or wage change makes a difference. Each tax or social security or unemployment compensation or medical program change is a change in the distribution system. Each manpower training program, minimum-wage law, and anti-poverty program exerts some influence. Yes, people are always trying to work through the political process to change the distribution system. And sure enough, it's being changed all the time.

The issues we're talking about now could take us far beyond the pure theory of income distribution. This book will not be able to go very deeply into all of them. But later on there's a chapter that deals with real-world income distribution problems. For

I want more income! Howbout you? Don't you spoze that's always true?

now, be sure you understand what the "distributive forces" are and how they work in the "model pure market system."

MICROECONOMICS, PURE COMPETITION, AND THE REAL WORLD

For the past three chapters you have been studying and learning about "the pure theory of microeconomics." You have found out how demand and supply work to set prices and how prices work to ration things and to motivate the production of things. You also know a lot about how the forces of the market process influence income distribution in the society. In fact, you know quite a lot of microeconomics!

Almost all of the principles explained in these "micro-theory" chapters rest on the assumption of pure competition. That means there must be many buyers and sellers, all responding to price, freely entering and leaving all markets—all the product markets and all the factor markets. The prices respond to demand changes and cost changes. Then the buyers and sellers respond to the price changes. Everything works out just right. That's the way it works in the model.

The model system, made up of markets with "pure competition," is different in many respects from the real world. The chapter coming up now will explain what happens when we don't have pure competition. But first, be sure you understand the pure theory. Then go on into Part Six and find out about some of the things that are going on in the real world.

REVIEW EXERCISES   • **MAJOR CONCEPTS, PRINCIPLES, TERMS (Explain each carefully.)**

    law of diminishing returns
    law of variable proportions
    how MVP influences factor demand
    how the law of diminishing returns influences factor demand
    how time influences factor demand
    how "output demand elasticity" influences factor demand
    how factor prices influence economic growth and change
    how relative scarcity influences factor prices
    how factor prices influence factor productivity
    how factor demand is determined by other factor supplies

• **OTHER CONCEPTS AND TERMS (Explain each briefly.)**

    marginal value product (MVP)
    marginal input cost (MIC)
    derived demand
    variable inputs
    fixed inputs
    the normative question of income distribution

• CURVES AND GRAPHS (Draw, label, and explain each.)

Demand for a Factor of Production
The Supply and Demand for Labor
The Supply and Demand for a Factor of Production

• QUESTIONS (Write the answers, or jot down key points.)

1. In the real world, each "factor of production" (labor, land, capital) is really made up of a great number of different factors of production. Each *kind* of labor is really a different "factor of production." How different is your "labor" today than it was five years ago? How about five years from now? What are you doing these days to try to develop a more productive, more highly valued kind of labor, so the "price" you can get for your labor will be higher in the future? Discuss.

2. Explain as much as you can about what influences (1) the demand for a factor of production and (2) the supply of a factor of production.

3. Suppose we're talking about a completely planned economy—the market process has no influence whatsoever. In planning the production activities for each industry, should the planners try to use each kind of labor, land, and capital in the same proportions as the market process would direct? or not? Also, do you think the planners should try to distribute the income among the members of the society in the same way the market process would direct? Explain.

4. Now that you know something about how the "prices" of labor and of capital are influenced by relative scarcity, think back over the past 100 years or so in the history and growth of the United States. What do you think was the effect of the "open immigration" policy on the wage rates? and on the returns to the owners of capital? and on the rate of economic growth? And today, what do you think are the effects of the *more restrictive* immigration policies? Discuss.

PART 6

MICRO PRINCIPLES, PROBLEMS, AND POLICIES: CRITICAL ISSUES OF THE MODERN WORLD

IF IT'S SUPPLY AND DEMAND THAT SETS PRICES, HOW COME SO MANY PRICES TURN OUT TO BE $4.98?

19 Monopoly Power, Administered Prices, and Antitrust Policy

The various kinds of competition and market structure have a lot to do with the way the market process really works.

The neatness and beauty of the pure market process is a delight to behold. We are all free to do as we please, yet just the right amount of everything gets produced. All of us get our shares of the output as determined by our productivity. It's so great it's just unreal. And that's true. It really is unreal. This chapter will explain to you some of the reasons why it's so unreal.

PURE COMPETITION AND MONOPOLY POWER

You know a lot about how the model market system works. You know how changes in the demand and the supply change the market price. You know how prices move freely, responding to shifts of demand or supply. But all those things won't happen that way unless there is pure competition in all the markets. Unless the market has something like "pure competition" the adjustment process can't work out the way the pure market model says it will.

Competition Protects the Buyer

Back in our "island economy" there was a big demand for tuba (coconut-palm wine). Remember? The northside chief, King Ratukabua, was the only seller of tuba. In response to the great demand for tuba, he might have simply raised the price (instead of increasing the output). But suppose he had lots of competitors all selling tuba. Then he couldn't just raise the price and make lots of profits. Right? Of course not.

Competition is the thing which prevents businesses from limiting their output and raising the price sky high. Suppose there's competition and one factory limits its output and holds up the price. What happens? Nobody buys! Everybody buys from the lower-priced sellers. If there are *many* buyers and sellers of a product we say the "market structure" is one of pure competition. Remember? Here's a brief review.

> Competition forces all sellers to do a good job of serving the buyers!

Pure Competition Again

In a market of pure competition *no producer thinks of cutting back output to hold up the price.*

Suppose you're growing corn and selling it in a roadside stand. Would you cut back your corn production to keep the price of corn from falling? No. Then you are selling under conditions of pure competition. Would any one of your customers stop buying corn to force the price to go down? No. So the buyers are buying under conditions of pure competition.

Buyers and sellers simply "react" to the market price. They don't try to change the price. So it's a market of pure competition. But *as they all react, "the market" changes the price.*

In a market of pure competition, the price moves upward only if many buyers are trying to buy more (or if there are a lot more buyers) or if many sellers are selling less (or if there are a lot fewer sellers). With pure competition, the price is a true reflection of society's demand (reflecting the society's marginal utility of the product) and of society's supply (reflecting the cost of production of the product). But if any buyer or seller gets big enough to create a shortage or surplus in the market then pure competition no longer exists.

A Producer with Monopoly Power Is Free to Set the Price

Without pure competition, no longer can we say that the price is a true reflection of society's demand for and cost of the product. Suppose one seller gets large enough to influence the total supply for a product. Then that seller can restrict output and keep the price up high and make big profits. This power to restrict output and hold up the price is called market power or monopoly power. Remember?

Is pure competition the usual thing? You know it isn't. In all the modern economies in which "free markets" play an important role—the United States, Canada, Western Europe, Japan, and most of the other nations of the modern world—pure competition usually exists only in the markets for farm and fishery products. Most manufactured products are made by a few large producers.

Sometimes there is strong competition among these big manufacturers. But the competition is very different and brings different results than pure competition would bring. Outputs still adjust to changes in demand. But *the adjustment process is very different.* Also the equilibrium price and the quantity flowing across the market may be quite different from the results described in the "model market structure of pure competition."

Producers Can Respond Directly to Demand Changes

Manufacturing firms usually set the selling prices of their products. They try to set and hold the prices at levels they believe will cover their costs and bring in some profits. Once the price is set it will not change in response to every little change in demand, or cost. The price stays constant.

This does not mean that the buyers have no influence on the amounts produced. If the buyers demand a large amount of something, a large amount of it will be produced and sold; if they demand a smaller amount, production will be cut back. A smaller amount will be produced and sold. But the adjustment doesn't come about through the "price mechanism," as described in the market model of pure competition.

In the markets for almost everything you buy, *outputs respond directly to demand.* Prices stay about the same. In a market of pure competition a demand change causes a price change. Then production responds to the price change (as was the case in our egg market and corn market examples). But in the markets for manufactured products (toothpaste, TV sets, automobiles, ball-point pens, economics books and almost anything else you can think of) output usually responds directly to the strength of the demand. The manufacturer sets the price and doesn't change it very often. Of course, if the demand for some product turns out to be especially strong the producer probably will find some excuse to move the price up to get more profits.

There Are Subtle Ways to "Raise the Price"

No producer likes to be thought of as a selfish and ruthless profiteer. But if the demand for some product is really strong the producer probably will find a way to raise the price. There are all sorts of ways to do this—perhaps stop producing the cheaper line and only produce the more expensive line; then soon the expensive line begins to look very much like the old cheap line.

There are all sorts of ways of "raising the price" without coming right out and announcing that you are raising the price. But suppose the demand falls? If it turns out that much of what has been produced cannot be sold at the set price, what does the manufacturer do? Cut back production? Of course. But it's also necessary to find some special way to reduce the price to get rid of the surplus.

What would you do? You might use a special sale or larger trade-in allowances or perhaps remove the brand labels and sell the entire surplus to a discount outlet. There are many ways to lower the price without announcing that you are lowering the price!

Figure 19-1 illustrates the situation in which the individual producer is producing a brand-name product—perhaps Ford Pintos or Bobbie Brooks knitwear, or whatever. The producer fixes the price and then adjusts the output in response to the quantity people are buying. Take a few minutes now to study Figure 19-1.

Competition Always Limits Monopoly Power

What keeps the business from setting the "usual price" very high? One thing is competition. Competition usually isn't "pure." But it still can't be ignored. Someone is always trying to take away your customers. Or the business might fear charges of "monopoly"— and then government intervention. Or what about bad publicity from consumer groups? No one wants a bad public image! Or maybe workers will strike for higher wages if they see such high profits.

There are many forces in the real world which work against individual firms setting exorbitantly high prices or making exorbitantly high profits. Probably the most important force is *the role of actual and potential competition*—that is, *the threat of acceptable substitutes from other producers.*

Any one steel company, automobile manufacturer, television producer, or other manufacturer who sets prices very much above the others in the industry is likely to lose sales and profits. Customers will buy other (substitute) brands instead.

But wait! Why don't the producers get together and decide to all raise their prices at the same time? This could be *very* profitable! But alas: There's a law against it. Several laws, really. The "antitrust laws" which try to protect the consumer by keeping businesses from monopolizing markets.

Administered Prices? Or "Competitive" Prices?

How different the markets are in the real world from the market model of pure competition! In markets of pure competition the price moves freely in response to changes in demand and supply. It's the *price* as it moves up or down, which carries the message from the consumers to the producers. It's the *price increase* which pulls the factors into the

Fig. 19-1   The Administered Price (Horizontal) Supply Curve

The price is set by the producer and the amount produced and offered for sale responds directly to changes in demand.

This illustrates the supply of a manufactured product marketed under normal circumstances in an economy like the United States. For a broad range of output, the *price* will stay the same.

If the quantity people are buying is large, production will be stepped up; if the quantity people are buying is small, production will be cut back. The producer would go on a four-day work week, or perhaps close down for one week each month rather than lower the price.

If the demand is low the output is low; if the demand is high, the output is high. The price stays the same. But notice that if the demand goes very high (shifts far to the right) the price *will* go up. Or if the demand goes very low (shifts far to the left) the price will go down. Sales and discounts and other gimmicks will be used to get rid of the surpluses. If the demand does not soon pick up, the business will stop producing this unprofitable product.

industries which society wants expanded and it is the *price decrease* which moves the factors out of those industries which society wants contracted. But in the real world very few prices are free to move around like that.

The prices for almost everything you can think of are set by someone. The economist calls these "set prices": *administered prices.* Manufacturers, wholesalers, retailers, barber shops, doctors, lawyers, taxicab companies and airlines all sell their products and services at "administered prices." The wages received by most people are "administered prices." Interest rates are "administered prices." Even many of the farm products are now sold at prices which are "administered" either by government or by farmers' organizations.

All administered prices reflect demand and cost conditions, at least to some extent. The administered prices for manufactured products generally are set on the basis of cost and demand estimates. Then the prices are held firm and the output is expanded or contracted, depending on how much is being sold. You just saw that in Figure 19-1.

Yes, administered prices *are* influenced by demand and cost conditions. But the extent of the influence and the results obtained are not the same—and in some cases are greatly different—from the "pure competitive market model."

The Effects of Adminstered Prices

Economists have spent a lot of effort and have written many volumes on the issue of "administered prices." Yet we still don't know for sure exactly how to assess the effects of administered prices in the real world. We know that administered prices reduce the immediate responsiveness of the market price to a shift of demand. But that isn't always bad.

Violent fluctuations resulting from sharp changes in demand don't do anybody any good. Administered prices do introduce a degree of stability. That's desirable. But *administered prices permit sellers to bend the economic choices of the society toward their own interests.* This would not be possible in the pure competitive model.

Another problem is that *administered prices tend to inch upward year after year.* Workers want bigger paychecks. Businesses want increasing profits. Everyone who is selling anything would like to get more money year after year. When prices are administered, sellers usually have the opportunity to inch up their prices—so they do. So what happens? There's a tendency for a *continual upward movement* of prices.

Now you have an overview of the issues of pure competition, market power, and administered pricing. But there's a lot more to it than that. Not that it's difficult or complicated or hard to understand. It isn't. In fact it's all very "real-worldly." When we dig into it you will recognize many familiar things—advertising for example. So let's go back and start at the beginning and talk about "market structure."

"COMPETITION" IS DETERMINED BY MARKET STRUCTURE

The market is not a place or a thing. It's just a concept. Remember? So how could it have a structure?

The "structure" of something is: "how it's put together." The *structure* of a house is *how it is built.* When you study human anatomy you learn about the structure of the human body—how it is put together—how many bones there are and how many muscles and where they are and how big they are and all that. You learn what all the parts are and how they fit together. When we are looking at the *structure* of something we are not concerned with how it works—only with how it is built: What are the pieces? How do they fit together?

You already know that each market is "made up of"—that is, built of, or structured out of—buyers on one side and sellers on the other. All the buyers and all the sellers are not standing there glaring at each other, of course! But they are there just the same.

No more than two people—one buyer and one seller—may meet face to face at any one time. But if each buyer and each seller knows that there are a thousand other buyers and a thousand other sellers just waiting to appear, then we have a "market structure" of pure competition.

Pure Competition Is a Form of Market Structure

Whenever there are many small buyers on one side of the market and many small sellers on the other, no *one buyer* and no *one seller* can go into the market and start throwing his or her weight around. With a thousand buyers and a thousand sellers, if one seller gets mad and goes home there will be no noticeable effect on the market—on the price or on the quantity flowing across the market.

Suppose one buyer decides to buy twice as many eggs this week. That won't have any effect on the price or quantity either. With pure competition the "natural market process" determines the price and regulates the quantity flowing across the market from the sellers to the buyers.

When we talk about "pure competition" we are talking about one form of "market structure"—a structure of *many buyers and sellers—so many that no one of them acting alone could have any noticeable effect on the market—either on the price or on the quantity flow.* You've heard quite a bit about pure competition already. But now here are some other kinds of market structures that you don't yet know much about.

Bilateral Monopoly Means One Seller and One Buyer

What kind of market structure would be the complete opposite of pure competition? Complete monopoly, of course! It would be a market where there is only one buyer and one seller. This market structure is sometimes called bilateral monopoly. Other times it is called monopsony-monopoly (one buyer-one seller).

When the steel workers' union bargains with the steel industry that's a labor market of "bilateral monopoly" or "monopsony-monopoly." The union has complete control of the supply. It's the only seller. The steel industry has complete control of the demand. It's the only buyer. You can see how ridiculous it would be to assume that the wage rate for steelworkers will be set by "the natural and impersonal forces" of the pure competitive market!

Whenever a market structure of bilateral monopoly exists, both the buyer and the seller must consider their market power. Anything either one does will change conditions in the market. Both must take this important fact into consideration. So the monopolist's decision-making process is more complicated than that of the "pure competitor." The monopolist must consider costs and revenues, just as a "pure competitor" would. But *the monopolist must also figure out what effect each decision will have on the market price!*

Now you have seen the two most extreme forms of market structure. All other market structures are variations of these extremes. There's one seller and many buyers (monopoly), one buyer and many sellers (monopsony), a few on each side of the market, and so on. All kinds of variations in the sizes and numbers of buyers and sellers are possible. Most of the rest of this chapter will be talking about some of the variations.

Most Product Markets Have Few Sellers and Many Buyers

Many (most) consumer product markets in the real world consist of a few sellers and many buyers. All the *buyers* know that no matter how much they buy, it won't force the price up. But all the *sellers* know that if they increase their output very much they will have to reduce the price to sell all of the output. They can all set their prices and as long as each seller's prices are not higher than the prices of the other producers (competitors) then each seller can continue to hold a share of the market.

How many products and services can you think of which are produced and sold by "a few sellers"? How about metals—steel, aluminum, copper, etc.? Or coal, oil, and natural gas? And what about the railroads, trucking companies, bus companies, airlines? Producers of automobiles, washing machines, refrigerators, TV sets, tires, paints, chemicals? Local building contractors, shipbuilding firms, computer companies? Toothpaste, deodorants, hair spray, after-shave lotion, headache pills? Just about everything you can think of, right?

All Producers Must Keep Their Prices "In Line"

Most of the products you buy are produced and sold by a few large sellers. Each company determines the price it will charge for its product. But each company knows that the price it charges must not be very far out of line with the prices other companies are charging for similar products. If one company's price is so high that it's out of line, no one will buy that company's product.

If one company is selling only half as much as it would like to, one way it could sell more would be to lower the price. But any company that lowers its price will take customers away from its competitors. The competitors would not be very happy about that! So what would they do?

They would lower their prices too, just like in a gasoline "price war." In the end where will they all wind up? In about the same place except that everybody's prices will be lower and probably everybody will be losing money. Suppose you were a producer in this industry. What good would it do to lower your price? No good. You would wind up hurting your competitors and yourself, too. Every producer

already knows that. So usually, nobody lowers the price.

All Producers Limit Their Outputs

In the kind of market structure we are talking about (where there are a few sellers and many buyers) does each firm produce as many as it can? Not on your life! The rate at which each plant operates is determined by the rate at which people are buying the output. Each business keeps its production regulated so that no unwanted surpluses will be produced and no price cutting will occur.

This is very different from what would happen in a "pure competition" market. Here, each firm is responsive to demand. But their responsiveness does not result from *price movements* in the market. Each firm responds *directly* to the strength of the demand. If their customers are buying more they produce more. If their customers are buying less they produce less. No producer will keep on producing if no one is buying the product! Of course not.

In the egg market, how did the producers know that they should start producing more eggs? Because the price of eggs went up, offering excess profits! But the way that General Motors knows to cut back on the production of the Olds 88 and increase the production of the Vega station wagon is by seeing how many of each the people are buying. The response of production to demand is *direct*, rather than through the movement of price. If Bethlehem Steel finds that people aren't buying as many hot rolled sheets as before, Bethelehem doesn't wait around and let a glut on the market push the price down. Production is cut back immediately!

OLIGOPOLY IS A MARKET WITH FEW SELLERS

This kind of market structure we have been talking about is one with lots of buyers but only a few sellers. Each seller must be very careful not to push the price down. Economists call this kind of market structure oligopoly.

"Oligopoly" is an important kind of market structure in the world today. You need a good understanding of what it is and how it works. So let's resurrect our island example and talk some more about "palm-tree wine." What do we call it? Tuba! Of course.

The Island Example Again

Remember in the beginning when the northside chief King Ratukabua had the monopoly on tuba? That was a market structure of complete monopoly on one side and several buyers on the other. The northside chief (monopolist) had the power to restrict the output, raise the price and make profits. Why should he produce a lot of tuba and force the price way down? His maximum profit will come if he limits output and sells his tuba at a high price.

That's a very important thing about a market structure of monopoly. Once King Ratukabua has it he *cannot ignore the fact that he has it.* He cannot ignore the effect of his actions on the market—on the price and quantity. If he does ignore his monopoly position he loses the opportunity for more profits. What kind of businessman would he be if he didn't take advantage of his profit opportunities? That's a problem with monopoly. *Once monopoly exists, the seller must restrict output to keep from pushing the price down.*

In order to introduce *oligopoly* to our island we need more people. So let's assume there are several more islands just like our island, all scattered within easy trading distance. Soon trade develops among all these islands. Also, let's suppose that the only island on which the people know how to make tuba is *our* little island—Tubaland Island. (You knew I named it that for some reason. Right?)

Suppose that as the years have passed, all of the families on our island have learned to make tuba. Now there are four big tuba-making operatings on the island—north,

south, east, and west. All the operations are approximately the same size, and all four families are selling tuba to the people on the other nearby islands.

Oligopoly Discourages Price Competition

The northside chief always sells his tuba at the "going price." He is wise enough to know that if he tries to charge more than that, no one will buy from him. They will buy from the eastside, westside, and southside islanders, but not from him. He realizes also that if he tries to sell more by cutting his price, his "oligopolistic competitors" will lower their prices too. Otherwise they would lose all of their customers! In the end all of the producers would be worse off. So he doesn't cut his price either.

Is there "competition" in the tuba market? Yes. Oligopolistic competition. But notice how different this "oligopolistic competition" is from pure competition! Remember the case of the egg market? One egg producer doesn't care if the next farmer down the road goes into the egg business or not. Each producer knows that one more or less producer isn't going to have any effect on the market. But what about the "oligopolistic competition?" That's very different. Each seller is acutely aware of the interdependence in the market. You know that everything your competitors do will affect you. Everything you do will affect your competitors. Each seller is very careful to restrict output to that amount which can be sold at the going price.

What Happens If Someone Cuts the Price?

Suppose the westside islanders are not careful enough about limiting their production of tuba. One day the westside chief (Queen Isaleilani) realizes that they have produced so much tuba that the only way they can sell it is to cut the price. So she decides to pull a quick price cut and sell off the surpluses before the other tuba sellers know what's up.

She decides to cut the price from eight fishsticks (FS 8.00) to six fishsticks (FS 6.00) per jugful. She sends out a boatload of tuba. As the boat approaches a neighboring island the crew unfurls a huge banner saying: "SPECIAL PRICE! TUBA FS 6.00 A JUGFUL!" The minute the boat gets to the beach the people begin to clamor for the tuba. In less than an hour all the tuba is sold. The boat heads back home for a new supply.

It just so happens that about two hours after the westside boat leaves, an eastside boat arrives and tries to sell tuba for FS 8.00. No one will buy. They explain that they can now get tuba at FS 6.00 from the westside islanders and that they are not going to buy any more tuba from anyone else unless they can get it for FS 6.00 a jugful.

The eastside islanders realize immediately that they can't sell any tuba on that island unless they lower their price to six fishsticks. Those westside islanders! Trying to get away with a trick like that! They should know that *with a market structure of oligopoly, "price competition" only lowers the profits for everybody*!

Everyone Must Cut the Price

The eastside islanders reluctantly agree to sell their boatload of tuba for FS 6.00 a jug. They would rather do this than to take back a boatload of tuba or to try to make the long run to the next island before nightfall. By the time they arrive home the eastsiders are in the mood to convince the westsiders of the error of their ways—by fair means or foul!

By the time the eastside chief, King Tuituranga, arrives at the westside village, Queen Isaleilani has already been thinking about this thing. She begins to realize that it probably would be more profitable for her (and for everybody) if she would just dump the

surplus tuba in the lagoon and keep the price at FS 8.00. She is already planning to send a messenger around saying that she made a mistake and announcing that from now on all westside tuba will be sold for no less than FS 8.00 a jugful.

Since the demand for tuba is not very elastic, the total amount people would buy at a price of FS 6.00 probably isn't very much greater than the total amount they would buy at a price of FS 8.00. As the price moved down to six fishsticks, the producers would be able to sell a little more—but not much more. They wouldn't sell enough to make up for the loss (FS 2.00 a jug) caused by lowering the price. Everybody would get less revenue. So no one is ever going to be so foolish as to cut the price of tuba again!

Oligopoly Generates Price Leadership

Will anyone ever *raise* the price of tuba? Maybe. If one seller raises the price, all the others must also raise their prices or else the initial price increase will be withdrawn in a hurry! Suppose the northside chief raises the price to nine fishsticks a jugful. Unless everyone else immediately does the same, the northside chief will not be able to sell any tuba.

Here's a new idea. Perhaps the northside chief can become recognized as the "price leader" in the tuba market. If so, he can raise the price to FS 9.00 and be confident that all the other tuba makers will immediately follow. Then all will get more profits at the higher price. Can you see why price leadership usually develops in oligopolistic industries? Sort of obvious, isn't it?

In the United States, if Bethlehem Steel announces a ten percent price increase for hot rolled plates, unless the other steel companies soon announce similar price increases Bethlehem will probably announce that it isn't going to raise the prices after all. Bethlehem doesn't want to lose all of its customers! They know that no one is going to buy steel from Bethlehem when they could get the same product from USS, Republic, Inland, J & L (or maybe from Germany or Japan) for ten percent less!

Characteristics of Oligopoly Markets

All oligopoly markets have three special characteristics:
1. All producers must quote prices which are identical (or nearly identical).
2. No producer can profit by using price competition—by cutting the price to less than the "going price."
3. The only way any producer can raise the price and then stick to the higher price is for all the other producers to follow along and move their prices up, too.

If you understand why these three things are true, then you have a good basic understanding of oligopoly. You can see how each seller must be very careful in a market of "pure oligopoly" (where the product of all sellers is identical). Each seller must always be mindful of what those other sellers are doing. It's a watchful, nervous kind of situation!

Oligopolists Would Like to Form a Cartel

Producers don't like the limitations and restrictions imposed on them by this "pure kind" of oligopoly. No producer can change the price without considering what the other producers are going to do. Producers like to escape from such restricting influences. One way to escape is to have a little conference with all the other oligopolists and agree on what prices to charge. You might even agree which market territories each one will sell in. A "cartel" agreement like this surely would relieve some of the pressure!

An agreement among the oligopoly sellers would let all of them know just how everything is going to go. Everybody can have high prices

and carefully restrict outputs and make high profits. How? By eliminating the nervous, watchful kind of "oligopolistic competition" and replacing it with an agreement which, in effect, creates a "pure monopoly." When all the big sellers get together and form a cartel and plan market stategy, they become "one seller."

An "oligopolistic conspiracy" is great for the big producers. But it can be expensive for all the rest of us. This is the kind of agreement "in restraint of trade" (to limit the amount sold and hold up the price) which the U.S. antitrust laws are designed to prohibit. I suppose you already knew this would be an "illegal conspiracy"—one of the things prohibited by the Sherman Antitrust Act of 1890.

A GRAPHIC EXPLANATION OF OLIGOPOLY

As you have been reading all this about oligopoly you may have been wondering about the strange nature of the demand for tuba as seen by each seller:
—If you lower the price, everybody else is going to lower the price. So you aren't going to sell very much more. Inelastic demand. Right? Sure.
—But what if you raise the price? Other sellers probably won't raise their prices So who will buy from you, with your price so high? Maybe nobody! Everybody may buy from other sellers whose prices are lower.

So your little increase in price causes your quantity sold to drop maybe all the way to zero. Highly elastic demand? Right?

Can you see what this is saying? Inelastic demand if you lower the price (you don't sell much more). Elastic demand if you raise the price (you sell a lot less)! How can that be?

Look at Figure 19-2 and you'll find out about it. After that go on to Figure 19-3 and you'll find out even more about oligopoly markets.

Fig. 19-2 Oligopoly I: Demand as Seen by the Individual Seller

The demand is very elastic if you raise the price (you lose your customers) and not very elastic if you lower the price (you don't sell much more.)

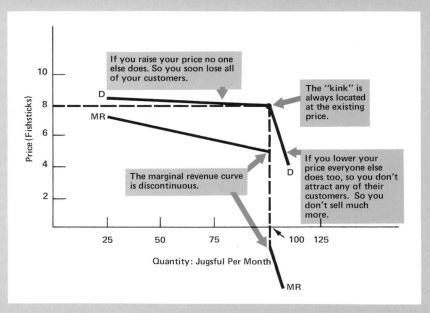

Why is there a kink in the demand curve? With the upper segment "price elastic" and the lower segment "price inelastic"? It's simple. There are really two demand curves put together.

The upper segment is "the demand curve for your product assuming all other sellers keep their price the same." The lower segment of the curve is "the demand for your product assuming that any price you choose will also be the price chosen by all the other sellers."

Why do we build the demand curve for the oligopolist using the lower segment of one of the curves and the upper segment of the other? Because that's realistic. That's the way it works in oligopoly markets.

If you raise your price it's profitable for the other producers *not* to raise their prices. They get your customers and make more profits. But if you lower your price the other sellers must lower theirs or else you will get all their customers!

So when you lower the price, everyone follows so that's the demand curve that applies. When you raise the price, no one follows, so the other demand curve applies. Get the idea?

Now you can understand why the marginal revenue curve is discontinuous. The upper segment of the marginal revenue curve really goes with the "nobody follows" demand curve. The lower segment of the marginal revenue curve goes with the "everybody follows" demand curve.

So when should an oligopolist either raise or lower the price? According to this, never! The next graph tells more about that.

Fig. 19-3   Oligopoly II: Total Market Demand, and Sales by Each Seller

If all the sellers get together and raise their prices, everyone can make more profits. They can escape from the "frozen situation" of the kinked demand curve.

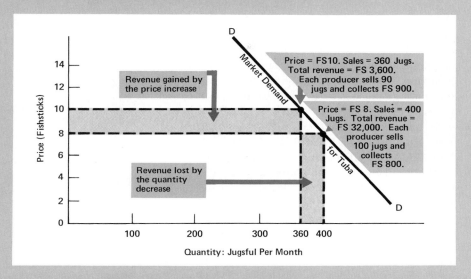

At the higher price, everyone gets more revenue! And since they are all selling less, their total costs also must be less. It's obviously very profitable to raise the price *if everyone raises the price at the same time*!

Here it is assumed that each seller will have one fourth of the entire market. As long as all of the sellers increase their price at the same time there is no reason why the price increase should disturb the "market shares" of any of the sellers. But if any one seller raises the price and the others don't? Then we have a kinked demand curve again!

You can see that the market demand for tuba between the prices of FS8 and FS10 is price inelastic. Each increase in price brings an increase in total revenue. All the producers will make more money (but all the buyers will be worse off) when the price goes up to FS10. The buyers will get less tuba and pay more money. The sellers will produce less tuba and will get more money.

What about a price of FS12? It looks like a price of FS12 about 320 jugsful would be bought. So would it be good business to raise the price of FS12? It sure would! The total revenue received would go up to FS 3,840. The revenue each producer would receive would increase to FS 960. And what about the producer's costs? They would go down even more! When you produce less, your total cost is lower!

PRODUCT DIFFERENTIATION GENERATES MONOPOLISTIC COMPETITION

There is another way—a legal way—which producers may be able to escape from the nervous, watchful conditions of "oligopolistic competition." One day the northside chief decides to order from Japan some beautifully designed, multicolored tuba bottles with interesting figurines on the bottle caps. Then when the new bottles arrive he fills them with tuba and labels them with the slogan THE ONLY MONEY-VAULT-AGED AND DECORATIVELY-BOTTLED TUBA IN THE WORLD. Then he makes a ceremonial trip to the other islands and donates one bottle to the chief of each village.

Now Advertising Becomes Important

On each island the northside chief makes a speech. He says: "Of all the very, very finest things in the entire world, by far the most outstanding and regal is this. This is the only Money-Vault-Aged and Decoratively-Bottled Tuba in the world. This tuba should be used only by those who have that highly developed sense of taste which will enable them to appreciate the very finest. You should never give this tuba to anyone unless you care enough to give the very best!" The northside chief then announces that the price of this special money-vault-aged tuba will be 22 fishsticks a jugful and that he can supply only 12 jugsful per month.

You wouldn't believe the reaction! Everyone wants some vault-aged tuba. The high price appears to be no deterrent at all. There is a long waiting list of people who want some of this special tuba. In actual fact the tuba is no different than the other tuba. But in *economics* it is different. If the people think something is different, it will carry a higher price. So *from the point of view of economics, it is different!*

The northside chief is making beautiful profits. How did he swing it? He escaped from the "oligopolistic competition" by product differentiation—by making his product different from those of his oligopolistic competitors. Now, he has escaped from that nervous, cautious oligopolistic competition!

The northside chief is still selling ordinary tuba in the "oligopoly" market. But in his special "vault-aged tuba," he has himself a little monopoly, all his own. He has hit upon a truly profitable scheme—a scheme recognized by business people all over the world—"differentiate your product, and advertise!" But how long do you suppose he is going to be able to enjoy this great special advantage? Can he keep this "separate little monopoly" all his own? Forever?

Other Producers Differentiate their Products

The other tuba producers are not stupid. They too are going to think up some special brand names, get some special bottles, differentiate their products, advertise, and create some little monopolies of their own. Soon they will start cutting in on the northside chief's little monopoly. Just watch.

Soon Queen Isaleilani gets a bright idea and orders some pink food coloring from Japan, mixes it with some of her tuba, bottles the tuba in smaller containers of clear glass so the pink can be clearly seen, puts on a label showing a strong man with big muscles, and the words: WESTSIDE TUBA FOR HEALTH, STRENGTH, VITALITY. She runs her own advertising campaign, complete with two giant-type strong men borrowed from a traveling carnival. She prices the bottles at 27 fishsticks each and announces that because of the great difficulty of producing this special tuba she can only supply 14 bottles a month. Soon she too has a long waiting list of customers for her special "health-type" tuba.

You can guess what happens from now on. Soon the eastsiders develop their own brand; then the southsiders develop their own brand. As all this going on the northside chief asks himself, "Why have only one brand? Why not one brand to sell for FS 100.00, in a gold-plated jug, and only sell two each month? Maybe have another brand to sell for FS 15.00? And several others?"

Soon There Are Many Brands of Tuba. Before long each family has five or six or eight or ten different brands of tuba, all sort of competing with each other, but no two brands exactly alike in the minds of the buy-

ers. The northside chief still has his monopoly in "money-vault-aged" tuba and the westside chief still has her monopoly in "health, strength, and vitality" tuba. Each family has, in effect, a "little monopoly" in each of their brand name products. What the producers are doing now is *competing by advertising*.

Each family is trying to convince the people that their kinds of tuba are the best kinds. But by now the island people are beginning to get a little immune to all the advertising and "medicine shows." Several people are beginning to suspect that the different kinds of tuba really aren't that different after all. Some strong-willed people are beginning to buy the brands that are priced lowest—and without even being apologetic about it.

Price-Consciousness Must Be Carefully Undermined! The producers do all kinds of things to try to stop this intelligent "price consciousness" on the part of their customers. They pay people to put on fancy clothes and go around drinking expensive tuba. They spread the word that only "low-class" people drink low-priced tuba. They put on "educational programs"—movies and guest speakers and free wall posters and all that—for the school children to convince them early in life about such "truths" as:

> "You get what you pay for"—"expensive things are good things and show good breeding and good taste"—"low-priced things are shoddy and only the very poor or the 'country clods' would buy such things"—"a truly refined person never asks about the price"—"anyone who is really intelligent will be glad if the price is high because high prices signify *good* goods."

So goes the propaganda campaign. You would be absolutely astonished how many otherwise intelligent people fall for it! The sales of the higher priced brands of tuba increase quite a bit, then stabilize.

Each family is now competing with all the other families in selling tuba at each "price level." Each family continues to have its own little monopoly in each of its brands, but each brand is in close competition with other brands. This kind of market structure should not seem strange to you. You've been living with it all your life! You have been bombarded with it by radio and TV ever since you were old enough to hear and see!

The kind of market structure we are talking about now is called monopolistic competition. "Monopolistic competition" is simply competition among "little monopolies." Each "little monopoly" is a "brand name" or "differentiated product" monopoly, just as in our island example. With monopolistic competition, most of the competing is done through advertising and trying to improve (or differentiate) the product.

Monopolistic Competition Is Everywhere

In the United States and throughout the world, monopolistic competition exists almost everywhere you look. We find it in toothpaste and cigarettes and soaps and detergents and candy bars and beer and cola drinks and gasoline and swimming pools and TV dinners and almost everything else. It exists with big, nationally known products, and also on the main street of every town and village.

Each store is trying to advertise a little better, trying to compete for customers, trying to display its products better, to run attractive sales and do all kinds of things to get more customers to come in and buy. Each of these businesses, just like each of the brand name products, is really a "little monopoly." The amount of "monopoly power" or "market power" each holds is really very small. Why? Because there are so many "little monopolies," all with similar products and services and all trying to take customers away from each other.

Is "monopolistic competition" a kind of market structure? Sure. But it isn't quite as neat and easy to describe as the market structures of pure competition or pure monopoly or pure oligopoly. Why? Because with monopolistic competition, instead of having one product we have many *slightly different* products. The competing products are very much alike. Still, the products aren't *exactly* alike.

With Monopolistic Competition, Each Producer Has Some Freedom

A "monopolistic competitor" has a little bit of freedom to change the price. Once you differentiate your product, you will have customers who will stay with your product even though you raise the price some. All producers would prefer to have "brand name loyalty" among their customers because this gives them more freedom from competition. It lets them raise prices without losing much business.

Just think how profitable it can be to advertise effectively. How long will people continue to pay 30¢ or more for a dozen aspirin when they could buy a different brand and get a

hundred aspirin for 25¢ or less? For a long time, I suppose. The difference which advertising can create in the minds of your customers is as real to them as if the difference *really was real*! So it pays to advertise. That's the way it is with monopolistic competition.

MONOPOLY POWER IN THE REAL WORLD

How does the market process really work, when we get away from pure competition? Does the market still get the choices made *in response to the wishes of society?* Or does the market process *serve the producers, at the expense of the rest of the society?* This is a difficult question. Many aspects of the "real world" answer aren't even known—not by anyone.

No producer, not even one with *pure monopoly,* can completely escape the influence of consumer demand. At prices which are too high, the monopolist will lose customers. Also, at high prices, if the monopolist is making high profits, the magnetism of these profits to potential competitors is very strong. So we might say that no producer, no seller ever has complete, *absolute* "monopoly power." Some kind of actual or potential competition—either in the same product or in some substitute product—seems to always be lurking there, somewhere.

"Bigness" Is Not All "Badness"

Another fact to consider is that "bigness" is not all "badness." Specialization is limited by the size of the market. You can't specialize in something unless the market is large enough to use up all of your specialized output. If the market will only buy half an acre of corn from you, you certainly can't specialize and produce seven acres of corn. It takes large markets to support large firms. Large firms can introduce new technology and can spend money for research and development and for new, more efficient machines and techniques and processes.

A big firm can look more to the long run than to the short run. It can smooth out some of the ups and downs in its production operations by stockpiling things during times of slack demand and then selling out of inventory when demand picks up. There are several very real economic advantages of bigness, both in production and in marketing. But the problem of "market power" always exists when a few big firms make up the seller's side of the market.

The modern societies of "mixed capitalism" are faced with this dilemma:

Each society wants all the advantages which bigness can bring: good management, effective planning, production efficiency, stability, sound financing, industrial growth and all that. Yet each society wants each business to have many competitors, so that no one will have much monopoly power.

See the dilemma? What should the public policy be? How far should the government go in trying to pass and enforce laws and regulations to prevent businesses from getting big, from joining together, from doing things which the businesses themselves claim are necessary for increased efficiency? Where and how should the lines be drawn? This is the dilemma.

We Want to Have Our Cake and Eat It Too

The "market model" tells us that the best interests of the society will be served by markets in which there are many competitors. With pure competition, each producer will be forced to respond to market prices which reflect (a) the wishes of the buyers in the market, and (b) the true cost conditions in the society. Any producer who doesn't respond to market prices soon goes out of business.

If we absolutely prevent bigness we will force inefficiency on our economic system. The standards of living of all the people will suffer. There isn't much logic in that! On the other hand we can hardly afford to let the markets become monopolized. The market model tells us that sellers with a lot of monopoly power can (and will) guarantee themselves large profits at the expense of society. So what do we do?

The "Monopoly Power" Question Is Unresolved

Are we certain that the market model really is close enough to the real world to be trusted as our guide on this vital matter? The honest answer is that we don't know. A good understanding of basic economic concepts can be of great help in approaching the problem. But the truth of the matter is that we don't yet have a body of "real-world theory" which is capable of taking us all the way to clear and indisputable answers on these vital public policy issues.

This is but one example of the many kinds of problems facing modern society which are simply unresolved at our present state of knowledge. If you want to do something important in the world while you are making your journey through life, and if this kind of thing appeals to you, perhaps you will help us to work out answers to some of these questions.

Government Policies Toward Big Business and Monopoly Power

We have gone into quite a bit of detail on this problem of monopoly power, and on two real world variations: oligopoly, and monopolistic competition. If you have a general understanding of how the sellers behave in these two kinds of market structures, and if you can tie all this in with the idea of administered pricing, then you understand the concepts.

Also, you understand some of the public policy issues and problems. Now, before we set this subject aside, here's a quick look at governmental attitudes toward monopoly power.

***All Market-Oriented Nations Limit Monopoly
Power.*** What has been the public policy toward
monopoly power, in the nations of mixed
socio-capitalism? No nation permits the unlimited creation and exercise of monopoly
power. Of course not! You can understand
why.

Even before the first antimonopoly ("antitrust") laws, if sellers got together and agreed
to limit their output and keep their prices up,
this was held to be illegal by the courts. It was
considered to be a "conspiracy" against the
public— *conspiracy to restrain trade*.

U.S. Antitrust Policy. In the latter 1800s in
the United States, there was rising sentiment
against the economic power of big business.
In 1887, the *Interstate Commerce Act* was
passed to limit the monopoly powers of the
railroads. Then three years later (1890) the
Sherman Antitrust Act was passed to prohibit
all businesses from trying to monopolize any
market, either by joining together in some sort
of "trust" arrangement, or by merger, or by
any other means.

The Sherman Act was not very strictly enforced. In fact, it was hardly enforced at all.
Only a few of the most obvious and flagrant
violations were prosecuted. By the early
1900s Standard Oil had managed to get control of most of the oil companies in the country, and American Tobacco had managed to
monopolize the tobacco industry. Then, in
1911, the U.S. Supreme Court forced both
these companies to split up—but not until
after the Rockefeller family (Standard Oil) and
the Duke family (American Tobacco) had
made many millions of dollars in profits!

In 1914, two new laws, the Clayton Antitrust
Act and the Federal Trade Commission Act,
were passed to strengthen the government's
position against monopoly. After that, enforcement was somewhat better. Since 1914
there have been several additional laws and a
great many court cases. Some have
strengthened the government's antimonopoly
position. Some have weakened it.

A part of the inconsistency in U.S. antitrust
policy results from political pressures which
are so strong that they are certain to have
some influence. But perhaps the major cause
of the inconsistency is the uncomfortable fact
that we really don't know what we want. We
want all the advantages of bigness and all the
advantages of smallness. Which to give up?
and which to have? That's the question. Sound
familiar? The economic problem—the problem of choosing. Right?

Antitrust enforcement became much more
effective during the 1950s and 60s. New laws
were passed, and the courts prohibited
several mergers between competing
businesses—mergers about which, in earlier
decades, the courts would have said: "Not
too bad. Let's let them go ahead."

What About "Conglomerate" Corporations?
During the 1960s, a new kind of "big business" problem arose (or exploded!) on the
scene. What problem? The problem of the
rapid growth of giant conglomerate
corporations—corporations producing everything from oil and chemicals and building materials and aircraft engines and agricultural
machinery, to soft drinks, record albums, cake
mixes and shampoo! And each "conglomerate
corporation" was always looking for more and
more new and different partners to merge
with.

What to do about the problem of "conglomerate mergers"? Is it a problem? Each merger
is between *non-competing* firms (aircraft engines don't compete with record albums!) so
why worry? But what about all that financial
power and economic control falling into the
hands of one corporation? Controlled by one
board of directors? Isn't that bad? And if so,
what should be done?

The courts soon took the position that conglomerate corporations can't be permitted to
keep on merging with and absorbing more and
more other corporations. The courts began
prohibiting some of the attempted mergers
and some of the conglomerates were required

to split off some of their merged units. So in the 1970s the "urge to merge" has been much more restrained. Still, a lot of mergers continue to occur.

Big Business Is a Fact of Life

Today multi-billion dollar corporations (conglomerates, and others) make up a major segment of the U.S. economy and of all the other modern economic systems. Certainly that doesn't surprise you.

To be sure, big business is a permanent part of the modern world. And sometimes that creates problems. But there are several other problems at least as bad and maybe even a lot worse. The next two chapters will be talking about several of the other problems. But first, the review exercises? Sure.

REVIEW EXERCISES

● **MAJOR CONCEPTS, PRINCIPLES, TERMS (Explain each carefully.)**

pure competition
pure monopoly
oligopolistic competition
monopolistic competition

● **OTHER CONCEPTS AND TERMS (Explain each briefly.)**

market power
monopoly power
antitrust laws
administered prices
bilateral monopoly
monopsony-monopoly
oligopoly

cartel
price leadership
product differentiation
conglomerate corporation
Sherman Antitrust Act (1890)
Clayton Act (1914)
FTC Act (1914)

● **CURVES AND GRAPHS (Draw, label, and explain.)**

The "Administered Price" (Horizontal) Supply Curve
Oligopoly I: Demand as Seen by the Individual Seller
Oligopoly II: Total Market Demand and Sales by Each Seller

● **QUESTIONS (Write out answers or jot down key points.)**

1. Explain why pure competition is essential to the functioning of the "model market system."
2. Discuss some of the advantages and disadvantages of administered prices.
3. Can you think of any specific ways you have seen businesses "raise the price, without *announcing* that they were raising the price?" Discuss.

4. Explain why oligopoly tends to eliminate price competition and to generate price leadership.
5. Explain why, when oligopoly exists, there is a strong incentive for product differentiation to arise and for the market structure to gravitate toward monopolistic competition.
6. Discuss some of the advantages and disadvantages of business "bigness."
7. Discuss the highlights of the "evolution of public policy toward big business" in the United States.

20 The Problems of Progress, Pollution, Population

*The modern world must change
its directions of progress
to respond to the urgent needs
of modern society.*

In an economy like the United States the microeconomic forces do a lot to direct things and to protect things for the society. But these microeconomic forces don't take care of everything.

Some of the serious problems these microeconomic forces don't take care of for us are: pollution, population growth, urban blight, poverty, and discrimination. All these problems are already serious. Some are getting more serious. This chapter and the following one will give you some insight into the economics of these issues.

PROGRESS AND PROBLEMS: WHICH OBJECTIVES SHOULD SOCIETY PURSUE?

Many of the *problems* which have become so serious in the advanced modern nations seem to be related to all the *progress* which has occurred in these nations. Does progress create more problems than it solves? Some people are saying "maybe so."

But it's really a question of what we mean by progress—that is, of which objectives we want to pursue. Modern society's objectives must reflect its changing ideas about what's important and what isn't. More on that in a minute. But first, a little more introduction to this chapter and the next.

The Economic Considerations: Alternatives and Opportunity Costs

In the discussion in this chapter and the next you'll be reading about the *economics* of real-world problems. A few statistics describing the problems will be presented, but not many. What I want you to get from all this is a good understanding of the *nature of each problem* and of the *economic influences at work.*

If you can really see the choices available to society as we tackle these problems—if you can recognize the difficulties involved and the opportunity costs which the choices will require—then you'll be far ahead of most people. And you'll know a lot more about the basic economic forces working in the real world, too.

For now, please don't worry about memorizing a lot of detailed statistics on pollution or population or urban problems or poverty or discrimination or any such things. Textbook statistics are always out of date anyway. And up-to-date statistics are easy to find.

From time to time as you go along I'll tell you where you can find current figures. But in general, remember this: The *Statistical Abstract of the United States* is an excellent place to go to find statistics when you don't know where else to look. (I'm sure your friendly librarian would be glad to help.)

All of Us Are to Blame for the Major Problems of Our Society

When something is going wrong we usually try to find someone to "blame it on." It's frustrating to discover there's *nobody* to blame it on! But in this case you're going to find out that's the way it is.

If the problem is poverty or population or pollution or unemployment or inflation or a balance of payments deficit or whatever, you're going to find that you can't "blame it on" the rich people or the labor unions or the landowners or the government or big business or the foreigners or the southerners or the northerners or the younger generation or "the system" or any other easily available scapegoat. Why not? Because mostly, for all of these problems *all of us are to blame.*

What I'm trying to say is this: There aren't any easy answers. The answers are *tough* answers. The opportunity costs are high. You can't have your cake and eat it too, remember? Even if we all decided that we were willing to pay the opportunity costs—to make the sacrifices needed to overcome all of the these problems—most of the problems still couldn't be solved very fast. The problems are *too big*. *Quick solutions are physically impossible*! (As this chapter and the next unfold, you will see just how true this is.)

Progress Uncovers or Creates New Problems

People and societies have always faced problems. Now that modern societies have pushed back the age-old problems of hunger and disease, new problems are coming to the surface. So now modern society's objectives are having to change.

As one set of problems is solved, new problems are uncovered or created. We solve the problems of hunger and disease. So what happens? People stay alive longer, live better, consume more. Population explosion? Yes. Environmental problem? Sure! Who's to blame? High technology and high productivity have done it. So let's get rid of high technology and high productivity? We'd better not!

Without our high technology and high productivity we wouldn't have a chance of handling the environmental effects of the world's exploding population! Not nearly enough progress has yet been made in bringing the population explosion under control or in dealing with the environmental crisis. Everybody knows we've barely scratched the surface. But we've made more progress than we ever could have made without our high technology and high productivity to help us.

Sometimes people suggest that because of the environmental problem, we should try to stop economic progress—have "zero economic growth" (ZEG). But surely zero growth isn't the answer. Even if it was a good idea it wouldn't work. People always try to change the things they don't like—that is, to improve things. That's what progress is all about—making things better—moving toward the objectives we desire.

Progress Means Moving Toward the Desired Objectives

What "progress" means to each person depends on what that person wants most. Think about William Wellsford, an unemployed worker whose family has been subsisting on nothing but dandelion greens and corn meal mush. Mr. Wellsford is a lot more interested in seeing a new factory open up where he can get a job than he is in protecting the clean air in the valley or the pure water in the stream. To him, a new factory would bring progress.

But what about the retired stockbroker who lives in the valley or the local school teacher who heads the environmental protection committee or the wealthy family that owns most of the land and raises horses? A new factory that might mess up the water and air? And bring a lot of low-class outsiders who might have Saturday night brawls in our peaceful little city? That's progress? Forget it!

Suppose there's a public hearing on the issue of re-zoning some land to permit the new factory to be built in the area. Will all the local people agree? Of course not! What a tough situation this creates!

Each of us will work for the things that are most important to us. We will try to change those conditions which we see as problems. But is a problem to *me* a problem to *you*? That all depends on *your own* point of view!

Many choices have to be made by "society as a whole"—by the government. Whenever this happens, disagreements are inevitable. In every society, no matter what the economic or political system, people disagree about issues such as these. Only when a problem becomes very obvious and very serious will everyone agree that something must be done. Even then they still will disagree about exactly *what* should be done, and *how much*, and *how*.

There are many kinds of economic issues and "public policy" problems which fit into this discussion. This chapter talks about only two: pollution and population. First, the pollution problem.

THE ENVIRONMENTAL CRISIS: THE ECONOMICS OF THE POLLUTION PROBLEM

I suppose everybody knows that the pollution problem is bad. And it has been getting worse. All of us are in on it.

The Pollution Problem Is Already Serious

All of us are dumping cans and bottles and garbage and trash and all kinds of junk ("solid wastes") into the environment. And that's only the beginning. We're dumping liquid wastes (effluents) from all the industrial plants and processing plants and from all the sewage systems of all the cities all over the country and all over the world. All these effluents wind up in our streams and lakes and rivers and oceans and everywhere.

We're spreading all kinds of chemicals all over the landscape to control insects and weeds and all. We're puffing out smoke and all kinds of "gaseous emissions" into the air from the smokestacks of all the factories and from the exhaust pipes of all the automobiles and trucks and from city incinerators and home furnaces—even from burning steak fat from the backyard barbecue grills.

We're pulling fresh water out of the rivers and streams: to drink, to bathe in, to use for industrial purposes. So now less fresh water is flowing into the salt water estuaries—Cheasapeake Bay and Galveston Bay and Pudget Sound and Pamlico Sound and all the others. So the water in the estuaries is getting more salty. Maybe it's getting too salty to continue to serve as a breeding ground for many kinds of marine life. That's bad. At the same time the power plants and other plants are dumping warm water into the streams and increasing the temperatures. That may be upsetting the natural balance of life there.

I know figures like this are hard to comprehend. But to get some idea of the extent of the problem, consider this:

—The United States has about a quarter of a million miles of rivers and streams in its major watersheds. More than one fourth of that mileage is polluted.

—More than 100 million tons of carbon monoxide are being released into the air every year. Other air pollutants: hydrocarbon, sulphur oxides, nitrogen oxides, and others amount to millions of tons each, per year.

—There's more than 150 million tons of garbage and trash being thrown away every year. And billions of tin cans, billions of bottles, and even *several million junk cars* every year.

It isn't a question of whether or not these pollutants and junk will be thrown away. They must be thrown away. It's a question of *where* they will be thrown, and how—that is, of what we will do to make them clean and safe before we throw them away.

Another way of getting at the seriousness of the pollution problem is to figure what it is costing American industry to try to control it. More than $5 billion a year is being spent. But many people say that isn't enough. Certainly it hasn't stopped pollution!

It would take a lot of polluting to pollute all the land and water and air of the earth and kill off all the wild life and marine life—and human life. But some scientists say we are moving in that direction at a rapid clip! Everyone knows that the trend can't be allowed to continue. Something must be done. But what? And how? These are tough questions.

We All Contribute to the Pollution Problem

Who pollutes? Everybody. Every living person. Every organization, every business, every school, every factory, every store. Everybody!

We are all responsible for this pollution problem.

All pollution results from either final consumption activities or from production. If it results from final consumption activities, the final consumers are the ones who are *directly* responsible. If it results from productive activities then the final consumers are the ones who are *indirectly* responsible. You might say that all pollution is either final pollution or derived pollution.

"Ask not for whom the industrial plant pollutes. It pollutes for thee!" And who is going to make the sacrifices required to pay the cost of overcoming the problem? Make no mistake about it. "Thou art."

All industrial activity and all of the normal processes of life require some "environmental destruction" and some "waste disposal." Until recently everyone has been thinking of the "environmental destruction effects" and the "waste disposal task" as sort of trivial aggravations—to be ignored—to be dealt with only when absolutely necessary.

Throughout history the task of environmental protection and waste disposal has been treated as "an afterthought in the total economic process of life." But now that isn't good enough. Not anymore. With so many people on the earth, consuming so many things, environmental protection has become critical. It's becoming more critical every day.

We Are "Living High" by Not Fully Paying Our Way

In the past, most of the environmental costs—the costs of waste disposal and resource destruction and all that—have been external to the market. In adding up their costs, businesses haven't had to pay much attention to the resource destruction and waste disposal effects of their activities. Consumers have been able to buy all kinds of products without having to pay for the "full social cost" of producing them.

Also, people have been getting by without having to pay the full cost of disposing of their trash and garbage and sewage. All of us have been enjoying the temporary pleasure of "living high" at the expense of our environment. But it won't be long before we aren't going to be able to do that any more.

What does all this mean? It means that some things which have always been thought of as "cheap" are suddenly going to become expensive. Why? Because the cost of environmental protection from now on is going to be included in the price of things. It's already beginning. But it still has a long way to go.

In recent years paper manufacturers have been putting many millions of dollars into equipment and processes to protect the environment. You helped to pay for some of that when you paid the high price of this book! Get the point? Already we're beginning to feel the pinch. But it's only just begun. We will all grumble. But we will pay. We just don't have any choice.

Cleaning Up Is Part of the Job

The environmental protection task must become an important part of every productive activity—really, *of every aspect of life*. A larger and larger percentage of the national output will be directed toward enviromental protection. A lot more labor and equipment and power and other resources will have to be directed toward this task. Maybe before it's all over with we will have to learn to get along with less—fewer cars, less electricity, less gasoline, less plush college buildings, less of lots of things. Maybe. We can't have our cake and eat it too. Remember?

How much more of the GNP will have to go for environmental protection? How much are we going to have to transform "consumer goods" and "industrial goods" into "environmental protection goods"? Nobody knows. But we do know that the cost will be high. And we know that all of us are going to have to give

up some things (things we otherwise could have had) to help to pay for it. There's no doubt about it. There's just no other way.

How Much Pollution Should be Allowed?

How much "gaseous emissions" or "liquid effluents" or "solid wastes" should be permitted? And by whom? And under what circumstances? Absolutely none? Zero? That's really going to be tough! Be careful. Don't exhale and pollute the atmosphere with your used breath! Don't drive your car because if you do you'll pollute the air with exhaust fumes and you'll support the "derived polluion" of all those gasoline and tire companies! Don't eat or drink anything out of cans or bottles or paper bags. And please! No trips to the bathroom!

Zero pollution? No. That can't be the answer. So how much then? That's a tough question. Nobody really knows the answer. The biologists and chemists and other scientists are working on it.

Luckily the environment has much ability to rejuvenate itself. It can give up a lot of resources and absorb a lot of wastes before the effect becomes cumulative. But everybody knows that in the big cities and in the industrialized areas we have gone too far. We've got to cut back. But to zero? No. That would be an impossible, unnecessary, ridiculous objective. But we must cut way back from where we are now. Some scientists are saying that if we do the very best our technology will permit, that will be barely good enough.

The Political Process Must Solve This Problem

The environmental protection problem is "external" to the market. That's why the problem must be solved through the political process. There's just no other way it could be done. But that doesn't mean that the market mechanism can't be used to help. Of course it can. And it will be.

Essentially there are three different ways the government can approach this problem:

1. By a system of direct regulations, with constant policing to see that everyone follows the law,

2. By charging "prices" for the use of the society's environment (that is, selling nature's "waste disposal services") and letting the rationing function of price take care of the problem, or

3. By subsidizing the business by giving them tax concessions or direct payments to pay for the installation and operation of pollution control equipment.

The first two of these approaches will internalize the externalities and pass along the "environmental protection costs" to all of us who buy the products. The third approach will charge the general public. Economists generally favor approach number 2. Why?

Approach number 3 is usually rejected because it doesn't internalize the externalities. Consumers buy the good for less than its true social cost. That's socially wasteful.

Approach number 1 usually is not preferred because the policing problem is not easy to handle, and because it's difficult to adjust the anti-pollution regulations to suit the economics of the individual firms.

For example, suppose regulations are established. The firm which can clean up its pollution at relatively low cost is placed in the same situation as the firm which can clean up its wastes only at very high cost. Perhaps the high cost firm will have to go out of business. Perhaps its production processes make it impossible for it to reduce its pollution to the required minimum.

But suppose the firm which could clean up its pollution completely would do so. Then it might not be necessary for the other firm to go out of business. It could simply reduce its pollution and that would be sufficient. Get the idea?

There's no reason why all firms should have to meet the same "standard of cleanliness" if what we're aiming for is optimum social efficiency in our economic system. You'll be reading more about this later in this chapter. But now, here's an example to illustrate the differences between approach number 1 and approach number 2.

As you drive along the highway you see signs saying: DO NOT LITTER. $50 FINE. That's the first approach. It's against the law to throw beer cans out of your car window.

Another approach might be for the government to require a nickel deposit on each beer can. Then when you turn in the used can for proper disposal or recycling you get your nickel back. If you throw the beer can beside the highway or in the lake it costs you a nickel. If people still throw away too many beer cans, raise the price to a dime, or a quarter—or to a dollar, or two, or five! Can you see how effective this approach might be? (But be careful! Someone may set up a factory to produce used beer cans and make millions!)

Internalizing the Environmental Externalities

Which approach should the government use? regulations and policing? or the price mechanism? Probably both. Whenever the price mechanism can be used, it's likely to cut down on the "policing cost." But no matter which approach is used, the results are going to be far from perfect.

There will be all kinds of special interest groups pushing for more protection or less protection, for tighter or easier regulations, for stricter or more lenient enforcement, for higher or lower "environmental protection prices." That's the way the political process always operates.

Suppose Mr. Wellsford is an unemployed father of five who can only afford to feed his family on dandelion greens and corn meal mush. He certainly wants a new local factory so he can get a job! He detests the environmental protection program because it discourages new factories from starting up in his area. He writes nasty letters to the mayor and to the governor and to Congress.

The local gas station operator and the local real estate agent do the same. They want to see business pick up. What about investors who want to build the factory? They write letters, too. All these people want to kill (or soften) the environmental protection program.

But what about the people who want to preserve the natural beauty of the area? They get together and visit city hall and the state capital and Washington. They're urging that the environmental protection programs be tightened!

Who will win out? Who knows. If we're lucky the final decision will be made with an eye to *what ought to be done.* But the final decision is almost certain to depend partly on who is a member of which political party, who contributed how much to the last political campaign and such things as that. That's too bad, I suppose. But that's the way it is. Such is the nature of the political process.

How Fast Should the Government Move on Environmental Protection?

What ought to be done? And how quickly? Nobody knows, really. The "doomsday prophets" say it's already too late. We've blown it. Human life on earth is on the way out. Others say that we must move as fast as we can because there's no time to lose.

At the other end of the range are those who say that this whole problem has been blown completely out of proportion—that we are working on it too fast already. They say we're distorting the progress of our economy by turning too much effort toward environmental protection.

Many people seem to agree that we should work on the environmental

protection issue as fast as we reasonably can. But how fast is that? We could impose enough controls to absolutely "shut down" the economic system! We might say: "Okay. Let's do it." But after we've been going without food or water for a few days we might all decide to change our minds.

This is a tough question, with opportunity costs staring us in the face every step of the way. As long as we recognize that, and go after the problem realistically, I think we'll find the ways to handle it. We'd better all hope so!

The Problem Provides the Means for Its Own Solution

One thing is sure. The great human population is going to have to become compatible with its limited environment—with its city, its nation, its "spaceship earth." Solutions will not be easy to find. The cost is going to be higher than most people would like to admit. But *the cost must be paid.* Soon everyone will realize that we don't have any choice about that.

Can we do it? Sure. High technology and economic growth have let the problem arise. That same high technology and economic growth will now provide us the means to solve it.

So is the solution to the environmental problem at hand? No. Far from it. But we have the means to develop the solutions. Now it's time for the economic system, through the political process, to redirect much more energy and effort toward environmental objectives. "Progress" in the decades ahead is going to have to be redefined, and *aimed much more toward achieving environmental objectives and less toward other objectives.*

It's good that we have the means. Now let's hope we will be wise enough to pay the opportunity costs and take care of the problem. Try

The political process might work fine if everyone could **agree** on everything.... But they can't!

not to grumble too much as more and more of the costs come to rest on you. Sorry, but there's just no other way. Let's all pay the cost and be glad we got around to it in time! (I hope.)

AN ECONOMIC ANALYSIS OF "ENVIRONMENTAL EXTERNALITIES"

Can the tools of economic analysis help in deciding what to do about pollution? Or in understanding who bears the burden of pollution control? Or deciding how much pollution we should put up with? How clean the air and water and landscape should be? Sure.

If the environmental problem was not external to the market, then the market forces would take care of it. If *production costs* really did reflect *social costs* then the rationing function of price would limit the use of the natural environment for waste disposal.

If it cost something to pollute the rivers, then there would be an incentive to develop techniques to *prevent* polluting the rivers. But since the "waste-disposal services of the ecosystem" have been offered as a free good, there has been no incentive to limit the use of those "waste-disposal services."

When the waste-disposal services of the ecosystem are available free, then they will be used right to the point where the last little bit used has zero marginal value. Why not? Nobody restricts or conserves or limits the use of free goods! You have known that ever since Chapter 1. Right?

So we must prevent people and businesses and communities and cities from using the "waste disposal services of the ecosystem" as a free good! We can pass laws prohibiting them from doing it. Or we can charge prices for "nature's waste disposal services."

The Increasing Cost of Cleaning Up Wastes

Suppose we decided to levy a charge for using nature's waste disposal services. Even a low charge might result in a lot of cleaning up.

Why? Because a lot of cleaning up can be done at low cost.

Think of it this way. Suppose a factory is putting out a lot of very dirty smoke and very dirty effluent. It wouldn't be difficult or expensive to remove a lot of pollutants from the very dirty smoke and effluent. But as the smoke and effluent get cleaner it becomes more difficult to clean it up even more.

So if the government puts a "pollution measurement meter" on the smoke stack and one on the effluent discharge pipe and places even a low charge per unit of pollution, suddenly it becomes profitable for the firm to clean up more. So the "demand for nature's waste-disposal services" probably would be fairly elastic when the prices (charges for nature's waste-disposal services) are low. At higher prices where firms have already cleaned up a lot and it's difficult to clean up more, demand probably would be much less elastic. In Figure 20-1 you'll see all this on a graph.

When you see a smoke stack, something's coming out of it. Usually you can't see the smoke anymore. It isn't really smoke. But something's coming out other than pure clean air. Or when you see an effluent pipe flowing into the river, it may look like it's dumping clear water. But I don't think you'd want to drink it.

What would have to be done to make the smoke stack release nothing but pure clean air? Or the pipe release nothing but pure drinkable water?—and at normal river temperature? That's what would be necessary to go all the way to "zero pollution."

It would be very expensive. When you look at the four figures coming up you'll see that zero pollution wouldn't make much sense. The social cost of "total clean-up" would be much greater than the social cost of allowing tolerable amounts of pollutants to enter the atmosphere and the water. Now take time to study Figures 20-1, -2, -3, and -4, and you'll find out a lot more about the economics of pollution controls.

Fig. 20-1 The Increasing Cost of Cleaning Up Wastes

The cleaner the wastes become, the more expensive it may get to clean them up even more.

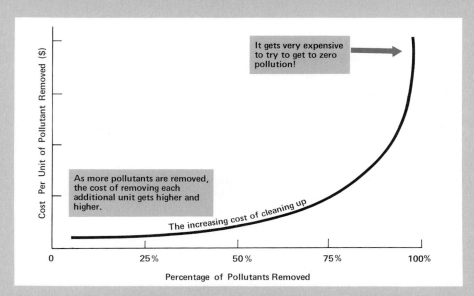

It gets very expensive to try to get to zero pollution!

As more pollutants are removed, the cost of removing each additional unit gets higher and higher.

The increasing cost of cleaning up

Cost Per Unit of Pollutant Removed ($)

Percentage of Pollutants Removed

On this graph, as you move to the right you get less pollution, but a lot more clean-up cost per unit of pollution removed.

For liquid effluents there are stages in the clean-up process. "Primary treatment" takes the large particles out. Primary treatment is not very expensive and gets rid of a lot of pollutants. But then secondary treatment costs a lot more. It takes out a lot less pollutants per dollar spent.

The same principles apply to smoke stacks. The cleaner you get the "air" coming out of the stack, the more expensive it may get to clean it up even more.

Would this same principle hold for the society as a whole? Could society go a long way toward cleaning up pollution at a fairly low cost? Then would it become terribly expensive to get all the way to zero pollution? Right!

The U.S. Environmental Protection Agency has estimated that about $60 billion would be sufficient to remove more than 85 percent of the water pollutants of industries and municipalities by 1982. But to reduce the pollutants to zero? That would cost $320 billion! That's *more than five times the cost, to clean up about one-seventh as much!*

Fig. 20-2   The Producer's Demand for Nature's Waste-Disposal Services

At a price of zero the producer will dump everything. So even a low pollution charge will make it profitable to clean up quite a lot.

On this graph as you go to the right you get more pollution—that is, more demand for the use of nature's waste-disposal services.

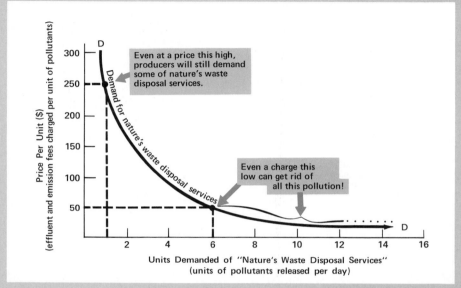

This graph derives from the previous one. If the cost of polluting is zero, then a great amount of nature's waste-disposal services will be used. It's a free good. Why not use it?

A low charge on pollution will provide an incentive for firms to eliminate all those kinds of pollution which can be easily eliminated. But after that, what happens?

As the pollution charges get higher and higher and the businesses get their effluents and emissions cleaner and cleaner, it becomes more and more expensive for them to clean up even more. That's why it would be so very expensive to try to get to zero pollution—either for a firm or for a society.

You can see that this demand curve, just as the increasing-cost curve on the previous graph, applies to the society as well as it applies to the individual firm. Society can clean up quite a lot of pollution without very much cost. But as it gets closer to zero pollution the marginal cost gets higher and higher for each additional unit of "pollution removal."

Fig. 20-3 The Supply and Demand for Nature's Waste-Disposal Services

The government could decide how much liquid and gaseous "dumping" to permit, and then auction off that number of "dumping rights."

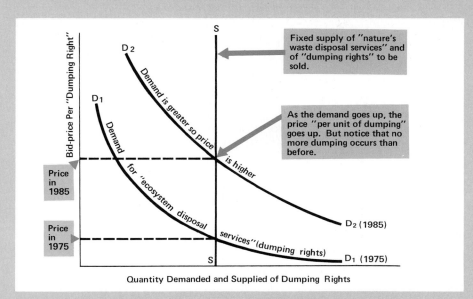

Bid-price Per "Dumping Right"

S

D 2

D 1

Demand is greater so price

Demand

for "ecosystem disposal

services" (dumping rights)

is higher

Fixed supply of "nature's waste disposal services" and of "dumping rights" to be sold.

As the demand goes up, the price "per unit of dumping" goes up. But notice that no more dumping occurs than before.

Price in 1985

Price in 1975

D₂ (1985)

D₁ (1975)

S

Quantity Demanded and Supplied of Dumping Rights

Each "dumping right" would permit the holder to release one unit of pollutant into the ecosystem.

Would it be possible for governments to find out how much "dumping" into the air and water could be permitted without seriously undesirable results? And then allow that much dumping? and no more? And could they sell the "rights to dump" to the highest bidder? Probably. It would be hard to get people to agree. But it would be a very efficient way to internalize the externalities and protect the environment.

You can see from the graph that as industrial activity in some area expands and the demand for the disposal services of the ecosystem go up, the price of the fixed supply of "dumping rights" would go up. The cost of production in that area would go up, too. It would be necessary to spend more on pollution control equipment in that area. Perhaps firms would move to other areas where "dumping rights" could be obtained at lower cost because the pressure on the environment there was not so great.

With this approach, producers who could use cheaper equipment to clean up their wastes instead of buying dumping rights, would do so.

It won't be easy to work out the details. It won't be easy to get people to agree on the quantity and kinds of dumping to be permitted in each area. Some will say "none." Others will say "much more." But the approach (if it can be made to work) is a good one.

Fig. 20-4   Finding the Optimum Social Level of Dumping into the Ecosystem

Society should try to minimize social cost. If the social cost of cleaning up pollution gets greater than the social cost of the pollution itself, then we've gone too far.

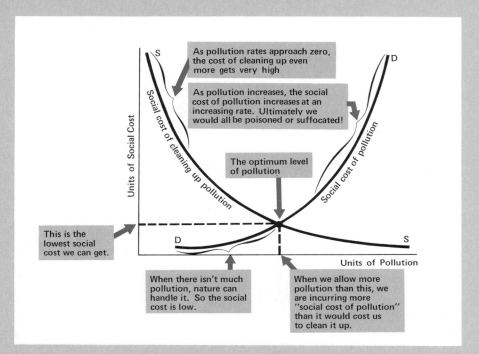

On this graph, as you go to the right you get more pollution.

As pollution gets worse and worse, the social cost goes up very fast. But going the other way, as pollution gets lower and lower, the social cost of cleaning up even more gets higher and higher. So what is the "optimum pollution level"? Where the social cost is at a minimum. Of course.

If the amount of pollution in an area gets greater than the "optimum" level, then society can improve its welfare by cleaning up. The "social cleanup cost" is less than the "social pollution cost."

But suppose pollution is held to less than the optimal level. That means the society is incurring greater cleanup costs than the pollution costs they're preventing! That's not a very good deal.

This looks all very clear and straightforward on a graph. But wait until you try to get people like the environmentalists of the Sierra Club and the business leaders in the public utilities and heavy industries to agree on where to put this "social cost of pollution" curve! It isn't easy to assess the social cost of different levels of pollution!

A major advantage of using pollution fees or selling "dumping rights" is that this approach allows each firm to decide how far it should go in cleaning up. For some firms, the cleaning up process may be very expensive. For others it may be very easy. The firms which can clean up at low cost certainly should and certainly will.

The firms which can clean up only at very high cost should be permitted to dump wastes within tolerable limits. If not, *the social cost of prohibiting the dumping will be greater than the social cost of the dumping would have been.*

What happens when a producer's costs go up, either because of anti-pollution regulations or because of effluent and emissions charges or "dumping rights"? The next section explains that. Then there are some graphs that show how it works.

Who Pays the Cost of Pollution Control?

Earlier in this chapter you already heard that "thou art" going to pay the cost of protecting the environment. Ultimately it's the people who must pay. But what about the steps in the process? How does it come about?

Suppose the government requires a local manufacturing plant to put "scrubbers" or "electronic precipitators" into their smokestacks to reduce air pollution. Who is going to pay the cost?

The Model Market System. First look back at the model pure market system. You know that in the "long-run equilibrium situation" the price is just high enough to cover the cost of production, including a "normal profit" for the producer. So the increased waste disposal cost is going to force the firms into a loss position. The increased cost is going to reduce the supply.

The reduced supply will push the price up so some of the cost will be shifted to the buyers

right away. Then some firms will start leaving this high cost industry. They will lay off workers and sell off equipment.

See what's happening? During the short-run adjustment period some of the cost is being borne by the firm. Some is being borne by the workers who are losing their jobs and by the firms who supply the industry. Only part of it is being borne by the consumers.

What about the long run? In the model market system you know exactly what will happen. The firms remaining in the industry once again will be making normal profits. All of the input factors remaining in the industry will be receiving their normal returns. So who will be paying the cost of the pollution controls? The consumers of the product? Of course.

What About the Real World? In real-world markets it usually works the same way, only quicker. When producers see the cost go up that gives them an immediate excuse to increase the price. So they do.

But then don't they lose their customers to other sellers? Not usually. The other sellers are faced with the same problem. So they raise their "administered prices" too. Otherwise all of them would lose money. But sometimes producers in other parts of the country may not have to clean up so much and that may give them an advantage.

As all the prices go up to reflect the higher cost, don't the buyers buy less? And doesn't that result in reduced profit for the producers? Maybe so. In the short run the cost probably is shared by both the consumer-buyers and the producer-sellers.

What about the workers and other input suppliers for this industry? As this industry produces less, some of the workers will lose their jobs. Some of the suppliers will sell less and maybe lose money, too. You can see that some of the workers and suppliers may bear a part of the burden too.

What about the long run? That's going to be different? Of course. The demand is going to be much more elastic. People who were buying the output of the "high polluting" industry are going to find other acceptable substitutes to use instead.

The supply will adjust, too. The industry is going to decline. How much the industry declines will depend a lot on the *relative seriousness* of the pollution problem in the industry. An industry which is by nature very "dirty" and difficult and expensive to clean up is going to be hit much harder than one which is naturally cleaner.

Some of the dirty industries may be put out of business entirely! Then who is hurt? Who bears the ultimate cost? All three: the consumers (who can't get the product), the producers (who are forced out of business) and the workers and other input suppliers (who lose their sources of income).

Of course, in the very long run there will be time for the workers to be relocated elsewhere, for all the suppliers to shift over and start supplying other industries, and for the producers who were losing money in this industry to get out and go into something else.

Here's the point: For a while the producers and the workers and the suppliers are likely to share the increased waste disposal cost with the consumers of the product. But if you wait long enough, things will all shift around so that the buyers are the ones who will be paying the cost.

In the Long Run
It's the People Who Pay

You'll probably get a truer picture of the situation if you'll think of it as "the society" paying the cost. People in general are going to experience a somewhat lower standard of living than otherwise would have been attainable. The increased costs of waste disposal are going to be shared by all of us.

The waste disposal and environmental protection cost is going to become an important part of just about everything being produced— either directly or indirectly. Some pollution control cost is going to be embodied in just about everything.

Textbook publishing companies certainly don't pollute the environment. But the paper companies which supply them paper? and the gasoline companies which supply them fuel? and the petrochemical companies which supply them ink? and the utility companies which provide them electricity? The list could go on and on. Get the point? The cost of protecting the environment is going to get embodied in everything. We are all going to pay for it.

When production cost for everything goes up, that means we can't produce as many things as before. So we can't have as many things as before. More of our output is going to be shifted from consumer goods and industrial goods into environmental protection and waste disposal goods. And you can't eat those things!

Figure 20-5 shows the market for a product which is suddenly hit with an increase in waste-disposal cost. I think this figure will round out your understanding of the economics of the pollution problem. Now would be a good time for you to stop and study it.

How Much Pollution?
It's a Matter of Choice

It's not easy to keep the questions of pollution, environmental protection, external diseconomies, and all that in proper perspective. It is easy to argue for zero pollution. But now you know the idea of zero pollution just doesn't make sense.

It's easy to blame environmental problems on economic growth. It's easy to see that as economic growth has occurred, the environment has gotten messed up. But it didn't have to be that way. The defect wasn't in the economic process of growth. The defect was in our own socio-economic institutions.

The problem was that the environment was outside the protection of the market system. We were depending on the market system to

Fig. 20-5   How Output Markets React to the Cost Increase When Pollution Controls Are Imposed

This shows the short-run and long-run effects of the increased cost from pollution controls, or from effluent fees.

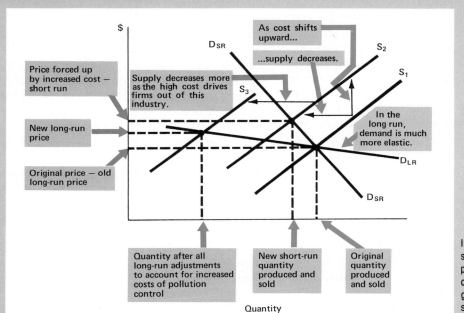

Quantity

In the long run the social effects of the pollution control costs are much greater than in the short run.

How much smaller the output of this industry is, if you wait long enough for the buyers to find acceptable substitutes! Less than half as much of this product is produced! But isn't that the way it should be?

This is a product which generates a lot of pollution. The cost of the pollution has been included in the price of the product and in the long run the rationing function of price is taking care of the pollution problem for us.

As you look at this graph you can see the adjustment problem for the people in this industry. It will be tough. More than half the workers will lose their jobs. The towns and cities where this industry is located are going to lose jobs and tax revenues. Investors in these businesses are going to lose money. All these people will be unhappy about this and they will fight hard to prevent it from happening to them. Wouldn't you?

It's one thing to be "highly in favor of" a clean environment. It's quite another thing to know that a specific regulation is going to wipe out your life's savings or throw you out of a job or make you lose your house or lose your ability to help your kids through college.

Some of the social costs of cleaning up pollution are going to be very high. We must get on with the task of course. But we shouldn't make believe that it's going to be easy.

take care of things which it couldn't possibly take care of!

There is no reason to conclude from the past that we must now stop all economic growth in order to stop pollution. No. That isn't the answer. It's just a matter of choice among alternative directions of progress.

The economic, social and political processes which have permitted the pollution and environmental destruction to occur now must be turned toward solving the problem and preventing it in the future. That's all.

It's only recently that the United States and most other countries began to take a serious interest in the problem. For many years environmental protection groups—the Sierra Club and others—have been pushing to get something done. But it's only in the last decade or so that some definite action has been taken.

In 1969 the Council on Environmental Quality was set up. In 1970 the Federal Environmental Protection Agency was established. If you want to find out something about the seriousness of the pollution problem and about what's being done, go to your library and find the annual reports of these two agencies. Or write either of these agencies in Washington—or to your Congressional Representative or Senator. You'll get a wealth of interesting things. Why not try it?

New Technology Can Help: the Example of the Coal Scrubber

Environmental protection in an economy like the United States is a very complex thing. There aren't any easy approaches. And no easy answers. But definite progress is being made. New pollution control-waste disposal technologies are being developed.

Take the example of the coal scrubber. It's a system for removing sulphur oxides so they won't escape from smokestacks and pollute the atmosphere. The Environmental Protection Agency has been pushing for the coal-scrubber, but as recently as 1975 the major electric power companies were fighting against it as "unproved and unreliable."

But by early 1976 there were more than 100 of these systems being installed. The system is admittedly high cost. But consider this: It makes it possible for the power companies to use high-sulphur coal without polluting the atmosphere. That kind of coal happens to make up 90 percent of the coal in this country. It produces more energy than low-sulphur coal and it is located in the eastern part of the country where most of it is needed.

Furthermore, the high-sulphur coal can be taken from deep mines. This doesn't destroy the landscape as does the surface-cut "strip-mine" operation which is used in the West to produce most of the low-sulphur coal.

The externalities of waste disposal and environmental destruction are being internalized. So incentives and efforts to develop new technologies are being greatly increased. You may be quite sure that a lot of progress is going to be made.

All is not yet perfect with the coal scrubber, of course. But this example is good enough to illustrate the idea that technology can go a long way in helping us to solve the problem.

What About the Population Question?

Some people have blamed the pollution problem on the fact that population has been expanding too fast. We know that population has been expanding too fast. No question about that. But it isn't just a question of population size.

Population can continue to expand and the environmental problem can still be solved. Again, it's a question of choice among alternatives. But the population issue is a serious one. If it could be solved that would help on the environmental problem. So what about the population issue? The next section talks about that.

THE POPULATION CRUSH: THE ECONOMIC PROBLEM OF WALL-TO-WALL PEOPLE

Human beings have been on earth for thousands of centuries. But it was "only yesterday" that suddenly there were *lots of people* on the earth. At the time of the first Crusade (about 1100 A.D.) the population of the world only amounted to about 300 million people. Then in the 4 centuries between the first crusade and the time Columbus discovered America, the world's population expanded by about 50 percent—to about 450 million.

Then in the next 3 centuries (by the time the United States was created as a nation) the world's population *doubled*—to about 900 million. Then in the next *one* century (the 1800's) it almost doubled again! Now it appears that the number of people in the world may double again (may increase by *three billion*) in only 40 years (1960-2000). You can see what is happening!

The World's Population Is Exploding

Just think. In 1900 when the world entered this century there were about 1.5 billion people on earth. By 1960 there were about 3 billion. By the end of this century (by the year 2000) the number could reach 6 billion. Three fourths of the total (4.5 billion) is being added just during this century. Explosion? You bet. Is there any wonder we have a pollution problem? And lots of other serious problems?

It has been said that "of all the people who have ever been alive on earth since the beginning of time, half of them are alive today." That's a sobering thought. Here's another. The number of children who will be born during *your* lifetime will be greater than the total number of children who have been born before you, *since the beginning of time!*

It's just hard to conceive of the dimensions and seriousness of the population problem. Unless mankind can work out the means for drastically curtailing the number of births, then nature will take care of the problem for us—probably by arranging for most of us to die off!

People Are Pouring into the Cities

Where are all these people? These three billion, going on six billion, most of whom are in their teens and younger? They're all over the world. They're in the high-income advanced countries, they're in the low-income advancing countries, and they're in the poverty-stricken underdeveloped countries. They're everywhere. They're in India and China, Mexico and Brazil, Japan, western Europe, the United States, Canada, Russia, Australia, Africa, South America, Indonesia—everywhere.

Wherever they are, masses of them are moving to the cities—thousands every day—a constant, steady, increasing stream. Why do they pour into the cities? Because there's nowhere else for them to go. The greatest migration the world has ever known is the one that's going on right now—the millions of people pouring into the cities. It's happening everywhere the world over. Every day it gets larger.

Suppose a peasant farmer has enough land to get by on. Then there are six or eight or a dozen children. Maybe all of them can eke out a semi-starvation existence from the little bit of land. But then by the time the children are in their mid-teens the girls start having babies and raising families of their own—perhaps each of them having six or eight or a dozen children.

Where can all these people go? What can they do? They go to the cities to try to find something to do—some means of existence. But wherever they go, whatever they do, they keep having children. Babies, babies, babies, everywhere babies.

Yes, it's true that more than half of the people alive on the earth right now are in their teens or younger. In China the number of children under ten is greater than the total population of the United States! In most countries most of those in their teens are already having more babies. And the flood of surplus population keeps pouring faster and faster into the already overburdened cities. How long can it continue? Not very long, now. Not very long at all.

Population Growth
Is Very Difficult to Control

The flood of babies pouring into the world is going to have to be stopped. But how? Every individual has feelings about this. Every society has its taboos, its restrictions, its religious beliefs about the "right" or the "obligation" to bear children. Getting around all of that is going to be a tough task.

Here's another tough one. Some people, some organizations, some groups, some nations see *strength in numbers*. Having lots of children can provide a kind of "social security"—the children can care for their aging parents. Or if a "good Democrat" or a "good Episcopalian" raises a dozen children, chances are most of them will turn out to be good Democrats or good Episcopalians. If the French-Canadians or the Irish Catholics or the Southern Blacks want to gain political control of some area, if they just keep having enough babies, sooner or later they "tip the balance"—especially if all the other people are all trying to have small families and slow down the population boom. Even the leaders of some nations still see "strength in numbers" and hesitate to curb the baby boom.

"Everybody just like me, who agrees with me, who wants what I want, should have lots of babies. Everyone else should stop!" See the problem?

Cooperative and Decisive Action
Is Essential

Several of the nations of the world are aware of what must be done. Many of them are trying. The U.N. is working on it. In India where

the problem is very serious, the government has been trying to slow the birthrate but without much success. In 1976 Mrs. Gandhi's government announced that several of a person's rights, privileges, and government benefits would be removed if they had a third child. Also, government employment would be denied.

Drastic measures such as this may help some. But they don't reach into the remote rural areas where most of the problem stems from.

The technology of birth control is just now getting good enough so that a solution is becoming *technically* possible. But technology is not enough. The socio-cultural problems are going to be really tough to overcome. Multi-billion dollar programs—a massive thrust of energy and effort to bring down the birth rate—are going to be required. Nobody knows where these billions of dollars' worth of energy and effort are going to come from.

What's the ultimate answer? First a lot of people are going to have to become aware of the imperative need for population control. The international community, all nations, must work together to convince the people of what must be done. Then the governments must provide the assistance and the incentives required to do the job. The *political process* must direct resources toward this objective.

The tidal wave of new babies will be brought under control, because it must. The only questions are: how soon? and in what ways? In the meantime, what happens to the ones who already have been born? and to the ones who will be born? What about today's little babies, young children, teenagers?

They will continue to grow up. Many of them will pour into the already overcrowded cities. The population crush in the metropolitan areas—just from those who are already born—will continue to get worse. It's in the cities where the full force of the population explosion does its damage. It's going to get a lot worse before it gets better.

The next chapter is going to begin by talking about the problems of the urban areas. Then it will go into the problems of poverty and discrimination.

But before you go on, be sure you understand the nature of the environmental problem. That's really a critical issue for modern society. It's an issue on which popular discussion often generates more heat than light. Spend enough time to really understand it. That will put you far ahead of most people.

REVIEW EXERCISES

• **MAJOR CONCEPTS, PRINCIPLES, TERMS (Explain each carefully.)**

the meaning of "progress"
progress and problems
the population explosion
who will pay for pollution controls

• **OTHER CONCEPTS AND TERMS (Explain each briefly.)**

final pollution
derived pollution
dumping rights
Environmental Protection Agency
Council on Environmental Quality

• **CURVES AND GRAPHS (Draw, label, and explain each.)**

The Increasing Cost of Cleaning Up Wastes
The Producer's Demand for Nature's Waste-Disposal Services
The Supply and Demand for Nature's Waste-Disposal Services
Finding the Optimum Social Level of Dumping into the Ecosystem
How Output Markets React to the Cost Increase When Pollution Controls
   Are Imposed

• **QUESTIONS (Write out answers or jot down key points.)**

1. The "desired directions of progress" in a society are always changing some. In recent years the desired directions have been changing very rapidly. Can you think of several shifts in the directions of progress, just during the last few years? Discuss.
2. "We have all been 'living high' by not paying the full costs of the things we've been using up." Explain.
3. Can you think of several ways in which you personally are helping to pay some of the cost of environmental protection? Can you think of ways in which you are likely to have to pay more of those costs as time goes on? Discuss.

4. "The reason the environmental problem has grown so rapidly and become so serious is that in the 'market directed' economies, most of the things which create and contribute to the environmental problem are free from the major control mechanism of the society—that is, are external to the market process." Discuss.

5. "Two ways the environmental problems can be handled are these: (a) force the social costs of each bit of 'environmental destruction' to be reflected in the market process, or (b) establish regulations and prohibitions to protect the environment. Both these approaches require decisive (and sometimes unpopular) actions by the political process." Discuss.

6. Explain some of the reasons why the population problem is so difficult to control.

21 The Problems of Urbanization, Poverty, Discrimination

These problems are complex — not easy to understand, even more difficult to solve — but some progress is being made.

This chapter continues just where the last one left off. First it centers in on the places where the population crush is serious: the urban areas. Then it goes on to talk about poverty and about the unequal economic opportunities which result from discrimination. First, the urban areas.

FOCUS OF THE POPULATION CRUSH: THE URBAN AREAS

We don't have to wait for a serious problem to appear in the urban areas. That problem is already here. Acute. Demanding attention *now*. As the *chronic* problem of the population explosion continues to infect more and more areas and further threaten the future of man on earth, the acute problem of the urban areas will continue to become more acute, more urgent.

In the urban areas the population crush and all of the other problems of modern society come into sharp focus. We need to spend a while talking about these urban places—these places where the *acute* symptoms of the *chronic* "population disease" weigh so heavily on so many people.

The Explosive Growth of Urban Areas

About three fourths of the people in the United States are living in urban areas now. More are pouring in all the time. Some forecasters estimate that in the United States, by the end of the present century another 100 million people will be living in urban areas.

That's enough people to make up ten metropolitan areas as large as New York City! Can you picture that? Or it would make up fifteen metropolitan areas the size of Chicago, or Los Angeles-Long Beach. It would make twenty more Philadelphias or Detroits. It would make up between fifty and a hundred Buffalos or Cincinnatis or Dallases or Denvers or Indianapolises or Kansas Citys or Miamis or Milwaukees or New Orleanses or San Diegos or Seattles.

If you live in a city of only 100,000 population it would take a *thousand more* cities like yours just to accommodate all these people! Get the picture? All this is likely to be happening just during the next four decades of your lifetime!

All over the world the same thing is going to be happening. In many countries it will happen much faster and be much more severe than in the United States. The United States and other advanced countries have the technology, skills, education, governmental stability, everything needed to somehow handle the problem. But many nations don't have what it's going to take. Much human suffering is likely to result and there doesn't seem to be much that anybody can do about it.

The Problems of the Urban Areas

The problems of the urban areas are the problems of modern society. Not that all the people with problems are located in the urban areas. Of course not. Many people live in rural areas and some of them face serious problems, to be sure. In the United States there are several government programs aimed toward overcoming the poverty of people who live in Appalachia, the Ozarks, and in other rural areas. The rural area problems can be very stubborn and difficult to solve. But the really tough challenge to the wisdom, the ingenuity, and the technology of modern society is the challenge of the exploding urban areas.

It is in the urban areas where the serious problems of modern society are concentrated and magnified—expanded into crisis proportions. It is in the urban areas that the environmental crisis is most acute. It's there that the problems of unemployment, inadequate education, inadequate medical and health facilities, inadequate housing, high crime rates—all the things which are heralded as the "major problems of our society"—come into focus. And it is in the urban areas that the problems are so frustratingly resistant—so difficult to overcome.

One problem of the urban area is that it is made up of such different parts. Urban areas contain healthy places and sick places. There are the wealthy suburbs and there are the poverty-ridden ghettos. It is in the ghettos—these "isolated cities within the cities" where all the problems come most sharply into focus. It is in the ghettos where the solutions to the urban problem will be most difficult. But it's in the ghettos where the solutions are most needed and where most of the effort is going to have to be applied.

The Problem of "Population Spillover"

Yesterday, there was a city. It had its boundary and its people lived within the boundary. Then suddenly, almost overnight the population of the city exploded—spread itself out beyond its own boundaries. When that happened, the city lost control of itself. It lost the means for governing itself, for working out its problems.

Why Did People Move to the Suburbs? As low income people began moving into the city seeking jobs, residential property values began to go down. Then more people began moving out to the suburbs.

Everybody had a car. Highways were built up rapidly connecting the suburbs with the central city so commuting was no serious problem. Once this trend began, the "natural forces of the market" guaranteed that it would continue. The "laws of positive economics" can explain it.

Suppose you live in a neighborhood where the people next door have sold their house and the house has now been subdivided into four apartments. Now there are four families living next door.

As more people move into your neighborhood there's overcrowding in the schools. There are more social welfare costs. There's more congestion. More noise on your street. Life there isn't so pleasant anymore. Then to provide the additional services needed, city tax rates go up.

This is the last straw! You move to the suburbs. You sell your house. Soon it is subdivided into apartments. The process continues.

Do the buyers of your house and the other houses keep up all this real estate in tip-top condition to "protect their investment"? Of course not. The market value of each one of these places depends more on what happens to the neighborhood than it depends on what the owner does to the property. So each owner lets the property "go with the neighborhood." So what happens? The neighborhood goes down. It's absolutely guaranteed!

Once it starts, what can reverse this trend? Local governments try to use zoning laws to prevent the single family residences from becoming apartment houses and to require that property be maintained. This may slow the process. But once the process gets going, it isn't likely that much private money is going to be risked on the future of such a neighborhood!

The people moving out will go to the suburbs and establish zoning laws to limit the building of cheap housing and to require each house to be built on a large lot. If all your neighbors' properties are as expensive as yours then your neighbors will carry as much of the local government property tax burden as you do. Also, it isn't likely that there will be expensive welfare programs or the high cost crime control programs, fire prevention programs or other high cost programs associated with the central city.

The Fragmentation of the Metropolitan Area.

All over the country and all over the world we see metropolitan areas sliced up into many local government jurisdictions—people living in the county, working in the "central city," visiting their friends in another "little city" nearby—when really it's all one metropolitan area. Usually there's not much coordination among all these local government units. Each "local government unit" has its own leadership, its own tax system, its own local programs, its own little problems to take care of. But the metropolitan area as a whole really doesn't have a "government." Nobody is in charge of the whole thing!

The metro-area really doesn't have a government!

For example, the New York City metropolitan area is made up of some 1,400 different local governments. The San Francisco area includes about 1,000 and the St. Louis metropolitan area includes almost 500 with half of them in Illinois and half of them in Missouri. The pattern is the same in the big metropolitan areas all over the country.

Most of the problems of a metro-area can't be solved in little pieces. The problems are area-wide. It's obvious that the transportation problem, or the problems of education, law enforcement, fire protection, welfare, housing, air and water pollution, employment and such things just can't be solved piecemeal. So what can be done? In the United States, the federal government tries to force some coordination and area-wide program planning in the metropolitan areas.

The federal government now requires that "councils of government" (COG's) or "regional planning councils" be set up to coordinate the programs and plans for the entire metropolitan area—either that, or else the federal government will cut off the grants for the sewer systems, and the urban transit systems and such things. The "COG movement" has helped quite a bit—more in some places than in others, but the problem still is far from being solved.

The "Metro Government" Approach.

The city of Toronto, Canada, and a few other cities in the world have established "super governments" that encompass the entire metro-area. The results appear to be very good—but apparently not good enough to convince the "small town" residents of any U.S. metro-area to give up their own independence and toss in with a "metro-area government."

While the urban areas have been growing and their problems multiplying, a financial crisis has been emerging. The "financial base" of the city has been eroding from two sides: (1) the more wealthy taxpayers have moved outside the city where they no longer pay city taxes, while (2) the cost of providing city services have been going higher and higher. So now the cities can't make it on their own. They just can't!

The Urban Transportation Problem

You'll be surprised how much the urban area problem is tied in with urban area transportation. Without the development of the massive freeways and everyone except the very poor owning a car, the suburban development wouldn't have occurred.

If, instead of the development of freeways, urban mass transit systems had been developed linking the downtown areas with the outlying areas, then the whole pattern of urban development would have been very different.

Congestion in the downtown areas has become more acute. Tax rates and property costs and costs of utilities and other services have gone up. Many of the commercial and industrial firms have moved to the outlying areas to escape all this.

But what of the low-paid workers living in the ghettos and other areas of the central city? When the firms move, how do these people get to work? Many don't own cars. If they did they would have no place to park them and they couldn't afford to operate them.

Why don't they move out near the jobs? They can't do that either. They can't afford to. And there are various kinds of regulations to prevent them from coming out and "breaking down" the new suburban neighborhoods. Many are locked into the central city with no way to get out.

As urban areas grow in future years, the pattern of the transportation links throughout each urban area will be of critical importance.

But what will that pattern be? That's hard to forecast.

Everyone seems to agree that there should be mass transit. But most of those who are driving their automobiles don't want to go to mass transit and give up the personal convenience of driving their own cars. If no one is going to ride the mass transit except the poor, then mass transit is going to be a losing proposition. Are the taxpayers going to want to pay for it? And maintain adequate standards? Just so the poor can ride? These are important issues. They won't be solved easily.

Federal Government Programs

In the 1950s as things got worse the federal government began to get involved. The Department of Housing and Urban Development (HUD) was set up. Various "urban renewal" programs have been undertaken. Hundreds of thousands of ghetto housing units have been demolished in various cities throughout the country. Low cost housing has been built.

Urban throughways have been built to speed automobile traffic. More recently (1964, 1966, and later) urban mass transit acts were passed providing federal funds to help provide mass transit systems. In 1975 the federal government for the first time subsidized operating expenses on some urban mass transit systems.

Federal grants have been given to the cities for many different purposes. The programs have been expanded over the past 25 years. Several approaches have been tried—urban renewal, community renewal, model cities, various housing programs and others.

There is no question that some impressive things have been done. A look at Atlanta or Norfolk or Buffalo or Philadelphia or Dallas or Houston or St. Louis or many other cities throughout the nation shows the physical success of several urban renewal programs. Still, most of what has been done so far has been more "panic relief" than carefully planned, long-range problem-solving.

Some progress has been made, but we haven't yet aimed enough resources, enough effort at this "urban problem" to get very many things really "solved." In the future, more permanent solutions are going to be required. Many people are worrying about it and working on it. That's a good sign, I suppose.

The U.S. Advisory Committee on Intergovernmental Relations has recommended (1) that some kind of effective coordination among the local governmental units— between the cities and villages and counties and townships and all the others which make up each "metro-area"—be worked out; (2) that the cost of public education be taken over entirely by the state government; (3) that the cost of the welfare program be taken over entirely by the federal government; and (4) that the federal government give "no strings attached" grants to help out the local governments in the urban areas.

Developing "New Towns"

Another recommendation of the Advisory Committee (and of others) is that we plan for and develop many more "new towns" to take some of the population pressures off the existing cities. This means that we go out into the rural areas and find suitable undeveloped sites and develop new cities. In recent years several "new towns" have been developed in the United States and in other countries. It's likely that many more "new towns" will be developed, and that these new towns will absorb some of the (perhaps 100 million) people who will pour into U.S. urban areas (and some of the thousands of millions who will pour into urban areas throughout the world) during the next few decades.

New towns will help. But they won't solve the problem. For one thing, "new towns" won't necessarily be "better towns." But more serious than that, it's the already overburdened *existing* cities which are going to feel most of the pressure. They are going to have to be greatly strengthened, both politically and economically, if they are going to be able to handle the task without worsening "the mess" which we have already allowed most of them to get into.

The Impediments Are Many and Serious

The problems of the urban areas will not be solved by economics alone. Some of the major impediments are political, social, traditional, psychological, cultural. The key individuals in each little borough or suburb or county government don't want to give up their positions of status or power. Racial, nationality, religious, and cultural groups within the metropolitan area don't want to give up whatever "local government control" they may have and toss in with some distant, impersonal "metrogovernment."

Many people fear change. The people who feel at home in the ghetto may be very wary about those "social planners" who are out to tear down their neighborhoods and disrupt their familiar pattern of life—the only pattern of life they have ever known.

Not only that. What about this? After the urban renewal demolishers come through, where will these people live? The government may provide "low cost housing" at maybe $100 a month. But in their slum dwellings some of these families have been paying less than half that much!

So maybe they did have to walk down a dark hallway to get to the cold-water bathroom. And maybe they would step on a cockroach on the way. Not very pleasant, true. But at least they could pay the rent and have money left for enough food to get by on. After they move into the government "low cost housing" how are they going to make it? They were already living on a malnutrition budget!

Don't forget why all these people drifted into the ghetto in the first place. It isn't necessarily because they prefer the surroundings. It's because *they can afford to live there.*

A person who only has $100 a month to live on would rather give up housing than food. If urban renewal means forcing more housing (and less food) on the poverty stricken people, then it isn't a very humanitarian program. It may make the city look prettier for visiting dignitaries. But it doesn't solve the problem of people who inhabit the central city. Sometimes urban renewal programs have not given enough attention to this problem.

Fixing up the cities will not be easy. Just think of the many billions of dollars worth of resources it's going to take just to get the "physical plant" in shape: all the tearing down and rebuilding; the development of transit systems; greatly improved waste disposal and anti-pollution services; better housing, schools, hospitals—and what about the "people oriented" programs? Better education, training, manpower development, health, recreation, job development and all that? And with the constant relentless flood of new people pouring into the area, while the costs keep going higher and higher? This is going to be a tough one, all right!

The 1975-76 Financial Crisis of the Cities

In 1975 there was a serious recession. The state and local governments were hit hard—as if they didn't already have enough problems!

The "Bankruptcy" of New York City. I suppose everyone knows that New York City actually went "bankrupt." It couldn't meet its outstanding debts. It couldn't borrow the money it needed to keep the city services going because its credit was no good. It was bailed out by the federal government. A "stewardship" was created to exercise final authority over the city's budget.

More than 40,000 municipal jobs were eliminated. Taxes were raised on sales, incomes and cigarettes. Capital expenditures were cut back to levels lower than at any time during the previous 8 years. Deep personnel cuts were made in education, hospitals, police, fire, social services, and sanitation. The greatest percentage cuts were in the "nonessential" functions: resorts, recreation, and cultural affairs.

How are the problems of a major urban area like New York City going to be solved, with cutbacks like that going on? They will be lucky to be able to hang on and keep things from getting worse! But that's the way is was in New York City in 1975 and 1976.

Problems in Other Cities. When New York's trouble hit, other cities around the nation felt the shock. If New York couldn't meet its debt obligations, then investors might not be so interested in investing in the bonds of other cities either! In Los Angeles the largest urban renewal project in the nation's history was cut back because of the shock of what happened in New York. The city of Seattle had to pay hundreds of thousands of additional dollars in interest in order to sell their bonds following New York's crisis.

In October, 1975, the city of Buffalo was near defaulting on some of its debt obligations. But it managed to work things out. Then early in 1976 Philadelphia announced a big budget deficit and the need for many millions in short-term loans to prevent having to lay off thousands of city employees.

Nationwide there seemed to develop (in the 1975-76 period) a public reaction against heavy government spending and an awareness of the danger of city or state bankruptcy. Federal Reserve Board Chairman Arthur F. Burns referred to this change of attitude as the "rediscovery of the need for prudence in the conduct of fiscal affairs" and said it was the most beneficial economic development of 1975. (Of course there weren't many beneficial economic developments in 1975! It was a tough year.)

All this financial trouble certainly doesn't take us any closer to solutions to the problems of the urban areas! What it does is to re-emphasize the fact that there are opportunity costs involved and that those costs are high. It seems that the opportunity costs may be higher than most people have been willing to admit—or to pay. So progress may not be as rapid as some people might have wished—and expected.

Ultimately it could help a lot if the *population problem* could be solved. That's a major cause of the urban problem and the pollution problem and of most of the other problems of our society. It would be difficult to find a problem anywhere in modern society to which the population explosion is not an important contributing factor. When the flood of births is brought into check, many of our problems will become more manageable.

While we are waiting to get the flow of births slowed down we must keep working on the problems in the urban areas, and on the environmental crisis. Another is the *poverty problem*. It's time to talk about that now.

POVERTY: WHAT IS IT?
AND HOW BAD IS IT
IN THE UNITED STATES?

What is poverty? Poverty is not being able to have what most people have—not being able to live like most people live. It's like hearing the jingle of the ice cream truck and peeking out from behind the curtain, watching the other kids buying ice cream and knowing that you can't have any. Not today. Not ever.

It's like hearing your mother in the bedroom crying because she has no money to give you for lunch. It's like having to be always pleading with people not to disconnect the electricity or the telephone or to repossess the car or the TV set—like being forced to move from one shabby apartment to another because you

can't pay the rent—like trying to hide from your "well-off" friends so they won't see how poor you are and feel sorry for you.

The kind of poverty I'm talking about is the poverty of an affluent society like the United States. In less developed countries poverty means something quite different. It may mean having no home, sleeping in the streets, getting wet when it rains—going for days with no food—having no access to medical care—someday dying of sickness and malnutrition.

Poverty Is Always Relative

Poverty is always "relative to the people around you." It means "being deprived of the things the people around you have." It may be defined as: "not having enough to meet basic needs." It's easy for everyone to agree on that.

But what do we mean by "basic needs"? And how much money does that take? That's where people disagree. In the United States in the early 1970s the government defined the "basic needs" income as being about $2000 for a person living alone, or about $4500 for a family of four, with about $1000 more for each additional person over four in the family.

You can see that these minimum basic income figures couldn't be very exact. Picture a family of six living on a farm, growing much of their own food and living in their own house and receiving a cash income of a little less than $6000 a year. By the government's definition they might be living in poverty. But they might think of themselves as quite well-to-do. Probably they're living as well as (or better than) most of their neighbors and friends!

Now put that same family in a tenement house in the heart of a big city where they must pay for everything, with no relatives or friends to share vegetables and hand-me-downs. Suddenly they're poor. Where you live and how you live and who your neighbors are can make all the difference! Also it makes a lot of difference whether the family includes young children or teenagers or grandparents and whether or not any of them have chronic illnesses.

Any income definition of "the poverty line" is bound to be too high for some families and too low for others. Still, if we're going to set up any practical programs to cure poverty we must have some way of deciding who qualifies and who doesn't! We must have some measurable definitions. Since there is no "right" definition let's hope our programs can be flexible enough to take care of the injustices which will result from the definitions we choose.

In the United States the Social Security Administration has developed measurements of "basic needs" and estimates of how much income is required for a family to be above the "poverty level." In their measurement, the Social Security Administration makes an adjustment to account for the rural or urban location of the family.

If you would like to see what some of the current estimates are of the income required for "basic needs" and of the numbers of people who fall below this "poverty line," go to your library and look in the *Current Population Reports*, published by the U.S. Department of Commerce.

How Many Americans Are Living in Poverty?

Using these (admittedly inexact) "minimum income" definitions of poverty, how many people in the United States are "living in poverty"? More than one family in ten. More than five million families. A lot of people, to be sure. If you look just at the black and other minority families, you see about one family in four with incomes below the poverty line. Also, if you look at families headed by very young men or very old men or by women, you will see a high incidence of poverty.

About a third of all the Americans living in poverty are living in fatherless households. Most of them, of course, are children. There

are about ten million children and teenagers under 18 living in households with incomes below the goverment's poverty line.

None of these measures or indicators of poverty is very precise or accurate. Still, there's enough evidence to be convincing. Yes, we can be quite sure that a very real poverty problem does exist in our affluent American society.

Changing Patterns of Income Distribution in the United States

If you look at the trend in income distribution over the past several decades, there are two clear conclusions:

(1) The percentage of the population living in poverty has gone down greatly since World War II. In 1947 about 30 percent of Americans were living below the poverty line. By 1960 the percentage was down to about 20 percent. By the early 1970s the number had dropped to about 12 percent.

   That kind of reduction in the percentage of people in poverty is gratifying, of course. But it still leaves some 25 million Americans living with less than a "basic needs" income. Many of these are victims of some kind of disability, or are living in a household where there is no husband to help to support the family.

(2) Since World War II, the extent of inequality of income distribution in the United States hasn't changed significantly. Rising incomes, supplemented by the social security program and other programs have done a lot to overcome the poverty at the low end of the income scale.

   But in terms of "percentage of income received" the 20 percent of the people who receive the lowest incomes are still receiving about the same percentage of the total as they were receiving 30 years ago (between 5 and 6 percent of the total income.) The 20 percent of the people who receive the highest incomes are still receiving about the same percentage of the total as they were receiving 30 years ago (about 40 percent of the total income.)

We use a Lorenz curve to show the percentage breakdown of income distribution. A "Lorenz curve" showing the income distribution pattern for the United States in the 1970s is explained in Figure 21-1. If you will study that Figure now I think all of this will become very clear.

Profiles in Poverty

It's difficult for most people to visualize a poverty situation. If you're from a middle or upper income family, how can you picture a family in poverty? If you begin by picturing a family like *your* family, you'll never make it. A family like your family wouldn't be in poverty.

Try to picture what your family would have been like if your father had died before you were old enough to remember. Or suppose he had contracted some kind of disabling disease that required a lot of medical expense. And suppose there were no well-to-do relatives to help out. And suppose there were already three young children ahead of you, and another due in a few months. What would life have been like for you, then? Very different. Right?

The most frequent, most serious profile of a poverty family is the profile of a fatherless household where there are small children. Other "profiles in poverty" would include families with disabled or otherwise unproductive fathers, and families of high school dropouts who get married in their teens, start producing children and try to make it on their own.

For another profile, you might picture a household headed by a middle-aged or older man, perhaps not too bright, not too flexible, whose skills have been made obsolete by changing times. If the man happens to be a member of a minority race or has a poor employment record or a prison record or some other "undesirable characteristics" (or even if he doesn't) he may not be able to get another job. After months or maybe years of looking, he may just give up. Many do.

Other profiles in poverty would show you families living on seasonal employment, working at part-time jobs, temporary jobs, low-paying jobs. Often the poverty is worsened by a large number of people depending on one low-wage earner. If the family includes aging relatives, plus several children, the paycheck just won't meet the needs.

The Poor: Who Are They? Where Are They?
A lot of poor people are old people—people who can no longer be self-supporting who are living on what they can get from relatives, savings, and government assistance programs. About one in every twelve people over 65 in the United States is living in poverty.

There is a lot of poverty in agriculture, especially in the South. About one-fourth of all the rural people in the country are poor.

You will find poverty in homes where health problems (physical or mental) are interfering with the ability of the adults to earn money. Sometimes unemployment is responsible. Some jobs—in hotels and motels and retail stores and some others—pay such low wages that even a full-time worker couldn't earn enough to lift the family income above the poverty level.

Poverty occurs four times as often among non-whites as among whites. About one third of all Southern blacks and about one fifth of all Northern blacks are living in poverty.

About one third of all of the poor people in the United States live in households which have no man—no husband, no father—to help to support the family. In our society when the mother attempts to take care of the children

Fig. 21-1   Income Distribution in the United States by Population and Income Groups: the Lorenz Curve

This income distribution pattern has been approximately the same for the past 30 years.

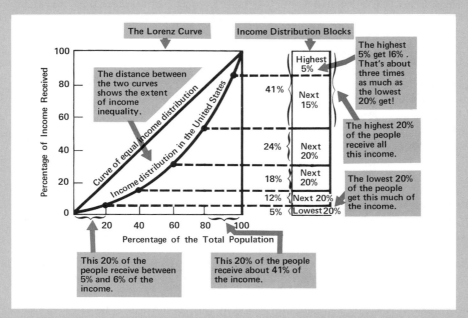

The Lorenz curve keeps adding more people as you go to the right along the horizontal axis, and adding more income as you go up along the vertical axis. You add the low income people first. So as you start at the zero point and go to the right along the horizontal axis the curve doesn't go up very much. Then as you go farther to the right along the horizontal axis you begin to add people with higher incomes. So the curve gets steeper.

For the last few people added, the curve goes almost straight up. Those people are making millions! But look over near the zero corner at how little income is earned by the first few people. The lowest five percent of the people have almost no income at all!

Generally speaking, there isn't much mobility of individuals or families along the horizontal scale of this graph. The poor usually stay poor and the rich usually stay rich. But there are many exceptions to this general rule. Poor people sometimes work their way into better income situations. And some affluent families are struck by disaster and forced down into poverty.

Before the 1930s, income distribution in the United States was more unequal than it is now. In 1929 the top 5 percent of the population received 30 percent of all the income. These days the top 5 percent receive about 16 percent.

This curve shows income before taxes. What about after taxes? Do taxes reduce income inequality in the United States? Not much. Economists disagree about how much. There are some progressive (soak the rich) taxes like the income tax. But there are lots of regressive (soak the poor) taxes like sales taxes, too.

and earn enough money to provide for the family she is faced with a herculean task. Throw into the picture the sex discrimination which exists in the American labor market and the task for most husbandless mothers becomes impossible.

Poverty Is Self-Perpetuating

An important *cause* of poverty is the *existence* of poverty. Poverty begets poverty. Many people are born and raised in poverty, in neighborhoods where poverty is a way of life. All the influences point toward the poverty pattern of life rather than toward ways to get out of poverty. Avenues of escape are difficult to find. Many people feel beaten before they start—so why try?

A person who is bright, strong, healthy, and capable will find a way to get out of poverty. But only a certain percentage of the people born in any generation are going to be bright, strong, healthy and capable. The others, if they had been lucky enough to be born into affluent middle class families, would have been able to do okay. They would have been educated and trained and given all the necessary advantages and "conditioned to succeed." They would have succeeded. But when born in the ghetto and conditioned to the poverty way of life their chances for success are very slim. They will just stay in the ghetto and be the "perpetuating group" left behind when the strongest and most capable ones break out and leave. The ones left behind are trapped by and are the ones who perpetuate the "vicious circle of inherited poverty."

What Can Be Done About Poverty?

When you look at the poverty profiles it's easy to see that simple solutions are not going to solve the problem. No longer is it possible to quip: "If people are poor, let them go to work. If they are unskilled, offer them training and then let them go to work. If they won't take the training and won't go to work then let them go hungry."

How simple this solution seems to be! But how do you apply it to the widowed or unwed or deserted pregnant mother of four small children? How do you apply it to the aged person? or couple? Or to the worker who is not too old to work but is too old to be able to get a job? Or to the men and women who are physically or mentally incapable?

Much, probably *most* of the poverty in the United States can't be "cured" by getting people to go to work. In so many poverty families there just *isn't anybody* to go to work! Often, even if there is someone who possibly *could* work, there's no *feasible* way to train them and fit them into an available job.

We need to emphasize manpower training and job development. Obviously. We need such programs as worker education and skill development and on-the-job training, supplemented by job placement services, and subsidies to stimulate new employment opportunities. Of course! Many such programs are already operating, and progress is being made in overcoming some of the "curable" kinds of poverty. But no matter how far we go in job development, this approach cannot *completely eliminate* the poverty problem. Obviously not. So what can be done?

What's the most serious "profile in poverty" we see in this country? The fatherless home with small children. Do you suppose the population problem is lurking under the surface here, somewhere? You know it is. If the number of children born into these homes could be reduced, that would help a lot. Improved birth control technology and liberalized abortion laws may lessen the seriousness of this "profile in poverty." But still the problem isn't going to be completely solved that way.

The only way we can really hope to handle the incurable kinds of poverty is to have some programs which will provide money to the families who have no way to generate their own incomes. There's just no other way. What kinds of programs? And how much money? To whom? Under what circumstances? Those are the tough questions. The choices usually reflect more political and social considerations than economic ones. Near the end of this chapter there's a section that talks about programs for overcoming poverty. But first we need to get into the issue of discrimination.

THE PROBLEM OF DISCRIMINATION BY RACE AND SEX

Discrimination is one important cause of poverty. But discrimination is a deep issue. It goes far beyond the problem of poverty. How serious is discrimination as a cause of poverty? It's hard to say. One problem is: it isn't easy to separate present discrimination from the results of past discrimination.

Discrimination Against Blacks

We know that less than 10 percent of the whites and about 30 percent of the blacks live in poverty. Does that mean the blacks are poor because of discrimination? We can't conclude that unless we know more about the situation. Beware of *post hoc ergo propter hoc!* Remember? (But we do know more about the situation.)

We know that blacks generally have not had past opportunities for education, development of skills, job experience, etc., as have whites. And we are seeing some of the results of that, now. Also we know that in almost every field of work blacks have usually received less for doing the same jobs.

But progress has been made.

Less than 20 years ago the "average" (median income) black family only earned a little more than half as much as the "average" (median income) white family. By the early 1970s the average black family was earning three fourths as much as the average white family. That shows a lot of progress. But it's still a long way from equality.

In 1972 the median income for a white family was about $11,000. For a black family it was about $7,000. Unemployment among blacks was about double the unemployment rate for whites.

Blacks have been discriminated against by being hired last and fired first, denied education and training and access to other programs which would permit them to advance. And discrimination in housing helps to lock them into the ghettos where their economic opportunities are seriously limited.

The New Economic Role of Women

Since World War II the role of women in the American economy has really changed! Before World War II, back in the 20s and before, women never made up more than about 20 percent of the labor force.

What about now? The percentage of women in the labor force has gone up from about 20 percent to about 40 percent. These days, *two out of every five employed people in the United States are women.*

More than 45 percent of all working-age women now are in the labor force. That's almost one out of every two. In the mid-1970s there are more than 36,000 women in the labor force.

These figures show the very important role that women are playing in the American economic system. No longer can "working women" be thought of as being "at the fringe" of the economic system, to be taken not too seriously and to be discriminated against.

Discrimination Against Women

In 1971, the average female worker was only making about 60 percent as much as the average male worker. Job segregation is an important cause. Women often are employed in "appropriate female tasks" such as retail sales, clerical work, elementary teaching, nursing, etc., while men are the doctors and lawyers and dentists and engineers and craftsmen and the important business decision makers.

This kind of job separation makes it easy to maintain wage differentials between men and women because "it has traditionally been that way." But even in occupations where men and women compete openly, the men earn much more than the women.

In the early 1970s while men sales workers were averaging more than $10,000 a year, women sales workers were averaging less than $5,000. Men school teachers were averaging more than $10,000 while women were averaging only $8,000. The same patterns existed among clerical workers and among service workers.

As in the case of discrimination against blacks, discrimination against women is under serious attack. The Equal Pay Act of 1963 and the Civil Rights Act of 1964 bar discrimination in hiring and firing and in other job practices and require equal pay for equal work. The actions of the women's liberation movement in court cases have made some significant progress in getting equal pay and job rights for women.

Progress is being made to be sure. But the barriers and impediments and traditions are strong. The road is much more open for women and for blacks and other minorities today than in the past. But there are several stretches of that road which are still very rocky for one of unfamiliar sex or color who tries to travel it.

Now it's time to talk about what government has been doing to overcome poverty—about programs we have now and other programs we might have. That's the subject of the next section.

PROGRAMS FOR OVERCOMING POVERTY

Essentially, there are two ways to approach the poverty problem. One way is to try to "cure the disease"—that is, to help the poor people become more productive so they can lift themselves out of poverty and be self-sufficient. The other is to redistribute some of the income from those who earn it to those who need it. Government agencies, private charities and various religious and other organizations are working on this problem, both ways. I'm sure you know that. This section will be talking about government programs, but don't forget that the efforts of the private charities and religious organizations also are important.

Curing "the Disease of Poverty": Manpower Development

The United States has a long tradition of manpower training and development through public education, vocational education, extension services and many other programs. Since the "New Deal" days of the 1930s, the U.S. government has become more involved in these programs. During World War II the government undertook a massive manpower training effort, not to cure poverty, but to increase the output of the economy. But the wartime manpower program cured a lot of poverty. You can be quite sure of that!

In the latter 1940s and throughout the 1950s, traditional kinds of manpower training were continued. Then in the early 1960s the Manpower Development and Training Act increased the size and scope of this effort. But it wasn't until the mid-1960s that the *Economic Opportunity Act* was passed, setting up the "anti-poverty program"—that is, the "war on poverty."

The "Economic Opportunity" Program–The "War on Poverty." The thrust of this new program was to get local people, including poor people, involved in working out innovative ways to overcome poverty. Many things were tried—neighborhood information and help centers, legal aid for the poor, "black capitalism" programs to help small businesses, job development activities, volunteer counseling and help for the poor, and of course, education and training and manpower development.

Several of the efforts supported by OEO (the U.S. Office of Economic Opportunity) failed miserably. Others, including some of the legal aid and counseling and education programs, were generally thought to be very successful. The OEO-sponsored "headstart" program— pre-schooling to help "culturally deprived" children to get ready for school—was a most popular and apparently very successful program.

The OEO also sponsored educational programs—Sesame Street, the Electric Company, and several programs offering special help (in primary and secondary schools and in college) for students from poor and minority families. In 1973 the Democrat-born Office of Economic Opportunity was "phased out" by the Republican administration and its surviving programs were distributed among other agencies.

There's no question that governments have been making increased efforts to "cure the disease of poverty." Progress has been made, sure. But much more could be done. It seems likely that more *will* be done, and that more success will be achieved. But one thing is certain. Complete success in "curing the disease of poverty" will never be achieved. It just isn't possible.

Some Poverty Is Not "Curable." There will always be some people who can't be productive enough to stand on their own. Some will be "down" only temporarily. They will need only temporary help. Others will be permanently incapable of self-support. They will need continuing help for as long as they live. For the people who can't stand alone, their only chance for a share of the society's output is for the society to donate something to them—a gift from the productive people to the unproductive people of the society. No matter how effective the "poverty curing" programs may become there always will be a need for some income redistribution to take care of those who are either temporarily or permanently incapable of self-support.

Lessening the Discomfort of Poverty: Income Redistribution

In the United States we have three big "income redistribution" programs: (1) the "social security" program, (2) the "unemployment compensation" program, and (3) the "welfare" program.

Social Security. The social security program is the largest income redistribution program in the country. It was set up during the depression of the 1930s and has been growing ever since. This is the so-called "Old Age, Survivors, Disability and Health Insurance" (OASDHI) program. This is the same as the "Retirement, Survivors, and Disability Insurance and Medicare" program.

Under the social security program, taxes are automatically deducted from people's paychecks and payments are automatically made to people who qualify—by retirement, disability, or poor health. If the wage earner dies, payments automatically go to the dependents. You can see that this program would help a lot to soothe the hurt of lost income. This is a federal government program and the taxes and benefits are the same nationwide.

In the early 1970s there were more than 30 million people receiving monthly checks averaging around $150 under the social security program. By 1977, expenditures under the program were more than $100 billion. The program is financed by social security taxes which are paid both by workers and employers. This is the payroll tax which you probably already know about.

In 1976 the tax rate was 5.8 percent of the first $15,300 of salary or wages. Both the rate and the maximum amount of taxable salary were scheduled to go up again in 1977.

Medicare. The Social Security Program was initially set up back in the 1930s. But it has been expanded frequently since then. In 1965 there was a major new addition to the program: Medicare.

This is a program of hospital insurance which covers people over 65 and pays almost all of their hospital costs for up to 90 days. The program also provides a low-cost (optional) insurance program to help on doctors' fees.

Unemployment Insurance. The unemployment insurance or "unemployment compensation" program gives payments (for a limited number of weeks) to anyone who gets laid off. This is a federal-sponsored, state-administered program. The amount of money you get per week and the number of weeks you can get it depends on rules adopted by your state. The program is financed by a tax on employers. It usually pays around $50 a week but there are wide variations among the states.

People "sign up" for their unemployment payments at the state employment office in their area. Usually the only requirement is that they be ready to take any appropriate job that might become available. If you're interested in how the program is working in your state, go down to the local employment office and ask. I'm sure someone there would be glad to explain it to you.

There are many things to complain about, about the social security and unemployment compensation programs. The payments aren't high enough to provide for basic needs, and what does a person do after the unemployment payments run out? There are other questions, but generally these two programs seem to be functioning reasonably well. It's in the welfare program where most of the serious problems seem to arise.

The Welfare, or Public Assistance Program

The welfare program includes several kinds of aid. "Aid for Dependent Children" (ADC) (to families without a father's support) and Medicaid take most of the "welfare" money, but some is also paid to others. This "welfare program" is supported with federal and state money and some local money. Generally, the federal government sets up the guidelines and each state sets up the rules for its own program. The procedures and the benefits are a lot different from one state to another. (I suppose everyone has heard stories about poor families moving from one state to another so they can get more welfare benefits.)

The costs of the "welfare" or "public assistance" program have been growing very rapidly in recent years. In the early 1970s more than seven million children (about eight percent of all the children in the United States) were being supported under this program. In New York and California this program supports about *twelve percent* of the children in the state. In other states the percentages are smaller.

In addition to "aid for dependent children," welfare payments go to "needy" people who are elderly, blind, disabled, or otherwise unable to work and who for some reason don't qualify for payments under the social security program. A person must be able to really prove a need for the money. How hard that is to do may depend a lot on which state you happen to be in and which person at the public assistance office you happen to be talking to.

In 1974 a new federally financed and administered program called the Supplemental Security Income (SSI) program was initiated. It provides payments to the aged, the blind, and the disabled. More than 3 million people are covered under this SSI program.

Another recent addition to the welfare program supported by the federal government (with some matching funds paid by the states) is *Medicaid*. This is a medical care program for the poor who would not be eligible for Medicare. Before Medicaid, aid to families with dependent children (ADC) was the biggest user of welfare money. But it didn't take Medicaid long to take the lead.

In 1977, of the total expected federal welfare expenditure of about 28 billion, Medicaid was expected to use up about $14 billion. ADC was expected to cost about $9.5 billion, with day care centers and emergency support amounting to another $4.5 billion.

In addition, there are the food stamp programs costing about $5 to $6 billion a year, school lunch programs and various other programs operated by several different departments of the federal government and by the state and local governments, all aimed toward relieving some part of the poverty problem.

There is a lot of confusion about who does what on the anti-poverty front. The federal programs are administered by the departments of Health, Education, and Welfare; Agriculture; and Housing and Urban Development. Each has different criteria for eligibility. In some cases eligibility is left up to the states. Requirements differ greatly from one place to another.

Early in 1976 President Ford was talking about asking Congress to do something to coordinate all these programs. Also, the idea of some "new and different" approach to the welfare program is still very much alive. But this book will be going to press before any "bold new action" is likely to be taken.

Everyone seems to agree that we need to reform our "public welfare" program. One suggested approach is the "guaranteed annual income"; one suggested way to achieve it is the "negative income tax."

The Guaranteed Annual Income and the Negative Income Tax

Maybe the government should stop providing welfare payments and simply guarantee each family a minimum income. People whose paychecks were large could still have taxes deducted, but people with paychecks too small could have "taxes" *added!* People with no job (no paycheck) could receive checks from the government. If your income is high, you pay. If it's low, you receive. See how this approach can be called the "negative income tax"?

Another approach might be to give *everyone in the country* a certain sum of money (say $1,000 a year) and call the money "taxable income." People who had no other income wouldn't have to pay any taxes on the grant but those with high incomes would have to repay most of it in taxes. Senator George McGovern suggested some such program when he was campaigning for the presidency in 1972.

Previously, President Nixon had recommended a guaranteeed annual income program, with the minimum income being $1600 for a family of four, plus $300 for each additional person. Under the proposed program, a family of four with no income would receive $1600 from the government. The family could earn up to $720 a year without any reduction at all in the subsidy payment, but as their earnings went above that, the subsidy would be reduced. When the family's earnings got up to about $4,000, the subsidy would be zero.

As part of the President's proposed program, any able-bodied recipient would be required to register for work, and/or to participate in a job training program. Day care centers would be set up to permit mothers of dependent children to take jobs and/or training. The continuation of the family's "guaranteed annual income" would require that a person take any suitable job that became available.

What about this "guaranteed annual income" approach to getting rid of the "welfare mess"? Is it a good approach? Can it be made to work? The answer is "probably, yes" to both questions. But it isn't going to be easy to work out, not only because of the economics involved, but even more, because of the political and administrative problems. Unless it's done right it could turn into an administrative nightmare of red tape, high costs, and injustices. That would be no improvement! That's what we're trying to get rid of now.

There Is No Easy Solution to the Poverty Problem

The poverty problem isn't going to be easy to solve. Much progress has been made, sure. The number of people classified as "living in poverty" has decreased considerably—by about *half*—over the past twenty years. That isn't enough, but the more we reduce the number in poverty the more difficult it becomes to do more. The more we succeed, the closer we get to the "hard core" of families who have no way of becoming self-supporting—families which have no choice but to depend on the "social process" or the "political process" to provide them a distributive share of society's output.

Proposals for overcoming the poverty problem are among the most controversial public policy proposals of our time. It's obvious that the U.S. economy is productive enough to provide for everybody. There's enough so that the rich can still be rich and the middle income people can keep on living well, while the poor can be brought up above the poverty level. The physical means to solve the problem certainly exist. But to try to design a realistic program or plan to put it all together—that's really tough. It involves hard choices—difficult trade-offs.

How do we serve the needs of the "honestly poor" without indulging the "fast buck artist"? and without destroying the incentives, and the feelings of personal worth of the recipients? How do we get the needed flexibility into our programs? And withstand selfish political pressures and bypass entangling bureaucracy? How do we balance off the insensitive snobbism of the "hard-nosed" against the unworkable idealism of the "willing-bleeders"?

Can we go far enough to really take care of the problem without perpetuating it? Or without creating other problems more serious than the one we're trying to solve? Are we endangering any golden-egg-laying geese by trying to reach the best of all possible worlds?

Anyone who is sure what the ultimate answer is either has great wisdom—or else doesn't understand the complexity of the problem! So far, all we have been able to do is creep along, experimenting, taking various steps as they have become politically feasible. Probably that's what we will continue to do. There will be tough choices every step of the way and it isn't likely that anybody will be completely satisfied with the results. But that seems to be the way it is with the income distribution problem. Remember?

SUMMARY

This chapter and the previous one haven't given you any answers—only tough questions—questions that your generation and mine are going to have to struggle with. What's going to happen? We will direct more effort and make more progress toward these "new" microeconomic objectives: protecting the environment, bringing the population explosion under control, working out the problems of the urban areas, overcoming the problem of poverty. We *will* make progress toward these new objectives because we *must*.

The purpose of these two chapters has been to sharpen your awareness of these problems—to let you see what's involved and to let you see a few of the kinds of tough choices that are going to be required. In these chapters you have taken a quick look at some of the most pressing "*microeconomic* public policy issues" of our time. Before you go on, think about these micro-issues for awhile. The better you understand these micro-problems the more likely it is that your gereration and mine will succeed in working out better solutions than we've been able to come up with, so far. We must, of course. We have no choice.

REVIEW EXERCISES

• MAJOR CONCEPTS, PRINCIPLES, TERMS (Explain each carefully.)

the neighborhood deterioration problem
the urban transportation issue
the metro-government approach
poverty
U.S. Social Security program
the U.S. welfare program
negative income tax

• OTHER CONCEPTS AND TERMS (Explain each briefly.)

population spillover
urban renewal
HUD
Lorenz curve
Civil Rights Act of 1964

Unemployment insurance
Medicare
ADC
Medicaid
SSI

• CURVES AND GRAPHS (Draw, label, and explain each.)

Income Distribution in the United States by Population and Income Groups: the Lorenz Curve

• QUESTIONS (Write out answers or jot down key points.)

1. Discuss some of the characteristics—the "nature"—of the urban problem. Explain some of the reasons why the problem is not going to be easy to handle. Can you see examples of any of these characteristics and impediments in *your own* local area? Discuss.
2. Do you think New York City's financial crisis will have much effect on the speed with which the urban problems are worked out in the United States? Discuss.
3. Explain some of the important causes of, and impediments to overcoming poverty in the "affluent societies."

4. What are some indications of discrimination in the U.S. labor markets? Do you think these indications are conclusive? Discuss.

5. Do you think the negative income tax would be a good idea? Why or why not? Discuss.

6. The poverty problem is *especially* difficult to handle, because just about everything you can think of to *overcome* poverty, seems to interfere with something else—seems to generate reflex effects: "Adequate" payments to support fatherless children may result in more fatherless children; "adequate" payments to the unemployed may result in more unemployment. When a person receives "adequate" payments to eliminate the discomfort of poverty that automatically takes the pressure off. It relieves the urgency to work out a permanent solution to the uncomfortable situation. It tends to perpetuate the problem. This basic dilemma is inherent in all "anti-poverty" programs. It's because of this dilemma that the "degree of success" in overcoming poverty is likely to always fall short of the "desired social objective." Discuss.

22 Economic Systems of the 1970s: Evolving Blends of Economic Planning and the Market Process

Revolution and evolution in this stormy century have brought the emergence of autocratic planned economies and democratic socio-capitalism.

Throughout this book, you've been reading about economic systems, either directly or indirectly. When you think about it, almost all you've been studying in microeconomics and in macroeconomics is concerned with how a market-directed economic system works.

You know that the concepts and principles of economics can be applied to an individual, to a business, or to the whole society. When concepts and principles are applied to the whole society we're talking about the economic system—what it is, how it's put together, how it works.

Different Kinds of Economic Systems: An Overview

A society's economic system makes a lot of difference in how the society works and what it's like to live there. You bet it does! Back in the beginning, in Chapter 3 you read about the three different processes at work in all economic systems: the social process (tradition), the political process (government), and the market process (the price mechanism).

You also read about the real-world economic systems: those which are mostly market-directed and those which are not. In the real world there are really only economies of mixed socio-capitalism and the non-market economies of the communist countries. You remember that from Chapter 3, of course.

What Is an Economic System?

Every society has an economic system. It's what gets the people fed and housed and clothed and all. The economic system is what gets the society's economic choices made and carried out.

The economic system is what organizes and directs all of the natural resources and all of the factories and machines and equipment—and all of the people who operate and manage the factories and machines and equipment and everything. Everyone involved in the production of anything is a part of the economic system.

How are the basic economic questions answered? Who decides what goods and services are going to be produced? How much will be available to consumers? What kinds of production methods will be used? And how does each person get a share of all this output of goods and services?

How are all those decisions made? And then how are the decisions carried out? When you know the answers to these questions you understand the basic nature of the economic system.

The economic system is the organized set of procedures the society uses for working out the answers to the basic production and distribution questions. It's the systematic way the society solves its economic problem!

Most of what you have been reading about in this book has been talking about the "mostly market-directed" systems of "mixed socio-capitalism." But in this chapter you'll be reading more about the non-market "planned economies" of the communist countries.

Economic planning—that is, economic choice making by the political process—has become an important feature of the modern world. The communist countries rely on economic planning and government direction of the nation's productive resources much more than the non-communist countries do. But still there is no country in the world today in which governmental economic planning is not important. Why?

MODERN PROBLEMS REQUIRE MORE "POLITICAL PROCESS" CHOICES

Just think about all of the modern-world economic problems you've been reading about in this book. Lots of them, right? How are they going to be taken care of? By government? Mostly, yes.

Think about the macroeconomic problems. The problems of keeping the economy stable and running at acceptable speed—not too much unemployment, not too much inflation. Is the government going to be getting involved in things like that? Of course.

What about the microeconomic problems? There's too much environmental destruction and too much poverty and monopoly power and several other socially unacceptable conditions. Who is going to do anything about that? The government? Of course.

And what about the world problems? What about such problems as working out international trade arrangements and foreign aid programs for the LDCs, and all that? Who is going to take the lead in getting these worked out? The governments? Of course. The political process must do it. Who else?

The choice-making role of government has been increasing in all of the "mostly market-directed" economies of "mixed socio-capitalism." I'm sure you understand *why* this has been happening and I'm sure you also understand that this trend will continue. Why? Because it *must* continue.

Society is demanding that something be done about the major problems. So the role of the state must continue to expand. There's just no other way to get at these problems of modern society.

As Objectives Change, "Progress" Must Take New Directions

There were times not very long ago, when the major economic problem was how to meet the basic needs of the people. That's still the way it is in the less developed countries. But in the advanced nations, not so. Not anymore.

The economic problems have changed so now our objectives must change. "Progress" must be aimed toward the new, emerging problems—toward a new set of objectives. But how can that be done? Only through the political process. Only by government choice-making.

For those of us who live in the rich nations, progress is going to have to be less "consumption-oriented," more oriented toward longer range objectives. We are already well fed and highly productive. So now we have the opportunity to do something about the "rough spots" in our society.

But in the societies where affluence has not arrived, people aren't worring about such things. To the people who are poor, "progress" still means material things—more and better food, clothing, shelter, clean water, sanitation, medical care.

As economies grow—become more productive, more specialized, more interdependent, more "modern"—the problems change. As the problems change, the directions of progress change. You already know that. But as all this happens, the *procedures for approaching solutions* must change, too.

The State Must Make More of the Choices

In the economic systems which rely on the market process—that is, in the advanced economies of mixed socio-capitalism—the "new" problems and objectives require more and more government action. The state makes more and more of the economic choices. That just seems to be "in the nature of things." There doesn't seem to be any other way.

Modern society has more and more people, living closer and closer together, becoming more and more interdependent, influencing each other's opportunities for employment and income. All of these people are infringing on each other's freedoms, using up each other's resources, polluting each other's water and air and land.

It's sort of obvious that as all this happens, the society (through its political processes) must get more involved in deciding who gets to do what. Nothing difficult to understand about that!

In the economies of mixed socio-capitalism, the role of the state—the political process—expands. In the communist countries the role of the state can't very well expand. The state is running just about everything already!

The political process will play a major role in the LDCs too, of course. The governments of those countries will try to stimulate development.

The Trend Toward More Choices by Government

Governments everywhere in the "mostly market-directed" economies of socio-capitalism are playing an increasing role. It's a trend that got going in Europe in the 1920s, after World War I.

In the United States the trend toward the increasing role of government in the economy didn't get going until the 1930s. The New Deal days? Right. And it has been going that way ever since.

It's only during this century—since the time of World War I, in fact—that the several so-called "communist" economic systems have been set up. Most of those countries have gone through revolutions. The revolutionary governments have taken tight control over the economic system and have exercised the production and distribution choices.

Governments Are Doing "Economic Planning"

How does it work when the government directs the economy? Either partly, as in the mostly market-directed economies, or totally, as in the communist countries? What is the *process* of economic planning? If you were to look at a government which was doing economic planning, what would you see?

In practice, economic planning can look very complex. There are so many details that must be taken care of! But in overview it's really quite simple. It works like this: The government makes some choices and works out some economic plans which reflect those choices. Then it proceeds to try to carry out the plans.

Why is "government economic planning" or "central economic planning" or just "economic planning" so very important in the world today? Because economic planning *is the alternative to the market process* for getting the society's economic choices made and carried out.

"Economic planning" is the mechanism of the political process." It's going on everywhere. In some places it's in almost complete control. In other places it isn't. But it's very important everywhere. So you really need a good understanding of economic planning. You'll get that in the next section.

ECONOMIC PLANNING

Economic planning means about what you would think. It means deciding how to use (how to economize and optimize) the productive resources of the society. But it also includes the idea of implementing, or carrying out the plans.

There are several approaches to economic planning, of course. This section gives an overview of how it works.

Designing the Plan

The Soviet Union and other communist countries and several non-communist countries (including many LDCs) operate on a "five-year plan." The idea is that a set of objectives is laid out in detail, to be achieved during the coming five years. Then all the resources are aimed toward fulfilling the plan.

For example, the plan would include (as objectives) the completion of certain additions to the total highway network, construction of new buildings, houses, and all that; opening up new mines for coal, iron ore, and other things; new railroads; added productive capacity in steel, chemicals, and other industrial products; total amounts of consumer goods in each category (clothing, food, etc.) for each year within the planning period.

The plan would include construction and operation of schools and hospitals; numbers of people to be educated in various ways; numbers and kinds of motor vehicles to be produced; amounts of output to be produced for export to get the foreign exchange to buy the things wanted from other countries; num-bers of people to be moved from one industrial center or activity to another, and on and on.

The five-year plan attempts to figure out just exactly how much of each of the various kinds of resources and products the economy will be capable of producing, and then plans exactly how each of these should be used—for consumption, or for further production; and if for further production, for the further production of which things.

Planning Is a Big "Production Possiblity" Exercise. You can see that this is like a big "production possibility" or "transformation curve" exercise. Only instead of having only two choices, the choices are almost infinite; and instead of knowing for sure exactly how much we can produce with the available resources, these things can only be estimated.

How are all these things decided? Through the political process, of course! The government experts (economists) work with the political leaders to get the plans worked out.

All Economic Systems Use Some Planning. Without economic planning, do you suppose there would be any public schools in your state? or a highway system? or any police or fire protection in your town?

Or do you suppose there would be a United States flag on the moon? or an intracoastal waterway running from Maine to Mexico? or a Saint Lawrence Seaway? or national parks and recreation areas? None of these would exist without economic planning.

The amount of "economic planning" going on in a society indicates the extent to which the political process is making the economic choices. If the government makes most of the choices then there is a lot of economic planning. But when the choices are left up to the market process, economic planning isn't necessary. Resources and products and workers automatically flow to where they are demanded.

Economic Planning Reduces the Individual's Choices

Economic planning can make a lot of difference in the lives of the people. It matters whether there is a little or a lot of planning and it matters how the plans are made.

How much democracy is used in designing the plan? Who gets to have an influence on the objectives? Who decides which resources will be used in which way? If there's a lot of planning, everyone's life is patterned by the plan. So in a society which has a highly planned economy, these questions become very important.

If there is very little economic planning then the market process will be in control of most of the choices. People will respond to the market. The ones who are able to get a lot of money will have a lot of infuence. Each person who can get more money can have more influence and can have more things.

In an economy controlled by economic planning, individuals have less freedom of choice. If the government of the United States decides to use more resources for medicare (and to tax you to pay for it) then the society is not going to be able to produce that sporty little car you had wanted to buy—but which because of the high taxes you aren't going to be able to pay for now anyway!

In the Soviet Union, suppose you wanted some new gloves and a warmer coat but the government decided to put more of its resources into the production of a new steel mill. Then the new gloves and warmer coat are not going to be available to you no matter how much you would like to have them.

See how economic planning thwarts the individual's desires for things? This is not to say that economic planning is always undesirable. Of course not! No intelligent person would suggest that "maximum individual freedom of choice in all things" is the paramount objective!

But the farther we go with economic planning the more we cut down on the individual's freedom of choice. That's a fact we should recognize.

Implementing the Plan

It makes a lot of difference how the plan is carried out, too. Essentially there are two kinds of approaches: (1) the resources can be allocated directly—that is, "ordered" or "directed" to go where and do what the plan requires; or (2) the resources can be "enticed" to do as the plan requires by offering rewards (money).

The first approach can be called "allocation by direct order" or simply "direct allocation." The second might be called "allocation by incentive." It means using the price mechanism to direct the people and resources.

Using the Market Mechanism. In an economic system which relies mostly on the market process, it's just natural for the government's economic plans to be carried out through the "market mechanism."

If the government wants a canal dug, a highway built, or someone to teach in the local school, what does it do? It doesn't *order people* to do these things. Instead, the government *offers to pay* to get the job done.

In the case of the highway, the government can pay a contractor. Then the contractor will hire the labor and buy all the needed things, then build the highway. Or the government might hire the people, buy the rocks and gravel and steel and cement and graders and all the other things and build the highway itself.

In each of these cases you can see that the market mechanism is being used to carry out the plan. People are automatically responding to the "price and profit incentives" offered by the government.

Most of the economic planning decisions in the United States and in the other modern non-communist countries are carried out by the market mechanism. This means that if you look at the total amounts of money being spent by the national, state, and various local (county, township, city, village) governments, you will get some idea of the total amount of resource use which is being directed by the political process—by governmental "economic plans."

You know that in the United States total government spending amounts to about one third of GNP. A lot of economic planning? Right.

Direct Allocation. Many of the "political process choices" even in a country like the United States are carried out by direct allocation. Many of the "direct allocations" consist of limitations on the private uses of resources.

For example, the uses of almost all of the land in the urban areas of the United States (and in many rural areas too) are restricted by some kind of "zoning" or "land use restrictions." This means the local government tells you what you can do (and what you cannot do) with "your" (the society's) land.

Governments limit the kinds of activities you can undertake in various places and the kinds of resources you can use for what purposes. Government regulations and restrictions are influencing the economic decisions—the resource-use choices—of all of the people all of the time.

As population expands and as technology develops, we all become more interdependent. As more and more people live closer and closer together the actions of each person have more influence on everyone else. So the government can be expected to come in and play a larger role. That's the way it has been happening. It seems likely to keep on moving in that direction.

So people will lose more of their individual freedom. Our "private property rights" will be limited more and more. But all things considered, what are the alternatives? More

economic planning may be the only realistic alternative.

Economic Planning in the "Non-Market" Economies

In the Soviet Union and Maoist China and the other so-called "communist" countries, economic planning gets into every aspect of life. The plan includes not only choices of final products. It also includes choices of which resources and which techniques will be used. The plan shows how industry and agriculture will be organized: what kinds of machinery and other inputs will be used, and all the other production details.

But each person's income is not predetermined by the plan. In the Soviet Union and in the other communist countries the productivity principle of distribution is used just as it is in the United States and in the other "mostly market-directed" economies.

One important difference between the non-market economies and our kind of economy is that they use resource administration a lot more than we do to carry out the plans. What is resource administration? We need to talk about that.

RESOURCE ADMINISTRATION? OR THE MARKET MECHANISM?

You already have had a lot of experience with "resource administration." Your college administrators decide how each classroom will be used at each hour of the day, who will live in which dorm, how much land space will be used for athletic fields and how much for parking lots, and who will get to play in which fields and who will get to park in which lots.

They decide how much floor space will be used for the library, how much for study areas, for student lounges and for faculty lounges, which professors will teach which courses with how many students in which rooms at which times, which students will get to use which of the college's resources, to take which courses. . . On and on the list could go. This is what it's like with resource administration.

At your college, all of the resource-use choices may be made through very democratic processes. The students and faculty may be the ones who have the ultimate say on all of these issues. If so, then everything may be going just fine. But, likely as not, many of these decisions will be made undemocratically—will be imposed by someone "from above"—who knows what's best for the good of your college and is going to give it to you whether you like it or not.

Sometimes your own college administration may be the the "dictator." Or it may be your state legislature. Or maybe both. But whoever does it, whenever "autocratic resource-use planning and administration" happens, unless it's done with great wisdom—with great awareness of and sensitivity to the people and issues involved—then problems will arise. Things won't go smoothly. Morale will be low.

The power to order people around is an essential part of any system of "resource administration." If the administrators are wise and just and if they use effective leadership techniques and all that, it can work out just fine. But unfortunately there just don't seem to be enough wise, just, sensitive administrators to go around. So it isn't unusual for problems to arise.

How "Market-Mechanism-Type" Incentives Could Be Used

Do you begin to get the idea of what "resource administration" is? When your dad hands you a bucket of paint and tells you to paint the bathroom or when your mom hands you a broom and tells you to sweep the steps—and if you feel that you *must* do it (or else face unpleasant consequences)—that's resource administration.

How might "market-mechanism-type" incentives be used instead? Your dad might offer to pay to get the bathroom painted. He could keep raising the "price" until you (or someone) will gladly grab the brush and start slopping paint all over. Or your mom could pay to get the steps swept. Obviously.

But what about your college? You know that your college is sort of an "administered economic system." How could it use "market-mechanism-type" incentives, instead of "direct allocation"? instead of resource administration? For many things, it couldn't. For some things, it does.

Raises and promotions go to the professors who do a good job (and/or to the ones who please the administrators). Sometimes parking fees are low for the distant lots and high for the close-in ones. But these examples don't really get into the basic resource-use choices for your college. Let's take one that does.

A Price System for the "Planned Economy" at Your College. Most colleges need more facilities—more and better buildings, classrooms, listening booths, study areas, and other facilities. But did you ever stop to think of the amount of wasted excess capacity that exists on the college campus at three a.m.? Wow!

Why don't our resource administrators start scheduling classes all night long? Because the faculty and students would revolt, that's why! And because administrators don't like to work nights, either.

Suppose someone began to think about the millions of dollars of saving which might result from running the college all night. Is there any way that people might be *induced* to go to college on the "midnight shift"? Some of the savings might be offered as "bonuses" to the professors and as "scholarships" to the students.

Do you suppose that could work? You bet it could! All it would require is that administrators set the right "price incentives"—the right "bonus" and "scholarship" payments.

Price Adjustments to "Fine-Tune" the Resource Flows. If too many professors and students volunteered for the night shift, the bonuses and scholarships could be reduced. If not enough volunteered, the payments could be raised. Maybe it really ought to be tried. It might work!

The administrators could assign "penalty charges" to professors and students who chose the most desirable class times (like 10:00 a.m., M.W.F.) and offer "bonus payments" to those who chose the less desirable times.

Eight a.m. and four p.m. classes might carry a two percent bonus; 9:00 a.m., noon, and 3:00 p.m. classes, no bonus and no penalty charge. Then evening and night classes would all carry bonuses of various sizes.

The bonuses and penalties would have to be adjusted to get just the right number of professors and students to volunteer at each time. For some hours—like midnight on Saturday night, or 8:00 a.m. Sunday—perhaps the bonus payments would need to be so high that those hours would have to be left idle.

Do you think a system like this could be made to work on your campus? How about all over the country? It's interesting to think about. The savings might run into several millions! But the purpose here is not to recommend it. It's just to show how "market-type" incentives might be used.

Once we get going on this "market-mechanism-type" incentive program we might just as well keep going. We could build in bonus payments and penalty charges for professors on the basis of their productivity—how many students they deal with, how much they publish, or whatever measure of productivity is decided on. Each student could make "large-class or small-class" choices and "high-paid prof or low-paid prof" choices and could get rebates or pay extra according to the choices made.

See how it might work? There would be some problems, of course. This approach might not meet our ideas of "equity and justice." But it sure would take care of the problem of being ordered around by your college administrators! Many professors and students and administrators would perform quite differently under such a system.

Now you know how the price mechanism might be used to carry out economic plans. Prices are adjusted to get the right people to go to the right places and do the right things. This makes it unnecessary to order people around, so *policing* (watching to see that everyone follows orders) become unnecessary.

The price mechanism is very efficient in getting the resources to do what the plan calls for. Everthing just moves automatically!

Do Communist Countries Use the Price Mechanism?

Now that you see what an efficient "resource director" the price mechanism can be, you may wonder why the communist countries use resource administration (direct allocation) instead. One reason is philosophical. They associate wage and profit incentives with their philosophical adversary: capitalism.

Anything that looks like capitalism is bad. Anyone who suggests using profit incentives to get resources to move around, soon may be scheduled to go on a long trip—one way.

A second reason is that the communist party planners haven't been fully aware of the advantages. Understanding the price mechanism and how it works isn't exactly the communist party leader's cup of tea!

But the truth is that the communist countries *are* using market-mechanism-type incentives (the price mechanism) more and more. They are beginning to appreciate the great efficiency of the market mechanism as a tool for carrying out economic plans.

They're finding out that an efficient way to get a hole dug is to offer money to anyone who will dig it—and let the digger try to make a "profit" on the job. A good way to get a factory or a hotel or a restaurant or anything else operated *efficiently* is to let the manager work to try to make a profit.

Sometimes Communist Countries Use Profit Incentives. The Soviet Union and its satellite countries are discovering that enterprises which cannot be operated efficiently by government resource-administrators can sometimes be operated very efficiently by a private individual seeking profit.

What the difference? The profit seeker has a very strong incentive to economize and optimize! The November 15, 1971 issue of *U.S. News and World Report* carries the article: "Why Reds Are Turning to Capitalism."

This article describes several instances in which serious inefficiencies had existed in hotels and other service establishments. Then individual managers were allowed to take over the establishments, run them as their own businesses and try to make profits. In most cases the improvements in services and reductions in costs were dramatic!

The Influence of Pragmatism. Are the "Reds turning to capitalism" as the title of the *U.S. News* article says? No, not really. But there seems to be a movement away from the philosophy that "anything that looks like capitalism must be despised and shunned."

The communist countries aren't becoming "capitalist." They are simply indicating their ability to use an approach which has been a hallmark of American life—in economics, in politics, in everything. What approach? Pragmatism.

The pragmatic approach aims for results. Try something. If it works that's good. Do it some more. If it doesn't work, stop doing it. Try something else. Pragmatism recognizes only *effectiveness*.

Pragmatism has been leading the Soviet Union and other communist countries to use the market mechanism. Why? For philosophical reasons? Of course not! Why then? Because for some things, it's effective. It's efficient. It works too well to be ignored.

What about the United States, with its strong laissez-faire, anti-government philosophy? We have been hastily introducing economic planning techniques which the communist (and other) countries have been developing. Why? For philosophical reasons? Are we swinging over to communism? Of course not! Then why are we using more and more economic planning? Because *it works*, that's why!

Are Economic Systems Becoming More Alike?

So can we say that the economic systems in the real world are becoming more alike? It seems sort of logical to assume that they would. If one system starts out with a very extreme position—using all dictatorial economic planning and direct-order resource administration—and then begins to change, which way *can* it change?

Or suppose if a system starts out "laissez faire and pure market process all the way." Which way *can* it change? If the two systems are as far apart as they can get, then as they change we might expect them to move closer together—to become more alike. That seems to be what's happening.

What's the ultimate result of all these "economic system changes" going to be? Will all the nations eventually wind up with the same kind of economic system? A system with some blend of the market process and government planning? I don't know. Nobody knows. But it doesn't seem likely to happen anytime soon.

We'll talk more about this question later. First let's take a closer look at what's been going on in some of the "non-market" economies—the economic systems of the communist countries.

THE PLANNED ECONOMIES OF THE USSR AND MAOIST CHINA

There are two really big countries which have so-called "communist" economic systems. Which countries? The People's Republic of China and the Soviet Union, of course.

The economic systems of both of these countries have one very basic thing in common: central economic planning and administration of the system from the top. Let's talk about how these two systems have been doing. First, the USSR.

The Economy of the USSR

After the Bolshevik (Communist) revolution in 1917 the Soviet system sort of fell apart. The Communist leaders imposed rigid controls, but they didn't know how to get the system put together again.

Lenin's "New Economic Policy." In 1921 Lenin announced his "New Economic Policy"—a "temporary step backward toward capitalism"—and urged people to produce for themselves and to trade and try to make profits. The purpose was to overcome the complete economic collapse following the Communist take-over. Remember in the book (or the movie) *Dr. Zhivago,* how tough things were?

Beginning in 1928 with the first five-year plan, rigid economic controls were imposed again. That was about a half a century ago. Today the Soviet economy is still rigidly controlled. No doubt about that! But it's considerably different.

Present-day Planning in the USSR. Consumers now get to have more things. People are ordered around less. Wage and price incentives are used more. The economic plan now reponds more to the people's demands for consumer goods—but apparently not very much more.

The question of which goods are to be produced is answered in the plan. Then the managers of the factories and mines and railroads and everything else are given their production quotas. How does it all work out? Sometimes very well. Sometimes not so well.

Sometimes the consumers don't want the kinds of consumer goods the planners have decided to produce! So what do the managers do? Would you believe advertising to try to sell surplus products to the consumers in the USSR? Yes! These days sometimes it's happening!

Of course the major effort of the Soviet economy has not been in the production of consumer goods. The emphasis has been and still is on building capital in basic industries: electric power, transport, mines, chemicals and fertilizers, etc.

There also has been a lot of effort to overcome the great inefficiency of Soviet agriculture. I'm sure you've heard about Russia's "wheat deals" with the United States. In the mid-1970s it brought millions of tons of wheat from us because its own wheat output was so low.

How Efficient Is the Soviet System?

In the USSR, factories are run by managers just as they are in the United States. There, the managers have their planned quotas to meet. When the managers are efficient and when all of the raw materials and other inputs arrive on time, things may go just fine. But it doesn't always happen that way.

There are many stories about the things managers do to try to avoid the penalties of falling behind their quotas: hoarding materials, giving false records, holding down output so future quotas won't be too high.

Then there's the story (fictitious, of course) of the Soviet nail factory which met its quota in tons of nails by producing one gigantic nail! And the story (true, they say) of the transportation company which met its quota of "ton-miles hauled'' by hauling carloads of water back and forth!

There are always bound to be ridiculous examples in every economic system, of course. How does the Soviet economy work, overall? That's hard to answer.

We know that Soviet agriculture has been very unproductive. About one fourth of the Soviet labor force is employed in farming—as compared with about one twentieth in the United States. And still they haven't been able to produce enough to feed the people.

Productivity per person in Soviet agriculture is far below that of the United States. Still the planners and administrators go on following the same patterns, year after year.

What about industry? Can we believe the statements of Nobel prize winner Solzhenitzyn? the writer who left Russia and has been proceeding to ''tell the world the truth'' about what goes on there? Solzhenitzyn says the productivity in manufacturing is incredibly low—as bad as in agriculture. Other reports seem to agree with this.

Recently, Planned Outputs Have Not Been Achieved. During the period 1970-75, both industrial production and national income fell quite a bit below the amounts planned. Planned increases in industrial production were about 8 percent per year but the actual increase was only about 6.5 percent. National income was planned to rise by 6.8 percent and actually rose by about 5.2 percent.

According to figures presented in the Soviet newspaper *Pravda* (February 1, 1976) in some products, output quotas were met or exceeded in the 1970-75 plan. This happened with coal and with eggs. But in electric power, oil, gas, steel, cement, and most agricultural products (grain, meat, milk) outputs fell behind the amounts planned.

Clearly, the performance of an economy like the USSR depends on the efficiency with which the economy is planned and then the efficiency with which the plans are administered. Some people are saying that the Brezhnev administration has been shelving problems rather than solving them. In the mid-1970s the long lines of people waiting for their food rations would seem to indicate that all was not well.

The Soviet Growth Rate Has Slowed. Back in 1961 Nikita Khrushchev said that by 1980 the Soviet Union would have the highest per capita GNP in the world. If the growth trends of that time had continued he would have been right. But they didn't.

The Soviet economy in the mid-1970s is advancing at less than half the pace it achieved in the 1950s. So there's no way that Krushchev's target could now be reached.

What of the future? Can the ''science of planning and administration'' be improved in the USSR to overcome the inefficiencies? To get growth speeded up again? And to plan the outputs of consumer goods so that the workers will want to buy the things the planners decide to produce?

Maybe so. But maybe not. Anyway, it's easy to look at the USSR and see some of the problems of trying to operate a massive thing like a modern economic system by the political process—by economic planning and resource administration. And now, a quick look at the planned economy of China.

The Economy of Maoist China

The People's Republic of China has a tightly controlled economy, planned from the top, just as does the USSR. In that respect the two economic systems are very much alike. But there are lots of really great differences between the two countries.

China Is One of the LDCs. The USSR is classed as one of the world's highly developed countries. China is ranked as one of the LDCs. Also there are strong ideological differences between the two—differences about the best directions to aim for, and about the best ways to get there.

But from the point of view of the economic system, the two countries are quite similar. In both, the political process—economic planning and resource administration—is the name of the game.

China certainly has one thing that every LDC needs: a strong and gutsy government! The government seems to have been quite successful in transforming the traditional way of life of the people. The people seem to be under control and mobilized and working—being productive. That's very good for a big LDC like China! But it hasn't always been working out well.

For one thing, there has been an "anti-expert" attitude. Some observers have said that capable management has been replaced by "revolutionary mass enthusiasm." Enthusiasm is great. But you can't run an economic system on enthusiasm alone!

Some observers claim that the Chinese production statistics are greatly overstated—that over the past 20 years there have been times when China's output has gone down because of inefficiency.

China Has Outdistanced Most of the LDCs. In the mid-1970s there seems to be general agreement that China is moving forward. Great gains have been made in medicine, public health, and education—and the minimum needs of the population seem to have been supplied. In China you don't see millions of people starving.

There has been a good bit of capital investment and modernization of industry. Some of the other LDCs have done as well and a few may have done better. But it seems clear that China has outdistanced most of them.

What About the Future? In 1976 amid the turmoil following the death of Chou En-lai, China set out on a new 5-year plan under a new leader: Hua Kuo-feng. The new plan is dedicated to some impressive goals: 70 percent mechanization of farming by 1980, for example.

The new plan reaffirms strict control by Party committees and detailed supervised planning of almost everything in the economy. So there's no question about what kind of economic system exists in the People's Republic of China!

Much is still up in the air about what's happening in the Chinese economy. It will take a while before the world will know for sure what's going on there.

But meanwhile, one thing is sure. It's providing the world another interesting and informative example of some methods and problems of economic planning and resource administration.

ECONOMIC PLANNING AND THE MARKET PROCESS IN THE WORLD TODAY

If we want to find out about the basic nature of an economic system, what do we look at? At the processes at work in the system? Of course!

We try to find out the extent to which the market process influences the resource choices as compared with the extent to which economic planning is in charge of things. Then, for the "economic planning" kinds of choices we ask questions about how the plans are made and what techniques are used for carrying out the plans.

If we can get answers to these questions then we can see what the economic system is like—what it's doing, how it functions. Suppose we look at the world today using this approach. What do we see?

The Economies of Mixed Socio-Capitalism

First, we see that in every non-communist nation, many of the major resource-use decisions are made by the political process—that is, by government plan.

In most of the economies of mixed socio-capitalism these decisions are made through some kind of (more or less) democratic process. Then the decisions are carried out by the market mechanism—by using wage, price and profit incentives to get the job done.

There are several differences among these various economies of socio-capitalism, of course. But the economies of these countries are much more alike than different. The market process plays a major role in all of them. And all of them do a lot of "political process" choosing—that is, "economic planning."

If you take a close look at the economies of such different countries as Britain, France, Japan, Sweden, Italy, West Germany, Mexico, Australia, Thailand, Canada, Brazil, Argentina, Ethiopia, the United States (or almost any other non-communist country), in all of them you will find a basic reliance on the market process for making most of the economic choices. But always the political process plays a very important role, too.

The Non-Market Economies of the Communist Countries

What about the economies of the Soviet Union, Maoist China, Cuba, the East European countries and the other communist countries? Are they really different from the economies of mixed socio-captialism? Yes they are! They are different on all three counts:

1. They *do not rely on the market process* to make any significant economic choices;

2. The economic plans *are not responsive to the wishes of the people;* and

3. The plans usually *are carried out by resource administration–not by the market mechanism.*

In the non-market economies, just about all of the economic choices are made by government and are carried out by resource administration. Yes, those systems really are different. But, just as the systems of socio-capitalism, they too are changing.

Economic Systems Are Always Changing

All economic systems are changing all the time. The communist countries are finding more ways to use the market mechanism. The economies of mixed socio-capitalism are using more planning—more choice-making by the political process.

All nations face the same economic problems, more or less—problems of choosing what to do with the scarce resources of the nation, of saving some output and turning it into capital, of controlling population size, of designing programs for education and training, of taking care of the incapable ones, of keeping the economy running smoothly and keeping prices stable, etc.

Want to know about the economic system? Then look to see the **processes at work.**

All nations approach these problems somewhat differently. Some do a better job than others. But all nations keep changing their approaches (their "economic systems") as time goes by.

Economic systems are "living systems"—always changing. They never "arrive someplace." There's no "ultimate shape" of something like an economic system. Of course not!

Certainly we don't need to be worrying about some "ultimate arrival place for an economic system"! But it's nice to know about such things as the directions and speed and processes of change. Which way are we headed? how fast? and how is it all happening? Those are the things we need to be thinking about.

Do Economic Systems Change as the Stage of Development Changes?

Could it be that the "stage of economic development" in a society will influence the kind of economic system the society will have? Perhaps so.

A Primitive Society May Require "Resource Administration." In a primitive society, custom and tradition seem to do the best job of making the economic choices—of ensuring the survival of the society. But if the economy is ever going to grow, the system must change.

The only way economic development is likely to get started in the tradition-bound primitive societies is for the political process to come in and do something to change things. The LDCs need a lot of planning and direction by the political process. What would you call such a system? Mixed socio-capitalism? Maybe so. There's no name that fits very well, really.

Economic planning certainly can help an economy on its way up the development path. But as development proceeds, conditions change.

A Complex Economy Is Not Easy to Administer. As a planned economy gets more developed and specialized, the complexity of the planning process may get overwhelming. The task of planning and directing and controlling all the people and resources and things—and doing it efficiently—becomes just about impossible.

In a highly complex "mature modern economy" some indirect way is needed to get all the thousands—no, millions—of little daily choices made and carried out. What "indirect way"? The price mechanism? Of course!

Does this explain why the USSR and some other communist countries are changing their economic systems? Placing more reliance on the production-motivating and rationing functions of price? Of course it does.

So is it now time for people to start talking about the Soviet economy as "mixed capitalo-communism"? No. I don't think it's time to go that far!

But I don't suppose it makes much difference what you call the Soviet economic system, really. Why not? Because we don't have any names that tell us much about what an economic system really is like anyway!

The "Changing Mix" in the Systems of "Mixed Socio-Capitalism"

What about countries like the United States and Canada and the countries of Western Europe and all the other countries of mixed socio-capitalism? These countries experienced their "economic growth breakthroughs" in another era. Another time. Another world, really!

From Laissez-Faire to Economic Planning. The "capitalist" economies grew up basking in the philosophies and policies of nineteenth century liberalism: of laissez-faire, strong property rights, individualism, the Protestant ethic—of the inalienable rights (and duties) of all individuals. Economic growth was rapid.

In these countries the market process and the price mechanism seemed to work just fine. But now we see these systems changing rapidly. The "role of the state" is increasing by leaps and bounds! Does the stage of development have something to do with it? So it seems.

The "capitalist" economies have become highly industrialized. Population has expanded and become concentrated in the urban areas. These economies have become highly complex, highly interdependent.

Most of the basic economic needs of most of the people have been taken care of. But now we have a new set of problems and needs—problems and needs which the market process can't take care of very well.

The Market Process Can't Solve Today's Problems. The expanding demands of modern society for better "public goods and services"—education, police and fire protection, public health and sanitation, recreation areas, highways, urban transit systems, etc., etc., etc.—require more "political process" choices.

The political process is going to have to be used to tackle the "externalities" problem and the poverty problem and the whole complex of urban problems. Almost any "problem of modern society" you can think of is going to require some involvement by the political process—some increase in "the role of the state."

So economic systems are changing. There's more government planning and control. The rights of private property and individual freedom are being reduced.

The system called "capitalism" has become something else. That's why I've been calling it "mixed socio-capitalism." The word "capitalism" doesn't describe it very well anymore.

WHAT ABOUT THE SURVIVAL OF CAPITALISM?

Sometimes people talk about the question of "the survival of capitalism." What nonsense. Capitalism was the economic system of the mid-nineteenth century, observed and attacked (and incidentally, named) by Karl Marx. That kind of economic system doesn't exist anywhere in the world. It hasn't for more than forty years!

Suppose we stretch the word "capitalism" to mean "any system in which the market process plays an important role." What then? As time goes on will the market process continue to be one of the important ways societies make their economic choices? Yes.

The Market Process Will Continue to Be Important

For the foreseeable future the market process will continue to play an important role. No question about it. So if that's the way you want

to define capitalism, then okay. Capitalism will survive.

As long as people have individual desires and as long as incentives and rewards are effective ways of motivating people, the market process will keep on influencing social choices. But forevermore? Until the end of time? Who can say? Who cares, anyway?

Consumer demand will never completely direct the resources of any society. But consumer demand won't ever be completely ignored, either.

The market mechanism will continue to be used as an "implementation tool" to carry out political process choices, too. As more planners come to understand the efficiency of the market mechanism you can expect to see it being used more and more as a "plan-implementation device."

Will Private Property Survive?

The market process can't work without some rights of private property. Will private property survive? Of course.

You know that private property rights will never be complete and unlimited in any society—but they won't ever be totally revoked, either. Just about everybody in every society gets to own something!

In the United States and the other economies of mixed socio-capitalism we can expect more limitations on our private property rights. That's what will happen as the political process makes more of the choices and takes on more of the problems.

What problems? Externalities must be internalized. Income must be redistributed. That means some loss of private property rights.

As the society's productive efforts shift direction—from the old problems of yesterday to the new problems of tomorrow—much of the shift will be a shift from "private" objectives to "social" objectives. As the shift continues, the individual is going to lose more private property rights—rights to choose what to do with what.

In the communist countries, private property rights are likely to be expanding. Why? Because as these countries learn more ways to use the market mechanism to carry out their plans they're going to have to let people receive more personal rewards—more "private property."

The income earner must be able to keep the money earned!—or to spend it for things and keep the things! Of course. Otherwise, why work so hard?

Some increases in private property rights are already being allowed in some of the communist countries, just as the rights of private property are being cut back in the economies of mixed socio-capitalism.

Will Individual Freedom Survive?

What about the freedom of the individual? Are we all going to be free to go our own way? and to claim the rewards of our successes or suffer the hardships of our failures? Will that sort of "individual freedom and responsiblity" survive? You already know the answer.

In the "free economies," personal freedom will be reduced. It's already happening, of course. In the "controlled economies," individual freedom probably will be increased.

When millions of people are crowded together in a little space called "an urban area," then the society can't let each of us do our own thing. We must work things out together through the political process. All of us have to go along with the restrictions decided on by the group. That's the way it is in the complex modern world.

Our "Worldly Religions": Capitalism, Socialism, Communism

By now you can see the nonsense of talking about the "survival" of some kind of economic system. When we use labels like "capitalism" or "socialism" or "communism" we spread a blanket over the economic system and hide all the things that are going on!

But then people get identified with the name. The label becomes "the name of our team." Everyone begins to think of it as something to believe in, to cherish, to fight for. These labels—capitalism, socialism, communism—words coined by nineteenth century "social protest philosopher-prophets"—have become our "banners" in our "struggle of worldly religions."

It would be better to just forget about the words "capitalism" and "socialism" and "communism." The labels don't describe any of the world's economic systems anyway. If you want to see what the system really is you need to know how the choices are made and carried out. How much social process? political process? and market process? and how does each process work?

If you know these things then you know what kind of economic system the society has. If you don't, then you don't. And whatever it is today, you can be sure that tomorrow it will be different.

Economic Philosophies? or Economic Systems?

The words "capitalism," "socialism," and "communism," refer to economic philosophies much more than they refer to economic systems.

The Philosophy of Capitalism. The philosophy of capitalism is the philosophy of the market process—the philosophy of Adam Smith's laissez-faire—of "consumer sovereignty and the invisible hand." It's the philosophy of individual freedom, of private property, of rewards for productivity. The idea is that if people and businesses are left free to make their own choices, everything will come out better for everybody.

This "individual freedom" philosophy of capitalism is strong in the United States. It is also strong in the other non-communist countries, even though most of those countries call themselves "socialist." But there's no real-world economic system anywhere which even comes close to reproducing in the real world the "rugged individualism" philosophy of pure capitalism.

This unmodified "law of the jungle, survival of the fittest" philosophy of capitalism was accepted and followed by most business and political leaders of the western world in the last century. This philosophy and the harsh 19th century system was what Marx attacked. He predicted its downfall.

The "downfall" of the system didn't come the way Marx predicted, but it came just the same. Not by revolution but by evolution—by (more or less) orderly change.

No real-world economic system will ever again be built on the "rugged individualist" philosophy of unmodified capitalism. Certainly not. But all real-world systems embody some of the philosophy of capitalism. Even the communist countries use one of the most basic concepts of capitalist philosophy—incentives and rewards—more income for more productivity.

Any system based on the capitalist philosophy, today, must also embody much of the philosophy of socialism. There are still some people in the United States and other countries who don't like socialist philosophy creeping into their societies and influencing the evolution of their "capitalist" economic systems. Some cry out against it. But that's the way thing seem to be going just the same.

The Philosophies of Socialism and Communism.
What is the philosophy of socialism? It's a philosophy of working together and sharing, of giving up individual freedoms for the benefit of society. The society (government) should own most of the means of production and the people should work, not for their own betterment, but for the betterment of everybody.

The philosophy of socialism seems more "philosophically appealing" to most people than the "self-centered, dog-eat-dog" ideology of capitalism. Everybody knows it's good

to be benevolent and to share with others. But when it gets down to the real world, the "benevolent sharing" of socialist philosophy doesn't seem to work out.

No modern economic system has ever been able to run on "benevolent sharing." Most people seem to be more productive and do more to help the society toward its objectives if there's a system of incentives and rewards.

What a far cry the philosophy of socialism is from the real-world economic systems called "socialism"! Even farther than the real-world capitalist systems are from the philosophy of capitalism. Real-world systems of "democratic socialism" really are more capitalist than socialist!

So what's a "socialist economic system"? It's a system in which the leaders (and maybe most of the people) proclaim their belief in some version of the socialist philosophy? Right! And a "capitalist economic system" is a system in which the leaders (and maybe most of the people) proclaim their belief in some version of the capitalist philosophy? Sure.

What about communism? Is that more "philosophy"—more "worldly religion" than economic system, too? Of course. Communism is a system in which the leaders (and perhaps most of the people) proclaim their belief in the philosophies of communism. But one communist system can be very different from another, of course.

"Pronouncements of philosophy" don't tell you much about what an economic system looks like! You can see why it's necessary to forget the label. If you want to know what kind of system really exists you have to look and see.

THE MARKET PROCESS: FROM MASTER TO SERVANT OF SOCIAL CHOICE?

Did you ever stop to think of the great impact which the market process has had on the world? Truly, it was the market process that created the modern world!

The Market Process Generated the Modern World

The market process provided the power that thrust the world through the industrial revolution. It stimulated savings and investment and great increases in output.

The harshness of it all!—denying things to unproductive people—while the powerful rationing and production motivating functions of price exercised control—that's what brought the economic breakthroughs which generated the modern world. But now, everywhere you look in the market-directed economies, the "role of the market" is being reduced. Why?

You know why. The results of the market process are often unacceptable these days. Also, society seeks "new-type objectives" which cannot be approached through the market process—cannot be decided on the basis of how people spend their money.

So the market proces must be bypassed. The political process must get involved. You already know all about that.

In a brief few hundred years the market process succeeded in ripping out the social control mechanisms that kept society stable and alive for thousands of years. How quickly it broke down the past! And how quickly it generated the modern world!

Is that all over now? Must the market process now be pushed offstage after such a short and brilliant performance? Not entirely. But to some extent, yes.

In the past the market process performed two functions: (1) it made the decisions, and (2) it carried out the decisions. But now that's being changed. More and more the market process is being used to *carry out decisions which it didn't make*. Decisions made how? By the political process, of course!

For the past few centuries the market process really has been in control. Truly, it has been the "master mechanism" of social choice. But now? The market process is being broken to harness—forced into the role of servant to carry out the deliberate choices of the political process.

The Decision-Making and Implementation Questions

You know that the society's economic problem can be broken down into the "production" and "distribution" questions.

How about breaking down the society's economic problem into: (1) making the choices and (2) carrying out the choices? Maybe it's important to separate these two functions.

One process (the political process) can be used to make the decisions, while another process (the market process) can be used to carry out the decisions. Of course! More and more that's just what has been happening.

In the societies of "traditional capitalism" the market process has been in charge of both the decision-making and the implementation functions. In the non-market "communist" economies the political process has been used both to decide and to carry out the economic choices. But what's been happening recently?

In the "capitalist" societies the political process has been taking over more and more of the decision-making functions, leaving the market process with only the implementation function. In the non-market economies the political process continues to exercise tight control over the decisions but more and more ways are being found to use the powerful forces of the market mechanism to implement the decisions.

What About the Future of the Market Process?

So what's the future for the market process? The market process will never be stripped of all of its decision-making functions. To be sure, products will still be produced in response to what the people are buying!

As an implementation device it seems that

the market process will be playing an even more important role in the future. Why? Because it's so efficient, of course!

People and resources move automatically. Price adjustments can be used to adjust the flows of resources—of inputs and outputs. It all works so efficiently, yet no one needs to be ordered around. Fantastic!

The world's economic systems will continue to evolve. As they do the market process will continue to play an important role in most of them. It will continue to play some role in all of them.

Chances are that as the years go by, economic systems will become somewhat more alike. People always seem to like to steal each other's secrets—and they try to learn from each others' successes and failures.

Over the next several years I think it's a safe bet that the United States and the other economies of "mixed socio-capitalism" will be doing more economic planning. And the rigidly planned (communist) economies are likely to be using the market mechanism more and more. How far will it all go? Only time will tell.

I Wish Everybody Knew As Much Economics As You Do

I only wish that all of those who will be influencing the economic decisions—the leaders of the countries all over the world—knew as much basic economics as you do. Just the economics you've learned from this one book, if understood and applied by all the people making the decisions, could make a better world for all of us.

"But," you say, "I really don't know all that much economics." Maybe not. Relative to what you could know or to what you might like to know, maybe not. But you know a lot more useful economics than you think.

Right now you know a lot more economics than most people in the world. You know a lot more than some government officials who will be making decisions and choosing policies that will influence the lives of thousands, maybe millions of people.

Some political leaders have very little understanding of basic economic concepts. That's very unfortunate—especially since it seems to be necessary for the political process to get more and more involved in making the choices for society.

Some of the "economically illiterate" leaders are in the underdeveloped countries. But not all of them are. Not by a long shot! Many of them are right here—in the federal government and in the government of your own state, city, county, township, school district— everywhere.

It's too bad that so many policy makers know so little about basic economics—about the "science of common sense." But that's the way it is. Some bad choices are bound to result. Be sorry that they don't know more economics. But at the same time, be glad that you do.

This is the end of the last chapter. A short epilogue follows—no big deal—I just wanted to share some parting thoughts with you. But before you go on to that, stop and do some serious thinking about the crucial issues in this chapter—about economic planning and the market process, and the evolution of the world's economic systems.

REVIEW EXERCISES

● **MAJOR CONCEPTS, PRINCIPLES, TERMS (Explain each carefully.)**

how mixed socio-capitalism works
how a "non-market economy" works
economic planning

resource administration
the changing directions of progress
the increasing role of the state
the economy of the USSR
the economy of Maoist China

• OTHER CONCEPTS AND TERMS (Explain each briefly.)

economic system
pragmatism
direct allocation
allocation by incentive
Lenin's "New Economic Policy"
the "five-year plan"

• QUESTIONS (Write out answers or jot down key points.)

1. "Capitalism—the economic system which was named by and attacked by Karl Marx—no longer exists. So Marx must have been right, after all!" Do you agree? or disagree? Discuss.
2. Think of some things which are now being "administered" at your college, but which might be handled by the "price mechanism" instead. Would you like to see any of these things handled by some kind of "price incentive, reward system"? Discuss.
3. Could it be that economic systems change as the stage of development changes? Discuss.
4. Is it always true that economic planning reduces the choices of individuals? Discuss.
5. What are some of the problems the Soviet economic system has been facing recently? Describe briefly.
6. It seems inevitable that in the "free economies" of mixed socio-capitalism the role of the state is going to increase more and more. Can you explain why this seems to be true? What kinds of additional things (which "social changes") is the state likely to get involved in ? Discuss.
7. It seems likely that in the rigidly-controlled economies of "communism," the market mechanism is going to be used, more and more. Can you explain why this seems likely?
8. Describe capitalism, not as an economic system, but as a philosophy. Do the same for socialism and communism. Now, think back to the last time you heard some people arguing over some economic issue. From listening to what each person said, could you tell how much of which economic philosophies each believed in? Think about it.
9. This chapter suggests that we might all be better off if we could just get rid of the "blanket labels"—the names for our "worldly religions"—capitalism, socialism, communism—and refer to economic systems by describing the highlights instead. What do you think about this idea? Discuss.

Epilogue: Some Parting Words About Economics and You

Welcome to the end of the book. If you've read the whole thing you've seen a lot of economics. If you've learned the concepts well, your eyes are now open to a lot of things you couldn't see before.

You've done a lot of work. Yes. And you're well on your way. So relax for a minute "Enjoy your achievements. . ." Smile and feel good. You have a right to be proud of yourself.

If you've really been studying hard and learning it well, by now I'm sure you have some new awareness of the world—some sharpened ability to conceptualize reality. You have a new "feel" for things that are going on around you.

You'll be carrying several of these concepts with you, using them as "a way of looking at things" for as long as you live. You have a sound framework that will help you as you further develop your own good common sense, day after day, year after year.

The World Is Your "Econ Lab"

The world is full of illustrations and examples of economic concepts. I'm sure you remember when I said, back in the beginning of the book: "there's no real-world issue or problem that is *purely* economic." Remember? Sure. It's very true, too.

But almost every real-world issue or problem you can think of has *some* important economic aspects. Yes, you can be sure that you will be running into real-world illustrations of economic concepts, all the time.

Everywhere you go (now that you have built this new "window through which to observe the world") you will keep on seeing things you never noticed before. Whenever you go into a bank you'll know a lot more about what's going on. You'll know that when the teller is pushing those accounting machine buttons to print a deposit receipt for you, somewhere in the bank a figure is automatically being added to your checking account. And you'll know that the figure is your money!

As you leave the bank you'll see your friendly branch manager sitting there behind the desk and you'll be tempted to go over and ask if they have created any money today. Go ahead! Ask! I dare you.

Whenever you go into your favorite shoe store you'll see those shoe boxes all around and you'll wonder how much the store keeps in inventory. And you might wonder if the inventory is expanding or contracting.

From now on, whenever you hear the news about employment and unemployment, about Americans spending too much money abroad, about the price of wheat or oil or steel going up, about the increasing GNP, about interest rates going up and bond prices going down, and about all such things, you'll have the good feeling of being "in the know."

From now on **you** are an economist.

Whenever you hear a political demagogue promising to do all kinds of

408

great things for the people, you'll wonder where all the scarce resources needed to do all those great things will come from. You'll always be aware that choices to use our scarce resources in one way are also choices to *not use* our resources in some other way.

Whenever laws are passed influencing wages or prices, or restricting or subsidizing the supply of something, or regulating market conditions in any way, you will have some idea about whether we will soon be seeing surpluses or shortages.

From now on, whenever you choose corn flakes instead of eggs for breakfast, you might think about how you're influencing the resource-use choices in the economy—about how you're supporting the "Kellogg team" and deserting the "egg team." (You might even wonder if everybody else is switching to corn flakes today, and if, pretty soon, we're all going to be up to someplace in eggs!)

From now on, whenever you have a worrisome choice to make, you'll be aware that you're weighing alternatives, considering opportunity costs—thinking marginally. That's good. Some of your choices may come out better if you think about them that way. I hope so.

You know a lot of economics. You really do! Not enough to handle all the problems economists deal with. Of course not. But as you go through life with your mind turned on you'll be learning more and more economics all the time.

Someday you may understand more economics than some people who majored in it! (You can get there quicker by being an econ major—but anyone who knows anything at all about "the science of common sense," knows that a person can't major in everything!)

It Takes Scarce Resources to Solve Most Problems

Now that you know some economics, does that make you "materialistic"? There's plenty

of talk going around these days against materialism. Everybody knows that big money and big houses and big cars and big steaks and long trips on big airplanes don't bring happiness. No argument on that score.

But everyone who thinks about it will realize that if we want to try to seek an objective—*any* objective—it's going to require some scarce resources—energy, thought, effort, capital, other resources. *"Material inputs" are essential in order to move toward almost any objective you can think of.* That's just the way it is.

Energy is required to move things, to do things, to make things, to change things, to achieve things. And energy is scarce. So we aren't going to be able to move and do and make and change and achieve all the things you might wish plus all the things I might wish plus all the things everyone else might wish.

It's likely that *every major problem you can think of could be at least partly solved if enough scarce resources (material inputs) could be turned in its direction.*

And it's almost just as certain that *no progress toward solving any of these problems is going to be made without the use of some scarce resources (material inputs.)*

If it is true that some scarce resources are needed, then we can't possibly solve all the problems we would like to solve—at least, not all right now. Not all at once. That's the way it is with scarcity.

There just aren't enough resources, enough inputs to do all the things all the people want done. So what can we do? What *must* we do? We must *choose*. Of course. We must decide which problems to solve and which to tolerate for a while.

The Stark Reality of Economics

When you learn economics you experience a stark confrontation with reality. You come face to face with scarcity—and *scarcity is the natural condition of reality.* Once you face it, confront it, recognize it—from then on you live with an awareness of opportunity costs, of substitution, of having to choose between things.

You become painfully aware that every time labor or building materials or electric energy or any other factors are shifted to aim at a new objective or to attack a new problem, someone must pay the cost. Someone must *give up* something.

People *don't like* to give up things! None of us wants to choose this or that. It's so much nicer to have this *and* that. But we can't have this *and* that, *of everything!*

Who Will Make the Sacrifices?

Oh, it's so easy to choose to give up things we never had! "I'll give up the luxury of driving a big car if it will bring a better school system. So everyone else ought to be willing to give up their big cars, too! Of course, I don't happen to have a big car. I only have a motor bike. I sure don't plan to give *that* up! That's not a luxury. It's a necessity!"

Everyone wants someone else to make the sacrifices. Sure. But we aren't going to solve any of society's problems by "volunteering away" the things other people have, while clinging to our own. We aren't going to solve the pollution problem by wishing it on the big businesses or the local governments or the federal government or anyone else. The same is true of education and law enforcement and everything else.

These problems are society's problems. We're *all* sharing in the benefits of high productivity and individual freedom. And *we're all going to share in the costs.* You can be sure of it.

Solutions to society's problems are not going to be coming along any faster than we ourselves are willing to pay the costs—in taxes, in product prices, in the opportunity costs of *other* goods and services we forfeit, and sometimes in giving up some of our freedoms. It's too bad we're going to have to pay the costs. But we are. You know that now. You

know that these are the facts of economics—the facts of the real world—the facts of life.

A Word of Farewell

Now that you are turned on to some of the basic economic concepts, your thoughts never again will be able to escape the fact of scarcity. You'll always have some awareness, now, of the discomfort of opportunity cost.

You'll always be aware that realistic plans and programs to improve anything or to solve any problem, require some means—some effort—some resources—some "scarce factors of production." You will never forget that these factors must come from somewhere. But from where? And then to be used to meet *which* urgent need? These are the really tough questions.

Answering these tough questions can be a very difficult and trying task. If you stop and think about it for a minute you will realize that this difficult and trying task is the thing we've been talking about all along. Sure. It's the economic problem! It's the basic problem of economics—the problem of choosing.

It's the problem of scarcity—of not being able to do all the things we'd like to do—the problem of having to decide, to choose which things to do when we can't do everything—the problem of choosing which objectives to pursue and which to forego, which things to have and which to give up. That's what economics is all about. Surely you'll never forget that.

I hope you will go further in economics. This one book couldn't take you but just so far. But no matter where you go, no matter which objectives you seek, no matter which paths you choose, I hope your choices turn out to be *truly* the right ones, for you.

The right choices are the ones which, many years from now, will let you look back and say:

"How lucky I am to have been wise enough then, to make the right choices—for me." I wish you wisdom in all your choices. Today, and always.

Index